DYNAMICS OF TRIAL PRACTICE: PROBLEMS AND MATERIALS

Third Edition

By

Ronald L. Carlson
Fuller E. Callaway Professor of Law
University of Georgia

Edward J. Imwinkelried
Professor of Law
University of California at Davis

AMERICAN CASEBOOK SERIES®

Mat #40061901

American Casebook Series and West Group are
registered trademarks used herein under license.

ISBN 0–314–26479–5

 TEXT IS PRINTED ON 10% POST CONSUMER RECYCLED PAPER

1st Reprint — 2004

Professor Carlson dedicates his work on this project to the memory of Mason Ladd.

Professor Imwinkelried dedicates his work on this project to every adjunct trial advocacy professor he has been privileged to work with at the University of California, Washington University, and the University of San Diego.

*

Preface

THE CENTENNIAL HISTORY OF HARVARD LAW SCHOOL 84–85 (1918) reported that "[e]fforts have been made from time to time to give students some experience in the trial of cases by substituting a trial . . . before a jury for the argument of questions of law . . . ." However, THE HISTORY added that those efforts succeeded primarily "in affording amusement [rather] than in substantial benefit to the participants." *Id.* THE HISTORY concluded that although a mock trial "now and then is . . . worth while," its value is "only as a relief to the tedium of serious work." *Id.*

Trial practice teaching has made great strides since the publication of THE HISTORY early this century. In part in response to former Chief Justice Burger's criticism of the quality of trial advocacy in the United States, both the bar and law schools have substantially revised their programs for training litigators. As Professor Steve Lubet has pointed out, "Over the last fifteen years trial advocacy teaching has matured from a sideline into a discipline." Lubet, *What We Should Teach (But Don't) When We Teach Trial Advocacy,* 37 J.LEGAL EDUC. 123, 124 (1987). There are numerous signs of that maturation. To begin with, although the trial practice course was formerly "largely the province of part-time instructors," at most schools the course is "now taught by full-time tenured faculty." *Id.* Moreover, the past fifteen years have witnessed a dramatic growth in the body of literature on trial advocacy. Law professors, litigators, psychologists, and communications experts all have contributed to that growth.

Despite the progress made to date, however, there are those who are skeptical of the value of contemporary trial practice instruction. Bellow, *Clinical Legal Education Undergoes Changes,* 13 SYLLABUS 7 (Dec. 1982). Traditionalists emphasize that "[t]rial practice has remained a course that deals essentially in [forensic] technique . . . ." Lubet, *supra* at 126. The course seems to slight the development of analytic skills. The thrust of the criticism is that every law school course must contribute to the school's primary academic mission of developing students' analytic ability. In the skeptics' minds, if the trial practice course does not do so, the course does not deserve a "place in the academy." *Id.* at 130. To meet this criticism, an "injection of analytic instruction" is imperative. *Id.* at 135.

Our hope is that the publication of this text will help bring the trial practice course squarely into the mainstream of the law school curriculum. To be sure, this text discusses the forensic techniques of witness examination and jury speech. However, this text attempts to teach the student far more than forensic technique. Throughout this text, we have emphasized the need for strategic evaluation of the case—rational, sys-

tematic planning. Since the release of our first edition, we have conducted a series of continuing legal education programs, based on this text,
throughout the country. The attendees' comments at these conferences
have convinced us that we are on the right track; again and again attendees remarked that they found the program useful precisely because the
topic of strategic case evaluation was largely neglected in their law school
advocacy course. Strategic planning demands the type of precise fact
analysis and predictive judgment which Karl Llewellyn described as the
raison d'etre of the law school curriculum. For an instructions conference
in law reform litigation, the trial attorney must draft a jury instruction
on his or her legal theory. To do so, the attorney must be able to identify
the facts triggering the social policies which will motivate the trial and
appellate courts to reform the law—an analytic skill learned in the most
Socratic law school courses. In making such decisions such as the choice
of a theory of the case and the exercise of strikes during jury selection,
the litigator makes difficult predictive judgments. Llewellyn himself
wrote that one of the most important lessons for law students to learn is
that the so-called rules of law are essentially predictions of legal behavior.
K. LLEWELLYN, THE BRAMBLE BUSH 77 (1960).

We have stressed fact evaluation in this text to help achieve the objective of making the trial practice course a "linchpin of the curriculum."
Lubet, *supra* at 126. In this respect, we share Professor Llewellyn's opti-
mism:

> It is worthwhile to mark off a course in . . . trial practice . . . and set
> [it] apart. . . . [I]t should be marked off for the most intensive
> study. . . . because [it is] of such transcendent importance as to need
> special emphasis. [I]t should be marked off not to be kept apart and
> distinct, but solely in order that [it] may be more firmly learned,
> more firmly ingrained into the student.

LLEWELLYN, *supra* at 17.

RONALD L. CARLSON
EDWARD J. IMWINKELRIED

August, 2002

Acknowledgements

The authors would like to express their thanks to several distinguished colleagues who contributed materials for the case files in the appendices to this text: Professor James Smith of Georgia, Professor Paul Bergman of U.C.L.A., Ms. Robin Craig-Olson of the firm of Boornazian, Jensen & Garthe, Professor Richard Gonzales of the University of New Mexico, Professor Thomas Mauet of the University of Arizona, Professor Leonard Packel of Villanova University, Professor Roger Park of the Hastings College of Law, Dean Rex Perschbacher of the University of California, at Davis, Mr. Richard Seltzer of Seltzer & Cody and the Honorable Warren Wolfson.

Professor Imwinkelried would like to thank the secretarial staff of the University of California, at Davis Law School: Ms. Paula Buchignani, Ms. Saralee Buck, Steven Dunn, Ms. Helen Forsythe, Ms. Alice Gonzalez, Ms. Ann Graham, Ms. Kathy Houston, Ms. Kelly Humphreys, Ms. Berta Lewin, and Ms. Glenda McGlashan. They prepared the entire manuscript for this text.

Professor Imwinkelried would like to extend special thanks to two good friends: Mr. Merle Silverstein of Rosenblum, Goldenhersh, Silverstein & Zafft and Ms. Sonya Urquhart of Directed Verdict. Mr. Silverstein and Ms. Urquhart were kind enough to review and critique the draft manuscript.

Professor Carlson acknowledges the influence on theories of evidence and trial practice imparted by Dean Mason Ladd, who was born in 1898 and died in 1980. Dean Ladd served the legal profession as Dean of the Law School at the University of Iowa from 1939 until 1966. After completing a career at Iowa that began in 1929, first as professor and then as dean, he became the first dean of the Florida State University Law School. He established an outstanding evidence program at Florida State, and the Mason Ladd Memorial Lecture Series at both schools—Iowa and Florida State—are tributes to his memory.

When the Fellows of the American Bar Foundation conferred the 1979 Fellows Research Award on Dean Ladd, they stated in part: "Few law academicians have equalled the productivity and excellence of Dean Ladd's contributions. His research work, including chairmanship of the American Bar Foundation Research Committee, has been of inestimable value to scholars and practitioners."

Whether writing or teaching, Dean Ladd always warmed to subjects that involved discussion of trial proof and practice. The mix of insight and good will that Dean Ladd brought to teaching and scholarly writing is almost unequalled. He made a lasting impact and matchless impressions upon the law as well as his family, friends, students, and other teachers.

Ronald L. Carlson
Edward J. Imwinkelried

August, 2002

Summary of Contents

---

*

Table of Contents

*

Table of Cases

DYNAMICS OF TRIAL PRACTICE: PROBLEMS AND MATERIALS

Third Edition

*

Chapter 1

INTRODUCTION

Table of Sections

§ 1.1 THE IMPORTANCE OF THE LITIGATION SYSTEM

The Preamble to the United States Constitution lists the fundamental objectives that the Founding Fathers had in mind when they drafted that document. The list of objectives includes "establish[ing] Justice [and] insur[ing] domestic Tranquility...." U.S.CONST. preamble. To achieve those objectives, the drafters established a government, including a judicial system described in Article III of the Constitution. The functions of that system are corollaries of the drafters' objectives: to dispense justice to litigants and to insure domestic tranquility by serving as a public mechanism for peaceful dispute resolution. As Hobbes wrote in the 17th century, when people feel the need to resort to private, violent methods of dispute resolution, "the life of man" is likely to be "poor, nasty, brutish, and short." A. CASTELL, AN INTRODUCTION TO MODERN PHILOSOPHY 360 (2d ed. 1963). Further, in a society lacking pacific mechanisms for resolving controversies, "notions of ... justice ... have ... no place." *Id.* In short, an effective litigation system is a *sine qua non* for a just, orderly society. In our republic, the right to access to the litigation system is considered so valuable that the Supreme Court has elevated the right to constitutional status. *Bounds v. Smith,* 430 U.S. 817 (1977); *Boddie v. Connecticut,* 401 U.S. 371 (1971).

§ 1.2 COUNSEL'S ROLE WITHIN THE LITIGATION SYSTEM

§ 1.2(A) Protecting Private Interests

Just as the litigation system serves a vital function within society, the attorney performs a critical function within the system. It is true

1

that the attorney's systemic role has several dimensions. For example, to some extent the attorney is treated as an officer of the court. Burger, *Standards of Conduct for Prosecution and Defense Personnel,* 5 AM. CRIM.L.Q. 11, 12–13 (1966). However, the primary conception of the trial attorney's role is that she functions as a representative of and advocate for a client involved in litigation. The American Bar Association's Model Rules of Professional Conduct, originally adopted in 1983, reflect that conception. The Rules' Preamble lists all the variegated roles the attorney plays in contemporary American society, but the first role listed is that of "a representative of clients." The Rules are divided into eight different sets of regulations, but all the duties highlighted in the initial set are obligations which the attorney owes her client.

In a case of any consequence, the client desperately needs "the guiding hand of counsel." *Powell v. Alabama,* 287 U.S. 45, 69 (1932). To begin with, the law is so complex that "[t]he right to be heard would be, in many cases, of little avail if it did not comprehend the right to be heard by counsel. Even the intelligent and educated layman has small and sometimes no skill in the science of law." *Id.* at 68–69. Moreover, modern litigation has reached such staggering proportions that the client requires a trained representative who can devote full time to analyzing and organizing the factual material for trial. In *United States v. I.B.M.,* the attorneys produced over 64 million pages of documents in the first five years of discovery. Pope, *Rule 34: Controlling the Paper Avalanche,* 7 LITIGATION 28 (Spr. 1981). Another federal case, the Washington Public Power Supply System Securities Litigation (the WPPSS) suit, involved a default on $2.25 billion in bonds sold to finance the construction of two nuclear power plants. "During discovery in the WPPSS case, ... more than 200 million pages of documents were produced." Sugarman, *Coordinating Complex Discovery,* 15 LITIGATION 41 (Fall 1988). This phenomenon is not confined to federal court. In one case in Texas state court, the parties exchanged over 40 million pages of documents before settling. Arthurs, *Decision Tree Sprouts into King–Size Settlement: In Complex Case, the Theme Is the Key,* LEGAL TIMES, July 29, 1985, at p. 4 (discussing *Houston Lighting & Power Co. v. The Brown & Root, Inc.*). Clients who find themselves enmeshed in this type of litigation must call on full-time professional litigators for guidance.

§ 1.2(B) Advancing Public Interests

By guiding private clients, the attorney advances a number of public interests: contributing to accurate fact-finding in the adversary system, helping maintain the public's perception of the litigation system as legitimate, and vindicating such democratic values as the individual's autonomy.

The most obvious public interest is the societal stake in the effective operation of the adversary system. One of the assumptions underlying that system is that it is a superior method of determining the merits of factual disputes between litigants. *See generally* Joint American Bar Association—American Association of Law Schools Conference on Professional Responsibility, *Professional Responsibility*, 44 A.B.A.J. 1159 (1958). Since the adversary parties have primary responsibility for gathering information before trial and presenting it at trial, they have the maximum incentive to develop a full factual record—a stronger incentive than a government-appointed magistrate or judge would presumably have. S. LANDSMAN, READINGS ON ADVERSARIAL JUSTICE: THE AMERICAN APPROACH TO LITIGATION 3, 34 (1988); Landsman, *The Rise of the Contentious Spirit: Adversary Procedure in Eighteenth Century England*, 75 CORNELL L.REV. 497 (1990); Landsman, *From Gilbert to Bentham: The Reconceptualization of Evidence Theory*, 36 WAYNE L.REV. 1149 (1990). Conversely, since the judge has little responsibility for evidence collection and presentation, the system minimizes the risk that the judge will develop a pretrial bias. S. LANDSMAN, READINGS ON ADVERSARIAL JUSTICE, *supra* at 2–3, 15–16, 34–35. Ideally, the net effects are a more impartial decision-maker and a more complete record.[1]

However, the adversary system can operate in this fashion only when all sides have a meaningful opportunity to prepare for and participate at trial. Goldstein, *The State and the Accused: Balance of Advantage in Criminal Procedure*, 69 YALE L.J. 1149 (1960); Younger, *Sovereign Admissions: A Comment on* United States v. Santos, 43 N.Y.U.L.REV. 108 (1968). If one side or all sides are denied this opportunity, the system can easily malfunction, yielding an inaccurate, unjust decision. In any substantial case, the litigant needs counsel to make the pretrial opportunities and the trial presentation meaningful. Ignorant of the discovery rules, a counselless litigant may overlook key evidence in her pretrial investigation. Or, ignorant of the evidentiary rules, a *pro se* litigant may be unable to present the key evidence to the trier of fact. In either event, the verdict can be a miscarriage of justice. As we have seen, the lawyer's expertise is the reason why the individual litigant needs the lawyer's assistance; the same expertise helps explain why the attorney's involvement is vital to the functioning of the adversary system as a fact-finding mechanism.

Attorneys' participation in the litigation system not only objectively increases the probability of the system's proper functioning; their involvement also contributes to the public's acceptance of the system as legitimate. As Hobbes noted, one of the essential purposes of the litigation system is to remove the incentive for persons to resort to private, violent means of dispute resolution. If that purpose is to be realized, the system must not only yield accurate, just decisions; there must also be a widespread public perception that the system operates fairly. J. BIES-

---

1. There have been some empirical studies of the hypotheses that the adversary system leads to a more complete factual record and a more impartial judge. The data on the completeness of the factual record is inconclusive, but data does support the "claim ... that an adversary presentation significantly counteracts decisionmaker bias." Thebaut, Walker & Lind, *Adversary Presentation and Bias in Legal Decisionmaking*, 86 HARV. L.REV. 386, 397 (1972); Lund, Thebaut & Walker, *Discovery and Presentation of Evidence in Adversary and Nonadversary Proceeding*, 71 MICH.L.REV. 1129, 1143 (1973).

ANZ & M. BIESANZ, INTRODUCTION TO SOCIOLOGY 586 (1969); Lipset & Schneider, *Political Sociology,* in SOCIOLOGY: AN INTRODUCTION 399, 406 (N. Smelser ed. 1973). The public at large must be willing to accept and abide by decisions rendered by the system. Nesson, *The Evidence or the Event? On Judicial Proof and the Acceptability of Verdicts,* 98 HARV.L.REV. 1357 (1985).

Attorneys' participation helps to maintain that legitimacy and acceptability. The general public is sophisticated enough to appreciate the complexity of contemporary law. It would undoubtedly strike most members of public as unfair and unacceptable to deny litigants the right to be represented by counsel in any but the simplest of cases. Concededly, in some states the party to a small claims case may not be represented by counsel at the hearing. *E.g.,* CAL. CODE CIVIL PROCEDURE § 117g. However, this apparent exception proves the rule; these jurisdictions bar attorneys from small claims courts in part because the stakes in those trials are so small and because the normal, complex evidentiary and procedural rules do not apply to those trials. We tolerate a denial of counsel in these proceedings because their informality removes the need for counsel. The Founding Fathers themselves shared the belief that counsel is needed for a fair, adversary hearing when the stakes are significant. More than any other provision of the Constitution, the sixth amendment epitomizes the adversary system; that amendment guarantees defendants both the right to confront opposing witnesses and the right to compulsory process to call favorable witnesses. U.S.CONST. amend. VI. It is no accident that the same amendment safeguards the right to counsel. *Id.*

Lastly, counsel's participation vindicates democratic values. The vindication is evident in criminal cases. In that setting, the defendant's attorney stands between the individual client and the state to protect the individual's civil liberties. Lubet, *What We Should Teach (But Don't) When We Teach Trial Advocacy,* 37 J. LEGAL EDUC. 123, 132 (1987). However, counsel's involvement upholds the democratic tradition in a broader sense. *Id.* One of the premises of our democracy is respect for the individual's autonomy and liberty. John Stuart Mill championed that premise in the 19th century, and it remains a central tenet of our democratic ethos. In a liberal democracy, autonomy is or at least approaches the status of an ultimate value. G. DWORKIN, THE THEORY AND PRACTICE OF AUTONOMY (1988); Strauss, *Toward a Revised Model of Attorney–Client Relationship,* 65 N.C.L.REV. 315, 336 n. 92, 339 (1987). The individual's ability to use counsel as a representative in litigation promotes the individual's autonomy; it enables the individual to exercise more effective control over the course of the litigation-and, therefore, more practical control over his own future. *Id.* Goodpaster, *On the Theory of American Adversary Criminal Trial,* 78 J. CRIM.L. & CRIMINOLOGY 118, 125 (1987). The individual is no longer totally dependent on the decisions of a judge or magistrate; aided by counsel, the individual himself can make informed decisions to protect his personal, private interests.

§ 1.3 THE REQUISITES FOR EFFECTIVE ASSISTANCE OF COUNSEL

Counsel's participation in litigation will serve the private and public interests discussed in the last section only when counsel's representation is competent. As the American Bar Association Committee on Evaluation of Professional Standards pointed out, "[l]awyer competence has been studied and debated extensively in recent years." PROPOSED FINAL DRAFT MODEL RULES OF PROFESSIONAL CONDUCT 8 (1981). The Committee underscored the need for upgrading attorney competence by prescribing the duty of competence in the very first rule in the Model Code of Professional Responsibility. ABA MODEL RULES OF PROFESSIONAL CONDUCT Rule 1.1 (1983). Incompetent counsel can neither protect their client's private interests nor help insure the effective operation of the system.

The purpose of this text is to help law students become competent trial counsel. The question then naturally arises: What bodies of knowledge and skills must a competent litigator possess?

The litigator unquestionably must understand the psychological dynamics of the courtroom. The available empirical data demonstrates that jurors are sensitive to the courtroom demeanor of attorneys and witnesses. *See generally* J. FREDERICK, THE PSYCHOLOGY OF THE AMERICAN JURY (1988); D. HERBERT & R. BARRETT, ATTORNEY'S MASTER GUIDE TO COURTROOM PSYCHOLOGY: HOW TO APPLY BEHAVIORAL SCIENCE TECHNIQUES FOR NEW TRIAL SUCCESS (1981); N. NELSON, A WINNING CASE (1991). L. SMITH & L. MALANDRO, COURTROOM COMMUNICATION STRATEGIES (1985); K. TAYLOR, R. BUCHANAN & D. STRAWN, COMMUNICATION STRATEGIES FOR TRIAL ATTORNEYS (1984); D. VINSON, JURY TRIALS: THE PSYCHOLOGY OF WINNING STRATEGY (1986); Timothy, *Demeanor Credibility,* 49 CATH.U.L.REV. 903 (2000). To be sure, it is debatable whether a person's demeanor is a reliable indicator of the truthfulness or truth of their testimony. Wellborn, *Demeanor,* 76 CORNELL L.REV. 1075 (1991). However, it seems undeniable that lay jurors attach a good deal of significance to witnesses' demeanor. Communications experts commonly assert that when one person speaks to another, the speaker's nonverbal conduct accounts for more than 50% of the information communicated. J. KESTLER, QUESTIONING TECHNIQUES AND TACTICS § 2.49 (1982). If the speaker's statement is laden with emotion, more than 90% of the message can be communicated nonverbally. K. TAYLOR, *supra* at 49. The subject-matter of many cases—the loss of a child in a wrongful death action or a vicious beating in a prosecution—is likely to generate emotion. A case can be lost if the attorney overlooks the psychological dimension of persuasive trial advocacy.

A litigator must also have a working knowledge of evidence law and procedure. Evidentiary rules and procedural devices are tools of the litigator's craft. However, standing alone, that legal knowledge does not guarantee competent representation at trial. Suppose, for instance, that on the very eve of trial, an attorney with a mastery of evidence and procedure agreed to appear as counsel to try a case like *United States v. I.B.M., WPPSS,* or *Houston Lighting & Power Co.*—a "documents" case involving millions of pages of writing. It is virtually a foregone conclusion that notwithstanding his superior knowledge of evidence and procedure, the attorney's representation will be inadequate. To represent the client adequately, the attorney must have a thorough understanding of the facts. Even a master of evidence and procedure could not digest the facts in a case of that magnitude in such a short time.

But even an attorney who knows both the relevant law and facts may not serve her client well. For example, assume in the last hypothetical that the attorney trying the I.B.M. case closely monitored the discovery in the case and is thoroughly conversant with the facts. Does the attorney's grasp of the law and facts guarantee success at trial? The answer is No. The evidentiary standard for admissibility at trial is quite liberal. The Federal Rules of Evidence define logical relevance as "having any tendency to make the existence of any fact that is of consequence to the determination of the action more probable or less probable than it would be without the evidence." FED.R.EVID. 401, 28 U.S.C.A. That definition is so lax that in a large case, the attorney might be permitted to offer "tens or even hundreds of thousands" of documents into evidence. Quinn, *Documents at Trial Require Careful Preparation,* LEGAL TIMES, Aug. 19, 1985, at p. 11. In all likelihood that volume of information would overwhelm the trier of fact. In an American Bar Association survey of jurors in complex cases, the jurors' primary complaint was that the attorneys overtried the case and deluged the jury with marginally relevant information. SPEC. COMM. ON JURY COMPREHENSION, A.B.A. LITIGATION SECTION, JURY COMPREHENSION IN COMPLEX CASES 27–28, 31 (1990). The attorney must reduce the quantity of evidence to manageable proportions for the trier. For that matter, even drastically reducing the volume of information is not enough; if the trier of fact is to understand and remember the evidence, the order of presentation must be logical. One of the litigator's worst enemies is confusion. McElhaney, *The Risk of Confusion,* 74 A.B.A.J. 100 (Jan. 1988). The trial presentation must have simplicity and continuity. Above all else, like an office attorney structuring a real estate transaction, a litigator must be an effective planner. *See* L. BROWN & E. DAUER, PERSPECTIVES ON THE LAWYER AS PLANNER (1978). To be a competent litigator, an attorney must develop both planning skills and the prudential, professional judgment needed to exercise those skills.

In summary, a competent trial attorney must: be sensitive to the psychology of the courtroom; know the relevant evidentiary and procedural law; master the facts of the case; and carefully plan the trial presentation at the strategic and tactical levels.[2]

---

2. In truth, a competent trial attorney needs an additional attribute: a good sense of humor. As the saying goes in the litigation trade, you have to be able "to take a

§ 1.4 THE STRUCTURE OF THIS TEXT

Having identified the requisites of competent counsel, we have attempted to design a text that will help law students acquire those requisites. The text is systems engineered with that purpose in mind. Educational systems engineering is an approach to curriculum design. According to that approach, after identifying the knowledge and skills needed in a particular professional position, the curriculum planner should tailor the course of instruction to give the students precisely that knowledge and those skills.

This text is tailored to achieve that objective within the framework of a typical Trial Practice course at a good law school. In our experience, the Trial Practice courses at most law schools have a number of common characteristics. Rather than expecting students to try full cases at the outset of the course, most instructors proceed step by step and introduce the students to one major stage of the trial at a time: voir dire, opening statements, direct examination, etc. In addition, although there may be some regular class discussion hours, the bulk of the learning occurs in laboratory sessions. The laboratory sessions are conducted by a full-time or adjunct professor, and the sessions include student performances, critiques by the other students, and critiques by the professor. Many courses culminate with a full trial at the end of the semester.

Just as this text makes an assumption about the structure of the Trial Practice course, it makes an assumption about the content of the balance of the curriculum at the law school. We presume that the course is not the primary teaching vehicle for evidence or procedure. This text takes as a given that the student is familiar with evidence and procedure; the student has taken those courses or is taking them concurrently with Trial Practice. This text is not a reprise of evidence or procedure; rather, as the following paragraphs explain, this text concentrates on the other skills requisite for competent trial advocacy.

Courtroom Psychology

Section 1.3 noted that one of those requisites is sensitivity to the psychology of the courtroom. Chapters 4–15 of this text deal with the individual stages of the trial. Each chapter discusses the psychological considerations arising at that stage. For example, Chapter 10 on cross-examination considers the techniques the cross-examiner can use to pressure the witness into unfavorable demeanor, nonverbal conduct suggesting uncertainty or guilt that can effectively impeach the witness in the jurors' eyes. Several chapters refer to the empirical studies that have been conducted to refine attorneys' understanding of the dynamics of advocacy. The chapters are replete with references to S. HAMLIN, WHAT MAKES JURIES LISTEN (1985).[3]

joke." To help the reader develop the necessary sense of humor, we have interspersed artwork from CHARLES BRAGG ON THE LAW (1984) throughout this text. The art-work is reprinted with the kind permission of Warner Books/New York.

3. There is an excellent summary of the available empirical studies in Appendix 10 to JURY COMPREHENSION IN COM-

Mastery of the Facts

Another requisite is mastery of the facts. The text employs several techniques to aid students in developing that mastery. One of the early chapters, Chapter 3, is devoted to strategic planning. That chapter includes an assignment requiring the students to write a case evaluation memorandum, analyzing their case to identify their best trial theory and theme. That assignment will necessitate that the students become intimately familiar with the facts in their case file early in the course. (If the professor assigns you a new case file for the full trial at the end of the semester, the professor might require you to rewrite a second case evaluation memorandum for the case file.)

The laboratory exercises and final trials reinforce the point that the attorney must thoroughly digest the case file. As previously stated, Chapters 4–15 dissect the trial process and analyze the various stages of the trial. Each chapter contains laboratory exercises. Each chapter emphasizes that effective advocacy at that stage requires a thorough understanding of the facts in the file. For instance, Chapter 5 on opening statement observes that the most common objection to remarks in opening is that a remark is "argumentative;" during opening—as opposed to closing argument—the attorney must refrain from inviting the jury to draw inferences from the expected testimony. The chapter explains that to avoid the argumentative objection, the attorney delivering the opening statement must engage in an exercise of *res ipsa loquitur*, making the facts speak for themselves. The attorney must know the facts and the plausible inferences from the facts so well that she can marshal the facts to make the desired inferences obvious without expressly stating the inferences. In the laboratory session based on Chapter 5, the student must be particularly conscious of the argumentative objection.

In addition, to encourage students to master the facts in their case files, we urge the instructor to require the students in the laboratory sessions to deliver their jury speeches and conduct their witness examinations while holding at most a single sheet of paper. Each chapter contains an illustration of the attorney's presentation for that trial stage. All the illustrations are based on the *Scott* case file set out in Chapter 2. For example, Chapter 5 contains a sample opening statement in the *Scott* case. The initial part of the sample is a verbatim text of an opening statement. The last part of the sample is an illustrative, one-page set of handwritten notes that an attorney would use to deliver that opening. A trial attorney cannot maintain effective eye contact with the jury during an opening if he attempts to read from a multi-page script. The student must know the facts so well that he can work from a compact outline during the laboratories.

PLEX CASES, the 1990 report of the Special Committee on Jury Comprehension of   the A.B.A. Section of Litigation.

Like the laboratory exercises, the final trials underscore the imperative that the trial attorney master the factual data in the file. Appendix A sets out the case files for the laboratory sessions on the various stages of the trial discussed in Chapters 4–15. The case files in that appendix are relatively short. Appendix B contains the files for the final trials at the end of the semester. Most of those files are lengthier and more complex. As in the laboratory sessions, the student should be required to make each jury address and conduct each witness examination while working from a concise outline. To fulfill that requirement, the student will have to plumb the case file in depth.

Strategic and Tactical Planning

Lastly, each chapter of the text develops the thesis that litigation is a planning process. The primary thrust of this text is to introduce the student to a strategic philosophy of litigation planning. Chapter 3 introduces the student to the concepts of trial theory and theme used in strategic planning. Unfortunately, in the past, law schools have largely neglected the topic of strategic planning; the focus of the curriculum has been "narrowly doctrinal." Neumann, *On Strategy,* 59 FORDHAM L.REV. 299, 318, 345 (1990). In both litigation and transactional work, the client needs more than a legal technician who can tell the client what the client's legal rights are; the client needs a counselor who can help the client make wise tactical and strategic decisions as to whether and how to exercise legal rights. Chapter 3 leads the student through the strategic steps a litigator progresses through in selecting a theory and theme for trial. Chapters 4–15 shift to the tactical level. Those chapters discuss the planning and structuring of the attorney's presentation at each trial stage. The chapters demonstrate that the early planning step, the choice of theory and theme, should dictate every word the attorney utters during the trial. The old bromides about trial tactics make much more sense understood against the backdrop of the strategic concepts of theory and theme. One bromide is that the attorney ought to end a direct examination on a "high" note. Chapter 9 explains that the "high" note should be the witness's testimony that most directly supports the attorney's theme. Another trial practice adage is that the attorney should begin an opposing witness's cross-examination by eliciting "favorable" admissions. Chapter 10 points out that the expression, "favorable" admissions, is best understood as testimony establishing the cross-examiner's theory of the case. The text discusses these bromides and adages to illustrate the tactical considerations which the planner must be cognizant of. Like evidentiary doctrines, tactics and strategies undergo change and refinement. In practice, to follow those changes, the litigator must keep abreast of the trial practice literature. To familiarize the student with that body of literature, this text includes numerous references to such sources as TRIAL, LITIGATION, THE AMERICAN JOURNAL OF TRIAL ADVOCACY, and THE REVIEW OF LITIGATION.

In each chapter—at each step in the planning process—the text also highlights the relevant ethical constraints. The essence of strategic and tactical planning is making choices. However, the rules of ethics can limit the range of choice. Like an office attorney, a litigator is subject to the ethical code in effect in her jurisdiction. In many respects, the office attorney and the litigator operate under the same ethical rules. Thus, both types of attorneys owe a duty of confidentiality to their client. However, there are also rules applicable only to litigators. For example, Model Rule of Professional Conduct 3.2 imposes a duty on trial attorneys to expedite litigation, and Rule 3.6 regulates trial publicity. Although this text touches primarily upon issues of formal legal ethics, we must add an important caveat. Increasingly, courts are making it clear that they expect civility as well as ethical conduct of counsel. The adversary system is not an excuse for nastiness in dealing with opposing counsel. Many observers have decried a trend toward "Rambo" litigation tactics. 77 A.B.A.J. 63 (Dec. 1991). The late Supreme Court Justice Thurgood Marshall lamented the trend. 78 A.B.A.J. 61 (June 1992). We previously stated that this course is not a reprise of evidence or procedure. Neither is it a review of legal ethics. The text covers only the ethical rules of special interest to the litigator. Even more narrowly, we focus on ethical quandaries facing a planner working within an adversary system of litigation.

As the reader proceeds from chapter to chapter, the reader ought to keep in mind the three basic course objectives: becoming more conscious of the psychological dimension of trial advocacy, learning techniques for mastering the facts in the case file, and developing an understanding of litigation as a strategic and tactical planning process. It would be foolish to assert that at the end of this course, every student will be competent to try a major case. However, the student should appreciate the requisites for competent trial advocacy and have begun the career-long task of perfecting those skills.

Chapter 2

A CASE FILE

Table of Sections

§ 2.1 INTRODUCTION

This chapter sets out the file for the *Scott* case. As Chapter 1 indicated, Chapters 3–15 discuss the various strategic and tactical steps in planning a trial. Those chapters not only describe the planning steps; they also illustrate the steps. Almost all of the illustrations are based on the facts in the *Scott* case. We decided to base the illustrations on a single case file for several pedagogic reasons. The use of a single file saves time. If we had used different cases to exemplify the various steps, the chapter would have to pause to give you the factual background about the new case. Once you have read this case file, you will be oriented to the setting for most of the concrete illustrations in the following chapters. Moreover, the use of a single file is more realistic. As you progress from chapter to chapter, you will have the experience of working with a case file for an extended period of time,as you do in practice. As each week passes, you should gain additional, more sophisticated insights into the significance of the facts in the file. As the semester wears on, subtler inferences should emerge from the facts. Many insights come to a litigator by virtue of associational logic. You are reading a newspaper article in the morning or listening to a news broadcast at night, and suddenly something "clicks"—a chance association between the article and the facts of your case suggests an argument for the case. The longer you live with a single case file in this course, the more likely you are to have an associational logic experience.

The file is named after Robert Scott. He is the defendant in a civil action and a prosecution. A Mr. Peter Williams claims that Scott and a third party, Richard Rogers, attacked Williams in the hallway of the second floor of the Senator Hotel. The hotel is located in the city of

11

Morena, the largest city in El Dorado. Rogers fled town shortly after the alleged attack. Williams has initiated a tort action against Scott. In addition, the local prosecutor has filed an information, charging Scott with various violations of the Penal Code of the State of El Dorado. Williams has answered in the tort action and entered a not guilty plea in the prosecution. Scott insists that he had nothing to do with the attack on Williams.

The litigation arises in the State of El Dorado. El Dorado is the newly admitted 51st state of the Union. It generally follows modern common law. El Dorado resorts to the common law of crimes to supplement its Penal Code. However, pursuant to its authority under the state constitution, the El Dorado Supreme Court has adopted state court rules identical to the Federal Rules of Civil Procedure, Criminal Procedure, and Evidence.

To keep the case file current, we have used the following dating system. The case comes to trial this year, 19YR. The attack allegedly occurred in the immediately preceding year, 19YR–1. For example, if you are using this text in 2002, 2002 would be 19YR; but the date of the alleged attack would fall in 2001. If a date in the file is designated as 19YR–10, that date would be 1992.

§ 2.2　THE *SCOTT* CASE FILE

PEOPLE OF THE STATE OF EL DORADO v. SCOTT

WILLIAMS v. SCOTT

The criminal case involves mayhem and assault with a deadly weapon. The civil case involves the torts of assault and battery. The following witnesses will give the following testimony:

PETER WILLIAMS

Williams is a 65–year-old night desk clerk at the Senator Hotel at 105 West F Street in a slum area of Morena. He will testify that at approximately 1:20 a.m. on the morning of January 19, 19YR–1, while he was on duty at the hotel desk, he heard a bottle hit the sidewalk outside the hotel. He went out, observed the glass on the sidewalk, and looked up. He determined that the bottle had come from room 212; the room was directly above and the only room with a light on. He could not see anyone in the room at the time. However, he thought he heard music coming from the room and decided to go up to see what was going on. As he got off the elevator on the second floor, he met two men who immediately began beating him with their feet and fists. Although there was no light in the hallway, Williams can positively identify the two men as Robert Scott, the defendant, and Dick Rogers. In Williams' first statement to the police, however, he was unable to make a positive identification. He said, "I know it was Rogers and I think it was Scott because it kind of looked like him and I've had trouble with the two of them before, and besides they always hang around together."

Williams was knocked to the ground where the assailants attempted to stomp on his head with their feet. They then dragged him into the restroom where they continued beating him. At one point, Rogers attempted to choke Williams with his own necktie. Finally, Rogers and Scott stopped beating Williams but told him, "Keep quiet, or we'll kill you." They left Williams lying there on the floor in the bathroom. Williams received a torn right ear, severe swelling to the right side of the face, a badly bruised and swollen right eye, and numerous contusions over his body.

Williams feels that there was absolutely no provocation for the attack. The only thing he did was ask, "What about that bottle?" Williams has had very little contact with Scott or Rogers other than telling them on numerous occasions that they could not use the employees-only elevator. On one such occasion, Scott made a derogatory remark about Williams' old age. Williams is very sensitive about his age; he considers himself to be in very good shape for a 65–year-old. Williams drinks regularly but does not consider himself an alcoholic. On the morning in question, Williams had consumed three boilermakers approximately 30 minutes before the incident.

Williams can testify about the physical layout of the hotel. He can draw or verify a diagram of the layout.

JAN TAYLOR

Ms. Taylor is a 25–year-old policewoman. On January 19, she was assigned to regular patrol duty in the downtown area. At about 1:30 a.m., she received a dispatch to go to the Senator Hotel, 105 West F Street, a seedy area, to investigate an assault. She first observed the victim, Peter Williams, sitting behind the front desk in the hotel. She saw that he was bleeding profusely from his right ear, was badly bruised, and had a swollen right eye. At that time, Williams stated, "I was beat up by two guys, one of them was definitely Dick Rogers, and the other, I'm not sure, but it might have been Robert Scott in room 212."

Taylor then proceeded to Rogers' room, 302, and entered after knocking. Taylor discovered that Rogers had apparently fled the scene without taking his personal property. Taylor immediately went to Scott's room, 212, and knocked on the door. There was no answer at first, but Scott then opened the door from the side. Scott was bare-chested and dressed only in shorts; he seemed to have just gotten out of bed. Taylor identified herself and advised Scott of his constitutional rights per P.D. Form 115 before any questioning. Scott stated that he understood his rights and was willing to speak to Taylor. He stated that he was a trucker, had been in Morena for a little over four weeks, and was leaving the following day. Scott stated that he had been awakened by some commotion and shouting in the hall. He had not gotten out of bed and did not know what was going on.

Taylor then asked Scott to get dressed. He asked her to hand him his shoes, a pair of brown loafers. As Taylor picked up one of the shoes near her, she observed red stains on the bottom. The stains appeared to be blood. When Taylor asked Scott about the stains, he said, "Maybe I lent them to someone." Scott was then arrested for mayhem and assault with a deadly weapon. Taylor seized the following items from the room: one pair of brown loafers with red stains found to the left of the bed; one plastic glass found on the nightstand to the left of the bed; and one bottle of Hiram Walker Ten High with amber fluid found on the floor on the left side of the bed. Scott and the seized evidence were then transported to the jail. The shoes and blood samples were preserved in a plastic bag and held in the evidence locker until January 21. At that time, they were turned over for laboratory analysis to Steve Sykes, police chemist. They were later picked up that same day and returned to the evidence locker. They will remain in the locker until the date of trial when Officer Taylor will bring them to the courtroom.

Officer Taylor returned to the hotel during the day of January 19th. She observed the hallway and bathroom in which the alleged beating occurred. She took two photographs showing blood on the floor and wall of the bathroom. Taylor can identify each of the items of physical evidence listed above by her initials, "JT," and the date, "1/19," which she placed on the articles when she seized them.

STEVE SYKES

Sykes is a 35–year-old chemist for the Morena Police Department. On January 21st, he received a plastic bag containing two brown loafers with stains on the soles from Officer Jan Taylor. Sykes performed a laboratory analysis on the stains. He determined that the stains were blood of the type AB grouping. He then placed the shoes back in the plastic bag and returned the bag to Officer Taylor who was waiting.

JOAN FREEMAN

Ms. Freeman is a 23–year-old, unemployed social worker. On January 19, 19YR–1, she was living in room 213 of the Senator Hotel. She had just arrived from New York and had been staying in the hotel for approximately one week. She was acquainted with Peter Williams, Robert Scott, and Dick Rogers. With the exception of Rogers and Scott, most of the people living in the hotel were elderly. She had spent considerable time with Rogers and Scott since her arrival in Morena. Earlier that evening, she had been in Scott's room; she was drinking with Scott and Rogers. However, she left about 11:30 p.m.

That morning she was awakened by yelling and fighting in the hallway. She looked at the clock and noticed that it was about 1:20 a.m. Although she stuck her head out, the hall was so dark that she could not visually identify any of the people involved. She did see that there were definitely three people fighting. They seemed to be right on top of each other. She feels relatively certain that two were Williams and Rogers; she recognized the voices. However, she did not recognize the third voice at all. She is familiar with Scott's voice and believes that the third person involved in the fight was not Scott. He has a pronounced New York accent. She would not lie to protect Scott. However, she feels that Scott is getting a raw deal. She hates to see Scott, a fellow New Yorker, go to jail for something that someone else did.

ROBERT SCOTT

Scott is a 21–year-old trucker from New York. On January 19, he was staying at the Senator Hotel in room 212. He had been there for approximately four weeks and was scheduled to leave that day, January 19, in the afternoon on a cross country trip. Earlier on the night of January 18th, he, Joan Freeman, and Dick Rogers had been in his room drinking and talking about New York. Joan left at about 11:00 p.m., but he and Rogers continued drinking until about 12:00 when Rogers left and Scott went to bed. Sometime later Scott was awakened by shouting in the hall. The noise did not sound too serious, and he just rolled over and tried to go back to sleep. However, after the noise stopped, he became concerned and went into the hall to see what had happened. There was no one in the hallway, and he went back to his room and to bed.

A very short time later, he was again awakened by knocking at his door. The door opened, and there was a policewoman standing in the doorway. Scott was still drowsy and somewhat embarrassed by the fact that he had on only his underwear. The policewoman said something about an aggravated assault and asked what he knew about it. She did not advise him of his rights until he was in the police car on the way to the jail. Scott told her that he knew absolutely nothing about any assault. She then said that he was a suspect and that he was under arrest. She proceeded to search the room, allegedly for Rogers. She searched under the bed and pulled out his brown loafers. She turned the loafers over and observed some red stains on the soles. When the policewoman asked Scott about the stains, Scott said, "Maybe I lent the shoes to a friend." He now realizes that the answer was rather ill-conceived. However, at the time, he was drowsy, surprised, and a bit angry at the intrusion. He believes that when he was walking in the hallway, he must have stepped in the blood without knowing it.

Scott was then transported to the jail. After being advised of his rights, he made no further statements to the police. He made the following statement to his attorney: I was born in New York City and grew up there with my father, mother, and three brothers. When I was 17, I joined the Navy. I was stationed in Long Beach with the Navy. I had never been in any trouble until 19YR–4 when some of my buddies and I got drunk and decided to rip off a bakery because we were hungry and needed some money. I pled guilty to second degree burglary. The deal was that the charge was supposed to be dropped to a misdemeanor after I finished my probation period, but I don't know whether the charge actually was reduced. I did 30 days in jail on the charge. As much as I dislike the old man, I didn't beat him up on January 19th or any other time. I don't know whether Dick did or not, but I wouldn't blame him if he did. The old guy was constantly hassling us. I want to get this whole thing cleared up. I have to get back to my van line. This thing is costing me a lot of money to sit around and wait for trial.

> Attorney for Plaintiff Peter Williams

SUPERIOR COURT OF EL DORADO COUNTY OF MORENA

PETER WILLIAMS,	)	
Plaintiff	)	NO. 402177
vs.	)	COMPLAINT FOR
ROBERT SCOTT AND RICHARD	)	DAMAGES
ROGERS a.k.a. DICK ROGERS,	)	(Assault)
Defendants	)	

Plaintiff alleges:

I

The defendants, ROBERT SCOTT and RICHARD ROGERS, are and at all times mentioned herein were residents of Morena, El Dorado.

II

The cause of action sued upon is a cause of action in tort which accrued in Morena County, El Dorado.

III

On or about January 19, 19YR–1, at or near 105 West F Street in Morena, the defendants assaulted and battered the plaintiff by threatening to strike the plaintiff and violently striking the plaintiff in and about his face, head, and body.

IV

By reason of the defendants' acts, the plaintiff was placed in great fear for his life and physical well-being.

V

By reason of the wrongful and malicious acts of the defendants and each of them and the fright caused the plaintiff, the plaintiff has suffered extreme and severe mental anguish and physical pain and has been injured in mind and body as follows: severe contusions and lacerations around the head, face, and right ear; permanent impairment of hearing and vision, all to the plaintiff's damage in the sum of $15,000.

VI

By reason of the defendants' wrongful and malicious acts, the plaintiff was required to and did expend money and incur obligations for medical services, drugs, and sundries reasonably required in the treatment and relief of the emotional disturbance and injuries he sustained in the sum of $2,000.

VII

By reason of the defendants' wrongful and malicious acts, the plaintiff was prevented from attending to his usual occupation and thereby lost earnings during the period of January 19, 19YR–1, to the present. The plaintiff is informed and believes and, on such information and belief, alleges that he will be prevented from attending to his usual occupation for a future period he cannot now ascertain and will thereby suffer further loss of earnings in an amount which has not yet been ascertained. Plaintiff will ask leave of court to amend his complaint when the sum has been ascertained.

VIII

In making this unprovoked attack on plaintiff defendants acted willfully, wantonly, maliciously, and oppressively. The acts justify the award of exemplary and punitive damages in the amount of $100,000.

WHEREFORE, the plaintiff prays judgment as follows:

(1) For general damages in the sum of $15,000;

(2) For medical and related expenses according to the proof;

(3) For lost earnings, past and future, according to the proof;

(4) For exemplary and punitive damages in the sum of $100,000;

(5) For costs of suit incurred herein; and

(6) For such other and further relief as the Court may deem proper.

Dated: August 17, 19YR–1

_____
Attorney for Plaintiff
Attorney for Defendant Robert Scott

SUPERIOR COURT OF EL DORADO COUNTY OF MORENA

PETER WILLIAMS,	)	
Plaintiff	)	
vs.	)	NO. 402177
ROBERT SCOTT and RICHARD	)	ANSWER
ROGERS a.k.a. DICK ROGERS,	)	
Defendants	)	

Comes now the defendant ROBERT SCOTT and, severing himself from his co-defendants, admits, denies, and avers as follows:

I

This answering defendant admits that he is now a resident of Morena, El Dorado. The defendant has no information or belief sufficient to enable him to answer the remaining allegations of paragraph I and, basing his denial on that ground, denies those allegations.

II

This defendant has no information or belief sufficient to enable him to answer the allegations of paragraph II and, basing his denial on that ground, denies those allegations.

III

This answering defendant denies the allegations of paragraph III. This answering defendant specifically denies that he injured the plaintiff in any manner.

IV

This answering defendant has no information or belief sufficient to enable him to answer the allegations of paragraph IV and, basing his denial on that ground, denies those allegations.

V

This answering defendant denies the allegations of paragraphs V, VI, VII, and VIII. This answering defendant specifically denies that the plaintiff was damaged in any manner or sum alleged or to be alleged by any conduct of this answering defendant.

WHEREFORE, the defendant prays that the suit be dismissed as against him and for costs of suit incurred.

DATED: August 29, 19YR–1

_____
Attorney for Defendant
Robert Scott

ACTION NO. 4776 DEFENDANT Robert Scott

VIOLATION 203.245 Penal Code

THE PEOPLE OF THE STATE OF EL DORADO
vs. THE DEFENDANT ABOVE NAMED

IN THE MUNICIPAL COURT
IN THE CITY AND COUNTY OF MORENA
STATE OF EL DORADO

COMPLAINT

STATE OF EL DORADO   )
CITY AND COUNTY OF MORENA   )

PETER WILLIAMS, being duly sworn deposes and says on information and belief that:

COUNT I.   The said defendant did in the City and County of Morena, on or about the 19th day of January A.D. 19YR–1, commit the crime of Felony, to wit: Violating Section 203 of the Penal Code of the State of El Dorado, in that the said defendant did then and there wilfully, unlawfully, and maliciously split the ear of Peter Williams, a human being.

COUNT II.   The said defendant did in the City and County of Morena, on or about the 19th day of January A.D. 19YR–1, commit the crime of Felony, to wit: Violating Section 245(a) of the Penal Code of the State of El Dorado, in that said defendant did then and there wilfully and unlawfully commit an assault upon Peter Williams with means of force likely to produce great bodily injury, to wit, fists and shoes.

Subscribed and sworn to before me on   )
)   /s/   Peter Williams
)   Address 4700 Bryant
/s/   Ronald Clark   )   Telephone 291–6722
        Deputy District Attorney   )
        City and County of Morena   )
        State of El Dorado   )

1 TYPE OF REPORT	2 CSI NOTIFIED	3	PARTIAL RECOVERY		POLICE DEPARTMENT		✓ IF KEY REPORT
1 ☒ CRIME			COMPLETE RECOVERY		CRIME REPORT		5 REPORT NUMBER
2 ☐ CASUALTY ☒ YES		4	ALL SUSPECTS ARRESTED				4776
3 ☐ BOTH ☐ NO			☒ SUSPECTS OUTSTANDING				

6 CRIME CODE SECTION 203, 245   **SOURCE**   **7 CRIME DEFINITION** assault, battery, mayhem   **8 CRIME CLASS CODE**

9 LAST NAME, FIRST, MIDDLE	10 FIRM NAME IF CRIME AGAINST BUSINESS
Williams Peter NMI	Senator Hotel

11 RESIDENCE ADDRESS			12 RESIDENCE PHONE
4700 Bryant	CITY Morena	E.D. ZIP CODE	291-6722

13 BUSINESS ADDRESS (IF STUDENT, NAME OF SCHOOL)		14 BUSINESS PHONE
Senator Hotel	CITY 105 West F St., Morena ZIP CODE	985-0199

15 SEX	16 DESC	17 AGE	19 IF VICTIM WAS INJURED, INDICATE CASUALTY DISPOSITION: CHECK (✓) APPROPRIATE BOX
M	C	65	A ☒ TAKEN TO SMC B ☐ TAKEN HOME C ☐ CORONER D ☐ REFUSED AID E ☐ OTHER: (SPECIFY)

18 DATE OF BIRTH	20 SPECIFY EXTENT OF INJURY	21 TRANSPORTING UNIT OR AGENCY
19YR-65	torn ear, swelling face, bruised eye, contusions	ambulance

☐ CHECK (✓) IF REPORTING PERSON IS SAME AS VICTIM AND DO NOT COMPLETE THIS SECTION.

22 LAST NAME, FIRST, MIDDLE	23 SEX	24 DESC	25 AGE	26 DATE OF BIRTH	27 RESIDENCE PHONE	28 BUSINESS PHONE

29 RESIDENCE ADDRESS	30 BUSINESS ADDRESS

31 LOCATION OF OCCURRENCE (INCLUDE CROSS STREETS)	32 LOCATION CODE
Senator Hotel	Downtown

33 DATE OCCURRED	34 TIME OCCURRED	35 DAY OCCURRED	36 DATE REPORTED	37 TIME REPORTED	38 DAY REPORTED
Jan 19-20, 19YR-1	1:30 a.m.	Sat	Sat	2:00 a.m.	Sat.

39 ROBBERY/ASSAULTS ONLY: MEANS OF ATTACK (CHECK (✓) APPROPRIATE BOX)
A ☐ FIREARM   B ☐ KNIFE   C ☐ PHYSICAL/NO WEAPON   D ☒ OTHER WEAPON: (SPECIFY) shoes and fists, necktie

40 CHECK (✓) WHERE APPLICABLE

RESIDENCE	BUSINESS	PUBLIC PREMISES
A ☐ HOUSE	A ☐ BANK/SAVINGS & LOAN J ☐ DEPARTMENT STORE S ☐ THEATER/DRIVE-IN	A ☐ STREET/HIGHWAY/ALLEY
B ☐ APARTMENT/CONDOMINIUM	☐ CREDIT UNION K ☐ CLOTHING STORE T ☐ GAS STATION/GARAGE	B ☐ SCHOOL
C ☒ MOTEL/HOTEL ROOM	B ☐ OFFICE BUILDING L ☐ JEWELRY STORE U ☐ MOTEL/HOTEL	C ☐ PARK/PLAYGROUND
D ☐ DUPLEX/FOURPLEX	C ☐ MEDICAL OFFICE M ☐ SPORTING GOODS/GUNS V ☐ WAREHOUSE	D ☐ PARKING LOT
E ☐ MOBILE HOME	D ☐ DRUG STORE N ☐ TV/RADIO/APPLIANCES W ☐ MANUFACTURING FIRM	E ☐ PUBLIC BUILDING
F ☐ GARAGE ATTACHED	E ☐ BAR O ☐ CAR, MOTORCYCLE OR X ☐ CONSTRUCTION SITE	F ☐ CHURCH
G ☐ GARAGE DETACHED	F ☐ LIQUOR STORE BICYCLE SALES Y ☐ FENCED STORAGE	G ☐ HOSPITAL
H ☐ OTHER:	G ☐ RESTAURANT/FAST FOODS P ☐ PAWNSHOP/SECONDHAND Z ☐ BOX CAR	H ☐ DOWNTOWN MALL
	H ☐ SUPERMARKET Q ☐ LAUNDROMAT/CLEANERS 1 ☐ LONGHAUL TRAILER	I ☐ OTHER:
	I ☐ CONVENIENCE STORE R ☐ COIN OPERATED MACHINES/ 2 ☐ OTHER: PHONE BOOTH	

VEHICLE -- IF CRIME AGAINST VICTIM'S VEHICLE OR INCIDENT OCCURRED IN A VEHICLE, COMPLETE THE FOLLOWING BOXES:

41 A ☐ AUTO C ☐ MOTORCYCLE B ☐ TRUCK D ☐ OTHER	42 MAKE	43 MODEL	44 YEAR	45 LICENSE NO.	46 STATE	47 YEAR	48 VEHICLE COLOR(S)

CHECK (✓) WHERE APPLICABLE	● 49 POINT OF ENTRY		● 50 LOCATION OF ENTRY	● 51 METHOD OF ENTRY	● 52 ALARMS
	WINDOW DOOR OTHER		A ☐ FRONT	A ☐ UNLOCKED/OPEN G ☐ CUT PADLOCK	A ☐ NONE
	A ☐ NONMOVABLE F ☐ SINGLE SWING K ☐ FLOOR		B ☐ REAR	B ☐ PRIED H ☐ REMOVED	B ☐ RINGER
	B ☐ SLIDING G ☐ DOUBLE SWING L ☐ ROOF		C ☐ SIDE	C ☐ BROKE GLASS I ☐ EXPLOSIVE	C ☐ SILENT
	C ☐ CRANK TYPE H ☐ SLIDING M ☐ WALL		D ☐ OTHER	D ☐ CHANNEL LOCKS J ☐ VEHICLE FORCE	D ☐ SILENT/RINGER
	D ☐ DOUBLE HUNG I ☐ OVERHEAD GARAGE N ☒ ALREADY ON			E ☐ PASS KEY/SLIPLOCK K ☐ UNKNOWN	E ☐ NOT SET
	E ☐ LOUVERED OR J ☐ OTHER: PREMISES			F ☐ BODY FORCE L ☐ OTHER:	F ☐ BYPASSED
	☐ WIND-WING O ☐ UNKNOWN				G ☐ DISABLED

	53 CURRENCY/ NOTES	54 JEWELRY/ METALS	55 CLOTHING/ FURS	56 OFFICE EQUIPMENT	57 TV/RADIO ETC	58 FIREARMS	59 HOUSEHOLD GOODS	60 CONSUMABLE GOODS	61 LIVESTOCK	62 MISC.
STOLEN	$	$	$	$	$	$	$	$	$	$
RECOVERED	$	$	$	$	$	$	$	$	$	$

63 ACTIONS TAKEN WHEN INCIDENT REPORTED	1 ☐ CLEARED BY ARREST 3 ☒ MEDICAL RELEASE (BACK OF P.3) 5 ☒ EVIDENCE BOOKED-PROPERTY RECORD NO. 2476
	2 ☒ CLEARED BY CITATION 4 ☐ VEHICLE STORED/IMPOUNDED 6 ☐ FIELD EVIDENCE RELEASE (BACK OF P.3)

64 IF INCLUDED IN REPORT	1 ☒ SUSPECT(S) 3 ☐ ADDITIONAL VICTIM(S) 5 ☐ PROPERTY DESCRIPTION(S) 7 ☒ VICTIM STATEMENT(S) 9 ☒ SUSPECT STATEMENT(S)
	2 ☒ WITNESS(ES) 4 ☒ SUSPECT VEHICLE(S) 6 ☒ PHYSICAL EVIDENCE 8 ☐ WITNESS STATEMENT(S) 10 ☒ OBSERVATIONS

65 REPORT PREPARED BY	66 BADGE	67 DIV	71 APPROVED BY
Officer J. Taylor	42175	Dwntn	Clyde Swindell, 37916

68 ASSISTING OFFICER	69 BADGE	70 DIV	72 BADGE	73 DATE	74 TIME
				Jan 21	1800 hours

FOR RECORDS DIVISION USE ONLY				79 CONNECT-UP NUMBERS
75 CLEARED BY ARREST OTHER	76 RECOVERY	77 UNFOUNDED	78 RECLASSIFICATION	
DATE	DATE	DATE	DATE	

SPD 041 REV 8-77

CRIME REPORT   PAGE 1 OF ____

[E0555]

POLICE

DEPARTMENT OF POLICE   813 Sixth Street

↓ AUTHORIZATION FOR RELEASE OF MEDICAL INFORMATION ↓

TO WHOM IT MAY CONCERN:

I, the undersigned, authorize any sworn representative of the Morena Police Department or the Morena County District Attorney's Office to obtain any of my medical records they deem necessary to assist in the investigation of an incident which occurred on ___January 20_____ , 19 _YR-1_

I hereby relieve you, your organization, or others from any and all civil and/or criminal liability which might result from the disclosure of the information requested. A photocopy of this authorization shall be as valid as the original.

___Peter Williams_____ Date___January 21, 19-YR-1___
Patient's Signature or Parent/Guardian's Signature
if Patient is Under 18 Years of Age

___Fred Houts_____ Date___January 21, 19YR-1___
Witness Signature

Please send the above records to the attention of
___Sergeant Clyde Swindell_____ and
refer to Report No. ___4776_____ .

NOTE: You may retain this copy for your files.

↓ FIELD EVIDENCE RELEASE ↓

I, _____ hereby acknowledge the return to me by the Morena Police Department of the property listed below.

I have been advised that should the property itself be required for evidence in the criminal proceedings in connection with which it was recovered, I should be able to produce it for that purpose.

I understand that should I not be able to produce the property if the same is required by the courts, there is a serious risk that the criminal case involved may have to be dismissed thereby resulting in a considerable waste of time and money and the release of the suspects who have been charged with criminal dealings with my property.

Date: _____ Signed _____

LIST OF PROPERTY ITEMS:

_____
_____
_____
_____
_____

1 ☐ CRIME REPORT SUPPLEMENT	POLICE	3 REPORT NUMBER ● 4776
☐ MOTOR VEHICLE REPORT SUPPLEMENT		
2 CRIME CODE SECTION OR TYPE OF INCIDENT 203, 245	SOURCE	ADDITIONAL PERSONS / SUSPECT VEHICLE

VICTIM OR COMPLAINANT

4 LAST NAME, FIRST MIDDLE (FIRM NAME IF CRIME AGAINST BUSINESS) Williams Peter NMI	5 RESIDENCE PHONE 291-6722	6 BUSINESS PHONE 985-0199
7 ADDRESS WHERE INCIDENT OCCURRED Senator Hotel, 105 West F Street, Morena		8 DATE INCIDENT REPORTED January 20, 19YR-1

SPECIAL INSTRUCTIONS: If it is indicated that the person listed below was BOOKED or CITED, a Clear-Up Report (SPD 100) should NOT be filed.

ADDITIONAL PERSONS

9 SUSPECT ONLY ☒
ARRESTED ☒ BOOKED ☒ CITED
WITNESS ☐
ADDITIONAL VICTIM ☐ INJURED ☐ NON-INJURED

10 LAST NAME, FIRST, MIDDLE Scott Robert A	11 ARREST REPORT/CITATION # 5551	12 CHARGES battery, mayhem
13 RESIDENCE ADDRESS Senator Hotel, above (originally NY, NY)		14 RESIDENCE PHONE above
15 BUSINESS ADDRESS (IF STUDENT, NAME OF SCHOOL) N/A		16 BUSINESS PHONE

17 SEX	18 DESC	19 AGE	20 DATE OF BIRTH	21 HEIGHT	22 WEIGHT	23 BUILD	24 EYES	25 HAIR COLOR/STYLE
M	C	22	19-YR-22	5'11"	150	aver	brn	brn

26 WEAPON: A REVOLVER B AUTOMATIC C RIFLE D SHOTGUN E KNIFE F OTHER — DESCRIBE: shoes
27 OTHER PHYSICAL DESCRIPTION (INCLUDE CLOTHING, FACIAL FEATURES, ETC.) / CASUALTY INFORMATION

9 SUSPECT ONLY ☒
ARRESTED ☐ BOOKED ☐ CITED
WITNESS ☐
ADDITIONAL VICTIM ☐ INJURED ☐ NON-INJURED

10 LAST NAME, FIRST, MIDDLE Rogers Richard	11 ARREST REPORT/CITATION #	12 CHARGES battery, mayhem
13 RESIDENCE ADDRESS same as above (originally Denver, Colorado)		14 RESIDENCE PHONE above
15 BUSINESS ADDRESS (IF STUDENT, NAME OF SCHOOL) N/A		16 BUSINESS PHONE

17 SEX	18 DESC	19 AGE	20 DATE OF BIRTH	21 HEIGHT	22 WEIGHT	23 BUILD	24 EYES	25 HAIR COLOR/STYLE
M	C	25	19YR-25	6'	180	stocky	blue	blonde

26 WEAPON: A REVOLVER B AUTOMATIC C RIFLE D SHOTGUN E KNIFE F OTHER — DESCRIBE:
27 OTHER PHYSICAL DESCRIPTION (INCLUDE CLOTHING, FACIAL FEATURES, ETC.) / CASUALTY INFORMATION

9 SUSPECT ONLY ☐
ARRESTED ☐ BOOKED ☐ CITED
WITNESS ☒
ADDITIONAL VICTIM ☐ INJURED ☐ NON-INJURED

10 LAST NAME, FIRST, MIDDLE Freeman Joan L	11 ARREST REPORT/CITATION #	12 CHARGES
13 RESIDENCE ADDRESS same as above (originally NY, NY)		14 RESIDENCE PHONE
15 BUSINESS ADDRESS (IF STUDENT, NAME OF SCHOOL)		16 BUSINESS PHONE

17 SEX	18 DESC	19 AGE	20 DATE OF BIRTH	21 HEIGHT	22 WEIGHT	23 BUILD	24 EYES	25 HAIR COLOR/STYLE
F	C	23	19YR-23	5'2"	110	aver	Brn	Brn

26 WEAPON: A REVOLVER B AUTOMATIC C RIFLE D SHOTGUN E KNIFE F OTHER — DESCRIBE:
27 OTHER PHYSICAL DESCRIPTION (INCLUDE CLOTHING, FACIAL FEATURES, ETC.) / CASUALTY INFORMATION

SUSPECT VEHICLE

28 ✓ ONE ONLY: A AUTO B TRUCK C MOTORCYCLE D OTHER:

29 MAKE	30 MODEL	31 YEAR	32 BODY STYLE	33 VEHICLE COLOR(S)
34 LICENSE NUMBER	35 STATE	36 YEAR	38 DETAILS	
37 LICENSE COLOR(S)				

39 CHECK (✓) WHERE APPLICABLE

INTERIOR: Bucket Seats, Bench Seats, Custom, Tape, Unique Item, Sticker Decal, Stereo Tape, Floor Shift, Equip. Added or Missing, "List in Details (Box 38)"

EXTERIOR: Sticker/Decal, Rust/Primer, Vinyl Top, Custom Paint, Flocked, Painted Inscription

MODIFIED: Front, Rear, Lowered, Raised, Low Rider

BODY DAMAGE: Left, Right, Front, Rear, Top

GENERAL CONDITION: Poor, Fair, Good, Excellent — WHEELS: Mags, Chrome Rims, Unique Size

WINDOWS: Damage R/L Side, Damage Front/Rear, Tinted, Covered, Decal Plaque, Curtains

LIGHTS OUT: R Front, L Front, R Rear, L Rear, Front, Rear

40 REPORT PREPARED BY Officer J. Taylor	41 BADGE 42174	42 DIV DTN	6 DATE Jan.21, YR-1	48 APPROVED BY Clyde Swindell
43 ASSISTING OFFICER	44 BADGE	45 DIV	47 TIME	49 BADGE 3791b	50 DATE Jan 21	51 TIME 1800

SPD 174 (9-77)   ADDITIONAL PERSONS/SUSPECT VEHICLE   PAGE   OF   (E4483)

	CRIME REPORT SUPPLEMENT		MEMORANDUM	POLICE			REPORT NUMBER
	INCIDENT REPORT SUPPLEMENT MOTOR VEHICLE REPORT SUPPLEMENT		OTHER		SUPPLEMENTARY INVESTIGATION REPORT		

CRIME CODE SECTION OR TYPE OF INCIDENT — SOURCE

VICTIM OR COMPLAINANT

LAST NAME, FIRST, MIDDLE (FIRM NAME IF CRIME AGAINST BUSINESS) — RESIDENCE PHONE — BUSINESS PHONE

ADDRESS WHERE INCIDENT OCCURRED — DATE INCIDENT REPORTED

NARRATIVE SECTION / PROPERTY DESCRIPTION — DOLLAR VALUE

ITEM #		
1	The victim who was the night clerk at the hotel heard a bottle hit the side-	
2	walk outside the suspect's room. He went up to room #212 to find out what	
3	was going on. He was met by ROGERS, Dick, and SCOTT, Robert. They began	
4	beating him with their feet and fists. They knocked him to the ground and	
5	tried to stomp on his head with their feet. They then knocked him into the	
6	restroom where they continued beating him. The suspects made the above	
7	statement as they tried to choke the victim with his own necktie. SCOTT	
8	was arrested inside the hotel. ROGERS ran out the front door. The victim	
9	received a torn right ear, severe swelling to right side of face, badly	
10	bruised and swollen right eye, and numerous contusions.	
11	VICTIM'S NAME: WILLIAMS, Peter (night clerk, hotel)	
12	ADDRESS: 4700 Bryant	
13	STATEMENT: "I went upstairs to see about the bottle. Rogers and Scott	
14	started hitting me. They said, 'Shut up or we'll kill you.'"	
15	STATEMENT OF ARRESTED PERSON: After being advised of his rights, the de-	
16	fendant said, "What happened? Did the hotel get robbed? I don't know any-	
17	thing. I've been here about four weeks. I'm a teamster, and I've got to	
18	leave town with a load in a couple of hours. Those are my shoes. Maybe I	
19	let someone use them and my clothes."	
20	STATEMENT OF OFFICER: At approximately 0120, WILLIAMS went to the second	
21	floor of the Senator Hotel. WILLIAMS was checking for the person or persons	
22	who had thrown a bottle to the ground floor. WILLIAMS met SCOTT and ROGERS	
23	in the hallway and asked about the bottle. At this time, both suspects	
24	began to hit the victim with their fists and knocked him to the floor.	

REPORTING OFFICER		BADGE	DIV	DATE	APPROVED BY			
ASSISTING OFFICER		BADGE	DIV	TIME	BADGE	DATE	TIME	

NPD 105 (REV 3-77)

SUPPLEMENTARY INVESTIGATION REPORT   PAGE ____ OF ____

[E4404]

FORM COMPLETION INSTRUCTIONS

This form is provided for you to list information relating to the incident you have reported to the Sacramento Police Department.

It is only necessary for you to complete the Narrative Section on the front side of this form. All other sections will be completed by Police Department personnel. Type or print clearly using pencil or black pen. Please supply the required information according to the following instructions:

List any additional information available (such as brand or manufacturer's name, model name or number, serial number, etc.) for stolen or lost items which have already been reported *missing to the Sacramento Police Department*. List all other missing articles which were not included in the initial police report as follows:

- Item #: Number each item to be listed consecutively. This makes the report easier to read.
- Property Description: Use as many lines as necessary to describe the item as completely as possible. Give the name of the article. Where appropriate, describe the article as MAN'S, LADY'S, BOY'S, GIRL'S, CHILD'S, or INFANT'S. For each item listed include (when applicable) the number of articles missing, brand or manufacturer's name, model name or number, manufacturer's serial number, size, style, color, material, and condition. Show any initials, inscriptions, dates, engravings, or other marks of identification. List information regarding the purchase date and place of purchase if known. For bicycles: Indicate if the bicycle was licensed or not. If it was licensed, list the license number and include the name of the city (or county) where the bicycle was licensed.
- Dollar Value: List the estimated dollar value of the item. If the value is not known, write UNKNOWN in this column.

EXAMPLES:

ITEM #	NARRATIVE SECTION PROPERTY DESCRIPTION	DOLLAR VALUE
1	Color portable television, Sony, 15" screen, "Trinitron" model,	
2	serial #5257695, engraved Driver's License #P521350, dark brown wood case,	
3	built-in antenna, 2 years old, left side of case was scratched.	375.00
4		
5	Lady's dinner ring, size 7, silver setting with ¼ carat diamond. Shape of	
6	setting is similar to the number "9".	650.00
7		
8	Boy's bicycle, Schwinn, "Stingray" model, serial number S3217826, chrome	
9	frame, black seat, handlebars wrapped with black tape, Sacramento City	
10	license number 27812.	Unknown

After completing the list of missing property, enter your name and the other information requested below. Mail (or deliver) the completed form to the Sacramento Police Department, Public Counter, 813 6th Street, Sacramento, CA 95814.

LAST NAME, FIRST, MIDDLE		RESIDENCE PHONE	BUSINESS PHONE	
RESIDENCE ADDRESS				
NUMBER	STREET	CITY	STATE	ZIP CODE

_____   _____

Signature   Date

If you have any questions, phone 449-5476.

[E4485]

☐ 1 CRIME REPORT SUPPLEMENT ☐ 4 MEMORANDUM ☐ 2 INCIDENT REPORT SUPPLEMENT ☐ 5 OTHER: ☐ 3 MOTOR VEHICLE REPORT SUPPLEMENT	POLICE	**POLICE DEPARTMENT** **SUPPLEMENTARY INVESTIGATION REPORT**	3 REPORT NUMBER	

2 CRIME CODE SECTION OR TYPE OF INCIDENT	SOURCE

VICTIM OR COMPLAINANT

4 LAST NAME, FIRST, MIDDLE (FIRM NAME IF CRIME AGAINST BUSINESS)	5 RESIDENCE PHONE	6 BUSINESS PHONE
7 ADDRESS WHERE INCIDENT OCCURRED		8 DATE INCIDENT REPORTED

9 NARRATIVE SECTION

Both suspects began to kick the victim's head and chest area with their shoes. The victim was then pushed into the second floor restroom where the suspects continued the beating. The suspects told the victim to keep quiet or they would kill him. The suspects then left. The victim was able to get downstairs and call the police. Suspect ROGERS apparently came downstairs and fled out the front door. ROGERS left his belongings behind. SCOTT apparently returned to his room. I received a call to the hotel and contacted the victim in the lobby. There was blood all down the right side of the victim's shirt. His ear was extremely bloody and swollen as was his left eye. The victim stated that the suspects were staying in rooms #212 and 302. I then proceeded to room #212 with the other desk clerk. The sergeant knocked on the door but failed to receive an answer.

As the clerk started to use his key, suspect SCOTT opened the door. We asked to step into the room and were granted permission by the suspect. I then identified myself and asked to see his identification. SCOTT removed his ID from his wallet. At this time, SCOTT was bare-chested and dressed in only his shorts. I then advised him of his constitutional rights per PD Form 115 prior to any questioning. He then stated that he has been in Morena for a little over four weeks and was unemployed. He stated that he had been in the Navy and was trying to become a teamster. I then asked SCOTT to get dressed. SCOTT asked that I hand him his shoes, a pair of brown loafers. There were two pairs of shoes on the floor. I picked up one of the brown shoes nearest him. I asked if this was the one he wanted.

10 REPORTING OFFICER	11 BADGE	12 DIV	16 DATE	18 APPROVED BY		
12 ASSISTING OFFICER	14 BADGE	15 DIV	17 TIME	19 BADGE	20 DATE	21 TIME

SPD 106 (REV 3-77)   SUPPLEMENTARY INVESTIGATION REPORT   PAGE ____ OF ____

	POLICE DEPARTMENT	
☐ CRIME REPORT SUPPLEMENT ☐ MEMORANDUM ☐ INCIDENT REPORT SUPPLEMENT ☐ OTHER: ☐ MOTOR VEHICLE REPORT SUPPLEMENT	SUPPLEMENTARY INVESTIGATION REPORT	3 REPORT NUMBER

2 CRIME CODE SECTION OR TYPE OF INCIDENT   SOURCE

VICTIM OR COMPLAINANT

4 LAST NAME, FIRST, MIDDLE (FIRM NAME IF CRIME AGAINST BUSINESS)   5 RESIDENCE PHONE   6 BUSINESS PHONE

7 ADDRESS WHERE INCIDENT OCCURRED   8 DATE INCIDENT REPORTED

9 NARRATIVE SECTION

He stated yes. At this time, I turned the shoe over and observed red stains

on the bottom. I then picked up the mate and observed similar stains on the

bottom of that shoe. SCOTT said that maybe he had lent the shoes to some-

one. I then advised SCOTT that he was under arrest for ADW, P.C. 245.

Since the victim's ear was badly damaged, the suspect was also arrested for

565.050. SCOTT was then transported to city jail.

PHYSICAL EVIDENCE:

While in the presence of SCOTT, I impounded the following items: One (1)

pair of brown loafers with red stains on the sole. These were found on

the floor to the left of the bed. One (1) brown jacket, size 40, with the

name, "Exclusive Europe Craft Import. Made in Austria," found next to the

chair left of the bed. One (1) rust colored shirt, short sleeve with

horizontal blue stripes. Found in the same location as the jacket. One

(1) bottle of Hiram Walker 10 High with amber fluid, found on the floor on

the left side of the bed. One (1) slip of paper, on how to obtain seaman's

papers, found in the top right hand drawer of the dresser on the right

side of the bed. The above items were impounded on tags 114180-181.

These items were transported to the Lab by myself and placed in the

evidence room.

Four pictures were taken by Officer A.M. Aldrich #180. One shows the

restroom on the second floor of the Senator Hotel. The other three are

of the victim at the hospital. I also prepared a diagram of the

layout of Scott's room at the hotel.

10 REPORTING OFFICER		11 BADGE	12 DIV	16 DATE	18 APPROVED BY		
13 ASSISTING OFFICER		14 BADGE	15 DIV	17 TIME	19 BADGE	20 DATE	21 TIME

SFD 186 (REV 3-77)

SUPPLEMENTARY INVESTIGATION REPORT   PAGE _____ OF _____

[E4486]

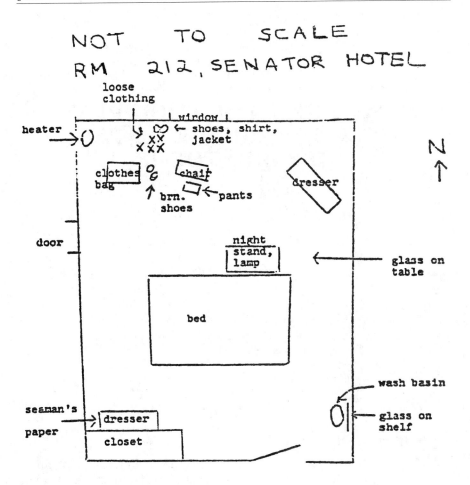

NOT TO SCALE
RM 212, SENATOR HOTEL

JAN TAYLOR
BADGE # 42174

[E4487]

Chapter 3

STRATEGIC LITIGATION PLANNING: THE CHOICE OF THEORY AND THEME

Table of Sections

§ 3.1   INTRODUCTION

Chapter 1 pointed out that a litigator should be an effective planner. To achieve a simple, coherent trial presentation, the litigator must plan her case strategically and tactically. The essence of strategic planning is the choice of a trial theory and a trial theme. As we shall see, at trial the attorney uses the theory to make her presentation simple and the theme to give the presentation continuity.[1] As a generalization, like a plaintiff or prosecutor, a defense attorney must develop a positive theory and theme:

> In a defense of a civil action, says Howard J. Privet, the burden of proof is on the plaintiff. But to win at trial, [as a practical matter] the defense counsel has to go beyond chipping away at the other side's case. "You don't have to prove anything as matter of law," he notes. But as a matter of reality, "to win, you have to make an affirmative assertion. You can't just rely on the technicality of the burden of proof."

1. This chapter is based in part on Imwinkelried, *The Development of Professional Judgment in Law School Litigation Courses: The Concepts of Trial Theory and* *Theme,* 39 VAND.L.REV. 59 (1986). Copyright Vanderbilt Law Review. Reprinted with permission.

Privet, *The Defense Must Make a Positive Statement,* NAT'L L.J., Feb. 8, 1993. As a general proposition, jurors are more comfortable taking a stand for something positive rather casting an essentially negative vote, based on the weakness of the opponent's evidence. It is especially important to think through a theory and theme when the case will be a bench trial. The judge is likely to be impatient for counsel to get to "the heart of the case." McElhaney, *Judge Trials: Litigation Techniques for Trying the Case to the Court,* 78, A.B.A.J. 69 (Mar. 1992). The attorney cannot do so unless she has completed a strategic evaluation of the case in terms of theory and theme.

§ 3.2   THE DEFINITIONS OF THEORY AND THEME

The literature on trial advocacy is replete with references to "theory" and "theme," but the writers rarely define those terms. The literature sometimes suggests that the terms are synonymous. In reality, there is a profound difference between the two concepts.

§ 3.2(A)   A Trial Theory

A trial attorney is a storyteller. As one experienced trial attorney has commented,

> Studying ... video tapes of real-life jury deliberations in ... criminal trials (filmed with the permission of the courts), I made a[n important] discovery: [During deliberations] jurors primarily argue with one another in story format. Trials are essentially story-battles.

Sunwolf, *Talking Story in Trial: The Power of Narrative Persuasion,* 24 THE CHAMPION 26, 26–27 (Oct. 2000). The available psychological research indicates that "[t]he jury seems to organize and remember evidence in narrative form." Burns, *Some Realism (and Idealism) About the Trial,* 31 GA.L.REV. 725, 751 (1997); Call, *Jury Persuasion: Making the Research Work for You,* 32 TRIAL 20 (Apr. 1996)("The Hastie, Penrod and Pennington study ... found that 90 percent of jurors decide on a story model of what happened.... [J]urors ... developed an understanding of the case using [a] story model"); Koski, *Jury Decision-making in Rape Trials: A Review and Empirical Assessment,* 38 CRIM. L.BULL. 21, 26 (Jan.-Feb. 2002)(collecting the literature on jury story construction). The theory is the attorney's story.

For our purposes, a trial theory is the complete set of ultimate facts that the attorney must prove to justify the outcome or legal consequence her client desires. Lubet, *The Trial as a Persuasive Story,* 14 AM.J.TRIAL ADVOC. 77 (1990). Suppose, for example, that the prosecutor in *Scott* selected a battery theory. That theory would necessitate proof of the following ultimate facts: On January 19, 19YR–1, at the Senator Hotel in downtown Morena, two men punched and kicked Peter Williams (the actus reus); they did so unlawfully—without provocation or Williams' consent; they intended to strike Williams (the mens rea); and one of the attackers was Robert Scott (the defendant's identity as the person who committed the actus reus). Or assume that in a contracts lawsuit, the plaintiff is Mr. Pollet and the defendant Ms. Rowland. Mr. Pollet's trial theory might be: On January 1, 19YR, in Morena, Mr. Pollet and Ms. Rowland entered into an agreement; under the agreement, Mr. Pollet promised to pay Ms. Rowland's company $90,000.00, and Ms. Rowland promised to deliver a certain custom generator to Mr. Pollet's plant on March 1; on February 1, Mr. Pollet paid Ms. Rowland the $90,000.00; Ms. Rowland's firm failed to deliver the generator on March 1; due to the lack of the generator, Mr. Pollet's firm had to shut down between March 1 and April 15; and during that period, Mr. Pollet's firm lost $40,000.00 in profits.

The theory must include all the essential legal elements of the cause of action, crime, or defense. There are several ways of learning the elements. The most reliable—but the most expensive and time-consuming—method is legal research into the relevant cases, statutes, and constitutional provisions. More commonly, though, the attorney will refer to a book of pattern jury instructions. For example, a California practitioner might turn to CALJIC, CALIFORNIA JURY INSTRUCTIONS CRIMINAL (6th rev. ed. 1996). There she would find a substantive criminal law instruction on battery, and the instruction would list the actus reus, mens rea, and identity elements of the crime. There are also specialized texts which dissect substantive law doctrines into lists of their essential elements. West Group markets a treatise entitled CAUSES OF ACTION, and Callaghan and Company has a similar set including PLAINTIFF'S PROOF OF A PRIMA FACIE CASE (1987) and DEFENSE AGAINST A PRIMA FACIE CASE (1987). An attorney might consult PLAINTIFF'S PROOF OF A PRIMA FACIE CASE to ascertain the elements of a breach of contract cause of action. That text would tell the attorney that to prove breach of contract, she must establish that: The plaintiff and defendant formed a contract; under the contract, the defendant assumed a particular duty; the plaintiff fulfilled all the conditions to the duty, or the conditions were excused; the defendant breached the duty; and the plaintiff suffered damage because of the breach.

Although jury instruction books and texts such as CAUSES OF ACTION aid the attorney in developing a theory, there is an important difference between a theory and the lists of essential legal elements that are included in those books and texts. The theory is more fact specific than those lists. The lists are couched in abstract, impersonal language. In contrast, the theory should be formulated with the specificity of a pleading. The information that the prosecutor filed against Scott is illustrative. The information does not refer generically to a "victim;" it specifies Peter Williams as the victim. In a contracts suit, while describing his theory in opening statement, the plaintiff's attorney would not be content to state that "the plaintiff and defendant formed a contract." Rather, the attorney would tell the jury that "on January 1, 19YR, at an office in downtown Morena, my client and the defendant entered into an agreement for my client to buy a $90,000.00 generator manufactured at the defendant's upstate plant." To develop a trial theory, the attorney can start with an abstractly worded list of essential legal elements from a book of approved jury instructions; but the attorney must then particularize the theory to the specific facts of her case. The instruction gives you the bare bones of the legal theory, but you must add the flesh of the facts of your case.

In fleshing out your theory, remember that your story must be complete in a human sense as well as a legal sense. Although the law rarely requires that you prove the motive for relevant conduct, jurors want to know why the key actors engaged in the conduct you allege. Cole, *Psychodrama and the Training of Trial Lawyers: Finding the Story,* 21 NO.ILL.L.REV. 1, 4–5 (2001). "Understanding why the actor might do something gives ... meaning to the action and makes the action more likely to have occurred." *Id.* at 5. Before embracing your theory, the jury will want to know the reasons for the human behavior. The defendant breached the contract to deliver the generator because, the day after the parties signed the contract, the market shifted and the bargain turned out to be a terrible deal for the defendant. Or the plaintiff was driving very carefully because she had just purchased an expensive, antique vase and the vase was sitting on the passenger seat. Your theory should posit motives in accord with the jurors' beliefs about the way people act. Ohlbaum, *Basic Instinct: Case Theory and Courtroom Performance,* 66 TEMPLE L.REV. 1, 20 (1993).

§ 3.2(B) A Trial Theme

A trial theme functions as the recurring motif that the attorney uses at trial. The theme is the title or label incorporating the attorney's strongest argument on the pivotal element of his best trial theory.

Revisit the contracts hypothetical. Before choosing a theme, the attorney must select the best trial theory. Suppose that at the outset of the litigation, Mr. Pollet's attorney thought that there were three possible theories: promissory estoppel, an express written contract, and an express oral contract. However, after accepting the case, the attorney conducts some legal research and discovers that El Dorado is one of the jurisdictions which refuses to apply promissory estoppel to commercial transactions. J. CALAMARI & J. PERILLO, THE LAW OF CONTRACTS § 6.3 (4th ed.1998). Upon that discovery, the attorney should abandon the promissory estoppel theory; the theory would be vulnerable to a motion to dismiss under Rule of Civil Procedure 12. The attorney then moves into the discovery stage of the case. Based on some statements by Mr. Pollet in the initial attorney-client interview, the attorney hoped that discovery would unearth a letter from the defendant accepting the terms of an earlier written offer by Mr. Pollet. Unfortunately, that hope did not materialize. Mr. Pollet's attorney should now jettison the express written contract theory; that theory would be vulnerable to a summary judgment motion under Rule 56. By process of elimination, the attorney selects the express oral contract as the theory for trial.

Next, the attorney must identify the pivotal element of the theory: Which element of the theory will be the real battleground at trial? To identify that element, the attorney must carefully review the developments during pretrial discovery. Those developments are vital clues to help you identify the central issue. When Ms. Rowland's attorney deposed Mr. Pollet, the overwhelming majority of the questions related to the issue of contract formation. Later, when Pollet's attorney served Rowland with a set of requests for admissions, the defendant refused to admit the facts relevant to contract formation. However, the defendant readily admitted receipt of the $90,000.00 payment and the fact that her firm never delivered the generator. At the pretrial conference on the eve of trial when the judge pressured the parties for stipulations, Ms. Rowland's attorney confirmed the defense's willingness to make those admissions. It should now be evident to Pollet's attorney that at trial, the linchpin issue will be contract formation. Ms. Rowland may claim that the $90,000.00 was a payment on a debt that Pollet already owed her firm, but she will undoubtedly deny that there was a firm oral agreement to sell Pollet the generator.

Pollet's attorney faces the task of developing an argument to prevail on the pivotal issue of contract formation. During the discovery stage, Pollet deposed Mr. Silverstein, the shipping superintendent of Ms. Rowland's firm. During the hearing, he conceded that: The "almost invariable" practice at the firm is to box merchandise for shipment only after the firm has entered into a final contract to sell the merchandise; on February 15, 19YR, Mr. Raduenz, one of the firm's vice-presidents, ordered him to prepare the generator for shipment to Pollet; he readied the generator for shipment; but late in the afternoon of February 28, Mr. Raduenz countermanded the order. Silverstein's concessions at the deposition give Pollet a powerful argument that the conduct of the defendant's employees evidenced the existence of a final contract.

The last step in formulating a theme is to reduce the best argument to a short, memorable expression that the attorney can use as a motif at trial. The theme "is the common thread that unifies the case." Feder, *Effective Trial Preparation,* 28 TRIAL 79 (July 1992). A trial theme functions in somewhat the same fashion as an effective television or radio advertisement. A good advertisement does not merely repeat the product name over and over again; more importantly, the advertisement highlights the most important reason why consumers should prefer that product over competing products—"the 70,000 mile warranty" or "lowest tar and nicotine." Just as the advertiser attempts to capture the single most attractive feature of the product in the jingle, the attorney tries to encapsulize her most potent argument in the theme. The theme "distills the essence of the case. Like an advertising slogan, it is easy to understand and recall. National advertisers recognize the value of defining their products in a few memorable words, and they pay ad agencies millions of dollars to do it." Booth, *Arguing Damages: The Power of Preparation,* 17 TRIAL 28 (Mar. 1991).

In this case, the attorney might use the old bromide, "Actions speak louder than words." The thrust of the argument will be that although Ms. Rowland now denies the existence of a contract, at the critical time,

February 19YR, all the key personnel at her firm were acting on the assumption that there was a contract. During voir dire examination, opening statement, and closing argument, Pollet's attorney can employ that bromide to highlight the importance of the concessions at Silverstein's deposition. Doing so will help the jurors remember Silverstein's concessions during their deliberations. Pollet's attorney's judgment is that those concessions are Pollet's best hope for winning the contract formation issue; and if that judgment is correct, the use of the theme, "Actions speak louder than words," maximizes the probability of a plaintiff's verdict.

This theme increases the probability precisely because it will help the jury remember Pollet's most persuasive argument on the key issue in the case. Contrast this theme with other possible themes such as "a firm understanding" or "a clear agreement." Those expressions would be ineffective themes. They merely repeat the conclusion that Pollet's attorney wants the jury to reach: There was "a firm understanding" or "clear agreement" between Pollet and Rowland. Unless both Rowland's attorney and the jury are exceptionally weak-willed, Pollet's attorney cannot expect to win a verdict by the simple expedient of repeating the desired conclusion over and over again. "Actions speak louder than words" is preferable because it embodies a common sense argument to convince the jury to come to the conclusion. Just as an effective advertisement tells the consumer *why* to buy a particular product, a good theme incorporates an argument answering the question *why* should the jury resolve the pivotal issue in favor of the attorney's client. That is the argument that you want the jurors to focus on in the deliberation room. Tierney, *A Little Different View of Final Argument,* THE PRACTICAL PROSECUTOR, Fall 2000, at 25. If the argument is one that lay jurors are comfortable with and the theme aids the jurors to remember the argument, the theme will help the jurors "recall and restate" the argument "during deliberations." Crawford, *Make the Listening Easy for Jurors,* TRIAL, 54, 56 (June 1996). Thus, the theme can carry the day during deliberations.

§ 3.3   THE PRETRIAL CHOICE OF THEORY AND THEME

On the eve of trial, the attorney must formalize make the choice of theory and theme. This section describes the analytic process that the attorney should work through to make that choice. The process spans the pretrial intake, pleading, discovery, and motion stages.

§ 3.3(A)   The Intake Stage

At this stage, the attorney accepts the case and first interviews the client. At this early juncture, one of the attorney's principal goals is to identify every conceivable theory of the case. D. BINDER & P. BERGMAN, FACT INVESTIGATION: FROM HYPOTHESIS TO PROOF (1984). Perhaps the worst sin the attorney can commit at this stage is premature diagnosis. D. BINDER & S. PRICE, LEGAL INTERVIEWING AND COUNSELING: A CLIENT CENTERED APPROACH 86

(1977). The client probably has not disclosed to the attorney all the information the client possesses; the client may forget some facts and withhold others until the attorney wins the client's trust. Further, the attorney has not yet spoken with other witnesses who can furnish additional or conflicting information. Finally, the attorney may know little or nothing about the areas of law involved in the case. For all these reasons, the attorney should use this stage primarily to develop a list of plausible theories. The attorney should brainstorm and engage in the type of imaginative factual analysis expected of law students on first-year examinations. *See* S. KINYON, INTRODUCTION TO LAW STUDY AND LAW EXAMINATIONS 126 (1971).

Adopt the perspective of the prosecutor in *Scott*. Functionally, the prosecutor's client is Peter Williams. After interviewing Williams, the prosecutor ought to review the facts with a view to identifying every conceivable theory raised by those facts. Those facts should alert the prosecutor that at least four crimes have possibly been committed: assault with a deadly weapon (ADW), attempted murder, battery, and maiming.

§ 3.3(B) The Pleading Stage

The next major stage in pretrial processing is pleading. The function of the pleading stage is to eliminate theories lacking legal merit. The attorney should abandon any theory that cannot withstand a demurrer or a motion to dismiss or strike. By this point, the attorney has had an opportunity to conduct legal research, and she can now evaluate the legal merits of the pled causes of action, crimes, and defenses.

Again, consider the *Scott* case from the prosecutor's point of view. Suppose that the prosecutor originally included an ADW count in the information. After filing the information, the prosecutor researches the scope of the definition of "deadly weapon" under El Dorado law. She finds a recent El Dorado Supreme Court decision squarely holding that fists and shoes do not constitute deadly weapons. The prosecutor ought to abandon the ADW theory. The prosecutor should do so even if the defense counsel neglects to move to dismiss. Most jurisdictions subscribe to the view that even when a defendant fails to make a pretrial motion to dismiss a legally insufficient count, the issue of its legal sufficiency can be raised for the first time at trial or on appeal. 71 C.J.S. *Pleading* § 560 (1951). This view obtains in both civil and criminal cases. *E.g., Ex parte Seaton*, 580 S.W.2d 593 (Tex.Crim.App.1979) (post-conviction proceeding). If you take that theory to trial, you are building a ground for appeal into your record. Worse still, the very mention of that theory at trial will detract from the overall credibility of your trial presentation. If the judge dismisses that count during trial after your mention of the theory in opening, the jurors may conclude that the judge questions the strength of your case.

§ 3.3(C) The Discovery/Motion Stage

The function of this stage parallels that of the pleading stage. The purpose of this stage is to winnow out theories lacking factual merit.

Suppose that it becomes clear to the attorney before trial that one of her theories is vulnerable to a summary judgment motion. She should discard that theory even if the defense fails to move for summary judgment. Notwithstanding that failure, the opposing attorney can attack the legal sufficiency of her evidence at trial. 88 C.J.S. *Trial* § 252 (1955). The attorney could suffer a directed verdict on that count during trial. Worse still, a directed verdict on one count reduces the likelihood of obtaining a favorable judgment on other, sound counts. The unsupportable count is a strawman the opponent can easily destroy. The presence of the weak count in the case may lower the overall credibility of the attorney's case in the jurors' eyes. After rejecting the unsupported count, the jurors may leap quickly—and incorrectly—to the conclusion that the other counts are equally meritless.

Revisit the *Scott* case. Assume that the prosecutor decided to include a maiming count in the information. After filing the information and conducting legal research, the prosecutor undertakes an intensive factual investigation. During the investigation, the prosecutor speaks to the two physicians who have treated Williams for his injuries. The physicians tell the prosecutor that Williams' torn ear was certainly caused by the attack. However, they concur that the prognosis is excellent and that Williams will not have any permanent damage to the ear. The offense of maiming or mayhem requires proof of a permanent injury. R. PERKINS & R. BOYCE, CRIMINAL LAW 242 (3d ed. 1982). Consequently, the prosecutor should not take the maiming theory to trial; as a matter of law, proof of an essential element is missing.

§ 3.3(D) Final Pretrial Case Evaluation

On the eve of trial, the attorney must review the mass of information collected during discovery to answer three questions: What is my best theory? Which element of the theory will be the real battleground at trial? What is the best theme to use to prevail on that element?

The Determination of the Best Theory

The easy case is the one in which only one theory remains after the pleading and discovery stages. In the contracts hypothetical discussed earlier, Mr. Pollet's attorney discovered that the promissory estoppel theory lacked legal merit and that the written contract theory was vulnerable to summary judgment. Simple process of elimination led the attorney to select the express oral contract theory. There is no need for a choice.

However, often there are several theories that have both legal and factual merit. In a major antitrust or securities regulation suit, the plaintiff's attorney may have ten theories to choose from on the eve of trial. The threshold question is whether the attorney should urge all those theories at trial. Most experienced attorneys answer that question in the negative. Reliance on a single theory is the most powerful technique for radically simplifying the case. In one case, Maxwell Blecher won a $72 million verdict for the plaintiffs in a lawsuit against Eastman

Kokak. *Organize Complex Cases Clearly,* NAT'L L.J., May 13, 1996, at p. D3. Another attorney had drafted a "shotgun" complaint for the plaintiffs. However, at trial Mr. Blecher decided to "abandon[] all but the monopoly claim." He explained: "The more claims you pile on, the more you can confuse. You go in with a rifle, not a shotgun. My style is to give the jury the simplest possible case."

The answer should certainly be in the negative when the theories are factually inconsistent. It is true that with their law school training, most lawyers and judges are comfortable with "even if" arguments: The defendant has an alibi; even if he was present at the crime scene, he was insane; and even if he was present and sane, he was entrapped. However, laypersons find such arguments curious and suspect. Common sense tells them that the defendant either was or was not present. When an attorney relies on inconsistent arguments, the jurors understandably doubt the attorney's candor. The jurors know that you have had the benefit of confidential conversations with your client; and even if you cannot divulge the content of the communications, the jurors believe that you know the Truth in the singular.

There is even a grave risk in taking multiple consistent theories to trial. Urging secondary theories can "weaken your primary contention." R. KEETON, TRIAL TACTICS AND METHODS § 10.6 (2d ed. 1973). "(E)ven the subtle suggestion of alternative positions is harmful. The advocate who tries to sell two ideas at once robs each of a measure of conviction and appears less than credible for the effort." Goldberg, *What Your Opening Statement Should and Shouldn't Do,* 2 CRIM. JUST. 10, 12 (Fall 1987). The jurors may treat the attorney's invocation of other theories as evidence of the attorney's lack of faith in the primary theory. Finally, during closing argument an astute opposing counsel can make you pay for urging multiple theories. The opponent may poke fun at you and tell the jury that even at that late point in the case, you evidently "cannot decide" which version of the facts is the truth. The jurors are likely to be especially skeptical when the testimony indicates that your client has personal knowledge of the events.

For all these reasons, in the opinion of most seasoned litigators, when faced with multiple theories, the attorney must choose a single theory for trial. The consensus among veteran litigators is so extensive that in criminal cases, appellate defense counsel are beginning to argue that a trial defense counsel's reliance on multiple theories, especially inconsistent theories, amounts to ineffective assistance of counsel under the sixth amendment. *E.g., Brown v. Dixon,* 891 F.2d 490 (4th Cir.1989).

How should the attorney make the choice? Different attorneys use different approaches. Some attorneys are gifted with brilliant insight into the lay juror's psychology, and they tend to make intuitive choices. At the other extreme—especially at large firms handling major cases— litigators use surrogate jurors to help them choose their theory. Clifford, *Simulated Juries Can Be Used Most Effectively Early in the Litigation Process to Develop the Theory of the Case,* NAT'L L.J., Feb. 27, 1995, at

p. B8; Gidmark, *The Verdict on Surrogate Jury Research,* 74 A.B.A.J. 82 (Mar. 1, 1988). The surrogates may be referred to as a mock jury. Schaefer, *Low-Cost Shadow Juries,* 22 TRIAL 58 (Dec. 1986); Call, *The Trial as Story,* 22 TRIAL 84, 86–87 (Nov. 1986). They listen to abbreviated presentations by the attorneys and give the attorneys their reactions to various possible theories. Their reactions help the attorneys predict the reactions of the real jurors and thereby aid the attorneys in selecting a theory. Andrews, *Mind Control in the Courtroom,* PSYCHOLOGY TODAY 66, 73 (Mar. 1982). In effect, the attorneys pretest the possible theories on the surrogate jurors. Call, *Jury Research: Improving Trial Results,* 18 TRIAL LAWYERS Q. 33, 34 (Sum./Fall 1987). The use of a surrogate jury for this purpose is similar to test marketing a product. The feedback from the surrogate jurors helps the attorney choose the optimal theory.

Most attorneys have neither the time nor the resources to use surrogate jurors in this fashion. Unless these attorneys are confident of their ability to intuit the correct choice of theory, they must make their choice on the basis of their prudential judgment informed by the following factors, *inter alia:*

(**1**)   Which theory will afford the client relief that is adequate for the client's personal or business needs? Suppose that the original complaint in *Pollet v. Rowland* had included a fraud count. Assume further that during discovery, Pollet's attorney uncovered enough evidence of deceit on the defendant's part to survive a summary judgment motion on that theory. However, during their final consultation before trial, Pollet tells his attorney that he desperately needs the generator and that Rowland's firm is the only company that manufactures that type of generator. At the beginning of the litigation there were other potential sources for the generator; but while the litigation was pending, the other potential sources went out of business. Even if now all the other factors are equal, Pollet's attorney should select a contract theory and abandon the tort theory. As a matter of remedy law, only the contract theory will support a decree of specific performance. D. DOBBS, HANDBOOK ON THE LAW OF REMEDIES § 12.8 (2d ed. 1993). Pollet's business needs dictate the choice of the contract theory. Clients usually engage in litigation instrumentally as a means to a real world end. As a counselor, you need to learn that end objective.

(**2**)   If the relief my client desires is an award of money damages, which theory will yield the largest net recovery, considering the relevant tax law? Prior to 1996, the courts tended to construe the pertinent Internal Revenue Code section, 26 U.S.C. § 104(a)(2), as excluding tort recoveries of compensatory damage from gross income. However, in that year the Small Business Job Protection Act amended the statute to refer to "damages ... received ... on account of personal physical injuries or physical sickness." The amendment also generally provided that "emotional distress shall not be treated as a physical injury or physical sickness." Tax considerations are virtually ubiquitous in transactional legal work, but those considerations are by no means confined to that setting.

(3) Which theory has the largest volume of and most cogent corroboration? Our hypothesis is that all the remaining theories have bare factual merit in the sense that they could defeat a summary judgment motion. However, if one theory has superior corroboration—disinterested, unequivocal lay eyewitness testimony or testimony by an eminently credentialed expert—the availability of the corroboration cuts in favor of that theory.

(4) Is the theory based on substantial justice rather than a rule that may strike the jurors as a legal technicality? Suppose that Ms. Rowland has tenable fraud and Statute of Frauds defenses against Mr. Pollet's claim. Both defenses could survive a motion to strike, and there is enough evidence supporting each defensive theory that at trial, the judge would have to instruct the jury on the defense. A lay juror, however, would likely find the latter defense unattractive. If the defense relies on the Statute of Frauds, a layperson might conclude that the defendant is invoking a legal technicality to walk away from a freely bargained agreement. At a subconscious level, the juror might find it difficult to excuse nonperformance ("welshing") for the apparently trivial reason that the parties did not document the agreement. As Professor Llewellyn stressed in THE BRAMBLE BUSH (1960), the attorney must not only build a sound technical ladder. *Id.* at 69, 72. The attorney must also attempt to predict the trier of fact's probable reaction to each potential theory. Your objective is to influence the jury debate. Googasian, *Some Tips on Litigation,* 25 TRIAL 74 (May 1989). If you can fashion a theory resting on substantial justice, the jury is more likely to rely on that theory during their deliberations. You want to find a theory which a lay juror will be comfortable presenting to other lay jurors during deliberations. Is the theory one which a layperson would feel at ease urging in an argument "at a cocktail party, a club luncheon, or a church dinner"? Dodd, *Innovative Techniques: Parlor Tricks for the Courtroom,* 26 TRIAL 38–39 (Apr. 1990). Do not be content with a legalistic approach. Rench, *We Win by Being Persuaders—Not the Legal Technicians the Law Schools Taught Us to Be,* 15 THE CHAMPION 51, 52 (July 1991). You need a theory "that satisfies both the head and the heart." McElhaney, *Briefs That Sing: A Winning Argument is More than a Stack of Legal Issues,* 83 A.B.A.J. 80 (Mar. 1997). The legendary New York trial attorney, Moe Levine, once remarked that at trial, the attorney's challenge is to give the jurors a reason to feel proud about returning a verdict in the client's favor. A theory resting on substantial justice can make the jurors proud of voting for your client.

There is a further reason for selecting a theory resting on substantial justice: As an advocate, you will probably feel more comfortable arguing for the theory. It is true that the rules of ethics and evidence prohibit you from expressing your personal opinion as to the merits of the case during the trial. However, the jury thinks that you know the truth in the case; you have had the benefit of privileged conversations with your client. For that reason, they may treat your nonverbal demeanor as evidence of the merit of your client's claim. Your "very presence" in the courtroom must convince the jurors that you believe that "fundamental justice [is] on your side." McElhaney, *Goals in Opening Statements,* 16 LITIGATION 47, 48 (Wint. 1990). When you have chosen a theory resting on substantial justice, you will find it easier to project sincerity to the jurors. *See also* McElhaney, *The Most Important Witness,* 77 A.B.A.J. 86 (Aug. 1991) (in your demeanor, the jurors "get glimpses of . . . how much you believe in your case"). As Ralph Waldo Emerson once remarked, "[T]hat which we do not believe, we cannot adequately say." *Quoted in* R. WAICKAUSKI, P. SANDLER & J. EPPS, THE WINNING ARGUMENT 42 (2001).

(**5**) Will the judge give the jury a favorably worded instruction about the theory? The jurors know that the attorneys are partisan advocates,"hired guns." Consequently, the jurors tend to discount what the attorneys say during trial. Dombroff, *Jury Instructions Can Be Crucial in Trial Process,* LEGAL TIMES, Feb. 25, 1985, at p. 26. The jurors accord far more significance to what the judge says at trial, including the judge's statements in the final jury charge. If there is a pattern instruction with favorable language on one theory, during summation an astute attorney can exploit the instruction to convince the jury that in some sense, the judge approves of the attorney's theory. Assume that for other possible theories, the pattern instructions contain bland language or, worse, no pattern instruction exists. The attorney will have to overcome the judge's reluctance to give a special instruction. The availability of a favorable instruction on the other theory points toward the choice of that theory for trial. If you anticipate such an instruction, you should attempt to incorporate some of the wording of the instruction into the very phrasing of your theory. Klein & Shayne, *A Soup-to-Nuts Jury Selection and Opening Statement Primer,* 4 THE PRACT. LITIGATOR 29, 39 (Mar. 1993).

(**6**) Does the theory cast the client in a role with which the jurors can easily identify? Begam, *Opening Statement: Some Psychological Considerations,* 16 TRIAL 33, 34–36 (July 1980). You want to project an image of your client which the jurors can identify with. Gutman, *Image Creation An Important Part of Trials,* NAT'L L.J., May 23, 1988, at p. 21. Suppose that a commercial litigator must choose between the theories of breach of contract and breach of warranty. If she opts for the former theory, the jurors may view the case as a contest between two large businesses. On the other hand, if she selects the warranty theory, she can portray her client in the role of a consumer with whom many jurors can empathize.

(**7**) Does the theory require that the jurors find intentional misconduct by the opposing party? This consideration is sometimes dubbed the "congeniality" factor. Ohlbaum, *Basic Instinct: Case Theory and Courtroom Performance,* 66 TEMPLE L.REV. 1, 21 (1993).

Many commentators have pointed out that jurors are loath to conclude that a witness has committed perjury. P. BERGMAN, TRIAL ADVOCACY 288–89 (1979). A contention that the witness is mistaken ordinarily is more palatable. K. HEGLAND, TRIAL AND PRACTICE 47 (1978). By the same token, a juror may be hesitant to find that the opposing party perpetrated an intentional misdeed. Therefore, it may be preferable for Ms. Rowland to defend against Pollet's claim on the ground of mutual mistake rather than outright fraud. As a practical matter, you cannot rely on a theory requiring a finding of deliberate misconduct unless you have strong evidence of the person's motive to engage in such behavior. McElhaney, *Finding the Right Script*, 81 A.B.A.J. 90 (Aug. 1995). You need to have "the goods" on that person.

(**8**)   Which theory will justify the admission of the items of evidence that are most damning to the opposition? McElhaney, *Don't Be Locked Out: The Right Strategy Can Open Doors to Evidence That Might Otherwise Be Inadmissible at Trial*, 85 A.B.A.J. 64 (May 1999)("Sue a trucking company for its driver's negligent injury of a pedestrian, and the driver's bad record for speeding and reckless driving is inadmissible in evidence. But change your pleadings to add a count of negligent entrustment of a truck to someone the company should have known was a terrible driver, and the driver's record is admissible"). In Professor McElhaney's words,

> Don't just start with your legal theory and then look for the evidence to support it. Think about your best evidence—what is going to make a serious impact—and look for the theories that will make it admissible.

Litigating in Theory, 81 A.B.A.J. 94 (June 1995). One of the most damaging types of evidence is testimony about the opposing client's other misdeeds—for example, testimony about other assaults that Scott might have committed. In a study conducted by the National Science Foundation Law and Social Science Program, researchers found that evidence of a party's uncharged misconduct was one of the few types of testimony consistently rated prejudicial by surrogate jurors. Teitelbaum, Sutton–Barbere & Johnson, *Evaluating the Prejudicial Effect of Evidence: Can Judges Identify the Impact of Improper Evidence on Juries?* 1983 WIS.L.REV. 1147, 1162. Under Federal Rule of Evidence 404(b), uncharged misconduct evidence can be admitted when it is logically relevant on a non-character theory to prove intent. However, the courts admit the evidence much more liberally to prove a special mens rea than to establish general mens rea. *E.g., Young v. Rabideau*, 821 F.2d 373, 380 n. 5 (7th Cir.1987). If the other factors are equally balanced and the prosecution has devastating uncharged misconduct evidence, the prosecutor might opt for the theory of a special mens rea crime to ensure the admission of the evidence.

(**9**)   Which theory is consistent with the largest number of seemingly unfavorable but incontrovertible facts? You not only want a theory which enables you to justify introducing facts which damage the opposition; you also want a theory which permits you to effectively neutralize the facts which seem to damage your case. The theory should account for the facts that as a practical matter, you cannot deny or refute. LARRY S. POZNER & ROGER J. DODD, CROSS–EXAMINATION: SCIENCE AND TECHNIQUES 41 (1993) ("facts beyond change"); French, *KISS in the Courtroom,* 28 TRIAL 130, 132 (Nov. 1992); Lubet, *Objecting,* 16 AM.J.TRIAL ADVOC. 213, 221 (1992). The theory must pass muster under this test as well as being able to survive a summary judgment motion.

(**10**)   Does the theory require the jurors to assume an extraordinary coincidence or an implausible occurrence? In the privacy of the deliberation room, the jurors' natural inclination is to rely on their everyday experience to help them choose between the competing versions of the facts urged by the parties. Henringer, *Persuasive Proof,* 36 TRIAL 55 (Apr. 2000). That experience is the default basis for a jury's decision. Moreover, in most jurisdictions, the judge will instruct the jurors that they may draw on that experience in evaluating the testimony in the case. Suppose that you represent the defendant in a personal injury action resulting from a collision. Before trial, an accident reconstruction expert tells you that a third party driver merging from a freeway onramp could have caused the accident by driving either too slow or too fast. Other testimony indicates that the third party driver was probably a teenager. Relying on stereotypes, the lay jurors are more likely to accept the hypothesis that the teenage driver was speeding.

Suppose that the *Scott* prosecutor attempts to apply this multi-factor approach to choosing a trial theme. The choice facing the prosecutor is between an attempted murder theory and a battery theory. In most respects, the theories are equally desirable. However, the second factor, the availability of corroboration, cuts against the former theory. The prosecutor may have enough evidence to eke out a permissive inference of an intent to kill, but the inference is a weak one. The prosecutor could point out that one assailant told Mr. Williams, "Keep quiet, or we'll kill you." However, the threat was not only conditional; the threat was also made after the attackers had finished beating Williams. More importantly, they did not stop the attack because they were interrupted by another hotel resident or the police; they evidently could have continued the beating and killed Williams if they had wanted to. In contrast, the inference of the mens rea element needed for battery is overpowering; if the attackers voluntarily committed the acts Williams describes, they unquestionably had at least general mens rea. Furthermore, while reliance on a special mens rea theory might make it easier to introduce evidence of Scott's similar uncharged misconduct, the case file makes no mention of such misconduct. This line of reasoning would probably lead the prosecutor to opt for the battery theory.

The Identification of the Pivotal Element of the Theory

The next step in case evaluation is the identification of the element of the theory that will be decisive at trial. "Every case without exception has a main controlling issue." Beasley, *Closing Statements,* in TRIAL PRACTICE FOR THE GENERAL PRACTITIONER 98, 99 (L. Packel ed. 1980). In a major case in which there are detailed pretrial stipulations or requests for admissions, it can be relatively simple to single out the element of the theory that will be the central focus at trial. The stipulations may practically eliminate every element but one. In other cases, the attorney must carefully review the course of pretrial discovery to forecast the issue. The key clue frequently is the focus of the opposing attorney's questions at the deposition of the attorney's client. When the vast majority of the questions dealt with contract formation, as was true at Mr. Pollet's deposition, in our hypothetical case one can expect that that element of the plaintiff's theory will be the contested issue at trial. Although criminal discovery is not as extensive as civil discovery, it is becoming easier for prosecutors to predict the nature of the defense's trial theory. For example, Federal Rule of Criminal Procedure 12.1 now requires defendants to give the prosecution pretrial notice of an alibi defense, and Rule 12.1 similarly requires pretrial notice of an insanity theory.

If the *Scott* prosecutor engages in this type of analysis, the prosecutor should conclude that the critical issue at trial will be the question of identity. The treating physicians would probably attest that given the nature and location of Williams' injuries, he must have been beaten; the hypothesis that Williams was drunk and fell down the stairs could not account for the injuries. The physicians' testimony thus would establish the actus reus. Moreover, the nature of the crime virtually compels the conclusion that there was the requisite mens rea. Battery is a general mens rea crime, and general mens rea is the intent to commit the actus reus. If the jury finds that two men voluntarily attacked Williams, they will naturally conclude that those attackers had the required guilty state of mind. Thus, it is predictable that Scott will defend on the theory that he was not one of the attackers.

The Formulation of a Theme

After isolating the pivotal element of the theory, the attorney must devise a theme for that element. The attorney must identify the argument that has the greatest common sense appeal to the jurors on the pivotal element. Just as attorneys differ in their approach to choosing a theory, they vary in the method in which they select their themes. Some rely heavily on intuition, and others go to the length of hiring focus groups and trying possible themes out on these surrogate jurors. Howie, *Bringing Case Issues into Focus,* 31 TRIAL 32 (Jan. 1995); Singer, *Jury-Validated Trial Themes,* 30 TRIAL 74 (Oct. 1994); Varinsky, *Try Out Your Case on a Focus Group,* 8 CAL. LAW. 47 (Mar. 1988). In the past, trial attorneys hired jury consultants to convene and conduct such groups. However, do-it-yourself and Internet focus groups are now coming into vogue. Hsieh, *Trial Lawyers Are Cutting Costs of Focus Groups Via the Internet,* LAWYERS WEEKLY USA, Feb. 5, 2001, at p. 1; Twiggs, *Do-It-Yourself Focus Groups: Big Benefits, Modest Cost,* 30 TRIAL 42 (Sep. 1994). Still others—perhaps the majority—consciously weigh the same types of factors that they consider in selecting a theory. Is corroborating evidence available to support the theme? Does the theme embody an argument that seems grounded in substantial justice? Will the argument resonate with the jurors' values and beliefs? Is there a favorably worded pattern instruction about the theme?

Which theme should the *Scott* prosecutor use? It would be ineffective to use a theme of "a reliable identification" or "a trustworthy identification." Like the "clear agreement" theme that we rejected in *Pollet v. Rowland,* these proposed themes merely restate the conclusion that the prosecutor wants the jurors to reach. However, they do not tell the jurors *why* they should come to that conclusion. Probably the best theme for the prosecution would be "so close for so long"—Williams was so close to his attackers for so long that his identification is undoubtedly reliable. Prosecutors are well aware of the numerous studies showing that jurors tend to attach great weight to lay eyewitness testimony. *See generally* E. LOFTUS, & J. DOYLE EYEWITNESS TESTIMONY: CIVIL AND CRIMINAL (3d ed. 1997); A. YARMEY, THE PSYCHOLOGY OF EYEWITNESS TESTIMONY (1979). Furthermore, many of the pattern jury instructions on eyewitness identification specifically direct the jury to consider how close the witness was to the perpetrator and how long the witness had to view the perpetrator. *United States v. Telfaire,* 469 F.2d 552 (D.C.Cir.1972); *People v. Guzman,* 47 Cal.App.3d 380, 121 Cal.Rptr. 69 (1975). That instruction dovetails beautifully with a "so close for so long" theme.

At this point, we must add a caveat. As carefully as you think through the pretrial choice of theory and theme, the choice is necessarily only a tentative one. At trial, things may go better or worse than you expected; if the unexpected occurs at trial, you must be flexible enough to adapt to the unforeseen development. You may need to "refocus your case as you move along." Fisk, *Ten Diverse Keys to Winning Suits,* NAT'L L.J., Feb. 3, 1993, p. S1. In particular, you might revise your theory or theme after jury selection; you may need to fine tune the theory or theme in light of what you have learned about the jurors' backgrounds and attitudes. Klein & Shayne, *A Soup-to-Nuts Jury Selection and Opening Statement Primer,* 4 THE PRACT. LITIGATOR 29, 36 (Mar. 1993). In major cases, some litigators use shadow juries during the trial. Strong & Baber, *How We Use a Shadow Jury,* 47 J. MO.BAR 144 (Mar. 1991). During the trial, the shadow jurors sit in the spectators' area of the courtroom and listen to the testimony. The shadow jurors periodically report to the attorneys about their reactions to the testimony; and on the basis of those reports, the attorneys can adjust their trial strategy, perhaps modifying their theory or theme. *Id.* at 146–48. Thus, even if you tentatively rejected a particular theory or theme before trial, at trial you may have to shift to that theory or theme. During the pretrial planning you will likely consider many possible theories and themes; even if you provisionally discard them, do not put them entirely out of mind. At trial, you need contingency plans and fall back positions.

§ 3.4   THE USE OF THE THEORY AND THEME AT TRIAL

§ 3.4(A) The Functions of the Theory and Theme

Chapter 1 underscored that the trial attorney must plan her trial presentation to give the presentation simplicity and continuity. The theory and theme are the devices the attorney uses to achieve those qualities. Together, the theory and theme dictate virtually every word the attorney utters at trial.

The foremost function of the theory is to simplify the trial presentation. One prominent trial attorney, Gerry Spence, has written:

> I never have tried a complex case. I have tried cases with many exhibits, cases that took months in which scores of witnesses were called, cases with jury instructions as thick as the Monkey–Ward catalog.... But I never have tried a complex case. [A]ll cases are reducible to the simplest of stories.

Spence, *How to Make a Complex Case Come Alive for a Jury,* 72 A.B.A.J. 62, 64–65 (Apr. 1, 1986).

The use of a single story at trial helps simplify the trial, and that story is the theory. On the eve of trial, after collecting 1,000 documents during discovery relevant to 12 possible theories, the litigator should choose a single theory to rely on. Perhaps only 85 of the documents pertain to that theory. Reliance on that theory drastically decreases the volume of information to present to the jury. Relevance to that theory becomes the litmus test determining whether the attorney considers offering an item of evidence at trial; the attorney should proffer the item if and only if it will contribute to the development of the theory. As Chapter 1 noted, jurors in complex cases often complain that the litigators go overboard and swamp the jury with information, particularly an excessive number of exhibits. SPEC. COMM. ON JURY COMPREHENSION, A.B.A. LITIGATION SECTION, JURY COMPREHENSION IN COMPLEX CASES 27–28, 31 (1990). In the *Simpson* case, the prosecution deluged the jury with 99 days of testimony. *O.J. Trivia,* NAT'L L.J., Oct. 16, 1995. In the earlier *McMartin* child abuse prosecution, the prosecution called 124 witnesses and introduced 974 exhibits, requiring over 33 months of trial and consuming nearly 64,000 pages of transcript. Benedictis, *McMartin Preschool Lessons: Abuse Case Plagued by Botched Investigation, Too Many Counts,* 76 A.B.A.J. 28 (Apr. 1990). The theory helps the attorney eliminate the "clutter" in his or her case. McElhaney, *Clutter,* 77 A.B.A.J. 73 (Mar. 1991). *See also* Reasoner, *Juries Need Guidance Without Condescension,* NAT'L L.J., Feb. 3, 1992, at p. S8 ("In complex civil litigation, ..., the key to winning is being able to simplify in a clear and powerful way. It's the single most important thing to accomplish in a trial. Nothing succeeds like simplicity.")

While the choice of a single theory lends simplicity to the case, the theme is the attorney's tool for giving the trial presentation continuity. The attorney can: insinuate the theme during voir dire, state the theme during opening, incorporate some of the wording of the theme into the phrasing of questions, and hammer at the theme during summation. In short, the attorney can employ the theme to pull the whole case together in the jury's mind. The theme can serve as a psychological anchor to "reduce the complexity [of the case] to [a] satisfying order." Vinson, *What Makes Jurors Tick?*, 24 TRIAL 58, 62 (June 1988). The theme helps the trier of fact to maintain focus during the trial. McElhaney, *Focus,* 77 A.B.A.J. 78 (May 1991).

If anything, in the foreseeable future it will be more important to formulate a trial theory and theme. In February 1998, the A.B.A. Section of Litigation released its Civil Trial Standards. Although the standards do not have the force of law, in all likelihood many federal and state trial judges will follow the practices commended by the standards. Standard 2 encourages trial judges to use jury notebooks in complex cases. The notebooks will be distributed to the jurors even before opening statement. In particular, Standard 2.a.iv.D urges trial judges to allow parties to include "[a] short statement of the parties' claims and defenses...." Further, Standard 12.b.i points out that in a lengthy case, it is in the interest of judicial economy for the judge to impose limits on "[t]he total time to be allowed each party or side...." Especially when the judge prescribes such restrictions, the litigants must make the optimal use of their limited time. If the judge permits the trial attorneys to include "[a] short statement" of their position in a trial notebook, the attorney should incorporate the theory and theme into the wording of the statement. The time limits increase the need for a theory and theme, and the use of the notebook gives the attorney the opportunity to put the theory and theme to use early in the proceeding.

§ 3.4(B) Explaining Tactical Maxims in Terms of Theory and Theme

The theory and theme are not only the key concepts in strategic planning; they also help explain many of the maxims that are used in planning at the tactical level.

As we shall see in Chapter 4, one maxim is that during voir dire examination, the attorney should attempt to indoctrinate the venire on "favorable" jury instructions. What is a favorable instruction? The obvious answer is an instruction that seems to place the judicial *imprimatur* on the theme. Suppose that in *Scott,* the prosecutor is confident that in the final jury charge on eyewitness identification, the judge will use the words, "how close" and "how long." The prosecutor might question the venire in this fashion:

Q Later in this case, her Honor may instruct you that in deciding whether to believe Mr. Williams' identification of the defendant, you should consider "how close" Mr. Williams was to his attackers. If she does do so, can you promise me that you'll follow that instruction?

Q And you'll do your very best to carry out that instruction?

> **Q** And will you promise me that you'll carefully consider Mr.
> Williams' testimony about how close he was to those two men?

The judge is likely to give the attorney very little time to question the
venire; and if the attorney contemplates spending any time exposing the
jury to favorable instructions, that time is best spent previewing the
instruction that dovetails with the theme.

Another maxim is that the attorney ought to conclude the client's
direct examination on a "high" note. What is a high note? The best
interpretation of that expression is the testimony that most directly
supports the theme. The end of the direct examination is a naturally
emphatic position. If the theme embodies the strongest argument for
winning the pivotal issue in the case, the testimony supporting the
theme is the evidence that should be highlighted. Suppose that the
prosecutor is planning Mr. Williams' direct testimony. The prosecutor
should conclude the testimony by having Mr. Williams make it clear how
close he was to the attackers and how long a period of time he had to
view them. Structuring the direct examination in this manner may
deviate from strict, chronological order. However, if the theme is "so
close for so long," the deviation is warranted.

There is another tactical bromide that the attorney should generally
elicit "favorable" admissions at the beginning of the cross-examination
of a hostile witness. At that point, before any attempted impeachment,
the witness is more likely to be cooperative. The rub is defining "favorable" admissions. However, it is relatively easy to define the term once
the attorney has formulated a theme: The most favorable admission is
the hostile witness's testimony lending support to the theme. In *Scott,* a
key defense witness will be Joan Freeman. She will testify that: She
heard the scuffle in the hallway, looked into the hallway and saw three
figures fighting, could identify two voices as that of Williams and Rogers,
but is confident that the last voice was not Scott's. Suppose, though, that
based on his pretrial interview with Freeman, the prosecutor is confident
that she will concede that when she looked into the hallway, the three
men were "right on top of each other." That testimony is powerful
ammunition for the prosecution. During summation, after restating
Williams' testimony about his proximity to his attackers, the prosecutor
could continue:

> And, ladies and gentlemen, you don't have to accept Mr. Williams'
> word for that. The defense's very own witness, Ms. Freeman, corrob-
> orated that. I want you to think back to the beginning of my cross-
> examination of Ms. Freeman. I asked her how close the three figures
> were in the hallway. She said that they were "right on top of each
> other." "Right on top of each other"—those are the exact words of
> the defense's very own witness.

That would be a persuasive summation, and it is a summation the
prosecutor can deliver in *Scott* if he elicits the "right on top of each
other" testimony at the outset of Ms. Freeman's cross-examination.

These are only a few of the tactical maxims that take on new meaning in light of the concepts of theory and theme. The choice of theory and theme is not only the essence of strategic litigation; that choice also facilitates planning at the tactical level. Simply stated, at trial the attorney plays out the theory and theme.

§ 3.5　ETHICAL QUESTIONS

In an adversary system, the most visible conflicts are usually conflicts between the two sides. However, the most difficult tensions to resolve are often conflicts between the client and the attorney on the same side. Suppose initially that during the final pretrial case evaluation, the attorney concludes that a particular claim or defense lacks legal or factual merit. The client nevertheless demands that the attorney present the claim at trial. Must the attorney comply with the demand? Consider the guidance given in A.B.A. Model Rule of Professional Conduct 3.1:

> A lawyer shall not bring or defend a proceeding, or assert or controvert an issue therein, unless there is a basis for doing so that is not frivolous, which includes a good faith argument for an extension, modification, or reversal of existing law. A lawyer for a defendant in a criminal proceeding, or the respondent in a proceeding that could result in incarceration, may nevertheless so defend the proceeding as to require that every element of the case be established.

As amended in 1983, Federal Rule of Civil Procedure 11 provides that when an attorney signs any filed "pleading [or] motion," his signature represents "a certificate ... that to the best of his knowledge, information, and belief formed after reasonable inquiry it is well grounded in fact and is warranted by existing law or a good faith argument for the extension, modification, or reversal of existing law...." Do these rules furnish an answer to the question posed? How far does the second sentence of Rule 3.1 permit a criminal defense attorney to go?

Assume alternatively that on the eve of trial, there are several theories with both legal and factual merit but the attorney concludes that one theory is unquestionably the best for trial. May the attorney opt for that theory without consulting the client? What if the attorney consults the client and the client demands that the attorney rely on another trial theory? Must the attorney comply with that demand? Lubet, *Ethics and Theory Choice in Advocacy Education*, 44 J.LEGAL EDUCAT. 81 (Mar. 1994).

Model Rule 1.2(a) states:

> A lawyer shall abide by a client's decisions concerning the objectives of representation ... and shall consult with the client as to the means by which they are to be pursued. In a criminal case, the lawyer shall abide by the client's decision, after consultation with the lawyer, as to a plea to be entered, whether to waive jury trial, and whether the client will testify.

Standard 4–5.2(a) of the A.B.A. Standards Relating to the Defense Function is to the same effect. However, Standard 4–5.2(b) amplifies:

> The decisions on what witnesses to call, whether and how to conduct cross-examination, what jurors to accept, or strike, what trial motions should be made, and all other strategic and tactical decisions are the exclusive province of the lawyer after consultation with the client.

The Supreme Court has approvingly cited both the rule and the standard. *Jones v. Barnes,* 463 U.S. 745, 753 (1983).

Although that citation suggests that the client has the ultimate authority to choose the theory, other language in *Jones* points to a contrary conclusion. The Court noted that "[e]xperienced advocates since time beyond memory have emphasized the importance of winnowing out weaker arguments ... and focusing on one central issue if possible...." *Id.* at 751. In *Jones,* the Court announced that an appellate counsel has no duty to "press nonfrivolous points requested by the client, if counsel, as a matter of professional judgment, decides not to present those points." *Id.* In cases involving claims of ineffective assistance by trial counsel, lower courts have concluded that counsel has the right to forego a defense so long as there is a reasonable basis for counsel's decision. *Keys v. Duckworth,* 761 F.2d 390 (7th Cir.1985); *Harris v. Clusen,* 487 F.Supp. 616 (E.D.Wis.1980) (inconsistent alibi and insanity defenses); *Ivey v. Commonwealth,* 655 S.W.2d 506 (Ky.App. 1983). However, some commentators have challenged that interpretation of *Jones:*

> Certainly it may be argued that the winnowing of issues on appeal is strategic, while the choice of a defense is more akin to the "fundamental" issues such as how the defendant should plead, or whether he should testify. [T]here is a line of ethical precepts and cases which persuasively suggest that at trial, the attorney should be required to implement his client's defense, regardless of the wisdom of the client's choice or the extent of the attorney's professional reservations.

Epstein, *Choice of Defense and the Attorney–Client Relationship: Whose Call Is It?,* 18 THE CHAMPION 30 (Nov. 1994).

Consider the policy issue as a question of first impression. Is the lay client sufficiently sophisticated to weigh the factors listed in § 3.3(D) governing the choice of theory? On the other hand, do the courts allocating the decision to the attorney give sufficient weight to the client's democratic interest in personal autonomy, the right to make decisions that affect his or her own future? *See* C. WOLFRAM, MODERN LEGAL ETHICS § 4.3 (1986).

§ 3.6 TRIAL TECHNIQUE EXERCISES

All student attorneys in all cases have the same assignment for this chapter. You are a young trial attorney assigned to second chair the trial of your case. In the criminal cases, the students with prosecutor roles will be assisting a senior Deputy District Attorney, and the students with defense roles are working with a senior Deputy Public Defender. In the civil cases, you are working with a junior partner, a litigator with extensive trial experience. The case is scheduled to go to trial in two weeks. The attorney you are assisting has tasked you to write a case evaluation memorandum for trial. The memorandum should be addressed to that attorney. Your professor may announce maximum or minimum length requirements. The memorandum should answer the following questions: What are all the possible theories which have both legal and factual merit? Which is the best theory for trial—and why? What are the elements of that theory? Which element is likely to be the real battleground at trial? What is the best theme for prevailing on that element—and why?

Chapter 4

JURY SELECTION—THE STRATEGY OF JURY DESELECTION

Reprinted by permission of Warner Books/New York from *The Law as Seen by Charles Bragg*. Copyright © 1983 by Charles Bragg.

Table of Sections

---

§ 4.1   INTRODUCTION

The trial now begins. The first order of business is choosing the petit jurors. The jury selection phase of the case is a critical stage. If the judge permits the attorneys to question the jurors directly, jury selection will be your initial personal contact with the prospective jurors. This contact occurs early in the trial when the trial is a novel experience for most venirepersons and they are likely to be interested and attentive. Further, voir dire examination is arguably your best contact with the jurors. In the later phases of the case, you can speak to them. However, this is the only phase of the case at which you can speak *with* them. During the questioning, you can engage in a dialogue with the jury and develop personal rapport with them.

§ 4.2   THE DECISION WHETHER TO REQUEST A JURY

You should not automatically assume that you desire a jury. The truth of the matter is that most cases tried in the United States are bench trials. In some types of cases, there is no right to a jury. Moreover, even in many cases in which attorneys could request a jury, they decide to waive the jury. Assume that you have a constitutional or statutory right to jury trial. Should you exercise that right? If you waive the right, you can try the case to a judge, a bench trial. The question is whether you would prefer laypersons as the trier of fact. In answering this question, there are three key factors to consider.

One factor is the complexity of the case. When the case is very complex, some attorneys prefer a bench trial. The available empirical research generally supports the conclusion that lay jurors are capable of evaluating the evidence presented to them. *See* H. KALVEN & H.

ZEISEL, THE AMERICAN JURY Ch. 11 (1966); V. HANS & N. VID-MAR, JUDGING THE JURY (1986). However, many attorneys assume that a judge is more expert at sorting through mountains of evidence. In addition, complex trials tend to be lengthier; and these attorneys fear that many laypersons will become resentful if the trial keeps them away from their normal jobs and activities for weeks or months. This factor is especially important for the plaintiff or prosecutor with the burden of proof.

Another factor is the nature of your theory of the case. Suppose that you must rely on an argument such as the Statute of Frauds or entrapment. These defenses may strike some lay jurors as legal technicalities; at least at a subconscious level, they may be tempted to nullify the law and find liability or responsibility even if you have established the defense. You may decide that you can be more confident that the legally trained judge will sustain the defense when the facts warrant.

The last factor is your knowledge of the predilections of the judge in question. In some cases, you will learn the identity of the judge assigned to the trial before you must decide whether to request a jury. In many other cases, you can predict the identity of the judge who will probably be assigned. Your decision is not an absolute judgment on the jury's ability to effectively decide your case; the decision is a comparative choice. Suppose, for example, that you are an insurance defense attorney in a personal injury action. You contemplate presenting a complex, technical defense at trial. Ordinarily, the nature of that defense would cut in favor of a bench trial. However, assume further that the judge assigned to your case was a plaintiff's personal injury attorney for 20 years before he became a judge. Moreover, several of your friends in the defense bar have tried cases before him, and they all tell you that he seemed quite biased in favor of the plaintiff's side of the docket. Given that knowledge, you might opt for a jury trial.

§ 4.3　AN OVERVIEW OF JURY SELECTION PROCEDURES

We shall assume for the balance of this chapter that you have made the tactical decision to request a jury. Before examining in detail the attorney's role during jury selection, you should have an overview of jury selection procedure. The procedures vary from jurisdiction to jurisdiction; in some states, the judge is not even present in the courtroom during jury selection. L. WRIGHTSMAN, PSYCHOLOGY AND THE LEGAL SYSTEM 228 (1987). (The *Batson* line of authority, *infra*, has reduced the number of jurisdictions following that practice.) However, some generalizations hold true for most jurisdictions.

Many of the key events occur before trial. In many cases, as we shall see, the judge conducts the entire verbal interrogation of the jury panel. If so, before trial, the attorney must draft proposed questions for the jury and submit them to the judge. After reviewing the submissions by both sides, the judge decides which questions to pose to the panel. Furthermore, in a growing number of cases, the judge submits a pretrial questionnaire to the members of the panel assigned to the case. In these instances, the attorney submits draft questions for inclusion in the questionnaire.

At the beginning of the procedure at trial, a bailiff or other court official escorts the panel of venirepersons into the courtroom. The number of venirepersons usually slightly exceeds the sum of the number of: jurors needed to fill the jury box, alternates, and peremptory challenges available to all the parties. Suppose, for instance, that in a criminal case, there will be 12 jurors, 2 alternates, and 20 possible peremptory challenges. You need at least 34 jurors: 12 + 2 + 20. Since there might be challenges for cause, the panel would probably include at least 36 or 38 venirepersons.

Immediately after escorting the panel into the room, the judge, clerk, or bailiff may seat six or 12 in the jury box and announce their names. Some attorneys have a wonderful memory for names and quickly commit the names to memory. However, most attorneys use a jury box diagram such as Figure 4–1 (on following page). Alternatively, you can place six or 12 yellow stickum tabs on a large sheet of paper. As soon as the venireperson is seated and her name called out, write the name in the appropriate box. Many attorneys write down the phonetic pronunciation of the venireperson's name. W. BROCKETT & J. KEKER, EFFECTIVE DIRECT AND CROSS–EXAMINATION § 10.16, at 224 (1986). When you question the individual venire members, it is ideal if you address them by name. It damages your credibility if you forget or mispronounce the person's name.

Formerly, it was merely helpful to use a diagram such as Figure 4–1. Hours or days might elapse between your questioning of a particular panelist and the judge's call for peremptory challenges; during that time lapse, you could forget the answer or conduct which makes it advisable to strike a particular panelist. However, modernly the use of such diagrams is a virtual necessity. In the *Batson* line of authority, the Supreme Court has announced that it is unconstitutional for any litigant—prosecutor, criminal defense attorney, or civil party—to exercise peremptory strikes on racist or sexist grounds. *Batson v. Kentucky*, 476 U.S. 79 (1986); *Edmonson v. Leesville Concrete Co.*, 500 U.S. 614 (1991); *Georgia v. McCollum*, 505 U.S. 42 (1992); *J.E.B. v. Alabama ex rel T.B.*, 511 U.S. 127 (1994). Several lower courts have ruled that like race and sex, religion is an improper basis for a peremptory challenge. Bianchi, *Jurors Cannot Be Struck Because of Religious Beliefs,* LAWYERS WEEKLY USA, Apr. 19, 1999, at p. 1 (collecting cases from California, Connecticut, Florida, Hawaii, Massachusetts, Mississippi, New Jersey, New York, and North Carolina). If the opposing attorney accuses you of striking panelists on such unconstitutional grounds, you need to articulate a legitimate reason for removing the panelist. *Purkett v. Elem,* 514 U.S. 765 (1995). To substantiate that reason, you can insert your marked diagram into the record. *E.g., McCrory v. Henderson,* 871 F.Supp. 597 (W.D.N.Y.1995); *Echlin v. LeCureux,* 800 F.Supp. 515 (E.D.Mich.1992). The diagram will document your legitimate basis for exercising a strike against the panelist. The stakes are high. In some jurisdictions, on appeal a single *Batson* error is per se reversible error. *United States v. Annigoni,* 96 F.3d 1132 (9th Cir.1996); *State v. Huerta,* 175 Ariz. 262, 855 P.2d 776 (1993).

At this point in the proceeding, your jurisdiction will follow one of three basic approaches.

The one-by-one system. In some jurisdictions, jury selection proceeds one juror at a time. The venirepersons may remain in the jury box or spectator area, or one by one they might enter the jury box. One venireperson is questioned, and the judge immediately entertains challenges for cause and then peremptory challenges to that person. Jury selection is complete as soon as the required number of jurors (for example, six or 12) have completed the process.

The sequential or "jury box" system. In contrast, most states follow the sequential or jury box system. Suppose that you need a 12–person jury. Twelve persons would initially enter the jury box. As an over-simplification, jury selection then proceeds in three stages: one stage primarily questioning, another phase dominated by challenges for cause, and a final stage of primarily peremptory challenges.

The process begins by questioning the first 12 venirepersons who enter the box. After they all have been questioned, some judges give the attorneys an opportunity to make challenges for cause. Other judges require the attorney to make cause challenges as soon as the ground surfaces or at least before the attorney moves on to question another panelist. If a cause challenge is sustained, that venireperson exits the box; and a replacement takes her seat. The replacement is questioned, and the judge then entertains challenges for cause to the replacement. This phase continues until 12 venirepersons either have been passed for cause or have survived cause challenges.

The final stage is peremptory challenges. Suppose that one party exercises a peremptory and strikes one of the 12 people in the box. The stricken venireperson exits the box, and a replacement takes his seat. The replacement is questioned, and then in sequence the judge allows cause challenges and finally peremptory challenges to that person. Jury selection is complete when the parties exhaust their peremptory challenges or when all parties pass for peremptory challenges.

Note the disadvantage of this system: You must exercise your peremptory strike against a venireperson before you have an opportunity to question the replacement venireperson. Suppose, for example, that you are a plaintiff's attorney in a personal injury action. You may be inclined to use your last strike against a venireperson who is distantly related to an insurance claims investigator; but if you do, to your horror you may discover that the replacement is the chairperson of the board of a liability insurance company. Thus, in this system, you must husband your strikes.

Figure 4-1

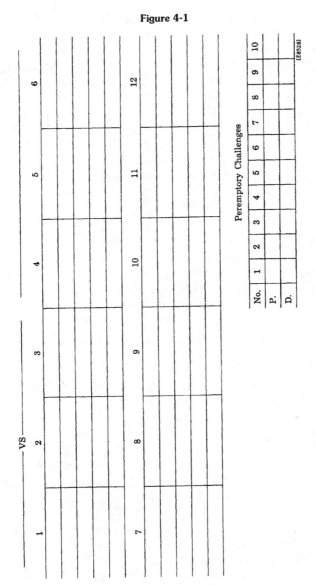

The "struck jury" system. Most federal courts use a different system. After the panel has been led into the courtroom, the judge or the attorneys question the entire panel before challenges are made. When the questioning is complete, the judge entertains cause challenges and then peremptory challenges.

The advantage of this system is that you can question all venirepersons before exercising strikes. In this respect, the struck jury system is the mirror image of the sequential or jury box system. However, this system can be more time-consuming than the sequential procedure, particularly when the attorneys are primarily responsible for the questioning. Moreover, unlike the jury box method, this system does not allow you to "observe the chemistry of the" six or twelve people who will be working together as the jury. *United States v. Broxton,* 926 F.2d 1180, 1182 (D.C.Cir.), *cert. denied,* 499 U.S. 911 (1991). When you are a prosecutor (who needs every vote) or a plaintiff (who needs a supermajority), you want panelists who can cooperate and reach consensus.

§ 4.4 THE ATTORNEY'S ROLE

With this overview in mind, we shall now examine your role as an attorney in jury selection. We shall do so initially from the perspective of the questioning attorney who may want to challenge a venireperson. That role can entail: preparing a pretrial questionnaire (§ 4.6), making preliminary remarks at trial before questioning (§ 4.7), the actual questioning (§ 4.8), and lastly making challenges (§ 4.9). In § 4.10, we shall shift to the point of view of the opposing attorney who wants to keep the venireperson on the jury.

§ 4.5 THE PERSPECTIVE OF THE QUESTIONING ATTORNEY—THE STRATEGY OF JURY DESELECTION

The expression, "jury selection," is misleading. "Jury deselection" would be more accurate. In truth, given the time constraints and the small number of peremptory challenges, you cannot select an ideal jury. If a panelist is an ideal juror for you and the opposing attorney has any sense, the opponent will presumably strike that panelist. However, if you use your limited time and strikes wisely, you can usually deselect the potential jurors you least want. Perlman, *Jury Selection,* 12 THE DOCKET 1, 5 (Spr. 1988); 54 U.S.L.W. (BNA) 2096 (Aug. 13, 1985) (Lisa Blue, a Dallas psychologist-lawyer, commented that realistically "[t]he best that you can hope to do is to eliminate the worst of the jury panel...."); Corboy, *Final Argument: Earning the Jury's Trust,* 28 TRIAL 60, 63 (Feb. 1992). "At most you can 'unpick' some of the worst jurors." McElhaney, *Picking a Jury,* 18 LITIGATION 43, 44 (Wint. 1992). You do not want an "audience" which is positively hostile to your case. Bennett & Hirschhorn, *Conducting Meaningful, Effective Voir Dire in Criminal Cases,* 17 THE CHAMPION 18, 19 (June 1993). However, if your strike any panelist who is not a "dream" juror for your case, you may run out of strikes early before the "nightmare" panelist takes his or her seat in the jury box.

By way of example, in the Mitchell/Stans trial in 1974, the defense team attempted to develop "a profile of the persons who would seem to be the most prejudiced against [the] defendants...." L. WRIGHTSMAN, PSYCHOLOGY AND THE LEGAL SYSTEM 223 (1987). Later, Dan K. Webb served as the prosecutor at the trial of former national security adviser John Poindexter for his role in the Iran–Contra affair. Lieutenant Colonel North had already been convicted. Before the Poindexter trial, Mr. Webb decided that his theme was going to be that Poindexter was North's "boss" and that North "could not have done the things he did without his boss's approval." *Simplify! Simplify! Simplify!,* NAT'L L.J., Feb. 11, 1991, at p. S11. Given his theme, Mr. Webb identified the persons he did not want sitting on the jury: "I decided that I didn't want any bosses on my jury, I wanted employees. I would pick working-class people, who understood that the boss has to accept responsibility." *Id.*

In a nutshell, the essence of the jury deselection strategy is the pretrial development of the profile of the juror you would least want— the set of demographic characteristics and attitudes which would strongly incline the panel member to reject you, your client, or your theme. (Note that if both sides pursue this strategy and identify the right set of characteristics, the end result will be a relatively fair, open-minded jury. Johnson & Haney, *Felony Voir Dire: An Exploratory Study of Its Content and Effect,* 18 LAW & HUM.BEHAV. 487, 502 (1994).) The question that then arises is the optimal method of identifying that set of characteristics.

There are many different approaches to developing this profile. Pavalon, *Jury Selection Theories,* 23 TRIAL 26 (June 1987). On occasion, attorneys have even resorted to astrology and handwriting analysis as aids in jury selection. M. SAKS & R. HASTIE, SOCIAL PSYCHOLOGY IN COURT 60 (1986). However, there are two leading schools of thought.

The traditional school relies primarily on stereotyping. Clarence Darrow popularized the practice of stereotyping, developing generalizations about ethnic and occupational groups' biases that might affect voting behavior during deliberation. In a 1936 interview in *Esquire,* Darrow stated:

> An Englishman is not so good as an Irishman, but still, he has come through a long tradition of individual rights, and is not afraid to stand alone; the fact is he is never sure he is right unless the great majority is against him. The German is not so keen about individual rights except where they concern his own way of life.... Still, he wants to do what is right, he is not afraid. If he is Catholic, then he loves music and art; he must be emotional, and will want to help you; give him a chance.

Some of these generalizations have merit. For example, accountants are accustomed to work with precise numbers. "Some prosecutors do not like to have as a juror an accountant ... on the theory that he will be too strict in determining whether your case meets the burden of proof." Bouska, *Selecting a Jury,* in THE PROSECUTOR'S DESKBOOK 371, 373 (1971). However, as one commentator has noted, if you take all these stereotypes seriously, "the [only acceptable] juror [is] a Spanish carpenter",—the type of juror you are likely never to encounter in practice.

Pavalon, *Jury Selection: Art? Science? Guessing Game?*, 21 TRIAL LAW.Q. 56, 63 (1990). Every other ethnic or occupational group is undesirable according to some stereotype. Some generalizations are simplistic to the point of being silly: "I never let an older woman sit on my jury who wears a hat." Younger, Compton & Fletcher, *Jury Selection,* in THE PROSECUTOR'S DESKBOOK 361, 369 (1971).

Suppose that in the *Scott* prosecution, the prosecutor follows the traditional approach. The prosecutor should strike any panel member who will have serious difficulty accepting the prosecutor's theme, the prosecutor's formal or functional clients, or the prosecutor herself. During the pretrial planning, the prosecutor concluded that an undergraduate psychology major could reject the "so close for so long" theme. The prosecutor might assume that a person with that background has read a large number of the studies allegedly establishing the unreliability of eyewitness identification. The prosecutor would likely use strikes to remove that type of person from the jury. Thus, the prosecutor would start with a rebuttable presumption that he or she should strike any panelist who was an undergraduate Psychology major. Further, it is predictable that certain categories of persons will have difficulty relating to the prosecutor's functional clients, Williams and Taylor. Panel members who are opposed to drinking may dislike Williams, and male members with a chauvinist attitude may not give Taylor's testimony appropriate weight. For that reason, the prosecutor might use strikes to eliminate members of anti-drinking or all-male organizations. Finally, the prosecutor should consider his or her own race, gender, and personality type. Who is likely to react adversely to the prosecutor? The bottomline is that the prosecutor must develop a profile of venirepersons who will have substantial difficulty relating to the prosecutor, the prosecutor's clients, or the prosecutor's theme.

Although most litigators still follow this traditional approach, there is growing support for the so-called scientific method of jury selection. Scientific jury selection was first employed in the Harrisburg Seven trial in 1971–72. M. SAKS & R. HASTIE, SOCIAL PSYCHOLOGY IN COURT 55 (1986); Green & Maxwell, *Jury Research: Reading the Road Map of Jury Thinking*, 16 AM.J.TRIAL ADVOC. 795 (1993). Philip Berrigan and his codefendants were charged with raiding draft boards, conspiring to destroy draft records, and plotting to kidnap Henry Kissinger. The case was tried in Harrisburg, Pennsylvania, a fairly conservative venue. Yet, with the help of social scientists, the defense gained a hung jury, split 10–2 in favor of acquittal. *Id.* at 56. The defense teams also used scientific jury selection techniques in the O.J. Simpson, William Kennedy Smith, and Rodney King cases. Strasser, *Smith Jury Consultant Reflects*, NAT'L L.J., Dec. 30, 1991, at p. 3 (the jury consultant was the late Cathy Bennett); Cox, *L.A. Cop Defense: Experts Helped Pick King Jury*, NAT'L L.J., May 25, 1992 (the defense consulted Litigation Science, Inc.). The use of these techniques is becoming so widespread that in the case of the three defendants accused of attacking trucker Reginald Denny during the 1992 Los Angeles riot, the trial judge approved the use of public funds to permit the defense to hire Litigation Science as jury consultants. Hayes, *Aid for Denny Defendants,* WALL ST.J., Apr. 26, 1993, at p. B6.

This approach relies on social science research techniques. *See generally* C. BENNETT & R. HIRSCHHORN, BENNETT'S GUIDE TO JURY SELECTION AND TRIAL DYNAMICS IN CIVIL AND CRIMINAL LITIGATION (1993); NATIONAL JURY PROJECT, JURYWORK: SYSTEMATIC TECHNIQUES (2d ed. 1983). The basic thrust of this approach is to identify demographic characteristics that correlate strongly with relevant undesirable attitudes and beliefs. Assume, by way of example, that you are defending a left-wing political activist in a prosecution for an act of civil disobedience. As a defense attorney, you certainly would not want jurors with an authoritarian attitude. However, at trial it would be impractical to question the venirepersons bluntly about their political beliefs. Direct questions about that sensitive subject are not only unlikely to elicit frank answers; there is an additional risk of offending panel members. Instead, you might hire a group of researchers to canvass the community the venire is drawn from. The researchers would sample that community to attempt to identify the demographic characteristics—neighborhood, line of work, marital status, etc.—which most strongly correlate with authoritarian attitudes. The result would be the profile of the juror you least wanted. At trial, you would question the panel members about those demographic characteristics: Where do they live? What line of work are they in? Are they married? If the answers to those questions indicate that the panel member fits the profile, that member would be a good candidate for a strike.

The prospect of a truly scientific approach to jury selection is an exciting one. However, there are two important caveats. One is cost. One consultant estimates that any decent survey will cost the attorney at least $5,000.00. Many clients cannot afford that expense. Further, there remain doubts about the validity of this profiling approach. Pavalon, *Jury Selection Theories,* 23 TRIAL 26 (June 1987). To date, there has been no definitive experimental verification of the accuracy of this approach. Some attorneys continue to believe that the "judgment of an experienced trial lawyer is as good as or better than the judgment of any psychologist." *Id.* Even some leading psychologists believe that the image of "jury consultant as shaman" is a "fable." Koski, *Jury Decisionmaking in Rape Trials: A Review and Empirical Assessment,* 38 CRIM. L.BULL. 21, 150 (Jan.-Feb. 2002).

Even if a profile is carefully prepared, its "predictive power is relatively weak." M. SAKS & R. HASTIE, SOCIAL PSYCHOLOGY IN COURT 65 (1986). Whether you rely on stereotyping or scientific jury selection, at most your pretrial deselection profile gives you a rebuttable presumption: If the panelist fits the profile and does and says nothing to rebut the presumption, you ought to strike the panelist. However, during the actual questioning, you need to give the panelist an opportunity to rebut the presumption. Get the panelist talking and find out whether he or she possesses the undesirable attitudes and beliefs that normally accompany the demographic characteristics in the profile. Even though the panelist fits every element of the deselection profile, he or she might be the maverick who would be a wonderful juror for your case.

§ 4.6 THE PERSPECTIVE OF THE QUESTIONING ATTORNEY—PRETRIAL QUESTIONNAIRES

The process of interrogating the panel can begin before trial. In almost all jurisdictions, the courts have standard forms such as Figure 4–2. The form is prepared by the court itself and poses a few elementary questions designed to ensure that the panelist possesses the minimal qualifications such as English language proficiency needed to be eligible for jury service. The attorney plays no role in the preparation of these standard forms.

However, in a growing number of cases, courts are submitting forms such as Figure 4–3 to panelists before trial. These questionnaires differ in both their form and content from standard forms such as Figure 4–2. These questionnaires tend to be much longer than the traditional standard forms. In the O.J. Simpson case, prospective jurors had to fill out a 294–question, 80–page survey. These questionnaires are not only more detailed than the old standard forms; unlike the standard forms, the questionnaires are tailored to the specific facts of the case which the panelist has tentatively been assigned to. In the *King* case, question #109 asked: "What was your personal reaction to the verdicts in the state court trial?" Levenson, *The Future of State and Federal Civil Rights Prosecutions: The Lessons of the Rodney King Trial,* 41 U.C.L.A.L.Rev. 509, 530 n. 115 (1994). Some courts have permitted inquiry about the acquittal in O.J. Simpson's prosecution. *Shelling v. State,* 52 S.W.3d 213 (Tex.App.2001). Although it is the judge who finally orders the questionnaire submitted to the panelists, the attorneys are primarily responsible for drafting the questionnaire. Each attorney has an opportunity to submit proposed questions for inclusion in the questionnaire.

Tailored questionnaires such as those employed in the *Simpson* and *King* cases are now in widespread use. Fargo, *Juror Questionnaires Can Supplement Voir Dire,* 29 TRIAL 23 (Oct. 1993); James, *Voir Dire in the '90s,* 6 THE PRACT. LITIGATOR 29 (Jan. 1995)(including a sample questionnaire). The American Bar Association has revised its STANDARDS FOR CRIMINAL JUSTICE: TRIAL BY JURY to regulate the content of questionnaires. Standard 15–2.2 now provides:

(a) Basic questionnaire.

Before voir dire examination begins, the court and counsel shall be provided with data pertinent to the qualifications of the prospective jurors and to matters ordinarily raised in voir dire examination.

(1) The questionnaire should include information about the juror's name, sex, age, residence, marital status, education level, occupation, and occupation history, employment address, previous

service as a juror, and present or past involvement as a party to civil or criminal litigation.

(2) Such data should be obtained from prospective jurors by means of a questionnaire furnished to prospective jurors with the jury summons, and to be returned by the prospective jurors before the time of jury selection.

(b) Specialized questionnaire.

In appropriate cases, the court, with the assistance of counsel, should prepare a specialized questionnaire, addressing particular issues that may arise.

(1) The questionnaire should be specific enough to provide appropriate information for utilization by counsel, but not be unnecessarily embarrassing or overly intrusive.

In 1998, the A.B.A. Section of Litigation released its new Civil Trial Practice Standards. Standard 1.a.i encourages trial judges to use specialized questionnaires in complex cases.

As a general proposition, in drafting proposed questions, the attorney should follow the planning process described in § 4.8 of this chapter. However, there are common-sense differences between questions intended to be posed in open court and those designed for insertion in a written pretrial questionnaire. The medium may not be the message, but it importantly influences the message.

On the one hand, as Figure 4–3 suggests, written pretrial questionnaires are ordinarily restricted to hard factual data. Although the attorney is often interested in the panelists' attitudes as well as their demographic characteristics, a written questionnaire can be an awkward medium for exploring certain types of attitudes and beliefs. Questioning about such topics can be difficult. If the panelist is reluctant to discuss the topic, the attorney may have to prod and encourage a complete, candid answer. Effective questioning about attitudes sometimes requires following up on initial, unsatisfactory answers; and followup is impractical in the context of a written questionnaire. It is usually best to reserve questioning about attitudes until the oral interrogation at trial.

On the other hand, as the length of the Rodney King questionnaire suggests, the judge often permits more questions in written pretrial form than she would during oral interrogation at trial. As § 4.8 indicates, there has been a marked trend toward judicial control of voir dire questioning. In part, the trend reflects a widespread judicial belief that attorneys abuse the questioning in order to indoctrinate panelists, that is, to bias the panel rather than to gather information from the panel. However, the trend also reflects an even wider judicial consensus that jury selection has become too time-consuming. That concern evaporates, however, when the questioning takes the form of a written pretrial questionnaire; the use of the questionnaire does not consume any trial time. For that reason, many judges will permit you to include more questions in the pretrial questionnaire than they would ever permit you to orally pose at trial. The use of a juror questionnaire might not only enable you to ask more questions; some judges will also allow you to ask especially probing questions. For example, in one of the prosecutions of Dr. Jack Kevorkian, the questionnaire included such queries as "Can you think of any situations where you would consider assisted suicide as an option for yourself?" Sherman, *Kevorkian Voir Dire Astonishes*, NAT'L L.J., May 2, 1994. FInally, there are indications that absent the pressure of having to speak in open court, some panelists give more candid answers in their questionnaire responses. Green, *Juror Anxiety Can Be a Wild Card During Trial*, NAT'L L.J., Sept. 26, 1994, at p. A22; Heaney, *Jury Selection: Utilizing Juror Questionnaires*, 20 CACJ FORUM 14, 15–16 (1993); Lilley, *Techniques for Targeting Juror Bias*, 30 TRIAL 74, 77 (Nov. 1994).

Figure 4-2

Notice to Appear for Examination for Jury Duty on:

At:

If impossible to appear on the above date you may report on any of the following dates:

Mo.Day Mo.Day Mo.Day Mo.Day Mo.Day

Dear Citizen:

By direction of the Superior Court your name has been drawn and included on the court list of prospective jurors.

You are hereby requested to present this letter between the hours of 8:30 A.M. and 3:00 P.M. at the location and on the date listed above. If you use glasses, please bring them with you.

Only the reasons set forth on the reverse side of this letter can be considered as proper for failure to appear. If you wish to claim exemption, please comply with the instructions on the reverse side of this letter.

You will not be summoned for actual jury service until after 3 to 6 months from the date of examination. Ordinarily, jury service on cases will not exceed twenty days.

Yours very truly,

By direction of the Court   (s) William A. Goodwin
Jury Commissioner

(s) Donald R. Wright
Presiding Judge

INSTRUCTIONS

If you are physically unable to perform jury duty, lack supervision for your minor children, or are exempt by reason of your occupation as lawyer, physician, dentist, clergyman or pharmacist, or have served on the jury within the past two years, satisfactory completion and return by mail of the certificate on this page to the Jury Commissioner's office will excuse you from jury duty until further notice.

If you are a legal resident of Los Angeles County, but temporarily absent from the County, you may so state on this letter and return it to the Jury Commissioner for deferment. If you are no longer a legal resident of Los Angeles County, you may complete the certificate on this page and mail it to the Jury Commissioner in order that you may be excused from jury service.

STATE OF CALIFORNIA
County of Los Angeles   CERTIFICATE

1. FULL NAME (Mr. Mrs. Miss) _____
                              LAST NAME   FIRST NAME

2. HOME ADDRESS _____
                 NUMBER   STREET   ZONE   CITY

3. ARE YOU A CITIZEN OF THE
   UNITED STATES?   YES ☐ NO ☐ (check one)

4. AGE _____ BIRTHPLACE _____
                              (STATE OR NATION)

Figure 4-2—Continued

5. HAVE YOU EVER SERVED AS A JUROR
   IN THIS COUNTY?   YES ☐ NO ☐ (check one)

   (a) If your answer is yes, check the court or court in which you have served

federal court		municipal court	
superior court		justice court	

   (b) when were you last discharged from jury service? _____
6. WHAT IS YOUR OCCUPATION, TRADE OR PROFESSION? _____

7. IF EMPLOYED, BY WHOM? _____
8. STATE NUMBER AND AGES OF MINOR CHILDREN _____

9. STATEMENT OF ADDITIONAL FACTS:

   _____
   _____
   _____
   _____
   _____

   I declare, under penalty of perjury, that the above statements are true and correct.

   _____   _____
        (DATE)   (CITY)   [E8531]

Figure 4-3

Juror Questionnaire

Name_____
1. Place of birth_____
2. Age_____ and sex_____
3. Marital Status Married _____, Single _____, Divorced_____,
   Widowed _____. If married, how long? _____
4. Children, Their Ages _____
   sexes_____, and occupations_____
   _____
5. Please state your education. Highest grade completed: _____
   Degrees:_____; Other educational programs
   (vocational, night school, part-time study, certification program):_____
   _____
6. Please state your present occupation_____
   job description_____
   Employer_____
   Length of employment_____
7. Please state your previous occupation_____
   job description_____

Figure 4-3—*Continued*

Employer_____

8. Please state the present occupation of your spouse or significant other

_____

Employer_____

9. Their previous occupation_____

Employer_____

10. Have you ever served on a jury trial before? _____

If yes, please state the type of trial (Criminal or Civil)_____

How many times have you served?_____

11. What city do you live in or near?_____

How long have you lived there?_____

12. Do any other adults live in your household?_____

(Voluntary) if yes, please state occupation_____,

educational background_____

13. Are you, a close friend or relative employed by a federal, state, or local law enforcement agency?_____If yes, who and what agency?

_____

14. Have you, a close friend or relative ever been involved in a criminal case?_____, If yes, please check one of the following:

Victim____, Defendant____, Witness____.

15. Do you have any moral or religious principles, opinions, or feelings which would make it difficult or impossible to judge whether someone is guilty or innocent of a crime?_____

_____

16. Have you, a close friend or relative ever been involved in a law suit or legal action of any kind?_____ If yes, who was involved and in what manner?_____

_____

17. What social, civic, religious, or other organizations are you affiliated with?

_____

Please describe your activities and offices you have held, this includes volunteer work._____

_____

18. What are your hobbies and leisure interests?_____

_____

_____

19. Have you taken any courses or had training in any legal field, e.g. law, law enforcement, corrections, etc.?_____

If yes, which area?_____

20. Please circle one of the following . . . would you describe yourself as a leader: infrequently, occasionally, frequently

21. In your work, do you have management or supervisory responsibilities?_____

Figure 4-3—Continued

Have you had them in the past?_____ If yes, please describe,_____

_____

22. Have you, a close friend or relative ever suffered from severe injury
    or accident?_____ If yes, please describe briefly,_____

_____

23. Do you have any close friends or relatives in the legal profession?____
24. Please name the newspapers or other periodicals you read.

_____

25. What are your favorite televisions shows? _____

_____

26. Is there any reason why you would or would not like to sit on the jury in
    this particular case?_____

_____

Are there any pressing issues in your life that may cause a distraction?

_____

Please inform the court of any additional information you feel affects
your ability to serve as a juror._____

§ 4.7 THE PERSPECTIVE OF THE QUESTIONING ATTOR-NEY—PRELIMINARY REMARKS AT TRIAL

In some jurisdictions, at trial the judge makes all the preliminary remarks to the jury. However, in many jurisdictions, the judge permits the attorneys to make brief, prefatory remarks before the questioning begins.

Assume that you are the first attorney to deliver preliminary remarks. What should you tell the jury? (1) At the outset, introduce yourself and your client. Some attorneys ask their client to stand and face the panel during the introduction. (2) Next, explain the purpose of voir dire examination. You may have to question the jurors about sensitive subjects such as sexual practices and political or religious beliefs. The jurors can resent the questions. You want the jurors to understand that you are not simply prying into their privacy. Rather, tell them that you are questioning them simply to ensure that both sides receive a fair trial from an impartial jury. (3) Then, identify all the participants in the trial: the judge, the court officials, the opposing attorney, his firm, the opposing client, and the witnesses. If a venireperson is personally acquainted with any of those persons, he might be subject to challenge for cause; his impartiality would certainly be suspect. (Moreover, by introducing all the other participants in the trial, to some extent you "take command" of the courtroom.) (4) Finally, in simple, lay terms, state a thumbnail sketch of your theory of the case. You want the panel to learn that theory as early in the case as possible. At the same time, single out the key element of your theory—the element that you expect to be the real battleground during the trial. These preliminary remarks enable you to give the jury "the big picture" or synopsis of your case early in the trial. Klein & Shayne, *A Soup-to-Nuts Jury Selection and Opening Statement Primer*, 4 THE PRACT. LITIGATOR 29, 32 (Mar. 1993); O'Quinn, *State the Case Simply, Starting With Voir Dire*, NAT'L L.J., Feb. 8, 1993. To give the jury "the big picture," both state the theory and single out the key, disputed element of the theory.

You can easily tie all four elements of the preliminary statement together: "Ladies and gentlemen, my name is _____, and I represent the People of the State of El Dorado in this criminal case. As her Honor just indicated, we are now beginning jury selection in the case. At this point, I have to ask you some questions. I want to explain why I'm going to do that. I'm not asking these questions just because I'm nosy and want to pry into your private lives. Rather, we have to make sure that you can sit as impartial jurors in this case and give both sides a fair trial. For example, it would obviously be difficult for you to be impartial if you were well acquainted with one of the key participants in the trial. For that reason, I'm now going to introduce to you all the key participants in this case. This morning we're in the courtroom of her Honor, Judge Lisa Farnsworth. Her court clerk is James Wilson, and the court reporter is Marcia Wiley. For the People, I'll be calling several witnesses: Peter Williams, Morena Police Officer Janice Taylor, and Dr. Miles Stacey. The defense attorney in this case is Mr. Albert Hewitt seated to my immediate left; and the defendant, Robert Scott, is with Mr. Hewitt at the other table. The defense will be calling Ms. Joan Freeman as a witness in this case. The jury in this case will listen to these witnesses; and, based on their testimony, it will have to decide whether the defendant is guilty of the crime of battery. The key issue in this case will be identity—whether the defendant is one of the men who attacked the victim, Mr. Peter Williams. The People believe the evidence will show that the defendant attacked Mr. Williams at the Senator Hotel in the early morning of January 19, 19YR–1. The defendant denies that he did so. That's the case in a nutshell, and we need an impartial jury to decide this case."

Even if you are the second attorney to address the jury, the judge may also allow you to make some prefatory remarks. You should obviously introduce yourself and your client. If the opposing attorney did not do a good job of explaining the purpose of voir dire, you may want to say a few words about that topic. You may have to ask more delicate questions than the opposing attorney, and you might want to elaborate on the purpose of voir dire to encourage the venirepersons to be candid in their answers. Of course, it is unnecessary for you to reintroduce the other participants if the judge or opposing attorney has already done so. However, you will certainly want to state your theory of the case and identify its pivotal element before you start questioning.

These preliminary remarks should be short. The judge may tolerate two or three minutes of remarks, but this is not the occasion for your opening statement in the case.

§ 4.8 THE PERSPECTIVE OF THE QUESTIONING ATTORNEY—PLANNING AND CONDUCTING THE QUESTIONING AT TRIAL

Just as the jurisdictions use different overall procedures for jury selection, they employ various procedures for the questioning. Specifically, the division of labor between the judge and the attorneys varies.

In some states, the attorneys do all the questioning. In fact, in a few jurisdictions, the judge does not even attend the questioning.

In other jurisdictions, the judge does all the questioning. This is the pattern in roughly two thirds of the federal judicial districts and a fifth of the states. Fahringer, *"In the Valley of the Blind"-Jury Selection in a Criminal Case,* 3 TRIAL DIPL. J. 34, 36 n. 3 (Sum. 1980). Bills have been submitted in recent sessions of the United States Senate to amend the Federal Civil and Criminal Rules to require judges to permit attorneys to directly question prospective jurors, but it is doubtful that the bills will be enacted. McMillion, *Advocating Voir Dire Reform,* 77 A.B.A.J. 114 (Nov. 1991). In this system, before trial, the attorneys can submit proposed questions in writing to the judge; but the judge conducts all the personal interrogation of the panel. In drafting proposed questions for use at trial, follow the guidelines outlined in § 4–8(D), *infra.* This system arguably lowers the quality of the questioning. The judge knows less about the case than the attorneys, and for that reason the questions may be less tailored to the facts. In addition, the judge is an authority figure; and the jurors could be less frank in answering a question posed by the judge. However, the counterarguments are that attorneys misuse voir dire to bias the jury and that attorney voir dire tends to be too time-consuming. "Horror stories abound on how long it takes to pick a jury in California criminal cases: almost four months in the 'Hillside Strangler' case, seven months in David Carpenter's trial in Santa Cruz, [and] nine months in the Los Angeles murder trial of Steven Jackson." Duncan, *Putting a Cap on Voir Dire,* 7 CAL. LAW. 14 (Oct. 1987); L. WRIGHTSMAN, PSYCHOLOGY AND THE LEGAL SYSTEM 244 (1987) ("in the highly publicized 'Hillside Strangler' trial in Los Angeles, the voir dire alone took 49 court days").

In still other jurisdictions—the majority of states—the judge and attorneys share responsibility for questioning the venire. The judge conducts the initial questioning, typically concentrating on possible grounds for challenge for cause. The judge then turns the panel over to the attorneys to complete the interrogation. In its 1998 Civil Trial Practice Standards, the A.B.A. Section of Litigation encourages trial judges to allow counsel to directly question the panelists. Standard 1.b.i states that the "trial judge should conduct an initial voir dire dire examination. Counsel should then be permitted to question panel members for a reasonable period of time." In some jurisdictions, though, the counsel may need to file a formal motion to obtain permission to supplement the judge's questioning. Hennenberg & DeVan, *Conducting a Defense Voir Dire Through the Judge in Federal District Court,* 11 THE CHAMPION 20, 22–23 (Mar. 1987)(including a sample motion). For the remainder of this section, we shall assume that the judge will permit allow the attorneys to conduct some of the questioning. If allowed to directly question the panel, the attorney must decide: which questions to ask, how to phrase the questions, and whom to pose the questions to. Subsections 8.4(A)-(C) address the initial topic, § 8–4(D) discusses the phrasing of voir dire questions, and § 8–4(E) takes up the final subject.

§ 4.8(A) Listing All the Types of Questions That the Attorney Would Like to Ask

The initial planning step for the attorney is listing all the types of questions that the attorney would ideally like to pose to the panel. There are four different types of questions.

Challenges for cause. One type is designed to determine whether there is any ground to challenge the venireperson for cause. Many jurisdictions have statutes or court rules detailing the grounds for challenge for cause. For example, in California, Code of Civil Procedure §§ 228–29 list the various grounds. Assume that in Morena, a venireperson is challengeable for cause if she is related to a party or witness. You are the prosecutor in the *Scott* case. You want to know whether the panel members are related to the defendant or Joan Freeman.

Peremptory challenges. Another type of question is calculated to help you intelligently exercise your peremptory strikes. There is a great deal of mythology about the persons you should strike from the jury. As we analyzed case strategy in Chapter 3, the essence of your trial presentation will be a theory and theme. Section 4.5 pointed out that you should strike venirepersons whose background would predispose them to reject either the theme, your client, or you. These questions implement the jury deselection strategy. You need to identify the venirepersons who would not be receptive members of the "audience" for your theory and theme. Bennett & Hirschhorn, *Conducting Meaningful and Effective Voir Dire in Criminal Cases,* 17 THE CHAMPION 18, 19 (June 1993). In *Scott,* the prosecutor's theme will be "so close for so long." As previously stated, the juror the prosecutor least wants is a person who believes the various psychology studies supposedly establishing the unreliability of eyewitness testimony. Many undergraduate psychology majors have been exposed to those studies. For that reason, the prosecutor will want to question the panel about their educational background. If they indicate that they attended college, the prosecutor should probe further to determine their major. Although formally the prosecutor's client is the government, functionally the prosecutor's clients are Officer Taylor and Mr. Williams. Since the prosecutor must rely on Officer Taylor's testimony, he does not want any jurors with chauvinist biases against female police officers. Consequently, the prosecutor will also want to question the male panel members to determine whether any of them belong to all-male organizations such as athletic clubs, business associations, or fraternal orders.

Factual indoctrination. Third, the attorney can use questions for factual indoctrination. The conventional wisdom is that the attorney should expose the principal factual weaknesses in his case during voir dire. Candidly tell the jury about "the most worrisome" aspect of your case. Smith, *Challenges of Jury Selection,* 88 A.B.A.J. 35 (Apr. 2002). In some cases, your client's unsavory appearance, complete with tattoos, can pose a problem. Bowden, *Representing "Unsavory" Clients in Criminal Cases,* LAWYERS WEEKLY USA, Apr. 29, 2002, at p. 19. In a personal injury action, a defense attorney might fear that the major problem at trial will be the sympathy generated by the severity of the plaintiff's injuries. With the court's permission, the defense attorney might show the panel a photograph of the plaintiff's injuries or even part of the plaintiff's day-in-the-life film. Fullenweider, *Exposing Your Warts,* 17 LITIGATION 22, 24 (Wint. 1991); *Roberts v. Sisters of St. Francis Health Servs., Inc.,* 198 Ill.App.3d 891, 145 Ill.Dec. 44, 556 N.E.2d 662 (1990). If you bury your head in the sand like an ostrich and ignore the weakness, the opposing attorney may be the first to mention the weakness to the jury. If so, the weakness may sound twice as damning; and the venirepersons might begin to doubt your candor. The prosecutor in *Scott* might want to mention that there will be evidence that Williams was drinking just before the attack. The prosecutor may then seek a commitment from the jurors—"a contract"—that they will not disbelieve Williams simply because he had been drinking.

Although veteran litigators have long believed that it is wise to attempt to expose your factual weaknesses during voir dire, another school of thought is emerging. Two commentators argue that as a general proposition, it is unwise to volunteer your weaknesses. R. KLONOFF & P. COLBY, SPONSORSHIP STRATEGY; EVIDENTIARY TACTICS FOR WINNING JURY TRIALS 12, 88 (1990); Colby & Klonoff, *Sponsoring Strategy,* 17 LITIGATION 1 (Spr. 1991). These commentators fear that by volunteering the weakness, the advocate will magnify its importance in the jurors' minds. These commentators argue that by "sponsoring" the fact, the advocate in effect concedes to the jury that the fact is material to the case. Having made that earlier concession, the advocate may find it difficult during closing argument to convince the jury that the fact is unimportant. These commentators favor exposing factual weaknesses only when "the jury is apt to conclude that . . . the advocate, by . . . unusual efforts, went out of his way to omit" the damaging fact. *Id.* at 88. In the exceptional situation in which the jurors perceive that "the advocate went out of his way to hide a weakness, [the jury] may view the advocate's entire case with greater skepticism. . . ." *Id.* at 89.

Professor Michael Saks, one of the leading authorities on law and psychology, has questioned the Klonff–Colby thesis. According to Professor Saks, several empirical studies indicate that by exposing a decisionmaker to an opponent's argument before the opponent has a chance to state the argument in more damning terms, to some extent an advocate can "inoculate" the decisionmaker against the argument. Saks, *Turning Practice into Progress: Better Lawyering Through Experimentation,* 66 NOTRE DAME L.REV. 801, 807 n. 28 (1991) ("Research on the 'inoculation' theory of resistance to persuasion supports the defanging strategy"); Lawson, *Experimental Research on the Organization of Persuasive Arguments: An Application to Courtroom Communications,* 1970 LAW & SOC.ORDER 463, 464–65, 478–79; McGuire, *Inducing Resistance to Persuasion,* in 1 L. BERKOWITZ, ADVANCES IN EXPERIMENTAL PSYCHOLOGY (1964). Professor Saks elaborated his criticism in a review of the Klonoff–Colby text, *Flying Blind in the Courtroom: Trying Cases Without Knowing What Works or Why,* 101 YALE L.J. 1177 (1992).

Floyd Abrams joined in the criticism in a companion book review, *Trial Tactics: Sponsorship Costs of the Adversary System,* 101 YALE L.J. 1159 (1992). While Saks leveled the criticism that the sponsorship strategy theory is at odds with psychological research, Abrams argues that the theory is inconsistent with the experience of successful litigators in cases such as the trials of Alger Hiss (*id.* at 1165–69), Jean Harris (*id.* at 1169–72), and Wayne Newton. *Id.* at 1172–75.

It seems clear that the traditional view still has a large number of adherents. Fullenweider, *Exposing Your Warts,* 17 LITIGATION 22, 59 (Wint. 1991) (describing several trials of his partner, Richard "Racehorse" Haynes); Jamail, *Keeping the Case Rolling and Jurors Will Follow,* NAT'L L., Feb. 8, 1993, at p. S8 (the article quotes Joseph Jamail as stating that during voir dire, "[t]here's a race for disclosure because I tell my weaknesses right off the bat;" "by disclosing problems first, he can take the sting out of the revelation. . . ."). In one survey of successful litigators, all the trial attorneys commenting on their voir dire strategy voiced the traditional view. For instance, one eminently successful litigator, Willie E. Gary, stated that during voir dire, he "admits any problems with his case. 'You have to steal their thunder.' " *He Works Hard to Win Cases Before They Are Filed,* NAT'L L.J., Feb. 14, 1994, at p. S8. A 2001 text released by the A.B.A. Section of Litigation flatly recommends the traditional view. R. WAICUKAUSKI, P. SANDLER & J. EPPS, THE WINNING ARGUMENT Ch. 12 (2001). At least for the foreseeable future, many, if not most, litigators will attempt factual indoctrination on the weaknesses of their case during voir dire.

Legal indoctrination. Finally, the attorney can use questions for legal indoctrination. Some attorneys recommend exposing the panel during voir dire to legal doctrines that may surprise them such as vicarious liability or responsibility. When the plaintiff's attorney suspects that the jurors may be surprised by and shocked at the large size of the verdict which damages law permits the plaintiff to seek in this type of case, the attorney may raise that issue during voir dire examination. Other attorneys suggest exposing the jurors to disfavored legal doctrines such as entrapment or insanity. After the *Hinckley* verdict, the insanity defense is unpopular in many circles. If the defendant is going to rely on that defense, the defense attorney may want to broach the defense early in the case. If you are forced to rely on a disfavored doctrine at trial, try to minimize the risk that the jurors will succumb to the temptation to nullify the law and disregard the doctrine. Finally, the attorney ought to briefly but vigorously stress any instruction supporting the theme in the case. One of the reasons the *Scott* prosecutor chose the "so close for so long" theme was that the judge will probably give a pattern instruction on eyewitness identification, containing the language "how close" and "how long." The prosecutor may want to mention that instruction and solicit the venireperson's commitment to follow that instruction.

§ 4.8(B) Determining the Types of Questions That You Need to Ask in Court

It may be unnecessary for you to ask a question in court. First, the judge may ask the question for you. As previously stated, in many jurisdictions the judge begins the questioning by interrogating the panel about potential grounds for challenge for cause. In some jurisdictions, you can even predict the phrasing of the judge's questions because there are pattern questions the judge uses. For example, § 8 of the Judicial Administration Standards of the California Rules of Court, promulgated by the Judicial Council, sets out a complete set of voir dire questions for civil cases. Section 8.5 contains a similar set of voir dire questions for criminal cases.

Second, you may not need to ask a question because you already know the answer. You can gather information about the panel members before trial. As § 4.6 noted, some courts submit questionnaires such as Figures 4–2 or 4–3 to potential venirepersons before trial, and then routinely distribute the completed forms to the attorneys. In other courts, you can obtain pretrial discovery of the answers to the questionnaires. The questionnaire answers may give you information that you would otherwise have to question the panel to obtain. Or there may be a jury book containing information about panel members, at least if they have already served on a local jury. There are commercial services that publish such books, and large offices such as district attorney's and public defender offices sometimes maintain their own jury books. In addition, if you have the resources, you may conduct a background investigation of the panel members. American Bar Association Disciplinary Rule 7–108(A) and Model Rule 3.5(b) forbid personal contact with the panel members; but your investigator may contact other persons, including associates and neighbors, to gather information about the panel member. Finally, if you obtain the names of the panel members before trial, you can contact public agencies with information about the members' backgrounds. For example, in many states, by contacting the registrar of voters, you can learn each panel member's political affiliation. When you obtain the needed background information from one of these sources, it is a waste of time to question the panel member in court.

By process of elimination, you have identified the types of questions that you would not only like to ask but need to ask in the courtroom. If, for example, it is predictable that the judge will cover all the possible grounds for challenge for cause with the panel, you will need to ask only the remaining three types of questions: those tailored for peremptory challenges, factual indoctrination, and legal indoctrination.

§ 4.8(C) Identifying the Types of Questions the Judge Will Allow You to Ask

The next question that arises is whether the judge will allow you to ask the types of questions that you identified in the last planning step.

The judge must allow you to ask the question if by statute or case law, you have a right to ask that type of question. All courts agree that if attorney questioning is permitted at all, you have a right to interrogate the venire about possible grounds for challenge for cause. At one extreme, there is a minority view that you also have the right to ask questions needed to enable you to intelligently exercise peremptory challenges. *People v. Williams,* 29 Cal.3d 392, 628 P.2d 869, 174 Cal. Rptr. 317 (1981); *Mares v. State,* 83 N.M. 225, 490 P.2d 667 (1971); *Mauldin v. State,* 874 S.W.2d 692 (Tex.Ct.App.1993); *Powell v. State,* 631 S.W.2d 169 (Tex.Crim.App.1982); Tanford, *An Introduction to Trial Law,* 51 MO.L.REV. 623, 642–43 (1986).

However, the majority view is that even if you do not have an absolute right to ask a particular type of question, in her discretion the judge may permit you to do so. *Id.* at 643. Thus, even though you may not be entitled to ask questions to allow you to intelligently exercise peremptory strikes, the judge has discretion to permit you to do so. You should contact other attorneys who have appeared before the same judge and attempt to learn whether the judge permits factual or legal indoctrination and, if so, to what extent. If your trial is in federal court, you might consult the latest edition of the ALMANAC OF THE FEDERAL JUDICIARY. You may find, for example, that your judge allows factual indoctrination but prohibits legal indoctrination; the judge happens to be very jealous of her prerogative of instructing the jury on the law.

There is another minority view which narrowly restricts the range of questioning; under this view, the attorneys may not ask questions for any purpose other than establishing a ground for challenge for cause. *Davis v. Maryland,* 93 Md.App. 89, 611 A.2d 1008 (1992). In 1992, by an initiative, the California electorate amended the pertinent statutes to provide that in criminal cases, "[e]xamination of prospective jurors shall be conducted only in aid of the exercise of challenges for cause." This language seems to deny the judge discretion to even permit questioning for any other purpose.

§ 4.8(D) Drafting the Voir Dire Questions

The prior three planning steps determine the types of questions you need to and will be permitted to ask. At the conclusion of the analysis described in § 4.8(B), for example, you conclude that there is no need to question about challenges for cause because the judge will adequately cover that topic. Further, at the end of the analysis outlined in § 4.8(C), you might discover that your judge flatly forbids legal indoctrination. By process of elimination, you have to pose only the two remaining types of questions: those enabling you to intelligently exercise peremptory strikes and those calculated for factual indoctrination. The next task is drafting the questions.

Whatever the type of question—challenge for cause, factual indoctrination, etc.—you should keep the question simple, short, and clear. You want to encourage the jurors to speak with you; and if you want to attain that objective, you must use the language they are accustomed to hearing and conversing in. We shall discuss courtroom language in greater detail in the next chapter. It suffices now to stress that simplicity, brevity, and clarity should be common denominators of all your voir dire questions. However, while the questions ought to share those qualities, the phrasing of the question should vary with the purpose of the question.

Questions designed to determine whether the venireperson is subject to challenge for cause. This type of question should ordinarily be phrased in a mildly leading fashion: "Are you related to any parties to this suit?" or "Do you know any of the witnesses I just listed?" As these examples suggest, the phrasing should also be closed-ended, specifying a particular ground for challenge for cause.

Questions designed to enable the attorney to intelligently exercise peremptory challenges. There are two different schools of thought on the proper wording of this category of question.

One school of thought is that these questions ought to be non-leading and open-ended in the extreme: "In your own words, tell us something about yourself." Social scientists tend to support this school. They reason that the attorney should make the question extremely open-ended because there are so many psychological inhibitors to candid answers by the venirepersons. To begin with, they have to answer questions in the presence of the judge, an authority figure. Moreover, there is usually a substantial distance—often 12 or more feet—between them and the questioning attorneys. Frank conversations are ordinarily conducted at the "intimate" distance of three feet or fewer, permitting the conversants to speak softly. When the distance between the conversants reaches a "public" distance, it is difficult to carry on a candid conversation. Further, the venirepersons must speak in the presence of their peers. Their peers' presence generates a pressure to give the socially acceptable answer. Finally, the voir dire examination occurs in a formal, ritualistic environment replete with black robes, flags, and armed police officers. Social scientists contend that the only way to counteract these inhibitors is to go to the extreme of asking open-ended questions.

Most experienced trial attorneys agree that you must get the panel members talking to make the voir dire examination worthwhile. You must invite the panel members to open up to obtain valuable insights into their personalities. However, many seasoned litigators reject social scientists' recommendation that the questions be completely open-ended; there is no telling what the venirepersons will say in response to a truly open-ended question, and you may exhaust the judge's patience with a parade of irrelevant answers. For that reason, the majority of experienced trial attorneys recommend that this type of question be phrased in a non-leading but closed-ended manner. The question should at least specify the topic that you want the panel member to talk about: "Tell us something about your schooling," "What organizations do you belong to?," or "In your own words, describe your job for us." Pursue your jury deselection strategy, and target the demographic characteristics which make up the profile of the juror you *least* want. If the judge is especially tolerant, the attorney might also ask about the newspapers and magazines they read, the television programs they regularly watch, the magazines they like to read, and perhaps even the bumper stickers they have on their car. What political initiatives have they signed within the past year? The areas of their lives "where people choose—where they select what they do, . . . read, like, and believe—these are the places for you to explore." S. HAMLIN, WHAT MAKES JURIES LISTEN 79 (1985); Conlin, *Effective Voir Dire in Sex Discrimination Cases,* 29 TRIAL 22, 24 (July 1993)(the charities they contribute to, the television shows they watch, and the social organizations they belong to).

Determining whether the venireperson possesses an attitude justifying the use of a strike to remove the person from the jury is a challenging task. To do so, some attorneys employ "spectrum" questions: "Mrs. Jones, some people feel that. . . . However, other people think that. . . . What do you think?" Herman, *In Trial with Lender Liability* 14 (unpublished article). This type of question "gives the juror the two poles of the spectrum and then allows the juror to position herself toward one pole or the other on the attitude spectrum." *Id.* "[E]ncourage the expression of different attitudes and experiences" by the various panel members. Heaney & Lunsford, *Voir Dire: How to Avoid the Improper Question as Defined by the New Law,* 18 CALIFORNIA ATTORNEYS FOR CRIMINAL JUSTICE FORUM 12, 15 (Jan./Feb. 1991). If a recent event in the national, state, or local news might trigger the same attitude as one you are probing about, ask the panelist "What was your first reaction to the story?" or "How did you feel when you read about it?" Bennett, Hirschhorn & Epstein, *How to Conduct a Meaningful & Effective Voir Dire in Criminal Cases,* 46 S.M.U.L.REV. 659, 667 (1992).

Questions calculated to indoctrinate on the facts. As previously stated, you can use voir dire examination to expose the factual weaknesses in your case and solicit the panel members' commitment not to decide the case against you simply because of those weaknesses. This type of questioning typically follows a three-step pattern.

Initially, the attorney exposes the problem in a declarative sentence or two: "There will be evidence in this case that just before the attack, Mr. Williams had several drinks. There will also be testimony that he drinks regularly." Put the bad cards on the table.

Next, some judges will permit you to attempt to discover the venireperson's relevant attitudes and beliefs. In *Scott,* the prosecutor wants to know whether the panel members are violently opposed to drinking or belong to any anti-drinking organizations: "How do you feel about people who drink regularly?" "How strongly do you feel that?" and "What anti-drinking organizations, if any, do you belong to?" These questions are non-leading but closed-ended.

Assume that the panel member gives you a favorable or neutral answer. For instance, she might say to the prosecutor, "It's O.K. to drink if you can hold your liquor" or "Honestly, I haven't given much thought to it." If so, you can finally proceed to solicit the commitment not to decide the case against you simply because of that factual weakness: "If a person drinks, do you necessarily think that they can't make an accurate identification? Before deciding whether to believe the identification, would you consider all the other facts? Can you promise me that you won't reject Mr. Williams' identification of his attackers simply because he had some drinks before the attack?" The phrasing ought to be leading, and it should incorporate language such as "necessarily reject," "automatically disbelieve," or "reject simply because." The judge may allow you to seek that limited, negative type of commitment, but the judge will usually disallow questions which seek an affirmative commitment that the panel member will believe or accept a particular proposition.

Questions calculated to indoctrinate on the law. We noted earlier that during voir dire, you may want to expose the panel to probable instructions that support your theme or that relate to surprise or disfavored legal doctrines. This type of questioning follows a three-step pattern similar to that for factual indoctrination.

You begin with a declarative sentence paraphrasing the anticipated instruction: "Later in this case, her Honor may instruct you that...."

Then, especially when the instruction embodies a surprise or disfavored legal doctrine, you may want to question the venireperson about his attitude toward the doctrine. In a criminal case, a defense counsel might ask "What do you think about the legal doctrine that a jury must acquit a person of a crime if the person was insane at the time?" The phrasing is non-leading but closed-ended.

Again assume that the member gives a favorable or neutral answer: "Well, you can't convict somebody of something when they couldn't control their actions" or "If that's the law, you've got to follow it." If so, you can conclude by seeking an affirmative commitment to apply the instruction: "If her Honor instructs you to consider how long Mr. Williams had to observe his attackers, can you promise me that you'll follow her instruction? And you'll carefully consider how close Mr. Williams was to the men?"[1] The phrasing of the commitment question should be leading.

Some attorneys rely on neuro-linguistic theory to help them word their voir dire questions. Lisnek, *Stepping Inside the Courtroom and Jurors' Minds: Meaningful Jury Selection,* 41 THE TRIAL LAWYER'S GUIDE 39, 50–52 (1997). According to this theory, different persons process information differently. Some are primarily visual processors, others are hearing-oriented, and still others are feeling-based. The panel

---

1. Some judges limit the questioning to the prospective juror's present state of mind. In these courtrooms, you might ask: "As you sit now, do you have any problem with that instruction that might prevent you from following it?"

member's nonverbal demeanor can be a clue to the panelist's orientation:

— "When asked a question, a vision-based juror will flick the eyes up ... to find an answer." *Id.* at 51. The upward eye movement "indicates a search for a visual answer."

— In contrast, "[h]earing-based persons move their eyes from side to side." *Id.* at 52.

— Finally, feeling-based persons "look down ... to access feelings." *Id.* The downward glance suggests that the panelist is endeavoring to "get in touch with the feelings related to" the information.

Having classified the panelist, the attorney can best elicit useful answers by tailoring the phrasing of the question to the manner in which the panelist processes information:

— In the case of vision-oriented panelists, the attorney can use graphic phrasing such as "I see what you mean" or "Picture this." *Id.* at 51.

— When the panelist is hearing-oriented, the attorney selects sound-based words such as "I hear what you mean," "That sounds good to me," or "That rings a bell." *Id.* at 52.

— When the panelist is feeling-based, the attorney should employ tactile words such as "feel," "grasp," and "handle." *Id.*

§ 4.8(E) Deciding Whom to Put the Questions to

In the planning steps discussed in §§ 4–8(A)-(D) you decided which questions to ask. You must also decide whom to put the questions to. More specifically, you must decide whether to pose the questions to the group as a whole or to individual panel members.

There is no one, right decision. However, you should consider these factors. The general consensus among trial attorneys is that the first and fourth types of questions (questions relating to challenges for cause and questions calculated to indoctrinate on the law) are better suited for group questioning. Further, individual questions are more threatening to the panel members. Individual questions pry more into their personal privacy. Finally, if the judge questions the panel before turning the panel over to the attorneys, the judge may have "warmed the panel up" and put them at ease. When the judge conducts the initial interrogation and does a good job of it, you can begin immediately with individual questioning. However, when the judge foregoes any questioning or does it mechanically, it may be safer to start with group questions about challenge for cause and relevant legal doctrines.

In planning the voir dire examination, it is critical to realize that the judge may impose severe time constraints. Consequently, you must get right to the point. In *Scott,* with as little delay as possible the prosecutor should: learn the panel members' educational backgrounds and determine whether they belong to any male-only organizations (to help him exercise peremptory challenges); expose the factual weakness of

Williams' drinking before the attack; and mention the instruction that in deciding whether to accept Williams' testimony, the jurors must consider "how close" he was to the attackers and "how long" he had to observe them. The prosecutor must ask those questions to ensure that she has a jury which is at least open-minded about accepting her theory, theme, and client. The sample voir dires in § 4.11 are illustrative.

§ 4.8(F) Conducting the Questioning at Trial

The pretrial planning is now complete, and we shift to trial. At trial, when you question the venirepersons, strive for a conversational tone. Voir dire examination is not the time for oratory. You want the panel members to relax, open up, and give you candid answers. To achieve that objective, you must put them at ease.

Project friendliness and strike a low-key tone. Smith, *Challenges of Jury Selection*, 88 A.B.A.J. 35, 36, 39 (Apr. 2002). To help put the panel at ease, many attorneys make it a practice to remain seated during voir dire. S. HAMLIN, WHAT MAKES JURIES LISTEN 55 (1985). "Sitting at a table looks more relaxed...." *Id.* If the jurors feel that you are relaxed, that feeling may help them to do likewise.

Consider using a visual aid during voir dire examination. Although attorneys rarely do so, in most jurisdictions the judge has discretion to allow you to do so. For example, if you intend to question the jurors about legal doctrines or a particular jury instruction, you might use a chart listing the names of the doctrines or summarizing the instruction. A chart will not only help the panel members understand your questions; the use of the chart may also help you sustain the panel's interest throughout a long voir dire.

When you put questions to individual venirepersons at trial, start with the most outgoing panelist. You are not only more likely to obtain candid answers early if you begin with the most extroverted panel member; that panel member will also set a good example for the more reticent members. Observe the panel intently from the moment they enter the courtroom. Which panelists were smiling or even joking as they walked into the room? Those panelists are the best to question initially. Try to preface the question with their surname. Do not address them as "Juror #3." Rather, refer to them as "Mr. Martinez" or "Ms. Wilson." As previously stated, when the judge or bailiff reads off the venirepersons' names before questioning begins, note the phonetic pronunciations of each surname on the jury box diagram, Figure 4–1. Consult the diagram before you pose a question to a venireperson.

After questioning the initial panel member, move randomly through the panel. If you "go down the row" and question in order, the members who do not expect to be called next tend to become inattentive. (The same phenomenon sometimes occurs in law school classes!) As the voir dire examination progresses, you can use more and more open-ended questions; as the questioning continues, the panel members should become more at ease and conversational. When you have to pose essentially the same question to several panelists, vary the wording of the question. By doing so, you both reduce the likelihood of an objection and minimize the risk of boring the panel. Heaney, *Jury Selection in the Era of "Tort Reform,"* 31 TRIAL 72, 74 (Nov. 1995).

Listen intently to the verbal answer given. If the answer is telling, you may want to note it on the diagram. To save time during voir dire, before trial develop a set of "initials, abbreviations and symbols . . . that define the various things you are looking for. For example, 'A' could stand for prior accident; 'LS' for prior law suit . . . and so on." S. HAMLIN, WHAT MAKES JURIES LISTEN 47 (1985). There is only a small space for entries about each panel member on a typical diagram such as Figure 4–1. However, you ordinarily need to make only a few, short entries about each member to help you remember whether to challenge that member. You may have to question a large number of venirepersons before the judge entertains peremptory challenges. Unless you have an exceptional memory, you should notate important answers on the diagram to help you remember them later.

When the venireperson answers, be responsive. Urquhart, *Voir Dire . . . When They Speak, Do You Listen?* 23 TRIAL 106 (Nov. 1987). "By word or gesture, encourage the speaker to further explain. . . ." *Id.* Make it clear to the panel member that you are interested in what they have to say: "Mr. Grant, you just said that. . . ." If you want the panel members to open up, you must convince them that you are a receptive audience. Incorporate some of the panelist's words into the phrasing of your next question.

If you sense that the panelist is reticent to disclose sensitive information, consider using

> the Gerry Spence method of voir dire—I have to show you mine before you show me yours. I can't just ask them if they have alcoholics in their family, I've got to admit that people I love are alcoholics.

Digges, *Visualizing the Invisible Injury,* LAWYERS WEEKLY USA, June 25, 2001, at p. B5. The attorney's self-disclosure can clear the air. It signals the panelist that it is socially acceptable to give an honest answer to the question.

In contrast, when the verbal answer is especially candid, "reward" it. Stout, *The Problem with Jury Selection, or Raise Your Hand if You are Prejudiced and Unfair,* 11 THE CHAMPION 19, 23 (Nov. 1987). Tell the panel member that you "really appreciate" her candor. McElhaney, *Picking a Jury,* 18 LITIGATION 43, 62 (Wint. 1992) ("Thank you. That's exactly the sort of [honest answer] we are looking for"). Roy Black used this tactic in the William Kennedy Smith trial. Heller, *Rating the Kennedys; Family Matters in Jury Selection for Smith Trial,* LEGAL TIMES, Dec. 2, 1991, at p. 15 ("Black rewarded jurors who gave responses he considered favorable with comments such as 'You did an excellent job.' And he encouraged those who spoke openly of their feelings about the case by thanking them for their honesty").

You should not only listen intently to the verbal answer; you should also closely watch the venireperson's nonverbal demeanor. *See generally* Fahringer, *"Mirror, Mirror on the Wall....": Body Language, Intuition, and the Art of Jury Selection,* 17 AM.J.TRIAL ADVOC. 197 (1993); Suggs & Sales, *Using Communication Cues to Evaluate Prospective Jurors During the Voir Dire,* 20 ARIZ.L.REV. 629 (1978). You must be attentive to paralinguistic as well as kinesic behavior. If a question prompts a panel member to speak much more rapidly or to change the pitch of his voice, the paralinguistic change suggests that the question troubled the panelist. Or suppose that as soon as you put the question to the panel member, she frowns, averts her eyes, contorts her face, folds her hands, or adopts a more rigid posture. *See* Branson & Branson, *Successful Voir Dire,* 28 TRIAL 21, 23 (Feb. 1992) ("Open-arm positions are associated with warmth and acceptance of the communicatee; closed-arm positions, coldness, rejection, and passivity"). That kinesic behavior is a clue that the member is uncomfortable answering the question. Compare the member's behavior during your questioning with her behavior when questioned by the judge and opposing attorney. If her behavior seems more relaxed when the opposing attorney questions them, she may be more empathetic with the opposition. You should suspect such empathy especially when she begins to "mirror" the opposing attorney's gestures and posture. Klein, *Winning Cases with Body Language,* 29 TRIAL 56, 57 (Oct. 1993). While you are observing the questioned panel member, you should also try to scan the jury box. Another panel member may register a noticeable, nonverbal reaction to the question. If any panel member does so, you ought to note the reaction on the jury box diagram. Based on that reaction, you may decide later to strike that member. As a prosecutor, you need every vote to gain a conviction; and even as a plaintiff, you need a supermajority. You need to drink in the demeanor of the entire panel.

Finally, suppose that the member's answer betrays a possible ground for challenge for cause. Assume, for example, that in response to the prosecutor's question, a venireperson in *Scott* says that he thinks that all drinking is immoral. The venireperson adds that he is an active, contributing member of three different anti-drinking organizations. The venireperson's anti-drinking beliefs may be so intense that he may be unable to dispassionately decide the question of the reliability of Williams' identification. If so, the prosecutor should question the venireperson to establish the relevant bias so clearly that the opposing attorney cannot rehabilitate the venireperson by further questioning. Firm up the record to maximize the probability that your cause challenge will be sustained. "If you attack the king, you must kill the king;" when you challenge a venireperson, you must be prepared to spend a peremptory strike to remove him if the judge denies the cause challenge.

How can you maximize the probability that the judge will uphold your challenge for cause? One thing is clear: To establish a panelist's bias, you cannot simply ask panelists whether they are "biased" or "prejudiced." Stout, *The Problem With Jury Selection or Raise Your*

Hand If You are Prejudiced and Unfair, 14 N.MEX. TRIAL LAW. No. 11, 147 (1986). The questioning has to be subtler. Give the panel member a graceful way to remove himself or herself from the panel. Suppose that during the initial phase of the questioning, the venireperson has admitted facts strongly suggesting a biased attitude or belief. Reflect the facts back to the venireperson. Herman, *In Trial With Lender Liability* 20 (unpublished article). In effect, "throw the juror's cumulative answers back at him...." (*id.*): "Mr. Jones, you've already told us that.... You also said that.... Finally, you added that...." After reflecting those facts back to the panelist, ask the member whether his beliefs would make him "a bit uncomfortable" sitting in the case. "Given what you've said, do you understand why Mr. Williams might be comfortable if you served on this jury?" Then add: "Considering that, do you think it might be better if you served as a juror in some other case" that did not involve testimony about drinking. W. BROCKETT & J. KEKER, EFFECTIVE DIRECT AND CROSS–EXAMINATION § 10.17, at 229 (1986); McElhaney, *Picking a Jury,* 18 LITIGATION 43, 62 (Wint. 1992) (" 'Well, in view of that, Mr. Compton, would you feel it would be better if you were to sit in judgment in some other kind of case—one that was not quite so close to home?' [The panelist might say,] 'I guess maybe so.' That is about as close as you are likely to get with a lot of panelists"). If the venireperson frankly answers those questions, the opposing attorney will find it difficult to rehabilitate the venireperson; and the judge will be hard pressed to deny a cause challenge.

As the preceding paragraph suggests, once you begin questioning the panelist to challenge the panelist for cause, you have the passed the "fail safe" point. The questions may antagonize the panelist; and if the judge denies the challenge, you will probably have to use one of your precious, few strikes to remove the panelist from the jury. Thus, you cannot be content with a record that supports a bare, permissive inference of bias. As § 4–10(B) notes, before the judge rules, the judge may give the opposing counsel an opportunity to question the panelist and rehabilitate the panelist's qualification. Once you start down the road to challenging the panelist, try to carry the questioning past any realistic possibility that the opponent will be able to rehabilitate the panelist.

If the judge denies the cause challenge, make the record for appeal. The prevailing view is that later in the jury selection, either at sidebar or in chambers, you must "advise the court of two things.... (1) ... [the attorney] would exhaust all peremptory challenges and (2) ... after exercising such strikes, objectionable jurors ... remain on the jury.... [T]he lawyer must demonstrate the 'objectionable' ... nature of the juror allowed to remain because of lack of additional peremptory strikes. Absent such an objection, any error in disqualification of a juror is waived and may not be argued ... on appeal." Perdue, *Defusing Jury Bias,* 27 TRIAL 50, 51 (Apr. 1991); *United States v. Hardy,* 941 F.2d 893 (9th Cir.1991). According to the majority of courts, you may complain on appeal about a denial of a challenge for cause only if you have exhausted all your peremptory challenges. Carlson, *Meaningful Examination of Trial Jurors,* 2 TRIAL PRACTICE NEWSLETTER 5, 6 (Jan. 1988).

§ 4.9 THE PERSPECTIVE OF THE QUESTIONING ATTORNEY—CHALLENGES

After the questioning, the judge entertains challenges to the panel. The topic of challenges raises several questions: When do you announce the challenge? Whom should you challenge? And how should you phrase the announcement of the challenge?

§ 4.9(A) When to Challenge

In most jurisdictions, cause challenges precede peremptory challenges. At one point during jury selection, some judges call for peremptory challenges: "Does either side wish to make a peremptory challenge?" However, many judges expect you to make a cause challenge on your own motion as soon as the possible ground appears during the questioning. If you move on to another venireperson, you may have waived the cause challenge. In short, if the judge follows this procedure, as soon as there is an inkling of a ground for cause challenge, you should pursue the questioning and announce the challenge before beginning the questioning of another panel member.

§ 4.9(B) Whom to Challenge

During challenges, the attorneys can pursue several strategies. For example, since the prosecutor and the plaintiff need either a unanimous vote or a supermajority, the defense typically prefers a heterogeneous group of panelists. The greater the differences among the panelists, the more likely they are to disagree. Further, the defense may want jurors with a "maverick" streak, capable of resisting social pressure and holding out against a majority. Perlstein, *Effects of Social Pressure on Jury Decisions,* J.MO.BAR, Sep.-Oct. 1994, at 269, 270. However, the primary strategy should be jury deselection.

Section 4.5 discussed the strategy of jury deselection. Again, the essence of the strategy is developing the profile of the juror you least want, the juror who will have real difficulty accepting your theme or identifying with you or your client. As that section points out, you can develop the profile either by stereotyping or by relying on "scientific" jury selection. In either event, the profile gives you at most a generalization. In effect, you have two rebuttable presumptions. One is that a juror is unacceptable—and should be struck—if he or she fits the profile. The other is that a juror is acceptable if he or she does not fit the profile. However, the generalization has limited predictive value. M. SAKS & R. HASTIE, SOCIAL PSYCHOLOGY IN COURT 65 (1986). At trial, before deciding whether to strike a particular panelist, you must supplement the generalization by considering the panelist's verbal answers and nonverbal demeanor. *Id.* at 59.

Assume, for example, that a panelist does not fit the profile. However, you notice that when you questioned the panelist, he exhibited negative demeanor; his facial expression became grim, he folded his arms, and his posture became much more rigid. That conduct may be sufficient to rebut the presumption that he is an acceptable juror.

Alternatively, suppose that a panelist does fit the profile; she possesses all the demographic characteristics normally correlated with attitudes that would incline her to reject your theme. However, her answers to your voir dire questions strongly indicate that she is the maverick; she is the exceptional person who possesses those traits but lacks the biases that typically accompany those traits. Again, the presumption may have been rebutted.

The profile you developed gives you the starting point for analyzing the question of whether you should strike a particular panelist, but you must complete the analysis by considering everything you hear and see at trial. Keep your eyes and ears open during the questioning.

§ 4.9(C) How to Phrase the Challenge

In many jurisdictions, you must announce your challenges in open court in the panel's hearing. Suppose that you decide to strike a particular panel member. You could announce, "We would like to challenge (or strike) juror #7 Ms. McMillan." However, using that phrasing is dangerous. Juror #7 (Ms. McMillan) may have a number of friends among the remaining panel members; one of the remaining members may be the person she has had lunch with at the courthouse every day for the past week. Announcing that you "challenge" Ms. McMillan may offend her friend, Ms. Giannelli. The preferable phrasing is, "We would like to excuse Ms. McMillan." Better still, state: "We would like her Honor to excuse Ms. McMillan;" try to create the impression that the judge is the person removing the panel member. You might add that you "thank Ms. McMillan for her time today."

Conversely, assume that you do not want to challenge a particular juror. You could state that you "waive" or "pass." However, if you do so, you forego an opportunity to establish rapport with the jury. It is better to announce that you are "happy" or "satisfied" with the panel. Moreover, do not say that you are satisfied with the panel; indicate that your client is happy with the panel. After visibly consulting with your client, state that "Mr. Williams is satisfied with this panel of jurors."

As the last paragraph indicated, you should at least purport to consult with your client before announcing whether you want to make or forego a challenge. Some attorneys do only that; they merely go through the motions of consulting with the client in order to make the statement, "Mr. Williams is satisfied with this panel of jurors," appear more credible to the panel. Other attorneys believe that you should actually solicit the client's view and give great weight to that view. To begin with, some clients have better intuition than their attorneys. Your client may be a much better judge of character. Moreover, if the client feels uneasy about a particular panel member and that member remains on the jury, that person's presence on the jury might make your client uncomfortable during the trial. An uncomfortable client may display negative demeanor to the jury. That demeanor may be the most damaging "evidence" presented against your client at trial.

In a minority of jurisdictions, there is no need to announce the challenge in the hearing of the panel members. The "Arizona" practice is that after questioning, the bailiff circulates a list of panel members to the attorneys. The attorneys indicate the strikes by checking or lining through names on the list. The attorneys then return the list to the judge, and the judge announces the strikes. The panel members do not learn which side struck a particular venireperson.

§ 4.10   THE PERSPECTIVE OF THE OPPOSING ATTORNEY

Now adopt the point of view of the opposing attorney. You listen to the questioning attorney interrogate the venirepersons. The attorney even challenges a particular venireperson. Can you object to the questions? How do you resist the challenge?

§ 4.10(A)   Objecting to Voir Dire Questions

In a short text such as this one, we cannot go into detail about the law governing objections to voir dire questions. For that matter, little has been written on this subject. We do recommend one source, though: Chapter 6 of E. HEAFEY, CALIFORNIA TRIAL OBJECTIONS (9th ed.2002). That text lists the following possible objections to voir dire questions:

— Objection, Your Honor. The question is not related to any ground for challenge for cause. Nor will the question assist counsel in the intelligent exercise of a peremptory challenge. *Id.* at § 6.42.

— Objection, Your Honor. The purpose of the question is to preinstruct the jurors on the law. *Id.* at § 6.34.

— Objection, Your Honor. The question does not correctly state the law. *Id.* at § 6.36.

— Objection, Your Honor. The question asks the juror to prejudge the evidence. *Id.* at § 6.38.

— Objection, Your Honor. The question introduces inadmissible prejudicial matter. I assign counsel's asking that question as misconduct. *Id.* at § 6.40.

As the above list indicates, in her discretion the judge can sustain the objection that the question preinstructs the panel on the law or asks the panel member to prejudge the facts in the case. In many trials, however, when both parties are attempting to indoctrinate the panel on the law and facts, there will be few, if any, objections on these grounds. The explanation is obvious. Both sides want the judge to allow them to indoctrinate to some extent, and they consciously forego objections. Their hope is that if they do not object to similar questions by the opposing attorney, out of fairness the judge will permit them to pose similar questions to the panel.

§ 4.10(B) Questioning the Venirepersons to Rehabilitate Them

Suppose that the opposing attorney challenges for cause a venireperson you would like to retain on the jury. The judge will usually permit you to question the venireperson before making a final ruling on the challenge. Assume, for example, that the attackers had killed Williams and that Scott is now on trial for capital murder. You are the defense attorney for Scott. The prosecutor has just completed questioning a panel member. During the questioning, the panel member indicated that he has general ethical scruples against the death penalty. Based on that indication, the prosecutor challenges the panel member under *Witherspoon v. Illinois,* 391 U.S. 510 (1968). Before the judge rules, you could request permission to question the panel member further:

Q A few moments ago while the prosecutor was questioning you, you said that you have "moral reservations" about the death penalty. Is that correct?

Q When you said that, did you mean you would *never* vote to impose the death penalty?

Q So that in an *extreme* case, you might be willing to vote for the death penalty?

Q Can you promise us that you'll do your level best to follow whatever instructions his Honor gives you about the death penalty in this case?

The short-term objectives of this line of questioning are two-fold. One objective is to defeat the challenge and keep that panel member on the jury. The other short-term objective is to force the prosecutor to expend a peremptory strike to remove that panel member. Again, the reality is that "if you attack the king, you must kill the king." The long-term objective of this line is educational. In effect, you teach the other similarly inclined panel members that the prosecutor can remove them from the jury for cause only if they make sweeping, blanket statements of opposition to capital punishment.

§ 4.11 SAMPLE VOIR DIRE EXAMINATIONS

§ 4.11(A) Short Form Voir Dire Examination

You are the prosecutor in the *Scott* case. The trial judge has imposed severe time constraints and told you to get right to the point. You therefore conduct the following voir dire examination:

(Preliminary Remarks)

"Good morning, ladies and gentlemen. My name is _____. I am the Deputy District Attorney representing the People of the State of El Dorado in this case. This is the part of the case called jury selection or voir dire examination. We'll be asking you some questions about your background and opinions. I want to make it clear that we're not asking these questions just to pry into your privacy. I want to apologize in advance if any question I ask offends you.

"I know you've all received this little pamphlet about jury service. It talks about the purpose of these questions. We have to make certain that both the defendant and the People of the State of El Dorado receive a fair trial in this case. The People will offer proof that the defendant is guilty of a crime called battery. We believe that the evidence in this case will show that on January 19, 19YR–1, the defendant beat up a Mr. Peter Williams. Mr. Williams is the desk clerk at the Senator Hotel in downtown Morena. The People intend to prove that together with a man named Dick Rogers, the defendant attacked Mr. Williams. The defendant has entered a not guilty plea; the defendant claims he had nothing to do with the attack. We've come here today to choose a jury to decide whether the defendant attacked Mr. Williams. The basic issue is going to be the identity of the second attacker. You'll have to decide whether the defendant was the second man who beat Mr. Williams. We need fair, impartial jurors to make that decision. I have to ask you some questions now to help us determine whether you could sit as open-minded, objective jurors in this case.

(Questions Relating to Challenges for Cause)

"To begin with, we've got to find out whether any of you know any of the people who will be involved in this case. As I'm sure you can understand, it's usually easier to be an impartial juror if you don't know anyone involved in the case. I'm going to list and introduce the people who'll be participating in this trial. This morning we're in the courtroom of the Honorable Jack Levitt, Judge of the Superior Court. The court reporter will be John Merton, the gentleman sitting at the small desk over there. The bailiff is Joseph Napoli, the officer in the blue uniform by the door. Seated at the other counsel table to my left are the defendant, Robert Scott, and his attorney, Mr. Martinez. During the People's case, I'll be calling several witnesses. One witness will be Officer Janice Taylor of the Morena Police Department. Another will be Mr. Stephen Sykes, a chemist who works for the Morena Police Department Crime Laboratory. The final witness will be the victim of the crime, Mr. Peter Williams. We believe that the defense will call Ms. Joan Freeman as a witness. Do any of you know any of the people I've just named? If you do, please raise your hand. Your Honor, please let the record reflect that none of the members of the panel raised his or her hand.

"I have one other question for you as a group. Have any of you read anything about this case in the newspapers or heard anything about it on radio or television? Again, if you have, just raise your hand. Thank you. Your Honor, once again please let the record reflect that no one raised a hand.

"Now I'd like to talk to you individually. Mr. Stern, I'd like to start with you.

"Am I pronouncing your name correctly?

(Questions Relating to Peremptory Challenges—Determining Whether the Panelist Fits the Profile of the Juror You Least Want)

"Where do you live?

"How long have you lived there?

"What line of work are you in?

"Who do you work for?

"How long have you worked for them?

"In your own words, tell us about your educational background.

"What was your major in college?

"Are you married?

"Does your wife work outside the home?

"Has she ever worked outside the home?

"What organizations do you belong to?

"When you have free time, what types of television shows do you like to watch?

"What sorts of books or magazines do you like to read?

(Factual Indoctrination—Exposing Your Weaknesses on the Key Element of Your Theory)

"Mr. Stern, there is going to be evidence in this case that about half an hour before the attack, the victim, Mr. Williams, had been drinking. To be specific, he had three boilermakers—a shot and a beer.

"What do you think about people who drink liquor?

"Do you have any religious objections to drinking?

"Do you belong to any organizations that oppose drinking?

"Have you ever belonged to such an organization?

"Do you think that Mr. Williams' identification of his attackers is automatically wrong because Mr. Williams had those three drinks?

"Would you consider all the evidence before deciding whether Mr. Williams' identification is reliable?

"Would you carefully listen, for example, to the evidence about how well Mr. Williams tolerates liquor—how well he holds his liquor?

"Can you promise me—can you promise the People of the State of El Dorado—that you won't reject Mr. Williams' testimony simply because he had been drinking?

(Legal Indoctrination—Exposing the Panel to the Instruction Supporting Your Theme)

"Mr. Stern, there's one final topic I'd like to discuss with you. At the end of this case, her Honor may give you an instruction about the law in El Dorado on eyewitness identification. It's an instruction that tells you how to decide whether to believe an identification like Mr. Williams' identification of the defendant.

"Her Honor may tell you that you're supposed to consider how close Mr. Williams was to his attackers. If she tells you that, will you do your best to follow her instruction?

"Will you carefully consider the testimony about how close Mr. Williams was to the two men who attacked him?

"Her Honor may also instruct you that you're supposed to consider how long Mr. Williams had to view his attackers. If her Honor gives you that instruction, will you do your level best to follow it?

"Can you promise the People that you'll pay close attention to the evidence about how long Mr. Williams had to observe his attackers?

"Thank you very much, Mr. Stern.

(Challenges)

"Your Honor, we have no challenges at all against Mr. Stern. The People will be happy to have Mr. Stern as a juror in this case."

§ 4.11(B) Long Form Voir Dire Examination

Suppose alternatively that the judge allows a lengthier voir dire examination.

(To the entire jury panel after it has been sworn and seated) Ladies and gentlemen, I am Judge Smith. I am now going to question all of you prospective jurors who are seated in the jury box concerning your qualifications to serve as jurors in this case. However, all members of this jury panel, whether in the jury box or those of you seated elsewhere in the courtroom, should pay close attention to my questions. You ought to make note of the answers you would give if these questions were put to you personally. If and when any other member of this panel is called to the jury box, he or she will be asked to give their answers to these questions.

In the trial of this case the parties are entitled to have a fair and unbiased jury. If there is any reason why any of you might be biased or prejudiced in any way, you must disclose that reason when you are asked to do so. It is your legal duty to make this disclosure.

This trial will likely take four days to complete, but it may take longer. Do any of you have any responsibilities at home or at work that would make it difficult or impossible to give us your full attention for this period of time? If you would, please raise your hand at this time.

(No hands are raised.)

The record will reflect that no panelist raised a hand.

Now let me give you some background about this case. This case is a personal injury action. The plaintiff, Mr. Peter Williams, is a desk clerk at the Senator Hotel in downtown Morena. The defendant, Mr. Robert Scott, was a guest staying at the hotel in January, 19YR–1. The plaintiff alleges that on January 19th of that year, the defendant and another man by the name of Richard Rogers attacked and beat him. The plaintiff also alleges that he suffered certain injuries in the attack. I want to emphasize that the plaintiffs' allegations are not evidence. The plaintiff will not only have to allege those things; he will also have the burden of proving those things at this trial.

At this point, we need to find out whether you can serve as a fair juror in this case. We're not trying to pry, but we need to know whether you can be an impartial juror for this trial. For that reason, I'm going to ask you some questions; and then the attorneys will have a chance to question you. Before we do that, though, we need to put you under oath. Madame Bailiff, would you please administer the oath to the panel?

Yes, Your Honor. Ladies and gentlemen, all members of the panel, please stand. "Do you and each of you understand and agree that you will accurately and truthfully answer, under penalty of perjury, all questions propounded to you concerning your qualifications and competency to serve as a trial juror in a matter pending before this court and that failure to do so may subject you to criminal prosecution?" If so, say, "I do."

(All panelists respond, "I do.")

You may be seated.

The parties to this case and their respective attorneys are: Mr. Kenneth Clark representing the plaintiff Mr. Williams and Ms. Jill Peterson representing the defendant Mr. Scott. I would like all the parties and their attorneys to stand. (to the jury panel) Ladies and gentlemen, have you heard of or been acquainted with any of these parties or their attorneys? Again, if you do, please raise your hand.

Do any of these people even look familiar to you? If so, just raise your hand.

During the trial of this case, the following witnesses may be called to testify on behalf of the parties. These witnesses are: Dr. Fred Amerson, Professor Anna Dulay, Police Officer Janice Taylor, Dr. Gina Jackson, Ms. Joan Freeman, and Mr. William K.S. Wang. Have any of you heard of or been otherwise acquainted with any of the witnesses just named?

Do any of those names even sound familiar to you?

Have any of you heard of, or have you any knowledge of, the facts or events in this case?

Do any of you have any belief or feeling toward any of the parties, attorneys, or witnesses that might be regarded as a prejudice for or against any of them?

Do you have any interest, financial or otherwise, in the outcome of this case?

Have any of you served as a juror or witness involving any of these parties, attorneys or witnesses?

Have any of you served as a juror in any case?

(A juror raises her hand.)

What is your name?

Ms. Palumbo, Your Honor.

Was it a civil or criminal case?

It was a criminal case, Your Honor.

You must understand that there is a basic difference between a civil case and a criminal case. In a criminal case a defendant must be found guilty beyond a reasonable doubt; in a civil case such as this, you need find only that the evidence you accept as the basis of your decision is more convincing, and thus has the greater probability of truth than the contrary evidence. The standard in this trial is lower than in a criminal case. The standard here is just a preponderance of the evidence. Do you understand the difference between the two types of cases?

Yes, Your Honor.

And you realize that the plaintiff in this case doesn't have the same burden of proof as the prosecution in the earlier criminal case you sat on. Correct?

Yes.

Very well. Let's shift to another topic then. Have any of you, or any member of your family or close friends to your knowledge, ever sued anyone, or has there ever been a claim presented against any of you, or to your knowledge against any member of your family or close friends, in connection with a matter similar to this case?

Are any of you, or any member of your family or close friends to your knowledge, presently involved in a lawsuit of any kind?

Have any of you, or any member of your family or close friends, had any special training in investigating criminal offenses?

In this case, you may be called upon to award damages for the plaintiff's claimed personal injury, including pain and suffering. Do any of you have any religious or other belief that pain and suffering are not real or any belief that would prevent you from awarding damages for pain and suffering if the defendant's liability for them is established?

Are there any of you who would not employ a medical doctor?

To your knowledge, have you or any member of your family ever been involved in an incident with the result that a claim for personal injuries or for substantial property damage was made by someone involved in that incident, whether or not a lawsuit was filed?

Have you or they, to your knowledge, ever been involved in a situation in which someone died or received serious personal injuries, whether or not a lawsuit was filed?

In this case, Mr. Williams claims that he has suffered permanent injuries to his arms, legs, and back. Do any of you, or any member of your family or close friends to your knowledge, currently suffer from similar injuries? Have you or they, to your knowledge, suffered from similar injuries in the past?

It is important that I have your assurance that you will, without reservation, follow my instructions on the law and will apply that law to this case. To put it somewhat differently, whether you approve or disapprove of the court's instructions, it is your solemn duty to accept them as correct statements of the law. You may not substitute your own idea of what you think the law ought to be. Will all of you follow the law as given to you by me in this case?

I am now going to allow the attorneys to ask you some questions. Before they do that, though, would each of you should now state the information listed on the chalkboard over there. As you can see, it asks you to state your name, where you live, your marital status—whether married, single, widowed or divorced—the number and ages of your children if any, your occupational history, and the name of your present employer. If you are married, you should also describe briefly your spouse's occupational history and present employer, if any. Please begin with juror number one.

My name is Margaret Marcetti. I reside at 347 San Benito Way in Morena. I work for State Farm Insurance Company. I'm divorced, and I have one child, a nine year old son.

Now juror number two.

Yes, Your Honor. My name is Harvey Leader. I live at 1051 Felton St. here in Morena. I'm single with no dependents. I work at a Circuit City warehouse.

Juror number three.

My name is Reverend Wiley Morris. I live and work at the New Life Evangelistic Center on the 2200 block of Mission Street here in town. I'm married and have two children. My wife is also a counselor at the center.

Juror number four.

My name is Elaine Palumbo. I'm a graduate student in psychology at the University of El Dorado. I live in an apartment near campus. I'm engaged to be married to Brandon Lowenthal. He's a physician at Morena Med School.

Juror number five.

My name is Jan Gilligan. I'm retired military. I spent 30 years on active duty with the Marine Corps. I'm a widower. I live in Condo Unit C, 239 Castro Street. I have two kids. They're both grown. One lives in Hong Kong, and the other is in Palo Alto, California.

Now juror number six.

Right, Your Honor. My name is Jesus Castro. I live at 3344 18th Avenue in Morena. I have my own business, a small specialized computer programming firm. I've been married for ten years. My wife Elizabeth and I have two kids, Tomas and Teresa.

Ladies and gentlemen, please think carefully. Do any of you know of any factor, whether or not I have asked about it, that might influence your view of this case? Has anything occurred during this questioning period that might make you doubt whether you would be a completely fair and impartial juror in this case? If there is, it is your legal duty to disclose the reason at this time.

All right. Mr. Clark, you may question the panel.

(Plaintiff's Questions)

Thank you, Your Honor. Ladies and gentlemen, my name is Kenneth Clark. I represent the plaintiff in this case, Mr. Peter Williams. Mr. Williams contends that on January 19, 19YR–1, the defendant and a Dick Rogers punched and kicked him at the Senator Hotel. The defendant denies that he was involved in the attack. That's why you're here today—to decide that dispute. The jury in this case is going to have to decide who attacked Mr. Williams. As her Honor indicated, I'm going to ask you a few questions now. At the very beginning, I want to make it clear that Ms. Peterson and I need to ask you these questions just to ensure that you can be fair to both Mr. Williams and the defendant. I want to apologize in advance if any of my questions seem to pry into your privacy. I want to assure you that we're questioning you just to make certain that you can be an impartial juror to decide this dispute.

Ms. Marcetti, let's start with you. I'd like to ask you a few questions now.

You said that you work for State Farm Insurance Company. How long have you worked for them?

About nine years now.

Specifically, what is your job?

I handle earthquake and flood insurance for this area.

Do you handle personal liability claims like claims for injuries resulting from incidents such as fights?

No.

Have you ever handled personal liability claims?

No.

Does anyone in your office handle that type of claim?

No. There are a couple of State Farm offices in Morena. We're out in the Avenues. There's another office downtown, and that's where they take care of all the personal stuff.

Having worked for an insurance company for so long, do you think that you'd tend to side with the defense in this case?

No. Not necessarily.

You said "not necessarily". In your mind, what would it depend on?

The facts. Some good claims come across my desk, and I see some bad ones too. I try to be fair. If the facts show that it's a bad claim, I turn it down. But if the facts show that it's a good claim, I pay it. I have insurance too, and I resent it when I'm in the right and my insurer drags it feet paying the claim. Like I said, it all depends on the facts.

Let's talk for a moment about some of the facts in this case. Ms. Marcetti, in this case there's going to be evidence that about half an hour before the attack, Mr. Williams had been drinking. To be specific, he had three boilermakers, a shot and a beer. What do you think about people who drink?

It's O.K., I drink sometimes. It all depends on how much you drink and the social setting. As I said, it depends.

Do you have any religious objections to drinking?

No.

Do you belong to any organizations that oppose drinking? You know—organizations like MADD, Mothers Against Drunk Driving.

No.

Have you ever belonged to such an organization?

Never.

Do you think that Mr. Williams' identification of his attackers is automatically wrong just because he had those three drinks?

Of course not.

Would you consider all the evidence before deciding whether Mr. Williams' identification is reliable?

Yes.

For example, would you listen carefully to the evidence about how well Mr. Williams tolerates liquor—how well he "holds" his liquor?

Yes.

Can you promise Mr. Williams that you won't reject his testimony simply because he had been drinking?

Yes.

At the end of this case, Judge Smith will give you an instruction about the law in the State of El Dorado on eyewitness identification. It's an instruction that tells you how to decide whether to believe an identification such as Mr. Williams' identification of the attackers. Her Honor is going to tell you that you're supposed to consider how close Mr. Williams was to his attackers? Will you do your best to follow her Honor's instruction?

Yes.

Will you carefully consider the testimony about how close Mr. Williams was to the two men who attacked him?

Yes.

Her Honor may also instruct you that you're supposed to consider how long Mr. Williams had to view his attackers. If her Honor gives you that instruction, will you do your level best to follow it?

Yes.

Can you promise us that you'll pay close attention to the evidence of how long Mr. Williams had to observe his attackers?

I'll certainly try.

We appreciate that. Thank you very much, Ms. Marcetti.

Mr. Leader, I'd like to speak with you next. A few moments ago you heard Judge Smith describe the incident involving the plaintiff. I notice from your juror questionnaire that you live near the Senator Hotel. Are you familiar with the hotel?

Sure. It's one of the oldest hotels in downtown, and that's pretty near where I work.

Did you happen to witness any attack at the hotel in January of 19YR–1?

No.

As far as you know, did any of your friends and neighbors happen to witness this incident?

No, not as far as I know.

Have you read anything in the newspapers about the facts of this case?

If I did, I sure don't remember doing that.

Have you heard any reports on the radio or television about the facts of this case?

Nope.

O.K. Mr. Leader, could you please tell us something about your line of work.

I work as a warehouseman.

How long have you worked as a warehouseman?

About 10 years.

Exactly what are your duties as a warehouseman?

Well, let's put it this way. I'm not the white collar guy who sits in the office and shuffles paper. I'm the blue collar guy who actually pushes the boxes around in the warehouse. I do the manual labor.

While you've worked as a warehouseman, did you know of any co-workers who suffered from back pain?

Sure.

Did they ever put in a day's work even though they had that type of pain?

Of course.

Have you yourself ever had a day when you had sharp back pain?

If it was really sharp, I'd get the day off; but in that job, it's pretty common to have some back pain.

Did you work despite the pain?

Sure. I need the paycheck.

Given your experience, what do you think about awarding money damages to plaintiffs for pain and suffering? Mr. Williams is asking for money damages for pain and suffering. Do you think that's fair?

I'm not sure I understand the question.

I'm sorry. Let me put it this way. Some people don't think courts have any business awarding money for something like pain. Other people believe that you should treat pain like any other injury caused by an accident—you should give money damages for pain in the same way you give them for lost wages. As between those two views, who would you tend to agree with?

I guess I'd have to agree with the second group of people. It's one thing if you have to put up with the pain because it's your line of work. That's part of what you get paid for. But it's different if someone is at fault and causes you to suffer the pain. In a way, I can see how you should be paid for that.

Thank for, Mr. Leader. Suppose that at the end of this trial, Judge Smith instructs you that if you find Mr. Scott liable, you must award Mr. Williams money damages for pain and suffering. Can you promise me that you'd follow that instruction?

Yes, sir.

And will you listen carefully to the testimony you'll hear during the trial about the extent of Mr. Williams' pain and suffering?

Yeah.

Mr. Leader, let's talk a bit more about Mr. Williams' injuries. In this case, to prove his injuries, Mr. Williams is going to call a number of doctors, medical experts. They're going to testify about "soft tissue" injuries—injuries you're not going to be able to see on any chart or X-ray.

Think back. Have you ever accidentally banged your arm or leg against a door? You hit it real hard, but you didn't cut yourself. That ever happen to you?

I guess so.

In that situation, you couldn't see any blood. Could you?

No. Not unless it was a real bad one.

And you didn't necessarily develop a black-and-blue bruise. Did you?

No.

But was the pain real? Did you really feel the pain even though you couldn't see any blood or bruise?

Sure.

You've had that personal experience. Would you then reject the expert's testimony about "soft tissue" injuries simply because the doctors won't be able to produce any X-rays to show you the injuries?

I don't think so. I'd try to listen to what the doc had to say.

At the end of the trial, Judge Smith will give you some instructions about the damages which Mr. Williams suffered. If Judge Smith instructs you that you should award Mr. Williams money damages for "soft tissue" injuries, can you assure Mr. Williams that you'll try to carry out Judge Smith's instruction?

Yes, I would. I'd do my best to do what the judge says.

And can you promise Mr. Williams that you'll listen carefully to what his doctors have to say about those injuries?

I'll try.

Thank you. Reverend Morris, I'd like to chat with you now. I have just a couple of questions. Now as I recall, a few minutes ago you said that you are affiliated with the New Life Evangelistic Center. Is that correct?

Yes.

I have to confess that I'm unfamiliar with that center. Could you tell us a little about it?

I'd be glad to. We are a Christian church organization. We have a shelter for the homeless, and on a daily basis we provide free meals for the poor. We also provide counseling services. I work primarily in the counseling function.

And you're a minister in this organization?

Yes. I am.

Now I know that some Christian organizations have scruples against using physicians. They believe in faith healing. My client, Mr. Williams, used a physician after this incident, and he's going to be asking the jury in this case to compensate for thousands of dollars in medical expenses. Do you personally believe in faith healing?

As a Christian, I do believe in miracles. I think that sometimes prayer can bring about miraculous medical recoveries.

Have you ever personally been acquainted with someone who you thought experienced a miraculous cure?

No. I can't say that I have.

Do you have any religious problems with people consulting physicians about medical problems?

None at all.

You said that you counsel people who come to the center. Do you ever counsel people with medical problems?

Of course.

Have you ever recommended that any of them seek professional medical help for those problems?

On many occasions. I do some work with people who have substance abuse problems. I strongly recommend that they go to see physicians, psychiatrists, and psychologists. I believe in that.

I take it then that you wouldn't have any problems awarding money damages for medical expenses?

No, at least not if I thought that the defendant was liable and the medical expenses were reasonable.

One last topic, Reverend Morris. A couple of minutes ago I was speaking with Ms. Marcetti. We were talking about the fact that Mr. Williams had had some drinks. She told us that she had no religious scruples against drinking. Do you?

No. I'm like her. It all depends on whether a person drinks in moderation. If they go too far, I do think it's sinful.

Do you personally use alcohol?

Rarely but sometimes.

Do you ever have parties at the center?

Yes.

Do you ever serve beer or liquor at the parties?

Sometimes we serve beer.

Can you promise Mr. Williams that you'll listen carefully to his testimony and not reject it just because he had those drinks?

I can assure you of that in good conscience.

Thank you very much, Reverend. Ms. Palumbo, can I ask you a few questions now?

Certainly.

Ms. Palumbo, when her Honor was questioning you, you said that you're engaged to a physician at Morena Med School. Does my memory serve me well?

Yes, it does. My fiancé is Dr. Lowenthal.

What is Dr. Lowenthal's specialty?

He's a brain surgeon.

I assume that he had training in general surgery before he developed his specialty.

That's a safe assumption. I vaguely recall a rotation in general surgery.

In this case, my client, Mr. Williams, will be calling several orthopedic surgeons to testify about the extent of his injuries. To your knowledge, has your fiancé ever done that type of surgery?

I would suppose so.

To the best of your memory, has he ever discussed that type of surgery with you?

He might have, but I honestly can't recall.

So he's never made any statements to you that might influence your evaluation of the testimony by Mr. Williams' witnesses?

None that I can remember.

And you do understand that if you serve on the jury in this case and you have any questions about the testimony about those witnesses, you won't be permitted to put those questions to your fiancé?

Certainly.

Can you promise Mr. Williams that you'll base your evaluation of that testimony solely on the evidence you would hear in this courtroom?

Yes. I can give you that assurance.

There's one other topic I'd like to take up with you. Mr. Williams is 65 years old. Do you live with any elderly people?

I'm not sure that I understand the question.

I'm sorry. Let me put it this way. Have you ever lived in the same house with someone who was 60 years of age or older?

No. I guess not. When I left home, my parents were both in their 40's.

Do you think that elderly people necessarily have grudges against young people?

No. It depends on the person. I'd hate to generalize about something like that. I don't think stereotypes are very useful.

Do you think that elderly persons necessarily have difficulty making identifications?

Well, your vision sometimes deteriorates when you get older, but it doesn't necessarily happen. You've got to know the facts about the eyesight of the individual in question. Again, it largely depends on the person.

So you wouldn't reject Mr. Williams' identification simply because he was 65 at the time of this incident?

No. I certainly wouldn't do that.

Thank you, Ms. Palumbo. Mr. Williams appreciates that. Now Mr. Gilligan, I have some questions for you.

O.K.

Mr. Gilligan, as I recall, you said that you are a retired member of the Marine Corps.

Yup.

What was your military specialty?

I was an artillery officer.

Did you ever serve as a juror in a court-martial?

On several occasions.

Those were criminal trials. Correct?

Yes.

Do you understand that although the standard of proof is beyond a reasonable doubt in a criminal trial, the standard is only a preponderance of the evidence in a civil case like this one?

I realize that. The judge talked about that before.

And you won't hold Mr. Williams to the higher burden, proof beyond a reasonable doubt, in deciding whether he had proven his case?

Of course not.

Mr. Gilligan, when you were on active duty in the military, were women permitted to serve in combat roles?

Not at that time. That's changed since I left active duty.

Do you agree with that change?

To be frank, I was a little skeptical at first. However, the change has been in effect for a while now, and the feedback I've gotten from my friends still on active duty is that it's worked out real well.

In this case, Mr. Williams is going to calling Police Officer Janice Taylor as a witness. She's a female member of the Morena Police Department. What do you think about women in the police force?

I've got no problem with that. They might not be as good at stopping a violent crime, but that's only part of their job.

Let's talk about a specific part of a police officer's job, namely, investigating a crime. Officer Taylor is going to testify about her investigation of the attack on Mr. Williams. Do you have any doubts that a female police officer would be competent to handle that job?

No. I knew several female MPs—military police. They were highly competent. In one case in particular I was involved in, it was a female MP whose investigation cracked it. Her work in that case was just plain outstanding.

Mr. Gilligan, that's good to hear. Now have you listened carefully to the questions I've asked the other jurors—the questions, for example, about awarding money damages for personal injuries?

I tried to be attentive as best I could.

Would you have answered any of those questions differently than they did?

I don't believe so.

Thank you. Finally, Mr. Castro, I need to speak with for a while. You told us that you own your own business. Have you ever been sued?

No.

Have you ever had to sue one of your customers?

Thankfully no.

So do you have any general impressions of attorney who represent plaintiffs or attorneys who represent defendants at civil trials?

No. I haven't had any personal dealings in lawsuits. You read things in the papers, but I haven't had any direct contact with trial attorneys other than Ms. Marcus who does my legal work.

You said that you "read things in the papers." What things have you read?

Well, to be honest, there a lot of negative things in the papers about attorneys. Everyone knows that.

Like what?

You sometimes read that plaintiff's attorneys bring unfounded lawsuits against businesses.

Do you think those statements are true?

Sometimes, but you can't take what you read in the papers at face values. I've certainly learned that over the years. When you read the silly articles about computer technology in the papers, you realize how off base they are on the facts a lot of the time.

In this case Mr. Williams is the plaintiff. You don't necessarily think that he's in the wrong simply because he's the plaintiff who brought this suit and he's asking for money damages?

No, of course not. You have to consider the specific facts of the case before you make up your mind.

Fine, Mr. Castro. No other questions, Your Honor.

Court: Ms. Peterson, you may question now.

(Defense Questions)

Thank you, Your Honor.

Ms. Marcetti, my name is Jill Peterson. I represent the defendant in this case, Mr. Robert Scott. As plaintiff's counsel indicated, Mr. Scott denies he was at fault in injuring the plaintiff. Mr. Scott freely admits that he was at the hotel the night of the attack, but he maintains that he had nothing to do with the attack on the plaintiff. I want to ask you a couple of questions to see whether you'd be comfortable sitting as a juror in this dispute between Mr. Scott and the plaintiff.

A few minutes ago the plaintiff's attorney indicated that one of the witnesses in this case is likely to be Officer Janice Taylor. She's a member of the Morena Police Department. Have you ever worked for a police department?

No.

Do you have any relatives who work for a police department?

No.

Do you have any friends that work for a police department?

I've got a neighbor down the street who I think works for the police, but I'm not even sure about that.

Let's suppose that Officer Taylor testifies in this case. Do you think that police officers are generally more truthful than other people?

No. They're just human beings. There are good ones and bad ones.

Do you think that the testimony of police officers is entitled to more weight than the testimony of other citizens?

No. It all depends on the facts. I get statements from policemen in the files I process. Some of the statements are great, and some of them are just plain garbage. It depends on the person.

Later in this case Her Honor may instruct you that you are to judge Officer Taylor's testimony the same way you judge the testimony of all the other witnesses in the case. If she gives you that instruction, will you be able to follow it?

Sure.

And you won't give Officer Taylor's testimony any special consideration just because she works for the police?

No.

Let's take another step. Officer Taylor might end up giving some expert opinions in this case—conclusions that a normal layperson couldn't give on the witness stand. Do you think you should accept a person's opinion just because they're an expert?

Not at all.

In your work, do you often receive statements from people who call themselves experts?

All the time.

How do you go about deciding whether to rely on those statements?

I look at their qualifications. I see if they have any biases, and I try to figure out whether their conclusion makes sense in terms of the facts. Over the years in my job I've learned to trust the facts more than particular witnesses.

Her Honor may instruct that you are not to accept expert opinions at face value simply because the witness is an expert. Could you follow that instruction?

I'll have no difficulty with that one. I can guarantee you that.

Mr. Leader, let me ask you some questions now. As her Honor said a few minutes ago, there may be a large number of witnesses in this case. However, at this point we intend to call only two witnesses, Mr. Scott and a Ms. Joan Freeman.

Have you ever been in a situation where some of your friends were having a disagreement—a couple of friends said one thing but one friend said something else?

Oh, I suppose so.

When you were in that situation, did you think that the last friend was necessarily wrong just because he or she was outnumbered, just because there were more people on the other side of the argument?

No. Not necessarily. It depends on who's on which side and what they have to say. You have to use your common sense.

O.K. So you'd listen to what your friend had to say even if there were more people on the other side.

Sure.

Now, later in this case, Judge Smith is going to give you an instruction. She's going to tell you that you shouldn't decide this case simply on the basis of the number of witnesses called by the two sides. You can't decide who's right just by counting the number of witnesses on the two sides. Can you promise me that if Judge Smith gives you that instruction, you'll try your level best to follow it?

Yes.

And you won't reject the defense's testimony simply because the plaintiff may call more witnesses?

No.

Thank you, Mr. Leader. Let's turn to you now, Reverend Morris. Reverend, I was talking to Ms. Marcetti about Officer Taylor. There's going to be some evidence in this case about a statement Mr. Scott made to the officer. The evidence is going to show that when she awoke him from his sleep and asked him about his shoes, he said that he might have lent the shoes to a friend. He'll testify in this trial that he said that only because he was a bit sleepy and angry about being awakened. He'll admit that he didn't lend those shoes to anyone.

Would you reject his testimony in this case simply because he made that earlier statement to Officer Taylor?

I'm not sure I understand.

I'm sorry. Let's suppose that a person says one thing before trial and then says something else on the witness stand. Does that necessarily mean that they're lying on the stand?

No. You'd have to know all the facts.

What facts would you want to know?

Well, I'd want to know why they made the statement before trial.

So can you promise Mr. Scott that you'll listen to his testimony explaining his statement to Officer Taylor?

Certainly. You can't leap to judgments about people. That's one thing I've learned in my work.

Thank you, Reverend Morris. Ms. Palumbo, I have just a couple of questions for you. You told us that you're a graduate student in psychology at U.E.D.?

Yes.

What is the focus of your graduate research?

I'm reviewing the validity studies of intelligence tests. Specifically, I'm looking into the question of whether there really is racial bias in some or all of those tests.

Does your graduate course work include any research into the process of memory?

No.

I'd presume, though, that as an undergraduate psychology student, you spent some time studying the process of memory.

Sure. That's basic material in introductory psych courses.

Did you spend any time reviewing the studies of the reliability of eyewitness testimony?

A bit.

Did you form any strong opinions about the reliability of the memory of eyewitnesses to events?

Not really. Some psychologists believe that eyewitness memories are quite untrustworthy, but the research struck me as rather inconclusive. They need to investigate that further.

Now in this case, the plaintiff is going to be presenting his own testimony supposedly identifying Mr. Scott as one of the men who beat the plaintiff. At the end of the trial, her Honor is going to give you an instruction on eyewitness identification testimony. She's going to tell you that one of the factors you should consider is the state of mind of the person who made the identification. Would your educational background make it difficult for you to follow that instruction?

I don't see why it would. Quite apart from the research, it's just common sense that the person's frame of mind would be relevant.

So you'd listen carefully to the evidence about Mr. Williams' state of mind—for example, what he was thinking about just before he was attacked on the second floor. Right?

Sure.

Very well, Ms. Palumbo.

Now, Mr. Gilligan, you said that you have two grown children. What lines of work are they in?

My daughter, Denise, is the export-import business. She works for a Hong Kong firm, and she lives there. My son, Chris, is an attorney.

Where does he work?

He lives and works in Silicon Valley in California.

What type of work does he do?

He does legal work for some of the computer firms there.

Does he do trials? Is he involved in litigation?

Not as far as I can tell. He does what he calls "transactional work." He puts together deals. He almost never goes to court as far as I can tell.

Has he ever expressed any preference for plaintiffs, attorneys or defense attorneys?

No. As I said, he never gets involved in trials. That's just not his bag. He likes to draft documents and negotiate deals. He doesn't touch the trial work. He says that's "too messy."

Are there other attorneys in his firm who litigate—who go to trial?

No. My impression is that they refer the litigation to other firms. They don't become involved in trials. They farm that out.

One last topic. The evidence in this case is probably going to show that one of the men who attacked the plaintiff was a Dick Rogers. The evidence will also show that Mr. Scott knew Mr. Rogers. If the evidence shows that Rogers was at fault, would you automatically tend to think that Mr. Scott also had to be involved?

Just because they were friends?

Right.

No. I don't believe in guilt by association. If you're coming to find someone at fault, you've got to show that they were personally, individually responsible. I feel very strongly about that as a matter of principle.

Thank you very much, Mr. Gilligan. Mr. Castro, I'd like to speak with you now. What specifically does your business do?

We do specialized computer programming.

Are any of your past or present clients law firms?

A few.

Were they firms that do trial work?

I think some of them were. We put together some innovative litigation support programs for them.

Let's talk about these firms for a second. Were they all plaintiffs' firms, firms that represented plaintiffs in lawsuits?

I honestly can't tell you. When I was doing the job, I had to find out the type of information they wanted to extract from the database; but that didn't require me to find whom they represented. It was a matter of indifference to me. It never occurred me to ask.

Now you've sat here and listened to Mr. Clark and I question the other five potential jurors. I asked a lot of questions—for instance, whether you'd decide a case simply on the basis of the number of witnesses called by the two sides. Would you have answered any of the questions differently than the other panel members?

I don't believe so.

Is there anything in your personal background that might make it difficult for you to listen carefully to Mr. Scott's testimony in this case and evaluate it impartially?

Not that I can think of.

Thank you very much, Mr. Castro. No further questions, Your Honor.

Court: Attorneys, please approach. Are there any preemptory challenges for cause?

Attorneys: No.

Court: Very well. Please resume your seats.

(The attorneys return to their respective counsel tables.)

All right. Are there any peremptory challenges? Mr. Clark, you first.

Your Honor, we'd like you to thank and excuse Mr. Leader.

Mr. Leader, we're going to excuse you from service on this jury. I do want to thank you. I'd like you to return to the jury pool room. Juror number seven, Mr. Furnish, please take Mr. Leader's seat.

Mr. Furnish, before I allow the attorneys to question you, I'd like you to give us the items of information listed on the chalkboard.

Yes, Your Honor. My name is Don Furnish. I live at 28 Huntington Drive in Morena out in the Avenues. I'm single. I'm not married, and I never have been. I'm a native Morenan. I teach History at Riordan High School here in the City.

Mr. Clark, you may question, but please keep it brief. We're running out of the time allotted for jury selection. This has run a little longer that I expected. We have only a couple of minutes left.

Yes, Your Honor. I'll be brief.

Mr. Furnish, I've noticed that you've been listening carefully while we talked to the other members of the panel. As you know, we've asked questions about such things as people's beliefs about drinking and awarding money damages for pain and suffering? Please think carefully. Would you have answered any of those questions differently?

No.

Your Honor, I have no further questions of Mr. Furnish.

Court: Ms. Peterson?

Your Honor, Mr, Scott would be perfectly happy with Mr. Furnish as a juror.

Very well. Ladies and gentlemen, we've been questioning you for well over an hour. I know that we've asked you a lot of questions, but it's always possible that we've overlooked something. One last time I want you to think carefully. Is there any fact that we've neglected to ask about that would make it difficult for you to be a fair, impartial juror in this trial?

Very well. Mr. Clark, any further challenges?

No, Your Honor. Mr. Williams will be happy with this jury.

Ms. Peterson?

We pass for cause.

All right. Madame Bailiff, please swear the jury.

Yes, Your Honor. Please stand again. "Do you and each of you understand and agree that you will well and truly try the cause now pending before this court, and render a true verdict according only to the evidence presented to you and the instructions of the court?" If so, say, "I do."

(All the panelists respond, "I do.")

Ladies and gentlemen, we have our jury.

§ 4.12 ETHICAL QUESTIONS

As previously stated, in order to develop a profile of the type of juror they want or do not want, some attorneys hire social scientists to canvass the community. Section 4.8(B) described some of the ethical restraints on prevoir dire jury profile surveys. Are those restraints adequate to protect the impartiality of the jury ultimately chosen? *Compare United States v. Lehder–Rivas,* 669 F.Supp. 1563 (M.D.Fla. 1987) with *United States v. Lehder–Rivas,* 667 F.Supp. 827 (M.D.Fla. 1987). Remember that in an adversary system, an impartial decision-maker is essential.

Now assume that you have conducted an ethically proper pretrial investigation into the panel members' backgrounds. During voir dire, the opposing attorney is questioning a panel member; and you realize that the panel member has just given the opposing attorney a false answer. Do you have an ethical duty to call the false answer to the attention of the judge and opposing attorney? Suppose that the subject-matter of the question is an incident that is remote in time—one that the panel member might be innocently mistaken about. Does an ethical duty arise only when you are convinced that the panel member is lying? Suppose alternatively that the member did not tell an outright lie; he merely withheld relevant information. Should an incomplete answer by a panel member trigger an ethical duty on your part? Both Model Code of Professional Responsibility DR 7–102(A)(1) and Model Rule 3.3(a)(1) impose at least a limited duty on the attorney to come forward to disclose a fraud on the court perpetrated by the attorney's client. Do the existence of those rules cut in favor of or against imposing a duty on the attorney to come forward when the fraud is perpetrated by someone other than the attorney's client? Would the duty of confidentiality apply to your knowledge of the panel member's lie? Bear in mind that in some jurisdictions, an intentionally false answer by a venireperson during voir dire is a ground for a new trial.

§ 4.13 TRIAL TECHNIQUE EXERCISES

§ 4.13(A) Instructions for the Students Playing the Role of the Attorney

As your assignment for Chapter 3, we asked you to submit a memorandum identifying the theory and theme you intend to use at trial. You must now write a related memorandum. The purpose of this memorandum is to identify persons who would be likely candidates for your peremptory strikes during jury selection in your case. Apply the strategy of jury deselection. In one paragraph, state your theme, identify a background characteristic that might predisclose a panel member to reject your theme, and explain why that characteristic would incline the person to reject the theme. In a second paragraph, describe your formal or functional client, identify a background characteristic that would make it difficult for a panel member to empathize with your client, and explain why that characteristic would have that effect. In a third paragraph, describe yourself, and identify a characteristic which would make it difficult for a panel member to identify with you.

For your laboratory exercise this week, your instructor may simply require you to conduct jury selection in your case: preliminary remarks, questioning (both group and individual), and challenges. However, jury selection is such a complex procedure that your professor may decide to dissect the process and have you conduct only part of the procedure. For example, the instructor may announce that you are to conduct only group questioning. Your instructor will give you further guidance.

§ 4.13(B) Instructions for the Students Playing the Role of the Venirepersons

Your instructor will assign you one of the following roles. The roles state your basic profile. You should feel free to fill in the details of the profile. Please use discretion and tact in filling in the details; you want the profile to be as realistic as possible.

Juror A. You are very active in part-time religious work. You do door-to-door preaching in the local community. You work part-time at a religious bookstore owned by your church. The bookstore has a large number of texts dealing with the corruption of modern secular government, including the courts.

Juror B. While you were a youth, you were arrested several times on minor charges; none of the arrests resulted in convictions or adjudications of juvenile delinquency. Despite the arrests, you have no grudges against prosecutors. However, you do believe that occasionally police officers misuse criminal laws to harass youth and minority groups. You are the assistant director of the placement office at a local college.

Juror C. You are a relatively quiet, withdrawn person. You have always lived in this community. After high school you went to work at a local bank. You have worked for the same bank for the past 15 years, and you have worked your way up to the position of head teller. Your political views are generally conservative; for example, you strongly favor the death penalty and are quite concerned about the high crime rate. However, you view yourself as essentially apolitical; you do not even bother to vote.

Juror D. You have a large number of cousins you are quite close to. One is a police officer in a nearby town. You regard her as a thoroughly honest person. Another, who lives in Iowa, is a claims investigator for an insurance company. Although your family is a close one, you know little about the details of the work of either cousin. You remember reading something about this case in the *Morena Times,* the most popular local newspaper. However, you cannot recall precisely what you read; as best you recall, the article indicated merely that the case was going to trial.

Juror E. You graduated from the state university with both a basic degree and a master's degree in psychology. You work for a psychology institute in Morena. The institute provides services to both private patients and mentally ill prisoners incarcerated in the county jail. On 10 occasions, you have appeared as an expert witness in trials in local court. On six occasions, you testified for the prosecution. On one occasion, you appeared for a civil plaintiff; and on three occasions, you testified for a civil defendant. You believe that too many experts, especially people in your field, prostitute themselves for large fees from attorneys. You think that an expert should be an objective scientist and call the shots as he or she sees them.

Juror F. You own your own business, a small computer programming company in town. When you were a freshman in college, you were active in the Young Democrats organization. However, you eventually became disillusioned with politics. After college, you attained an M.B.A. After attaining that degree, you worked for I.B.M. in New York City for ten years. You then moved to this community. You are the secretary of the local Chamber of Commerce. You are very supportive of local charities; you give a good deal of your time and money to support the charities.

Chapter 5

OPENING STATEMENT—AN EXERCISE IN RES IPSA LOQUITUR

Reprinted by permission of Warner Books/New York from The Law as Seen By Charles Bragg. Copyright © 1983 by Charles Bragg.

Table of Sections

---

§ 5.1   INTRODUCTION

Chapter 4 dealt with the initial stage of the trial, jury selection. The next stage is opening statement. Like jury selection, this stage poses problems in tactical planning for the litigator. The litigator must grapple with such problems as whether to deliver an opening, when to deliver it, and how to structure it. This chapter addresses those problems.

§ 5.2   THE IMPORTANCE OF THE OPENING STATEMENT

Before discussing those problems, we must appreciate the importance of the opening statement. The Chicago Jury Project, conducted in the 1960s, is easily the most extensive and significant empirical study of the behavior of the American jury. The findings of the study are summarized in the classic text, H. KALVEN & H. ZEISEL, THE AMERICAN JURY (1966). It is often asserted that the Chicago researchers found that "80% of jurors make up their minds during opening and never change their opinions." Jossen, *Opening Statements: Win It in the Opening,* 10 THE DOCKET 1, 6 (Spr. 1986). However, that assertion is apocryphal. J. TANFORD, THE TRIAL PROCESS: LAW, TACTICS AND ETHICS 144–45 (2d ed. 1993); Anderson, *An Advocate's Guide to Effective Closing Argument,* 11 THE PRACT. LITIGATOR 13, 14 (Mar. 2000). Indeed, one of the lead researchers in the project, Hans Zeisel, has described the 80% figure as a hoax. Zeisel, *A Jury Hoax: The Superpower of the Opening Statement,* 14 LITIGATION 17–18 (Sum. 1988). It is true that the Chicago data suggests that most juries ultimately return the same verdict that they would have voted for immediately after opening. However, it is quite another matter to conclude that the majority of jurors form an unshakeable opinion during the openings. More recent research at the University of North Carolina indicates that most jurors are open-minded and can be persuaded to vote against the side that the opening statements inclined them to favor. Hughes & Hsaio, *Does the Opening Determine the Verdict?,* 22 TRIAL 66 (Feb. 1986). *See also Panelists Give Tips to Lawyers* NAT'L L.J., Feb. 22, 1993 (reporting on a national survey of jurors conducted by Donald Hubert & Associates at the request of The National Law Journal and LEXIS, one researcher stated that "only 6 percent of the jurors ma[d]e up their minds after opening statement. . . .").

Notwithstanding the inaccuracy of the 80% assertion, common sense and psychological theory point to the importance of the opening. The old saying is that "First impressions count." In many jurisdictions, the jurors' first opportunity to form an impression of the attorney and client will come during opening. As we saw in Chapter 4, in two thirds of the federal judicial districts and a fifth of the states, the judge conducts the entire voir dire examination. In these jurisdictions, the attorney's initial opportunity to address the jury will be the opening.

Psychological theory also suggests that the opening is a unique opportunity for advocacy. After the final challenges, the remaining jurors realize that they are the Chosen. They know that the preliminaries are over and that the "real" trial is about to begin. In theatrical terms, "the curtain" is about to go up. Herman, *Taking Center Stage in the Courtroom Drama: A Trial Lawyer's Short Course in Dramaturgy* 3 (unpublished article). In addition, the jurors are physically fresh; they have not yet lived through the tiring ordeal of weeks or months of trial. For all these reasons, the jurors tend to be in an attentive, receptive state of attention at the opening statement stage. Vinson, *Juries: Perception and the Decision–Making Process,* 18 TRIAL 52 (1982). Although they may not irrevocably reach a decision while they listen to the openings, "[m]ost jurors start to make up their minds early. . . . [P]eople do not enjoy stress, and indecision is stressful. Most will form a strong inclination to find a particular way early in the case just to relieve the pressure." Wilkens, *The Art of Opening Statement,* 25 TRIAL 56, 57 (Nov. 1989). *See also* McElhaney, *Taking Sides: What Happens in the Opening Statement,* 78 A.B.A.J. 80, 81 (May 1992) (although the jurors do not make up their minds during opening, they may begin to "side with" or "pull for" one side). Most litigation consultants, many of whom are psychologists, insist that "opening statements are important far out of proportion to the time they consume in trial." Vinson & Hanley, *Do Not Ignore This Opening Statement-or Any Others: A Reply to Professor Zeisel,* 15 LITIGATION 1, 55 (Wint. 1989). These consultants assert that their "conclusions are based primarily on thousands of interviews with actual and surrogate jurors." *Id.* at 2.

One of the strongest indications of the perceived importance of the openings is the number of cases which settle immediately after the opening statements. If one side delivers a markedly more persuasive opening, the other side often makes a much more attractive settlement offer even before the first witness is called. In the trial of the mammoth civil class action against Charles Keating, Jr., "[v]irtually all the big accounting firms and law firms began settling after" the plaintiffs' dramatic opening statement. Cotchett, *The Opening Statement Can Win the Case and Encourage Settlements,* NAT'L L.J., Feb. 8, 1993, at p. S6.

§ 5.3 WHETHER TO MAKE AN OPENING STATEMENT

Some attorneys routinely forego making an opening statement in bench trials (cases tried without a jury) when the facts are straightforward. However, it is a mistake to assume that there is no need to make an opening simply because the trier of fact is a judge. On the one hand, the judge might may know a good deal about the law governing the case; and the judge may even have presided at similar trials in the past. On the other hand, the judge may be a complete stranger to the facts in the instant case. Like a lay juror, the judge can comprehend the subsequent testimony more easily if he or she has the benefit of a preview of the testimony in the opening. As a general rule with only two exceptions, the attorney should not waive opening even in a bench trial. One exception is a case in which the judge indicates that he or she does not desire an opening. In that event, delivering an opening would probably succeed only in irritating the judge. The other exception is a case in which you know that the trial judge is intimately familiar with the facts. For example, the same judge may have supervised the extensive discovery in the case.

Even when you decide to deliver an opening in a bench trial, do not assume that you must make the same opening that you would deliver to a lay jury. The identity of the trier of fact affects the content of the opening. As we shall see in § 5.5 of this chapter, at the beginning of an opening statement it is customary for the attorney to describe the purpose of the opening. It is certainly unnecessary to include that statement in an opening intended for a judge. The same section points out that near the end of the opening, many attorneys routinely specify the verdict they want the trier of fact to return. Unless the case is very complex, there is probably no need to do so in an opening delivered to a judge. You should ordinarily make an opening in a bench trial, but the opening ought to be shorter and more to the point than it would be in a jury trial. Also, during bench trials some judges permit more references to legal doctrine in opening statement than they allow in jury trials.

§ 5.4 WHEN TO DELIVER THE OPENING STATEMENT

The party with the ultimate burden of proof, usually the plaintiff or prosecutor, goes first. In most jurisdictions, however, the defense counsel has a choice. Tanford, *An Introduction to Trial Law,* 51 MO.L. REV. 623, 646 (1986). The defense may either present an opening immediately after the plaintiff's or prosecutor's opening, or the defense can reserve opening until the beginning of the defense case-in-chief. There are different schools of thought on the question of the timing of the defense opening.

Some defense counsel favor waiting until the defense case. It is unquestionably easier to make the defense opening after the defense has heard all the plaintiff's or prosecutor's evidence. Further, if the defense hopes to win by a surprise theory, there is a risk that the defense will tip its hand in an opening delivered right after the plaintiff's or prosecutor's speech.

However, perhaps the majority of experienced defense attorneys prefer to make the opening right after the plaintiff's or prosecutor's.

Section 5.2 pointed out that the empirical research suggests that many jurors make a tentative decision in the case on the basis of the openings. By reserving the opening, the defense surrenders an important psychological advantage to the opposition. In addition, the defense opening can interrupt the smooth flow of the plaintiff's or prosecutor's case; a powerful plaintiff's opening, followed immediately by a convincing case-in-chief, may make a plaintiff's verdict virtually inevitable. The plaintiff or prosecutor might even apply pressure to the defense to make an immediate statement. Near the end of their opening, the plaintiff's attorney or prosecutor might tell the jury that "the defense will now have an opportunity to give you their view of the case." The more acute jurors may become suspicious if the defense does not respond immediately.

The need to make this tactical choice can disappear if there is more than one defendant and more than one defense attorney. The defense attorneys may be able to coordinate. One defense attorney makes an opening right after the plaintiff or prosecutor while another defers the opening until the beginning of the defense case-in-chief. This type of coordination can give the defense the best of both worlds. However, it is important to realize that as a practical matter, codefendants are often adversaries. One defendant may attempt to exculpate himself by inculpating the codefendant. Thus, coordination is risky and rare.

§ 5.5 THE STRUCTURE OF AN OPENING STATEMENT

There are two schools of thought on the optimal structure for an opening statement. Most attorneys still follow the traditional view. The bulk of this section outlines the structure of a traditional opening statement. At the very end of this section, however, we shall discuss the emerging, competing view that other attorneys follow.

§ 5.5(A) The Beginning

At the outset of an opening statement, the attorney should introduce the client, if this has not already been done, and describe the purpose of the opening.

The Introduction of the Client

From the outset, the attorney attempts to personalize his client and depersonalize the opposition. Before you rush to the historical merits of the case, "put a human face on [the] legal problem." Reidinger, *Spinning Yarns,* 82 A.B.A.J. 102 (June 1996). For instance, in the trial of the class action against Charles Keating, Jr., plaintiffs' attorney Joseph Cotchett made it clear in opening statement that the plaintiffs were sympathetic elderly persons—not "New York bond traders." Cotchett, *The Opening Statement Can Win the Case and Encourage Settlements,* NAT'L L.J., Feb. 8, 1993, at p. S6. In *Williams v. Scott,* the plaintiff's attorney would refer to the plaintiff as "Mr. Williams" or "Peter Williams" rather than as "the plaintiff." Conversely, the attorney would consistently refer to Scott as "the defendant."

At this point in the opening, the attorney might also physically associate with the client. The attorney could stand behind the client's chair and rest his hands on the client's shoulders. Physical association is especially important in two types of cases. One case is a prosecution in which the client is charged with a heinous offense. By showing the jury that she is willing to stand near her client and touch her client, in effect the attorney is suggesting that she regards the client as a decent person. If the jurors perceive the suggestion, they will find it more difficult to conclude that the defendant committed the alleged crime. The jurors think that the attorney knows the truth.; The attorney has presumably had the benefit of privileged conversations with the client. and Iif the attorney seems to physically distance herself from her client, the jurors may interpret the attorney's conduct as an indication of the client's guilt or fault.

The second type of case is an action in which the client is an entity such as a corporation. In the jurors' mind, this type of action can shape up as a contest between "the little guy" and "the giant corporation." The jurors might view the corporation as a "cold, unfeeling, powerful monolith." S. HAMLIN, WHAT MAKES JURIES LISTEN 7 (1985). To reduce that risk, the attorney should have a living, breathing representative of the entity seated at the counsel table and introduce the representative. After introducing the representative, Mr. Grant Miles, point out that your client is "a family corporation. Grandfather Miles founded the business in 1933, and the family members, including Mr. Grant Miles whom you've just met, still own over 70% of the stock." As Professor McElhaney has written, "When you talk about your corporation, talk about people. Talk about them as individuals, not job titles ..." McElhaney, *Goals in Opening Statements,* 16 LITIGATION 47, 64 (Wint. 1990).

It is particularly important to go into detail about the client's background when your formal or functional client will not testify. In a criminal case, your client may decide against testifying because he could be impeached during cross-examination by past convictions. In a wrongful death action, the decedent will obviously be unavailable to testify. You will have to rely on other witnesses' testimony to flesh out the client's background; but like other admissible testimony in the case, the testimony about your client's background can be previewed during opening.

A Description of the Purpose of the Opening Statement

Traditionally, after introducing the client, the attorney describes the purpose of an opening. The description is usually twofold. Negatively, the attorney states that an opening is not evidence. Affirmatively, the attorney uses an analogy such as the statement that an opening statement is like a roadmap to the evidence.

Although it is traditional to inform the jury that the opening is not evidence, it may not be good advocacy. As Professor Jeans has noted, making that statement to the jury virtually invites the jury not to listen. J. JEANS, TRIAL ADVOCACY § 10.12, at 314 (2d ed. 1993). Rather than unthinkingly including that statement in her opening, the attorney should ask whether it is tactically advisable to do so.

Initially, consider the question from the plaintiff's or prosecutor's point of view. If the judge preinstructs the jury and informs them that the opening is not evidence, there is no need to repeat the statement. Suppose, though, that the judge does not preinstruct. In this event, the advisability of including the statement in the opening turns on the attorney's assessment of opposing counsel. If the attorney fails to include the statement, in his opening an acute opposing attorney may stress that the first attorney "neglected to point out that what she said in her opening is not evidence." A competent opponent can make it sound as if the first attorney was attempting to hoodwink the jury.

Now consider the question from the defense perspective. The answer to the question turns on the basic thrust of the defense. If the thrust is merely emphasizing the weakness of the plaintiff's or prosecution's case, it makes sense for the defense to repeat the statement that the openings are not evidence. The less "evidence" the jury hears, the better off the defense is. However, when the defense has a strong, affirmative posture, the defense attorney ought to omit the statement. In this situation, the defense opening should stress the favorable facts; and it is counterproductive to tell the jury that everything said during opening is not evidence.

Even if the attorney omits the traditional negative statement, in most cases the attorney should give the jurors an analogy helping them understand the function of the opening. The commonly used analogies are: a roadmap, a thumbnail sketch, a blueprint, the table of contents of a book, coming attractions at a theatre, and the picture on the cover of a jigsaw puzzle box. Although all analogies are a bit trite, inexperienced lay jurors often find them helpful. However, before drafting the opening, the attorney should consult the court clerk to learn whether this jury has sat before. If the jury is a new one, the analogies will be effective. However, when the jury is experienced—for instance, if most of the jurors have already sat on a trial—they have probably heard many of the analogies before. The experienced jurors will think that the analogy rings insincere. Before an experienced jury, the attorney ought to simply state that he is presenting an outline or preview of the evidence.

Keep these introductory amenities short. Today the largest group represented in the jury pool consisted of Generation Xers, "most of whom grew up in the 1970s and '80s ...." Hansen, *Reaching Out to Jurors*, 88 A.B.A.J. 33 (Feb. 2002). As a general proposition, they are less patient than older jurors. *Id.* As a generation, they are accustomed to getting relevant information immediately. Gilden, *Reality Programming Lessons for Twenty-first-century Trial Lawyering*, 31 STET.L.REV. 61, 68–70 (2001). You need to get to the substance of the opening quickly.

§ 5.5(B) Naming the Theory of the Case

Before going into any detail about the case, the attorney should give the jury a one-sentence overview of the case. The attorney can do so by including in one sentence the name of both the theory and the client. The *Scott* prosecutor might state, "This case is about a battery, the beating of a Mr. Peter Williams on January 19th, last year, by the defendant." The defense attorney might assert, "This is a case of mistaken identification, the misidentification of my client, Robert Scott." The sentence serves the same function as a movie poster at a theatre: "Mel Gibson in *We Were Soldiers*" or "Leonardo DiCaprio in *Titanic*." The sentence gives the jury the basic plot line and identifies the star.

§ 5.5(C) The Simplification of the Theory

Whether the attorney represents the prosecution, plaintiff, or defense, the next stage in the opening ought to be a radical simplification of the case. The attorney should list the elements of the theory that are formally or virtually undisputed and then identify the remaining, pivotal element, the element that the theme relates to.

In *Williams v. Scott,* the plaintiff's attorney could say: "Ladies and gentlemen, during the next two days you're going to hear a lot of testimony. At times the testimony may seem confusing. However, I want to emphasize that in the final analysis, there's only one real issue in this case. There's not going to be any dispute that Mr. Williams was attacked in the hallway of the Senator Hotel last year. There's not going to be any argument over whether he was hurt. He certainly was injured. The only question for you to decide in this case is this—who were the men who punched and kicked him in that hallway." Scott's attorney might say: "We've just listened to the plaintiff's attorney's very dramatic description of the attack on the plaintiff. From the beginning of this trial, ladies and gentlemen, Mr. Scott and I want to make some things clear to you. We don't deny that the plaintiff was attacked. It was a vicious, unprovoked attack. Mr. Scott and I both believe that the men who beat the plaintiff ought to be prosecuted to the full extent of the law. But that's not the issue in the case. The only real issue for you to decide, ladies and gentlemen, is the identity of the two men who attacked the plaintiff. Our position is simply that Mr. Scott isn't liable for the plaintiff's injuries because Mr. Scott had absolutely nothing to do with the attack."

Although both sides should simplify the case at this juncture in the opening, they do so for different reasons. The plaintiff or prosecutor does so to clarify the issues. The plaintiff and prosecutor have the ultimate burden of proof; if the facts are unclear when the jury retires to deliberate, there is a good possibility of a defense verdict. For her part, the defense attorney wants to simplify the case for very different reasons. By making intelligent concessions, the defense can defuse some of the sympathy that normally operates in favor of the plaintiff or prosecutor. Further, the concessions tend to enhance the jurors' view of the defense's candor. If the defense doggedly denied every element of the plaintiff's or prosecutor's theory, including the elements that will be overwhelmingly proven, the jurors would be less likely to accept the defense's position on the crucial element of the theory. As Chapter 3 pointed, one of the key factors in choosing a theory is whether it enables you to neutralize the opposition's best evidence. The proper selection of a theory puts you in a position to make these concessions without "giving away the farm".

§ 5.5(D) The Preview of the Evidence

The heart of the opening, of course, is the preview of the anticipated evidence. The attorney should preview both the evidence about the client's background and the evidence relevant to the historical merits.

The Client's Background

After simplifying the case, the temptation is for the attorney to rush to the historical merits. Doing so is a grave mistake. Before going into detail about the merits, the attorney should spend a minute or two describing the client's personal background. By way of example, Mr. Scott's attorney might say: "The evidence is first going to tell you something about Mr. Scott. He was born in New York. He grew up there with his father, mother, and three brothers. When he was 18, he joined the Navy. He spent three years on active duty. When he finished his Navy duty six months ago, he moved here. He joined the Teamsters' Union and went right to work for Eureka Van Lines." This part of the opening serves several purposes. It helps to humanize the client in the jury's mind. In addition, it can help the jurors identify with the client. Voir dire has already concluded; and before delivering the opening, the attorney learns a good deal about the jurors' backgrounds. If the attorney knows that many of the jurors are union members or members' spouses, it is worth mentioning in the opening that Mr. Scott is a union member.

However, there are two caveats the attorney must observe. One is that the attorney should avoid undue familiarity. The attorney should refer to her client as "Mr. Williams" or "Peter Williams" rather than "Pete." Early in the case, while the jurors are still becoming acquainted with the parties, they may react negatively to undue familiarity. In addition, some judges—especially federal judges—flatly forbid attorneys from referring to their clients by their first name.

The other caveat is that the attorney must not violate the character evidence rules set out in Federal Rules of Evidence 404–05. Make the facts about the person's background speak for themselves—*res ipsa loquitur*. The art is marshalling neutral, background facts that cumulatively create an impression of good character without overstepping the rules. The attorney can mention the seemingly neutral facts about the client's personal background which make it clear that the client is a stable, responsible family person; but the attorney may not say that the client is "a stable, responsible family person." For example, the attorney can state that Mr. Scott served on active duty in the Navy, but it would be improper to mention any decorations that Scott earned while on active duty. In the same vein, she can mention that Scott has worked for the same company for a substantial period of time, but she may not add that he chairs the company's United Way campaign. The decorations and chair affirmatively imply good character, and references to those facts are subject to a motion to strike. Worse still, the judge might hold that they improperly inject Scott's character into issue in the case. On a curative admissibility theory, the judge might then allow the plaintiff or prosecutor to rebut with otherwise inadmissible evidence of Scott's bad character.

The Historical Merits

The discussion of the historical merits is usually the largest segment of the opening. Its content is governed by two norms, one legal and one tactical. The legal norm is that *the attorney must initially make it clear that she is merely presenting an accurate preview of the admissible testimony of her witnesses* and she should do only that. This summational sentence incorporates all the major legal restrictions on opening.

"The attorney must initially make it clear." At the beginning of this segment of the opening, the attorney ought to use the phrasing, "The evidence will show that. . . ." However, it is unnecessary to repeat that phrasing at the beginning of every succeeding sentence. The jurors find the repetition of that expression annoying in the extreme. (However, if the judge sustains an argumentative objection against you, it is advisable to begin the next sentence out of your mouth with "The evidence will show. . . .")

"An accurate preview." The attorney must avoid overstatement. Clifford, *Credibility of a Case Depends on a Lawyer's Personal Believability,* NAT'L L.J., Feb. 8, 1993 ("a lawyer must be sure not to promise more than he or she can deliver"). Overstatement is an acute danger for criminal defense counsel. They sometimes succumb to "the Perry Mason trap:" Rather than being content to exploit the prosecution's heavy burden of proof, they feel compelled to show the jury who really committed the crime. McElhaney, *The Perry Mason Trap,* 17 LITIGATION 49 (Fall 1990). Or with little factual support, some defense counsel foolishly suggest in opening that the prosecution is the product of "a giant conspiracy between the police and the FBI." *Id.* at 50.

As a general proposition, exaggeration is a dangerous tack. In many jurisdictions, the jurors can take notes during opening. If the attorney makes a statement exaggerating the strength of her case, a juror may note the statement and point it out to the other jurors during deliberation. There is an even greater risk that the opposing attorney will exploit the overstatement during closing argument. The opposing attorney might ask the court reporter to prepare a partial verbatim transcript of the attorney's opening remarks. The opposing attorney could quote the transcript and convince the jurors that there has been a failure of proof. (This factor explains why you must pay such close attention during the opposing attorney's opening. You can exploit the failure of proof during summation only if you are alert enough to catch the overstatement during opening.) An overstatement by the attorney may lower the juror's estimation of the attorney's credibility, and the jurors may transfer that unfavorable estimation to their assessment of the client's credibility.

Tigar, *Jury Argument: You, The Facts, and the Law,* 14 LITIGATION 19, 20 (Sum. 1988).

"Merely presenting a preview of the admissible testimony." The only thing the attorney has a right to do during opening is to preview the testimony. At this point, the attorney should not invite the jurors to draw inferences from the expected testimony; the attorney will have an opportunity to argue those inferences during closing argument. If the attorney attempts to draw those inferences during opening, there may be an objection that the attorney is becoming "argumentative." *United States v. Dinitz,* 424 U.S. 600, 612 (1976) (Burger, C.J., concurring); Perrin, *From O.J. to McVeigh: The Use of Argument in the Opening Statement,* 48 EMORY L.J. 107, 151–53 (1999). *But see* O'Connor & Schopp, *Opening Statement Restriction Lifted?,* J.MO.BAR. 35 (Jan.-Feb. 2002)(discussing recent case law liberalizing the former view restricting the scope of the opening). Professor Jean describes the objection:

> Opening statements should not be an argument. . . . It is objectionable, for instance, for your opponent to state that "the evidence will show that the defendant negligently drove at an excessive rate of speed" or "the poor plaintiff has suffered a most grievous injury that will severely affect her for the rest of her life." How best to recognize an objectionable argument? As you listen to your opponent's opening statement ask yourself, "Will a witness testify in such fashion?" Relating to the examples, who will testify that "the defendant was negligent and drove at an excessive rate of speed?" These are conclusions and as such inadmissible. The testimony will relate to "tearing down the road at seventy miles an hour," and this should be the verbiage employed in opening statement.

J. JEANS, TRIAL ADVOCACY § 10.14, at 315 (2d ed. 1993). As Professor Jeans indicates, the attorney cannot include the statement in opening unless there is an available witness who can make the same statement on the stand. In short, the objection usually turns on the opinion rules set out in Federal Rules of Evidence 701–05. As a rule of thumb if those rules would permit the witness to express an opinion on the stand, the attorney may use the same opinionated expression in opening.[1]

In the opening, argument can not only be objectionable; it is often also poor advocacy. Jurors realize that the attorneys are partisan advocates. When the jurors hear an excessive number of adjectives or adverbs, they suspect that they are hearing the attorney's "spin" on the case. McElhaney, *Balanced Persuasion,* 88 A.B.A.J. 60, 61 (Mar. 2002). The opening will be more persuasive if the facts themselves seem to tell the story.

---

1. The reader should realize that judges vary somewhat in the strictness with which they enforce the rule as described by Professor Jeans. J. SONSTENG, R. HAYDOCK & J. BOYD, THE TRIALBOOK 5-1-2 (1985). One commentator has even asserted that "the old strictures against argument in the opening statement are breaking down. . . ." W. MASTERSON, CIVIL TRIAL PRACTICE: STRATEGIES AND TECHNIQUES 117 (1986).

Objectionably argumentative statements usually take one of three forms. One is an improper comment about credibility. Suppose that during opening, Scott's attorney said, "Ms. Freeman's testimony will establish three good reasons why you should reject the plaintiff's identification of Mr. Scott." The lay opinion rule set out in Federal Rule 701 would not permit Ms. Freeman to testify that "there are three good reasons why you should reject Williams' identification." Since she cannot testify in those terms, the statement is improperly argumentative.

Next, the attorney may improperly draw an inference from the circumstantial evidence on the merits. During opening, Scott's attorney would love to say:

> Now, ladies and gentlemen, during his opening the plaintiff's attorney said that there'll be testimony that there was blood on Mr. Scott's shoes. I would like you to pay particular attention to that testimony. The testimony will be that there was blood on the *soles* of the shoes—but none on the sides of the shoes. Just on the *soles*. That fact is much more consistent with the conclusion that Mr. Scott got the blood on his shoes when he innocently walked into the hallway to investigate the noise. It's inconsistent with their theory that my client used those shoes to kick the plaintiff. If he had, doesn't it stand to reason that there'd also be blood on the sides of the shoes?

The rub is that under Federal Rules 701–05, no witness would be permitted to testify in those terms. For that reason, the statement is objectionable.[2]

Finally, the attorney ought to avoid any extended discussion of the law. The witnesses usually cannot testify about the law, and it is therefore improper for the attorney to go on at any length during opening about the law. As we shall see, near the end of the opening while she is expressing confidence in her case, the attorney can make a passing reference to the burden of proof. If the attorney's case rests on a statutory cause of action or defense which lay jurors are likely to be unfamiliar with, the judge has discretion to allow the attorney to read the statute during opening. Petrocelli, *Opening Statements in California Civil Cases,* 12 LOS ANGELES LAWYER 24, 25 (Mar. 1989) (citing *De*

---

2. Although lay opinion testimony can present this problem, more often the problem arises because of anticipated expert testimony in the case. Law students tend to have an unduly expansive view of the opinions that experts are permitted to testify to. Suppose that in a traffic accident case, the plaintiff calls an expert accident reconstructionist-a witness with a background in physics and the laws of motion. Under Federal Rules of Evidence 702–05, most judges would allow that expert to testify to direction of travel, speed, and point of impact. Those determinations lie within the witness's scientific expertise. However, the judge should not permit the witness to testify that the defendant was "negligent," "careless," "at fault," or "in violation of El Dorado Vehicle Code § 1376." Those expressions relate to mixed questions of law and fact. They exceed the witness's expertise. For that reason, in most jurisdictions it would be argumentative for the attorney to use those expressions in opening. However, some cases now permit expert opinions on mixed questions of law and fact. *E.g.,* Puente v. A.S.I. Signs, 821 S.W.2d 400, 402 (Tex.App.1991); Harvey v. Culpepper, 801 S.W.2d 596, 601 (Tex.App.1990).

Armas v. Dickerman, 108 Cal.App.2d 548, 239 P.2d 65 (1952)). However, if the attorney spends more than a few sentences discussing the law, the judge might intervene *sua sponte;* in the jury's presence, the judge may remind the attorney that it is the judge's province to instruct the jury on the law and admonish the attorney to refrain from legal instruction.

As when the attorney is marshalling the facts about the client's personal background, because of the possible argumentative objection, an opening statement should be an exercise in *res ipsa loquitur.* The attorney must select and sequence the facts to make the facts speak for themselves to make the desired inferences clear without explicitly stating the inferences. We have seen that the argumentative limitation would prohibit Scott's attorney from expressly asserting that the presence of the blood on the soles of Scott's shoes is "much more consistent" with Scott's claim that he walked in the hallway after the attack. However, the defense attorney could say this:

> Ladies and gentlemen, as the plaintiff's attorney pointed out, there was blood on Mr. Scott's shoes. But only on the soles of his shoes. Not on the top of the shoes or the sides. Only on the soles. Mr. Scott will admit that, but he'll also tell you this. He'll tell you that right after he heard that noise in the hallway, he put on his shoes, opened his door, and set foot in the hallway. He took a couple of steps in the hallway while he was trying to figure out what had caused the noise.

This version of the opening is unobjectionable. In this version, the attorney has simply juxtaposed the blood on the soles of the shoes with Scott's claim that he stepped into the hallway. The juxtaposition makes it evident to the jury that one fact furnishes an innocent explanation for the other. In effect, the juxtaposition makes the facts speak for themselves.

"Admissible testimony." If the attorney has a substantial doubt about the admissibility of a particular item of evidence, it is ordinarily best to avoid mentioning the evidence during opening. The practical risk is that if the judge excludes the evidence, during deliberation the jurors will realize that the attorney overstated the case. The legal risk is that the mention of the evidence increases the likelihood of a mistrial. Suppose that the judge ultimately rules the evidence inadmissible.[3] The jury has already been exposed to the evidence during opening. If the judge concludes that the exposure was so lengthy that a curative instruction to disregard will be ineffective, the judge may have to declare a mistrial.[4] (Mistrial motions are discussed in Chapter 15.)

---

3. The opposing counsel's failure to object during opening does not waive the right to later object when the proponent attempts to introduce the testimony during the trial. McCarter & Stolze, *Opening Statements in Civil Trials,* J.MO. BAR, Apr.-May 1991, at 187, 189.

4. The attorney can sometimes escape from this dilemma by making a pretrial motion *in limine* in the nature of a motion

to admit. The attorney can seek an advance ruling that the item of evidence will be admissible. If the judge entertains and grants the motion, there is no risk in mentioning the evidence during opening. For a form for the motion, *see* R. CARLSON, SUCCESSFUL TECHNIQUES FOR CIVIL TRIALS § 1:62 (2d ed.1992).

"The testimony of her witnesses." The jurisdictions are split over the proper scope of opening. Tanford, *An Introduction to Trial Law,* 51 MO.L.REV. 623, 651–53 (1986). Some jurisdictions allow the attorney to refer to any anticipated testimony even if the testimony will probably come out of the mouth of an opposing witness. Other jurisdictions generally confine the attorney to previewing her own witnesses' testimony. *State v. Eisenlord,* 137 Ariz. 385, 670 P.2d 1209 (1983); *State v. Stinson,* 113 Mich.App. 719, 318 N.W.2d 513 (1982).; Perrin, *From O.J. to McVeigh: The Use of Argument in the Opening Statement,* 48 EMORY L.J. 107, 151–53 (1999). *But see* O'Connor & Schopp, *Opening Statement Restriction Lifted?,* J.MO.BAR. 35 (Jan.-Feb. 2002)(discussing recent case law liberalizing the former view restricting the scope of the opening).

Suppose initially that your jurisdiction follows the former view that the attorney may refer to any anticipated testimony in the case. Even if the jurisdiction does so, it is dangerous to devote too much time to opposing witnesses' testimony. When the attorney's primary focus is on the adversary's case, the opening may sound defensive to the jury. The jurors might wonder why the attorney is spending so little time talking about her own case. The jurors may begin to suspect that the attorney has little evidence to substantiate his own case.

Suppose alternatively that your jurisdiction generally restricts the attorney to his own witnesses' testimony. Even in these jurisdictions, the judges often permit the attorney to make passing reference to the opposing witnesses' testimony. It is sometimes necessary to do so to clearly join the issues and make the opening coherent. In civil cases, under Federal Rule of Evidence 611(c), an attorney may call a hostile witness aligned with the opposition. When there is a scope objection to the attorney's reference to the witness's testimony, at sidebar the attorney can represent to the judge that if necessary, he will call the person as his own witness under Rule 611 and elicit the testimony at that time.

The tactical norm is that *the attorney should tell a simple, interesting story that states the theory, exposes the weaknesses in the theory, and emphasizes the theme.*

"A story." As Chapter 3 emphasized, the available research indicates that during a trial, jurors attempt to organize the evidence into narrative accounts of the events. As previously stated, the jury deliberation can become a battle between two stories; the jurors resolve the case by assessing the relative plausibility of the opposing stories. Allen, *Factual Ambiguity and a Theory of Evidence,* 87 NW.U.L.REV. 604, 605 (1994). Do not force the jurors to construct the narrative themselves; rather, get your story before the jury in opening. Tell the story in narrative format. A witness-by-witness organization is boring and ineffective. R. MARSH, WINNING IN COURT 21 (1992). Weave the names of the key witnesses into the story narrative. Lubet, *The Opening Moment,* 43 DEF.L.J. 1, 27 (1994).

"*A simple story.*" Even after voir dire examination, the jurors are still largely strangers to the facts of the case. They may be hearing about these persons, places, objects, and events for the very first time in their lives. For that reason, in opening the attorney should discuss only the absolutely essential details. Keep the detail down to the bare minimum. Give the jury the facts "in broad strokes" and avoid "over-informing" them. S. HAMLIN, WHAT MAKES JURIES LISTEN 113, 125 (1985). If the attorney restricts the opening to "broad strokes," he or she can keep the opening short. As one writer cautions,

> The shrinking attention span is a fact of life in the 1990s. The average TV news program takes only a minute and 30 seconds to cover a story—30 seconds to set the stage, 30 seconds to tell the details, and 30 seconds to wrap up. Yet, to express points no more complex, a trial lawyer sometimes consumes an hour or more in the courtroom.... The net effect is juror boredom.

Bailey, *Lessons from 'L.A. Law': Winning Through Cinematic Techniques,* 27 TRIAL 98 (Aug. 1991).

The attorney can use visual aids such as charts to simplify the story for the jury. If the case arose from a traffic accident, during opening the attorney could use a bare bones depiction of the intersection to help the jury visualize the story. The chart need not even be an exhibit which the attorney intends to introduce into evidence later. In even a simple contract dispute, the attorney should use a timeline during opening statement to highlight the key events. Help the jury visualize the chronology. As Marshall McLuhan observed,

> Most people find it difficult to understand purely verbal concepts. They suspect the ear; they don't trust it. In general, we feel more secure when things are visible, when we can "see for ourselves." We admonish children ... to "believe only half of what they see, and nothing of what they hear." We employ visual ... metaphors for a great many everyday expressions.... We are so visually based that we call our wisest men visionaries or seers.

M. McLUHAN & Q. FIORE, THE MEDIUM IS THE MESSAGE 117 (1967). If a particular exhibit plays a central role in your case, invoke the judge's discretion and seek permission to display the exhibit during opening. *People v. Green,* 47 Cal.2d 209, 302 P.2d 307 (1956), allowed the showing of a motion picture during opening. *People v. Kirk,* 43 Cal. App.3d 921, 117 Cal.Rptr. 345 (1974), permitted an attorney to play an audiotape during opening. When you invoke the judge's discretion, under Federal Rule of Evidence 103(a)(2) make a detailed offer of proof demonstrating that the exhibit will prove to be admissible during the trial.

"*An interesting story.*" The attorney delivering the opening is a storyteller or playwright. McElhaney, *Creating Tension,* 74 A.B.A.J. 84 (June 1, 1988); Lubet, *The Trial as a Persuasive Story,* 14 AM.J.TRIAL ADVOC. 77 (1990). Use "a hook" to grab the jury's attention. Perlman, *The Compelling Opening Statement,* 30 TRIAL 64, 67 (May 1994). There are a number of techniques the attorney can use to arrest and maintain the jury's interest. The attorney should paint a sensory image for the jury by using vivid diction—the sort of concrete nouns and active verbs that Steinbeck uses. In the words of Colorado judge Christopher Munch, employ "television English"—"impact words ... that tell the theory of the ... case in human terms." McElhaney, *Key Words,* 76 A.B.A.J. 76, 78 (July 1990). "Use words that naturally bring to mind images of force, impact, and action, such as 'collision,' 'mangled,' 'impaled,' and 'crushed.'" Perlman, *Opening Statement: Persuade Through Storytelling,* 28 TRIAL 25, 27 (Feb. 1992).

Consider using a flashback technique to make the opening more dramatic. The attorney can shift into the first person and act out key testimony to help the jury relive the event that the client experienced. For example, Scott's attorney might say: "Miss Freeman will testify that, 'I heard some noise in the hallway. I decided to check it out. I opened my door and stepped into the hallway....'" At the same time, the attorney could act out opening the door and stepping out. *See* Gabriel, *Dramatic Impact in the Courtroom Act II: Non–Verbal Communication,* CACJ/FORUM 57, 58 (July/Aug. 1991) ("if an attorney actually turns the handle of an imaginary door in describing a fight sequence, the action is reinforced in the non-verbal channel. This allows the audience to follow the sequence of events visually as well as aurally"). There are available props in the courtroom. A jury railing can simulate a wall, the jury box can be a car, and a counsel table could be the table where a contract was negotiated. Speak in the present tense. Make the event come alive for the jury. McElhaney, *It's Happening Now,* 79 A.B.A.J. 101 (Oct. 1993).

Try to highlight the element of "crisis" in your case. Googasian, *Some Tips on Litigation,* 25 TRIAL 74, 75 (May 1989):

> A breach of contract is the broken promise that shuts down a production line and puts men and women out of work. Patent infringement is the theft of another's work. Breach of fiduciary duty is an act of treachery that commits economic murder.

Id.

"*A simple, interesting story which states the theory.*" The story, of course, is the theory that the attorney selected in the pretrial evaluation of the case. The attorney gave the jury a thumbnail sketch of the theory during the preliminary remarks preceding voir dire examination. Later the attorney named the theory near the beginning of the opening. Now the attorney can go into more detail about the theory. The attorney should at least go into enough detail to establish that she will produce sufficient evidence to make out a submissible case for the jury. In some jurisdictions, if the attorney fails to do so, the judge may direct a verdict for the opposition at the end of the opening statements. McCarter & Stolze, *Opening Statement in Civil Trials,* J.MO. BAR 187, 188 (Apr.-May 1991).

Although the attorney ought to tell the story incorporating the theory, the attorney should not use the expression, "story" or "theory." "Story" smacks of unreality. In the minds of many jurors, there is a dichotomy between "theory" and "reality." The attorney should tell the story without labeling it a "story."

"*A story that exposes the weaknesses in the theory.*" During the pretrial case evaluation, the attorney identified the pivotal element of the theory-the issue that will be the main battleground at trial. In *Scott,* the prosecutor knows that the issue is the identity of the second attacker. In part, the prosecutor reached that conclusion because he knows that Williams' identification is assailable; Williams drank three boilermakers just before the attack, and his initial identification of Scott was tentative. The unsure identification and the testimony about the drinking are the key weaknesses in the prosecutor's theory. The conventional wisdom is that the prosecutor should attempt to beat the defense to the punch and mention those weaknesses before the defense does in its opening. Mentioning those weaknesses will not only enhance the jurors' perception of the prosecutor's candor. Preempting the defense also supposedly softens the blow; the weaknesses may strike the jurors as far more damning if they learn of them for the first time during the defense opening.

As Chapter 4 pointed out, while most experienced litigators still believe that it is wise to beat the opposition to the punch, two commentators question the wisdom of that tactic. R. KLONOFF & P. COLBY, SPONSORSHIP STRATEGY: EVIDENTIARY TACTICS FOR WINNING JURY TRIALS 12, 88, 166 (1990). As previously stated, these commentators argue that by mentioning and "sponsoring" the fact, the attorney implicitly tells the jury that the fact is significant. By doing so, the attorney may inadvertently increase the weight which the jury attaches to the fact. *Id.* at 166. Moreover, later during summation that attorney might be hard pressed to convince the jury that the damaging fact is unimportant to the disposition of the case. These commentators favor exposing damaging facts in opening statement only in "egregious" cases in which the jurors may suspect that the advocate has gone "out of his way to hide a weakness. . . ." *Id.* at 89.

"*A story that emphasizes the theme.*" There are a number of methods of stressing the theme during opening. The attorney may use the label for the theme "so close for so long" at least once. The attorney should probably place the mention of the label near the end of the opening. The label is almost always technically argumentative, but the judge usually tolerates a bit of argument near the end of the opening. In addition, the attorney ought to devote more time to the testimony supporting the theme than to the other testimony on the historical merits. For instance, the *Scott* prosecutor would slowly, methodically preview the testimony about how close Williams was to the attackers and how long he had to view them. Moreover, the attorney can make a call "for special attention." S. HAMLIN, WHAT MAKES JURIES LISTEN 124 (1985). The prosecutor might say, "And, ladies and gentlemen, I would like you to pay special attention to Mr. Williams' testimony about how close he was to those two men. When Mr. Williams testifies about that, you'll see five photographs—pictures taken in the emergency room that Mr. Williams was rushed to right after the attack. These emergency room photos will show you the number of injuries Mr. Williams suffered all over his body." Finally, the attorney can act out key testimony supporting the theme. More than any other evidence, that testimony deserves highlighting.

§ 5.5(E) The Conclusion

In concluding, the attorney usually does two things. First, the attorney expresses confidence in the case. The *Scott* prosecutor might say: "I'm confident that when you've heard all the evidence in this case, you'll be convinced beyond any reasonable doubt that the defendant was one of the men who attacked Mr. Williams." At this point, many attorneys refer directly to the legal doctrines involved in the case. For example, in a medical malpractice action, the defense attorney might conclude by asserting that the evidence will show that "Dr. Jones was not negligent and was not guilty of any malpractice here...." Higgins, *Defense of Medical Malpractice Cases,* in 16 MODEL TRIALS 471, 570 (1969). Judged by Professor Jeans' test, the references to "negligent" and "malpractice" are technically argumentative; but many judges routinely allow brief references to the pertinent legal doctrines near the end of the opening statement.

In addition, the attorney specifies the verdict that she wants the jury to return at the end of the case. The prosecutor continues: "When you've heard all this evidence, you'll know that the only just verdict in this case is a verdict of guilty, that the defendant is guilty of the crime of battery." The specification is especially important in a complex case in which the attorney anticipates that the judge will instruct on several theories. From the very beginning of the case, the attorney wants the jurors to realize which verdict the attorney's client prefers.

As we mentioned at the beginning of this section, there are two schools of thought on the best structure for an opening. Subsections (A)-(E) outline the traditional structure that probably the majority of attorneys still use. However, other attorneys and many jury consultants feel that it is largely a waste of time to talk about the function of an opening. These attorneys believe that the attorney must get to the heart of the matter as quickly as possible. In their view, the attorney should "instantly get [the jury] into the story." S. HAMLIN, WHAT MAKES JURIES LISTEN 120 (1985). Many of these attorneys omit a description of the opening's purpose and go straight to the naming of the theory (§ 5.5(B)) after introducing the client. Some of these attorneys go further; they believe that after introducing the client, the attorney should immediately jump to the preview of the evidence (§ 5.5(D)). If the parties were previously introduced during jury selection, the attorney can begin with a dramatic preview of the evidence. Which view do you prefer? Why? In which types of cases is the more traditional format likely to be the more effective?

§ 5.6 THE STYLE OF DELIVERING AN OPENING STATEMENT

In the 19th century, attorneys tended to be flamboyant and use flowery oratory in opening. Modernly, especially in commercial litigation, attorneys are more low key. The tone of contemporary litigation is more business-like. However, the attorney must still be cognizant of the rudiments of effective courtroom speaking style.

The attorney should use simple, lay diction. Avoid legal jargon. *See generally* S. HAMLIN, WHAT MAKES JURIES LISTEN 166–70 (1985). There is no reason to say "prior to" when "before" is available, just as there is no need to use "motor vehicle" when you can say "car." An opening is a test of your communicative skill, not your vocabulary. "Lawyers should ... emulate good writers. In most instances, good writers keep it simple. Some 70 to 80 percent of the words used by W. Somerset Maugham, Sinclair Lewis, Robert Louis Stevenson, and Charles Dickens have only one syllable." French, *KISS in the Courtroom: Keep It Short and Simple,* 28 TRIAL 130, 132 (Nov. 1992). In a juror survey conducted for The National Law Journal and LEXIS, researchers found that "the best-represented occupation" among the jurors was skilled blue-collar laborers (who are often high school graduates) rather than white-collar professionals (who tend to be college graduates). *A Profile of Those In the Poll,* NAT'L L.J., Feb. 22, 1993. You do not even have to use grammatically correct sentences in an opening; the use of sentence fragments can be very effective in an oral presentation. Jurors react negatively to formal, "hypercorrect" speech. Conley, O'Barr & Lind, *The Power of Language: Presentational Style in the Courtroom,* 1978 DUKE L.J. 1375, 1389. In Professor McElhaney's words, "Trial lawyers need to be bilingual. They need to be able to speak English as well as law." McElhaney, *Impact,* 17 LITIGATION 41 (Spr. 1991).

Put variety in your voice pattern. Everyone has at least several octaves of vocal range. A monotone can be deadly. The attorney should consciously vary her volume, pace, and pitch. "One of the best ways to inject vocal variety into your speech is to read aloud from children's books, complete with sound effects. Practice using your full vocal range, from the squeak of a mouse and the shriek of a siren to the booming of Papa Bear and the Big Bad Wolf. [T]he increased flexibility that comes from this exercise will allow you to use your voice in ways that can have a dramatic impact on the outcome of a case." Dickson, *Voice and Credibility in the Courtroom,* 26 TRIAL 70, 72 (Sept. 1990). *See also* McElhaney, *Reading Out Loud,* 78 A.B.A.J. 88, 89 (Oct. 1992) ("Volunteer to be a reader at church or at a civic organization. Read out loud to your children as much for you as for them. Reading Shakespeare out loud is great practice for reading legal material").

The attorney must maintain solid eye contact with the jury during the opening statement. The attorney does her client a horrible disservice by reading an opening. The attorney's eye contact with individual jurors is what convinces them that the attorney sincerely believes in the client's cause. The next section sets out a sample opening statement. At the end of the section you will find a one-page set of notes. Although in your first few cases you may want to write out the opening verbatim to prepare for trial, you should force yourself to deliver the opening from a one-page topical outline. It is a mistake to use index cards; you lose eye contact as you flip the cards. S. HAMLIN, WHAT MAKES JURIES LISTEN 131 (1985). The outline ought to be tailored as a speaking outline with only a handful of words per line. *Id.* at 132. You can glance at the outline occasionally. When you glance at the outline, the major headings should jump out at you; they should be capitalized, underlined, or in different color. *Id.* at 133–34. You must master the facts in your case so well that except for that occasional glance, you can look at the jurors and project sincerity to them.

You must also gesture effectively. Do not rivet your hands to the lectern or hold them behind you. A lectern is a physical barrier between you and the jury; it is a terrible impediment to developing rapport with the jury. If you constantly hold your hands behind your back or lock them in a prayer position, you project nervousness to the jury. Some jurors may suspect that you are nervous because you have doubts about your client's case. To gesture effectively, keep your hands free; you should not be holding a pen or pencil. *Id.* at 435.

Your posture should be straight and erect. Do not slouch or lean on a railing or table. Your weight ought to be evenly balanced with your feet slightly apart. *Id.* at 441. Straight, erect posture projects confidence to the jurors, and they may infer that you are confident because you have faith in your client's cause.

During the opening, do not position yourself too close to the jury. *Id.* at 454. Even when the voir dire was lengthy, you are still a virtual stranger to the jurors, and some may resent it if you invade "their territory." *Id.* If you stand approximately eight feet away from the jury railing, you will have a view of all the jurors. Stand back a good distance if you have an intimidating stature or "a large, deep, booming voice." *Id.*

Finally, your movement during the opening should be purposeful. Aimless pacing during the opening can be distracting to the jurors. Move at transitional points. "Going to another spot makes the jury turn over the page they're mentally writing on." *Id.* at 446. For example, as you shift from the description of your client's background to the historical merits, you might pause, take a step or two, change the volume of your voice, and announce: "Ladies and gentlemen, the evidence is also going to tell you what happened in that hallway of the Senator Hotel on January 19th last year."

In your first few openings, you may fear that you will forget to make a specific, important, planned gesture or to move at a particular point for punctuation. If so, add marginal notes to the outline as reminders. *Id.* at 349.

§ 5.7 SAMPLE OPENING STATEMENT

The attorney delivering this opening is the defense attorney in *Williams v. Scott.* Before trial, the attorney decided that the best theory is mistaken identification. The attorney knows that the battleground at trial will be the trustworthiness of Williams' identification of the defendant. The attorney decides against arguing that Williams is perjuring himself; as a 65–year-old beating victim, Williams is a sympathetic figure, and the jurors may balk at concluding that Williams is lying. The attorney must convince the jurors that Williams is innocently mistaken. After considering various possibilities, the attorney concludes that his best argument is that Williams thinks he saw Scott because he expected to see Scott there. At his deposition, Williams stated that after seeing the light on in Room 212, he believed that Scott had thrown the bottle down. Williams admitted that he had Scott on his mind as he boarded the elevator, pushed the button for the second floor, and exited the elevator. He also conceded that he usually saw Scott in Rogers' company. There is corroboration for the argument. In his statement to the police immediately after the attack, Williams said, "I know it was Rogers and I think it was Scott because ... they always hang around together." Further, although Williams asserts that he "heard music coming from" Room 212, the police diagram of Scott's room shows no radio, stereo, or television. The defense theme will be that Williams thinks he saw Scott because he "expected" to see Scott although Scott was not there. The following is a sample opening developing the alibi theory and that theme.

(Introduction of Client and Purpose of Opening)

"May it please the court. Good morning, ladies and gentlemen. My name is _____, and I represent the defendant in this case, Mr. Robert Scott. I'm now going to present to you an outline of the evidence in the case. I hope that this preview will help you better understand the testimony that you'll hear later.

(Naming the Theory of the Case)

"We've just listened to the plaintiff's opening statement. We heard the plaintiff's attorney very dramatically describe the attack on the plaintiff. Mr. Scott and I are confident that when you've heard all the evidence in this case, you'll conclude that Mr. Scott was not one of the attackers; this is a case of mistaken identification, the mistaken identification of my client, Mr. Scott.

(Simplification of the Theory)

"Ladies and gentlemen, Mr. Scott and I want to make it clear at the very beginning today that we don't deny that someone attacked the plaintiff. All the evidence we've seen shows that he was beaten and that he suffered some injuries. And we certainly agree that the attackers are liable for the plaintiff's damages. However, those aren't the issues in this case. At times the testimony you'll hear may seem confusing, but in fact the only question you've got to decide is who attacked the plaintiff. On that question, our position is that Mr. Scott isn't liable for the plaintiff's damages because Robert Scott had absolutely nothing to do with the attack.

(Client's Background)

"The evidence in this case will prove that. First, the evidence is going to tell you something about Mr. Scott himself. He's 21 years old. He's a member of the teamsters' union, a truck driver. He was born in New York. He grew up there with his father, mother, and three brothers. When he was 18, he volunteered for the Navy. He spent over three years on active duty. After completing his military service, he moved here to Morena and started working for Eureka Van Lines. He's worked there the whole time he's been in Morena. While he's lived here, he's stayed in Room 212 on the second floor of the Senator Hotel downtown.

(Historical Merits)

"In addition to telling you about Mr. Scott, the evidence in this case is going to show you what happened on the evening of January 18, 19YR–1 at the hotel. That's the night when the plaintiff was attacked in the hallway on the second floor of the hotel. The attack occurred after the plaintiff decided to go up to the second floor to talk to Mr. Scott about a bottle the plaintiff found broken on the sidewalk outside the hotel. That night, the evening of January 18, Mr. Scott was in his room with some acquaintances, Richard Rogers and Joan Freeman. Like Mr. Scott, they live at the hotel. The next morning, January 19, Mr. Scott was supposed to leave on a long, cross-country trip. He was going to take a load of freight to the East Coast. He naturally wanted to see his friends before he left. The three of them spent some time in Mr. Scott's room having a few drinks. Mr. Scott wasn't drunk; he was just having a drink with some people he knew before leaving on a long trip. Ms. Freeman left at about 11 in the evening. Rogers stayed until midnight. After Rogers left, Mr. Scott went to bed; he had to get up early the next morning to hit the road.

"Later Mr. Scott was awakened by some noise in the hallway. He was concerned that someone might need help, so he stepped into the hallway to investigate. The chart I'm pointing to now is a diagram of the second floor of the Senator Hotel. As you can see at the top of this chart, Mr. Scott's room, 212, is here near one end of the hallway. He opened the door, stepped out of the room, turned to his right, and walked a few feet down the hallway shown here. As you can see from the chart, there's a bathroom on this floor. Mr. Scott walked toward the bathroom. He couldn't see anything in the dark hallway and returned to his room. He tried to go back to sleep. During this trial Mr. Scott will testify and admit that there was blood on the soles of his shoes. But, again he'll tell you that after hearing the noise in the hallway, he put those shoes on and took a few steps in the hallway to check out the noise.

"A little later he was awakened again—this time by knocking on his door. He opened the door and was met by a policewoman, Officer Jan

Taylor whom the plaintiff's attorney mentioned. Mr. Scott's memory of this meeting is a little hazy. He was drowsy and a bit embarrassed. You see he was in his underwear when Officer Taylor entered the room. He didn't expect to find a female police officer at his door at that hour of the night. He remembers that Officer Taylor said something about an attack on the plaintiff. He spoke briefly with Officer Taylor, and then she grabbed some of his property and arrested him. At the time of the arrest, Mr. Scott said that he had nothing to do with the attack on the plaintiff. Mr. Scott will say the same thing from the witness stand today.

"After Mr. Scott testifies, we'll call Ms. Joan Freeman as a witness. The chart shows her room on the second floor-right here. She'll describe the party in Mr. Scott's room. Then she'll testify about what she heard in the hallway that night. About 1:20 in the morning, she heard noises in the hallway. She stuck her head out into the hallway, but it was so dark that she could only make out three figures apparently fighting. However, she was able to distinctly hear the voices of the persons in the hallway. She will testify that she is familiar with the voices of Mr. Scott, the plaintiff, and Rogers. And she will testify: 'I recognized the voices of the plaintiff and Mr. Rogers. I couldn't recognize the third voice, but I know that it wasn't Mr. Scott. I'm certain that the third voice wasn't Robert Scott. The third voice was not Bob Scott.'

(The Theme)

"As I said earlier, ladies and gentlemen, the real issue in this case is who attacked the plaintiff. Mr. Scott will flatly deny that he attacked the plaintiff. Ms. Freeman will say that she's positive that Mr. Scott wasn't one of the attackers. However, as we know, the plaintiff is probably going to testify that he thinks Mr. Scott was one of the men who beat him. When the plaintiff testifies today, I'd ask you to pay special attention to his testimony on both direct examination by his own attorney and on my cross-examination. The testimony will show that after Mr. Williams found the bottle on the sidewalk, he thought he heard loud music coming from Mr. Scott's room, 212. However, the evidence will show that there was no television, no stereo and no radio in Mr. Scott's room. In addition, the testimony will show that after concluding that the broken bottle came from Room 212, the plaintiff went straight to the elevator, pushed 2 for the second floor, and rode the elevator up to the second floor thinking—all the while that he was going to see Mr. Scott on the second floor—expecting to see Mr. Scott.

(Conclusion)

"Mr. Scott and I are confident that after you've heard all the testimony, you'll come to the only reasonable conclusion, namely, that Mr. Scott had nothing whatsoever to do with the attack on the plaintiff. You'll conclude that the plaintiff thinks he saw Mr. Scott because he expected to see Mr. Scott—not because Mr. Scott was really there. When you've heard all the testimony, I'll come back and speak with you once more during closing argument. At that time, I'll ask you to return the only possible fair, just verdict in this case, a verdict in favor of the defendant, Robert Scott. Thank you."

Figure 5-1

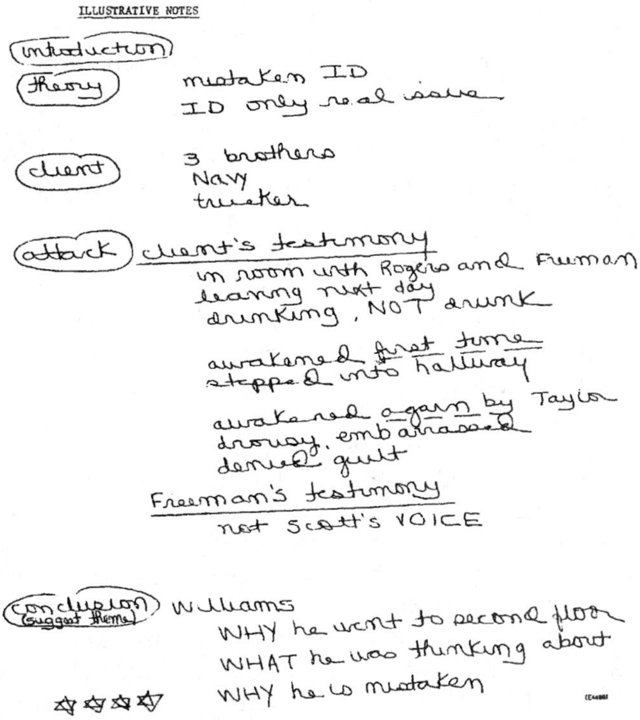

ILLUSTRATIVE NOTES

(Introduction)
(Theory)   mistaken ID
           ID only real issue

(client)   3 brothers
           Navy
           trucker

(attack)   client's testimony
           in room with Rogers and Freeman
           leaving next day
           drinking, NOT drunk

           awakened first time
           stepped into hallway

           awakened again by Taylor
           drowsy, embarrassed
           denied guilt

           Freeman's testimony
           not Scott's VOICE

(Conclusion) Williams
(Suggest theme) WHY he went to second floor
                 WHAT he was thinking about
✡ ✡ ✡ ✡   WHY he is mistaken

§ 5.8 ETHICAL QUESTIONS

One of the almost universally recognized ethical restrictions on opening statement is that the attorney should not refer to individual jurors by name. M. BRIGHT, R. CARLSON, & E. IMWINKELRIED, OBJECTIONS AT TRIAL 1–3 (4th ed. 2001).

The Model Rules of Professional Conduct set out additional restrictions on opening statement. For instance, Model Rule 3.4(e) states that "[a] lawyer shall not ... in trial ... allude to any matter that the lawyer does not reasonably believe is relevant or that will not be supported by admissible evidence...." (In February 1991, the A.B.A. House of Delegates approved a set of revised Standards for Criminal Justice. The wording of Model Rule 3.49(e) is similar to the language of revised Defense Function Standard 4–7.4: "Defense counsel's opening statement should be confined to a statement of ... the evidence defense counsel believes in good faith will be available and admissible. Defense counsel should not allude to any evidence unless there is a good faith and reasonable basis for believing such evidence will be tendered and admitted in evidence.") The rule certainly prescribes a reasonableness standard to determine the propriety of an attorney's belief that matter "is relevant." However, the phrasing of the sentence is a bit peculiar. Is reasonableness also the test to assess an attorney's belief that a matter "will ... be supported by admissible evidence"?

Assume that reasonableness is the standard. Suppose that in *People v. Scott,* during a conversation at the police station the detective in charge of the investigation candidly tells Scott that in her opinion, Williams' identification is "shaky." The detective tells Scott that she is "frankly surprised that the DA is even taking this one to trial." The detective will not testify at trial, but the defense attorney would love to offer Scott's testimony about the detective's statements as a vicarious admission against the government. The defense attorney would like to introduce the statements as substantive evidence of the unreliability of Williams' identification.

Assume for purposes of this question that in El Dorado, it is well-settled that vicarious admissions by agents can be phrased in opinionated terms and need not be based on personal knowledge. El Dorado has adopted verbatim Federal Rule of Evidence 410 excluding plea bargaining statements, but the El Dorado Advisory Committee Note makes it clear that only the defendant may invoke Rule 410. However, there is a remaining hurdle to the admission of the testimony about the detective's statements. In a line of cases beginning with *United States v. Santos,* 372 F.2d 177 (2d Cir.1967), many courts have held that statements by government agents cannot be offered as vicarious admissions against the prosecuting sovereign. The late Professor Irving Younger was the defense attorney in *Santos,* and he persuasively attacked that holding. Younger, *Sovereign Admissions: A Comment on* United States v. Santos, 43 N.Y.U.L.REV. 108 (1968). In his article, he pointed out that the courts routinely permit the prosecution to invoke the vicarious admission doctrine against the defendant; the courts liberally admit coconspirator declarations. Professor Younger asserted that in an adversary litigation system, "the rules of the game [should] be the same for both" parties. *Id.* at 108. The language of Federal Rule of Evidence 801(d)(2)(D) seems broad enough to allow the defendant to employ the vicarious admission doctrine against the government, but many courts have continued to follow *Santos. United States v. Durrani,* 659 F.Supp. 1183, 1185 (D.Conn.1987).

If the line of authority in other jurisdictions were unbroken but the El Dorado courts have not yet construed their version of Rule 801(d)(2)(D), may the defense attorney refer to the detective's statements during opening? Suppose that after the adoption of the El Dorado Rules of Evidence, an opinion following *Santos* was handed down by an intermediate El Dorado appellate court whose territorial jurisdiction does not include Morena. Lastly, suppose that 10 years before—but after the adoption of the El Dorado Rules, the El Dorado Supreme Court explicitly embraced *Santos.* On the varying assumptions, should the defense attorney be allowed to refer to the detective's statements so long as she is firmly convinced that the *Santos* doctrine is unsound?

§ 5.9 TRIAL TECHNIQUE EXERCISES

For this laboratory session, your assignment is to deliver an opening statement in your case. Your instructor will announce any maximum or minimum time requirements for the opening. You should assume that you and your client were introduced to the jurors during jury selection.

Your case file contains little background information about your client. For purposes of this exercise, you can invent some background facts about your client where he or she grew up, where they went to school, whether they served in the armed forces, etc. You ought to devote a minute or two of the opening to a discussion of your client's background. Fill in the gaps plausibly. In fleshing out your client's background, remember the caveat in § 5.5(D) against overreaching the character evidence rules.

Chapter 6

EVIDENTIARY OBJECTIONS —EFFECTIVELY URGING OBJECTIONS WHICH MAKE STRATEGIC OR TACTICAL SENSE

Objection Overruled

Reprinted by permission of Warner Books/New York from The Law as Seen by Charles Bragg. Copyright © 1983 by Charles Bragg.

Table of Sections

§ 6.1   INTRODUCTION

Chapter 5 discussed the opening statement. As that chapter explained, during the opening the attorneys give the jurors a preview of the evidence. The next seven chapters, 6–12, address the mechanics and tactics of presenting evidence. Chapters 7, 9, and 11 analyze problems that arise during direct examination while Chapters 8, 10, and 12 concern cross-examination. Whether the witness is testifying on direct or being subjected to cross, there is an opposing attorney with the right to raise evidentiary objections. This chapter focuses on evidentiary objections.

§ 6.2   RAISING EVIDENTIARY OBJECTIONS BEFORE TRIAL

Suppose that you anticipate that the opposing counsel will attempt to introduce a particular item of evidence at trial. In most cases, attorneys wait until trial to object to the admissibility of the evidence. However, there is a significant risk in delaying. When you wait and raise the issue at trial, the jurors might learn that the evidence exists and that you are attempting to prevent them from hearing the evidence. Some jurors may suspect that you are trying to hide the truth from them. From your perspective, it would be best if the jury never learned that the evidence existed. More importantly, the admissibility of a particular item of evidence might affect your choice of trial theory or theme. You will be in a much better position to make an informed choice if you know in advance how the judge will rule on the admissibility of the evidence.

There is a procedural device that you can use to raise an evidentiary issue before trial: a motion *in limine* in the nature of a motion to exclude. In criminal practice, defense attorneys routinely employ pretrial motions to suppress to attack the admissibility of evidence under the fourth, fifth, and sixth amendment exclusionary rules. Federal Rule of Criminal Procedure 41 specifically authorizes the use of suppression motions in federal practice. However, when the ground for excluding the evidence is non-constitutional (that is, a common-law or statutory rule of evidence), the *in limine* motion is the procedural tool for raising the evidentiary issue before trial.

Although trial judges are increasingly receptive to *in limine* motions, there are two caveats. One is that you must be selective. As a general proposition, the judge has discretion whether to entertain the motion. The larger the number of motions you file, the lower is the probability that the judge will rule on the merits of any motions. By this stage, you have at least tentatively identified your trial theory and theme. You should target items of the opposition's evidence that are arguably inadmissible and would do serious damage to your theory. File one or at most a handful of *in limine* motions challenging the admissibility of evidence.

The second caveat obtains in criminal practice. Suppose that your jurisdiction is one of the many that permit prosecutors to take extraordinary writs or interlocutory appeals from adverse rulings on defense *in limine* motions. You are familiar with the local bench, and you conclude that: The trial judge will likely exclude the evidence in question; if the evidence is excluded, you will probably win an acquittal or directed verdict motion; and the intermediate appellate court is more prosecution-minded than the trial judge. On this set of assumptions, it would be counterproductive to make a pretrial *in limine* motion. If the defense attorney made the motion, the trial judge might grant it. However, since double jeopardy has not yet attached, the prosecutor can take a writ or interlocutory appeal and ask the intermediate court to overturn the trial judge's order. In contrast, if the defense attorney waits until trial, the evidence will be excluded; and the result will be a defense victory, either an acquittal or a directed verdict. Moreover, jeopardy has now attached; and the fifth amendment will preclude the prosecutor from appealing the final defense judgment.

Assume that after weighing the above considerations, you decide to file a motion. In drafting the motion, you ought to not only specify the targeted item of the opposition's evidence and the evidentiary basis for excluding the evidence; you should also state the reason why you need a pretrial ruling. Explain to the court why a trial objection is an inadequate remedy. Suppose, for example, that your client has a previous conviction that the opposition might attempt to introduce under Federal Rule of Evidence 609 for impeachment. You have to decide whether to advise your client to take the stand at trial. If your client elects not to testify, his credibility does not come into issue; and the conviction would be inadmissible. You can point out to the judge that you are trying to decide whether to advise your client to testify and that the admissibility of the conviction will influence or even determine your decision. If the judge rules the conviction inadmissible, that ruling may prompt you to advise your client to testify; the ruling would eliminate one of the downside risks of testifying.

If you raise the issue before trial, when you describe the evidentiary basis you can go into more detail than you ordinarily can during trial. That advantage can be especially important if you are pressing an objection under Federal Rule of Evidence 403. Under that rule, the judge must weigh the probative value of the proffered evidence against any attendant probative dangers such as prejudice. If possible, minimize the probative value of the evidence by tendering a stipulation to the ultimate fact which the proponent is offering the item of evidence to prove. Suppose, for instance, that the accused is charged with being a felon in possession of a firearm and that the prosecution attempts to introduce the record of the accused's prior conviction for a heinous offense to establish his or her status as a felon. The defense attorney might offer to stipulate that a conviction occurred in order to bar the introduction of the full record. That was precisely the tactic employed by a defense attorney in a case that was resolved by the Supreme Court in 1997. The prosecutor had rejected the offer to stipulate, and the trial judge refused to compel the prosecutor to accept it. The Supreme Court found error in *Old Chief v. United States,* 519 U.S. 172 (1997).

In the memorandum supporting your *in limine* motion, do not simply cry "Wolf" or "Prejudice." Cite empirical studies establishing the prejudicial nature of the evidence proffered by the proponent. The Chicago Jury Project researchers found that the typical juror regards certain types of misconduct such as official corruption as particularly despicable. H. KALVEN & H. ZEISEL, THE AMERICAN JURY 396–401 (1966). Later, the Justice Department's Bureau of Justice Statistics conducted a National Survey of Crime Severity to determine how the public perceives the relative seriousness of various offenses. 60,000 citizens were surveyed. The survey found that homicides, rapes, and drug offenses were the highest rated offenses. The survey is detailed in the January 1984 issue of the Bureau of Justice Statistics Bulletin. Substantiate your claim of prejudice by pointing to social science research.

In addition, make certain that your motion requests comprehensive relief. If the judge decides to reach the merits of the motion, the judge's order can be final or preliminary; the judge can make a final ruling barring the evidence or at least require the opposing counsel to approach sidebar and request an admissibility ruling before mentioning the evidence in the jury's hearing. Even when the judge enters only a preliminary order, the order should state that the opposing counsel is forbidden from mentioning the evidence during jury selection or opening statement. R. CARLSON, SUCCESSFUL TECHNIQUES FOR CIVIL TRIALS § 1.3, at 7 n. 10 (2nd ed. 1992).

§ 6.3 TYPICAL EVIDENTIARY OBJECTIONS AT TRIAL

Although objections can be resolved before trial, in most cases they are disposed of at the trial. In some cases you decide that it is inadvisable as a matter of tactics to file an *in limine* motion, in other cases judge refuses to rule on the motion before trial, and in still other cases the objection arises unexpectedly at trial. The purpose of this section is to outline the procedure to follow at trial to make effective evidentiary objections.

§ 6.3(A) Listen and Watch Carefully

It seems obvious that the attorney must listen carefully at trial to make effective objections. However, most young counsel underestimate the difficulty of listening to the trial testimony. Suppose, for example, that you are the civil defense attorney in *Williams v. Scott*. Before trial, you may have: read Williams' statement to the police 10 times, deposed him, and reviewed the deposition transcript four times. Before Williams even mounts the witness stand, you have a firm expectation of the content of his testimony. The natural tendency is to hear what you expect to hear. One of the most difficult tasks for the trial attorney is to listen to a witness's trial testimony as if you are hearing the testimony for the first time. Do not divide your attention by reviewing your planned cross-examination questions as you listen to the direct testimony; put those notes aside, and concentrate on the testimony.

In addition to listening intently, you must watch carefully. Suppose that during Williams' direct testimony, his attorney has Williams mark a chart of the second-floor hallway. The attorney positions the chart blocking your view of Williams and the attorney. While your view is blocked, the attorney might use suggestive gestures or place leading notations such as "two feet" on the chart. Just as you can object to a leading question, you may object to a leading gesture or notation on a chart; the gesture or notation is the functional equivalent of a leading question. However, if your view is obstructed, you may not realize that the attorney is adding the notation to the exhibit. When the opposing attorney begins marking an exhibit out of your view, ask the judge to direct the attorney to reposition the exhibit. Of course, it may be infeasible to move the chart into your view by moving it closer to your counsel table; placing the chart there could make it difficult for the jury to read the chart. However, with the judge's permission, you can move to a position in the court from which you can view the exhibit.

If you are going to listen and watch carefully during the opposing witness's examination, you cannot afford to be distracted. One of the primary sources of distraction during a trial can be your client; as soon as she hears an item of testimony she disagrees with, your client may be tempted to tap you on the shoulder and discuss the testimony with you. If you engage in that conversation with your client, you may miss a critical evidentiary objection. Before trial, give your client a pad of paper and tell her to write notes to you during the trial. Explain to your client that it is imperative that you pay close attention to the opposing attorney's questions and the witness's answers.

§ 6.3(B) Recognize the Evidentiary Objection

At this step, you must determine whether Evidence law gives you a right to object. As Chapter 1 pointed out, the structure of this course assumes that you have already had an Evidence course or are taking the course concurrently with this class. Most evidentiary objections that arise at trial relate to the form of the question. The objection may be that the question is compound or leading. We encourage you to take the time to reread the pages of your Evidence casebook that deal with form objections.[1] If you feel that you need additional background in the law governing form objections, you might read Chapters 7–16 of E. HEAFEY, CALIFORNIA TRIAL OBJECTIONS (9th ed.2002). Each chapter focuses on a particular form objection; the chapter describes the nature of the objection and gives case illustrations of objectionable questions. As an aid to help you remember the possible objections at trial, you might use a checklist such as § 6–6(B) or a specialized handbook of objections. *E.g.,* MYRON H. BRIGHT, RONALD L. CARLSON, & E. IMWINKELRIED, OBJECTIONS AT TRIAL (4th ed. 2001); ROGER C. PARK, TRIAL OBJECTIONS HANDBOOK (1991); ROBERT A. WENKE, MAKING AND MEETING OBJECTIONS II (1986).

Although we cannot spend much time reviewing Evidence law in this class, the succeeding chapters will discuss three form objections in depth. The most important form problems on direct examination are the objections that the question is leading or calls for a narrative answer. Chapter 7 goes into some detail about those objections. The most important form problem on cross-examination is the objection that the question is argumentative. Chapter 8 analyzes that objection.

Before the right to object arises, the evidentiary violation must be complete. When the objection goes to the form of the question, the right accrues as soon as the question is asked. The opposing attorney must object after the conclusion of the question but before the beginning of the answer. However, suppose that the evidentiary rule being violated is a substantive doctrine such as authentication, best evidence, hearsay, or opinion. Those objections are foundational, and they may not be raised until the proponent attempts to offer the ultimate item of evidence. If

1. The listed pages in the following casebooks address the topic of form objections: R. ALLEN, R. KUHNS & E. SWIFT, EVIDENCE: TEXTS PROBLEMS, AND CASES 112–15, 117–19, 136 (3d ed. 2002); K. BROUN, R. MOSTELLER & P. GIANNELLI, EVIDENCE: CASES AND MATERIALS 501–09 (6th ed. 2002); R. CARLSON, E. IMWINKELRIED, E. KIONKA & K. STRACHAN, EVIDENCE: TEACHING MATERIALS FOR AN AGE OF SCIENCE AND STATUTES 78–85 (5th ed. 2002); S. FRIEDLAND, P. BERGMAN & A. TASLITZ, EVIDENCE LAW AND PRACTICE 194–95 (2000); M. GRAHAM, EVIDENCE: AN INTRODUCTORY PROBLEM APPROACH 48–52, 673–679 (2002); M. GRAHAM & E. OHLBAUM, COURTROOM EVIDENCE: A TEACHING COMMENTARY 48–54, 83–86 (1997); E. GREEN & C. NESSON, PROBLEMS, CASES, AND MATERIALS ON EVIDENCE 398–404 (2d ed. 1994); R. LEMPERT, S. GROSS & J. LIEBMAN, A MODERN APPROACH TO EVIDENCE 136–40, 145–46 (3d ed. 2000); M. MENDEZ, EVIDENCE: THE CALIFORNIA CODE AND THE FEDERAL RULES–A PROBLEM APPROACH 11–15 (2d ed. 1999); C. MUELLER & L. KIRKPATRICK, EVIDENCE UNDER THE RULES 557–66 (4th ed. 2000); D. PRATER, C. ARGUELLO, D. CAPRA, M. MARTIN & S. SALTZBURG, EVIDENCE: THE OBJECTION METHOD 6–18 (1997); P. RICE, EVIDENCE: COMMON LAW AND THE FEDERAL RULES OF EVIDENCE 8–12 (4th ed. 2000); P. ROTHSTEIN, M. RAEDER & D. CRUMP, EVIDENCE: CASES, MATERIALS, AND PROBLEMS 372–77 (2d ed. 1998); O. WELLBORN, CASES AND MATERIALS ON THE RULES OF EVIDENCE 335–43, 347–50 (2000); J. WALTZ & R. PARK, EVIDENCE: CASES AND MATERIALS 12–15, 27–28 (9th ed. 1999); J. WEINSTEIN, J. MANSFIELD, N. ABRAMS & M. BERGER, EVIDENCE: CASES AND MATERIALS 333–39 (9th ed. 1997); I. YOUNGER, M. GOLDSMITH & D. SONENSHEIN, PRINCIPLES OF EVIDENCE 134–40 (4th ed. 2000).

the objection is insufficient authentication of a letter or noncompliance with the best evidence rule, the opposing party cannot object until the proponent offers the document into evidence or invites the witness to quote the document. When the objection is inadmissible hearsay, the opposing party may not object until the proponent asks the $64 question calling for the content of the statement. It would be premature to object when the proponent asked, "Did you have a conversation with Mr. Williams?" The opponent must wait until the proponent asks, "And what did Mr. Williams tell you?" Similarly, if the objection is improper opinion, the opponent cannot object when the proponent asks, "Do you have an opinion about the blood grouping of the stain on the sole of the defendant's shoe?" The opponent must wait until the proponent asks, "And what is that opinion?"[2]

What if you jump the gun and object prematurely? If it is obvious to the judge that the testimony in question is substantively objectionable, the judge might be generous and sustain the objection. However, the judge would be perfectly within his or her rights overruling the objection on the ground of its prematurity—without either expressly stating that that was the only reason he or she was overruling the objection or having any obligation to invite you to repeat the objection later when it is timely. In short, the overruling might mislead you into thinking that your substantive objection was unsound. If you do not repeat that objection, you waive it.

§ 6.3(C) Decide Whether to Object

In the last step of analysis, you decided that under Evidence law, you have a right to object. The more important question is whether it is strategically or tactically advisable to exercise that right. You have precious little time to resolve that question. "In the heat of trial, the decision on whether to object to some item of evidence must usually be made literally on a split second basis. A typical question on either direct or cross-examination lasts less than ten seconds...." Lubet, *Objecting,* 16 AM.J. TRIAL ADVOC. 213, 218 (1992).

Waiving the Objection

You should not object to every technically improper question. Conti, *Trial Objections,* 14 LITIGATION 16, 17 (Fall 1987). As a matter of general social etiquette, it is impolite to interrupt. Moreover, the more often you object, the greater is the risk that you will alienate the jury; they may conclude that you are being petty or trying to suppress the

---

2. Note the interplay between this rule and mistrial motions. If the opponent must reserve foundational objections until the proponent offers the ultimate item of evidence, the jury may hear hours of what ultimately proves to be inadmissible material. Suppose that after four hours of proposed expert testimony, the judge eventually sustains the foundational objection. In light of that ruling, the four hours of earlier testimony may now be irrelevant and subject to a motion to strike. Worse still, if the testimony was prejudicial, it might be fanciful to think that the jury can follow a curative instruction to disregard the testimony. The domino effect may be that if the foundational objection is sustained, a mistrial will be necessary. Mistrial motions are discussed in Chapter 15.

truth. "A trial is not an evidence examination. You get no extra points for spotting every issue and making every [technically] proper objection." McElhaney, *Creative Objecting* , 80 A.B.A.J. 80, 81 (Aug. 1994). In a survey of jurors conducted for the National Law Journal and LEXIS, the researchers reported that:

> When a lawyer made an objection, 46 percent of the jurors thought that the lawyer was trying to hide something the jurors felt would have been helpful to know.... Young jurors were particularly suspicious of objections—59% of those in the 18 to 34 age group thought that lawyers had something to hide.

Panelists Give Tips to Lawyers, NAT'L L.J., Feb. 22, 1993. For that reason, most experienced litigators rarely object. One of the most successful modern litigators, Joseph Jamail, objects very little; "[h]e does this ... to give the jury the impression that nothing will harm his case." Jamail, *Keep the Case Rolling and Jurors Will Follow,* NAT'L L.J., Feb. 8, 1993, at p. S8. In one criminal appeal, the accused claimed that his trial defense attorney was incompetent because the attorney objected too frequently; the accused contended that any competent trial counsel would realize that frequent objections "serve to alienate and antagonize the jury...." *United States v. Shetterly,* 971 F.2d 67, 75 (7th Cir.1992).

You certainly should not object if the probable answer will be helpful to your theory of the case. Suppose that during Williams' direct examination, Williams' attorney asks, "Isn't it true that as you were riding up to the second floor, you were thinking about the defendant?" The question is patently leading and, hence, objectionable. However, the probable answer plays right into the defense theory that Williams mistakenly thinks he saw Scott because he expected to see Scott when he exited the elevator. It would be foolish to object. In your summation, you can point out that Williams not only gave that testimony but, even better, he gave that testimony on direct examination by his own attorney.

Or suppose that the probable answer will do only minimal damage to your case. Here too many veteran trial attorneys forego the objection. They fear that the argument over the question will only highlight the testimony and heighten the damage. The decision has to be made situationally on the spot. If the demeanor of most of the jurors indicates that they are paying little or no attention to the witness's testimony, it makes little sense to object.

Finally, it may be counterproductive to object. Suppose that Williams' attorney offers a letter allegedly written by Scott, containing a damaging admission. To authenticate the letter, the attorney has Williams identify Scott's handwriting style. Scott's attorney knows that as a matter of law, the foundation is inadequate; Williams' attorney never elicits Williams' testimony that he has seen Scott's handwriting on prior occasions. However, the deficiency in the foundation is curable. You know that in fact, Williams has seen exemplars of Scott's handwriting style; and if you force the issue by raising an objection, Williams' attorney will be able to adduce the missing testimony. Even here Scott's attorney should probably forego an objection. If the objection is sustained and Williams' attorney has any sense, the end result would be a better, more convincing authentication of the letter.

In many of these cases, before accepting an exhibit into evidence, the judge will turn to the opposing attorney and ask, "Any objection?" That question gives the opposing attorney a golden opportunity to impress the jury. Some attorneys merely sit at their counsel table and mumble, "No objection, your Honor." A more astute attorney will stand and respond, "We have no objection, your Honor. The jury may find the letter helpful." Seize on the judge's question as a chance to show the jury that you are not trying to hide the facts from them.

Asserting the Objection

When should you object? It is strategically worth objecting when the probable answer to the question will seriously damage your theory of the case. In the *Scott* prosecution, the prosecutor wants the jury to conclude that the second-floor restroom is well lit. Suppose that the defense calls Joan Freeman as a witness and that on direct examination, the defense attorney asks, "Ms. Freeman, isn't it true that most of the lightbulbs in that bathroom were burnt out the night of the fight in the hallway?" The question is objectionably leading, and the probable answer will hurt the prosecutor's theory. The likely damage to the theory warrants an objection. When the likely answer will do material damage to the argument embodied in your trial theme, it is imperative to object.

As a matter of tactics, many experienced attorneys advise objecting in two other situations as well. One situation is the case in which the examining attorney is a neophyte who might be rattled by the objection. Disrupt the examiner's train of thought. An inexperienced examining attorney may become frustrated and abandon an important line of questions after a series of sustained form objections.

The other situation is the case in which the witness is aligned with the objecting attorney and the witness needs "a breather." The attorney senses that the examining attorney is getting the best of the witness, and the witness may need a pause to regain his or her composure. Again, though, it would be unethical to object in these situations unless, under Evidence law, you have at least an arguable objection.

§ 6.3(D) Stand to Object

In courts of inferior jurisdiction, counsel often remain seated while they voice objections. However, in courts of general jurisdiction, especially federal District Courts, the usual custom is to stand to object.

§ 6.3(E) Object

There are several aspects of the objection process: the attorney's positioning, the attorney's demeanor, and the phrasing of the objection.

The Attorney's Position

If the matter is nonprejudicial and the legal argument over the objection will probably be short, you should object in open court in the jury's hearing. Almost all form objections are made in this fashion.

If the legal argument will probably be short but the matter is prejudicial, the objection is often made at sidebar. Suppose, for instance, that the prosecutor wants to question Scott about another alleged assault that may be inadmissible under Federal Rules of Evidence 404–05. The defense attorney could stand and say, "Your Honor, may we approach sidebar (or 'the bench')?" When both counsel had walked to the side of the bench away from the jury, the counsel and judge would discuss the objection. However, keep your requests for sidebar conferences to a minimum. The spectacle of you whispering to the judge on the other side of the bench may lead some jurors to conclude that you are conspiring to suppress the truth. Make certain that the record reflects the ruling made at sidebar. If the court reporter is not overhearing and recording the sidebar conference, ask the judge to instruct the reporter to reflect the ruling on the record. The judge can do so immediately or during the next break in which the jury temporarily exits the courtroom.

Lastly, suppose that the legal argument will be lengthy. We shall see in § 6.4 that the opponent sometimes has the right to voir dire a witness in support of an objection. The voir dire could include not only questioning that witness but also the presentation of other witnesses' testimony. In this event, the jury should be excused from the courtroom, or counsel and the judge could move into chambers out of the jury's hearing. To request the jury's excuse, counsel can move to sidebar, state the objection, and add that the objection may necessitate a prolonged voir dire examination.

Whenever the attorney stands to object, the attorney ought to face the judge and address all remarks to the judge. If the opposing counsel has just attempted to do something underhanded, the temptation may be to face and upbraid the counsel. However, judges quickly call a halt to "colloquies" between counsel. Although you should face the judge, you can "cheat out" a bit, turning slightly toward the jury box to upstage the examining attorney. Herman, *Taking Center Stage in the Courtroom Drama: A Trial Lawyer's Short Course in Dramaturgy* 27 (unpublished article).

The Attorney's Demeanor

In almost all cases, you should remain low-key and business-like when you object. Some attorneys occasionally resort to the so-called "explosive" objection. If the witness is a young child or timid person, the objecting attorney may attempt to intimidate the witness by virtually screaming out objections. When you encounter such tactics, move to sidebar. At sidebar, ask the judge to have the record reflect the attorney's behavior, and request that the judge admonish the attorney to refrain from such behavior. You have a duty to your client and your witness to protect the witness from such misconduct. On rare occasions when it is obvious to the jury that the questioning attorney has resorted to an underhanded tactic, you can object with righteous indignation. However, those occasions are infrequent. Save that demeanor for egregious misconduct by the questioner.

The Phrasing of the Objection

You should ordinarily word the objection in this manner: "Your Honor, I object to (blank #1) on the ground that (blank #2)." As a matter of courtroom etiquette, always preface the objection with "Your Honor. . . ."

In the first blank, specify the word, phrase, or sentence that you are objecting to. If only a particular part of the question is improper, a general objection to "the question" may not preserve the evidentiary issue for appeal. As § 6–3(A) notes, at trial you must listen carefully. The need to specify the objectionable word, phrase, or sentence is one of the reasons you must do so.

In the second blank, name the generic evidentiary rule that you believe is being violated: "insufficient authentication," "not the best evidence," "inadmissible hearsay," "improper opinion," or "calls for communications protected by the attorney-client privilege." These are the generic terms included in the titles of the various articles of the Federal Rules of Evidence. It is insufficient to assert that the question is "incompetent" or calls for "improper" or "inadmissible" matter; you must specify the evidentiary rule.

However, the prevailing view is that it is unnecessary to be any more specific. For example, there is no need to say, "The document is inadmissible hearsay because there's no proof that this business record was prepared in the regular course of business." It is not only unnecessary to be that specific; it is ordinarily unwise to do so. If your objection is that precise, the objection in effect tells the other attorney how to cure the problem. You have no obligation to educate your adversary. However, like most trial advocacy norms, this guideline is subject to exceptions. Suppose, for example, that the line of inquiry is prejudicial and that you know that there is an incurable defect in the foundation. In pretrial discovery, you learned that in fact, the document was not prepared in the regular course of business. In these circumstances, it makes sense to make a specific objection. The sooner you specify the incurable deficiency in the foundation, the sooner the judge will definitively sustain your objection and cut off the line of inquiry.

The wording of objections voiced during a jury trial should vary slightly from the phrasing of objections during a bench trial. In a bench trial without a jury, you can be content with technical, legal terminology such as "inadmissible hearsay" or "improperly leading." However, in a jury trial, to the extent possible you want to avoid creating the impression that you are attempting to suppress the truth. For that reason, you ought to phrase the objection to make it sound as if the other attorney is attempting to do something unfair or to elicit untrustworthy evidence. Before a jury, "inadmissible hearsay" becomes "unreliable hearsay;" and "improperly leading" becomes "leading, putting words in the witness's mouth." If the opposing attorney consistently leads on direct, ask the judge to admonish the attorney "so that we can hear" what the witness herself has to say. Conti, *Trial Objections*, 14 LITIGATION 16, 53 (Fall 1987); McElhaney, *You Can't Say That—Here's Why*, 85 A.B.A.J. 66, 66–67 (Apr. 1999)(rather than stating that a question is vague, say "Objection, your Honor, that question can be taken two ways;" or "Objection, your Honor, that question has a hidden double meaning;" rather than objecting that a question calls for an opinion on an ultimate fact, say "That's a question for the jury to decide, your Honor;" rather than merely citing the best evidence rule, say "Objection, your Honor. It's unfair for Mr. Beskind to talk about what's in a document and then not bring it to court;" and rather than objecting that a litigation report falls outside the business entry hearsay exception, say "They weren't making a real business record, your Honor. They were making a trial exhibit for this case"). Add an adjective or adverb to reduce the risk of alienating the jury. However, you must avoid long-winded, "speaking" objections. The judge wants to hear a single, short sentence succinctly stating the legal ground for the objection. Moreover, after you have taught the jury what "leading" means, you can use the technically correct phrasing for the balance of the trial.

As the preceding paragraphs suggest, when you are objecting to questions posed on direct examination, the basic theme of your objections ought to be that the proponent is attempting to introduce untrustworthy evidence. When you are challenging questions posed on cross-examination, the theme is often that the cross-examiner is treating the witness unfairly. Suppose, for example, that the cross-examiner inquires about an untruthful act under Federal Rule of Evidence 608(b) without a good faith basis in fact for believing that the witness committed the act. W. FORTUNE, H. UNDERWOOD & E. IMWINKELRIED, MODERN LITIGATION AND PROFESSIONAL RESPONSIBILITY HANDBOOK: THE LIMITS OF ZEALOUS ADVOCACY § 12.4.3 (2d ed. 2001). The cross-examiner has an obligation to question in good faith. *Sanders-El v. Wencewicz*, 987 F.2d 483 (8th Cir.1993)(while questioning a party about his prior criminal record, the cross-examiner "dramatically dropped in front of the jury ... what look[ed] like about 10 feet of paper"). In this situation, you should not only object; with righteous indignation in your voice, in the hearing of the jury you can accuse the cross-examiner of "bad faith misconduct." Carlson, *Objections at Trial: Putting New Wine in Old Wineskins*, 7 CR.L.ADV.RPTR. No. 5 (May 1997). In the jury's hearing, ask that the judge "admonish" the cross-examiner. When the proponent's misconduct is so blatant that the judge feels compelled to administer an admonition, you not only succeed in excluding the proffered evidence; even more importantly, you damage the opposing attorney's credibility in the eyes of the jury.

There is an additional tactic which you can use to impress the jury with your fairness and reasonableness. Make it clear to the jury that you do not object to the jury hearing relevant evidence; you merely want to ensure that the evidence is presented in a clear, understandable fashion.

Morton, *Making and Meeting Objections* 5 (unpublished article on file with the National College of District Attorneys, Columbia, South Carolina). Do not simply object that a question is ambiguous; in your next sentence, add:

And I ask that the question be clarified to avoid misunderstanding.

Similarly, do not merely object that a question is compound; in your next breath, state:

And I ask that the parts of the question be separated for better understanding.

§ 6.3(F) Obtain a Ruling on the Objection

In most cases, as soon as you object, the judge will explicitly announce a ruling: "Objection sustained" or "Objection overruled." However, if the judge is unsure about the ruling and fearful of reversal, the judge may attempt to move on and avoid ruling at all. Without ruling, the judge may simply encourage the attorneys to "proceed."[3] If the objection relates to critical evidence, you may have to insist on a ruling. Of course, you must do so politely and respectfully. You might, for instance, state, "Your Honor, before we continue, I did make an objection on the record. I would respectfully request a ruling on that objection."

§ 6.3(G) Respond to the Ruling

Your response to the ruling can be verbal as well as nonverbal. In many jurisdictions, it is customary for the objecting party to thank the judge for the ruling even when the judge overrules the objection. It may seem a bit silly to thank the judge for an adverse ruling, but that is well-established courtroom etiquette in many areas. Before trying a case in a jurisdiction, you should learn the local custom. Smith, *The Art and Etiquette of Stating Objections*, 31 TRIAL 72, 74 (May 1995).

Whatever the custom is with respect to verbal responses, your nonverbal response ought to be to remain poker-faced. You must do so even when the judge's ruling paves the way for the admission of devastating evidence against you. As Timothy Hallahan, a trial skills instructor for California Continuing Education of the Bar, has said, "You need to learn how to take a spear through the heart." If your face registers frustration or disappointment, some jurors may notice that facial expression; and they will then be inclined to attach even greater weight to the evidence. "After the ruling, take your seat with no outward emotion showing." S. HAMLIN, WHAT MAKES JURIES LISTEN 214 (1985). One of the most difficult tasks for a trial attorney is to maintain his or her professional composure. During a trial, a statement by the judge, the opposing attorney, or the witness might push one of your buttons and infuriate you. However, you owe it to your client to

---

3. However, there is authority that by directing the attorneys to "proceed," the judge has implicitly overruled the objection. Dunn v. Terminal Railroad, 285 S.W.2d 701, 709 (Mo.1956) (an objection made during closing argument).

keep your emotions in check—something, as you will find, that is much easier said than done.

§ 6.3(H) Request Reconsideration

It was once the rule that to preserve an evidentiary objection for appeal, the objecting party had to formally "except" to a judge's overruling of the objection. After the judge ruled, the attorney had to ask the judge to have the record reflect her exception to the ruling. Most jurisdictions have now abandoned that rule.

In a rare case, you may want the judge to reconsider her ruling. You ask to be heard further. You must do so very sparingly. You can easily irritate the judge by repeatedly requesting that she reconsider rulings. You ought to do so only when you are convinced *both* that the ruling is wrong and that the evidence in question will do grave damage to your theory. Moreover, even when you decide to request reconsideration, you should do so out of the jury's hearing. Seek permission to approach sidebar, and make the request there. The judge does not want the jury to know that you are challenging her last ruling. Making the request in the jury's hearing is another way of alienating the judge.

§ 6.3(I) The Sidebar Conference

At the sidebar conference, you should explain to the judge why you believe the ruling is erroneous. If you have a case or statute citation, do not merely give the judge the citation; offer to show the material itself to the judge. You must also remember to have the record reflect what occurred at the conference. The court reporter may be sitting on the other side of the bench. If so and the judge refuses to change the ruling, you should ask the judge to instruct the court reporter to have the record reflect the nature of your argument, including any cases or statutes you cited during the argument. The appellate court can review the ruling more intelligently when the record is complete.

§ 6.4 ATYPICAL EVIDENTIARY OBJECTIONS AT TRIAL— VOIR DIRE

Section 6.3 outlines the procedure for making most evidentiary objections. The judge listens to the earlier testimony and the proponent's question and, on those bases, immediately rules on the objection. The judge disposes of form objections in this manner.

Conditional Relevance Issues

The judge also rules on issues of conditional relevance in this fashion. Federal Rule of Evidence 104(b) prescribes the procedure for determining issues of conditional relevance; the rule reads:

> When the [logical] relevancy of evidence depends on the fulfillment of a condition of fact, the court shall admit it upon, or subject to, the introduction of evidence sufficient to support a finding of the fulfillment of the condition.

When Rule 104(b) applies, the judge: listens only to the proponent's foundational evidence; decides only the question of law whether, if accepted at face value, the evidence supports a permissive inference of the necessary fact; and allows the jury to finally decide whether the fact exists. *Determining Preliminary Facts Under Federal Rule 104*, in 45 AM.JUR. TRIALS 1 (1992). The two most common examples of conditional relevance issues are the authenticity of exhibits and a lay witness's personal knowledge. Federal Rules of Evidence 901 and 602 apply the Rule 104(b) procedure to these issues. Rule 901 governs the authentication of physical exhibits, and Rule 901(a) expressly states that "[t]he requirement of authentication or identification as a condition precedent to admissibility is satisfied by evidence sufficient to support a finding that the matter in question is what its proponent claims." For its part, Rule 602 imposes the requirement that lay witnesses have firsthand knowledge of the facts and events they propose testifying about. Rule 602 adds that the requirement is met when "evidence is introduced sufficient to support a finding that the witness has personal knowledge of the matter."

In other words, when the question is a conditional relevance issue, the judge need consider only the proponent's last question and the preceding foundational testimony. The judge does not have to consider any contrary testimony before ruling. Even if the opposing attorney has recruited questioned document examiners to testify that the document is a forgery, the judge need not listen to the examiners before ruling on the objection; the attorney calls those witnesses during a later phase of the case. Suppose that when the defense calls Ms. Freeman in the *Scott* prosecution, the prosecutor objects that a Mr. Martin is prepared to testify that he was with Ms. Freeman in another town the night of the attack. So long as Ms. Freeman testifies that she saw the attack and heard the voices, she can testify. The prosecutor would call Mr. Martin to give his contradictory testimony as a rebuttal witness later in the trial. In short, the procedure under Rule 104(b) entails two steps: The judge makes the initial, limited screening decision, and the jury later makes the final factual determination. In the final jury charge, on request the judge would instruct the jury that: The defense has the burden of convincing them by a preponderance of the evidence that Ms. Freeman actually observed the attack; the prosecution had presented contrary evidence that Ms. Freeman was in another town at the time of the attack; and the jury should disregard Ms. Freeman's testimony if they were not convinced that she witnessed the attack.

Competence Issues

However, there are other cases in which the objecting attorney has a right to present contrary evidence before the judge rules finally on the objection. These are cases governed by Rule of Evidence 104(a)—situations in which the objecting party has a right to conduct voir dire in support of the objection. The voir dire occurs after the objection but before the judge rules on the objection. We once again recommend that you reread the pertinent sections of your Evidence casebook, specifically the sections analyzing preliminary fact-finding procedures.[4] We cannot go into detail about that topic in this course, but we shall touch upon two aspects of the topic.

The initial question is when the objecting party has a right to conduct voir dire examination in support of an objection. The party generally has that right whenever the preliminary fact in question falls within the scope of Federal Rule of Evidence 104(a). That rule provides:

> Preliminary questions concerning the qualification of a person to be a witness, the existence of a privilege, or the admissibility of evidence shall be determined by the court, subject to the provisions of subdivision (b).

The courts have held that Rule 104(a) applies to these foundational facts, *inter alia:* Whether a prospective witness is married to the criminal defendant and, therefore, is entitled to refuse to testify against the defendant? Whether the witness is qualified as an expert to give opinion testimony? Whether the original document has been destroyed, permitting the introduction of secondary evidence under the best evidence rule? Whether a declarant had a hopeless expectation of imminent death, bringing her statement within the dying declaration hearsay exception? And whether a third party was present, negating the confidentiality needed for the attorney-client privilege? The judge rules finally on these factual issues; and to do so, the judge listens to both sides' evidence and weighs the credibility of the evidence before ruling.

---

4. We suggest that at this point, you review the pages of your Evidence casebook discussing preliminary fact-finding procedures under Federal Rule 104. The following pages in these casebooks address that topic: R. ALLEN, R. KUHNS & E. SWIFT, EVIDENCE: TEXTS, PROBLEMS, AND CASES 235–46 (3d ed. 2002); K. BROUN, R. MOSTELLER & P. GIANNELLI, EVIDENCE: CASES AND MATERIALS 16–29 (6th ed. 2002); R. CARLSON, E. IMWINKELRIED, E. KIONKA & K. STRACHAN, EVIDENCE: TEACHING MATERIALS FOR AN AGE OF SCIENCE AND STATUTES 101–16 (5th ed. 2002); S. FRIEDLAND, P. BERGMAN & A. TASLITZ, EVIDENCE LAW AND PRACTICE 14–15, 17–18, 33–36 (2000); M. GRAHAM, EVIDENCE: AN INTRODUCTORY PROBLEM APPROACH 626–33, 636–57 (2002); M. GRAHAM & E. OHLBAUM, COURTROOM EVIDENCE: A TEACHING COMMENTARY 54–63 (1997); E. GREEN & C. NESSON, PROBLEMS, CASES, AND MATERIALS ON EVIDENCE 52–60 (2d ed. 1994); R. LEMPERT, S. GROSS & J. LIEBMAN, A MODERN APPROACH TO EVIDENCE 156–64 (3d ed. 2000); M. MENDEZ, EVIDENCE: THE CALIFORNIA CODE AND THE FEDERAL RULES–A PROBLEM APPROACH 2.07–.08, Ch. 17 (2d ed. 1999); C. MUELLER & L. KIRKPATRICK, EVIDENCE UNDER THE RULES Ch. 10 (4th ed. 2000); D. PRATER, C. ARGUELLO, D. CAPRA, M. MARTIN & S. SALTZBURG, EVIDENCE: THE OBJECTION METHOD 139, 257–58, 532–38 (1997); P. RICE, EVIDENCE: COMMON LAW AND THE FEDERAL RULES OF EVIDENCE 28–31, 68–69, 884, 978–87, 1027, 1180, 1295 (4th ed. 2000); P. ROTHSTEIN, M. RAEDER & D. CRUMP, EVIDENCE: CASES, MATERIALS, AND PROBLEMS 3, 270–73 (2d ed. 1998); O. WELLBORN, CASES AND MATERIALS ON THE RULES OF EVIDENCE 39–40, 265–67 (2000); J. WALTZ & R. PARK, EVIDENCE: CASES AND MATERIALS 136–44, 170–74, 190–95, 413–18 (9th ed. 1999); J. WEINSTEIN, J. MANSFIELD, N. ABRAMS & M. BERGER, EVIDENCE: CASES AND MATERIALS 4–6, 195–200 (9th ed. 1997); I. YOUNGER, M. GOLDSMITH & D. SONENSHEIN, PRINCIPLES OF EVIDENCE 80–85 (4th ed. 2000). If you want a brief overview of these procedures, you can browse through *Judge Versus Jury: Who Should Decide Questions of Preliminary Facts Conditioning the Admissibility of Scientific Evidence?*, 25 WILLIAM & MARY LAW REVIEW 577, 586–98 (1984).

The other aspect of the topic we shall consider is how to initiate and conduct voir dire examination. To present her evidence to the judge, the objecting party should not only object but also request the opportunity to conduct "a voir dire in support of the objection." The voir dire can take two forms. The more common form is questioning the witness called by the proponent. Suppose, for example, that the *Scott* prosecutor calls Steven Sykes to testify as an expert on blood stain analysis. If the defense counsel doubts that Sykes qualifies as an expert, the counsel can take Sykes himself on voir dire; the counsel can question Sykes in the hope of exposing Sykes' lack of training in genetic marker analysis. The other form of testimony that can be presented during voir dire is extrinsic evidence. Assume that in El Dorado, a person is incompetent to be a witness if he is a psychotic suffering from schizophrenia. To be sure, the objecting attorney would take the proposed witness on voir dire to expose the witness's derangement. However, the attorney could also call an expert psychiatrist to testify to the witness's mental illness. The typical voir dire, though, consists of questioning the witness called by the proponent. In effect, this type of voir dire examination is a cross-examination during the direct examination. For that reason, the judge usually allows the objecting attorney to employ leading questions during the voir dire. However, the scope of the voir dire is strictly limited to the preliminary facts coming within Rule 104(a). The objecting attorney may not conduct a wide-ranging cross-examination of the witness at this point. The voir dire is often conducted out of the jury's hearing.

§ 6.5   MOTIONS TO STRIKE

In most instances in which you want to challenge the admissibility of an item of the opponent's evidence, the appropriate procedural device is an objection.[5] Sections 6.3 and 6.4 discuss the procedures for objections. However, in some cases the proper device is a motion to strike. You should use that device in three cases:

— The question is proper, but the answer is objectionable. The answer may be substantively objectionable; for example, it may unexpectedly inject inadmissible hearsay. More commonly, the answer may simply exceed the scope of the question and be at least partially nonresponsive. You must move to strike the objectionable or nonresponsive part of the answer.

— The question is objectionable, but the witness began her answer so quickly that you did not have a fair opportunity to object. In this situation, you must employ a two-step procedure. Initially, move to strike the answer "for the purpose of interposing an objection to the question." If the judge believes that the witness was too quick on the trigger, the judge will grant the motion. Next, make the objection to the question.

---

5. If the judge grants the motion, you should then request that the judge give the jury a curative instruction to disregard the inadmissible matter.

— The earlier testimony seemed properly based, but it later develops that the testimony was inadmissible. Suppose, for example, that an attorney asks a witness to tell the jury what the witness "knows" about a traffic accident. The lay witness interprets "knows" to include information she has learned from hearsay sources. On direct examination, she testifies in good faith about that information. On cross-examination, the witness finally makes it clear that she lacks personal knowledge. The attorney can now move to strike the earlier testimony.

Suppose that the answer is nonresponsive and subject to a motion to strike. Who has standing to make the motion? And must the judge grant the motion?

The majority rule in the United States is that only the questioning attorney has standing. She asked the question; and if the witness exceeds the scope of the question, the questioner is the only aggrieved party. However, a minority of states permit either attorney to move to strike. For example, California Evidence Code § 766 provides that the motion may be made by "any party." Of course, even if the noninterrogating attorney has no right to have nonresponsive testimony stricken, he can request that the judge admonish the witness to be responsive in the future. Day, *Getting More Than You Asked For: The Nonresponsive Answer,* 14 LITIGATION 18, 20 (Fall 1987).

The prevailing view is that the judge has discretion whether to grant the motion. Our hypothesis is that the only objection to the answer is that it exceeds the scope of the question; the answer contains logically relevant, otherwise admissible matter. If the judge wanted to, he could exercise his own power under Federal Rule of Evidence 614(b) to question the witness to elicit the very same information. However, again the jurisdictions are split. California Evidence Code § 766 illustrates the minority position on this issue. That section states that nonresponsive matter "shall" be stricken; and Evidence Code § 11 makes it clear that in the code, "shall" is a mandatory term.

§ 6.6 SAMPLE OBJECTIONS AND MOTIONS

§ 6.6(A) Sample Motion *In Limine*

In the *Scott* prosecution, the defense might file a motion to preclude any mention of the defendant's misdemeanor burglary conviction. The motion would consist of a notice of motion and a supporting memorandum of law.[6]

---

6. The following notice and memorandum are based in part on R. CARLSON, SUCCESSFUL TECHNIQUES FOR CIVIL TRIALS §§ 1:3–:4 (2d ed. 1992) and E. IM-WINKELRIED, UNCHARGED MISCON-DUCT EVIDENCE §§ 9:15–:16 (rev. ed. 1999). Reprinted with the kind permission of the Lawyers Co–Operative Publishing Co. and West Group.

NOTICE OF DEFENDANT'S MOTION *IN LIMINE* TO EXCLUDE EVIDENCE

Comes now the defendant in the above-entitled action and moves the court *in limine* for an order instructing the prosecutor to refrain from:

— making any mention of the defendant's 19YR–4 New York, misdemeanor burglary conviction during voir dire examination, opening statement, or final argument; and

— offering any evidence of the conviction or cross-examining any witness about the conviction.

For purposes of this motion, the defense offers to stipulate that in 19YR–4 in Rochester, New York, the defendant suffered a conviction for misdemeanor burglary. The defendant served his full, 30–day jail term and successfully completed a period of probation.

The defendant has reason to believe that the prosecutor will attempt to inject evidence of this conviction during the present trial for battery on Mr. Peter Williams. During pretrial discovery, the prosecutor informed the defense counsel that the prosecutor has a certified copy of the judgment of conviction. During a pretrial conversation with the defense counsel, she also indicated that if the defendant takes the stand to testify at trial, she intends to cross-examine him about the conviction.

The defendant moves for the exclusion of any reference to this conviction on the following grounds:

1. As the supporting Memorandum of Law points out, any mention or evidence of the conviction would be inadmissible under the El Dorado Rules of Evidence; and

2. An objection by the defendant at the time of trial would be an inadequate remedy to protect the defendant's rights. In the course of attempting to lay a foundation for the admission of the conviction, the prosecution would expose the jury to highly prejudicial, inadmissible matter. Even if the trial judge sustains a contemporaneous objection and grants a curative instruction to disregard, this matter is so inflammatory that it would nevertheless influence the jury's deliberations. Moreover, a pretrial ruling will aid the defense counsel in advising the defendant whether to testify at trial.

For the above reasons, any reference to or evidence of the 19YR–4 misdemeanor conviction should be excluded as a matter of pretrial adjudication under an order pursuant to this motion *in limine*. Wherefore, the defendant respectfully moves the Court to conduct a hearing on this motion and to enter an order enjoining any mention or evidence of the conviction.

_____

Attorney for Robert Scott

_____

MEMORANDUM OF LAW IN SUPPORT OF MOTION *IN LIMINE*

Introduction

This case is a battery prosecution. The prosecution alleges that on January 19, 19YR–1, the defendant and a Mr. Richard Rogers beat a Mr. Peter Williams. The prosecution alleges that the beating occurred on the second floor of the Senator Hotel in downtown Morena, El Dorado. The prosecution has filed a battery information against the defendant. The defendant has entered a not guilty plea. At trial, the defendant's position will be that the defendant had no involvement in the attack on Mr. Williams.

As the accompanying Notice of Motion states, the defense is willing to stipulate that in 19YR–4, the defendant suffered a misdemeanor burglary conviction in Rochester, New York. The prosecution has indicated that if the defendant testifies at trial, it intends to cross-examine him about the conviction. However, the controlling provisions of the El Dorado Rules of Evidence make it clear that any mention of the conviction during the instant battery trial would be improper. The provisions in point are El Dorado Rules of Evidence 404, 405, and 609.

Argument

I. EVIDENCE OF THE CONVICTION IS INADMISSIBLE UNDER EL DORADO RULE OF EVIDENCE 404(b).

It is true that under Rule 404(b), the courts sometimes admit evidence of a defendant's other crimes to show the defendant's identity as the perpetrator of the charged crime. However, the courts accept such evidence only when the charged and uncharged crimes involve a peculiar or unique modus operandi. *United States v. Guerrero*, 169 F.3d 933, 939 (5th Cir.1999); *United States v. Vavages,* 151 F.3d 1185, 1193 (9th Cir.1998). It is not enough that there are some similarities between the two crimes. *United States v. Carroll,* 207 F.3d 465 (8th Cir.2000). The two crimes must have such a startling resemblance that the judge can conclude that the same person committed both crimes. *United States v. Trenkler,* 61 F.3d 45, 53 (1st Cir.1995).

In the present case, there are virtually no similarities between the charged and uncharged crimes. The charged offense is a crime against the person while the prior conviction is for a crime against realty. In the present case, force was allegedly applied to the person of Peter Williams. The only force involved in the burglary offense was evidently the force needed to enter the premises. As a matter of law, the prosecutor cannot introduce evidence of the conviction under Rule 404.

II. EVIDENCE OF THE CONVICTION IS INADMISSIBLE UNDER EL DORADO RULE OF EVIDENCE 405.

El Dorado Rule 404(b) governs the admissibility of evidence offered on noncharacter theories of logical relevance such as proof of identity. However, Rule 405 controls when the parties attempt to use character as circumstantial proof of conduct. To begin with, 405 comes into play only when the defense elects to place the defendant's character in issue under Rule 404(a)(1). The defense does not contemplate doing so at this trial. Moreover, even if the defendant were to do so, Rule 405(a) restricts the methods of proving character to reputation and opinion. Neither party may use specific instances of conduct to prove character. The El Dorado Rules of Evidence are patterned after the Federal Rules. The Advisory Committee Note to Federal Rule 405 specifically states that even when a party offers a witness to give opinion testimony about the defendant's character, on direct examination the witness may not cite specific instances of the defendant's conduct as the basis for the opinion. The witness must confine the testimony to the general "nature and extent of observation and acquaintance. . . ." Adv. Comm. Note, Fed.R.Evid. 405, 28 U.S.C.A..

III.   EVIDENCE OF THE CONVICTION IS INADMISSIBLE UNDER EL DORADO RULE OF EVIDENCE 609.

The last possibility is that the prosecution may argue that the conviction is admissible to impeach the defendant's credibility under Rule 609. However, like the prosecution's Rule 404 and 405 arguments, this argument is flawed. Rule 609 allows the introduction of two categories of convictions; one category is governed by Rule 609 (a)(1) and the second by 609 (a)(2). The 19YR–4 conviction falls within neither category.

In the words of the federal Advisory Committee, Rule 609(a)(1) authorizes the admission of "felony grade" convictions. Adv. Comm. Note, Fed.R.Evid. 609, 28 U.S.C.A ... The only relevant evidence that the prosecution has disclosed to the defense is a certified copy of a judgment for a misdemeanor conviction.

In contrast, Rule 609(a)(2) permits the admission of any conviction for a crime of "dishonesty or false statement." There is substantial authority that this language includes only such *crimen falsi* offenses as perjury, false statement, or fraud. *See United States v. Carroll,* 663 F.Supp. 210 (D.Md.1986) (theft is not a crime of "dishonesty"). *United States v. Smith,* 551 F.2d 348 (D.C.Cir.1976) specifically holds that attempted burglary is not a crime of "dishonesty" within the meaning of that term in Rule 609(a)(2). The Reporter for the Federal Rules of Evidence, the late Professor Edward Cleary, stated that *Smith* represents a correct reading of the legislative history of Rule 609(a)(2). Cleary, "Preliminary Notes on Reading the Rules of Evidence," 57 NEB.L.REV. 908, 918–19 (1978). In 1990, Federal Rule 609 was amended. The amendment was accompanied by a new Advisory Committee Note. The next to last paragraph of the Note specifically criticizes cases which "take an unduly broad view of 'dishonesty,' admitting convictions such as for bank robbery or bank larceny."

CONCLUSION

For the foregoing reasons, the Court should bar any mention or evidence of the defendant's 19YR–4 conviction during the present battery prosecution.

_____

Attorney for Robert Scott

§ 6.6(B) Sample Trial Objections

Form Objections

Your Honor, I object to the question on the ground that the word, "trouble," is vague and confusing to the witness.

Your Honor, I object to the question on the ground that it is compound.

Your Honor, I object to the question on the ground that it is repetitive (or "it has already been asked and answered").

Your Honor, I object to the question on the ground that it is misleading, assuming facts not in evidence.

Your Honor, I object to the question on the ground that it calls for a narrative response.

Your Honor, I object to the question on the ground that it is leading.

Your Honor, I object to the question on the ground that it is argumentative.

Substantive Objections

Your Honor, I object to the admission of the exhibit on the ground that there has been insufficient authentication.

Your Honor, I object to the question on the ground that there has been no showing of the witness's personal knowledge of that fact.

Your Honor, I object to the admission of the exhibit on the ground that it is not the best evidence.

Your Honor, I object to that question on the ground that it calls for inadmissible hearsay.

Your Honor, I object to that question on the ground that it calls for improper opinion. I request permission to voir dire the witness in support of my objection.

Your Honor, I object to that question on the ground that it calls for confidential information protected by the physician-patient privilege. I request permission to voir dire the witness in support of my objection.

§ 6.6(C) Sample Motions to Strike

Your Honor, I move to strike the answer for the purpose of interposing an objection to the question.

Your Honor, I move to strike all the witness's direct testimony on the ground that it is now clear that the testimony is based on inadmissible hearsay rather than personal knowledge.

Your Honor, I move to strike the last sentence of the witness's answer on the ground that it is nonresponsive to my question. I request that you admonish the witness to merely answer the questions asked.

(You may want to Xerox §§ 6.6 (B)-(C) for use during the later exercises in direct and cross-examination. During these exercises, you might find it difficult to properly phrase your objections. Place a copy of §§ 6.6 (B)-(C) on the top of your counsel table, and glance at the copy when you stand to voice your objections.)

§ 6.7 ETHICAL QUESTIONS

To what extent must you reveal cases and statutes that your adversary has overlooked during legal research? American Bar Association Model Rule of Professional Conduct 3.3(a) declares: "A lawyer shall not knowingly . . . fail to disclose to the tribunal legal authority in the controlling jurisdiction known to the lawyer to be directly adverse to the position of the client and not disclosed by opposing counsel."

Is it significant that "controlling" modifies "jurisdiction" rather than "legal authority"? Suppose that during the legal research for her motion *in limine,* Scott's attorney discovers a decision by an intermediate El Dorado appellate court holding that burglary is a crime of "dishonesty" under Rule 609(a)(2). Must she disclose that case even if the territorial jurisdiction of that court does not include Morena? Suppose that she discovers a United States Supreme Court case authoritatively construing Federal Rule 609(a)(2). Does she have an obligation to reveal that case? Even if the wording of El Dorado Rule 609 (a)(2) is identical to that of Federal Rule 609(a)(2), is the Supreme Court's decision mandatory authority in El Dorado?

What does "directly adverse" mean? Suppose that during her legal research, she unearths an unpublished El Dorado Supreme Court decision sustaining the admission of a felony burglary conviction for impeachment under 609. In that case, the court first held that the conviction was admissible under 609(a)(1) as a felony and then added an alternative holding that burglary is a crime of dishonesty. Assume alternatively that the only holding in the case is that burglary is a crime of dishonesty but that in that case, the witness impeached was not a party. In the past, the El Dorado Supreme Court has been solicitous of criminal defendant's rights, and she believes that the court might well have reached a different result if the witness had been the defendant. Even if the case is arguably distinguishable on that basis, is the case nevertheless "directly adverse"?

§ 6.8 TRIAL TECHNIQUE EXERCISES

Your instructor will inform you which of the following exercises he or she wishes to prepare for this week.

§ 6.8(A) Motions *In Limine*

In the Trial Technique exercise for Chapter 3, you wrote a case evaluation memorandum. In that memorandum, you selected a theory and theme. In light of your theory and theme, target an item of the opposition's evidence that (1) is arguably inadmissible and (2) would do serious damage to your theory. Draft a short motion *in limine* attacking the admissibility of that item of evidence. The motion ought to include both a notice and a supporting memorandum of law. Your instructor will specify whether you should use federal law or the law of your state.

§ 6.8(B) Trial Objections: Form and Substantive

Be prepared to make all appropriate form and substantive objections to the following testimony. The case is the *Scott* prosecution, and the witness is Peter Williams. The prosecutor will conduct the direct examination, and the defense counsel will then cross-examine Williams.

Direct Examination

(Assume that the prosecutor has already elicited Williams' testimony describing the assault itself. Now the prosecutor turns to the identification of the defendant as one of the attackers.)

Q Mr. Williams, you've just testified about the assault. Was the hallway dark, or was it well lit by 100 watt globes spaced every ten feet or so?

A It was very well lit. We had a lot of 100 watt globes there. I could get a good view of the guys who were beating me up.

Q Then there was nothing obstructing your view?

A No.

Q Did you recognize the men who were attacking you?

A Yes.

Q And wasn't one of the assailants the defendant sitting at the defense table there?

A Yes.

Q Were you at the desk when the defendant checked into the hotel?

A Yes.

Q What name did the defendant register under when he checked in?

A He registered under the name of Robert Scott.

Q Now, Mr. Williams, the defendant's identification as your attacker is the key issue in this case. Are you sure that one of the men who attacked you was Robert Scott?

A Yes.

Q You're sure now?

A Yes.

Q In her opening statement, the defense attorney suggested that you weren't so sure right after the assault. Do you remember talking with Officer Taylor right after the assault?

A Yes.

Q And didn't you at that time-right after the attack—tell Officer Taylor that Robert Scott was one of the men who had just viciously attacked you?

A I certainly did. I told her that Scott was one of the guys.

Q Thank you, Mr. Williams. (Turning to the defense attorney) Your witness.

Cross-Examination

Q Mr. Williams, you were just testifying about your conversation with Officer Taylor. Isn't it true that you told Taylor that you weren't sure who attacked you?

A Maybe I did say that at the hotel, but later at the station I told her positively it was Scott.

Q I didn't ask you about what you told her at the station. I asked you what you said at the hotel. What did you say there?

A I said it was Scott.

Q Mr. Williams, don't try to evade my question. Didn't you say that you weren't sure it was Scott?

A I guess so.

Q All right. You told Officer Taylor you weren't sure. Now you tell us you are sure. Which story do you expect the jury to believe?

A This one I'm telling now because it's the truth.

Q How do you explain the inconsistency between what you say now and what you said then?

A Two men, including your client, had just beaten me to my knees. I was dazed, I was upset. What do you expect when you've just been through an experience like that?

Q Remember, Mr. Williams: I ask the questions. Let me ask you a few questions now about the conditions in the hallway. What was the lighting in the hallway?

A I already told you.

Q Tell us again. I would love to hear it another time.

A I already said that there were 100 watt globes every 10 or 15 feet or so and it was real well lit. It was certainly well lit enough for me to make out who was beating me up. They were right on top of me, and one of the guys was Scott.

Q Just tell us about the lighting. Were all the globes working? How good is your eyesight?

A Maybe one or two of the bulbs were out, but my eyesight's pretty good.

Q So a fair number of the bulbs were out, but your eyesight's good. Didn't you see your physician, Dr. Kuhns, about a month before the assault?

A Yeah.

Q And didn't you tell your physician then that you'd been having some eye problems. And didn't you ask her to examine your eyes?

A I most certainly didn't.

Q Mr. Williams, are your eyes really in good condition?

A The answer's the same as it was before. They were and are. They were in good condition at the time of the attack. They're in good condition now, and I can see that one of the guys who beat me up is sitting next to you right now, Scott.

Q You're certain of that?

A Yes.

Q Certain even though at the time of the attack you weren't wearing the glasses Dr. Kuhns told you you should wear?

A Kuhns didn't tell me that.

Q Your Honor, I have no further questions of this witness.

§ 6.8(C) Form Trial Objections

Your instructor may decide that he or she wants you to concentrate on form objections. Although most Evidence courses go into great depth discussing substantive evidentiary doctrines, the typical Evidence course makes short shrift of form problems. However, at trial the vast majority of evidentiary issues relate to the form of the question.

Be prepared to make all appropriate form objections to the following testimony. The case is the civil action, *Williams v. Scott*. The exercise includes questions posed to the plaintiff Williams, the defendant Scott, and Officer Taylor called as a plaintiff's witness.

TO WILLIAMS:

Direct Examination

1. You work as the night watchman at the Senator Hotel?

2. And you are 66 years old?

3. Tell us all your previous employers' names and what you did for them.

4. What did you do before working at the Senator Hotel?

5. Have you ever been in any sort of trouble before?

6. You've been arrested a couple of times, haven't you?

7. How heavily do you drink?

8. Do you drink?

9. In a typical week, how much do you drink?

10. Is there such a thing as a typical or average drinking week for you?

11. If you were to take the amount of drinks consumed over the four week period just prior to your being attacked at the hotel and divide that by the 28 days during those four weeks, about how many drinks would that average out to per day?

12. And that amount would not have affected you?

13. Would that amount have affected you at all?

14. Would that amount of liquor make you drunk, you know, tipsy or lightheaded?

15. At the time of the attack, was your hearing impaired? How?

16. Was your ability to identify someone impaired? How?

17. Was your vision impaired? How?

18. Did it affect your memory either at the time of the attack or the next day when you attempted to recall the incident?

19. You mean to say that you suffered no hangover?

20. Did you suffer a hangover?

21. You've been known to handle the effects of alcohol or liquor fairly well, haven't you?

22. You can drink a large amount of an alcoholic beverage without it impairing your senses or thinking abilities—I mean your ability to recall, to concentrate, and other general things affecting your alertness?

23. How much can you drink before you would say that your abilities—thought and sensory—are seriously impaired or affected?

24. How many drinks can you down without any significant effect on your abilities?

25. What effect would three drinks have upon your alertness, that is to say, your senses or sight and hearing, your mental alertness, concentration, et cetera?

26. What did you hear the night of the attack?

Cross-Examination

Assume that during cross-examination Williams has already testified that he considered that he had drunk the equivalent of only one drink because he used one third of the whiskey usually put in boilermakers.

27. In other words, when you add up the alcoholic content of the drinks, you had consumed the equivalent of one "standard" boilermaker?

28. And you felt then that you had consumed only one standard boilermaker?

29. The gist of your testimony is that you were not intoxicated—or drunk—to the point where your judgment was impaired?

30.   Was your judgment at least a bit impaired?

31.   So, your judgment was impaired, but it wasn't badly impaired, is that your story?

32.   So you've testified that your judgment was impaired. Would you say that your judgment was seriously impaired?

33.   Well, how much was your judgment affected by the alcohol?

34.   Did the alcohol affect your ability to identify Scott?

35.   Do you really believe that after consuming 10 drinks, you could still accurately identify your attackers?

36.   Do you expect us to believe that?

37.   Why should we believe you?

38.   Are there any other facts that would lend credence or bolster your story? What are they?

39.   Why didn't you call the police when you found the bottle on the sidewalk?

40.   Did you call the police? Why or why not?

41.   You've stated that you went up to Scott's room. Why?

42.   Where did the bottle on the street come from?

43.   What leads you to conclude that the bottle was thrown from Scott's room?

44.   What did you see or do before going upstairs to the second floor?

45.   You believe Scott was your assailant because he's hassled you before. Correct, Mr. Williams?

46.   You do not like Scott, do you?

47.   Did you conclude that there was a party upstairs?

48.   Why didn't you call the police first if there was a loud party?

49.   And from the crash alone, you knew that someone had thrown a bottle during a wild party?

50.   Then you went upstairs?

51.   Are you absolutely certain that the bottle was thrown from room 212, Scott's room?

52.   Maybe you just wanted to believe that Scott has thrown the bottle?

53.   You were looking for a confrontation with Scott, weren't you?

54.   You did not like Scott, did you?

55.   The alcohol made you feel brave, Mr. Williams?

56.   Did the alcohol relax you?

57.   Were you able to see if the assailant with Rogers was wearing a coat?

TO SCOTT:

Direct Examination

58.   After you went to sleep, what happened?

59.   Did anything disturb you?

60.   Did you hear anything?

61.   Then what did you do?

62.   You mean to say that you did not even get out of bed?

63.   Weren't you concerned?

64.   What did you think was happening in the hall?

65.   Did you think it might be a fight?

66.   Did you think that someone was being attacked?

67.   Well, did these ideas even cross your mind?

68.   You had to think something was happening. Do you mean that you don't remember?

69.   Did you think of calling the police?

70.   Did you call anybody?

71.   Who did you call?

72.   Did you hear any loud noises in the hallway?

73.   Did you hear something that sounded like people perhaps fighting in the hallway?

74.   Describe what, if anything, you heard in the hallway.

75.   Did you hear Rogers and anyone else say anything to Williams in the hallway?

76.   So you walked out the door, then what happened?

77.   What did you see in the hall?

78.   What were the conditions in the hall?

79.   Did you see Rogers and any other attackers?

80.   Were you able to identify anyone?

81.   Because of the poor lighting then, you were unable to see anyone?

82.   Did you notice stepping in anything on the floor of the hallway?

83.   Did you happen to notice anything on the floor, right then or when you looked at it later that morning?

84.   Describe the floor.

85.   Did you notice whether the floor was clean?

86.   As nervous as you were, your answers to the police officer were perhaps made in haste. Nevertheless, could you describe your conversation with her as best as your can recall it.

87.   And were all of those statement true?

88.   Which of the statements, if any, were not true?

89.   How do you think the blood got on the bottom of your shoes?

90.   Had you lent the shoes you were wearing that night to anyone within the week leading up to the incident?

91.   Can you explain your statement to the police officer that your shoes "must have been lent to a friend"?

TO OFFICER TAYLOR:

Direct Examination

92.   What did you see in the room?

93.   What happened after Scott admitted you into his room?

94.   What was Scott wearing?

95.   What admissible evidence did you take?

96.   What happened after you discovered Williams?

97.   Describe Williams' appearance or physical condition when you arrived at the scene.

98.   What did Williams do when you came there?

99.   Did he tell you anything? What?

Chapter 7

THE MICROCOSM OF DIRECT EXAMINATION: LAYING A FOUNDATION—TREATING THE WITNESS AS AN EXHIBIT AND PUTTING THE WITNESS'S HONESTY AND INTELLIGENCE ON OPTIMAL DISPLAY

Exhibit A

Reprinted by permission of Warner Books/New York from The Law as Seen by Charles Bragg.   Copyright © 1983 by Charles Bragg.

§ 7.1 INTRODUCTION

Chapter 6 is the first in a series of seven chapters devoted to evidentiary problems. This chapter also relates to evidentiary issues. The title of the chapter is "the microcosm of direct examination." By that expression, we mean the process of developing the complete set of foundational questions needed to introduce a particular item of evidence during a witness's direct examination. The item could be a physical exhibit such as a letter or testimony about a specific event such as the mailing of a letter. In Chapter 9, we shall turn to the macrocosm: organizing the direct examinations of all the witnesses you intend to call during your case-in-chief.

§ 7.2 DRAFTING A LINE OF QUESTIONS TO LAY A FOUNDA-TION FOR AN ITEM OF EVIDENCE

Chapter 3 emphasized that litigation is a planning process. In the present chapter, we shall dissect part of the process. Specifically, we want to study how the trial attorney plans the questions needed to justify the introduction of a specific item of evidence during the direct examination of one of his or her witnesses. Figure 7–1 is a worksheet illustrating the analytic steps that the attorney progresses through.

§ 7.2(A) Selection of the Trial Theory

As Chapter 3 pointed out, on the eve of trial you must select the theory that you will rely on at trial. That theory becomes a litmus test to determine whether you should offer an item of evidence at trial. Under Federal Rule of Civil Procedure 26, the outermost test for discoverability is logical relevance to the general subject-matter of the case-reaching even issues which the pleadings could be amended to include. Under Federal Rule of Evidence 401, the test for admissibility is logical relevance to the facts of consequence at trial, notably the issues alleged in the final pleadings. Both of those tests are far too inclusive. During the trial, you should attempt to prove only the facts that are elements of the chosen theory; and you ought to offer only items of evidence that contribute to the development of the theory. The theory helps give your trial presentation simplicity; it enables you to radically reduce the volume of information to present to the jury. In the Trial Technique exercise at the end of Chapter 3, you selected the theory for the case you are assigned for the laboratory sessions in this course. If you were using Figure 7–1 as a planning worksheet, you would specify the theory in the extreme, left-hand column.

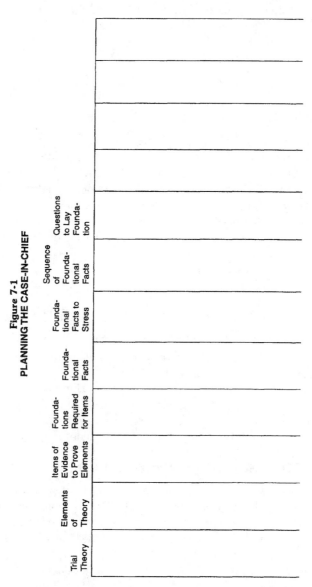

Figure 7–1
PLANNING THE CASE-IN-CHIEF

§ 7.2(B) Identification of the Factual Elements of the Theory

The next planning step is to identify the ultimate facts that serve as the essential elements of your theory. Chapter 3 discussed the use of pattern jury instruction books and texts such as PLAINTIFF'S PROOF OF A PRIMA FACIE CASE (1987) to help you determine those ultimate facts. In the exercise at the end of Chapter 3, you listed the factual elements of your theory. You could enter those ultimate facts in the second column on the worksheet. These are the facts on the historical merits of the case under Federal Rule of Evidence 401. One such fact might be whether your client purchased a substitute generator on a particular date. In contrast, § 7–2(E) discusses the preliminary or foundational facts needed under Rule 104 to permit the introduction of an item of evidence proffered to establish one of the ultimate facts on the merits. For instance, the foundation could include all the preliminary facts necessary to lay a business entry hearsay exception foundation for an invoice documenting the purchase of the generator.

§ 7.2(C) Choosing the Items of Evidence to Prove Each Factual Element

After identifying the facts on the historical merits, you must select the specific items of evidence to introduce at trial to prove each factual element of the theory. To make the selection, you must reach a quantitative and a qualitative judgment.

The Quantitative Judgment

How many items of evidence should you offer to prove each factual element? As a general proposition, you ought to offer only one—the very best—item of evidence to prove the factual element. Eliminate duplication and redundance. Jamail, *Keep the Case Rolling and Jurors Will Follow,* NAT'L L.J., Feb. 8, 1993, at p. S8. Offering cumulative evidence is both unnecessary and dangerous. It is unnecessary to offer cumulative evidence on most factual elements because most of the elements of your theory will be formally or virtually conceded. By the time of trial, the dispute often revolves around one, pivotal element of the theory. Overkilling on the other elements of the theory will only bore the jury.

Further, there are significant risks in offering cumulative evidence on those elements. The use of cumulative witnesses is an invitation to contradictions between the witnesses. They may give slightly different testimony about the element, and the differences may confuse the jury. This risk is especially acute for prosecutors. When government witnesses disagree, during closing argument, the defense counsel might assert: "You want to know where the reasonable doubt is in this case? All you have to do is compare the testimony of the two prosecution witnesses. They can't even agree with each other!" Moreover, when you present multiple items of evidence, the jurors may conclude that you are implicitly acknowledging that standing alone, even your strongest item of evidence is insufficient to prove the fact in issue. R. KLONOFF & P. COLBY, SPONSORSHIP STRATEGY: EVIDENTIARY TACTICS FOR WINNING JURY TRIALS 30–31 (1990). Finally, calling multiple expert witnesses may send the jury the wrong signal about your client's wealth:

> [From the perspective of a civil plaintiff,] the expert corps is often counterproductive for trial. Many jurors bring a David-versus-Goliath perception to a case in which an individual is trying to obtain justice from a huge institution. A battery of high-powered, highly

paid [plaintiff's] experts defeats this predisposition, which the plaintiff generally wants to cultivate.

Lundquist, *Selecting the Right Trial Witnesses,* 17 LITIGATION 25, 26 (Wint. 1991).

However, there are two important exceptions to the norm that you should offer only the best item of evidence to prove most factual elements of the theory. One exception relates to the pivotal element, the element that your theme focuses on. If your pretrial evaluation of the case is sound, that element will be the real battleground at trial. That element warrants cumulative evidence, additional corroboration to help you prevail on that central issue.

The other exception comes into play when you have to call a witness anyway to testify to another fact and it will be evident to the jury that he or she observed other facts about the case. Suppose, for example, that in *Williams v. Scott,* the plaintiff calls Officer Taylor to testify about the identification of the defendant that Williams made shortly after the attack. It will be obvious to the jury that Taylor had an opportunity to observe the extent of Williams' injuries. If he does not mention Williams' injuries, Taylor's testimony might strike the jurors as curiously incomplete. In the civil action, the extent of the injuries is an issue. The jurors may become suspicious if Williams puts Taylor on the stand and neglects to question her about Williams' injuries. Not only might some jurors wonder why the plaintiff neglected to do so. In addition, during closing argument, the defense might point out the oversight and invite the jury to infer that the plaintiff neglected to do so because the testimony would have been unfavorable. Especially when the witness in question is your client, you may have to question the witness about a fact even when the witness's testimony is not the best evidence of the fact. You need to preempt the adverse "missing evidence" inference. You cannot run the risk of raising doubts about your client's credibility.

However, with those two exceptions, you should ordinarily attempt to offer only one item of evidence to prove up most factual elements of the theory. Like the choice of a theory, following this norm helps to reduce the quantity of information that the jury must digest.

The Qualitative Judgment

Before concluding this planning step, you must make another judgment: a qualitative evaluation. If you are going to offer only one item of evidence to prove most elements of the theory, you must evaluate the possible items of evidence and select the best. Which item is the jury likely to find most persuasive?

There are some points of agreement among experienced trial attorneys. For instance, many, if not most, would concur that an admission by the party-opponent is probably the most convincing evidence. The jury realizes that in an adversary system, the party-opponent will attempt to present his case in the best possible light. R. KLONOFF & P. COLBY, SPONSORSHIP STRATEGY: EVIDENTIARY TACTICS FOR WIN-

NING JURY TRIALS 19–21 (1990). The jurors are therefore likely to attach great weight to an admission. If the opposing client admitted the fact during a deposition or in a written statement, you can offer the pertinent passage. Or you may want to exercise your right under Federal Rule of Evidence 611(c) to call the opposing client as an adverse witness.

Perhaps most litigators would agree that the next best type of evidence is physical evidence. Laypersons tend to think that physical evidence has superior credibility. Suppose that in a tort action arising from a collision, one issue is the location of the point of impact: Did the collision occur in the plaintiff's northbound lane or the defendant's southbound lane? Assume that the accident report, prepared by the investigating police officer, includes a diagram showing a gouge mark and most of the accident debris in the northbound lane. The plaintiff's attorney would undoubtedly stress that evidence. During closing, the attorney would probably argue that "physical evidence doesn't lie."

At this point, however, the consensus ends. When they have neither a helpful admission nor favorable physical evidence, many litigators turn to expert testimony. They think that the next most persuasive type of evidence is testimony by a well credentialed witness. They believe that expert testimony impresses jurors because the lay jurors tend to view the experts as authority figures. That belief helps explain the trend toward increased use of scientific testimony. *Study to Investigate Use of Scientific Evidence,* 7 NAT'L CENTER FOR STATE CTS. REP. 1 (Aug. 1980).

That belief, though, may be incorrect. Vidmar & Diamond, *Juries and Expert Evidence,* 66 BROOK.L.REV. 1121 (2001); Elacqua & Spears, *Technical Rules Call for Unique Strategies,* NAT'L L.J., June 6, 1994, at p. C2 ("To the jury, the most important witnesses are usually the [lay] witnesses who can explain ... what 'actually happened.' This is the information that is most influential when it is time for the jurors to make a decision on the issues"); Lunsford, *How Jurors Respond to Complex Commercial Cases,* 19 LITIGATION 50, 52 (Sum. 1993)("recent research shows that jurors usually have little trouble in discounting experts' testimony...."). Expert testimony is new to many jurors, and the natural distrust of the unfamiliar may come into play. Austin, *Jury Perceptions on Advocacy: A Case Study,* 8 LITIGATION 16 (Sum. 1982) (in an antitrust case involving a great deal of expert testimony about economics and electronics, the jurors were "skeptical of the experts"). In one study in the 1970's, researchers found that in cases in which the prosecution offered sound spectrography (voiceprint) evidence, the conviction rate was 11% lower than the average. Greene, *Voiceprint Identification: The Case in Favor of Admissibility,* 13 AM.CRIM.L.REV. 171, 190–91 (1975). In other research reported by Dr. Elizabeth Loftus in the early 1980s, the data suggested that lay jurors attach more weight to confident, impartial eyewitness testimony than to expert testimony. Loftus, *Psychological Aspects of Courtroom Testimony,* in 347 ANNALS N.Y. ACAD.SCI. 27, 32–33 (1980). Other research also indicates that if anything, jurors tend to underutilize expert testimony during deliberations. Thompson & Schumann, *Interpretation of Statistical Evidence in*

Criminals Trials, 11 LAW 7 HUMAN BEH. 167, 184 (1987). The research conducted to date does not furnish a definitive answer to the question; but the reader should realize that given a choice between an expert with extensive credentials and a lay witness with strong demeanor, the latter may be preferable.

Other things being equal, it is desirable to have a "mix" of types of witnesses. Overby, *Preparing Lay Witnesses,* 26 TRIAL 88, 90 (Apr. 1990). Call both lay and expert witnesses. Further, try to call different kinds of lay witnesses—"a cross-section of family members and people who have a more formal relationship with the plaintiff such as a banker, employer, or pastor." *Id.* The variety of types of witnesses will help maintain the jury's attention throughout the trial.

After completing the quantitative and qualitative evaluation, you can make the final selection of items of evidence. You could then list those items in the third column on Figure 7–1.

§ 7.2(D) Identifying the Foundations Needed to Introduce Each Item of Evidence

The next step is to identify all the foundations or predicates you will need to lay at trial to permit the introduction of the selected items of evidence. The identification requires the type of factual analysis you learn in the Evidence course. This course cannot be a reprise of Evidence, but at this point we want to remind you about several foundations. Whenever you contemplate introducing a document at trial, you should think of three evidentiary doctrines: authentication, best evidence, and hearsay. You will probably have to show that document is genuine. If you want to use the contents of the document, that use will trigger the best evidence rule. Lastly, when you want to offer a passage in the document as substantive evidence, that use will bring the hearsay rule into play. In addition, bear in mind that whenever you call a lay witness to testify to a fact or event, you must lay a personal or firsthand knowledge foundation. On Figure 7–1, the entries in the third column represent the items of evidence you contemplate offering. In the corresponding parts of the fourth column, you can list the necessary evidentiary foundations.

§ 7.2(E) Listing the Foundational Facts

Having identified the requisite foundations, you should now list the foundational or preliminary facts. These are not the facts on the historical merits under Federal Rule of Evidence 401, mentioned in § 7–2(B); rather, these are the historical facts that condition the admissibility of the item of evidence proffered to establish a fact on the merits. Chapter 6 discussed preliminary fact-finding under Federal Rule of Evidence 104(a)-(b). The facts falling under Rule 104(a)-(b) are the foundational facts.

Before drafting the list of foundational facts, you may want to refresh your recollection of Evidence law. You will obviously not have the time to thoroughly research every evidentiary issue that you anticipate arising during the trial. However, at least in your first few trials, you ought to make the time to research the evidentiary doctrines that will govern the admissibility of the evidence supporting your trial theme. The theme is the linchpin of your trial presentation. If you are going to spend time researching any evidentiary issues, you should devote that time to the issues concerning your evidence on the theme. If you have to conduct research on the Federal Rules of Evidence, you should be familiar with the following sources: the various volumes of C. WRIGHT & K. GRAHAM, FEDERAL PRACTICE AND PROCEDURE: EVIDENCE; the C. MUELLER, & L. KIRKPATRICK FEDERAL EVIDENCE treatise; the J. WEINSTEIN, WEINSTEIN'S FEDERAL EVIDENCE treatise (2nd ed.); M. GRAHAM, FEDERAL RULES OF EVIDENCE HANDBOOK (5th ed. 2001); S. SALTZBURG, & M. MARTIN, & D. CAPRA, FEDERAL RULES OF EVIDENCE MANUAL (8th ed. 2002); and G. WEISSENBERGER, FEDERAL EVIDENCE (2nd ed. 1995).

There are more specialized texts that contain lists of foundational facts: AMERICAN JURISPRUDENCE PROOF OF FACTS; R. CARLSON, 3 CRIMINAL LAW ADVOCACY–TRIAL PROOF (1982); E. IMWINKELRIED, EVIDENTIARY FOUNDATIONS (5th ed. 2002); R. KEETON, TRIAL TACTICS AND METHODS (2d ed. 1973); A. MORRILL, TRIAL DIPLOMACY (2d ed. 1972); E. SALCINES, TRIAL TECHNIQUE–PREDICATE QUESTIONS (1977); H. SPELLMAN, HOW TO PROVE A PRIMA FACIE CASE (3d ed. 1954); J. TARANTINO, TRIAL EVIDENCE FOUNDATIONS (1986); and J. WALTZ & J. KAPLAN, EVIDENCE–MAKING THE RECORD (1982).

These specialized texts illustrate the process of converting an evidentiary doctrine into a list of preliminary facts. Litigators do not think of evidentiary rules as abstractly worded sentences in a statute; rather, they conceive of the rules as the set of foundational facts that must be proven at trial to satisfy the rule. A simple example will suffice. Suppose that in the *Scott* prosecution, the prosecutor wants to offer a statement that Williams made after the attack. The prosecutor knows that proof of the statement will require a hearsay foundation, and she decides that the best argument to defeat the hearsay objection is that the statement qualifies as an excited or startled utterance under El Dorado Rule of Evidence 803(2). The El Dorado rule is identical to Federal Rule of Evidence 803(2): "The following are not excluded by the hearsay rule, even though the declarant is available as a witness: . . . [a] statement relating to a startling event or condition made while the declarant was under the stress of excitement caused by the event or condition." After consulting one of the specialized texts,[1] you would learn that to invoke 803(2), the prosecutor should establish these preliminary facts:

— An event occurred.

— The event was startling.

---

1. *See* E. IMWINKELRIED, EVIDENTIARY FOUNDATIONS § 10.08[2] (5th ed. 2002).

— The declarant had personal knowledge of the event.

— The declarant made a statement about the event.

— The declarant made the statement while he or she was in a state of nervous excitement.

A litigator equates the excited utterance doctrine with this list of preliminary facts. Every evidentiary doctrine can be broken down into a list of predicate facts in this fashion. Whether the doctrine relates to authentication, best evidence, privilege, witness competency, or hearsay, the doctrine can be reduced to a set of predicate facts. Again, browse through one or more of the specialized texts to familiarize yourself with them.

§ 7.2(F) Deciding Which Foundational Facts to Stress

You might think that after developing the list of foundational facts, you are ready to prepare the questions to lay the foundation. You could do so. You could, for example, draft a single question to establish each preliminary fact. However, a mechanical, one-to-one conversion—one question for each foundational fact—is unwise. Before drafting the questions, there is an additional step in analysis: determining which foundational facts to emphasize. J. TANFORD, THE TRIAL PROCESS: LAW, TACTICS AND ETHICS 254 (2d ed. 1993).

Many preliminary facts do not deserve emphasis. They ought to be established as quickly as possible; if one question will suffice, one question is all that you should ask to prove that fact. Typically, these facts are parts of the foundation for technical, legal reasons. Suppose, for instance, that you anticipate a privilege objection to a conversation that you want to question the witness about. To preempt the objection, your foundation should include proof of the preliminary fact that the conversation occurred in public; there was no privacy, and consequently the spousal privilege cannot attach. However, proof of the lack of privacy does little to enhance the trustworthiness of the evidence in the jury's mind. Consequently, you can dispose of that foundational fact with a single question: "Who else was present when you had this discussion with your wife?"

In contrast, some preliminary facts directly impact the jury's perception of the reliability of the evidence. In *Williams v. Scott,* the plaintiff will testify about the attack in the hallway. One of the preliminary facts is proof of personal knowledge. Chapter 6 pointed out that personal knowledge is a fact determining conditional relevance under Federal Rule of Evidence 104(b). As we have seen, the test under Rule 104(b) is lax; the judge accepts the foundational testimony at face value and asks only whether, if the jury accepts the testimony, there is a permissive inference of firsthand knowledge. Since the test is so minimal, the plaintiff's attorney could lay this foundational element with a single question: "How do you know about the attack?" However, it would be foolish and virtually malpractice to dispose of this foundational element so quickly. The outcome of the case will turn on whether the jury finds Williams' identification of Scott reliable. For that reason, the plaintiff's attorney should elaborate on this preliminary fact. Rather than asking a solitary question about personal knowledge, the attorney ought to go into detail:

Q Where were you?

Q How close were you to the two men?

Q How many feet away?

Q In what direction were you facing?

Q What, if anything, obstructed your view of their faces?

Q How good is your eyesight?

Q What were the lighting conditions?

The questioning should go into this preliminary fact in depth.

Whenever possible, amplify both on why the witness had such an excellent opportunity for observation and why the witness had such a powerful reason to remember the events or facts observed. Lutz, *Memory*, 26 LITIGATION 38 (Spr. 2000).

What about the event itself? Was it something most people would recall? A serious accident or an extended shouting match is likely to stick in the mind. . . .

Id. at 39. Ask the witness point blank:

Q How can you remember the facts so well?

Q Why does that event stick in your mind?

§ 7.2(G) Determining the Sequence of the Foundational Facts

In the last two planning steps, you identified all the foundational facts and the ones which warrant emphasis at trial. Before drafting the questions to prove the foundational facts, you must make still another decision: the sequence in which you will prove the foundational facts at trial. In most cases, it is best to use chronological order; the judge and jury will find that order easiest to follow. "[C]hronology is the order in which things happened." McElhaney, *Organizing Direct Examination,* 76 A.B.A.J. 92, 94 (Mar. 1990). For example, if you intend to question a police officer to lay part of a chain of custody foundation, you might initially establish the witness's receipt of the object, next the witness's safeguarding of the object, and finally the witness's transfer of the object to a laboratory technician for testing.

However, you should deviate from chronological order to make the foundational testimony more persuasive. In the preceding planning step, you identified the foundational fact or facts which deserve stress. The end of a line of questioning is a naturally emphatic position. Consider positioning that fact at the end of the line of foundational questioning. Assume, for instance, that you anticipate that the opposing attorney will challenge the adequacy of the witness's safeguarding of the object. There might been extensive questioning about the safeguarding at a pretrial deposition or preliminary hearing. On that assumption, you might deviate from chronological order and end the line of foundational questions with the testimony about safeguarding.

§ 7.2(H) Drafting the Foundational Questions

Now at last, you are ready to draft the questions to prove all the foundational facts that condition the admissibility of the item of evidence. In doing so, the most important tactical guideline is this: *Draft short, non-leading, open-ended questions that are phrased with simple, concrete words.*

"Short questions." The reading psychology studies indicate that reader comprehension drops off markedly when the sentence exceeds 25 words in length. It is generally more difficult to comprehend spoken sentences than written sentences. Many good litigators use the rule of thumb that a question should not exceed 15 words in length. Just as you edit the draft of a legal document, edit your draft questions. If a question is too long, rewrite. Subdivide the question into two or more shorter queries.

"Questions that are phrased with simple words." Like an opening statement, a line of questioning is a test of your communicative ability, not of your vocabulary. Resist the temptation to sound brilliant. Zemel, Resist *The Itch To Be Brilliant*, LAWYERS WEEKLY USA, Apr. 29, 2002, at p. 15. Use the language that the typical juror employs in everyday conversation. As Chapter 4 noted, in the 1992 National Law Journal–LEXIS juror survey, "the best-represented occupation" was skilled blue-collar workers who are often high school graduates. *A Profile of Those in the Poll*, NAT'L L.J., Feb. 22, 1993. Avoid words such as context, relate, surveillance, subject, in relation to, in regard to, and with respect to. Average citizens do not use those expressions in normal conversation, and you should likewise avoid them in drafting your questions.

"Questions that are phrased in concrete words." We have seen that negatively, you ought to avoid abstract terms and jargon. Affirmatively, you should use concrete words to paint a vivid picture for the jury. Williams should not testify that his assailants "withdrew" after the attack; he could tell the jury that they "ran away." Similarly, rather than informing the jury that the assailants "traumatized me from behind," Williams ought to tell the jury that they "kicked my back." Use words that help the jury visualize the events and facts that the witness is testifying to. Create a sensory image of the event. You should not only incorporate sensory imagery in the phrasing of your questions; even more importantly, the phrasing ought to encourage the witness to use such imagery. Consider these illustrations: "Could you help the jury see what you saw when you came around the corner?," Would you help us picture how cousin Charles was acting when Uncle Waldo signed his

will?," and "Ms. Williams, take us with you to that meeting. Could you show us how people reacted when the chairman announced that the company was going to start making assault rifles?" McElhaney, *Making Evidence,* 81 A.B.A.J. 84, 86 (Sep. 1995).

"Non-leading questions." There are several reasons why most foundational questions should be non-leading. The most obvious is that leading questions are usually objectionable on direct examination. Federal Rule of Evidence 611(a) continues the common-law tradition generally barring leading questions on direct testimony. However, more importantly, if you have a good witness, it is bad advocacy to use leading questions. *The witness is your most important exhibit.* Just as you would want to put a physical exhibit such as a knife or letter on optimal display for the jury, you want to give the witness an opportunity to put his or her honesty and intelligence on display for the jury. When you ask consistently leading questions, the predictable result is that the witness will give you a series of short answers such as "Yes" and "No." You want to invite the witness to open up to the jury and talk to the jury. Non-leading questions help to force the witness to do so.

How do you draft non-leading questions? Many judges follow the rule of thumb that questions beginning with natural interrogatory words such as Who, Which, Where, When, Why, and How are non-leading. Try to start as many questions as reasonably possible with those words. Another useful technique is the addition of the expression, "if any" or "if anything." By way of example, to elicit Williams' testimony that the attackers threatened to kill him, Williams' attorney might ask: "What, if anything, did they say to you before they ran away?"

"Open-ended questions." Asking non-leading questions helps ensure that the witness opens up to the jury. However, even a non-leading question can be closed-ended. For example, during his direct examination of Williams, the plaintiff's attorney might ask: "How many attackers were there?" The answer, of course, could be as short as "Two." If you want to put the witness on optimal display for the jury, you must choose open-ended questions. Researchers in the Duke University Law and Language Project studied the effect of varying question styles on the jury. Conley, *Language in the Courtroom,* 15 TRIAL 32, 35 (Sep. 1979). The researchers found that "the jurors believed that permitting the witness to use the narrative style was an expression of trust and belief on the part of the lawyer, and [the jurors] then adopted the lawyer's attitude as their own." *Id.* at 35. Why should the jurors make an act of faith in the witness and believe her testimony if they suspect that you lack faith in the witness? Ideally then, you want questions that will launch the witness into a medium-length narrative. Get out of the witness's way, and let the witness sell her honesty and intelligence to the jury.

Chapter 6 pointed out that a common objection during direct examination is that the question "calls for a narrative." In modern federal practice, the only express statutory form regulation is Rule 611(c), dealing with leading questions. There is no longer a categorical rule that such questions are objectionable. Federal Rule of Evidence 611(a) gives the judge discretionary control over "the mode ... of interrogating witnesses...." The Advisory Committee Note to Rule 611(a) states that that subsection governs the judge's ruling whether to permit the witness to testify "in the form of a free narrative or [in] responses to specific questions." Some empirical studies indicate that testimony elicited by narrative questions tends to be more accurate; when the questioner uses more specific questions, the phrasing of the questions influences the content of the answers. 1 C. McCORMICK, HANDBOOK OF THE LAW OF EVIDENCE § 5, at 14–15 (5th ed. 1999). If the witness has a good sense of the chronology and you have coached the witness to avoid referring to inadmissible matter, the judge may well allow questions calling for medium-length narratives. Realizing the advantages of narrative testimony, many judges in effect begin with a rebuttable presumption that they will exercise their discretion to allow the witness to testify in that fashion. However, the presumption is rebutted—and the judge will insist upon more specific questions—when the witness's testimony becomes confused or the witness makes numerous references to inadmissible matter such as hearsay. Proper pretrial preparation of the witness will help ensure that the presumption remains in effect throughout the witness's direct examination.

There is one other factor to consider in drafting your line of foundational questions. If the item of evidence you intend to offer is an object such as a letter or knife, the line of questions must comply with the mechanics for introducing exhibits at trial. The following is an overview of the mechanics:

— Keep the object out of view until you intend to use it during the examination of a witness. A.B.A. Prosecution Function 5.6(c) declares: "A prosecutor should not permit any tangible evidence to be displayed in the view of the judge or jury which would tend to prejudice fair consideration by the judge or jury until such time as a good faith tender of such evidence is made." Revised Defense Function 4–7.5(c) contains similar language.

— Initially request that the object be marked for identification: "I request that this be marked People's exhibit number one for identification." "Because of the oddities of judicial protocol, you ask the court reporter to mark the exhibit by talking to the judge: 'Your honor, I ask the court reporter to mark this as....' " McElhaney, *When Admissibility Is the Issue,* 81 A.B.A.J. 90, 92 (May 1995). In some jurisdictions, it is customary to premark exhibits before the trial begins. Alternatively, many judges permit counsel to premark at the beginning of the court day or during the break immediately before offering the exhibit. The plaintiff's and prosecutor's exhibits are often numbered while the defense exhibits are lettered.

You do not necessarily have to follow a strict alpha-numeric system. You can deviate from that system to make the relationship among exhibits clearer to the jury. Use your creativity. Suppose, for instance, that you have already entered a company cash deposit logbook as Exhibit A. Lines 11, 14, 19, and 20 of page 2 of the log refer to four important deposits. You next intend to offer into evidence four deposit envelopes corresponding to the entries. Ask that those exhibits be marked A–2–11, A–2–14, A–2–19, and A–2–20. Or assume that you want to enter two photographs of the front windshield of a car. You can ask that they be marked Collective Exhibit B. Or suppose that there are several issues in the case and that you want the deliberating jurors to understand which issue each exhibit relates to. All the designations of the exhibits related to one issue might begin with the letter A, *e.g.,* A–1, A–2, etc. The exhibits concerning another issue might start with the letter B, *e.g.,* B–1, B–2, etc. Wilson, *Making Complex Commercial Cases Come Alive,* 28 TRIAL 44, 48 (Dec. 1992).

— Pick the exhibit up. While you are handling the exhibit, try to evince the appropriate feeling toward the exhibit. If the exhibit is a photograph of the witness's child who was struck and killed by the defendant driver, you should handle the exhibit with care and reverence. When you are attempting to establish that the exhibit is a forgery, your demeanor should display a radically different feeling toward the exhibit. If you are a prosecutor handling the alleged murder weapon, hold the exhibit gingerly to signal the jury that the exhibit is an extremely dangerous instrumentality.

— Show the object to the opposing counsel before handing it to the witness. Some judges like the record to reflect this step: "Your Honor, please let the record reflect that I am showing People's exhibit number one for identification to the defense attorney." In a minority of jurisdictions, it is customary to show the exhibit to opposing counsel after the completion of the foundation but before the formal offer of the exhibit into evidence. When the record reflects that you showed the exhibit to the opposing counsel, you have a stronger waiver argument if the opponent does not expressly object.

— Ask for permission to approach the witness: "Your Honor, may I approach the witness." Many judges dispense with this formality.

— During the questioning of the witness, ask all the questions needed to prove all the predicate facts required to lay the applicable evidentiary foundations.

— After you have completed the questioning, make a formal tender of the exhibit: "Your Honor, I now offer People's exhibit number one for identification into evidence as People's exhibit number one." (Most trial courts still adhere to the procedure of delaying showing the exhibit to the judge until the formal tender. However, that procedure "evolved before the photocopy machine. Now that copies are inexpensive and convenient, there is usually no good reason to make the judge wait to look at the exhibit." McElhaney, *The Evidence Dance,* 76 A.B.A.J. 86, 88 (May 1990).)

— Respond to any objections. Even if the objection is ridiculous, look at the judge rather than the opposing counsel. Meet the objection head on with a short, simply worded response. Whenever possible, seize on the objection as an opportunity to remind the jury of your theory or theme. Ohlbaum, *Jacob's Voice, Esau's Hands: Evidence-speak for Trial Lawyers,* 31 STET.L.REV. 7, 13 (2001); Ohlbaum, *Objections and Offers: Tell It Again, Sam,* 25 LITIGATION 8 (Spr. 1999). Suppose, for example, that during the direct examination of the physician who treated Williams at the emergency room, the prosecutor attempts to introduce photographs showing the number of wounds Williams had sustained. Assume further that the defense objects on relevance grounds and notes that "since this is a criminal case, damages are not in issue." The prosecutor might respond: "Your Honor, the key issue in this case is identity, whether Mr. Williams has correctly identified the defendant as one of his attackers. These photographs show the large number of serious injuries Mr. Williams sustained in the attack. The photographs are relevant to show how close the attackers were to Mr. Williams and how long the attack must have lasted for him to suffer all those injuries."

— Suppose that the judge rules the exhibit admissible. If the exhibit is a document, hand the document back to the witness and request the judge's permission to have the witness read the relevant part to the jury: "Your Honor, I request permission for Mr. Williams to read this paragraph of this letter to the jury."[2] You may also want to seek the judge's permission to "publish" the exhibit to the jury: "Your Honor, I request permission to hand the exhibit to the jurors for their inspection." (Some attorneys prefer to defer the circulation of exhibits to the jurors until the end of the direct examination. Some judges permit the attorney to either read the exhibit to the jury or circulate the exhibit to the jurors but not both; these judges believe that it is cumulative to do both.) Other judges almost never allow the attorney to immediately publish exhibits; these judges either defer publication to the end of the attorney's case-in-chief or allow the exhibits to go to the jury only during deliberation.

— When you have finished using the exhibit, return the exhibit to the court reporter. Do NOT place the exhibit on your counsel table.

At first blush, these mechanics can sound complex and intimidating. However, in truth they are quite simple. Visualize the courtroom. The

---

2. When you make this request, the opposing attorney will sometimes object that "the document speaks for itself" or that "the document itself is the best evidence." This objection is bogus. W. BROCKETT & J. KEKER, EFFECTIVE DIRECT & CROSS–EXAMINATION § 11.11, at 248–49 (1986). The best evidence rule requires only that the best evidence be produced in the courtroom. The rule does not govern the procedure for handling the evidence after it has been produced and admitted. Under Federal Rule of Evidence 611(a), the judge has discretion to regulate that procedure. *See also* McElhaney, *Publishing the Exhibit,* 79 A.B.A.J. 82 (Nov. 1993)("This doesn't violate the Best Evidence Rule, your honor. We satisfied the rule when we introduced the document in evidence. So your honor has the absolute discretion to permit the document to be read or shown to the jury. . . ."); Moss, *Beyond the Fringe: Apocryphal Rules of Evidence in Texas,* 43 BAYLOR L.REV. 701, 726 (1991)("No Reading Documents to the Jury").

judge is sitting on the raised bench at the front of the room with the court reporter seated at a table below the judge. The witness stand is to the judge's left. The opposing counsel's table is across from the judge's bench. In effect, the mechanics of introducing an exhibit consist of making a triangle:

— Begin at the court reporter's table. Have the exhibit marked for identification there.

— Next complete one leg of the triangle by walking to the opposing counsel's table. There show the exhibit to your opponent and ask the judge to have the record reflect that you are doing so.

— Then, with the judge's permission, walk the next leg of the triangle to approach the witness. When you reach the witness stand, hand the exhibit to the witness and lay any necessary foundations.

— After you have laid the required foundations, close the triangle by walking back toward the judge to formally tender the exhibit into evidence.

The handling of charts poses several special problems for the attorney. If the judge permits, you should ordinarily place the chart in front of and near the middle of the jury box. When you ask a witness to mark a chart, have the record reflect that the witness is complying with your directions; you must make a record which the appellate court will understand in the event of an appeal. If you are going to ask the witness to mark the location of persons or objects, use a marking system indicating the identity of the person or object; if the witness is named Taylor, tell the witness to use T1 to indicate her first position on the chart or if the witness is going to indicate the defendant's initial position, direct her to indicate that position with D1. Movement lines should end with arrows. To avoid confusion with floorplan lines, movement lines should not be solid. When movement lines cross, consider using different colors. If you use a chart, another problem that arises is that the witness's body may block the jury's view of the chart. When the witness is righthanded, place the chart to his or her left; if they have to reach across their body to write on the chart, they will block less of the chart from the jury's view.

§ 7.3   SAMPLE LINE OF FOUNDATIONAL QUESTIONS

You are the defense attorney in *Williams v. Scott*. You are planning your case-in-chief. You plot the plan on Figure 7–2. The starting point is your theory, misidentification. One of the factual elements of that theory is that your client was not at the crime scene when the attack occurred. To prove that, you intend to offer two items of evidence. One is your client's flat, emphatic denial. However, since your client's involvement in the battery is the pivotal issue in the case, you cannot be content to offer only his testimony. For that reason, you decide to call Ms. Freeman as a corroborating witness. Specifically, you decide to offer her testimony that the third voice in the hallway was not your client's.

Having decided to offer her testimony, you must now identify the evidentiary foundations necessitated by that testimony. Federal Rule of Evidence 901(b)(5) states that any voice identification must be authenticated. Turning to one of the specialized texts on foundations,[3] you find this list of preliminary facts: (1) at a specific time and place, the witness heard a voice; (2) the witness recognized the voice; (3) the witness is familiar with that voice; and (4) the witness explains the basis for his or her familiarity with the voice. Common sense suggests that the first and fourth preliminary facts should be stressed; if the jury is going to accept Freeman's testimony, they must be persuaded that she had a good opportunity to hear the voices in the hallway and that she is very familiar with Scott's voice. You are now ready to draft the line of questions to lay the voice identification foundation. To highlight the process of converting preliminary facts into questions, we have annotated the questions to the facts. For instance, the questions designed to prove the third foundational element are followed by (3).

3.   E. IMWINKELRIED, EVIDENTIARY
FOUNDATIONS 50–51 § 4.05[2] (5th ed.
2002).

Figure 7-2
PLANNING THE CASE-IN-CHIEF

Trial Theory	Elements of Theory	Items of Evidence to Prove Elements	Foundations Required for Items	Foundational Facts	Foundational Facts to Stress	Sequence of Foundational Facts	Questions to Lay Foundation
Alibi	Not at crime scene	Freeman's ID of the voices	Lay opinion voice ID	—heard voices —recognized voices —basis for familiarity —how positive	—good opportunity to hear —very familiar with Scott's voice	position facts to stress near end of line of questions	

Assume that Ms. Freeman has already identified herself and testified that after hearing noises in the hall, she decided to investigate. Figure 7–3 is a set of notes for this part of the direct examination.

Q What did you do then? (1)

A I opened my door and set foot into the hallway.

Q What, if anything, happened when you stepped into the hallway? (1)

A I saw three figures fighting in the hallway, and I could hear the voices of the men who were fighting.

Q How well could you hear the three voices? (2)

A Very well.

Q How close were you to the men? (2)

A I was only 15 or so feet away. It was so dark that they must not have noticed me.

Q How long did you stay in the hallway listening to the fight? (2)

A I must have been there at least 30 or 40 seconds. I was so startled that I was just frozen in my tracks.

Q What other noise was there in the hallway at the time? (2)

A None. It was late at night, and everyone else had gone to sleep. The only noise was the fight and the men screaming at each other.

Q How good is your hearing? (2)

A Perfect, as far as I know.

Q How well could you make out what they were saying? (2)

A Perfectly. As well as I can hear what you're saying now. The one guy was begging the other two to stop, and the other two were cursing him and threatening the guy.

Q Whose voices were the voices in the hallway? (2)

A They were Williams, Rogers, and some other guy.

Q How do you know that two of the voices were those of Williams and Rogers? (3)

A I'm familiar with their voices.

Q How did you become familiar with those two voices? (4)

A I've been at the Senator Hotel for several weeks, and I've bumped into them almost every day. I ought to know their voices by now.

Q Ms. Freeman, how well do you know Mr. Scott's voice? (3)

A Real well.

Q How did you come to know his voice "real well"? (4)

A I'd see him almost every day. In fact, we'd every so often go out for a drink, and I know his voice even better than Williams' or Rogers'. I can pretty easily pick out Bob's voice—I mean Mr. Scott's voice.

Q Why can you pick his voice out so easily? (4)

A Like I said earlier, I'm originally from New York. And so is Bob. I have. It's sort of funny. It's probably the worst Big Apple accent I've heard since moving here to the West Coast. I used to kid him about that.In fact, he's got an even more pronounced New York accent than

Q Ms. Freeman, I want you to think very carefully before you answer the next question. You've testified that two of the voices in the hallway were the plaintiff and Rogers. Who was the third voice? (3)

A I honestly don't know. All I can tell you is that that night it wasn't Bob Scott.

Q How can you remember that night so well?

A It just made an incredible impression on me. I've never witnessed anything like this before in my entire life. It was so violent. I'll never forget what happened that night.

Q How positive are you that the third man was not Mr. Scott? (4)

A I'm absolutely certain.

Q Why are you so positive? (4)

A That voice didn't have anything like Bob's East Coast accent. I know his voice even better than Williams' or Rogers.' If that had been Bob in the hallway, I know I would have picked out his voice.

Figure 7-3

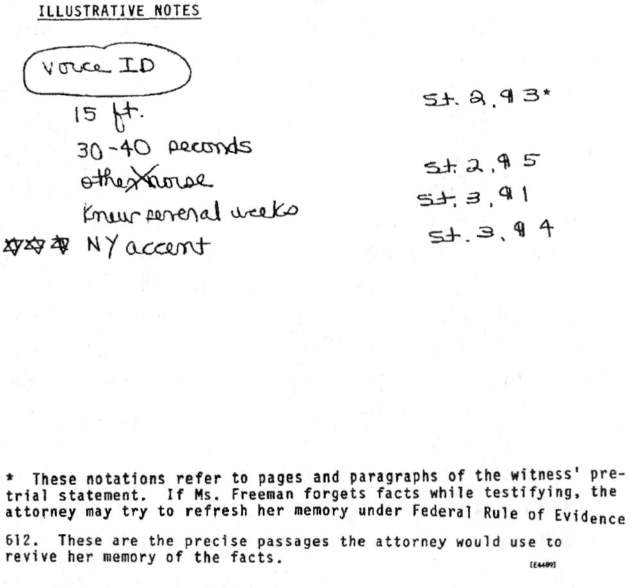

ILLUSTRATIVE NOTES

VOICE ID

15 ft.

30-40 seconds

other noise

knew several weeks

NY accent

St. 2.9 3*

St. 2.9 5

St. 3.9 1

St. 3.9 4

* These notations refer to pages and paragraphs of the witness' pre-trial statement. If Ms. Freeman forgets facts while testifying, the attorney may try to refresh her memory under Federal Rule of Evidence 612. These are the precise passages the attorney would use to revive her memory of the facts.

§ 7.4   ETHICAL QUESTIONS

May you ignore or "bend" evidentiary rules when you are opposed by a weak adversary? Model Rule of Professional Conduct 3.4 reads in part:

A lawyer shall not:

(c) knowingly disobey an obligation under the rules of a tribunal except for an open refusal based on an assertion that no valid obligation exists; [or]

(e) in trial, allude to any matter that the lawyer does not reasonably believe is relevant or that will not be supported by admissible evidence. . . .

What is the relationship between subsections (c) and (e)? The normal constructional preference is to interpret a statute or document in such a way as to give each part independent effect. In light of (e), should we interpret (c) as applying to "the rules of (evidence) of a tribunal"?

You are the prosecutor in the *Scott* case. You call Mr. Williams as a witness. You know that the defense attorney is weak and that his knowledge of evidence is deficient. Specifically, you know that even if you improperly lead Williams on direct, the defense attorney will probably not object. Like Federal Rule of Evidence 611(c), El Dorado Rule 611(c) states that "[l]eading questions should not be used on the direct examination of a witness except as may be necessary to develop the witness's testimony." In the face of this language, would it violate Rule 3.4(c) for you to ask consistently leading questions during Williams' direct? Would it violate Rule 3.4(e)? Would it make a difference if El Dorado Rule 611(c) used the verb, "shall," rather than "should"?

Change the facts. Now assume that the prosecutor suspects that the defense may claim that Williams fabricated the story about the attack and that he sustained the injuries when he became drunk and fell down a flight of stairs at the hotel. Two days after the attack, the prosecutor phones the emergency room at Memorial Hospital, the private hospital where Williams was taken on the morning of January 19. She speaks with Dr. Kelner who treated Williams. Kelner is a staff physician, and he is not in private practice. Kelner tells the prosecutor that in his opinion, the injuries could not have been caused by a fall; their location and nature show that they were caused by a beating. The prosecutor asks Dr. Kelner to prepare a report for trial to that effect. Kelner tells the prosecutor that under hospital staff procedure, he is supposed to prepare only one report immediately upon the patient's discharge. Kelner states that none of the emergency room staff physicians at Memorial has ever prepared the type of litigation report that the prosecutor is asking for. The prosecutor pleads with Kelner and tells him that she does not want to have to subpoena him to give live testimony. At that point, Kelner relents. He prepares the report and sends it to the prosecutor.

The prosecutor is now preparing for trial. On reading El Dorado Rule of Evidence 803(6), she discovers that a document can qualify as a business entry only "if it was the regular practice of that business activity to make the . . . report. . . ." Given the explicit requirements of Rule 803(6), would it violate Model Rule of Professional Conduct 3.4 for the prosecutor to attempt to introduce Dr. Kelner's report at trial? Is it relevant that El Dorado has adopted Rule of Evidence 807, the so-called residual hearsay exception? Suppose that as in Nevada, the El Dorado version of article VIII omitted a Rule 807 and that the El Dorado Advisory Committee Note to article VIII made it clear that the list of specific hearsay exceptions in article VIII was intended to be exhaustive.

§ 7.5 TRIAL TECHNIQUE EXERCISES

You will conduct a direct examination. Your instructor will announce any maximum or minimum length requirements for the direct. *Before drafting your line of questions, you should consult at least one of the specialized texts on foundations listed in § 7.2(E) of this chapter.* Your instructor may recommend a particular text. The designated opposing counsel may object and conduct any necessary voir dire examination in support of the objection. The instructor may also indicate that the opposing counsel should be prepared to conduct a cross-examination, following up on the direct.

Case file A–1. You will conduct a direct examination of Dr. James Maples. During the examination, you must attempt to introduce the entry in Mr. Alexander's patient chart. You must lay authentication, best evidence, and hearsay foundations for the chart.

Case file A–2. You will conduct a direct examination of Officer Randall Martinez. During the examination, you must attempt to elicit Officer Martinez' description of Ms. Barnes' statement, "Please don't arrest me. If you'll just let me go, I'll pay for the gloves." You must lay *Miranda* and due process voluntariness foundations for the statement.

Case file A–3. You will conduct a direct examination of Mr. J. J. Jacobs. During the examination, you will have Mr. Jacobs verify and use a chart of the Kingsbury–Williams intersection to illustrate his testimony. In addition, please assume that on the stand, Mr. Jacobs forgets the color of Mr. Paterson's car. You will resort to Mr. Jacobs' pretrial statement to revive his memory; in order to do so, you will have to lay a present recollection refreshed foundation.

Case file A–4. You will conduct a direct examination of Mr. Ladd. During the direct examination, you will attempt to introduce the lease, the termination of lease notice, and Ms. Valdez' letter to Ladd. You must lay authentication, best evidence, and hearsay foundations for all the documents.

Case file A–5. You will conduct a direct examination of Officer Krause. You will attempt to introduce his testimony about the other robberies Mr. McIver allegedly committed. Before drafting your line of questions, read Federal Rules of Evidence 404–06. During this direct examination, you should use the stipulation of facts listed in the Instructions at the beginning of the Case file.

Case file A–6. You will conduct a direct examination of Mr. Havens. During the direct examination, you will introduce the photograph of the orchard heater. In addition, using your body and Mr. Havens' body, you will conduct an in-court demonstration, showing the jury the positions of Mr. Pappas, Mr. Havens, and the heater when Mr. Pappas was injured.

Case file A–7. You will conduct a direct examination of Agent McNally. During the direct examination, you will attempt to establish a chain of custody for the introduction of the drugs analyzed by the laboratory. Please assume that because the holidays were so hectic, Agent McNally cannot recall the specific date when he returned to New York to pick up the exhibit; he cannot remember that date even after viewing his statement. Be prepared to lay a past recollection recorded foundation for that part of his statement.

Case file A–8. You will conduct a direct examination of Robert Green. During the direct examination, you will attempt to elicit lay opinions as to the state of mind of both the defendant and Ms. Kathy Lunda. Before drafting your line of questions, read Federal Rules of Evidence 602 and 701. *Compare United States v. Hoffner,* 777 F.2d 1423, 1425 (10th Cir.1985) *with United States v. Ruppel,* 666 F.2d 261, 270 (5th Cir.), *cert. denied,* 458 U.S. 1107 (1982).

Case file A–9. You will conduct a direct examination of Bonnie Blair. During the direct examination, you will attempt to lay a vicarious admission foundation for the witness's description of the statements made by Carol Johnson as well as the statements made by the public relations representative.

Case file A–10. You will conduct a direct examination of Rebecca Winters. During the direct examination, you will attempt to elicit her description of both Maxwell's statements during their meeting and negative, unfriendly demeanor she claims he displayed during the conversation.

Chapter 8

THE MICROCOSM OF CROSS–EXAMINATION: IMPEACHMENT—MAKING FACTUAL ASSERTIONS UNDER THE GUISE OF ASKING QUESTIONS

Cross-Examination

Reprinted by permission of Warner Books/New York from *The Law as Seen by Charles Bragg.* Copyright © 1983 by Charles Bragg.

Table of Sections

---

§ 8.1　INTRODUCTION

This chapter parallels the last; just as Chapter 7 analyzed the process of generating a set of questions to lay a foundation for an item of evidence on direct examination, this chapter addresses the parallel task of formulating questions for cross-examination.

On balance, mastering the art of direct examination is more important than learning the art of cross. Most cases are won by methodically prepared direct testimony rather than by divinely inspired cross-examination. However, in a close case, the cross-examination can be decisive. Cross-examination is an especially important skill for criminal defense attorneys who sometimes have few witnesses to call on their client's behalf. Moreover, in our experience, law students find it more difficult to master cross-examination. Masterful cross requires special discipline.

One of the keys to mastering cross is to appreciate that just as in the case of sound direct testimony, good cross-examination is the end product of a planning process. Section 8.2 of this chapter dissects many of the steps in that process. Figure 8–1 will help you visualize the planning steps. Note that the first four columns on Figure 8–1 have no headings. We are temporarily leaving those columns blank in this chapter. We are reserving them for the early steps in cross-examination planning: listing all the items of evidence that the witness can testify to; deciding whether to cross-examine the witness; if so, determining which purposes to pursue during the cross; and finally, choosing the specific items of evidence to elicit on cross. We shall address those steps in Chapter 10 devoted to the macrocosm of organizing all the cross-examinations. For purposes of this chapter, we shall assume that the attorney has decided to cross-examine to impeach and has already chosen an item of impeaching evidence to elicit. Suppose, for instance, that in *Williams v. Scott,* the plaintiff's attorney deposed Ms. Freeman before trial. At the deposition hearing, she wavered from her pretrial statement and indicated that she was uncertain whether the third voice in the hallway was Scott's. Williams' attorney decides to cross-examine her to elicit that inconsistent statement.

§ 8.2 DRAFTING A LINE OF QUESTIONS TO LAY A FOUNDATION FOR AN ITEM OF IMPEACHMENT EVIDENCE

The drafting process for cross-examination is analogous to the process for direct examination.

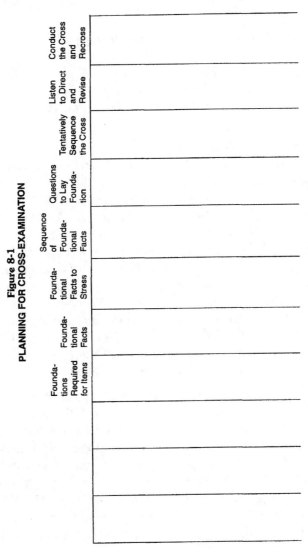

Figure 8-1
PLANNING FOR CROSS-EXAMINATION

§ 8.2(A) Identifying the Foundations Needed to Introduce Each Item of Impeachment Evidence

To lay a foundation on cross-examination for an item of impeachment evidence, the attorney must comply with several special rules as well as many of the normal foundational doctrines.

Suppose, for example, that during cross-examination, the attorney wants to offer a written statement by the witness as substantive proof of an assertion in the statement.[1] Chapter 7 observed that when the direct examiner contemplates offering a document as substantive evidence, she may have to lay foundations satisfying the authentication, best evidence, and hearsay rules. The same observation applies here. The cross-examiner does not have any special exemption from normal evidentiary requirements.

In addition, however, there are special impeachment doctrines that the cross-examiner must satisfy. Federal Rules of Evidence 607–13 set out many of those rules. For instance, Rule 609 contains detailed rules regulating the use of convictions for impeachment. Similarly, Rule 613 prescribes procedures for the use of prior inconsistent statements by the witness.

In our hypothetical, at trial Williams' attorney intends to cross-examine Ms. Freeman about her statement at the deposition hearing. The attorney ought to consult the pertinent El Dorado Rules of Evidence. The attorney should certainly review Rule 613 governing impeachment by prior inconsistent statement. Rule 613(a) allows the attorney to cross-examine the witness point blank about a written inconsistent statement without showing the writing to the witness. However, to an extent Rule 613(b) preserves the common-law requirement of a foundation on cross for the presentation of extrinsic evidence. Proof of the foundation usually consists of the witness's own testimony about the circumstances surrounding the inconsistent statement, including the time, place, addressee, and tenor of the statement. That foundation is the bare minimum predicate that Williams' attorney would probably want to establish during the cross of Ms. Freeman.

The attorney should also review Rule of Evidence 612. When Williams' attorney attempts to lay the Rule 613 foundation, Ms. Freeman may deny that she wavered at the deposition hearing; or she might claim that she does not remember her testimony at the hearing. In either event, Williams' attorney may want to use the deposition transcript to refresh her recollection of her testimony. Figure 8–2 is a sample excerpt from a deposition. The attorney would hand Ms. Freeman the transcript and show her the title page and her signature page. She could then identify the transcript as the record of her deposition testimony. The attorney would next direct her attention to the precise page and lines where the inconsistent statement appears ("page 33, lines 27 and 28") and have her read that passage silently to herself.

---

1. Some judges believe that it is *per se* beyond the proper scope of cross-examination to introduce exhibits as substantive evidence during that phase of the questioning. That belief is erroneous. Tanford, *Introduction to Trial Law,* 51 MO.L.REV. 623, 673 (1986). However, some respected commentators still treat that belief as good law. *E.g.,* R. HUNTER, FEDERAL TRIAL HANDBOOK § 22.3 (2d ed. 1984).

Figure 8-2

IN THE SUPERIOR COURT OF THE STATE OF EL DORADO
IN AND FOR THE COUNTY OF MORENA

PETER WILLIAMS,
Plaintiff

vs.

ROBERT SCOTT,
Defendant

REPORTER'S TRANSCRIPT

DEPOSITION OF JOAN FREEMAN

TUESDAY, MAY 23, 19YR

APPEARANCES:

For the Plaintiff: Andrew Hymes

For the Defendant: Maureen Haney

Cheryl E. Lux, Reporter

Q How long did you have to listen to those voices?

A Maybe 20 to 40 seconds. I can't be sure.

Q You can't be sure.

A Yeah.

Q Could it have been less—maybe 10 seconds?

A I guess that's possible. I'm not real good at estimating time.

Q You admit you are not real good at that?

A Yeah.

Q And what about the distance? How far away from you were the three men?

A I guess 15 feet.

Q You've told us you're not very good at estimating time. Are you as good at estimating distance?

A I'd have to say about the same.

Q So the distance could have been more?

A Looking back now, I'd say so.

Q Maybe 20 feet?

A Could have been.

Q Maybe 25 feet?

A It's possible, but I don't think so.

Q Well, let's put it all together now. The time could have been only 10 seconds. Right?

A I said that. Yeah.

Q And the distance could have been up to 25 or so feet. Correct?

A Right.

Q If that's so, are you certain that the third voice wasn't Scott?

A I'm not really certain, but I think so. At least that's what I think.

The proceedings were adjourned at 4:30 p.m., May 23, 19YR.

/s/ _____

Joan Freeman

STATE OF EL DORADO)
) ss.
COUNTY OF MORENA   )

I, *Cheryl Lux*, a Notary Public in and for the County of Morena, State of El Dorado, do hereby certify that the witness in the foregoing deposition,

JOAN FREEMAN

appeared before me on the date subscribed to below and that the witness read and corrected the deposition in all particulars desired. Each correction was duly initialed by me, and the deposition was then subscribed by this witness in my presence.

IN WITNESS WHEREOF, I have hereunto set my hand and affixed my notarial seal this *26th* day of *May*, 19YR.

/s/ _____

Notary Public

STATE OF EL DORADO)
) ss.
COUNTY OF MORENA   )

I, Cheryl E. Lux, a Certified Shorthand Reporter, Certificate No. 137, and a Notary Public in and for the County of Morena, State of El Dorado, do hereby certify that the witness in the foregoing deposition,

JOAN FREEMAN

was by name first duly sworn to testify to the truth, the whole truth, and nothing but the truth, in the foregoing cause; that the deposition was taken before me at the time and place herein named; that said deposition was reported by me in shorthand and then transcribed into typewriting under my direction, and the foregoing 49 pages contain a true, original record of the testimony of the witness.

I do further certify that I am a disinterested person and am in no way interested in the outcome of this action, or connected or related to any of the parties in this action or to their respective counsel.

IN WITNESS WHEREOF, I have set my hand and affixed my notarial seal on this 26th day of May, 19YR.

/s/ _____

(Notary Stamp)

_____

Finally, in the most extreme case, even after reviewing her deposition transcript tendered to her under Rule 612 to refresh her memory, Ms. Freeman may insist that the transcript is wrong or that she still cannot remember. In that case, while Ms. Freeman is on the stand or after she leaves the stand, Williams' attorney may want to offer the transcript itself as extrinsic evidence to prove her inconsistent statement. If so, the attorney must be prepared to lay authentication, best evidence, and hearsay foundations. As previously stated, the El Dorado Rules are identical to the Federal Rules. If the attorney has to resort to the deposition transcript, he may have to lay an authentication foundation to satisfy Rules 901–02. Assume that under El Dorado civil procedure, the court reporter taking the deposition is also a notary public authorized to attest to documents and affix an official notary seal. On that assumption, the original transcript would be self-authenticating under Rule 902(1); and a copy would also qualify for self-authenticating status under Rule 902(4). (When the passage relates to a critical issue in the case and the witness has suggested that the transcript is inaccurate, it may be more effective to call the court reporter as a witness and have the reporter read the original shorthand notes to the jury.)

The attorney can also satisfy the best evidence rule. The notary's attesting certificate at the end of the transcript will recite that the attached document is either the original transcript or a copy. The document will, hence, constitute either an "original" under Rule 1001(3) or at least a "duplicate" under Rule 1001(4).

The attorney can likewise surmount a hearsay objection if she decides to offer the deposition passage for a nonhearsay purpose. The use of the transcript to prove Ms. Freeman's statement is double hearsay under Rule 805. The transcript itself is an assertion by the reporter that certain statements were made and that particular events occurred at the hearing. However, that assertion falls within the official record hearsay exception under Rule 803(8). The judge can judicially notice the El Dorado statutes and court rules authorizing reporters to transcribe the proceedings at deposition hearings. The reporter is a public official for purposes of Rule 803(8). Under Rule 803(8), Williams' attorney can thus use the transcript to prove that Ms. Freeman made a particular statement at the hearing. It is true that a further hearsay exception would be needed if Williams' attorney wanted to offer Ms. Freeman's statement as substantive evidence in the case. However, if the attorney offers the passage for a purpose other than its truth, the passage would be nonhearsay under Rule 801(c). Offering the passage merely as a prior inconsistent statement is a classic example of a nonhearsay use. The fact that Freeman made an inconsistent statement is circumstantial evidence of her state of mind. She has made inconsistent statements about the same subject. Even if her prior statement is untrue, the fact that she made the statement gives the jury some insight into her frame of mind; she is either uncertain or lying. Under Rule 105, the defense would be entitled to a limiting instruction that the jury may consider Ms. Freeman's statement merely for the limited purpose of evaluating her credibility; but Williams' attorney could nevertheless read the passage to the jury.[2]

In summary, if Ms. Freeman acknowledges her inconsistent statement, the only absolutely necessary foundation would be a predicate under Rule 613(b). If Ms. Freeman admits her statement at the deposition hearing, it will be unnecessary for Williams' attorney to satisfy the present recollection refreshed, authentication, best evidence, and hearsay rules. The foundational, preliminary facts under Rule 613(b) are the circumstances surrounding the inconsistent statement. The key circumstances are the time, place, addressee, and tenor of the statement. *See generally* R. CARLSON, CRIMINAL LAW ADVOCACY: TRIAL PROOF 6.02[7], at 6–47–52 (1982).

§ 8.2(B) Listing the Foundational Facts

Chapter 7 catalogued several leading treatises on the Federal Rules of Evidence and the specialized texts listing foundational or predicate facts. The same treatise and texts that are aids in identifying the preliminary facts on direct examination are useful in developing the lists of foundational facts for cross.

§ 8.2(C) Deciding Which Foundational Elements to Stress

Chapter 7 noted that before drafting her questions, the direct examiner must pause and decide which foundational elements to stress.

---

2. If El Dorado had enacted Federal Rule of Evidence 801(d)(1)(A), the limiting instruction would be unnecessary. Under that provision, the passage would qualify as nonhearsay exempt from the hearsay rule and therefore be admissible as substantive evidence. The passage would be an "inconsistent" statement "given under oath subject to the penalty of perjury . . . in a deposition. . . ."

On direct examination, the attorney ought to elaborate on the elements determining the reliability of the evidence. In the same vein, before drafting her questions, the cross-examiner must choose the foundational elements to stress. On cross-examination, the attorney should embellish and go into detail about the elements which show the jury why the fact impeaches the witness's credibility.

Subsection 8.2(B) points out that as part of the foundation on the cross-examination of Ms. Freeman, Williams' attorney must elicit the circumstances surrounding her inconsistent statement at the deposition hearing. Under Evidence law, it would suffice for the attorney to elicit Ms. Freeman's testimony that: On a certain date, she came to the attorney's office for a "deposition hearing;" at the hearing, she was asked a particular question; and in response, she answered that she was a bit uncertain whether the third voice in the hallway was Scott's. However, any cross-examiner with a modicum of sense will realize that he must go at least a bit farther and have Ms. Freeman explain what a "deposition" is; that expression may be Greek to the average juror. You cannot be content with the bare bones facts required by evidence law; you must elicit *the specific aspects and features of those facts* which help the lay jurors understand why the line of testimony is impeaching. Hence, seasoned litigators elaborate on the circumstances surrounding the deposition testimony. They do so to make it clear to the jury that the inconsistent deposition statement was likely to be trustworthy. For example, they might include a number of additional questions forcing her to admit that:

— The opposing attorney was present at the hearing.

— The court reporter administered an oath to her—much like the oath she took before giving her trial testimony.

— At the beginning of the deposition, Williams' attorney asked her whether she was experiencing any physical or mental problem that would make it difficult for her to answer questions at the hearing.

— The attorney told her that if any of his questions were unclear, she should say so and ask him to reword the question.

— After the hearing, the court reporter prepared a booklet of her answers and sent the booklet to her to allow her to correct any errors.

— She made no corrections in the transcript.

By eliciting these additional circumstances about the deposition testimony, Williams' attorney might be able to convince the jury that that testimony is more trustworthy than the testimony they heard on direct examination. "Accrediting" or validating the earlier deposition testimony enhances the impeaching value of the inconsistency. Lubet, *Understanding Impeachment,* 15 AM.J.TRIAL ADVOC. 483, 507 (1992). In the above hypothetical, the cross-examiner elicited the fact that Freeman had a duty to tell the truth. *Id.* at 509. In other cases, the cross-examiner can establish that at the time of the earlier statement, the witness had "an important reason to be accurate" (*id.* at 507) or a substantially fresher memory. *Id.* at 510.

§ 8.2(D) Determining the Sequence of the Foundational Facts

As in the case of planning foundational questions for direct examination, you should determine the sequence of the foundational facts you intend to establish on cross-examination.

The general norm is that you ought to elicit the foundational facts in chronological order. That order is ordinarily easiest for the judge and jury to follow. For example, suppose that you want to force the witness to concede a particular encounter with your client, an encounter which you believe demonstrates the witness's bias against your client. When you question the witness about the event, you could lead the witness through the event step by step in chronological sequence.

However, as the last chapter noted, the end of a line of questioning is a naturally emphatic position. By way of example, in the last planning step, you identified the foundational fact which warrants stress. Assume, for instance, that you are questioning a witness about a prior conviction under Federal Rule of Evidence 609(a). If you followed strict chronological order, you would elicit the sentence as the last preliminary fact. However, the sentence may not be the most important fact. Rather, that fact may be the nature of the crime the witness was convicted of. If the witness was convicted of perjury, you should highlight that fact in the last foundational question. The climax ought to be the question, "And isn't it true that the crime you were convicted of was perjury—perjury as a witness in another trial in this state?"

A further example is effective sequencing of the foundation for prior inconsistent statement impeachment. In this impeachment technique, you need to cross-examine the witness about both her earlier statement and her present testimony. If you followed strict chronological sequence, you would first question her about the earlier pretrial statement; and you would then turn to the trial testimony. However, the consensus is that here again you should deviate from chronological sequence. At the outset, most cross-examiners endeavor to recommit the witness to her current testimony. Lubet, *Understanding Impeachment,* 15 AM.J.TRIAL ADVOC. 483, 499 (1992). If you do not lock her into the present testimony, she may claim that you misunderstood her or that she innocently misspoke. Once you have recommitted the witness to her current testimony, question the witness about the earlier pretrial statement.

§ 8.2(E) Drafting the Foundational Questions

As Figure 8–1 indicates, the next planning step is to draft the foundational questions for cross-examination. The general tactical guideline is this: *Draft plainly-worded, short, leading, non-argumentative questions designed to elicit facts that you are morally certain the witness will admit.* The following discussion reviews both the elements of the general guideline and some of the situations in which the attorney should seriously consider deviating from the guideline. Asbill, *The Ten Commandments of Cross–Examination Revisited: Should You Sin to Win When the Case Is Criminal?*, 8 CRIM.JUST. 2, 54 (Wint. 1994)(it is a serious mistake to treat the cross-examination guidelines as inflexible rules to be strictly followed; "There are very few absolute prescriptions [for cross-examination]"; it is much more a case of "situational" judgment); McElhaney, *Breaking the Rules of Cross*, 80 A.B.A.J. 95 (Apr. 1994).

"Plainly-worded questions." Chapter 7 pointed out that the direct examiner ought to use simple, concrete words in drafting his questions. The cross-examiner should do the same. In fact, there is even greater need for the cross-examiner to do so when the witness is hostile and intelligent. A hostile witness will strain to find ambiguities in the cross-examiner's questions, and an intelligent, hostile witness may succeed in doing so. Questions on cross-examination must be so clearly worded that even a hostile, intelligent witness cannot plausibly misconstrue them. Box the witness in. Give the witness only two options. The witness's only choices should be either giving you the concession you want or committing perjury.

"Short questions." Like direct questions, cross-examination questions should be short. Evidence law would permit Williams' attorney to pack the entire foundation for Ms. Freeman's prior inconsistent statement and the statement itself into a single question: "Isn't it true that at a deposition hearing at my office in downtown Morena on May 23, 19YR you testified that you were uncertain whether the third voice in the hallway was the defendant's?" However, it is preferable to stretch the impeachment out into several questions. There are a number of rationales for the preference.

To begin with, proceeding one short question—one discrete fact—at a time gives you better control over the witness. Suppose that one detail in the question is wrong; the deposition hearing was held on May 24. The witness can truthfully answer "No." Her general answer does not give you any clue to the specific defect in the phrasing of the question.

Further, drawing out the impeachment gives the jury more time to appreciate its significance. If Williams' attorney loads all the foundational facts into one question, the question and answer may flash by the jury in 15 seconds. By prolonging the impeachment to two or three minutes, the attorney increases the likelihood that the jury will realize that there is reason to doubt the witness's credibility. The cross-examiner sometimes succeeds in making a mountain out of a molehill.

In addition, a prolonged line of cross-examination may prompt unfavorable demeanor by the witness. In the Cleveland Jury Project, the researchers concluded that when witnesses disagree, jurors often decide the case by focusing on the witnesses' demeanor rather than the substantive content of their testimony. Austin, *Why Jurors Don't Heed the Trial*, NAT'L L.J., Aug. 12, 1985, at p. 18. If Williams' attorney asks Ms.

Freeman a single question about the deposition, the questioning will be over so quickly that there will be no time for her demeanor to change. However, by extending the questioning, the cross-examiner lets the impeachment "sink in;" and her demeanor may change from a confident one to a facial expression registering uncertainty—"death by a thousand cuts." Moritz & Harris, *Cross-examining the Accomplice Witness,* 14 LITIGATION 31, 34 (Fall 1987).

For all the above reasons, it is advisable to prolong a line of impeaching questions. When questioning a prosecution witness who has entered into a pretrial deal with the district attorney, to expose the witness's bias some defense attorneys rush through the impeachment with a few questions:

Q Isn't it true that you were charged with attempted sale of heroin?

Q And you knew that you could have received 30 years imprisonment for that crime. Didn't you?

Q But under your deal with the D.A.'s office, you'll serve only two years. Correct?

Other, more seasoned attorneys draw out the questioning:

Q The police arrested you for sale of heroin on January 10th last year. Right?

Q When they arrested you, you had the heroin on you. Didn't you?

Q The person you tried to make the sale to turned out to be an undercover police officer. Isn't that true?

Q Isn't it also true that you confessed on January 20th?

Q Then on February 10 you hired a lawyer. Right?

Q Didn't the lawyer tell you that your trial was set for March 20th?

Q Didn't he also tell you that if you were convicted, you might be sent to state prison?

Q For 30 years. Wasn't that the possible sentence for your crime your attorney told you about?

Q Then on March 10th before your trial, you and your attorney decided to make a phone call to the District Attorney's office. Right?

Q At that time you told the D.A. that you wanted to make a deal. Right?

Q The D.A.—the D.A. sitting at the table right over there—correct?

Q During that first phone conversation, you didn't mention my client, Mr. Scott. Did you?

Q And at that time the D.A. wasn't willing to make a deal. Was he?

Q But you and your attorney called again on March 17th, the Friday before your trial was supposed to begin. Correct?

Q And this time you were able to reach an agreement with the D.A. for a deal. Weren't you?

Q And under your deal, you're not going to serve 30 years in prison. Are you?

Q How long are you going to serve in state prison?

Q I see—only two years out of possible 30. Right?

Q This second time you called—the time you got your deal—this time you mentioned Mr. Scott. Didn't you?

Q And isn't it true that that was the first time you ever mentioned my client's name to the D.A.?

Q Now to get your deal with the D.A., you had to promise you'd do something for the D.A. Didn't you?

This extended line of questioning indicates how desperate the witness was to make a pretrial arrangement with the prosecutor—perhaps desperate enough to lie to cut a favorable deal. This line of questioning is much more likely to effectively impeach the witness's credibility in the jurors' minds.

"Leading questions." In some cases, the cross-examiner should use non-leading questions. Suppose, for example, that Williams' attorney suspects that Ms. Freeman has memorized her story about the night of the attack. When he interviewed her before trial, she used the very same words that she chose at the deposition hearing. She then repeated the story virtually verbatim on direct examination. In this situation, it may be advisable for Williams' attorney to ask non-leading questions inviting her to give the story verbatim once again. During closing argument, he can then invite the jury to reject her testimony precisely because it is "a memorized story." A case in point is

> Max Steuer's cross-examination in the Triangle Shirt Waist Company case. According to Irving Younger's engaging account, the prosecutor in that case "phoneyed up" the evidence and turned his witnesses into "human tape recorders" capable of parroting their narrative testimony over and over again without the slightest degree of variation.[3]

However, as a general proposition, the cross-examiner should lead the witness to maintain witness control. A leading question gives the witness "nowhere to run and nowhere to hide." There are three degrees of leading questions that give the examiner progressively more control over the witness. Mildly or gently leading questions begin with such words as Is, Are, Do, Did, Was, and Were. Fairly leading questions have a negative tone that make the desired answer even clearer. They often start with words such as Isn't, Aren't, Don't, Didn't, Wasn't, and Weren't. Finally, there are brutally leading questions. There are two

---

3. R. UNDERWOOD, & W. FORTUNE, & E. IMWINKELRIED, MODERN LITIGA-TION AND PROFESSIONAL RESPONSI-BILITY HANDBOOK § 11.4, at 398 (2d ed. 2001).

ways of making a question brutally leading. One is to preface the question with a phrase such as Isn't it true, Isn't it a fact, or Won't you admit. The other way is to use two sentences. One sentence is a simple declaration such as "The traffic light was red." The second sentence is called the tag: Correct? Right? Is that true?

Most questions asked on cross-examination ought to be mildly leading. However, as you shift from marginally relevant questions to the key questions, your phrasing should become more leading. The phrasing of the key questions ought to be brutally leading: "Isn't it true that at that deposition, you said that you weren't sure whether the third voice was the defendant's?" The principal caveat is that you should not habitually use brutally leading phrasing. The rhythm can become so repetitious that it lulls the jury into inattention. By the time the jurors have heard the fifth, consecutive question beginning "Won't you admit....," they may no longer be listening carefully.

"Non-argumentative questions that are designed to elicit facts." As Chapter 5 pointed out, perhaps the most common objection during cross-examination is that the question is argumentative. Unfortunately, little has been written about the definition of an argumentative question. The best article on the topic is Goff, *Argumentative Questions: Counsel, Protect Your Witness,* 49 CAL.ST.BAR J. 140 (1974). If you are unsure of the definition even after having taken an Evidence course, we recommend that you read Judge Goff's article. The article states that argumentative questions have two characteristics. First, they are not designed to elicit new data from the witness. Second, they are calculated to challenge the witness about an inference from data already in the record. Judge Goff gives the following examples of argumentative questions: Do you mean that seriously? How do you expect the jury to believe that? How can you reconcile those two statements?

There is no provision in the Federal Rules categorically forbidding the use of argumentative questions on cross. However, Rule 611(a) grants the judge discretionary control over "the mode ... of interrogating witnesses...." Given that control, most trial judges continue to prohibit the use of argumentative questions during cross-examination. Thus, if you become overtly argumentative, an objection may well be sustained.

There are more important, tactical reasons, though, for refraining from argumentative questions. One is that argumentative questions usually ask the witness for an inference and that in asking for an inference, the cross-examiner loses control of the witness. For example, during the cross-examination of Williams, Scott's attorney might ask, "And you seriously expect this jury to believe that you weren't drunk?" "Drunk" is an opinionated term. It would be better simply to force Williams to describe a boilermaker and to admit that he had three boilermakers in the half hour before the attack. Similarly, the attorney might ask Williams, "Won't you admit that that hallway was dark?" "Dark" represents an inference. Scott's attorney should ask narrowly-phrased questions eliciting the facts that: There are no windows in the hallway; there is at least 20 feet between each light fixture in the hallway; and on the morning of the attack, half the light bulbs were burnt out. Whenever possible, avoid using words that call for characterization or opinion: few, numerous, loud, soft, clear, careless, careful, significant, substantial, important, large, great, or small. Every time you resort to one of these terms, you give the witness an opening to hurt your case. "[P]hrase your question in terms of bedrock fact, making sure it contains nothing that approaches a characterization. The more factual the question, the less possible it is for the witness to deny you a simple answer." Lubet, *Cross-examination: ENDGAME,* 17 LITIGATION 40, 42 (Wint. 1991). Confine your questioning to constituent facts. Lubet, *Reasserting Control in Cross-examination,* 18 LITIGATION 24, 25 (Sum. 1992).

Another tactical reason for avoiding argumentative questions is that they often embroil you in argument with the witness and you usually come off the loser in the jurors' eyes. Most jurors sympathize with the witness at least at the outset of the cross-examination. The Duke University Law and Language Project researchers found that it ordinarily works to the attorney's detriment when the cross-examination degenerates into an argument between the attorney and the witness. Colley, *Style, Structure, and Semantics,* 19 TRIAL 86, 87 (July 1983). If the witness appears to win the argument, the jurors may perceive the attorney as weak and lacking faith in his or her case. When the attorney appears to dominate, some jurors may conclude that the attorney is unfairly preventing the witness from telling his or her story. Given the potential objection to an argumentative question and these tactical reasons, you should generally avoid argumentative questions during cross-examination. As previously stated, good cross requires special discipline. Get the factual ammunition you need for closing argument, and then STOP.

However, like most norms in trial advocacy, this norm is subject to exceptions. One exception comes into play when the witness has a particularly abrasive personality. When the witness does, arguing with the witness may be helpful. Doing so may expose the witness's personality. (The direct examiner might have used leading phrasing in order to keep the witness's personality under wraps as much as possible.) Once the jury appreciates how obnoxious the witness is, they may be less inclined to accept the witness's testimony. Frankly, you want to "goad" the witness "into a fight." McElhaney, *Prepping the CEO,* 82 A.B.A.J. 84 (Oct. 1996). In closing argument, you will then be able to tell the jurors that during cross, "they caught a glimpse of the real M. Clayton Ransom. . . ." *Id.*

Another exception comes into play when it is "safe" to ask the witness for an opinion. P. BERGMAN, TRIAL ADVOCACY 184–88 (1979). Suppose, for instance, that in a letter to an acquaintance after the attack, Williams wrote that the hallway was "pretty dark." Unbeknownst to Williams and his attorney, Scott's attorney has obtained a copy of the letter and has the acquaintance ready to authenticate it. It would ordinarily be foolish for Scott's attorney to ask Williams whether the hallway was "pretty dark." However, the availability of Williams' written statement largely removes the risk in posing the question. *Id.* at 188–201.

Finally, some attorneys ask argumentative questions designed to make their theory of the case clear to the jury. For instance, during Williams' cross-examination, Scott's attorney might ask, "Mr. Williams, isn't the real reason you think you saw Mr. Scott simply that you expected to see him when you stepped off that elevator?" Attorneys differ over the advisability of asking argumentative questions for this purpose. Some do so routinely. Others insist that you should never do so; they reason that if you intelligently use the opening statement and sequence the facts correctly on cross, you can make the conclusion clear without resorting to argument. A sensible, compromise view is that you ought to use this technique only when the witness's testimony relates to technical material and the point may not be readily apparent to lay jurors. S. HAMLIN, WHAT MAKES JURIES LISTEN 305 (1985). The witness might be a forensic pathologist or an accident reconstructionist. The testimony is likely to be scientific and somewhat confusing. In this situation, it may be necessary to ask an argumentative question on cross to ensure that the jurors understand how the cross-examination contributes to your theory of the case.

"Questions designed to elicit facts that you are morally certain the witness will admit." The late Professor Younger correctly cautioned young attorneys against going on "fishing expeditions" for favorable facts on cross-examination. More often than not, the witness uses the "fishing" questions as an opportunity to reaffirm the direct and compound the damage done to your case. Professor Younger's advice generally holds true in civil cases in which you have the benefit of virtually complete pretrial discovery.

However, there are times when you must deviate from this norm. In some cases, typically prosecutions, you are forced to trial even though you would rather settle. You may have virtually no ammunition for trial. If so, there is little to lose in resorting to desperate tactics. When you watched the jury during the opponent's direct examination, you could virtually see the adverse verdict sealed on their faces. It is obvious that they believed every word of the direct examination; and you realize that the testimony was so damning that if you do not cross-examine the witness, for all practical purposes the trial is over. A litigator has to trust his or her situational judgment and sometimes throw caution to the wind. The desperation tactics will probably be unsuccessful, but our hypothesis is that you were probably going to lose the trial in any event. In a few cases, the fishing expedition will unearth wonderful facts during cross-examination; and your willingness to launch the expedition will turn probable defeat into victory.

SUMMARY. As Chapter 7 stressed, when you are conducting the direct examination of a good witness, you want to treat the witness as an exhibit and put the witness on optimal display by allowing the witness to open up to the jury. On cross-examination, your objective is quite different. In this subsection, we have discussed a number of tactics in drafting cross-examination questions—the need for short questions, the desirability of leading, and the importance of avoiding argument. In addition to understanding these individual tactics, you must appreciate the cumulative effect of orchestrating these tactics. If you use narrowly-phrased, factual questions, you can virtually testify for the witness. One of the foremost cross-examiners in America, Mr. Albert Krieger, has remarked that when you properly phrase your cross-examination questions, you really are not asking questions on cross; under the guise of asking questions, you are making factual assertions and forcing the witness to express assent on the record. You reduce the witness to a soundingboard for your factual assertions. *See* Gonzalez, *Preparing and Conducting an Effective Cross–Examination of an Adverse Witness*, 27 LITIGATION 19 (Fall 2000)("The time to ask [real] questions is in deposition. Armed with the answers you get there, you should control the adverse witness in cross-examination like [the ventriloquist dummy] Charlie McCarthy, telling your story phrase by phrase, testifying for the witness, and asking him to agree").

§ 8.2(F) The Final Planning Steps for Cross–Examination

As Figure 8–1 indicates, there are three additional steps in cross-examination planning. We shall discuss those steps in greater detail in Chapter 10, but we shall touch on them now to help you prepare for the Trial Technique exercise for this chapter.

After drafting the questions for all the items of evidence you decide to elicit on cross, you must tentatively sequence the cross-examination. As we shall see in Chapter 10, in many cases, you will not only want to elicit some impeaching facts from the witness; you will also want to go after some admissions supporting your theory of the case. You usually seek those admissions before questioning the witness about the impeaching facts. Once you begin the impeachment, the witness may take offense and be less cooperative. If you want to elicit helpful admissions, you should ordinarily do so early in the cross-examination.

Although you can tentatively sequence the cross-examination before trial, you must be flexible enough to revise the cross-examination on the spot in light of the direct testimony. For some reason, the direct examiner may fail to have the witness testify to the fact that is most damaging to your case. The failure dictates a change in strategy; even if you have spent hours planning the cross of that witness, you may want to forego cross altogether. When you cross, the direct examiner will have the right to redirect; and by the time for redirect examination, the direct examiner may realize her oversight. Or the witness may deviate from his deposition testimony to a greater extent than you anticipated. The witness's deviation might force you to spend more time on prior inconsistent statement impeachment. You have to adapt to the direct testimony actually given in court.

Lastly, be conscious of your own demeanor. Suppose that you intend to spend the initial phase of the cross eliciting favorable admissions from the witness. A "snarling," "openly contemptuous" demeanor would backfire. Turow, *Crossing the Star,* 14 LITIGATION 40, 42 (Fall 1987). You should be friendly and low-key during this phase—in essentially the same fashion in which you conduct the direct examination of your own witnesses. The friendlier you are, the more cooperative the witness may be. Be genuinely courteous and considerate; "[t]he jury has a nose for phony friendliness." S. HAMLIN, WHAT MAKES JURIES LISTEN 244 (1985). However, when you shift to impeachment, you ought to change your demeanor and adopt a sterner attitude. During the impeachment phase of the cross-examination, the witness will probably resent your questions. You should adopt a stronger, more dominant demeanor to maintain control of the witness during the impeachment stage.

§ 8.3   SAMPLE LINE OF FOUNDATIONAL QUESTIONS

You are the defense attorney in *People v. Scott.* The prosecutor's witness list indicates that Richard Rogers will appear as a prosecution witness. The prosecution has given you a discovery packet. The packet includes the grand jury transcript and a copy of the plea bargain that Rogers has entered into with the prosecution. Rogers testified at the grand jury before striking the bargain. At the grand jury, Rogers testified that he left Scott's room at midnight and that he, Rogers, knew nothing about the attack on Williams.

You begin planning your cross-examination of Rogers. You decide to cross both to elicit favorable facts and to impeach. You will use the early phase of the cross of Rogers to corroborate Scott's testimony about how dark the hallway is. Then you will shift to impeachment. At the outset of the impeachment, you intend to use the grand jury transcript as a source of prior inconsistent statements. You plan to close by questioning Rogers about the plea bargain.

Having made those decisions, you use Figure 8–3 to plot out the cross. We shall focus on planning the use of the grand jury transcript. As we saw in § 8.2, the use of the transcript will require a prior inconsistent statement foundation satisfying Rule 613. Scott's attorney makes an appropriate entry in the column for required foundations. The next planning step is dissecting that foundation into the essential preliminary facts. Those facts are the circumstances surrounding the statement, notably the date, place, addressee, and tenor. Scott's attorney realizes that to make the impeachment effective, she should stress that Rogers testified under oath at the grand jury. She wants the jury to realize that a solemn oath is meaningless to Rogers. For that reason, she notes "OATH" as her last column entry. She is now ready to begin drafting her questions.

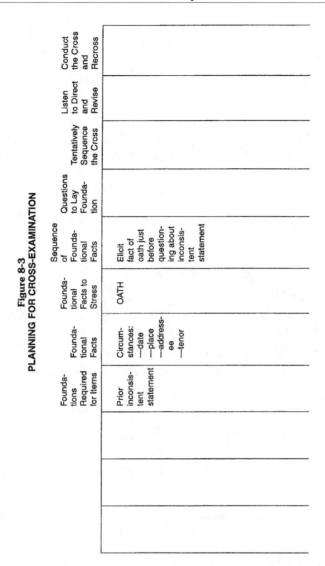

Figure 8-3
PLANNING FOR CROSS-EXAMINATION

Foundations Required for Items	Foundational Facts	Foundational Facts to Stress	Sequence of Foundational Facts	Questions to Lay Foundation	Tentatively Sequence the Cross	Listen to Direct and Revise	Conduct the Cross and Recross
Prior inconsistent statement	Circumstances: —date —place —addressee —tenor	OATH	Elicit fact of oath just before questioning about inconsistent statement				

For purposes of this sample cross-examination, assume that on direct examination, Rogers testified that on the morning of January 19, 19YR–1, he stayed in Scott's room until approximately 1:30 a.m. At that time, he and Scott decided to go out and buy more liquor. He further testifies that just as they stepped into the hallway, they saw Williams exiting the elevator. He finally testifies that on the spur of the moment, they decided to attack Williams.

During the early phase of the cross-examination, Scott's attorney forces Rogers to corroborate Scott's anticipated testimony about how dark the hallway is. The attorney now begins the use of the grand jury transcript. Initially, Scott's attorney will have Rogers briefly restate his direct testimony—he attempts to "lock" Rogers into that testimony—to help the jury realize the flat contradiction between that testimony and the grand jury statements she will next elicit.[4] Figure 8–4 is a set of notes for this part of the cross-examination.

Q Mr. Rogers, I've asked some questions about the hallway at the hotel. Now I'd like to ask you some questions about what happened on the morning of January 19, 19YR–1.

A You can just shoot your questions.

Q I want to make sure that I understand your testimony on direct examination. Was it your testimony that you stayed in Mr. Scott's room until about 1:30 that morning?

A Yeah.

Q Then, according to your direct testimony, the two of you stepped out into the hallway. Correct?

A Right.

Q And then you saw Mr. Williams. Right?

A Right again.

Q And was it your testimony that right then the two of you decided to beat up Mr. Williams?

A That's exactly what we did.

Q Mr. Rogers, this is your second visit to this court building. Isn't it?

A Yeah.

Q You were here once before. Correct?

A Right.

Q You came here on the afternoon of June 13, 19YR. Correct?

A Yeah.

Q That afternoon you went to the third floor and testified before our local grand jury. Isn't that true?

A That's right.

Q Mr. Trott, the prosecutor who's here in court today, was there then. Wasn't he?

A Yeah.

Q Wasn't he the attorney who questioned you that day before the grand jury?

A That's how I remember it.

Q And you testified before the grand jurors—about 20 citizens like the jurors here today—that afternoon. Right?

A Yeah.

---

4. For a detailed discussion of the mechanics of prior inconsistent statement impeachment, see Howerton, *CAPSTAR and* *The Kid: Impeaching with a Prior Statement,* 14 LITIGATION 21 (Fall 1987).

Q Before you testified, you took an oath. Didn't you?

A Yeah.

Q Like the oath you took today before your direct testimony?

A Uhm uhm.

Q Would you speak up please? The court reporter has to get all your answers. You took an oath that day. Yes or no?

A Yeah. I took an oath.

Q You swore to tell those grand jurors the truth. Right?

A Right.

Q The whole truth?

A Yeah.

Q Nothing but the truth?

A Yeah.

Q So help you God?

A Right.

Q During that grand jury hearing, didn't you say that you left Mr. Scott's room before midnight?

A Yeah.

Q Didn't you tell the grand jurors that you had nothing to do with the attack on Mr. Williams?

A That's what I said.

Q Didn't you also tell them that you had no idea where Mr. Scott was at 1:30 that morning?

A I'm not sure. I may have.

Q Your Honor, I request that this be marked Defense Exhibit C for identification.

J It will be so marked.

Q Your Honor, please let the record reflect that I am showing the exhibit, specifically page 124, to opposing counsel.

J It will so reflect.

Q Permission to approach the witness?

J Granted.

Q Mr. Rogers, I now hand you what has been marked Defense Exhibit C for identification. Please look at the cover page and this last page. (The defense attorney shows Rogers the title page and the page containing the reporter's signature and notarial seal.) What is this?

A It appears to be a record of what went on at the grand jury.

Q I'd like you to turn to page 124.

A Yeah.

Q Now I'd like you to read silently to yourself lines 10–17 on that page.

A O.K.

Q Does reading those lines refresh your memory of what you said at the grand jury?

A Yeah.

Q All right. Isn't it true that you told the jurors that you had "absolutely no idea" of where Mr. Scott was at 1:30 that morning?

A That's what I said then.

Q That's what you said on the afternoon of June 13. Correct?

A Yes.

Q (Scott's attorney now shifts to the last stage of the cross.) On June 13, you were facing charges for the same attack on Mr. Williams. Weren't you?

A Right.

Q And on June 13, you hadn't as yet entered into a deal—a plea bargain—with the prosecutor's office. Had you?

A No.

Q But isn't it true that you entered into a deal with the prosecutor on June 15 later the very same week?

A Yeah.

Q Two days later. Right?

A Yeah.

Q Now I'd like to ask you a few questions about that deal.

§ 8.4 ANOTHER SAMPLE LINE OF IMPEACHING QUESTIONS

Modernly, especially in civil cases, the most commonly used impeachment technique is proof that the witness made an inconsistent statement before trial at a deposition. Some passages in § 8.3 illustrate that technique. However, mastery of the technique is so important and many students find it so difficult to develop that mastery that we are devoting this entire section to a more detailed dissection of the mechanics of the technique. The mechanics of the technique can be reduced to a mnemonic, CLPR:

Figure 8-4

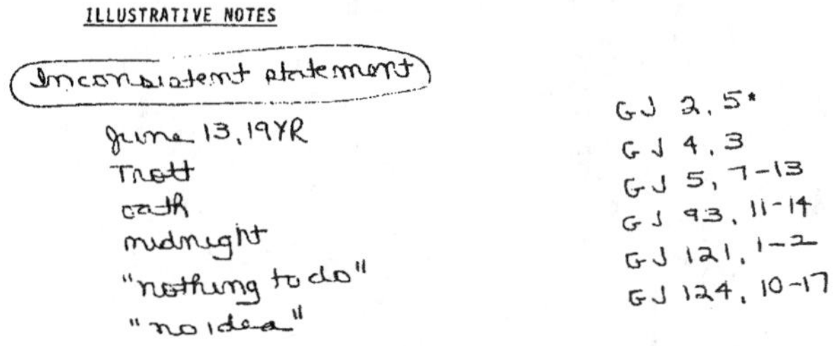

<u>ILLUSTRATIVE NOTES</u>

Inconsistent statement

June 13, 19YR
Trott
oath
midnight
"nothing to do"
"no idea"

GJ 2, 5*
GJ 4, 3
GJ 5, 7-13
GJ 93, 11-14
GJ 121, 1-2
GJ 124, 10-17

* These references indicate the page and lines in the grand jury transcript
where the defense attorney can find these statements. If Rogers denies or is
evasive, the defense attorney can turn immediately to these passages.

C—Commit the witness to the prior, inconsistent trial testimony.

L—Review the litany of facts accrediting the earlier pretrial statement—the facts suggesting that that statement is likely to be true.

P—Use present recollection refreshed to revive the witness's memory if the witness claims to be unable to remember the earlier pretrial statement.

R—Read the earlier pretrial statement into evidence if the witness refuses to acknowledge the earlier statement.

Figure 8–5 demonstrates the sequence of the mechanics. The remaining pages of this section discuss each step of the mechanics in greater depth.

THE INITIAL PHASE: LOCKING THE WITNESS INTO THE INCONSISTENT TESTIMONY (C—COMMIT)

Unless you commit the witness to the inconsistent testimony, the witness may attempt to weasel out of the inconsistency. In most cases, you can simply ask:

Q I want to make certain that I understand your testimony, Ms. Freeman. Your testimony now is that when you looked into the hallway, you couldn't tell how close the three men were to each other. Is that correct?

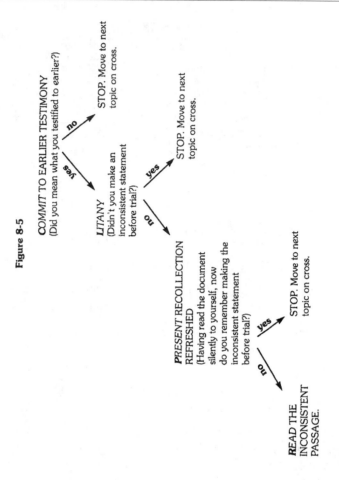

Figure 8-5

Suppose that you have surprise impeachment obtained during informal pretrial discovery. For example, Ms. Freeman made the statement that the three figures were "right on top of each other" in a letter to a friend, and she probably does not realize that you have a copy of the letter. In that event, you may want to ask the question several times. Each time you ask the question, the phrasing will come closer to the exact wording of the letter to her friend. The direct examiner may object that your questions are cumulative or "asked and answered." If so, request a sidebar conference and explain your purpose to the judge. The judge has discretion to permit you to proceed in order to expose possible perjury. The Federal Rules do not codify any prohibition against repetitive questioning. Rather, the matter is entrusted to the judge's discretionary control over the form of the question under Rule 611(a). You have a legitimate reason to be repetitive; it will help you expose suspected perjury. The first time you ask the question, you might use this phrasing:

Q You could see how close the men were to each other. Couldn't you?

A few minutes later you could revisit the issue and ask:

Q Weren't the three men right next to each other?

Finally, you would reask the question and virtually quote the letter:

Q Isn't it true that the three men were right on top of each other?

(IF THE WITNESS CHANGES HER TESTIMONY AND GIVES YOU THE FAVORABLE ANSWER YOU WANT—THE THREE MEN WERE RIGHT ON TOP OF EACH OTHER—TERMINATE THE LINE OF QUESTIONING.)

———————

(IF THE WITNESS REFUSES TO CHANGE HER TESTIMONY, CONTINUE THE IMPEACHMENT. YOU MAY EITHER:

— IMMEDIATELY CONFRONT THE WITNESS DURING THE BALANCE OF THE CROSS–EXAMINATION, OR

— EXCUSE THE WITNESS SUBJECT TO RECALL AND LATER OFFER EXTRINSIC EVIDENCE OF THE INCONSISTENT STATEMENT.)

IMMEDIATE CONFRONTATION WITH THE WITNESS DURING CROSS–EXAMINATION (L—LITANY)

(Many attorneys prefer immediate confrontation with the witness. Other attorneys reserve this technique for fact situations in which the contradiction between the pretrial statement and the trial testimony is so clear that there is a strong inference of perjury. If you are going to accuse the witness of lying, out of simple fairness many jurors expect you to personally confront the witness with the accusation.)

(Under Federal Rule of Evidence 613, you may question the witness point blank about a prior inconsistent written statement without showing the writing to the witness.)

Q This fight occurred on January 19, 19YR–1. Correct?

Q Do you remember giving a deposition in this case on March 19th of that year?

Q That was only two months after the fight?

Q You came to my office in downtown Morena. Correct?

Q Mr. Ahrens, the attorney representing Mr. Scott, was there. Wasn't he?

Q And I was there to question you?

Q There was also a court reporter. Wasn't there?

Q And she administered an oath to you. Didn't she?

Q An oath to tell the truth—just like the one you took today?

Q And didn't I tell you that if you had any physical or mental problems that made it difficult for you to testify, you should speak up?

Q And didn't I also tell you that if any question was unclear in any way, you could just say so and I'd reword it to make it clearer?

Q And then you testified.

Q After the deposition, the court reporter typed up your answers and gave you a copy of the written answers. Didn't she?

Q And she told you that you could make any corrections you wanted to. Is that true?

Q But you didn't make any. Did you?

Q Now please think carefully. At the deposition, didn't I ask you how close the three men were to each other?

Q At that time, didn't you say that they were right on top of each other?

(IF THE WITNESS FULLY ADMITS THE PRETRIAL STATEMENT, TERMINATE THE LINE OF QUESTIONING.)

(IF THE WITNESS DENIES THE STATEMENT OR IS EVASIVE, CONTINUE.)

REFRESHING THE WITNESS'S RECOLLECTION OF THE DE-POSITION STATEMENT (P—PRESENT RECOLLECTION REVIVED)

Q Can you remember exactly what you said at your deposition?

Q Do you think it would help if you took a look at the written transcript of your answers at the deposition?

Q All right. Your Honor, I request that this be marked Plaintiff's Exhibit number three for identification.

Q Please let the record reflect that I am showing the exhibit to opposing counsel.

Q Permission to approach the witness.

Q Ms. Freeman, I now hand you what has been marked Plaintiff's Exhibit number three for identification. (When you hand it to her, show her the title page and the page bearing her signature.) What is it?

Q How do you recognize it?

Q Please read page 44, lines 12–19, silently to yourself.

Q Does that refresh your memory of what you said at the deposition?

Q Then let me ask the question again. At the deposition, didn't you say that the men were right on top of each other?

(IF THE WITNESS NOW FULLY ADMITS THE PRETRIAL STATEMENT, TERMINATE THE LINE OF QUESTIONING.)

(IF THE WITNESS STILL DENIES THE STATEMENT OR PERSISTS IN EVASION, CONTINUE.)

(R—READ THE TRANSCRIPT)

Q Very well, Ms. Freeman. Your Honor, I now offer page 44, lines 12–19, of the witness's deposition transcript into evidence. (Like any document offered for substantive purposes, the transcript poses authentication, best evidence, and hearsay issues). If the opposing attorney objects, be prepared to make the following arguments.

Authentication. The transcript should include the notary's signature and seal. They make the transcript self-authenticating under Federal Rule of Evidence 902.

Best Evidence. The transcript is unquestionably a "writing" within the meaning of that expression in Federal Rule 1001(1). However, the facts recited in the notary's certificate ought to qualify the transcript as an "original" under the broad definition of that term in Rule 1001(3).

Hearsay. The transcript represents double hearsay. The transcript itself is a hearsay statement by the notary/court reporter, and the quotation of the witness's statements represents a second layer of hearsay.

The first layer of hearsay falls within the official record hearsay exception codified in Federal Evidence Rule 803(8). The judge may judicially notice the legal duty of stenographers to prepare such transcripts; and if the transcript is fair on its face—seemingly complete without evident erasures, the appearance of the transcript gives rise to a permissive inference that the stenographer properly discharged the duty.

The second layer of hearsay falls within the special exemption codified in Evidence Rule 801(d)(1)(A). (That subdivision provides that an inconsistent statement is admissible as substantive evidence if it was made under oath during a deposition.)

Q Your Honor, I request permission to read page 44, lines 12–19, of Ms. Freeman's deposition transcript to the jury.

(If you do not want to immediately confront the witness on cross, just before the witness leaves the stand, ask that the judge excuse the witness subject to recall. Most courts construe Federal Rule of Evidence 613(b) as meaning that even when the attorney does not lay a foundation on cross-examination, the attorney may later introduce extrinsic evidence of a prior inconsistent statement by the witness if the witness is excused subject to recall. It is true that on its face, Rule 613(b) requires that "the opposite party" be "afforded an opportunity to interrogate the witness" about the alleged inconsistent statement. However, the rule does not specify that the opportunity must be afforded before the introduction of the inconsistent statement; and if the witness is excused subject to recall, the opposing party may later recall the witness to explain away or deny the alleged inconsistent statement.)

EXTRINSIC EVIDENCE OF THE WITNESS'S INCONSISTENT PRETRIAL STATEMENT (R—READ THE TRANSCRIPT)

(Many attorneys almost never use the witness's deposition transcript after the witness has left the stand. However, others prefer to introduce extrinsic evidence rather than immediate confrontation—especially when the attorney is merely attempting to prove innocent misrecollection rather than outright perjury. In that event, the jurors' sense of fairness does not demand that you directly confront the witness.

If you want to offer a lengthy excerpt from the deposition transcript, consider putting a colleague, clerk, or secretary on the witness stand to read the witness's answers at the deposition hearing. That method of reading the transcript is not only livelier; it also makes it easier for the jury to distinguish between your deposition questions and the deponent's answers.)

Q Your Honor, I request that this be marked Plaintiff's Exhibit number three for identification. (Some judges will allow you to dispense with a formal offer if the transcript is already part of the official Case file.)

Q Please let the record reflect that I am showing the exhibit to opposing counsel.

Q Your Honor, may we approach the bench?

Q Your Honor, as you can see, this is the transcript of the deposition of Ms. Freeman who testified earlier for the defense. At this time, I want to offer into evidence page 44, lines 12–19, of the transcript.

(If there is an objection, be prepared to make the authentication, best evidence, and hearsay arguments previously outlined.)

Q Thank you, your Honor. I now request permission to read these lines to the jury.

Q Your Honor, before I read these lines to the jury, would you please give the jury a brief explanation of what a "deposition" is? I think that that would help the jury understand the significance of what they're about to hear.

Remember that in many cases, the prior inconsistent statement takes the form of an omission to mention a particular fact earlier. McElhaney, *Impeachment by Omission*, 14 LITIGATION 45 (Fall 1987). In that event, you must modify the Litany stage of the foundation. Assume, for example, that at trial, a police officer purports to remember an inculpatory fact which is mentioned nowhere in the official arrest report which she prepared. During the foundational questioning, the defense attorney would force the officer to concede that:

— at the police academy, she received formal training in the preparation of arrest reports;

— that training emphasized that an arrest report must be "complete;"

— at the time of the incident in question, it was obvious that this was a serious crime;

— the officer realized that this investigation might culminate in a trial; and

— the officer also realized that the arrest report might be needed as evidence at trial; and

— the arrest report in question contains a large number of details.

Straus, *The Most Powerful Impeachment Tool: Impeachment With Prior Inconsistent Statements,* THE PRACTICAL PROSECUTOR: SPECIAL CROSS–EXAM ISSUE 35 (2002).

Or suppose that at a civil trial, an expert purports to remember a fact which was not mentioned at his pretrial deposition. At the deposition, an experienced questioner would have posed a "vacuum cleaner" question to the witness: Are there "any other facts" supporting the opinion, or are there "any other reasons" for the opinion? The modified litany will suggest to the jury that the witness's sudden memory of the previously omitted fact is suspiciously convenient.

§ 8.5 ETHICAL QUESTIONS

In some cases, the bad faith of a cross-examiner is obvious. May a cross-examiner ask Rogers about "your prior convictions" while peering at an official looking document, and when Rogers denies any convictions simply put the document back in the examiner's briefcase? Or suppose that a prosecutor, cross-examining Scott, "accidentally" drops a lengthy "rap sheet" on the floor? In one case, while the civil defense counsel was cross-examining the plaintiff about prior criminal convictions, the counsel dramatically dropped a lengthy computer printout in front of the jury. Did the jury assume that was the plaintiff's "rap sheet"? The Court of Appeals was concerned with "not only the conscious impropriety of counsel here that we find troubling, but also the nature of the information counsel improperly intended to convey to the jury." The jury found for defendants in this civil rights suits against police. The Eighth Circuit Court of Appeals reversed and remanded for a new trial. *Sanders-El v. Wencewicz,* 987 F.2d 483 (8th Cir.1993) (the impression conveyed was that plaintiff was a hardened criminal with a long history of arrests; the display discussed in this paragraph was referred to by the court as the "computer printout fiasco").

In other cases, the question of good faith is more complex. Assume that before trial, Scott's attorney forms the suspicion that Rogers made several false statements on his 19YR–1 federal income tax return. The false statements have not as yet led to either formal charges or a conviction. However, she has heard from another defense attorney that Rogers was arrested and then released by the federal authorities for income tax evasion. She is trying to decide whether to cross-examine Rogers about the falsities.

Initially, suppose that El Dorado had adopted a statute identical to California Evidence Code § 787: "Subject to Section 788 (governing conviction impeachment), evidence of specific instances of his conduct relevant only as tending to prove a trait of his character is inadmissible to attack or support the credibility of a witness." Early in the trial, it becomes clear to Scott's attorney that the prosecutor does not know El Dorado Evidence law well. In the face of El Dorado Evidence Code § 787, may she question Rogers about the false statements on his income tax return? Turn back to § 7.4 in the last chapter and reread Model Rule of Professional Conduct 3.4.

Assume alternatively that El Dorado had adopted Federal Rule of Evidence 608(b)(1): "Specific instances of the conduct of a witness, for the purpose of attacking or supporting the witness' credibility, other than conviction of crime as provided in rule 609, may not be proved by extrinsic evidence. They may, however, in the discretion of the court, if probative of truthfulness or untruthfulness, be inquired into on cross-examination of the witness ... concerning the witness' character for truthfulness or untruthfulness...."

There is general agreement that the cross-examiner may resort to this method of impeachment under Rule 608 only if she has a good faith basis in fact. Tanford, *Keeping Cross–Examination Under Control,* 18 AM.J.TRIAL ADVOC. 245, 256 (1994); Annot., *Right to Impeach Witness in Criminal Case by Inquiry or Evidence as to Witness' Criminal Activity Not Having Resulted in Arrest or Charge–Modern State Cases,* 24 A.L.R.4th 333, 346–48 (1983). Does the information the attorney relies on have to be independently admissible? Will the attorney be presenting any of that information to the jury? In our hypothetical, there does not appear to be any pertinent hearsay exception for the other defense attorney's statement to Scott's attorney. Is it enough that Rogers was arrested for income tax fraud? Before questioning Rogers about the alleged fraud, must Scott's attorney inquire further about the incident? *See generally* Graham, *Impeachment-Contradiction; Partiality; Prior Acts of Misconduct; Character; Religious Beliefs,* 21 CRIM.L.BULL. 495, 500–04 (1985).

§ 8.6 TRIAL TECHNIQUE EXERCISES

You will conduct a cross-examination. Your instructor will announce any maximum or minimum length requirements for the cross. *Again, before drafting your line of questions, you should consult at least one of the specialized tests listed in § 7.2(E) of the previous chapter.* The designated opposing counsel may object and conduct any necessary voir dire examination in support of the objection. The instructor may also indicate that the opposing counsel should be prepared to conduct a redirect examination, following up on the cross-examination.

Case file A–1. You will conduct a cross-examination of Dr. Maples. With one exception, assume that on direct examination, he testified consistently with his declaration. The exception is that on direct examination, he stated that he probably spent at least ten minutes talking to Mr. Alexander about Mr. Alexander's symptoms. You must use Dr. Maples' declaration as a prior inconsistent statement.

Case file A–2. You will conduct a cross-examination of Officer Martinez. Assume that on direct examination, he testified consistently with his statement and investigation report. However, he added that at the end of her statement, Ms. Barnes said, "I knew the honest way would have been to pay for them."

Case file A–3. You will conduct a cross-examination of Mr. Jacobs. Assume that on direct examination, he testified consistently with his statement. You must attempt to impeach him with the material stated in the last paragraph of his statement. Before drafting your line of questions, read Federal Rules of Evidence 608–09.

Case file A–4. You will conduct a cross-examination of Mr. Thomas. Assume that on direct examination, he testified consistently with his statement. You will attempt to impeach him with the material stated in the last paragraph of his statement. Before drafting your line of questions, read Federal Rules of Evidence 608–09.

Case file A–5. You will conduct a cross-examination of Officer Krause. Assume that on direct examination, he testified consistently with his statement. On cross-examination, you will attempt to impeach his competency as an investigator. You may elicit such incidents as his failure to preserve the cigarette butt, misplacing the photograph of the defendant, and omitting the "wise remark" from the PD 100.

Case file A–6. You will conduct a cross-examination of Mr. Havens. With two exceptions, on direct examination he testified consistently with his pretrial affidavit. The exceptions are these: On direct examination, Mr. Havens testified that when Pappas picked up the "come-along" on the afternoon of February 2, he, Havens, saw a liquor bottle in Pappas' truck. In addition, Havens testified Pappas not only had the liquor bottle in his truck; Havens also saw Pappas "take a swig" from the bottle before Pappas drove off with the "come-along." You must use Havens' affidavit as the source of the prior inconsistent statements.

Case file A–7. You will conduct a cross-examination of Mr. Seymour. Assume that on direct examination, he testified consistently with his pretrial statement. On cross-examination, you could attempt to impeach him with evidence of: his past convictions, his drug addiction, and his pending charges. Choose two of these three impeaching items and attempt to elicit those facts during the cross-examination. In addition, be prepared to explain to the class why you decided against using the third item of possible impeachment.

Case file A–8. You will conduct a cross-examination of Robert Green. You will attempt to impeach him on the basis of bias. In addition, to the extent permissible under Article VI of the Federal Rule of Evidence, you will explore the material described in the last paragraph of Green's statement. Consider Federal Rules of Evidence 608(b) as well as Rules 404(a), 405, 608(a), and 609. Remember that Rules 608(a), 608(b), and 609 set out alternative impeachment techniques; even if the facts do not trigger one technique, you can resort to another technique.

Case file A–9. You will conduct a cross-examination of Bonnie Blair. You will attempt to impeach her for bias. In addition, you will question her about any conduct that you believe is provable under Federal Rule of Evidence 608(b).

Case file A–10. You will conduct a cross-examination of Rebecca Winters. You will attempt to use her letter to the editor to impeach her.

Chapter 9

THE MACROCOSM OF DIRECT–EXAMINATION: ORGANIZING THE CASE–IN–CHIEF—USING THE THEORY AND THEME TO BRACKET YOUR CASE

— The Witness —

Reprinted by permission of Warner Books/New York from *The Law as Seen by Charles Bragg*. Copyright © 1983 by Charles Bragg.

Table of Sections

§ 9.1   INTRODUCTION

In Chapter 7, we analyzed the microcosm of direct examination, drafting the set of questions needed to lay the foundation for a particular item of evidence. We used a worksheet to help plan the foundation. In Chapter 7, we left the last four columns of that worksheet blank. Figure 9–1 is a complete version of that worksheet. This chapter picks up where we left off in Chapter 7. We shall assume that we have formulated all the questions to lay the necessary foundations, and we shall now complete the process of planning your affirmative case, principally the case-in-chief.

§ 9.2   STRUCTURING THE DIRECT EXAMINATION OF EACH WITNESS

§ 9.2(A)   The Sequence of Topics on Direct

As Figure 9–1 indicates, the next step is structuring the direct examination of each witness. In effect, each item of evidence is a building block, and the structure we now want to erect is the direct examination of a particular witness. We already know which items of evidence we want to introduce during the direct examination. The question that naturally arises is the proper order for presenting those items during the witness's direct testimony. Although there are several points of agreement among veteran trial attorneys, there is also a major point of dispute.

Points of Agreement

When you are ready to present a witness at trial, stand and announce that "As the plaintiff's (People's) (defense's) next witness, we call _____." After the witness is sworn, it is customary that the first question should be: "Please state your full name and spell your last name for the record." Then ask the witness to state his or her current address. *But see* Siemer, *The Heart of a Trial: Direct Examination*, 28 TRIAL 48, 49 (Feb. 1992) ("Some lawyers start with a cold, formal opening like 'State your name for the record.' This fails to establish rapport. 'Tell us your name' or 'Let's begin with your name and address' is much better"). In some jurisdictions, the judge or clerk puts these questions to the witness.

The next point of agreement is that after the witness identifies herself, the direct examiner should elicit some facts about the witness's personal background.

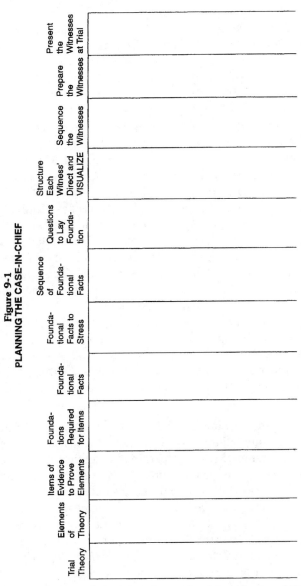

Figure 9-1
PLANNING THE CASE-IN-CHIEF

Do not rush to the testimony about the historical merits. You want to give the witness stature in the jurors' eyes. Without violating the character evidence rules, you can elicit neutral background facts that create a favorable impression of the witness. *United States v. Masino,* 275 F.2d 129, 133 (2d Cir.1960) ("What a [witness] is permitted to say about himself by way of introduction"); *United States v. Blackwell,* 853 F.2d 86 (2d Cir.1988) (on direct examination, the defendant may testify that he has no prior arrests without placing his character in issue); *Wilson v. Vermont Castings,* 977 F.Supp. 691, 699 (M.D.Pa.1997)("Information about a party's or a witness's background, job and education is certainly appropriate and admissible in every action. Juries cannot make assessment of credibility in a vacuum. Such information gives background on the witness and a point of reference in assessing that individual's credibility...."). This process is sometimes termed "accrediting the witness." Siemer, *The Heart of a Trial: Direct Examination,* 28 TRIAL 48, 49 (Feb. 1992). In the opening statement, you spent a short time describing the client's background. In a similar fashion, you should generally have each of your witnesses say a few words about their background.[1] For example, you might have a witness testify that: He grew up in Morena and has lived there his entire life; he went to work for a company right after high school and has been with the company for 15 years; and he is married with three children. The character evidence rules prohibit you from saying that this witness is "a stable, responsible family man"; but by carefully marshalling those seemingly neutral facts, you can give the jury precisely that impression. That impression will help the jurors conclude that the witness is worthy of their belief. Moreover, by covering the witness's background early in the direct, you relax the witness and put the witness at ease. The topic the witness knows best is his own background. By covering that topic first, you allow the witness to prove to himself that he can testify effectively. After gaining that confidence, the witness can testify more effectively about the historical merits. Finally, if you stress the characteristics in the witness's background in common with some or all of the jurors, it will be easier for the jurors to identify with the witness. At this point in the trial you should know something about the jurors' backgrounds. Capitalize on that knowledge.

The last point of consensus is that the direct examiner needs a proper exit—a concluding question that is objection proof. There is nothing worse than ending on a sustained objection. You want to ensure that the last question is proper substantively and in form. Some attorneys preface the questioning about the last point by announcing, "Now I'd like to ask you one last question." However, that technique is dangerous; the phrasing signals the opponent that you are about to end and may make the opponent even more alert to any possible objections. Siemer, *The Heart of a Trial: Direct Examination,* 28 TRIAL 48, 50 (Feb. 1992). Furthermore, the witness may give an unexpected response, necessitating one or more followup questions.

---

1. An exception obtains when you have called the person as a hostile witness under   Federal Rule of Evidence 611(c).

The Point of Dispute

The disagreement among trial attorneys relates to the optimal sequence for covering the historical merits during the witness's testimony.

One school of thought is that after eliciting the witness's background, you should ordinarily cover the witness's testimony about the merits in strict, chronological order. "After all, chronology is the order in which things happened[, and chronology] implies a sense of cause and effect." McElhaney, *Organizing Direct Examination,* 76 A.B.A.J. 92, 94 (Mar. 1990). The advantage of this approach is that in many cases, chronological order is the easiest for the jury to follow. However, a simple hypothetical will illustrate some of the weaknesses of this approach.

Suppose that the case is a prosecution for driving while under the influence (DWI). The witness is the arresting officer. The officer administered three tests to the arrestee. The arrestee flunked the first two tests but passed the last. If the prosecutor elicits the officer's testimony in unimaginative, chronological sequence, the direct examination will end with the testimony least helpful to the prosecution, namely, the defendant passed one of the tests. The end of the direct examination is a naturally emphatic position, and the prosecutor hardly wants to stress the test that the defendant passed.

The emerging school of thought is that the witness's testimony about the merits ought to be organized topically rather than chronologically. Professor Hegland has written:

> Corbin never said that you had to begin at the beginning. Neither did Williston. So why do beginners almost invariably begin there and flail away until they eventually reach the bloody end? The problem with this approach is that it's boring, confusing, and totally without pizzazz. Unless you are calling the witness to establish only one rather specific fact—"I served process on the defendant" or "I saw the defendant commit an impeachable offense"—realize that seldom is it best to present the testimony chronologically. Breaking from chronology allows you to organize the testimony around the points you wish to make. The point is this: you are to sculpt the testimony, not simply to present it. If clarity is increased by chronological presentation, use it. If not, you are free to use a different approach. [I]f the witness is to testify to many points, remember that the jury will best recall the first and the last. Points in the middle tend to be overlooked.

K. HEGLAND, TRIAL AND PRACTICE SKILLS 8–10 (1978).

The decisive question in the case may be whether the jury should draw a particular inference from the circumstantial evidence. A strictly chronological order might "scatter" the key circumstances throughout the witness's direct. Moore, *Inferential Streams: The Articulation and Illustration of the Trial Advocate's Evidentiary Intuitions,* 34 U.C.L.A.

L.REV. 611, 615 (1987). In contrast, topical organization allows the direct examiner to "juxtapose" the circumstances pointing to the critical inference *(id.)* and place the cluster of circumstances in an emphatic position.

Consider, for instance, the direct testimony of Peter Williams. You have chosen the theme of "so close for so long." His testimony supporting that theme belongs in the emphatic position at the end of his direct examination. Positioning the testimony there will necessitate deviating from chronological order. You may have him testify in the following order: his relationship with Scott before the attack, the attack itself, the developments after the attack (meeting with Officer Taylor and going to the hospital), and finally the facts indicating the reliability of his identification of Scott. If your judgment is correct that identity is the pivotal issue in the case and that the "so close for so long" theme represents your best hope for prevailing on that issue, the testimony underpinning the theme belongs at the end of the direct examination. Touch upon the attack earlier in the direct, but then circle back to that topic at the end of the direct and elaborate on the testimony supporting the "so close for so long" theme.

Or suppose that you are conducting the direct testimony of Robert Scott. Many seasoned criminal defense attorneys make it a routine practice to elicit their client's "unequivocal" denial of guilt just after the client's personal background and before the client's detailed version of the pertinent historical events. Jackson, *Defendants in Criminal Cases as Witnesses at Trial,* 14 AM.J.TRIAL ADVOC. 59, 73–74 (1990). Again, this practice represents something of a deviation from strict chronological order. However, these attorneys believe that it is critical for the defendant to look the jury in the eye "early in the examination" and forcefully assert innocence. *Id.* at 73.

§ 9.2(B) Ensuring that the Direct Testimony Is Visually Appealing

At this juncture, you have sequenced all the individual items of evidence that you plan on presenting during the witness's direct examination. You should review the planned direct testimony to ensure that overall, the direct examination will appeal to the jury visually.

Some learning psychologists estimate that we gather 85% of our data about the external world through the sense of sight and only 10% through hearing. Perlman, *Preparation and Presentation of Medical Proof,* 2 TRIAL DIPL. J. at 18 (Spr. 1979). They also estimate that the respective long-term retention rates are 20% of what we hear, 30% of what we see, and 50% of what we both hear and see. Briggs, *Real and Demonstrative Evidence* 4 (unpublished article on file with the National College of District Attorneys, Columbia, South Carolina). Imprinting in long-term memory is critical. You do not merely want to momentarily impress the jury when the testimony is presented in open court; much more importantly, you want the testimony to be remembered and influence the jurors when it matters—hours, days, or weeks later when the jurors vote. The moral is clear; if you want the jurors to understand the testimony in the short term and remember it in the long run, you should make the testimony of key witnesses visually appealing.

There are numerous ways of enhancing the visual appeal of direct testimony. You can, for example, integrate blow-ups of vital documents or commercially produced illustrations into the testimony. Your law library may include THE CIBA COLLECTION OF MEDICAL ILLUSTRATIONS or MEDICAL ATLAS FOR ATTORNEYS. These texts include anatomical diagrams that you can duplicate for courtroom use. Of course, you need not use an expensive, commercial chart. A simple cross diagram of an intersection can markedly improve a jury's comprehension of testimony about a traffic accident. Moreover, you can use the witness's body and your body as props during direct examination. Assume that Peter Williams is the witness. You want the jury to understand how close Williams was to his attackers. During his testimony, you could ask Williams to stand and position your body as close to him as his attackers were. Start out a good distance from Williams. Approach Williams in small steps, and have him repeatedly say that the attackers were "even closer." It is one thing for Williams to say that the two men were "only inches away." It is much more dramatic if the jury sees you standing virtually on top of Williams.[2] Modern technology gives the direct examiner a wide range of choice. Today the possibilities include such techniques as PowerPoint (D. SIEMER, F. ROTHSCHILD, E. STEIN & S. SOLOMON, POWERPOINT FOR LITIGATORS (2000)), magnetic boards (Bernstein, *Magnetic Board Exhibits*, LAWYERS WEEKLY USA, Sep. 17, 2001, at p. B9), multimedia systems (Lassiter, *Multimedia Trial Presentation Systems Win Cases*, NAT'L L.J., Oct. 10, 1994, at p. C10), video laserdisc, CD–ROM, 3D computer animations, paintbox animations, and visual presenters such as ELMO. Hout & de Bodo, *Technologies for Courtroom Presentation,* 7 THE PRACT.LITIGATOR 61 (July 1996).

In truth, it would be better to state more broadly that the direct examiner should ensure that the testimony has sensory appeal. Suppose, for example, that a plaintiff alleges that the cause of an accident was the defendant's drunken driving. The evidence establishes that the defendant consumed three glasses of Jack Daniels shortly before the accident. During the direct examination of the bartender, the trial judge might permit the direct examiner to have the bartender pour three glasses of Jack Daniels to help the jury appreciate how much liquor the defendant consumed. Doing so would not only enhance the visual appeal of the direct testimony; "[o]nce ... the smell of Jack Daniels [has] permeated

---

2. Remember that if you decide to use a chart or to conduct an in-court demonstration or exhibition, you must make the record for appeal. When a witness places a mark on a diagram to indicate her position, direct the witness to make the mark distinctive: "Please indicate your position on the chart with a capital P." Or when the witness is indicating a distance, complete the record to ensure that the appellate court will understand the testimony: "Your Honor, please let the record reflect that the distance the witness has indicated is approximately six inches."

the courtroom," the jurors may be more inclined to find that the defendant was intoxicated. Dodd, *Innovative Techniques: Parlor Tricks for the Courtroom,* 26 TRIAL 38, 40 (Apr. 1990).

§ 9.3 DETERMINING THE SEQUENCE OF THE WITNESSES

In the last section, we used the building blocks of individual items of evidence to construct a witness's direct examination. Now we must erect a larger structure, that is, the organization of the entire case-in-chief. The task is essentially one of determining the proper sequence for calling the witnesses. As in the case of the most effective order for organizing the individual witness's testimony, the subject of the optimal sequence for witnesses has produced two schools of thought.

Predictably, one school of thought is that you should almost always call the witnesses in chronological order. Suppose, for example, that the case is a prosecution. There are three witnesses available to the government: the accomplice who allegedly helped the defendant plan the crime, the victim of the crime, and the officer who later arrested the defendant. A proponent of this school would call the witnesses in that order. The accomplice knows what happened before the crime, the victim witnessed the crime itself, and the officer can testify about what happened after the crime. In the *Scott* case, the prosecution's order might be Rogers followed by Williams and lastly Taylor.

The weaknesses of this approach are obvious. To begin with, by slavishly following chronological sequence, the prosecutor might begin the case on a sour note. The accomplice may have an even longer criminal record than the defendant. Calling the accomplice first would violate the principle of primacy formulated by Lund in the 1920s. Parker, *Applied Psychology in Trial Practice,* 7 DEF.L.J. 33, 35, 37 (1960). That psychological principle is that the jurors tend to have the longest memory of whatever they hear first. In addition, if the prosecutor follows chronological order, the case-in-chief may end weakly—as T.S. Eliot wrote, "[n]ot with a bang but a whimper." *The Hollow Men.* The officer may have little critical testimony to give. If, as in the Scott case, the pivotal issue is identification, the victim's testimony should be highlighted at the end of the case. Closing with the officer violates the principle of recency. Colley, *Principles of Direct Examination,* 2 TRIAL DIPL.J. 13, 15 (Spr. 1979). According to that principle, it is easiest for the jurors to remember what they hear last. The prosecutor wants to make it easy for the jurors to remember the victim's testimony showing that the identification was reliable.

The second school of thought argues that the case-in-chief ought to be structured to capitalize on these principles of primacy and recency. This school of thought is sometimes referred to as the "sandwich" theory: You begin with a strong witness and end with a strong witness. Of course, there is an obvious definitional problem: What do we mean by the expression, a "strong" witness?

Perhaps the majority of attorneys who subscribe to this school of thought would say that a strong opening witness is the most dramatic witness. For instance, in medical malpractice cases, many plaintiffs' attorneys make it a practice to call the defendant doctor as the first witness in the plaintiff's case-in-chief. They reason that the jurors will be attentive during the direct confrontation between the defendant and the plaintiff's attorney. Similarly, many litigators of this persuasion believe that the best ending witness is the most sympathetic witness. In personal injury practice, the plaintiff's final witness is often the profoundly injured plaintiff. The obvious extent of the witness's injuries presumably generates jury sympathy. In the prosecution of Wayne Williams for the Atlanta child killings years ago, the defense concluded its case-in-chief by calling the defendant's mother. She had little to say about the historical merits of the case, but the defense hoped that she would generate sympathy for the defendant.

Although the authors tend to agree that the case-in-chief should be designed to exploit the principles of primacy and recency, we suggest a different definition of "strong witness." We submit that the ideal opening witness is the best theory witness, the witness who can give the jury the best overview of your theory of the case. In a commercial lawsuit, one of the corporate vice-presidents may know something about the formation of the contract, its breach, and your client's efforts to mitigate damages. It makes good sense to call that witness first. She can set the stage for all the other witnesses by giving the jury a conceptual framework for understanding the significance of the other witnesses' testimony. We likewise submit that the preferable closing witness is the best theme witness. The theme embodies your strongest argument for winning the central issue in the case. The best theme witness should therefore be your final witness. You want that witness's testimony ringing in the jurors' ears when they retire into the deliberation room. In effect, you can bracket your case-in-chief with the best theory and theme witnesses.

The sequence of witnesses between the first and last witnesses ought to make the testimony as clear as possible to the jury. As a general proposition, if you intend to call expert witnesses to base an opinion on facts established by lay witnesses, the lay witnesses ought to precede the expert to the stand:

> [T]he jurors will find it easier to follow an expert's testimony if they have first heard the underlying facts from lay witnesses. An expert's testimony can seem awkward ... if the expert must assume too many facts that have not already been presented to the jury.

Suplee & Woodruff, *Direct Examination of Experts,* 33 THE PRACT. LAW. 53, 54–55 (Dec. 1987). Similarly, in a civil action, you probably want to present the liability witnesses before calling the damages witnesses; that order is a natural, logical sequence.

After you have determined the order of your witnesses and exhibits, consider preparing an exhibit book for the jury. McElhaney, *Seeing the*

Facts, 78 A.B.A.J. 102, 103 (Dec. 1992). In some cases, you may be able to pre-mark and pre-admit all or virtually all of your exhibits before trial begins. When you can, assembling the exhibits in a notebook will make it easier for the jury to follow the testimony and understand the various exhibits. *Id.; United States v. Rana,* 944 F.2d 123 (3d Cir.1991).

We must add one final note at this point. Make a note to remind yourself that after you have presented all the evidence in your case-in-chief, you should stand to announce that "The plaintiff (People) (defense) rests." Do not mumble the announcement. Make the announcement with a confident tone in your voice—as if to say to the jury that you know that you have proven your case.

§ 9.4 PREPARING THE WITNESSES FOR TRIAL

As Figure 9–1 indicates, the next planning stage is readying all the witnesses for trial. Berg, *Preparing Witnesses,* 13 LITIGATION 13 (Wint. 1987). The direct trial testimony is only the tip of the iceberg. You may need to invest hours readying a witness for a few minutes of testimony. The central event at this stage is your pretrial conference with each witness. However, you may want or need to do other things before and after the conference itself.

To expedite your personal conference with the witness, before the conference you may decide to give the witness a preview of your guidance for direct and cross-examination. Some attorneys send the witness a letter, summarizing the guidance, before the conference.[3] Some large firms have a videotape, stating and illustrating the guidance, that the witness can view before the conference. There are now CD–ROM products which serve the same purpose. One such product, "Be Prepared! for Your Deposition," not only reviews the mechanics and techniques of testifying; the product even includes tests which the user can take after reviewing each segment to ensure that he or she understands the mechanics and techniques. Bayer & Cohen, *Preparing Your Client for Deposition,* LEGAL TIMES, June 3, 1996, at p. 28. Or the attorney may schedule a meeting between the witness and a paralegal or communications expert before the attorney confers directly with the witness.

The conference itself often consists of two parts. One part is a review of the chronology. You review the key facts and events with the witness. It is especially important to do so when you want the witness to

---

3. The letter typically advises the witness to: face the examiner when the question is asked; listen intently to the question; pause to think before answering; give the minimum, truthful, complete answer that the question calls for; be cautious in estimating speed, distance, or time; and address the answer to the jury. The letter often contains general advice as to what the witness should do in the event of an objection to the question. *See generally* Bracken, *Direct Examination: Lawyers Need to Prepare Both Witnesses and Themselves,* 23 TRIAL 63 (June 1987); Herman, *Direct Examination of Lay Witnesses,* 24 TRIAL 77 (Feb. 1988); McElhaney, *Horse-Shedding the Witness: Techniques for Witness Preparation,* 23 TRIAL 80 (Oct. 1987); Salman, *A Trial Testimony Guide for Witnesses,* 43 THE PRACT. LAWYER 15 (Dec. 1997). You should also give your client guidance about his or her behavior while they are off the witness stand but in the jurors' view. Ware, *What Your Client Does Off the Stand Matters, Too,* 35 THE PRACT. LAWYER 25 (Mar. 1989).

testify in narrative form at trial. As Chapter 7 pointed out, the judge will usually preclude a narrative if the witness testifies in disorganized fashion or makes repeated references to inadmissible matter. You must carefully review the facts with the witness to ensure that the witness (1) has a good enough grasp of the chronology to testify narratively and (2) understands which references such as hearsay and improper opinion to avoid unless he or she is asked point blank about that matter.

During the review of the chronology, it was formerly customary to show the witness all the documents that relate to the witness's testimony: the deposition transcript, the witness's statements, etc. However, modernly, there is a pitfall that you must be aware of. Federal Rule of Evidence 612 governs the practice of refreshing recollection. The rule states that even when the witness uses a document pretrial to refresh her recollection, the judge has discretion to order you to divulge the document to the opposition at trial. There is substantial authority that Rule 612 overrides both the work product and attorney-client privileges. Robinson, *Duet or Duel: Federal Rule of Evidence 612 and the Work Product Doctrine Codified in Civil Procedure Rule 26(b)(3),* 69 U.CIN.L.REV. 197, 198, 200, 244 (2000); Applegate, *Preparing for Rule 612,* 19 LITIG. 17 (Spr. 1993); Belcuore, *Use It and Lose It—Privileged Documents, Preparing Witnesses, and Rule 612 of the Federal Rules of Evidence,* 31 FED.BAR NEWS & J. 171 (1984). Hence, by showing a privileged document to a witness during this pretrial conference, you run the risk of waiving the privilege as to that document at trial. If your jurisdiction has already opted for this interpretation of Rule 612 and the document contains damaging information, you probably should not hand it to the witness during the conference. You may want to orally review the facts with the witness or prepare your own summary of the chronology for the witness to read—a—summary which you would be willing to divulge to the opposing attorney. McGanney & Seidel, *Rule 26(b)(3): Protecting Work Product,* 7 LITIGATION 24, 27 (Spr. 1981); Hamilton, *Taking and Defending Depositions,* 11 LITIGATION 20, (Wint. 1985).

The optional second part of the conference is a practice session. You may want to conduct a mock direct and cross-examination. With an experienced witness such as an expert, a practice may be unnecessary. However, if the witness has never testified before, a practice may be vital not only to polish the witness's testimony but also to allay the witness's fear about testifying. Although attorneys differ over this question, many litigators believe that in the typical case, it is probably unwise to tell the witness exactly the questions you will ask on direct examination at trial. If the cross-examiner inquires at trial, it may not only be embarrassing for the witness to admit that she knew the exact questions you would ask; worse still, the admission might lead the jury to conclude that the testimony is a rehearsed script rather than the truth. You do not want the direct testimony to appear "contrived." Purver, Young & Davis, *Winning the Trial Through Direct Examination,* 93 CASE & COMMENT 10, 13–14 (Jan.-Feb. 1988).

Even if you decide against practicing the direct examination, you should probably subject the witness to a mock cross-examination. It is best, though, to have another attorney conduct the cross; if you conduct the cross and the cross is too "effective," the experience may impair your working relationship with the witness.

In major litigation, some attorneys routinely videotape the practice sessions and later review them with the witness. It is particularly advisable to do so when the witness has marked, negative mannerisms. The witness may not even realize that she has the mannerism. Viewing the tape and discussing the mannerism can be an effective method of helping the witness overcome the problem.

Even after the conference, you may want to meet with the witness again before trial. Suppose, for example, that even at the end of the conference, you sense that the witness is still terrified at the prospect of testifying. You might suggest that at some later date you meet the witness at the courthouse. You can show the witness the courtroom and perhaps observe some testimony with the witness. If the courtroom is vacant, put the witness on the stand and allow him to get the perspective and "feel" of the witness stand. Ask him some questions while he is seated there. Doing so may help calm the witness down. As we have frequently emphasized, the jury is likely to attach a good deal of weight to the witness's demeanor on the stand. A terrified witness rarely displays positive, confident demeanor during his testimony.

§ 9.5 PRESENTING THE WITNESSES AT TRIAL

The last column on the worksheet is presenting the witnesses at trial. There are a number of aspects of the presentation.

§ 9.5(A) The Style of Presentation

Seat your client next to you at the counsel table. However, seat other witnesses in the spectator section of the courtroom. If non-party witnesses sit at the counsel table, their presence at the table can give the jurors the impression that the witnesses have become biased in favor of your side of the case. The non-party witnesses should not appear to be part of your "team".

When you want to call a witness, stand and announce firmly in a calm, loud voice, "As our next witness, we call...." Some attorneys state that they "would like to call ...," but that phrasing is weak.

In general, your demeanor toward your own witnesses should be friendly. Friendly demeanor puts the witness at ease. Further, it shows the jury that you like the witness. You are setting a psychological example for the jurors; if you want them to like the witness—to like the witness well enough to make an act of faith in his testimony—you ought to demonstrate that you regard the witness as a decent human being. This nonverbal conduct is especially important for defense attorneys representing defendants charged with serious crimes. The jury believes that you know the truth; you have presumably had the benefit of privileged attorney-client conversations with your client, and you know whether your client is guilty. The rules of ethics prohibit you from voicing your opinion of the merits of the case to the jury during trial. However, the jurors are sensitive to any clues of your opinion. If you act distant toward your own client, the jurors may infer that you believe him guilty; your demeanor can condemn your client to a conviction. Sound interested in the witness's answer. Again, you are setting a psychological example for the jury. You cannot expect the jurors to be interested in the witness's testimony unless you act as if you are. You must at least "affect genuine curiosity...." S. HAMLIN, WHAT MAKES JURIES LISTEN 187 (1985).

In the courtroom, you must be conscious of your positioning as well as your demeanor. Figure 9–2 illustrates the layout of a typical American courtroom. This courtroom happens to be left-handed—both the jury box and the witness stand are on the left side of the courtroom. Most seasoned trial attorneys recommend that the direct examiner stand at the end of the jury box. There are several reasons for the recommendation. One is that the suggested position helps ensure that the jurors can hear the witness; you are as far from the witness as any juror, and when you can hear the witness the odds are that all the jurors can likewise. Next, that position directs the witness's line of sight toward the jury. You want the witness to talk to the jury. If you have a good witness, one with evident intelligence and sincerity, you want to fade into the woodwork while the witness takes center stage. Finally, from that position, you can inconspicuously read the jurors' faces to determine whether they are registering comprehension or confusion. It is critical to do so when you are presenting expert testimony or demonstrative evidence. Ciresi, *The Case Can be Won During Discovery*, NAT'L L.J., Feb. 8, 1993 (the witness "would call up certain segments of the prepared animation, as he presented his testimony. 'I'd stand back and watch the jury,' Mr. Ciresi says, 'If I thought they didn't understand, I'd step in to ask questions' "). If several jurors' faces reflect confusion, you will want to back the witness up and force the witness to clarify the testimony.

Figure 9-2 *

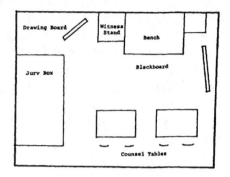

However, a number of communications specialists favor different positioning. For instance, Sonya Hamlin writes:

> Jurors can ... be distracted because they cannot see ... the interaction between the lawyer and the witness. Then, too, it is ... difficult to ask the jury to focus totally on one person, someone who may not be very eloquent or charismatic. It is more interesting to watch a dialogue between two people....

S. HAMLIN, WHAT MAKES JURIES LISTEN 203 (1985). According to this view, the attorney should stand in the jury's sight near the middle of the jury box. Regional styles of trial advocacy differ, and many successful litigators in the South and Southwest follow this practice.

In some jurisdictions, particularly federal courts, you may not stand at the end or near the middle of the jury box. The judge might insist that you question from a lectern in the middle of the courtroom, or there may be a court rule to that effect. Even when the judge does so, you can still verbally remind the witness to look at the jury while testifying to the key facts. For example, you can preface a question with: "Now, please tell the ladies and gentlemen of the jury...." At the same time you say that, gesture toward the jury box.

Be conscious of the pace of your question-and-answer dialogue with the witness. You want to create the impression of a natural conversation with the witness. If you begin your next question too quickly after the answer, the jury may suspect that the witness's direct examination has been carefully scripted by the attorney. If you allow too long a pause before posing the next question, you may lose the jury's concentration. It will also help to create the desired impression if, in phrasing your later questions, you include the same words or expressions that the witness used in earlier answers. Rather than employing the phrasing you planned to use, let the wording of the witness's prior answers shape the phrasing of your questions. Herman, *How to Master Direct Examination,*

31 TRIAL 70, 74 (Apr. 1995). You want the question-answer exchange to sound like a spontaneous dialogue.

In addition, punctuate the direct examination to help the jury appreciate the organization. Suppose, for example, that Peter Williams has just testified about the extent of his injuries. You want to conclude the direct examination on another topic, namely, the quality of his opportunity to observe his attackers. Pause for a moment after Williams' last answer about his injuries. A pause can be a powerful rhetorical device. If you briefly fall silent but nevertheless appear intense, the nonverbal signal to the jury is that you are about to broach an important topic. Take a step or two, and change a parameter of your voice such as volume. Then announce the shift in topics: "Mr. Williams, for the last few minutes you've been telling us about the injuries you suffered in the attack. Now I'd like to ask you a few questions about your opportunity to see the men who attacked you." The announcement acts as a headline for the ensuing story. McElhaney, *Emphasis on Direct,* 73 A.B.A.J. 116 (Nov. 1, 1987). The announcement serves essentially the same purpose as the topic sentence in a paragraph. McElhaney, *The Paragraph Method,* 75 A.B.A.J. 96 (Apr. 1989). Of course, the only thing you have a right to do during direct examination is ask questions, sentences ending with question marks. However, most judges understand how difficult it is for jurors to follow oral testimony. For that reason, they will tolerate a few declarative sentences to smooth the transition from one topic to another during direct examination.

Finally, emphasize key testimony. Pause after a critical answer to let the answer sink in with the jury. Again, silence can be dramatic. For additional stress, you can artfully repeat the testimony. On the one hand, if you merely reiterate key testimony in declarative sentences, the opposing attorney will probably object. On the other hand, there is an effective technique for underscoring key testimony. Michael Ficaro, the Chief of the Trial Division of the Illinois Attorney General's Office, gives this example:

Q What did the defendant say next?

A He told the girl and boy to "kiss their last kiss."

Q When he told them to "kiss their last kiss," what did they do?

A They began begging for their lives.

Q As the boy and girl begged for their lives, what did the defendant do?

A He shot them both—twice in the head.

Ficaro, *Direct Examination* (unpublished manuscript on file with the National College of District Attorneys, Columbia, South Carolina). This technique is sometimes called "looping back." The essence of the technique is incorporating part of the favorable answer in a phrase or dependent clause at the beginning of the next question. The technique allows you to avoid declarative sentences likely to draw objections. However, even this technique must be used sparingly. If you overuse the technique, it will become transparent; the opposing counsel will see through the technique and begin objecting to your repetition of the answers. *See also* McElhaney, *Say It Again,* 77 A.B.A.J. 7679 (July 1991) ("It . . . helps to introduce the question with something like, 'Let me see if I understand this . . .?' [D]o not overwork clarification questions. If you ask more than one every five or 10 minutes, you will be called to task").

As you proceed through the examination of each witness, keep track of the exhibits you offer. You or your assistant should make appropriate entries on an exhibit list like Figure 9–3 when you mark the exhibit for identification and when the judge finally rules on its admissibility.

§ 9.5(B) Readiness to Correct "Errors" by the Witness or Judge

If you have planned correctly and properly prepared your witness, the direct examination *should* go smoothly. However, as Robert Burns wrote, "The best laid schemes o'mice and men gang aft a-gley. . . ."

Assume that in response to your question, the witness says that he or she does not understand what you are asking about. A nervous witness might respond in that fashion even if before trial you told the witness exactly what you would be asking about.

> Don't try to save your own face at the cost of your case. Even if your question was a model of simplicity and elegance, if the witness doesn't understand it, don't blame him–blame yourself. "I'm sorry. I didn't put that very well. Let me rephrase that question."

McElhaney, *Helping the Witness,* 79 A.B.A.J. 85, 86 (Aug. 1993).

Suppose that the witness forgets or misstates an important fact. In light of that possibility, you must be ready to refresh the witness's recollection. When you stand to begin the direct examination, you should have not only your own notes for the direct examination; you also ought to have all the documents that you might need to resort to in case you have to revive the witness's memory under Federal Rule of Evidence 612. For example, you should take with you the witness's written statements and deposition transcripts. If you leave them at the counsel table and the need to refresh the witness's memory arises, you will waste time by walking back to the table to find the required memory joggers.

Even if the witness does not omit a fact, the witness's answer may be slightly different than the response you anticipated. Adapt the wording of the next question to the phrasing of the witness's answer. The answer should serve as a natural "springboard" for the next question. S. HAMLIN, WHAT MAKES JURIES LISTEN 206 (1985).

Figure 9-3

MASTER LIST OF EXHIBITS

Exhibit #	Exhibit Description	Admitted	Denied

Or suppose that the judge erroneously sustains an objection to one of your questions and blocks an important line of inquiry. You must be ready to make a proper offer of proof or avowal. Federal Rule of Evidence 103(a)(2) states:

> Error may not be predicated upon a ruling which ... excludes evidence unless ... [i]n case the ruling is one excluding evidence, the substance of the evidence was made known to the court by offer or was apparent from the context within which questions were asked.

Assume, for example, that Scott's attorney is questioning Officer Taylor to elicit the fact that the only bloodstains on Scott's shoes were located on the soles of the shoes. When Scott's attorney asks, "Where were the stains on the shoes?", Williams' attorney objects that the question is irrelevant. The judge immediately sustains the objection. Scott's attorney ought to request permission to approach sidebar. At sidebar, Scott's attorney should make an offer of proof: "Your Honor, I believe that if the witness is permitted to answer this question, she will say that the only stains were on the soles. I am offering this evidence to show that Mr. Scott did not participate in the attack on the plaintiff. The location of the stains on only the soles is logically relevant because it is more consistent with our theory that Mr. Scott picked up the blood when he walked in the hallway rather than with the plaintiff's theory that the shoes were used to kick the plaintiff." The offer thus predicts the answer, states the attorney's reason for asking the question, and explains why the objection is unsound. The direct examiner ordinarily must make an offer to preserve the issue for appeal. More importantly, in many cases the lightbulb goes on at sidebar; the offer persuades the judge to reconsider the ruling and permit the question. The judge may not know the facts of the case well. The judge might not have appreciated the logical relevance of your line of inquiry until you explained its relevance in the offer of proof.

If the opposing attorney objects to your question and the judge overrules the objection, in most cases you should reask the question after the judge's ruling. The witness or some of the jurors may have forgotten the precise wording of the question.

§ 9.5(C) Conducting Redirect Examination

In the last subsection, we saw that as a direct examiner, you must be prepared to adapt to any mistakes by the witness or judge. You must also be ready to adapt to the opposing counsel's cross-examination. The cross determines the content of your redirect. Although the direct examination can be planned well in advance, the redirect must be largely extemporaneous. The form rules that govern direct testimony also apply to redirect. Hence, just as you must avoid leading on direct, you should ask non-leading questions on redirect. However, some "judges are more lenient about leading on redirect examination.... They believe that leading, as long as it is not too blatant, helps things move more quickly." McElhaney, *Leading Questions*, 75 A.B.A.J. 104, 106 (Oct. 1989).

Substantively, the best use of redirect examination is to give the witness the opportunity to explain away seemingly impeaching facts elicited on cross. It is particularly important to conduct redirect examination when the cross-examiner cut off the witness's attempt to explain a seemingly impeaching fact. R. KLONOFF & P. COLBY, SPONSORSHIP STRATEGY: EVIDENTIARY TACTICS FOR WINNING JURY TRIALS 199 (1990). Ask the witness on redirect, "What were you trying to say when he (the cross-examiner) cut you off?" *Id.*

Many redirect examiners use the following three-step pattern: Initially, they refer the witness back to the impeaching fact; then they invite the witness to state a contrary inference; and finally they ask the witness to explain the reason for the contrary inference. In *Williams v. Scott,* during his cross-examination, Mr. Williams might be forced to admit that he drank three boilermakers just before the attack. A good cross-examiner would not argue with Williams and attempt to force him to admit he was too drunk to make a reliable identification; the cross-examiner would simply elicit the factual admission and wait until closing to explicitly draw the inference. Williams' attorney could attempt to blunt that inference on redirect:

Q Mr. Williams, a few minutes ago on cross-examination you told us that you had three drinks before the attack. Correct? (Step #1) (Although this question is leading, the judge usually permits the redirect examiner to modestly lead to refer back to the cross.)

A Yes.

Q After having those drinks, what condition were you in? (Step #2)

A I was still pretty in control and sober.

Q How can you explain that? (Step #3)

A Well, I'm not really proud of it, but I can hold my booze. I drink pretty regularly. I usually have two or three boilermakers just before I go on duty. I think it relaxes me and makes me a little sharper while I'm on duty at the desk. I take that number of drinks, and I can still handle all my job duties.

Save the most important redirect point for last. Redirect is the real end of the witness's direct examination. Hazel, *Direct Examination*, 6 LITIGATION 6, 9 (Fall 1987). Even if the formal direct examination had a powerful ending, a weak close for the redirect can ruin the overall impact of the witness's testimony.

As a matter of style, you should usually be very low key during redirect. If you are too intense, the jury may read your demeanor as a signal that you think that the cross-examination damaged your case. Act as if there are only a few minor points to be cleared up. Many attorneys conduct redirect examination while seated even though they always stand for direct examination.

In many cases, there is no recross after redirect. The redirect will be the final stage of the examination of the witness. If so, after the opposing attorney states that there will be no recross, the judge will ask whether the witness may be excused. In most cases, your response will be, "Your Honor, we have no further questions, and the witness may be excused." In a few cases, you may want to call the witness back for further testimony later in the case. In that event, ask that the witness be excused "subject to recall."

§ 9.5(D) Presenting a Rebuttal or Surrebuttal

You are not limited to your case-in-chief. The plaintiff or prosecutor may call witnesses in rebuttal after the defense case-in-chief. Similarly, the defense may call witnesses in surrebuttal after the plaintiff's or prosecutor's rebuttal.

Even when you have a right to present witnesses in rebuttal or surrebuttal, think carefully before exercising that right. By this juncture in the trial, the judge's and jurors' attention and patience may be exhausted; insisting on the last word can be counterproductive.

However, there are countervailing considerations. If you have a single rebuttal witness who will give brief, powerful testimony, it may be advisable to put that witness on the stand. Just as redirect is the real end of a witness's testimony, the rebuttal can serve as the real end for your case. Ending on a high note may leave the jury with a favorable impression of the strength of your case. Moreover, in some cases, the jurors expect rebuttal or surrebuttal witnesses. Suppose, for instance, that the concluding opposing witness accuses your client of misconduct. In effect, the opposition has thrown down a gauntlet. At your next opportunity, call your client to the stand to deny the accusation. If the client does so with a demeanor suggesting righteous indignation, the client's demeanor can make the difference between victory and defeat.

§ 9.6 SAMPLE DIRECT EXAMINATION

You are the prosecutor in the *Scott* case. You are planning Peter Williams' direct examination. You are using Figure 9–5 at the end of this chapter as a worksheet and Figure 9–4 as your courtroom notes. You decide to structure Williams' direct examination in this fashion:

I. Williams' Personal Background

II. The Historical Merits Organized Topically

    A. The physical setting of the attack

    B. The attack

    C. The initial tentative identification of Scott

    D. The in-court identification of Scott

    E. Ending on the testimony supporting the theme of "so close for so long"

To make the direct testimony visually appealing, you decide to use both exhibits and in-court demonstrations.

Figure 9-4

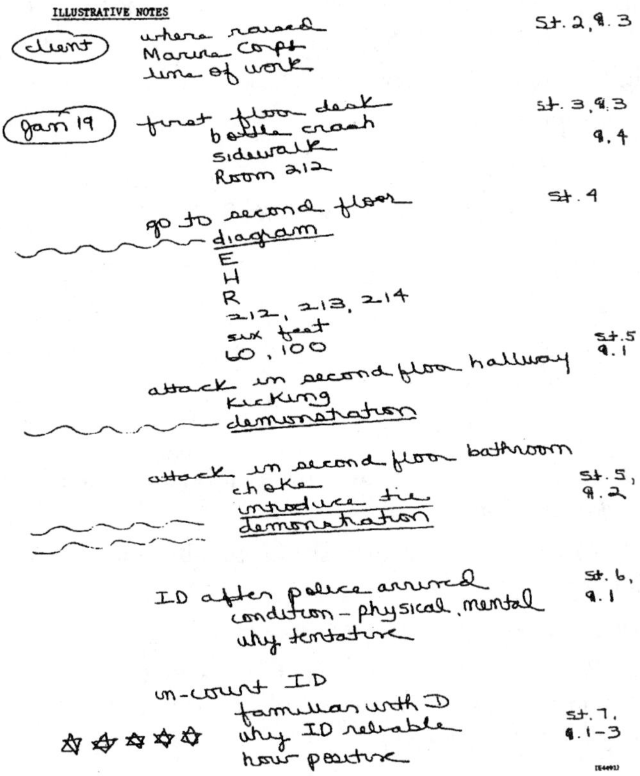

ILLUSTRATIVE NOTES

(client)   where raised   St. 2, 9.3
           Marine Corps
           line of work

(Jan 19)   first floor desk   St. 3, 9.3
           bottle crash   9.4
           sidewalk
           Room 212

           go to second floor   St. 4
           ───── diagram
               E
               H
               R
               212, 213, 214
               six feet
               60, 100
           attack in second floor hallway   St.5
               kicking   9.1
           ───── demonstration

           attack in second floor bathroom
               choke   St.5,
               introduce tie   9.2
           ───── demonstration

           ID after police arrived   St.6,
               condition – physical, mental   9.1
               why tentative

           in-court ID
               familiar with D
           ✡ ✡ ✡ ✡ ✡ why ID reliable   St.7,
               how positive   9.1–3

Q Please state your full name and spell your last name.

Q What is your current address?

(Personal Background)

Q Mr. Williams, how old are you?

Q Where were you born?

Q How long did you live there?

Q When did you leave South Bend?

Q Why did you leave?

Q Which armed force did you volunteer for?

Q How long did you serve on active duty with the Marines?

Q When did you leave the Marine Corps?

Q When did you move here to Morena?

Q What is your line of work?

Q How long have you worked as the desk clerk there?

Q Where is the hotel located?

Q Mr. Williams, now let me direct your attention to the evening of January 18 and the early morning of January 19, 19YR–1. Where were you then?

Q What, if anything, unusual happened?

Q What did you do after you saw the bottle broken on the sidewalk?

Q Which room was that?

Q How could you tell that it was room 212?

Q On January 19, who was the guest staying in room 212?

Q How do you know that?

Q What did you do after you saw the light on in room 212?

Q Where did you go?

(The Physical Setting of the Attack)

Q Your Honor, I request that this be marked People's Exhibit No. 3 for identification.

Q Please let the record reflect that I am showing the exhibit to the defense counsel.

Q Permission to approach the witness?

Q Mr. Williams, I'd like to set the scene for the rest of your testimony. I now hand you People's Exhibit No. 3 for identification. Can you recognize it?

Q What is it?

Q How can you tell that it is a diagram of the second floor of the hotel?

Q How many times have you been up on that floor?

Q How accurate is the diagram?

Q This line right here. What does it represent?

Q Please take this black marker and mark that line with a capital E for "elevator."[4]

Q Your Honor, please let the record reflect that Mr. Williams has complied with my request.

Q Where does the elevator go?

Q On the second floor what does the elevator open onto?

Q Please mark that with a capital H for "hallway."

Q What is this area over here on the chart?

Q Please mark that with a capital R for "restroom."

Q And what do these squares represent?

---

4. To ensure that the jurors will understand the chart during deliberations, some attorneys also direct the witness to add a legend at the bottom of the chart.

Q Please mark 212, 213, and 214 in those squares to show the room numbers.

Q Mr. Williams, how wide is the hallway marked H?

Q Please write "six feet" next to the H.

Q What lighting, if any, is there in the hallway?

Q Please take this red marker and mark the location of each 60 watt light with a "60."

Q What lighting, if any, is there in the restroom?

Q Please mark the location of each 100 watt light with a "100."

Q On the evening of January 18, how many of those lights—the lights in the hallway and restroom—were working?

Q Your Honor, I now offer People's Exhibit No. 3 for identification into evidence as People's Exhibit No. 3.

(The Attack)

Q Now, Mr. Williams, what happened when you stepped off the elevator onto the second floor?

Q How many men were there?

Q Where did the attack begin?

Q What were they using to attack you?

Q How did they kick you?

Q With her Honor's permission, would you please step from the stand, Mr. Williams, and show the jury how they kicked you?

Q Your Honor, please let the record reflect that Mr. Williams is raising his shoe approximately one and a half feet off the ground and then stomping straight down with his foot.

Q How many times did they kick you that way?

Q Thank you, Mr. Williams. You may return to your seat.

Q How long did the beating in the hallway last?

Q What happened next?

Q Where did they drag you?

Q How far did they have to drag you to get you to the restroom?

Q What, if anything, did they do to you after they dragged you into the restroom?

Q How long did the beating in the restroom last?

Q In the restroom, what did they use to attack you?

Q Your Honor, I request that this be marked People's Exhibit No. 4 for identification.

Q Please let the record reflect that I am showing the exhibit to opposing counsel.

Q Permission to approach the witness?

Q I now hand you People's Exhibit No. 4 for identification. Can you recognize it?

Q What is it?

Q How can you tell that it is your tie?

Q Your Honor, I now offer People's Exhibit No. 4 for identification into evidence as People's No. 4.

Q Mr. Williams, using the exhibit on my neck, please show the jury how the attackers used the tie to strangle you.

Q Your Honor, please let the record reflect that Mr. Williams wrapped the tie all the way around my neck, held one end in his right hand, had the other end in his left hand, and pulled in different directions.

Q What, if anything, did the men say to you during the attack in the restroom?

Q After they threatened to kill you, what happened next?

Q What did you do after they left?

(Initial Identification of Scott)

Q When did the police arrive?

Q How much time elapsed between the end of the beating and the arrival of the police?

Q What was the name of the officer?

Q What was your physical condition when she arrived?

Q What was your mental condition at that time?

Q What, if anything, did she ask you about your attackers?

Q What, if anything, did you say in answer to her question?

Q Why weren't you more definite then?

(In–Court Identification of Scott)

Q Mr. Williams, since the attack, you've had a chance to calm yourself and consider what happened. I want you to think very carefully before answering the next question. Who were the men who beat you on the morning of January 19 last year?

Q Before that night, how familiar were you with the defendant?

Q How many times had you seen him before the morning of January 19?

Q If you know, where is he now?

Q Where is he sitting in the courtroom?

Q Please describe him and his clothing.

Q Your Honor, please let the record reflect that Mr. Williams has identified the defendant.

(Testimony Supporting the Theme)

Q Mr. Williams, on the morning of January 19th, how long did the whole beating last?

Q How many minutes in total? Just give us a ballpark figure.

Q How good is your eyesight?

Q How well could you see in the hallway?

Q How well could you see in the restroom?

Q How does the lighting in the restroom compare to the lighting in this courtroom right now?

Q What, if anything, blocked your view of the men?

Q How close were you to those men?

Q Mr. Williams, I want you to assume that I was your attacker. I'm walking toward you now. I want you to tell me to stop when I'm as close to you as the defendant was that night.

Q This close?

Q This close?

Q How about this close?

Q This close?

Q Your Honor, please let the record reflect that Mr. Williams told me to stop when my face was approximately three inches from his face.

Q How positive are you that the defendant is one of the men who attacked you?

Q Thank you, Mr. Williams. No further questions at this time, Your Honor. Your witness.

§ 9.7   ETHICAL QUESTIONS

One of the thorniest problems of adversary ethics arises when you learn that your client contemplates perjury. On the one hand, you are the client's representative. As such, you owe your client a duty of loyalty; and disclosing your client's intent to the judge has all the appearance of an act of betrayal. Yet, on the other hand, as we saw in Chapter 1, one of the primary justifications for the adversary system is that it is a superior fact-finding mechanism. Permitting your client to present perjury flies in the face of that raison d'etre for the adversary system. Suppose that you represent Scott in the prosecution. During a pretrial conference with your client, Scott confides in you that he participated in the beating of Williams. However, by now, Scott has learned that Williams had been drinking and that his initial identification of Scott was uncertain. For those reasons, Scott is confident that he can "beat the rap" and insists on testifying.

A.B.A. Defense Function Standard 7.7(c) formerly prescribed the procedures the direct examiner was to follow when the direct examiner knew that the client contemplated perjury:

> The lawyer may identify the witness as the defendant and may ask appropriate questions of the defendant when it is believed that the defendant's answers will not be perjurious. As to matters for which it is believed the defendant will offer perjurious testimony, the lawyer should seek to avoid direct examination of the defendant in the conventional manner; instead, the lawyer should ask the defendant if he or she wishes to make any additional statement concerning the case to the trier or triers of fact.

This standard was withdrawn while the American Bar Association considered its new Model Rules of Professional Conduct. Model Rule 3.3(a)(4) now states that:

> A lawyer shall not knowingly ... offer evidence that the lawyer knows to be false. If a lawyer has offered material evidence and comes to know of its falsity, the lawyer shall take reasonable remedial measures.

How does Rule 3.3(a)(4) compare with Standard 7.7? *See* A.B.A. Formal Ethics Opinion 87–353 (Apr. 20, 1987), discussed in 41 Crim. L.Rep. (BNA) 1026, 2131 (May 13, 1987) and *Nix v. Whiteside,* 475 U.S. 157 (1986). Although Opinion 87–353 represents the official A.B.A. position, the courts are free to adopt a different approach. The former Chair of the A.B.A. Criminal Justice Section has urged the courts to continue to apply Standard 7.7(c). Lefstein, *Legal Ethics—Reflections on the Client Perjury Dilemma and* Nix v. Whiteside, 2 CRIM. JUST. 27 (Sum. 1986). The Delaware Supreme Court has opted to do so. *Shockley v. State,* 565 A.2d 1373, 1379–80 (Del.1989) ("Recently the ABA has eschewed the use of the narrative approach. Nevertheless, the narrative continues to be a commonly accepted method of dealing with client perjury"). Other courts concur with *Shockley. People v. Johnson,* 62 Cal.App.4th 608, 72 Cal.Rptr.2d 805, *cert. denied,* 525 U.S. 914 (1998); *People v. Gadson,* 19 Cal.App.4th 1700, 24 Cal.Rptr.2d 219, (1993).

Rule 3.3(a)(4) uses the expressions, "knowingly," "knows," and "know." The use of those expressions raises a difficult question of epistemology: When does the lawyer know that his client contemplates perjury? Standard 7.7 used an exacting test; under 7.7(a), the attorney knew only if "the defendant has admitted to defense counsel facts which establish guilt and counsel's independent investigation established that the admissions are true...." Is the knowledge standard for knowing receipt of stolen goods a helpful analogy? Even if the client does not admit guilt in so many words, might her nonverbal conduct be enough to convince the attorney that she is lying?

§ 9.8   TRIAL TECHNIQUE EXERCISES

You will conduct a direct examination. Your instructor will announce any maximum or minimum length requirements for the direct.

The designated opposing counsel may object and conduct any necessary voir dire in support of the objection. The instructor may also indicate that the opposing counsel should be prepared to conduct a cross-examination, following up on the direct.

Case file A–1. The witness is Mr. Alexander.

Case file A–2. The witness is Ms. Barnes.

Case file A–3. The witness is Ms. Crow.

Case file A–4. The witness is Ms. Valdez.

Case file A–5. The witness is Ms. Sandoval.

Case file A–6. The witness is Mr. Pappas.

Case file A–7. The witness is Mr. Williams.

Case file A–8. The witness is Ms. Lunda. *See People v. Hagan,* 145 Ill.2d 287, 164 Ill.Dec. 578, 583 N.E.2d 494 (1991).

Case file A–9. The witness is Mr. Trundale.

Case file A–10. The witness is Mr. Maxwell.

We want to reiterate a remark contained in 5.9 on the chapter on opening statement. Most of the case files contain little background information about your client. For purposes of this exercise, you should invent some background facts about your client. You should devote a minute or two at the beginning of the direct examination to develop your client's background. In fleshing out your client's background, remember the caveat in § 5.5(D) against overreaching the character evidence rules.

Before drafting your questions, it would be advisable to consult one of the specialized texts on evidentiary foundations mentioned in § 7.2(E).

Figure 9-5
PLANNING THE CASE-IN-CHIEF

Trial Theory	Elements of Theory	Items of Evidence to Prove Elements	Foundations Required for Items	Foundational Facts	Foundational Facts to Stress	Sequence of Foundational Facts	Questions to Lay Foundation	Structure Each Witness' Direct and VISUALIZE	Sequence the Witnesses	Prepare the Witnesses	Present the Witnesses at Trial
								Personal Background			
								Historical Merits Layout chart			
								Assault tie demo			
								Initial ID			
								In-court ID demo			

Chapter 10

THE MACROCOSM OF CROSS–EXAMINATION—USING THE OPPOSING WITNESSES TO SUPPORT YOUR THEORY AND THEME

Cross-Examination

Reprinted by permission of Warner Books/New York from *The Law as Seen by Charles Bragg*. Copyright © 1983 by Charles Bragg.

Table of Sections

§ 10.1   INTRODUCTION

In Chapter 8, we considered the microcosm of cross-examination, namely, the use of cross-examination to impeach a witness. This chapter takes a broader perspective and analyzes the entire process of planning and conducting a cross-examination. Chapter 8 used an abbreviated version of a planning worksheet. Figure 10–1 is the complete worksheet, and we shall use that worksheet to follow the sequence for planning and conducting a cross-examination and possible recross.

§ 10.2   PLANNING AND CONDUCTING A CROSS–EXAMINATION OR RECROSS

You are on the eve of trial. Discovery is complete. You may even have a list of the witnesses whom the opposing attorney intends to call. How do you plan the cross-examination of each witness?

§ 10.2(A)   Listing All the Facts the Witness Can Testify to

The initial step is listing all the facts that the opposing witness in question can testify to. You must review the entire work product of discovery to develop the list. At this step, litigation support companies and computer techniques can be of enormous utility. It can be time-consuming to manually correlate every potential witness with every fact they can testify to. However, the attorney can delegate this task to an outside company or an employee proficient in using litigation support computer equipment such as optical character readers (OCR).

§ 10.2(B)   Listing All the Facts that Evidence Law Will Permit the Witness to Testify to

Evidence law serves as a screen or filter at the next stage in planning. Evidence law may prohibit the witness from testifying to a fact relevant to the historical merits that the witness is perfectly willing to vouch for. For example, after reviewing the discovery, it might become clear that the opposing witness knows about many acts of misconduct committed by your client that are not mentioned in the pleadings. However, the character evidence rules set out in Federal Rules of Evidence 404–05 may bar offering those acts as evidence on the merits of the case. Likewise, Evidence law often limits your impeachment of the witness. In some states, the cross-examiner may question the witness about any prior conviction as a basis for impeachment. However, Federal Rule 609(a) permits the cross-examiner to use only two types of convictions. If the witness has suffered a conviction but it is not one of the two types of convictions listed in Rule 609(a), it would be improper to cross-examine the witness about it.

**Figure 10-1
PLANNING FOR CROSS-EXAMINATION**

Listing All Facts Witness Can Testify to	Listing All Admissible Facts	Predict Direct and Potential Cross	Cross At All?	If So, What Purposes?	Choose Items of Evidence	Foundations Required for Items	Foundational Facts	Foundational Facts to Stress	Sequence of Foundational Facts	Questions to Lay Foundation	Tentatively Sequence the Cross	Listen to Direct and Revise	Conduct the Cross and Recross

At the end of this step in analysis, you know all the facts that Evidence law will permit the witness to refer to on direct and cross at trial.

§ 10.2(C) Forecasting the Probable Direct and the Possible Cross

The next stage is forecasting the probable direct examination and the possible cross. In most cases, on the eve of trial, you will have a good sense of the opponent's theory of the case. When there has been thorough discovery, you and the opposing attorney have access to roughly the same factual database. Especially in civil actions, there are important clues to the opposition's theory—the focus of their depositions of your key witnesses, the content of their responses to requests for admission, and the stipulations they seek at the pretrial conference. Those developments are vital to helping you identify the opponent's theory. Admittedly, in predicting the probable direct examination, you are guessing; but it can be an informed, educated guess.

Federal Rule of Evidence 611(b) codifies the prevailing view that the scope of direct examination limits the scope of the cross. Once you have forecast the likely direct examination, you can therefore determine which facts may be elicited on cross-examination.

§ 10.2(D) Deciding Whether to Cross–Examine at All

The Potential Uses of Cross–Examination

In the prior step of analysis, you predicted the likely direct and the possible cross. That prediction puts you in a position to decide whether to cross-examine at all.

As a general proposition, you should not cross-examine unless you can *probably* attain one of the objectives of cross-examination. Chapter 8 addressed only one of those objectives. Suppose that on direct examination, the witness has given testimony that damaged your theory of the case. Effective impeachment of damaging testimony is one of the key objectives of cross-examination.

However, there are three other important objectives that you can pursue during cross. One is eliciting concessions on the historical merits that support your theory and theme. Assume that you are the plaintiff's attorney in *Williams v. Scott* and that you are cross-examining Ms. Freeman. She will probably concede that when she looked into the hallway, the three figures appeared to be "right on top of each other." That concession is helpful support for your theme of "so close for so long." Some attorneys refer to the practice of eliciting favorable admissions from an opposing witness as "hitchhiking." Baldwin, *Cross-Examination,* 17 TRIAL LAW. Q. 19, 20 (1986). Most prosecutors routinely devote the early phase of cross-examination to eliciting favorable testimony from defense witnesses. de la Garza, *Preparing Witnesses to Withstand Cross–Examinations,* 15 THE CHAMPION 41, 42 (Aug. 1991). Since pretrial discovery is limited in criminal cases, before trial the prosecution sometimes has relatively "sketchy information" about the crime. Especially in such cases, prosecutors use the initial stage of cross-examination to "fill in gaps" in their own case. In short, "tell your story by using their witnesses." Privett, *The Defense Must Make a Positive Statement,* NAT'L L.J., Feb. 8, 1993.

Another important cross-examination objective is using an opposing witness to rehabilitate the credibility of one of your witnesses. Suppose that during the cross-examination of Mr. Williams, Scott's attorney suggested that Williams told the ambulance driver that he, Williams, did not know who his two attackers were. Williams emphatically denies making such a statement. The cross-examination would amount to attempted impeachment by prior inconsistent statement. Ms. Freeman happened to be in the lobby when the ambulance came, and she was standing close enough to Mr. Williams to overhear his conversation with the attendant. Williams' attorney could elicit her testimony that although she was at most only three feet away from Williams at the time, she did not hear him tell the attendant that he could not recognize the attackers. Ms. Freeman's testimony would rehabilitate Williams' credibility by supporting his testimony that he never made the prior inconsistent statement. (This use of cross-examination explains why, during pretrial depositions and interviews of opposing witnesses, you must learn both what the witness knows and what she does *not* know.)

A final objective of cross-examination is putting the opposing witnesses at odds with each other, that is, using one opposing witness to impeach the other. Continue to assume that you are the plaintiff's attorney and further that on cross-examination, Scott insists that he had only one drink in his room before going to bed. Your pretrial interview with Ms. Freeman convinces you that she will testify that Scott had at least three drinks in her presence before she returned to her room. You could elicit that admission from her on cross-examination. Pitting the opposing witnesses at odds with each other allows you to argue during summation that the opposing witnesses "can't even agree among themselves." In criminal conspiracy cases, the prosecution sometimes calls several informants as witnesses. The informants often dislike each other, and the defense can frequently use one informant to impeach the other's credibility. In drug trafficking prosecutions in which several coconspirators testify for the government after entering into pretrial deals, one will sometimes testify that the other was high on drugs at the time of an event which the other testified about. In civil personal injury cases, the medical experts on the same side frequently disagree over some aspects of the plaintiff's condition. Moore, *Cross-Examining the Defense Expert,* 27 TRIAL 49 (May 1991). Likewise, in product liability cases, the safety expert for the defendant manufacturer can often be used by the plaintiff to attack the testimony of the safety expert for the defendant retailer.

Deciding Whether to Cross–Examine

You generally should not cross-examine unless you can probably attain one of the above objectives of cross-examination. There are grave dangers in conducting an exploratory cross-examination in the faint hope of eliciting a helpful admission. In many cases, the result is that the witness repeats and reaffirms the direct testimony—making it even more persuasive. In closing argument, the opposing counsel may point out that the witness "withstood" your cross-examination and "stuck to the same facts" that he had testified to on direct. Further, if you cross, the witness may blurt out another damaging fact during cross; or the direct examiner may elicit more damning facts on redirect. A "courtwise" opposing expert might deliberately hold back on direct examination in the hope that you will give him an opening on cross to emphatically add the damning fact. On direct examination by the prosecutor, a trace evidence expert might have mentioned only six points of similarity between the crime scene fiber sample and the carpet at the defendant's apartment but withheld the fact that there were four other points of similarity in the hope that an exploratory cross question will allow the expert to embarrass the defense counsel.

Given these dangers, most experienced attorneys recommend against fishing expeditions on cross-examination. Suppose, for instance, that in the *Scott* prosecution, the government calls the treating emergency room physician as a witness. The physician gives only a general description of Williams' injuries. The description tends to negate the possibility that Williams sustained the injuries by falling down a flight of stairs. You are willing to admit that Williams suffered the injuries in a fight. Your theory of the case is that although Williams was attacked, he has mistakenly identified your client as an assailant. There is no need to cross-examine the doctor. You might stand and state: "Thank you, Doctor. Your testimony has been very helpful. Your Honor, I see no need to detain the doctor any longer." The defense theory of the case effectively neutralizes the doctor's testimony. (Chapter 3 pointed out that in selecting a trial theory, one of the key factors to consider is the degree to which the theory allows you to neutralize otherwise damaging opposing testimony.) During closing argument, you can even integrate a snatch of the doctor's direct testimony into your review of the facts.

However, in one case, you should deviate from the norm and cross-examine even when it is unlikely that you can attain one of the objectives of cross-examination. As Chapter 8 pointed out, you are occasionally forced to trial even though you have little or no ammunition against key opposing witnesses. In that event, you may have to cross-examine even if the only thing you can do is conduct a fishing expedition. When the witness's testimony is devastating to your theory of the case, as a practical matter you must conduct some cross. Otherwise, the jurors will conclude that you implicitly concede the truth of the witness's testimony. *See* Weitz, *Cross-Examining the Expert at Trial*, 28 TRIAL 55 (Feb. 1992) ("If you decline to cross-examine, jurors may see this as a concession to the" opposition).

In some instances, when, the witness in question is an expert, you can conduct an "apparent" cross-examination. *See* McElhaney, *Phantom Cross–Examination*, 77 A.B.A.J. 102, 106 (Apr. 1991) ("One of the simplest ways to do a phantom cross-examination is to show what the witness does not know. For example, you can go through his deposition, picking out the questions he was unable to answer because of lack of information. Then the cross-examination is a laundry list of what the witness cannot say. And if he suddenly claims to know the answers, you have the deposition with which to impeach him"). That is, you can ask a series of questions designed to emphasize that the expert has no first-hand, personal knowledge of the relevant events. However, in other cases when the damning lay witness purports to have personal knowl-edge, you must resort to desperate tactics such as exploratory questions. You need to trust your own situational, "on the spot" judgment. If the jurors' demeanor convinces you that they believed every word of the direct and, if believed, the direct testimony virtually guarantees an adverse verdict, you need to either settle midtrial or launch a fishing expedition on cross.

With these exceptions, you ought to cross-examine only when, in your best professional judgment, you are *probably* going to achieve one of the four objectives of cross-examination: effectively impeaching damag-ing testimony, eliciting favorable admissions supporting your theory and theme, using an opposing witness to rehabilitate the credibility of one of your witnesses, and putting opposing witnesses at odds with each other. If you decide against questioning the witness, when the direct examiner tenders the witness to you simply thank the witness, turn to the judge, and state, "Your Honor, I see no need to question the witness. The witness may be excused." McElhaney, *Cross-Examination Choices,* 28 LITIGATION 57, 58 (Fall 2001).

§ 10.2(E) Choosing the Purposes to Pursue During Cross

Assume *arguendo* that you have decided to cross. The next question that arises is which purposes to pursue during the cross. Your case will fall into one of three categories.

In one category, there is only one goal to pursue on cross. You may discover, for instance, that the only purpose you can probably attain is impeaching the witness or eliciting facts supporting your theory. This is the simplest category; there is no choice to be made, and you should pursue that one purpose.

In the second category, there are multiple purposes to pursue; but all the purposes are consistent. Assume, for example, that you are Williams' attorney contemplating the cross-examination of Ms. Freeman. In the prior step of analysis, you conclude that in addition to impeaching her for bias, you can probably elicit some favorable admissions from her such as the concession that the men in the hallway were "right on top of each other." Should you pursue both objectives? The answer is Yes. There is a synergy between the bias impeachment and the favorable admissions. If she is biased, the impeachment is not only consistent with the favorable admissions; if anything, the bias would lead her to under-state the favorable facts. You can say so explicitly during summation. Bluntly tell the jury that if a biased opposing witness conceded that it was "dark, in all probability it was pitch black." You can simultaneously pursue the cross-examination objectives of eliciting favorable facts and impeaching the witness for bias.

The third category poses the most difficult problems for the cross-examiner: There are multiple purposes that could be pursued on cross-examination, but they are inconsistent. Change the last hypothetical in one respect. Assume that the available impeachment against Ms. Freeman was that she had limited perceptual ability; she has poor eyesight, and she forgot to put her glasses on before she looked out into the hallway. Evidence law would permit you to impeach on that basis while still attempting to elicit favorable admissions from her. However, the impeachment would undermine the value of her favorable admissions; if she has such poor eyesight, she may be mistaken in testifying that the three men were "right on top of each other." She may think that only because her poor vision causes her to see blurs rather than distinct images. It would be foolish to impeach her on that basis. "You do not want to impeach in a manner that will be at cross purposes with the rest of your case." Daniels, *Impeaching the Liar and the Fool,* 16 THE CHAMPION 6, 9 (Dec. 1992). Judge Goldstein counsels that eliciting favorable facts from an opposing witness is "the primary objective" of cross while impeachment is merely a "secondary" goal. Goldstein, *The Cardinal Principles of Cross–Examination,* in 1959 TRIAL LAWYER'S GUIDE 331, 338 (I. Goldstein ed.) One of the most successful trial attorneys of our time, Mr. Louis Nizer, usually stresses in closing that he has proven his case "out of the mouths of our very adversaries." *Trial Preparation: An Interview with Louis Nizer,* 2 TRIAL DIPL.J. 6, 11 (Spr. 1979). He can do so because he elicits as many favorable admissions as possible from opposing witnesses. That tactic is so effective that in most cases in which there are inconsistent purposes that you could pursue on cross, you should sacrifice impeachment and seek the concessions supporting your theory on the merits.

You ought to follow this general rule even when the result is a very short cross-examination. Do not be concerned that your planned cross will be relatively brief. "Cross-examination is . . . more impression than . . . information." McElhaney, *Mongo on the Loose: Following Primitive Instincts Can Lead to Traps in the Courtroom,* 81 A.B.A.J. 80, 82 (July 1995). A cross-examination need not be lengthy to be effective. Suppose that in the *Scott* prosecution, you represent Mr. Griffin, named as a codefendant with Scott and Rogers. The prosecution's theory is that Griffin was an accessory before the fact who helped Scott and Rogers plan an attack on Williams. Your theory is that your client Griffin merely knows Scott and Rogers; Griffin is otherwise completely innocent. The prosecution witness on the stand is a Mr. Phillips, a bartender who testifies on direct examination that he overheard Scott and Rogers talking about beating up Williams. Your entire cross-examination of Phillips might be:

Q Mr. Phillips, I have just a few questions to clarify your direct testimony. Now this meeting about beating up Mr. Williams occurred at the Buena Vista bar on the evening of January 14th. Is that correct?

A Yes.

Q The two people who were talking were the codefendants Scott and Rogers. Right?

A Yep.

Q Mr. Phillips, I want to introduce you to my client, Mr. Wayne Griffin.

A O.K.

Q I want you to think carefully, Mr. Phillips. Did Mr. Griffin say anything during that conversation at the Buena Vista bar?

A No.

Q Was he sitting next to the codefendants that night?

A No.

Q To the best of your knowledge, was he in the bar that night?

A No.

Q To the best of your knowledge, has he ever been in the bar?

A No.

Q Before you came to court today, had you ever seen Mr. Griffin face-to-face?

A No.

Q Thank you very much, Mr. Phillips. Your Honor, I have no further questions of this witness.

Even if you could impeach Phillips' memory or perceptual ability, it would be foolish to do so. His testimony is wonderful corroboration for the defense theory that Griffin did not help plan any attack on Williams. Griffin was nowhere in sight at the time of the conspiratorial meeting. It would be a grave mistake for the defense to attempt to undercut Phillips' credibility. Evidence law gives you the right to impeach Phillips, but you would be slitting your client's own throat by exercising that right.

There is, though, an important exception to that general proposition. Suppose that the opposing witness has given testimony that is highly damaging to your theme and that the only favorable admissions the witness could testify to would be helpful on virtually undisputed elements of your theory. These facts change the cost/benefit analysis. If your professional judgment is correct that the theme embodies your best argument for prevailing on the pivotal issue in the case, you must impeach the witness. In this situation, it is worth sacrificing the favorable admissions to attack the testimony damaging your theme.

§ 10.2(F) Choosing the Items of Evidence

Once you have selected the purposes to pursue on cross, you can choose the items of evidence for attaining those purposes. As in the case of choosing items of evidence for direct examination, you must make a quantitative and a qualitative judgment.

The Quantitative Judgment

As you review the list of facts you could elicit on cross-examination, you may find that the witness has made 17 prior inconsistent statements and has committed 20 acts of misconduct that could be used for impeachment. Should you use them all?

If the witness plays only a marginal role in the case, it is a mistake to pull out all the stops and attempt to elicit all the impeaching facts. If you did so, you might make the witness's testimony seem more important than it is. A lengthy cross-examination may serve to magnify the damaging impact of the testimony. The jurors might think that the direct testimony must have been harmful. Why else would you be spending so much time attacking the witness?

Even when the witness is a key witness for the other side, you should be selective. Professor Younger recommended that the cross-examiner strive to make no more than three telling points against the witness on cross-examination. Sometimes one point will suffice. The jury's decision whether to believe the witness usually turns on the overall impression left by the direct and cross. A cross-examination which quickly makes a handful of telling points is likely to create a better impression than a longer, more diffuse cross.

The Qualitative Judgment

If the cross-examiner must be selective, the next problem is a qualitative evaluation of the facts that potentially could be elicited on cross-examination.

Your choice of theme should help you choose the favorable facts on the historical merit to elicit on cross. Many of the favorable facts that the witness could testify to may relate to unimportant, virtually undisputed elements of your theory. However, a few of the concessions may lend support to your theme. Those are the helpful concessions that you ought to seek.

There are also guidelines for choosing among impeaching facts. How recent is the fact? The closer the fact is in point of time to the trial, the better insight the fact gives the jury to the witness's present credibility. If the fact is remote in point of time, the jury may resent dredging up "ancient history." How strong is the evidence connecting the witness to the impeaching fact? There may be sharp dispute whether the witness is the person who made the seemingly inconsistent statement or committed the fraudulent act. Impeachment is usually effective only when you have "the goods" on the witness. How directly does the fact relate to credibility? Even if your jurisdiction permits you to impeach a witness with any prior conviction, it is best to use convictions that bear directly on credibility. A prior conviction for perjury or false statement is the ideal. In the classic London School of Economics study of jury behavior, the researchers found that some jurors take offense when a cross-examiner attempts to impeach a witness with convictions for offenses that have little or nothing to do with credibility. Note, *Developments in Evidence of Other Crimes*, 7 U. Mich.J.L. REFORM 535, 544 n. 66 (1974). Similarly, although you may cross-examine the witness about a prior statement inconsistent with any testimony on direct, most experienced attorneys use only prior inconsistent statements that relate to important issues in the case. Suppose, for example, that in her police report, Officer Taylor had misstated either the address of the Senator Hotel or the number of minutes it took her to respond to the crime scene. Thus, she might have written "150" West F Street rather than the correct address, "105" West F Street. Those misstatements would strike most jurors as relatively trivial. The jurors might infer that the defense is so desperate that it is trying to discredit Officer Taylor on inconsequential issues; the jurors might conclude that the defense is resorting to trivial prior inconsistent statements because the heart of Officer Taylor's testimony is unassailable. In short, do not "nitpick." S. HAMLIN, WHAT MAKES JURIES LISTEN 306 (1985). Finally, does the item suggest that the witness is mistaken or lying? The jury is much more likely to infer a mistake. According to Neal Sonnett, the former chair of the A.B.A. Criminal Justice Section and president of the National Association of Criminal Defense Lawyers,

> In all but the most unusual situations, it does no good to cross by [characterizing] the law enforcement agents as lying. Instead, suggest that mistakes were made....

Sonnett, *Preparation Is the Key to Victory,* NAT'L L.J., Feb. 8, 1993.

§ 10.2(G) Intermediate Planning Steps

After selecting the items of evidence to seek during cross, you must complete the intermediate planning steps: identifying all the foundations needed to introduce the items, dissecting each foundation into a list of preliminary facts, choosing the foundational facts to stress, and then drafting the questions to lay the foundation. Chapter 8 analyzed all these intermediate steps.

§ 10.2(H) Tentatively Sequence the Cross–Examination

The Typical Case

Most trial attorneys would agree on the best structure for a cross-examination of the typical witness.

You should generally not begin on the same topic that the direct concludes on. Those facts are freshest in the witness's mind. Start on a different topic. Moreover, the initial part of the cross ought ordinarily to be devoted to eliciting favorable admissions supporting your theory. Once you have attempted to impeach the witness, the witness may be offended and become less cooperative. If you want to elicit favorable concessions, go after them early in the cross.

After seeking those concessions, shift to impeachment. You should realize, however, that there are two types of impeachment. Some impeaching facts relate to the merits such as prior inconsistent statements about relevant events. Other impeaching facts amount to *ad hominem* attacks on the witness. For example, if you question about a fraudulent act under Federal Rule 608(b) or a prior conviction under 609(a), the thrust of the impeachment is an attack on the witness rather than on the content of the witness's testimony. When you are going to use both of these types of impeachment, you should ordinarily save the *ad hominem* impeachment for the end of the cross-examination. Attacks on the witness himself or herself not only have a greater tendency to make the witness uncooperative; they also can be the most dramatic part of the cross-examination.

The ending questions on cross should have two characteristics. One is that they should be "can't miss" questions. You want to conclude on a high note. End with a crescendo. Reardon, *Cross-Examination—"To Sin or Not to Sin,"* 25 LITIGATION 30, 36 (Fall 1998). It is often effective to end by questioning about misconduct admissible under Federal Rule of Evidence 404(b) or 608(b). For instance, the high note or "zinger" for the conclusion of the cross-examination of the opposing party might be evidence indicating the opponent's consciousness of liability or guilt:

Q You received a letter of complaint from my client?

Q The very next day you destroyed one file? Correct?

Q The only file that you destroyed that day held all of your notes concerning this transaction? Right?

Q You didn't simply throw it in your wastebasket?

Q You shredded every document in the file, didn't you?

Lubet, *Cross-examination: ENDGAME,* 17 LITIGATION 40, 41 (Wint. 1991).

Second, the exit questions should be perfect in form. W. BROCKETT & M. KEKER, EFFECTIVE DIRECT AND CROSS–EXAMINATION § 4.14 (1986). You can ruin the effect of an otherwise fine cross-examination by ending on a sustained objection.

Atypical Cases

In some cases, even before trial you can anticipate that the witness will be evasive on cross-examination. The witness may have been, for example, difficult to pin down during a pretrial interview or deposition hearing. If so, you should vary from the normal sequence for cross-examination. Faced with an evasive witness, it is often best to begin with an item of surprise impeachment—some impeaching fact that the witness probably does not realize you know. (Such facts ordinarily have to be gathered by informal discovery such as through the efforts of a private investigator. The downside of formal discovery is that there is no element of surprise.) Doing so signals the witness that you know the facts better than she suspected and that you will not tolerate evasion on cross-examination. Once the witness reads that signal, the witness may abandon her earlier plan to try to evade your questions. You can then fall back to the normal sequence for cross, initially seeking favorable admissions and then shifting to impeachment.

§ 10.2(I) Listen to the Direct Examination and Revise

You must plan the cross-examination before trial, but you must be flexible enough to revise the plan in light of the direct testimony actually presented.

Suppose, for instance, that the direct examiner neglects to elicit the most damning fact that the witness can testify to. Even if you have spent hours planning a lengthy cross-examination about that fact, the wisest tactic may be altogether waiving cross-examination. If you conduct cross, the witness may nonresponsively blurt out the damning fact; or while the direct examiner is listening to your cross, she may realize her oversight and elicit the fact on redirect. Worse still, if your opponent is truly Machiavellian, she may have deliberately elicited only "the tip of the iceberg" on direct examination and primed the witness to mention the more damning facts on cross-examination. This strategy is often used with "courtwise" expert witnesses. Such witnesses take delight in embarrassing cross-examiners.

In other cases, you may want to omit a particular item of planned cross-examination. You may have assumed that the witness would testify to a damaging fact, and you may be ready to confront the witness with the inconsistent passages in the witness's statement and deposition. If the witness fails to testify to that particular fact, there is obviously no need to cross-examine about the statement and deposition.

Conversely, you may decide to cross-examine about additional topics that you did not plan on covering during cross. Suppose, for instance, that before trial, you learned that Scott had a number of prior arrests. As a prosecutor, you conclude that neither Federal Rule 608(b) nor Rule 609(a) would allow you to impeach Scott with the arrests. However, on direct examination, in violation of the rules which control proof of good character, Scott states that "I have never been in any trouble with the law." You can now resort to a curative admissibility theory and cross-examine Scott about the otherwise inadmissible arrests to contradict Scott's statement on direct examination.

The moral is obvious: You must listen intently to the direct. When you have prepared thoroughly for trial, the tendency is to hear what you expect to hear from the witness stand. You must attempt to listen as if you are hearing the witness's version of the facts for the very first time. You can extemporize effectively only if you listen carefully to the direct testimony the witness actually gives.

§ 10.2(J) Conduct the Cross and Re–Cross

There are several aspects to this problem.

The Style of Conducting the Cross–Examination

Picture the scene. The direct examination has just concluded. However, during the direct, the opposing counsel introduced a number of charts; and those charts are still standing in view of the jury. In some cases, you want to keep the charts in view. For instance, a chart might include a clear error that you can expose on cross. However, in most cases, you want to "clear the decks" before you begin cross-examination. Ask the opposing counsel to remove the exhibits from view. The exhibits may distract the jurors' attention. Worse still, if the exhibits describe key facts supporting the opposing counsel's theory, the presence of the exhibits in the jurors' view can serve as a constant, subliminal advertisement for the opposition's theory of the case. Clear away the exhibit, erase the chalkboard, and start with a clean slate.

When you stand to begin cross-examination, make certain that you have in hand all the exhibits that you could conceivably need during the cross-examination. In particular, you should have all the documents that you might need as a source of prior inconsistent statements—written statements, letters, and deposition transcripts. If the witness makes an inconsistent statement, you must immediately confront the witness and show the witness that you are so well prepared that the witness cannot play loose with the facts. If you leave the documents at the counsel table and have to walk back to the table to get them, the down time wasted walking back to the table and searching for the documents may break the jurors' concentration. Worse still, your seeming lack of preparation might embolden the witness to be uncooperative.

When you intend to spend the early part of the cross-examination eliciting favorable facts, your demeanor should be friendly and low key. "Self-control is even more important than witness control. Cross-examination does not mean angry examination." McElhaney, *Phantom Cross–Examination,* 77 A.B.A.J. 102 (Apr. 1991). Your demeanor at this point should be much the same as it is on the direct examination of your witnesses. The opposing counsel may have portrayed you as an ogre to the witness. If you are polite and friendly, the witness will tend to be more cooperative and give you the favorable concessions you want. Polite demeanor is particularly important with a sympathetic witness such as a young child, the bereaved widow, an elderly person, or the victim of a violent crime such as rape. In the early stage of the cross-examination of a sympathetic witness, you must handle the witness with kit gloves. A frontal attack will usually backfire. Some civil defense attorneys believe that a silly, mean-spirited attack on a sympathetic plaintiff can "easily triple the damages." McElhaney, *Losing Arguments,* 20 LITIGATION 55, 68 (Wint. 1994). If the witness begins to cry during cross-examination, do not bully or browbeat the witness. In the trial of William Kennedy Smith in Florida, when the complainant began to sob during cross-examination, the defense attorney Roy Black asked the judge to call a recess for the witness. As Chapter 8 noted, one of the legendary cross-examiners of our time is Mr. Albert Krieger. When he begins the cross-examination of a sympathetic witness, Mr. Krieger often states: "Ms. Grant, I know that this is difficult for you. I want to assure you at the outset that I'm going to ask only a few questions that are really necessary."

As you shift from eliciting favorable admissions to impeachment, you can change your demeanor. Your demeanor should become stronger and more dominant. If the witness makes a strikingly implausible statement, your demeanor ought to suggest your disbelief. Gaines, *Communicating with Juries: Episodic Representational Structure in Cross–Examination,* 67 TENN.L.REV. 599, 614 (2000). However, it may be a mistake to become too accusatory too early in the cross. In the jurors' eyes, you have the moral right to adopt that stance only after you have exposed a strong bias or possible perjury by the witness. Bender, *Cross-Examination Techniques,* 12 THE CHAMPION 6 (June 1988). The jurors normally side with the witness. If you become too combative with the witness, you may leave such an unfavorable impression that the jury will disregard all the substantively helpful admissions you elicited during cross. When you have adopted an accusatory demeanor and struck a telling blow, "pause long enough to allow its impact to be felt." Weitz, *Cross-Examining the Expert at Trial,* 28 TRIAL 55, 58 (Feb. 1992). Let the impact register in the witness's demeanor, and give the jurors ample time to see it register. You want the jury to note the uncertainty or guilt "written" on the witness's face.

Where should you stand during the cross-examination? Assume that the judge does not require that you cross-examine from the lectern. We discussed positioning for direct examination in Chapter 9. Figure 10–2 illustrates the normal positioning for direct: the dark circle indicates the attorney's position standing at the end of the jury box to direct the witness's line of sight to the jurors. In that position, the direct examiner is relatively inconspicuous; and the jurors naturally tend to focus on the witness. Experienced cross-examiners agree on one point: During cross-examination, the attorney should be

Figure 10-2 *

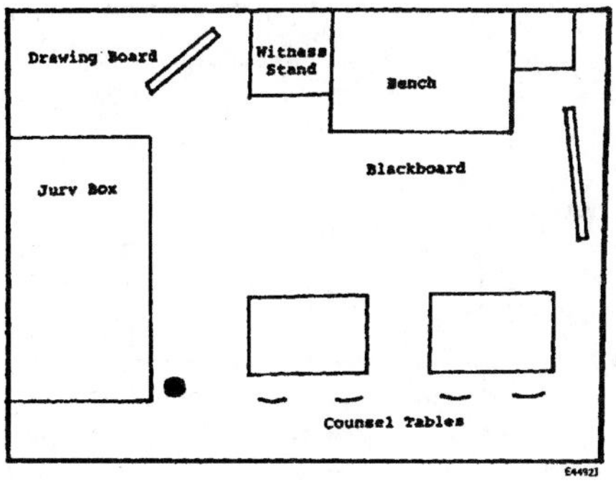

---

* Figures 10-2-6 all are reprinted with permission from 8 Am.J.Trial Advoc. 205 (Winter, 1984), copyright 1985, the American Journal of Trial Advocacy, Cumberland School of Law of Samford University, Birmingham, Alabama, 35229. All rights reserved.

more visible than on direct. The cross-examination should "star the lawyer...." S. HAMLIN, WHAT MAKES JURIES LISTEN 221 (1985). The cross-examiner ought to dominate the questioning visually and verbally. For that reason, the attorney should stand across from the middle of the jury box to permit most of the jurors to see the attorney.

However, cross-examiners disagree over other aspects of positioning during cross. Some say that the attorney should stand near the jury box as in Figure 10–3. Others say that the attorney ought to position himself near the middle of the courtroom, as in Figure 10–4. As should be evident by this point in the course, there are very few categorical rules in trial practice. The proper positioning arguably depends on your pretrial assessment of the witness's demeanor. If you believe that the witness will display helpful demeanor during cross-examination—for example, facial expressions suggesting uncertainty or guilt—you should probably position yourself as in Figure 10–3. You want to direct the witness's line of sight to the jury box; you want to make certain that jurors can see the unappealing demeanor. On the other hand, suppose that your pretrial contact with the witness convinces you that the witness will be unflappable; no matter what you do on cross-examination, the witness will maintain strong, confident demeanor. On that assumption, it makes more sense to position yourself as in Figure 10–4. You want to gain the helpful admissions from the witness, but you do not want the jury to see how well the witness stands up under your cross-examination.

Figure 10-3

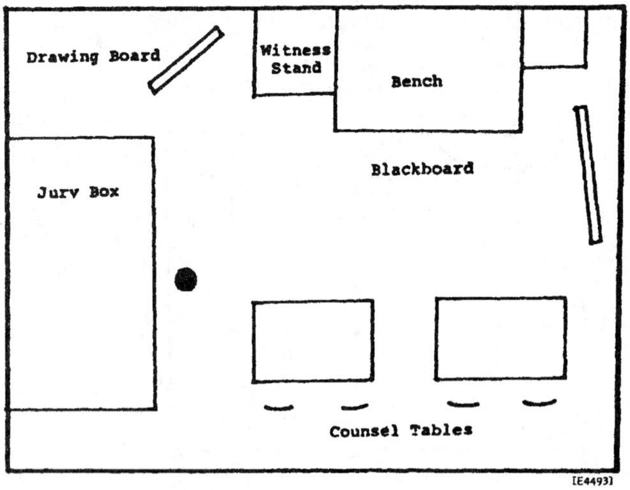

Figure 10-4

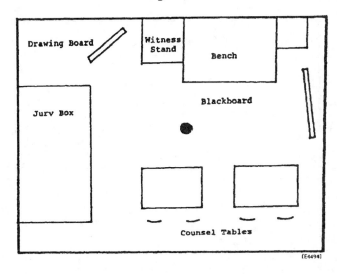

Suppose that you did not have a pretrial opportunity to assess the demeanor of the witness. For example, a prosecutor may not have a chance to evaluate the demeanor of a surprise defense witness. In that event, you may want to follow the pattern indicated in Figure 10–5. You can initially play it safe and adopt a position in the middle of the courtroom, much like the position in Figure 10–4. If it develops that the witness displays helpful demeanor, you can move toward the jury box to direct the witness's line of sight to the jury.

Finally, consider Figure 10–6. In the typical cross-examination, you will shift from eliciting favorable facts to impeachment. As you make the shift, if the judge permits, you may want to move closer to the witness. By doing so, you apply psychological pressure to the witness. Imwinkelried, *Demeanor Impeachment: Law and Tactics,* 9 AM.J.TRIAL ADVOC. 183, 225–26 (1985). Proxemics is the study of the effect of personal distancing on behavior. Proxemics experts claim that when the cross-examiner approaches the typical witness, the witness tends to become uncomfortable. The witness's anxiety often manifests itself as helpful demeanor that you can exploit during summation. By moving closer to the witness, you increase the probability that the witness will exhibit such demeanor.[1]

1. On the other hand, if your opponent is cross-examining and unduly "crowds" your witness, be ready to object and ask that counsel move back. You can cite Code of Trial Conduct 18(f), American College of Trial Lawyers (rev. 1987): "Examination of jurors and of witnesses should be conducted from the counsel table or from some other suitable distance except when handling documentary or physical evidence, or when a hearing impairment or other disability requires that he take a different position."

Figure 10-5

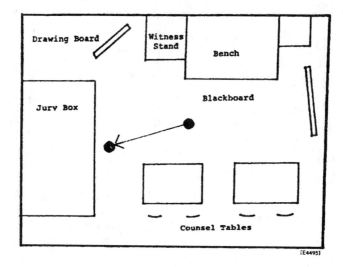

Figure 10-6

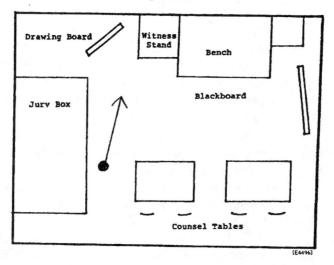

Dealing with the Nonresponsive Witness

In the last subsection, we saw that you must adapt to unforeseen developments on direct. You must also be prepared for unanticipated developments on cross such as nonresponsiveness by the witness. It is not enough to follow the guidelines set out in Chapter 8 and draft narrowly-phrased, factual questions. You must follow up and ensure that the witness restricts herself to the scope of the question you have asked.

How should you react if the witness becomes nonresponsive? The first time the witness does so, you may not want to react at all. Unless the nonresponsive material is damaging, the judge may not want to intervene yet; and at this early point, the jurors are unlikely to infer the witness's bias. Suppose, however, that the witness is nonresponsive again. The second time the witness does so, you may want to fight back. On the one hand, do not simply order the witness to answer Yes or No; some jurors may think you are being too curt, and others may suspect you are afraid of the truth. S. HAMLIN, WHAT MAKES JURIES LISTEN 255 (1985). On the other hand, you might use Richard "Racehorse" Haynes' ultrapolite technique: "Perhaps my question wasn't clear enough. If so, I apologize. Let me ask it again this way." Berg, *Cross-Examination,* 14 LITIGATION 25, 26–27 (Fall 1987). Notice the references to "my" and "I"—Mr. Haynes believes that the first time you ought to purport to accept some responsibility for the problem. The next time the witness ventures beyond the scope of the question, begin subtly shifting blame to the witness: "Excuse me. I don't think you understood my question." Pozner & Dodd, *Controlling the Runaway Witness: Tried and True Techniques for Cross–Examination,* 27 TRIAL 110, 112 (Jan. 1991). If the witness persists in being nonresponsive, try to cut the witness off politely: "Thank you. You've more than answered the question." "[S]tep forward with your left foot (if you are right-handed) and put up your right hand like a traffic officer stopping traffic." Dodd & Pozner, *Controlling the Runaway Witness,* 20 THE CHAMPION 33, 34 (May 1993). If the nonresponsiveness continues, ask the judge to intervene. If the judge sees that your courteous attempts to curb the nonresponsiveness have failed, she may be willing to step in. Make a motion to strike, and request the judge to admonish the witness to confine his answers to the scope of your questions. Once the judge intervenes, the jury is much more likely to discount the witness's credibility by inferring bias. You need an arsenal of different techniques to deal with the nonresponsive witness.[2] You must have several techniques because you will

---

2. Brockett and Keker recommend the following responses to a nonresponsive witness "in increasing order of aggressiveness:"

Q [Politely] You must have misunderstood my question. Did you see the light change?

Q You're answering a different question than the one I asked. Did you see the light change?

Q Yes or no, please. Did you see the light change?

Q You answered the question when you said "yes."

Q I take it your long answer means "yes, you did see the light change"?

Q In fairness to my client, please listen carefully to my question, and answer that question, and not another. Did you see the light change?

Q [To the reporter] Please read the answer back. What question were you answering?

Q I didn't ask you if it was raining. I asked if you saw the light change. Are you willing to answer the question?

Q Mr. Jones, you give the impression that you are deliberately avoiding giving a straight answer to a simple question. Please tell the jury, yes or no, did you see the light change?

Q Your Honor, I move to strike the last answer in its entirety and ask you to instruct the jury to disregard it.

Q Your Honor, please strike the last answer as nonresponsive, instruct the jury to disregard it, and admonish the witness to answer my question directly. W. BROCKETT & J. KEKER, EFFECTIVE DIRECT AND CROSS–EXAMINATION § 8.11, at 160 (1986).

In one case, after repeated stalling by the witness Jerry Spence walked to a chalkboard, wrote his question on the board, and told the witness, "*That's* the question I asked you." S. HAMLIN, WHAT MAKES

need to escalate if the witness persists in being non-responsive. For example, your normal arsenal might be: using Haynes' technique when the witness evades the first time, next asking the witness to "please just answer the question," and finally seeking the judge's intervention.

Whatever set of techniques you chose, remember that the most important thing you need to do is to control your own natural feeling of frustration with the witness. If you hope to maintain control of the opposing witness, you must maintain self-control. Campbell, *Walking the Tightrope: Cross–Examination of the Runaway Witness,* THE PRACTICAL PROSECUTOR 39, 41 (2002). When a witness is consistently nonresponsive, the normal human tendency is to become angry with the witness. However, as any good Jedi Knight knows, you cannot give in to the Dark Side. Effective cross-examination requires self-discipline, and you will lose that discipline if you succumb to an emotion of anger.

Sometimes, the witness's nonresponsiveness takes the form of undue delays before answering your question. In this situation, the natural temptation can be to press for an immediate answer. In most cases, though, you should resist the temptation. Suppose that on direct examination, the witness answered confidently without hesitation. On cross-examination, the witness's demeanor becomes more tentative; and the witness takes a much longer time before answering even simple questions. The witness is playing into your hands. Be patient. During summation, you can contrast the witness's behavior on direct with his or her conduct during cross. Do not rush the witness. Give the witness enough rope and time to hang himself or herself.

Dealing with Erroneous Rulings by the Trial Judge

Just as you must adapt to unexpected nonresponsiveness by the witness, you must be ready to adapt to unanticipated rulings by the judge. Suppose, for example, that you intend to introduce an exhibit during cross-examination. "Some judges think that a new exhibit is *per se* beyond the scope of the direct...." A. TANFORD, THE TRIAL PROCESS: LAW, TACTICS AND ETHICS 287 (2d ed. 1993). The better view is that an exhibit is admissible on cross so long as it relates to the topics covered on direct examination. *Id.* However, if your trial judge

JURIES LISTEN 256 (1985). If the witness, responds by putting a question to you, you can say, "I'm sorry, but the rules of evidence don't permit me to answer your question." McElhaney, *The Runaway: Seven Ways to Interrupt a Witness During Cross–Examination,* 74 A.B.A.J. 109 (Apr. 1, 1988). Doyle, *A Trying Experience for the Shy Lawyer,* 9 CALIFORNIA LAWYER 80, 81 (May 1989) illustrates still another technique for dealing with a nonresponsive witness:

Q Mr. Wright, did I ask you what my client was doing?

A No.

Q Did I ask you about stop signs?

A No.

Q I asked you what you were doing, didn't I?

A Yes.

Q Do you know the answer to that?

A Yes.

[**Q** Then please answer the question I asked you.]

enforces the former view, you may have to excuse the witness subject to recall and later recall the witness to offer the exhibit.

Or assume that as you are pursuing a line of inquiry, the judge sustains an objection blocking the inquiry. To be on the safe side, you may wish to make an offer of proof at sidebar. It is true that in some jurisdictions, there is no requirement for an offer of proof on cross-examination. *E.g.,* CAL. EVID. CODE § 354(c). However, there is no express exception for cross-examination in most jurisdictions. *Cf.* FED. R.EVID. 103(a)(2), 28 U.S.C.A. ... More importantly, as we saw in Chapter 9, offers of proof serve important, practical purposes in addition to the formal function of preserving issues for appeal. To the point, once the judge hears the offer of proof, the relevance of the line of questioning may finally dawn on the judge; the judge may reconsider and change the ruling. Thus, whether the erroneous ruling occurs on direct or cross, you ought to be ready to make an offer of proof to the trial judge.

Conducting Recross Examination

You should not automatically seek to conduct recross simply because there was a redirect. If the direct and cross have been lengthy, the jury and judge may be at the limit of their patience with the attorneys. If the redirect was ineffective, you might state in matter-of-fact fashion: "Your Honor, I see no need for any recross."

If you decide to recross, you can use roughly the same pattern that the redirect examiner uses. Initially, refer to the redirect testimony that you are attempting to counteract: "Ms. Freeman, was it your testimony on redirect that...." Then force the witness to admit the facts inconsistent with the redirect testimony: "But isn't it true that...."

Many attorneys remain seated for recross even though they routinely stand for cross-examination. The psychology is similar to the rationale for low-key demeanor on redirect examination. If you stand and act too concerned, the jury may leap to the conclusion that you think that the redirect effectively repaired the damage done by the cross. However, other attorneys prefer to stand at the counsel table for recross as a method of reasserting their psychological dominance over the witness.

When the questioning of the witness concludes, the judge will allow the witness to leave the stand. In some cases, you will want the witness excused subject to recall. For example, you may want to do so in order to ensure the admission of extrinsic evidence of the witness's prior inconsistent statement. Under California Evidence Code § 770(b), extrinsic evidence is admissible even though you have not laid a foundation on cross-examination when "[t]he witness has not been excused from giving further testimony in the action." The theory is that the witness's proponent can later recall the witness to deny or explain away the apparently inconsistent statement. Many courts construe Federal Rule of Evidence 613(b) in the same fashion as § 770(b). Although 613(b) states that "the opposite party" must be "afforded an opportunity to interrogate the witness's about the inconsistent statement, the statute does not specify that the opponent must be afforded that opportunity before you introduce the extrinsic evidence of the inconsistent statement. In most cases, though, you should consent to the witness's permanent excuse.

§ 10.3 SAMPLE CROSS–EXAMINATION

You are attorney for Peter Williams in *Williams v. Scott.* You are planning the cross-examination of the defendant, and you are using Figure 10–7 to plot the plan. You decide to devote the initial part of the cross to seeking helpful concessions from Scott: the layout of the second floor hallway, the lighting, Scott's relationship to Rogers and Freeman, and his drinking that night. You will then shift to impeachment. At first, you will try to attack the plausibility of his claim that he could not hear anything when he stepped into the hallway. (Assume that the trial judge will allow you to make some brief, passing references to Ms. Freeman's testimony during the cross-examination of Scott. Some judges forbid such references.) You intend to conclude the impeachment by forcing Scott to admit his inconsistent statement to Officer Taylor about lending the shoes to a friend.

Q Good afternoon, Mr. Scott. I have just a few questions that I'd like to ask you.

Q First, Mr. Scott, I'd like to show you what has been admitted as Plaintiff's Exhibit No. 2 in this case. Do you recognize it?

Q It's a diagram of the second floor of your hotel. Correct?

Q I want to review the diagram with you. The diagram shows that the hallway is only six feet wide. The hallway is that narrow. Isn't it?

Q The diagram also indicates that there are 60 watt light bulbs at all these locations in the hallway. That part of the diagram is also correct. Isn't it?

Figure 10-7
PLANNING FOR CROSS-EXAMINATION

Listing All Facts Witness Can Testify to	Listing All Admissible Facts	Predict Direct and Potential Cross	Cross At All?	If So, What Purposes?	Choose Items of Evidence	Foundations Required for Items	Foundational Facts	Foundational Facts to Stress	Sequence of Foundational Facts	Questions to Lay Foundation	Tentatively Sequence the Cross	Listen to Direct and Revise	Conduct the Cross and Recross
											Seek Helpful Admissions —hallway layout —lighting —relationships —drinking Impeachment —implausible he didn't hear —inconsistent statement to Taylor about shoes		

Q Finally, the diagram shows that there are all these 100 watt lights in the second-floor bathroom. Is that also correct?

Q Now I'd like to ask you a few questions about your stay at the hotel. You had lived there for about six weeks before the attack on the morning of January 19th. Right?

Q And you made some friends among the other hotel guests?

Q To be specific, you got to know both Richard Rogers and Joan Freeman. Correct?

Q Is that the same Joan Freeman who testified as the first defense witness today?

Q Did you hear her testify that she recognized the voice of one of Mr. Williams' attackers as that of Dick Rogers?

Q And isn't it true that that is the same Dick or Richard Rogers who was your friend?

Q Did you hear Ms. Freeman testify that at one time, she heard you tell Mr. Williams that he was an "old fart"?

Q Is that true? Did you make that remark to him?

Q Isn't it also true that on at least three occasions, you told her that you didn't like Mr. Williams?

Q All right, now let's turn to the night of January 18th and the morning of January 19th. That night you were with your friends, Dick Rogers and Joan Freeman. Right?

Q The three of you were in your room.

Q Room 212. Correct?

Q And the three of you were drinking?

Q Dick Rogers had more than one drink. Didn't he?

Q And you yourself—you had more than one drink. Right?

Q Now didn't Ms. Freeman leave at about 11:00 p.m.?

Q Did you hear her testify that she went straight back to her room and went right to bed?

Q But you didn't go to bed at 11:00 p.m ... Did you?

Q You kept drinking with Rogers until about midnight.

Q And then he left. Correct?

Q And you went to bed at around 12:30 a.m ... Right?

Q But you were awakened by a noise in the hallway?

Q Did you hear Ms. Freeman's testimony that she was also awakened by the noise in the hallway?

Q Did you hear her testify that when she looked into the hallway, she saw three men fighting?

Q And she says she heard three voices. Correct?

Q Now, when you looked into the hallway, did you see three men?

Q Did you see any men?

Q Is it your testimony that you saw absolutely nothing?

Q Did you hear any voices?

Q No voices at all?

Q Any noises at all?

Q Mr. Scott, isn't is true that your room is closer to the second-floor restroom than Ms. Freeman's is?

Q Isn't it a fact that the door to your room is only 15 feet from the door to that restroom?

Q Let's perform a little experiment with her Honor's permission. Mr. Scott, I'm walking off about 15 feet from the witness stand where you're sitting. Would you agree that this distance is approximately 15 feet?

Q And again that's the distance from your door to the door of the second-floor restroom?

Q You can hear me speaking. Can't you?

Q And you can hear me even though I'm speaking rather softly. Correct?

Q But that night when you went into the hallway, you didn't hear any noise. Is that your testimony?

Q No noise in the hallway?

Q No noise coming from the restroom?

Q Let's continue reviewing your testimony on direct examination.

Q After checking in the hallway, you went back to sleep. Right?

Q But you were arrested a short time later?

Q Isn't it true that just before the arrest, the arresting officer, Officer Taylor, took a pair of your shoes?

Q There were stains on those shoes. Isn't that a fact?

Q Bloodstains?

Q Wasn't it your testimony on direct examination by your attorney that you probably picked up those stains when you walked in the hallway?

Q Isn't it true that that night Officer Taylor asked you about the same shoes and stains?

Q Did you tell her that you picked up the stains walking in the hallway?

Q At that time, didn't you tell her that you thought you lent the shoes to a friend?

Q Did you lend the shoes to Joan Freeman?

Q Did you lend them to Dick Rogers?

Q Is it your testimony today before the ladies and gentlemen of this jury that you lent those shoes to some friend?

Q Your Honor, I have no further questions of the witness at this time.

§ 10.4　ETHICAL QUESTIONS

Some of the most troublesome issues of adversary ethics arise during cross-examination. You are the defense attorney in the *Scott* prosecution. For purposes of this section, assume that before trial, Scott admits to you that he helped Rogers beat Mr. Williams. At trial, the prosecution calls Ms. Freeman as a government witness. On direct examination, she testifies that she looked into the hallway and thinks she saw three men struggling. However, she honestly concedes that it was so dark that there might have been only two men. During your pretrial investigation, you discovered that Ms. Freeman has poor vision and that she was not wearing her glasses when she looked into the hallway. May you cross-examine her about her limited eyesight? Professor Monroe Freedman puts the question in this fashion: "Is it proper to cross-examine for the purpose of discrediting the reliability of a witness whom you know to be telling the truth?" Freedman, *Professional Responsibility of the Criminal Defense Attorney: The Three Hardest Questions,* 64 MICH.L.REV. 1469, 1474 (1966). Professor Freedman argues that the attorney has a duty to do so as a corollary to the attorney's duty of confidentiality to the client. The confidentiality duty "precludes the attorney from prejudicing his client's interest . . . because of knowledge gained in his professional capacity." *Id.* If that is the rationale for the duty to cross-examine about Freeman's restricted vision, may you cross-examine if you learn the truth about Scott's conduct from a source other than your client? *See also* A.B.A. Defense Function Standard 4–7.6(b), 49 Crim.L.Rep. (BNA) 2020 (1991) ("Defense counsel's belief or knowledge that the witness is telling the truth does not preclude cross-examination").

Now assume that you are Scott's attorney but that the prosecution witness is Williams. In this variation of the problem, Williams claims that he was not drinking before going on duty as desk clerk. Before the grand jury, Williams testified that he stopped by Ken's Tavern before going on duty but that he did so only to pay a debt he owed the bartender, John Furnish. The week before trial you stop by the bar and interview Furnish. He corroborates Williams' story but adds that he will be out of town the date of trial and has not been subpoenaed by the prosecution. At trial during Williams' cross-examination, could you ask, "Did you have anything to drink immediately before the [attack]?" J. JEANS, TRIAL ADVOCACY § 2.14, at 30 (2nd ed. 1993). Or could you inquire as follows:

Q How much intoxicating beverage had you consumed immediately before [the attack]?

A Why, none.

Q Well, you had just come from a tavern, hadn't you?

ILLUSTRATIVE NOTES

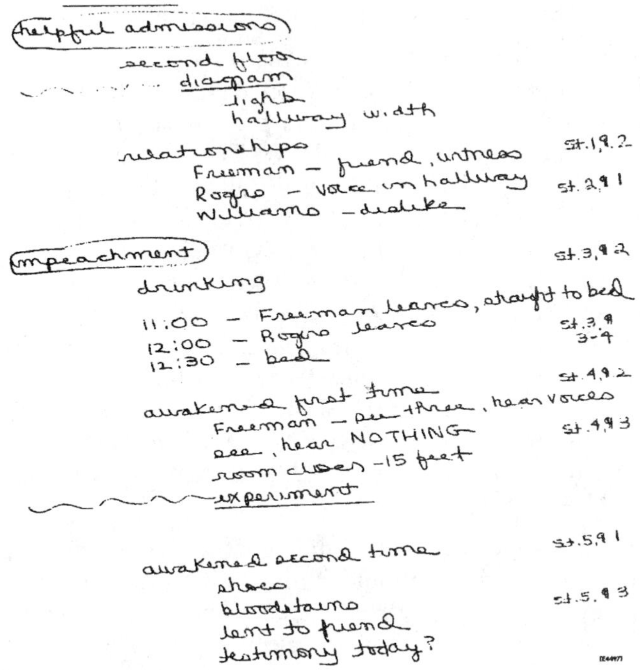

(handwritten illustrative notes)

> helpful admissions
>   second floor
>   diagram
>   lights
>   hallway width
>   relationships   St. 1, 9, 2
>   Freeman — friend, witness
>   Rogers — voice in hallway   St. 2, 9 1
>   Williams — dislike
>
> impeachment   St. 3, 9 2
>   drinking
>   11:00 — Freeman leaves, straight to bed
>   12:00 — Rogers leaves   St. 3, 9
>   12:30 — bed   3-4
>   awakened first time   St. 4, 9 2
>   Freeman — see three, hear voices
>   see, hear NOTHING   St. 4, 9 3
>   room closes - 15 feet
>   experiment
>
>   awakened second time   St. 5, 9 1
>   shoes
>   bloodstains   St. 5, 9 3
>   lent to friend
>   testimony today?

A Yes, but I didn't have anything to drink. I paid off a loan I had made with the bartender.

Q What is the name of the bartender?

A [John Furnish].

Q And is he a friend of yours?

A Enough to lend me ten bucks.

Q Does he know how much you had to drink that day?

A Yes. He knows I didn't drink anything.

Id. Could you then argue during summation that if Williams had not had anything to drink, the prosecutor should have called Furnish to corroborate Williams' story? "Missing witness's arguments sometimes take the form of rhetorical questions. Could you pose these questions during summation: "Where is John Furnish? Why didn't the prosecution call him to the stand? What could Furnish have been told us about Williams' drinking just before this incident?"?

Do you see a difference between the two hypotheticals? In the hypothetical involving Ms. Freeman, she in fact has limited vision. The fact you intend to elicit on cross-examination is true. However, in the second hypothetical, the questions seem to affirmatively suggest a fact that you know to be false. Professor Jeans calls this type of questioning "suggestive interrogation." *Id.* Yet it is arguable that merely eliciting the fact of Ms. Freeman's restricted vision is suggestive; it implies that her earlier testimony about viewing three men in the hallway might be mistaken. Are the two hypotheticals distinguishable?

Is it critical that these hypotheticals involve a criminal prosecution rather than a civil action. Two leading commentators state that "No general agreement seems to have emerged for the guidance of lawyers trying civil cases." R. UNDERWOOD, W. FORTUNE & E. IMWINKEL-RIED, MODERN LITIGATION AND PROFESSIONAL RESPONSIBIL-ITY HANDBOOK § 12.3, at 436 (2nd ed. 2001). They cite one respected authority, Professor Charles Wolfram, as taking the position that "it seems extremely doubtful that the practice of undermining truthful witnesses should be permitted in civil cases." *Id.* There is a good deal of authority that a prosecutor may not attempt to undermine the credibili-ty of a witness whom the prosecutor knows is telling the truth. Domin-guez, *Ethical Boundaries of Cross–Examination,* THE PRACTICAL PROSECUTOR 19,20 (2002), citing A.B.A. Standards for Criminal Pros-ecution 3–5.7(b) (3d ed. 1993) and N.D.A.A. National Prosecution Stan-dards 77.6 (2d ed. 1991).

Assume *arguendo* that you could elicit the above facts during the cross-examination of Freeman and Williams without violating any provi-sion of the Model Rules of Professional Conduct. However, you are a scrupulous person, and you find it troublesome to use these impeach-ment techniques. You discuss the matter with Scott, and he adamantly insists that you employ both techniques. At this point, do you have adequate grounds for seeking to withdraw from the case? Consider Model Rule 1.16(b)(3): "[A] lawyer may withdraw from representing a client if . . . a client insists upon pursuing an objective that the lawyer considers repugnant. . . ." Is your disagreement with Scott a disagree-ment over the ultimate "objective" (end) or means? How should we construe the term, "repugnant," in the Model Rule?

§ 10.5 TRIAL TECHNIQUE EXERCISES

You will conduct a cross-examination. Your instructor will announce any maximum or minimum length requirements for the cross. The designated opposing counsel may object and conduct any necessary voir dire in support of the objection. The instructor may also indicate that the opposing counsel should be prepared to conduct a redirect examina-tion, following up on the cross. In each case file, the witness to be cross-examined is the witness whose direct examination was conducted in the exercise at the end of Chapter 9.

Before drafting your questions, we recommend that you consult one of the specialized texts on evidentiary foundations mentioned in § 7.2(E).

Chapter 11

THE DIRECT EXAMINATION OF EXPERT WITNESSES—PRESENTING YOUR OPINION TESTIMONY IMPRESSIVELY BUT CLEARLY

Detail from the etching "Psychologist" by Charles Bragg.

Table of Sections

§ 11.1   INTRODUCTION

The last four chapters have discussed the direct and cross-examination of witnesses in general terms. This chapter and Chapter 12 focus on a specific type of witness, that is, the expert. The use of expert testimony is already widespread. In 1980, the National Center for State Courts released the results of a nation-wide survey of trial judges and attorneys. *Study to Investigate Use of Scientific Evidence,* 7 NAT'L CENTER FOR STATE CTS. REP. 1 (Aug. 1980). The Center found that almost half the judges and attorneys surveyed encountered scientific evidence in approximately one third of their trials. In the early 1990s Rand released a study of the use of expert testimony in California Superior Court civil trials. Gross, *Expert Evidence,* 1991 WIS.L.REV. 1113. Experts testified at 86% of the trials in the study, and on average there were 3.3 experts per trial. *Id.* at 1119. In personal injury actions, the attorneys routinely offer expert medical testimony. Similarly, scientific evidence is commonplace in prosecutions. As one prosecutor remarked, expert testimony has become "the backbone of every circumstantial evidence case." Clark, *Scientific Evidence,* in THE PROSECUTOR'S DESKBOOK 542 (P. Healy & J. Manak eds. 1969).

In all likelihood, the use of expert testimony will grow. Until recently, most jurisdictions applied a rigorous, conservative test to determine the admissibility of scientific evidence. That test was announced in *Frye v. United States,* 293 Fed. 1013 (App.D.C.1923). Under *Frye,* as part of the foundation for the admission of scientific evidence, the expert must testify that the theory has gained general acceptance within the relevant scientific circle. As recently as the mid 1970's, *Frye* was the controlling test in at least 45 states. Note, 40 OHIO ST.L.J. 757, 769 (1979). However, since that time, roughly a third of the American jurisdictions, including the federal courts, have moved toward a more liberal, validation standard to determine the admissibility of expert testimony. the Supreme Court's decision in *Daubert v. Merrell Dow Pharmaceuticals, Inc.*, 509 U.S. 579 (1993), roughly half the states have shifted to the new validation standard; and *Frye* remains entrenched in only a third of the states. 1 P. GIANNELLI *et al.*, SCIENTIFIC EVIDENCE § 1–6 (3d ed. 1999). The relaxation of the test for admitting expert testimony will make it easier to introduce novel scientific testimony in the future.

§ 11.2 THE VARIOUS USES OF EXPERT WITNESSES

There are four different ways in which an attorney can use an expert witness at trial. First, the attorney can use the witness to establish relevant facts. Suppose that immediately after arresting Scott, the police noticed that he had some bruises. After booking him, the police took him to the physician on call for the police station.[1] The physician notices Scott's bruises. At trial, the prosecutor could call the physician to testify to the bruises to suggest that Scott had just been in a fight. A lay witness would be permitted to testify to the existence of the bruises under Rule 602, and it would make no sense to disqualify the physician from testifying merely because she happens to be an expert.

At the polar extreme, the attorney can call an expert to testify solely about a scientific technique or theory. Assume that El Dorado admits polygraph testimony and that before trial, Scott passed a polygraph test about the assault on Williams. The defense would certainly call the polygraph examiner to testify to that effect. To enhance the weight of the examiner's testimony, the attorney might also call a leading expert on polygraphy. The expert could testify in general terms about the accuracy of the polygraph technique; the expert could do so even if the expert did not know any of the facts in the *Scott* prosecution.

Although the attorney can employ the expert to testify solely about facts or exclusively about a scientific theory, in most cases the attorney wants the expert to do more. The attorney wants to elicit an opinion about the significance of the facts in the case. In some cases, the expert can offer a lay opinion under Federal Rule of Evidence 701. Suppose, by way of example, that while subjecting Scott to a medical examination, a physician smelled alcohol on Scott's breath and noticed Scott's slurred speech. Like any layperson, on that basis the physician could opine that Scott was drunk at the time of the examination. Thus, the presentation of a lay opinion is the third use of an expert.

However, in most cases the attorney wants the witness to derive an expert opinion about the case by applying a scientific technique to the facts in the case. The attorney wants the expert to interpret the significance of the facts for the jury. The expert can do so because his knowledge or skill enables him to draw inferences beyond the lay jurors'

---

1. Under these circumstances, the physician-patient privilege would probably not attach to any information the physician gains from Scott. Indeed, in many states the privilege is altogether inapplicable in criminal cases.

capability. In a tort action, the plaintiff's attorney wants the physician to apply recognized symptomatology to the plaintiff's case history to derive a diagnosis. In the *Scott* case, the defense would want the polygraph examiner to apply the polygraph technique to Scott's interrogation to arrive at an opinion whether Scott truthfully denied attacking Williams. This is the most common use of expert testimony, and the balance of this chapter analyzes this use.

§ 11.3 THE STRUCTURE OF THE DIRECT EXAMINATION OF AN INTERPRETING EXPERT

You must plan the structure of an expert's direct examination. There are many methods of structuring the direct. This chapter discusses one simple format that is often effective. At the outset of the direct, you typically qualify the witness as an expert. The remainder of the direct examination proceeds as a syllogism. A syllogism requires a major premise and a minor premise, and the outcome of syllogistic reasoning is a conclusion. In the case of expert testimony, the major premise is the scientific technique or theory that the expert proposes to rely on. A physician might rely on a set of diagnostic criteria determining whether a patient is suffering from a particular illness. The minor premise is the data about the instant case. The data could be the patient's case history. When a forensic laboratory uses scientific techniques such as DNA typing or neutron activation analysis (NAA) to analyze physical evidence found at a crime scene, the minor premise is the physical evidence itself. The expert applies the major premise to the minor premise, and the result is an opinion relevant to the merits of the case. The opinion gives the jury an insight into the significance of the facts of the case.

The following seven sections dissect the direct examination of an interpreting expert. At the beginning of each section, there is a brief discussion of governing evidentiary rules. In addition, each section discusses the tactical considerations in conducting that part of the direct examination. In presenting expert testimony, you must strive for simplicity and brevity. To be sure, expert testimony can be impressive. However, expert testimony is a two-edged sword. Precisely because the testimony relates to a subject beyond the average layperson's comprehension, the testimony can easily confuse the jury. Especially when you have the ultimate burden of proof in the case, the presentation of complex, arcane expert testimony can be counterproductive. It is not worth offering expert testimony unless you take the time to make the testimony as straightforward and clear as possible.

§ 11.4 THE EXPERT'S QUALIFICATIONS

§ 11.4(A) The Law

Federal Rule of Evidence 702 governs the question of whether the witness qualifies as an expert. The rule refers to "a witness qualified as an expert by knowledge, skill, experience, training, or education...." Unfortunately, the rule mixes apples and oranges. A peculiar knowledge or skill is the ability that permits the expert to draw the inference. "[E]xperience, training, [and] education" are means of acquiring that ability. As a general proposition, the witness need not be a specialist to qualify as an expert.

In order to conserve trial time, many judges will allow you to mark the witness's written resume as an exhibit and introduce it into evidence. The judge may even permit you to distribute individual copies of the resume to each juror. The use of the resume can shorten the amount of time on direct examination needed to establish the witness's qualification as an expert.

In most jurisdictions after eliciting the witness's description of her qualifications, you proceed immediately to the expert testimony. However, in a few jurisdictions, after the witness's description, you must "tender" the witness as an expert or "move" that the judge accept the witness as an expert on a specified topic. Most federal judges follow the majority view.

§ 11.4(B) Tactics

If you use a written resume at trial, do not assume that you should use the resume that the witness circulates in professional or academic circles. To begin with, the latter resume will probably contain technical terms that are Greek to the jury. You will need to reword many of the resume entries to make them self-explanatory for the jury. Moreover, the typical academic's resume lists practical experience near the end of the resume. The witness's hands on experience may be the most important credential for the jury. In short, consider reorganizing the material on the witness's resume.

If you question the witness to establish her expert status, it is a mistake to rush to the witness's technical credentials. Like any other witness, the expert should be humanized. Spend a minute or two on the expert's personal background. As in the case of a lay witness, elicit neutral, background facts creating the impression that the expert is a decent human being worthy of the jury's belief. "The reason it took seven years for his Ph.D. is because he had to work his way through graduate school: she always wanted to be a doctor, like her father.... These humanizing factors in an expert's early life ... draw the jury closer to the expert as a human being." S. HAMLIN, WHAT MAKES JURIES LISTEN 300 (1985).

> Always be on the lookout for a human interest story buried in an expert's resume. For example, a surgeon I presented in a products liability case spent five years in a clinic in Africa after his medical school training. This was the only thing I touched upon in presenting the surgeon's qualifications, allowing the jury to see him as a devoted humanitarian. Another surgeon I called in a burn case described his wrenching experiences as an army surgeon in Vietnam, which caused him to dedicate his career to burn victims.

Bailey, *Expert Witnesses in the Sound–Bite Era,* 29 TRIAL 65, 66 (Feb. 1993).

Even in jurisdictions following the majority view described in § 11.4(A), some experienced litigators recommend that you move that the judge accept the witness as an expert. These attorneys believe that the judge's ruling increases the witness's credibility in the jurors' eyes. Precisely for that reason, though, some courts hold that it is improper for the judge to make such a ruling. *Compare United States v. Bartley,* 855 F.2d 547, 552 (8th Cir.1988) ("Although it is for the court to determine whether a witness is qualified to testify as an expert, there is no requirement that the court specifically make that finding in open court upon proffer of the offering party. Such an offer and finding by the court might influence the jury in its evaluation of the expert and the better procedure is to avoid an acknowledgment of the witness's expertise by the court"), Standard 17, SEC.LITIG., A.B.A., CIVIL TRIAL PRACTICE STANDARDS 46 (1998)("Except in ruling on an objection, the court should not, in the presence of the jury, declare that a witness is qualified as an expert or to render an expert opinion, and counsel should not ask the court to do so"), and Commentary, Ky.R.Evid. 702 (the official commentary states that "the practice of tendering a witness [as an expert] should be discontinued;" the commentary asserts that the judge's "anointing" or "approbation of the witness's improperly conveys the impression 'that the witness's testimony is especially believable' ") with *United States v. Vastola,* 899 F.2d 211, 234 (3d Cir.) ("the usual trial practice of moving for the admission of expert testimony"), *vacated on other grounds,* 497 U.S. 1001 (1990), and *Ingram v. State,* 178 Ga.App. 292, 342 S.E.2d 765 (1986)(preferred practice is to tender).

When you turn to the expert's credentials, do not be content to marginally satisfy Evidence law. Your real objective is to give the witness stature as a specialist in the jury's eyes. Malone, *Direct Examination of Experts,* 24 TRIAL 42, 44 (Apr. 1988). You might ask, "What courses did you take that *relate particularly* to your examination of the cause of Mr. Good's death?" *Id.* (Emphasis added). Or suppose that in a drug prosecution, the government calls a forensic chemist to testify that the substance found in the defendant's possession was cocaine. Do not be satisfied with the witness's testimony that she has a Master's degree in chemistry; in addition, have her testify that to obtain that degree, she had to write a lengthy thesis dealing with an aspect of cocaine identification. Similarly, do not merely elicit her testimony that she has qualified as an expert in 140 other trials; have her add that in each case, she testified as an expert on drug identification and that on over 100 occasions, she testified about cocaine analysis. Finally, do not stop when the expert says that she has published 20 articles in scientific journals; take the next step, and have her state that all 20 articles deal with cocaine identification.

You can enhance the witness's credibility at the same time that you establish the witness's expertise. You can do so, for example, by "associating your expert with a local[ly] or nationally respected institution."

Patterson, *Show and Tell,* 14 THE DOCKET 14 (Spr. 1990). You can also marshal facts creating the impression that the witness is an impartial "straight shooter." Under Rule 702, most judges will allow you to elicit the total number of times the witness has qualified as an expert in court. Rule 607 permits you to impeach your own witness and, thus, arguably to establish the number of prior occasions on which the witness has testified for the same side in litigation. If the jury hears that the witness testified 100 times but only 30 times for a criminal defendant like your client, the jury is likely to infer that your expert "calls them as she sees them."

§ 11.5   THE EXPERT'S MAJOR PREMISE

§ 11.5(A)   The Law

The *Frye* test is still the governing law in a substantial minority of the American jurisdictions. 1 GIANNELLI *et al,* SCIENTIFIC EVIDENCE § 1–15 (2001 Supp.)(17 states). Although only a minority of states adhere to *Frye,* that minority includes some of the most populous and litigious jurisdictions such as Arizona, California, Florida, Illinois, New York, Pennsylvania, and Washington. Most appellate opinions citing *Frye* are criminal cases involving instrumental techniques such as the polygraph. However, there are some criminal cases applying *Frye* to "soft" scientific techniques such as hypnotic enhancement of a witness's memory. *Compare People v. Shirley,* 31 Cal.3d 18, 723 P.2d 1354, 181 Cal.Rptr. 243, *cert. denied,* 459 U.S. 860 (1982) (applying *Frye* to hypnotically enhanced testimony) *with* Hanson, *James Alphonzo Frye Is Sixty–Five Years Old; Should He Retire?,* 16 WEST.ST.U.L.Rev. 357, 411 (1989) (asserting that the prevailing view is contra). Further, there are civil cases recognizing the *Frye* standard. *E.g., Huntingdon v. Crowley,* 64 Cal.2d 647, 414 P.2d 382, 51 Cal.Rptr. 254 (1966); Lipton, *The Results of Scientific Techniques as Evidence in Federal Courts: Evolution of the* Frye v. United States *Standard in the Period 1969–77,* 8 ENVIRONMENTAL L. 769 (1978). Peter Huber's controversial book, GALILEO'S REVENGE: JUNK SCIENCE IN THE COURTROOM (1991), popularized the issue of the applicability of *Frye* in civil cases. When *Frye* applies, you should elicit the expert's explicit voucher that the scientific technique or theory has gained widespread acceptance within his discipline:

Q How well accepted is that theory?

Q In general terms, what percentage of the specialists in your field accept that theory?

Assume alternatively that your trial is being conducted in a jurisdiction which has abandoned *Frye.* As previously stated, the majority of the American jurisdictions have jettisoned *Frye.* In *Daubert v. Merrell Dow Pharmaceuticals,* 509 U.S. 579 (1993), the Supreme Court held that Federal Rules 402 and 702 impliedly overrule *Frye.* The overruling of *Frye* does not mean that expert testimony can be admitted willy nilly. In *Daubert,* the Supreme Court announced that to qualify as "scientific knowledge" under Federal Rule 702, a proposition must be derived by sound scientific methodology. In his lead opinion, Justice Blackmun directed lower courts to consider the following factors, *inter alia,* in evaluating the soundness of the methodology: whether the proposition has been tested, whether there are standards for using the methodology, what is the margin of error in the methodology, and whether the methodology is generally accepted in the pertinent scientific field. Under *Daubert,* the focus shifts from the general acceptance of the expert's conclusion to the appropriateness of the methodology leading to the conclusion. To satisfy *Daubert,* the proponent should elicit foundational testimony about: the number of experiments conducted to validate the hypothesis, the size of the database, the composition of the database, the test conditions, and the accuracy rate attained in the experiments.

The Supreme Court and the lower courts have put real teeth in the *Daubert* standard. In many *Frye* jurisdictions, "soft" science such as psychological testimony is exempt from the general acceptance test. *People v. McDonald,* 37 Cal.3d 351, 690 P.2d 709, 208 Cal.Rptr. 236 (1984); Hanson, *James Alphonzo Frye Is Sixty–Five Years Old; Should He Retire?,* 16 WEST.ST.U.L.REV. 357, 411 (1989)("[t]he majority view"). In contrast, the prevailing view is that soft science does not enjoy any such exemption under the *Daubert* test. Comment, *Admissibility of Expert Psychological Testimony in the Federal Courts,* 27 ARIZ.ST.L.J. 1315 (1995). Furthermore, by its terms, the *Frye* test applies only to novel scientific theories and techniques. The *Daubert* test applies across the board to all purported scientific evidence. Hence, even traditional techniques such as questioned document examination and fingerprint analysis are subject to the empirical validation test. *United States v. Llera Plaza,* 188 F.Supp.2d 549 (E.D.Pa.2002); *United States v. Starzecpyzel,* 880 F.Supp. 1027 (S.D.N.Y.1995); Moenssens, *Handwriting Identification Evidence in the Post-*Daubert *World,* 66 U.M.K.C.L.REV. 251 (1997); Risinger, Denbeaux & Saks, *Brave New "Post-*Daubert *World"—A Reply to Professor Moenssens,* 29 SETON HALL L.REV. 405 (1998). Lastly, most *Frye* jurisdictions confine the scope of the rule to scientific testimony and take a relatively laissez-faire attitude toward the premises underlying non-scientific expert testimony. Strong, *Language and Logic in Expert Testimony: Limiting Expert Testimony by Restrictions of Function, Reliability, and Form,* 71 OR.L.REV. 349, 351–66 (1992). However, in *Kumho Tire Co., Ltd. v. Carmichael,* 526 U.S. 137 (1999), the Supreme Court ruled that like a proponent of scientific evidence, a party offering non-scientific expert testimony must show the reliability of the testimony. Whether the expert testimony is scientific or non-scientific in character, the trial judge must subject the evidence to a "*Daubert*-style inquiry."

§ 11.5(B) Tactics

There are several do's and don'ts for this phase of the direct examination.

Do not go into unnecessary detail. Again, expert testimony can be a two-edged sword. If the expert goes on at great length about the experiments verifying the scientific theory, the jury may be hopelessly confused. Expert testimony occasionally overloads the jury. Unfortunately, experts sometimes testify as if they were presenting a paper to colleagues at a scientific convention. Pare the direct examination down to the bare minimum. If the expert, for example, is going to testify about experiments, have her testify to the impressive, overall numbers: 50 experiments worldwide, 10,000 subjects, and a 99% accuracy rate. Confine the direct to such eye-popping numbers and eye-catching names such as "Harvard" and "the Mayo Clinic." All the other details can be saved for redirect examination.

Encourage explanations in plain language. Ladar, *Direct Examination: Tips and Techniques,* 87 CASE & COMMENT 7, 12, 13–14 (Mar.-Apr. 1982). Suppose that a professor of engineering has been asked by the trial lawyer about the reasons for collapse of a building:

A The supporting pylon exhibited fracture dimensions sufficient to indicate a failure of lateral bracing.

Q I'm sorry, Professor. What does that mean?

A The brace cracked and the whole roof fell in.

If the expert slips during her direct testimony and uses a confusing term, pause, back up, and ask the expert to explain to the jury what "[a]ll that means...." Greenwald, *In the Beginning–Examples of Winning Opening Statements,* 25 TRIAL 72, 73 (May 1989). If you see confusion registering on the jurors' faces, express puzzlement at the expert's statement and request a simpler explanation. Kinrich, *Dull Witnesses,* 19 LITIGATION 38, 42 (Spr. 1993).

There are several methods of attacking the problem of expert jargon at trial. At your informal pretrial conference with the expert, ask the expert which technical terms she intends to use during her testimony. Browse through a thesaurus, and see if you can find simple, lay substitutes for the terms. If not, consider preparing a chart of the definitions for the jury. Tell the judge at the later formal pretrial conference that your expert assures you that she needs to employ four different scientific terms of art during her direct. Show the judge a chart listing the definitions, and tell the judge that you are willing to accept any reasonable revisions of the definitions that the opposing attorney desires. Do not rely exclusively on the witness's oral definitions of the terms. Have the chart staring the jury in the face during the expert's direct examination. Simply stated, you need to translate the jargon for the jury.

More generally, use visual aids. If the expert is going to testify about a polygraph examination, bring into court a photograph or diagram of the machine. Help the jury visualize any instrumentation used by the expert. If it would be helpful for the jury to understand a scientific process, consider using a videotape or computer-generated animation (CGA) of the process. To make the testimony both more visual and more impressive, cite and produce learned treatises which support your expert's position. Schneider, *Using Enlargements of Learned Treatises*, 28 TRIAL 120 (Oct. 1992). On the one hand, Federal Rule 803(18) prohibits you from handing the treatises to the jurors for their physical inspection and reading. On the other hand, the cases construing Rule 803(18) allow you to show the jury enlargements of key passages. Further, by stacking the texts on your counsel table, you can in effect array a small army of experts who corroborate your expert's testimony.

Whenever possible, force the expert to give a simple example of the operation of the scientific theory she is relying on. "[E]xplain the ... process in a familiar context: "Gas can be deodorized by a chemical reaction in the same way kitchens can be deodorized by an aerosol spray." Bridgers, *The Selection, Preparing, and Direct Examination of Expert Witnesses*, 2 THE DOCKET 1, 20 (Fall 1987). Ask your witness:

> **Q** Doctor, what would be a simple, everyday example of how this scientific principle works?

The expert ought to be prepared to cite familiar analogies to help the jury understand any difficult, technical concepts. Wilson, *Making Complex Commercial Cases Come Alive*, 28 TRIAL 44, 46 (Dec. 1992). If a molecular biologist testifying about DNA typing refers to "restriction endonucleases," the witness should be primed to explain that an RE is like "a pair of biological scissors which cuts the DNA molecule."

§ 11.6 THE EXPERT'S MINOR PREMISE

§ 11.6(A) The Law

As previously stated, sometimes the minor premise takes the form of physical evidence. For instance, a criminalist might testify about an analysis of physical evidence such as hairs, fibers, or stains discovered at the crime scene. If so, the proponent of the criminalist's testimony ought to establish a chain of custody for the physical evidence. *See generally* Fed.R.Evid. 901, 28 U.S.C.A.; Giannelli, *Chain of Custody and the Handling of Real Evidence*, 20 AM.CRIM.L.L.REV. 527 (1983). The chain should run from the time of seizure at least until the time of the analysis. The testimony should cover the handling of the evidence by each link in the chain—each person who had physical custody of the object. The testimony ought to describe each link's initial receipt of the object, the ultimate disposition of the object (retention, transfer, or destruction), and the safeguarding of the object between receipt and disposition.

In other cases, the minor premise is testimonial information about the case. In *Williams v. Scott,* a physician testifying about Williams' prognosis would rely on various sources of information such as the physician's examination of Williams, Williams' oral statements, and medical records. Similarly, if Scott raised an insanity defense in the prosecution, the defense psychiatrist would base an opinion on information other than physical evidence. Federal Rule of Evidence 703 controls.

Under that rule, an expert may rely on personally observed facts, facts stated in hypothetical questions, and hearsay reports. Rule 703 permits the expert to base an opinion on hearsay reports when the reports are "of a type reasonably relied upon by experts in the particular field...." Fed.R.Evid. 703, 28 U.S.C.A. Most judges find Rule 703 satisfied if the expert testifies that it is the customary practice of specialists in her field to consider that type of report. Proof of the customary practice gives rise to a rebuttable presumption that it is objectively reasonable for the expert to rely on that source of information. For example, a forensic pathologist would give foundational testimony that pathologists routinely rely on toxicology reports in arriving at an opinion about cause of death. The pathologist should vouch that she regularly relies on toxicology reports in her day-to-day work.

Trial judges may allow expert opinions based on nonrecord material so long as the expert's reliance on the material is reasonable. In *Peabody Coal v. Director, Office of Work.Comp.*, 165 F.3d 1126 (7th Cir.1999), the court declared: "Rule 703 of the Federal Rules of Evidence is explicit that the materials on which an expert witness bases an opinion need not be admissible, let alone admitted, in evidence, provided that they are the sort of thing on which a responsible expert draws in formulating a professional opinion." In a minority of jurisdictions, the courts equate the term "reasonably" in Rule 703 with "customarily." In those jurisdictions, under Rule 104(a) the judge decides whether such a custom exists in the specialty; and if the judge finds as a matter of fact that there is such a custom, the judge must allow the expert to rely on that type of information. The support for that view is dwindling, though. *In re Paoli R.R. Yard PCB Litigation*, 35 F.3d 717, 748 (3d Cir.1994), *cert. denied sub nom. G.E. v. Ingram*, 513 U.S. 1190 (1995). The trend is toward the view that even when that is the customary practice among experts in that field, the judge has residual discretion to preclude reliance on that type of information if the judge believes that reliance on that kind of data is objectively unreasonable.

§ 11.6(B) Tactics

The expert's ultimate opinion is no more trustworthy than the minor premise which the opinion rests on. There is a large element of truth in the saying, "Garbage in, garbage out." Just as you should not be content to satisfy Evidence law by marginally qualifying your expert, you ought to strive to do more than barely satisfy Rule 703.

Suppose that you must prove the chain of custody of an object. Should you necessarily present the witness's testimony that he remembers handling the object? In some cases, that testimony would be perjury; the person may handle so many similar objects that he could not possibly remember the particular object. For example, a criminalist at the F.B.I. Laboratory might handle thousands of similar exhibits in a year. Even if the witness could remember, the purported memory might be too good to be believed; once the jury learns on cross-examination that the witness handles so many similar objects, the jury may doubt the direct examination. For this reason, you may want to use documentary evidence to prove the chain. Most laboratories employ some sort of chain-of-custody receipt. You can argue for the admission of the receipt as a business entry (Fed.R.Evid. 803(6)), past recollection recorded (Fed.R.Evid. 803(5)), or in some cases an official record. Fed.R.Evid. 803(8). The jurors may find reliance on the receipt more believable.

There are also pitfalls when your expert is relying on testimonial information. When the expert relies on the facts stated in a hypothetical question, it may seem to the jury that the expert is making a "snap judgment" on the spot at trial. For all the jury knows, this is the very first time the expert has heard the facts. Experienced attorneys make it clear that the expert has carefully studied the facts before trial:

Q When was the first time you heard these facts about Mr. Williams?

Q When did you begin studying these facts?

Q How many hours have you spent studying these facts?

When you set out the assumptions for a hypothetical question, you have a "chance to make a mini-summation while the trial is still in process." Suplee & Woodruff, *Direct Examination of Experts,* 33 THE PRACT. LAWYER 53, 58 (Dec. 1987). However, a lengthy hypothesis can backfire—especially if the expert cannot recall all the elements of the hypothesis on cross-examination. Keep the hypothesis as succinct as possible. *Id.* The primary risk in offering expert testimony is that you may confuse the jury. The longer the hypothesis, the graver is the risk.

When the information takes the form of a hearsay report, you ought to make it clear that the expert did not accept the report at face value. If the report indicated that a third person witnessed the same event, the expert should contact that person to verify the report. When the report refers to a document, ideally the expert should personally examine that document. The jury should come away with the impression that the expert carefully, critically evaluated the report and corroborated it before basing an opinion on the report. The minor premise must be "solid." *Id.* It would hardly be good medical practice to treat a patient on the basis of symptoms described in an uncorroborated hearsay report, and an expert who opines on that basis is vulnerable on cross-examination.

§ 11.7   THE MANNER IN WHICH THE EXPERT APPLIED THE MAJOR PREMISE TO THE MINOR PREMISE

§ 11.7(A) The Law

The most reliable scientific technique will not yield trustworthy results unless the expert applying the technique uses the correct procedures. For that reason, in most jurisdictions the use of proper procedures is another element of the foundation for offering expert testimony. A minority of jurisdictions have opted for the view that deficiencies in test procedure affect only the weight of the evidence. Harmon, *How Has DNA Evidence Fared? Beauty Is in the Eye of the Beholder,* 1 SHEP./ McG.-HILL EXPERT EVIDENCE REP. 149 (Feb. 1990). However, most courts continue to demand foundational proof of proper test protocol. *People v. Venegas,* 18 Cal.4th 47, 954 P.2d 525, 74 Cal.Rptr.2d 262 (1998). Moreover, effective December 1, 2000, Federal Rule of Evidence 702 was amended to explicitly require the proponent to show that "the [expert] witness has applied the principles and methods reliably to the facts of the case." For example, if a prosecutor contemplates introducing breathalyzer test results, the foundation should include the arresting officer's testimony that she used the proper procedure. *McClellan v. Colorado, Dept. of Revenue, Motor Vehicle Div.,* 731 P.2d 769 (Colo.App. 1986).

§ 11.7(B) Tactics

As a general proposition, elicit the bare minimum testimony needed to satisfy this foundational element. You want to keep the expert's direct examination as short and as simple as possible. It usually suffices to elicit the expert's conclusory testimony that she followed the "standard," "correct," or "recognized" procedure. However, there is one exception to this norm. Suppose that in a given case, you ultimately want to elicit the expert's testimony about a very exact, minute measurement such as a few millionths of a microgram of trace evidence found at a crime scene by neutron activation analysis (NAA). Before the jury is likely to accept that precise a measurement, the jury must be convinced that the expert meticulously followed correct procedure. In this instance, it is worth going into more detail about the procedures employed by the expert.

As in the case of the minor premise, in laying this element of the foundation you can encounter the problem of the memory that is too good to be believed. The expert may repetitively conduct this type of examination, and it might be difficult for the jury to believe that the expert actually remembers the occasion when he used the breathalyzer or reactor. When the expert cannot truthfully testify to remembering the occasion, there are two other ways of satisfying this foundational element. As in the case of the minor premise, you can use documents admitted under hearsay exceptions. The expert, for instance, might use a logbook or checklist describing the procedures for each test. You can urge the admission of the document as a business entry, past recollection recorded, or when appropriate an official record. Further, you can resort to a habit or routine theory under Federal Rule of Evidence 406. The expert can testify that it is his regular, habitual practice to operate the instrument in a particular fashion. That testimony is both admissible and sufficient to lay this foundational element. More importantly, that testimony may be more believable than an expert's claim that he remembers the specific occasion he tested this sample—out of the 1,500 similar tests he conducted in the same year.

§ 11.8 THE EXPERT'S FINDING AND OPINION

§ 11.8(A) The Law

When the expert applies the scientific technique to the minor premise, the immediate result is a test outcome or result. For example, neutron activation analysis of physical evidence discovered at a crime scene yields a measurement of the quantity of chemical elements in the sample analyzed. The instrumentation used may print out the numbers indicating the quantities. If the test result takes the form of a visual display, the display can become an exhibit at trial. The best evidence rule does not compel the introduction of the exhibit unless the exhibit qualifies as a writing. *United States v. Gavic,* 520 F.2d 1346 (8th Cir.1975) (chemist may testify to the results of a thin layer chromatography drug identification test without producing the TLC plates). The questioner has a choice whether to offer the exhibit to help the jury understand the testimony.

In some cases, the test result is self-explanatory. For example, suppose that the arresting officer administers a breathalyzer test to the defendant. This model breathalyzer has three readouts: Pass, Fail, and Warning. The jury does not need the assistance of an expert to understand the significance of a Fail reading. In other cases, however, the significance of the test outcome is not self-evident; and in addition to eliciting the expert's testimony about the result, you must invite the expert to opine about the significance of the test result. Suppose, for instance, that the model of breathalyzer used in a driving while intoxicated (DWI) case produces a digital readout such as 0.11. Absent a statutory presumption that any reading exceeding 0.08 indicates intoxication, the prosecutor would have to present expert testimony explaining that the typical person with a blood alcohol concentration of 0.11 displays clinical symptoms of intoxication.

You will often want the expert to explain the significance of the test result in quantitative terms. The test result might be, for example, a match between Williams' blood type and the type of the blood stains found on the soles of Scott's shoes. The prosecutor might want the jury to appreciate that Williams has a very rare blood type, one shared by only two or three percent of the population. After the expert testified to the match, the prosecutor would attempt to introduce the expert's testimony that only two percent of the population has that blood type. However, the expert must be prepared to cite a source for that percentage. Ideally, the source should qualify as a learned treatise, independently admissible under Federal Rule of Evidence 803(18). In any event, the expert must be prepared to cite the source for any population frequency statistic and to testify that the source is a reliable, recognized authority in her field.

The problem is relatively simple when the expert intends to use a population frequency statistic, generated by samples of the population. The problem becomes more complex when the expert intends to derive the ultimate statistic by probability calculations. *See People v. Collins,* 68 Cal.2d 319, 438 P.2d 33, 66 Cal.Rptr. 497 (1968). Assume, for example, that the expert typed a body tissue sample for two different white cell or human leukocyte antigen (HLA) systems. In one system, the sample exhibited a genetic marker possessed by one percent of the population; and in the other system, the sample displayed a marker possessed by ten percent of the population. May the expert use the product rule, multiply the two percentages, and testify that only one tenth of one percent of the populace would possess the same set of genetic markers? To give this testimony, the expert should be prepared to testify not only to the sources of the two population frequency statistics but also to the independence of the systems. 1 P. GIANNELLI *et al.*, SCIENTIFIC EVIDENCE § 17–9(A) (3d ed. 1999).

§ 11.8(B) Tactics

Even when the best evidence rule does not require the introduction of a visual display of the test result, it is usually advisable to offer the exhibit. A visual appeal to the jury can make the testimony more memorable. It may be dramatic for the jury to see the sharp leap on the polygraph chart accompanying the defendant's denial of guilt. In addition, as we shall see in the next section, the use of the exhibit can help the expert explain her reasoning process to the jury.

If the expert will also opine about the significance of the test result, on direct examination you should normally have the expert define the degree of certitude of the opinion. The early, common-law view was that the expert could testify to an opinion only if she was prepared to say that the opinion was a scientific or medical probability or certainty. The Federal Rules abandon that view, and modernly most jurisdictions permit experts to testify to possibilities. However, when the expert is prepared to testify only to a possibility and your opponent is competent, make that clear on direct examination. If your opponent forces the expert to concede that for the first time on cross-examination, the jury may think that you were attempting to mislead them.

When you intend to present a final opinion couched in statistical terms, proceed slowly and step by step. Statistical testimony epitomizes the risk that scientific testimony can confuse rather than impress. To minimize that risk,

— initially have the witness write out the formula used to derive the final opinion;

— ask the witness to explain every element of the formula including the symbols for the constants and variables;

— have the expert give a simple example of the use of the formula;

— force the witness to state every numerical value he or she fed into the formula in the present case and to identify the source of the value; and

— then and only then have the expert perform the computation, yielding the final opinion.

You do not want the jurors to think that the witness pulled the number out of thin air. Quite to the contrary, you should strive to create the impression that the computation was driven by inexorable logic.

§ 11.9 THE EXPLANATION OF THE REASONING PROCESS UNDERLYING THE EXPERT'S OPINION

Evidence law does not require that the expert explain his reasoning process. Yet, common sense suggests that you should invite the expert to do so before concluding the direct examination. If the expert is the Nobel Prize winner in the field, the jury may be willing to make an act of blind faith in the expert's opinion as *ipse dixit*. However, in the overwhelming majority of cases, the jury will be reluctant to do so—especially when your opponent calls an opposing expert. The jury will accept your expert's opinion only if it is clear that the opinion is based on the hard facts of the case.

Your goal is to convince the jury that the opinion is not only consistent with the facts but is virtually dictated by the hard facts in the case. Suppose that the expert testifies to a match in between fibers found on Williams' pants and fibers taken from the shirt Scott was wearing at the time of arrest. The expert often authenticates photographic enlargements of microscopic views of the two samples during the direct examination. Before concluding the direct testimony, the expert can identify and mark the points of similarity between the two fiber samples. The jurors can then see for themselves that the physical evidence shows a match.

A variation of this technique can be used even when the scientific technique in question does not yield a physical exhibit. Assume, for example, that Scott pleads insanity and calls a psychiatrist to testify in support of the defense. Before concluding the expert's direct examination, the defense attorney might invite the expert to explain her opinion by use of a chart. The left-hand column could be entitled "Sanity," the middle column "Scott's Case History," and the right-hand column "Insanity." The attorney would position the expert next to the chart and lead the expert through each salient factor in Scott's case history. The attorney would initially ask the expert to list the factor in the middle column on the chart. For each factor, the attorney would next ask the expert whether the factor points to sanity or insanity. Again and again, the expert would check the right-hand column for insanity. The jury would literally see that every key fact points to the same conclusion. During closing argument, you want to be in a position to rebut your opponent's argument that your expert's opinion is "pure theory and speculation." You want to be able to show the jury that the opinion is firmly grounded in the hard facts of the case.

§ 11.10 SAMPLE DIRECT EXAMINATION OF AN EXPERT

Steven Sykes is a criminalist employed by the Morena Police Department. The prosecutor calls him to the witness stand in the *Scott* prosecution. Earlier witnesses have established a chain of custody for: the shoes seized from Scott (People's Exhibit No. 2), a sample of Williams' blood (People's Exhibit No. 4), and a sample of Scott's blood

(People's Exhibit No. 6). The direct examination proceeds in this fashion:

> **Q** Please state your name and spell your last name.
>
> **A** My name is Stephen Sykes. My last name is spelled S—Y—K—E—S.
>
> **Q** What is your present address?

(Humanizing the Witness)

> **A** We live at 422 Oyster Bay Avenue here in Morena.
>
> **Q** You said "we" live on Oyster Bay Avenue. Who are "we"?
>
> **A** Myself, my wife, and our two kids.
>
> **Q** How long have you lived in Morena?
>
> **A** I've lived here my entire life. I was born in Morena and went to grammar school, high school, and college here.

(Qualifying the Witness as an Expert)

> **Q** Please tell us about your college education.
>
> **A** I was a science major. I graduated with a Bachelor of Science degree from the El Dorado State University campus in Morena in 19YR–12. I started at the campus in 19YR–18.
>
> **Q** Did you concentrate on any particular area in your studies?
>
> **A** Yes, biology and even more narrowly genetics.
>
> **Q** Why did it take you six years to get the degree?
>
> **A** I had to work my way through college.
>
> **Q** What did you do after you graduated from the University?
>
> **A** I immediately went to work for the Morena Police Department Crime Laboratory.
>
> **Q** How long have you worked there?
>
> **A** Ever since graduating from college.
>
> **Q** What sort of work do you do?
>
> **A** I work in the Genetic Marker section of the laboratory.
>
> **Q** What type of work is that?
>
> **A** We analyze body fluids and tissues. Most of my work is with blood samples. We analyze them to identify genetic markers like your blood type.
>
> **Q** How long have you worked in the Genetic Marker section of the laboratory?
>
> **A** The whole time I've been employed by the lab. Genetic marker analysis is my specialty.
>
> **Q** What writing, if any, have you done for scientific journals?
>
> **A** I've published over 30 articles in scientific journals.

Q What do those articles relate to?

A All of them deal with genetic marker analysis, in particular the analysis of red blood cells.

Q How many times, if any, have you testified in court as an expert?

A On over 200 occasions.

Q On how many of those occasions have you testified for the prosecution?

A I'd say 150 times.

Q Who else have you testified for?

A In about 30 cases, I've testified at civil trials—either for the plaintiff or the defense. In about 20 other cases, I've testified for criminal defendants in other cities and states. Our department permits you to appear as a witness for criminal defendants outside Morena.

Q What have you testified about as an expert?

A I always testify about genetic markers like blood types.

(The Major Premise)

Q You've told us something about yourself. Now I'd like to ask a few questions about genetic marker analysis. In general terms, how does it work?

A The simplest example—the one we're all familiar with—is red blood cell analysis. Everyone knows that you either have A, B, AB, or O type blood. You have a blood type, and that blood type remains constant throughout your life. It never changes.

Q How do you determine whether a person has one type of blood or another?

A The first thing you've got to do is to prepare the blood sample for the test.

Q I now show you what has previously been admitted as People's Exhibit No. 1 in this case. What is it?

A It's a list of the key terms in red blood cell analysis. It explains the terms.

Q How accurate are those definitions?

A They're good, general explanations of the terms. There are some wrinkles that an expert has to worry about—some exceptions to those general definitions, but none of those wrinkles is relevant here.

Q All right. Using those definitions, let me ask you some questions about red blood cell analysis. How do you get the sample ready for the analysis?

A The first thing you've got to do is extract the red blood cells.

Q What do you mean by "extract"?

A As the definition on the chart indicates, you separate them from the physical evidence that's delivered to the lab. The evidence could be a test tube of liquid blood or a dried blood stain on something like the soles of a pair of shoes.

Q How do you remove the red blood cells from the sample?

A It's a complicated process, but essentially you use heating to remove them.

Q What do you do after you've removed the red blood cells from the sample?

A You run an agglutination test.

Q Would you please explain, "agglutination," for the jury?

A Again, let me refer to the chart. It means clumping. The blood cell has an antigen like A or O. Clumping occurs when the antigen meets a certain type of antibody.

Q I now hand you what has previously been admitted as People's Exhibit 2. What is it?

A It's a chart showing two blood tests—one in which agglutination occurred and another where the reaction did not occur.

Q Which is which?

A The photo on the left shows a test in which there is no agglutination. You can plainly see that the fluids are still separate. The one on the right depicts agglutination. The contrast is obvious. You can see that there's a clumping together of the material in this test. Again, that's what happens when the antigen meets a certain type of antibody.

Q What is an antigen?

A It's like an identifying mark on the blood cell. The chart gives you a longer definition, but for our purposes it's enough to know that the antigen determines the blood type.

Q What is an antibody?

A The chart gives you an explanation of that too. To put it simply, it's the opposite or enemy of the antigen. Suppose you have A blood. If you mix it with anti-A antiserum, they react and clump together.

Q Can you explain this idea of clumping in simple terms?

A Sure. It's like two pieces of a jigsaw puzzle. If you get two pieces that are intended to be right next to each other, they lock together. A antigen and anti-A antiserum lock up. You mix the unknown red blood cells with anti-A antiserum. As Exhibit 2 demonstrates, you can see clumping with the naked eye. If they clump, you know that the blood contains A antigens.

Q How well accepted are these scientific principles for analyzing red blood cells?

A They're accepted universally. Landsteiner discovered this clumping reaction, and he won the Nobel Prize for it in 1930. All hospitals and blood banks use these techniques.

Q Why?

A These principles and techniques are used to determine whether a person can accept a blood transfusion. If you give the person the wrong type of blood—if you give someone with A blood a transfusion from someone with a different type of blood, you can get the clumping reaction. It would kill him. These techniques are used daily in thousands of hospitals throughout the world to save lives.

Q How many experiments have been conducted to prove the validity of these principles?

A Hundreds. Maybe thousands.

(The Minor Premise)

Q Now let me direct your attention to the afternoon of January 21, 19YR–1. Where were you that afternoon?

A I was in my office at the crime lab in downtown Morena.

Q What, if anything, happened while you were there?

A Officer Taylor stopped by and delivered some physical evidence to me.

Q What evidence?

A He gave me two test tubes of liquid blood and a pair of shoes that seemed to have blood stains on them.

Q I now hand you what have already admitted as People's Exhibits 3, 4, and 6. Do you recognize them?

A Yes.

Q What are they?

A They're the items of evidence that Officer Taylor gave me.

Q How can you recognize them?

A Each one of them has an evidence tag. I not only recognize the tags; as you can see, I've put my initials on each tag.

(The Application of the Major Premise to the Minor Premise)

Q What did you do after Officer Taylor gave you these exhibits?

A I ran a red blood cell test on each of them.

Q How did you do that?

A I used the extraction and agglutination procedures that I've already described to you.

Q How well do you remember the specific day when you tested these exhibits?

A The truth of the matter is that it would be difficult for me to remember without checking the logbook that I keep at the bench where I work.

Q Why would it be difficult for you to remember?

A As I said, genetic marker analysis is my specialty. I test a number of blood samples every day. I'd be lying if I said that I remembered every test.

Q What, if anything, might help you remember?

A Just like I said a couple of seconds ago, at the bench where I work I keep a log of every test that I run.

Q Your Honor, I request that this be marked People's Exhibit No. 8 for identification.

J It will be so marked.

Q Your Honor, please let the record reflect that I am showing the exhibit to the defense attorney.

J The record will so reflect.

Q Permission to approach the witness?

J Granted.

Q I now hand you what has just been marked People's Exhibit No. 8 for identification. What is it?

A It's the logbook I just described to you.

Q How can you recognize it?

A It's all in my handwriting.

Q Please turn to page 144. What does that page relate to?

A It's the test of these samples.

Q Please read that page silently to yourself.

A O.K.

Q Does that refresh your memory of the time you tested the physical evidence you received from Officer Riley?

A It sure does.

Q Please hand Exhibit No. 8 back to me.

A Sure.

Q Can you now tell us how you tested those samples?

A I used the standard procedures that I described earlier.

(Test Result)

Q What happened when you ran those tests?

A Well, the blood stains on the shoes turned out to be type AB. The blood in the tube that is People's Exhibit No. 4 was also AB.

Q What about Exhibit No. 6?

A Well, that was different. That was type O blood.

(Explanation of the Reasoning Process)

Q How do you know that those were the blood types?

A When I mixed the samples with the other antisera, nothing happened. There was absolutely no clumping. But when I mixed them with the antiserum for AB and then with O, I got classic clumping reactions.

(Opinion Explaining the Significance of the Test Result)

Q How common is type O blood?

A It's very common. Roughly 46% of the population has that blood type.

Q How do you know that?

A You can find that statistic in all the leading texts on blood work. That number was determined by blood bank studies from throughout the world.

Q How common is type AB blood?

A That's pretty rare.

Q How rare?

A The same studies show that only three percent of the population has that blood type.

Q Again, which of the exhibits had that type?

A Only the stains on the shoes and the fresh blood in the tube marked "Williams' Blood Sample."

Q Thank you. Your witness.

Figure 11-1

§ 11.11   ETHICAL QUESTIONS

Consider the following excerpt from F. FRANKFURTER, THE CASE OF SACCO AND VANZETTI 76–79 (1927)*:

"Vital to the identification of Sacco and Vanzetti as the murderers was the identification of one of the fatal bullets as a bullet coming from Sacco's pistol...."

"Proctor at the time of his testimony was head of the state police and had been in the Department of Public Safety for 23 years. On the witness stand he was qualified at length as an expert who had for 20 years been making examination of and experiments with bullets and revolvers and had testified in over a 100 capital cases.... On this crucial issue Captain Proctor testified as follows at the trial:

" Q. Have you an opinion as to whether bullet no. 3 [Exhibit 18] was fired from the Colt automatic, which is in evidence [Sacco's pistol]? A. I have.

" 'Q. And what is your opinion? A. My opinion is that it is consistent with being fired from that pistol. (R. 472).'

"After the conviction, Proctor, in an affidavit swore to the following account of his true views and the manner in which they were phrased for

* Reprinted with the permission of Little,   Frankfurter.
Brown and Company and Ms. Estelle S.

purposes of the trial. After giving his experience and stating the fact that he had the custody of the bullets, cartridges, shells, and pistols in the case, he swore that one of the bullets 'was, as I then testified and still believe, fired from *a* Colt automatic pistol of .32 calibre. During the preparation for the trial, my attention was repeatedly called by the District Attorney and his assistants to the question: whether I could find any evidence which would justify the opinion that the particular bullet taken from the body of Berardelli, which came from *a* Colt automatic pistol, came from the particular Colt automatic pistol taken from Sacco. I used every means available to me for forming an opinion on the subject. I conducted, with Captain Van Amburgh, certain tests . . . , about which I testified, consisting in firing certain cartridges through Sacco's pistol. At no time was I able to find any evidence which tended to convince me that the particular model bullet found in Berardelli's body, which came from *a* Colt automatic pistol, which I think was numbered 3 and had some other exhibit number, came from Sacco's pistol, and I so informed the District Attorney and his assistant before the trial. This bullet is commonly called a full metalpatch bullet. [A]lthough I repeatedly talked over with Captain Van Amburgh the scratch or scratches which he claimed tended to identify this bullet as one that must have gone through Sacco's pistol, his statements concerning the identifying markers seemed to be entirely unconvincing.

" 'At the trial, the District Attorney did not ask me whether I had found any evidence that the so-called mortal bullet which I have referred to as number 3 passed through Sacco's pistol, nor was I asked that question on cross-examination. The District Attorney desired to ask me that question, but I had *repeatedly* told him that if he did I should be obliged to answer in the negative; consequently, he put to me this question: Q. Have you an opinion as to whether bullet number 3 was fired from the Colt automatic which is in evidence? To which I answered, "I have." He then proceeded. Q. And what is your opinion. A. My opinion is that it is consistent with being fired by that pistol.' (Brief for Defendants on first appeal before Supreme Judicial Court, 161.)

"He then proceeded to state that he is still of the same opinion, 'but I do not intend by that answer to imply that I had found any evidence that the so-called mortal bullet had passed through this particular Colt automatic pistol and the District Attorney well knew that I did not so intend and framed his question accordingly. Had I been asked the direct question: whether I had found any affirmative evidence whatever that this so-called mortal bullet had passed through this particular Sacco's pistol, I should have answered then, as I do now without hesitation, in the negative.' (Brief for Defendants on first appeal before Supreme Judicial Court, 161.)"

Were any of the questions asked or answers given objectionable under Evidence law? Even if they were not, did the juxtaposition of the questions tend to create a misleading impression of the significance of the second answer? If a lay witness's direct testimony tends to mislead the jury, we normally assume that the cross-examiner can question to correct the misleading impression. However, since we are now dealing with expert testimony, it is more difficult for the opposing attorney to recognize the misleading character of the testimony. In *People v. Collins,* 68 Cal.2d 319, 327, 438 P.2d 33, 38, 66 Cal.Rptr. 497, 502 (1968), involving the erroneous admission of statistical evidence, the court stressed that the opposing attorney was "apparently unschooled in mathematical refinements...." Should we impose a special ethical duty on the attorney conducting an expert's direct examination? We ordinarily expect the opposing attorney to prepare for trial by learning enough about the scientific discipline in question to conduct an effective cross-examination. Further, even in jurisdictions which routinely sequester witnesses, the opposing attorney can request an exemption from the sequestration order for an "at the elbow" expert. *See* Fed. R. Evid. 615(3), 28 U.S.C.A. That expert sits next to the attorney at the counsel table while the attorney listens to the opposing expert's direct examination and helps the attorney prepare the cross-examination questions. Are the opportunities to prepare for cross-examination and to request an "at the elbow" expert sufficient antidotes to the risks of misleading expert testimony? Assume that the question arises in a jurisdiction which has adopted mandatory pre-discovery disclosure requirements for expert testimony, such as those set out in Federal Rule of Civil Procedure 26(a)(2). This incident in the Sacco and Vanzetti prosecution illustrates the sort of pressures—and temptations—which as human beings, trial attorneys are subjected to during litigation.

§ 11.12   TRIAL TECHNIQUE EXERCISES

You will conduct a direct examination. Your instructor will announce any maximum or minimum length requirements for the direct. The designated opposing counsel may object and conduct any necessary voir dire in support of the objection. Each witness is an expert. For the more technical subjects, we have cited a reference text to help you understand the subject area. Your research should lead you to more specialized texts, but these citations should serve as a good starting point for your research.

As in the case of the direct examination exercise at the end of Chapter 9, you may find it necessary to invent some details of the witness's personal background and credentials. The Case file may give you little information about those subjects, but you need to qualify and humanize the witness before proceeding to the technical merits.

Case file A–1. The witness is Dr. Jensen. The reference is Locke, *Failure of General Practitioner to Seek Consultation With or Refer Patient to Specialist,* in 1 AM.JUR.P.O.F.2d 373 (1974).

Case file A–2. The witness is Mr. Swift. The references are Bamberger, *The Dangerous Expert Witness,* 52 BROOK.L.REV. 855 (1986) and Note, *Criteria for the Admissibility of Expert Opinion Testimony on Criminal Modus Operandi,* 1978 UTAH L.REV. 547.

Case file A–3. The expert is Officer Solis. The reference is *Reconstruction of Accident,* in 10 AM.JUR.P.O.F. 137 (1961).

Case file A–4. The witness is Mr. Singer. You will attempt to introduce Mr. Singer's opinion that the amount he charged Ms. Valdez for his services was reasonable.

Case file A–5. The witness is Dr. Bertram. The references are Turner, *Eyewitness Identification,* in 20 AM.JUR.P.O.F. 539 (1968) and Taylor *Unreliability of Eyewitness Identification,* in 18 AM.JUR.P.O.F.2d 361 (1979).

Case file A–6. The witness is Ms. Felice. The references are *Blood Tests,* in 2 AM.JUR.P.O.F. 585 (1959), *Intoxication,* in 6 AM.JUR.P.O.F. 465 (1960), and Taylor, *Defense to Charge of Driving Under the Influence of Alcohol,* in 17 AM.JUR.P.O.F.2d 1 (1978).

Case file A–7. The witness is Mr. Pinto. The reference is Watkins & Watkins, *Identification of Substances by Instrumental Analysis,* in 22 AM.JUR.P.O.F. 385 (1969). Sections 6–17 deal with gas chromatography (GC) while §§ 36–48 address ultraviolet absorption (UV).

Case file A–8. The witness is Ms. von Heckmann. The reference is the collection of articles listed under the Legal Malpractice entry in volume 2 of the AM.JUR.P.O.F. GENERAL INDEX (1992).

Case file A–9. The witness is Ms. Brown. You will attempt to elicit her opinion that in checking the Davises' authorization to have the children accompany them to Australia, the Aussie Transcontinental attendants complied with both the degree of care customary in the industry and all applicable F.A.A. regulations.

Case file A–10. The witness is Mr. Short. You will attempt to elicit his opinion that: (1) the University of El Dorado has made below average progress in achieving gender equity in its athletic programs; and (2) the cause for U.E.D.'s lack of progress is a deep-seated chauvinist attitude that pervades its athletic department.

Chapter 12

THE CROSS–EXAMINATION OF EXPERT WITNESSES—DEMYSTIFYING THE OPPOSING EXPERTS

Table of Sections

§ 12.1 INTRODUCTION

In the last chapter, we noted that expert testimony is being offered with increasing frequency. The paradox is that that phenomenon is occurring at the same time that we are obtaining alarming insights into the rate of error in expert analysis. Some critics believe that in many cases, the expert testimony proffered in court amounts to "junk science." PETER W. HUBER, GALILEO'S REVENGE: JUNK SCIENCE IN THE COURTROOM (1991). In the mid 1970's, the Law Enforcement Assistance Administration conducted the Laboratory Proficiency Testing Program, involving 240 of the leading crime laboratories in America. PROJECT ADVISORY COMMITTEE, LABORATORY PROFICIENCY TESTING PROGRAM (1975–76). The Project Advisory Committee sent the participating laboratories blind samples for analysis. A distressingly high percentage of the laboratories submitted inaccurate or incomplete responses. On three of the 21 tests, fewer than half the laboratories arrived at a correct, complete analysis. LEAA NEWSLETTER, Sept. 1978, at p. 1, col. 1, at p. 5, col. 1. In 1980, Food and Drug Administration officials charged that of the 12,000 American clinical researchers, "perhaps as many as ten percent do something less than [honest research]." W. BROAD & N. WADE, BETRAYERS OF THE TRUTH 83 (1983). In January 1983, the JOURNAL OF FORENSIC SCIENCES published the results of a new survey of toxicology laboratories' proficiency. Peat, Finnigan & Finkle, *Proficiency Testing in Forensic Toxicology: A Feasibility Study*, 28 J. FORENSIC SCI. 139 (1983). One hundred five laboratories, representing 49 states, participated. The survey team described the laboratories' performance as "disappointing." *Id.* In the mid 1980s the Centers for Disease Control completed a study of the proficiency of drug testing laboratories and discovered significant error rates. Hansen, Caudill & Boone, *Crisis in Drug Testing: Results of CDC Blind Study*, 253 J.AM.MED.ASS'N 2382 (1985). The revelations of the Inspector General's 1997 report on the F.B.I. Crime Laboratory heated up the controversy. *Justice Department Investigation of FBI Laboratory: Executive Summary*, 61 U.S.L.W. (BNA) 2017 (Apr. 16, 1997); Johnson, *Report Criticizes Scientific Testing at F.B.I. Crime Lab: "Serious" Problems Cited*, N.Y. TIMES, Apr. 16, 1997, at p. A1. A 1995 proficiency study of fingerprint examiners is perhaps even more troubling, though. We have become accustomed to think that fingerprint testimony is virtually infallible. However, in the study conducted by Collaborative Testing Services, Inc., "[e]rroneous identifications constituted 22% of the total." Starrs, *Forensic Science on the Ropes: An Upper Cut to Fingerprinting*, 20 SCI. SLEUTHING REV. 1, 3 (Wint. 1996). Expert testimony is not infallible; and when the opposing attorney contemplates calling an expert, you should give serious thought to aggressively cross-examining the expert at trial.

Some courts believe that lay jurors routinely attribute "mystic infallibility" to expert testimony. *United States v. Addison*, 498 F.2d 741, 744 (D.C.Cir.1974). Indeed, in *Daubert*, the Supreme Court itself stated that the trial judge may exercise "more control over experts" because expert testimony "can be both powerful and quite misleading...." 509 U.S. at 595. However, if you critically evaluate the opposing experts' testimony, you can demystify the testimony for the jury. In deciding whether to attack the expert's testimony, you should follow the same planning step outlined in Chapter 10. Should you cross-examine at all? If so, should you cross-examine to impeach? What impeachment techniques are available? The following sections of this chapter address those questions.

§ 12.2   DECIDING WHETHER TO CROSS–EXAMINE

As in the case of opposing lay witnesses, it is a mistake to assume that you must cross-examine every expert called by the opposition. When the expert's testimony does not hurt you and there is no additional, helpful testimony that you can elicit on cross-examination, the wisest tack is usually waiving cross-examination. Precisely because the witness usually knows more about the subject which his or her expertise relates to, the cross-examination of an expert can be "the most dangerous part" of a trial. Weitz, *Cross-Examining the Expert at Trial,* 28 TRIAL 55 (Feb. 1992). Suppose, for instance, that in the *Scott* prosecution, the People call a physician to testify solely that in her opinion, Mr. Williams' injuries could not have been caused by a fall down the stairs at the hotel. As Scott's attorney, you have already chosen the theory that there was an attack on Williams but that Scott was not involved in the attack. Your theory of the case neutralizes the physician's testimony; the testimony is consistent with your theory. In part, you select your theory with a view to neutralizing the opposition's evidence. When the prosecutor turns the witness over to you, you might say, "Your Honor, Dr. Martell's testimony has been very helpful. I see no need to conduct any cross-examination."

§ 12.3 DECIDING WHETHER TO IMPEACH

Even if you decide to cross-examine, you do not necessarily have to impeach the opposing expert. Suppose that in *Williams v. Scott,* the plaintiff called Dr. Martell to testify about damages in the case. You know from reading Dr. Martell's report that she observed injuries near both of Williams' eyes—injuries severe enough to have impaired his vision during the attack. During your pretrial interview with the doctor, she told you that any normal person would have begun to suffer blurred vision as soon as those injuries were inflicted. In this situation, the best cross-examination of Dr. Martell may be eliciting those admissions supporting your theory that Williams has mistakenly identified Scott.

§ 12.4 IMPEACHING THE EXPERT—AN OVERVIEW

For the balance of this section, we shall assume that you have decided to cross-examine the opposing expert to impeach. What impeachment techniques are available to you? There are numerous methods of attacking an opposing expert. *See generally* R. HABUSH, ART OF ADVOCACY: CROSS EXAMINATION OF NONMEDICAL EXPERTS (1981); E. IMWINKELRIED, THE METHODS OF ATTACKING SCIENTIFIC EVIDENCE (3rd ed. 1997). A text of this size cannot hope to illustrate or even list all the possible methods. However, you should realize that when an opposing expert takes the stand, there are six basic targets to attack: the expert's credibility, the expert's qualifications, the scientific technique or theory the expert relies on, the expert's minor premise (the data about the instant case), the manner in which the expert applied the technique to that data, and finally the expert's opinion itself. Sections 12.5–.11 of this chapter discuss some of the most common attacks on these targets.

As you review these cross-examination attacks, give some thought to the style in which you would conduct the cross-examination. As a general proposition, "treat an expert respectfully." S. HAMLIN, WHAT MAKES

JURIES LISTEN 305 (1985). "[T]here is something in our culture that says honor is to be given to people of accomplishment...." *Id.* at 306. The typical juror views the expert as an authority figure entitled to a measure of respect. However, you can adopt a sterner demeanor when the witness is vulnerable to bias impeachment. If the facts strongly suggest that the witness has a venal, financial interest, your demeanor can become more accusatory. The next section discusses bias impeachment.

§ 12.5   ATTACKING THE EXPERT'S IMPARTIALITY

Like a lay witness, an expert places her credibility in issue. Therefore, like a lay witness, an expert can be impeached for bias.

In some cases, the source of the bias is financial interest. Suppose, for example, that in the *Scott* prosecution, the police found hair strands on Williams' clothing immediately after the attack. The prosecutor decides to hire an independent consultant to subject the strands to a new DNA fingerprinting technique to prove that Scott was the source of the hair strands; the prosecutor's theory is that the strands transferred to Williams' clothing during the attack. The prosecutor is in a rush and tells her clerk to draft the employment contract for the independent consultant. The contract of employment should state only that the consultant will analyze the hair strands and testify about his analysis at trial. However, if the clerk is inexperienced, the clerk might word the contract to provide that the consultant will testify that the hair strands in question came from the defendant. Ostroff, *Experts, A Few Fundamentals,* 8 LITIGATION 8, 9 (Wint. 1982). That provision makes the expert's fee contingent on testimony favorable to the prosecution. A contingent fee provision in a contract with an expert witness violates A.B.A. Disciplinary Rule 7–109(C). Moreover, if the expert signs the tendered contract, the expert is vulnerable to devastating cross-examination. The expert has committed to giving favorable testimony even before he examined the physical evidence.

Even when the contract of employment contains no objectionable provisions, the expert may be impeachable for bias. California Evidence Code § 722(b) states that "[t]he compensation and expenses paid or to be paid to an expert witness by the party calling him is a proper subject of inquiry by an adverse party as relevant to the credibility of the witness...." As a cross-examiner, you are entitled to expose the fact that the expert is receiving an extraordinarily large fee in the pending case. In addition, This attack is rarely effective unless the fee is truly outlandish. In most cases, you will also be calling an expert witness; and most jurors are realistic enough to realize that the experts will not donate their services. More importantly, though, you can inquire about the expert's fees in other cases when those fees demonstrate a pattern relevant to show bias. *United States v. Edwardo–Franco,* 885 F.2d 1002, 1009–10 (2d Cir.1989); *Collins v. Wayne Corp.,* 621 F.2d 777 (5th Cir.1980); Ford & Holmes, *Exposure of Doctors' Venal Testimony,* 1965 TRIAL LAW. GUIDE 75; Graham, *Impeaching the Professional Expert*

Witness, 53 IND.L.J. 35, 46 (1977). On direct examination, the proponent may have held the witness out as an objective, impartial searcher
for truth. However, assume that on cross-examination, an expert called
by Williams' attorney is forced to admit that: During the past three
years, she has testified in court 60 times; on each occasion, she testified
for a plaintiff; those appearances earned her roughly $400,000 in con-
sulting fees; and that amount represents over half of her total income for
that three year period. Those admissions create a powerful inference of
bias.

Financial interest is not the only possible cause of bias; in some
cases, the source of the bias is a doctrinal belief. In the prosecution of
Sirhan Sirhan for the killing of Robert Kennedy, the defense called a
psychiatrist to testify that the defendant had an irresistible impulse to
kill. During cross-examination, the psychiatrist admitted that "he considered the concept of free will . . . a delusion." Younger, *Diminished
Capacity: A Principle in Search of Refinement,* in THE PROSECUTOR'S
DESKBOOK 584, 586 (P. Healy & J. Manak, eds. 1971). Based on that
admission, during closing the prosecutor argued that the witness was
biased in favor of finding an irresistible impulse. In an extreme case, you
may be able to force the witness to admit that in every case in which he
has testified, he has concluded that the witness was insane. A witness
that biased might as well have "mailed" in an opinion rather than
taking the time to study the facts of the case. Weitz, *Cross-Examining
the Expert at Trial,* 28 TRIAL 55, 57 (Feb. 1992).

§ 12.6 ATTACKING THE EXPERT'S QUALIFICATIONS

Federal Rule of Evidence 702 states that a person can qualify as an
expert "by knowledge, skill, experience, training, or education. . . ." The
courts liberally apply Rule 702 and, in doubtful cases, usually resolve
doubt in favor of finding the person qualified as an expert. There are
some signs that in the wake of *Daubert,* the courts are tightening the
standards and more frequently demanding that the witness qualify as a
true specialist in the field. *Alexander v. Smith & Nephew,* 90 F.Supp.2d
1225 (N.D.Okla.2000); *Berry v. Crown Equipment Corp.,* 108 F.Supp.2d
743 (E.D.Mich.2000); *Broders v. Heise,* 924 S.W.2d 148 (Tex.1996). Yet,
altogether barring testimony by a witness with extensive credentials or
substantial experience is still a long shot. As Chapter 6 pointed out,
under Federal Rule of Evidence 104(a), the opposing attorney has the
right to take an alleged expert on voir dire examination to challenge the
witness's qualification as an expert.

However, as just stated, trial judges rarely hold the witness unquali-
fied. If you mount an unsuccessful voir dire challenge, the expert's
proponent may emphasize that your attack failed; immediately after the
judge's ruling, the expert's proponent might resume the questioning by
saying, "Doctor, now that you have told Mr. Richards [the defense
attorney] your qualifications, can you please tell him as well as the ladies
and gentlemen of the jury what the economic damages are in this case."
Langerman, *Making Sure Your Experts Shine: Effective Presentation of*

Expert Witnesses, 28 TRIAL 106, 109 (Jan. 1992). For that reason, in most cases it is inadvisable to formally challenge the alleged expert's qualification by voir dire. You will challenge in the jury's hearing, and you will lose. "If you attack the King, you must kill the King." It is ordinarily preferable to "sav[e the] attack for cross-examination." McElhaney, *The Evidence Dance,* 76 A.B.A.J. 86, 89 (May 1990).

Rule 702 governs only the admissibility of the person's testimony. Even if the person satisfies the minimal standard set out in Rule 702, the person's qualifications may be vulnerable on cross-examination. The qualifications can be assailable even when they sound quite impressive on direct examination. Assume, for example, that a DNA typing expert called by the prosecution in *People v. Scott* testifies on direct that: She has 20 hours of graduate course work; she has written a thesis; she has testified as an expert on 50 prior occasions; and she has published 20 articles in scientific journals. When the jury first hears this testimony, the jury will probably be impressed. However, suppose that you elicit the following admissions on cross-examination: None of the courses related to DNA analysis; the thesis has nothing to do with DNA analysis; she has never testified as an expert on DNA fingerprinting; and her articles likewise relate to other subjects. *See* Weitz, *Cross-Examining the Expert at Trial,* 28 TRIAL 55, 56 (Feb. 1992) (show that the witness's expertise "is just not applicable to the case"). These admissions not only impeach the witness's qualifications; more importantly, they tend to impeach the candor of the opposing attorney. The jurors will suspect that the opposing attorney was trying to foist off an expert with largely irrelevant credentials.

Even when the credentials are relevant, the witness may be impeachable because he does not qualify as a specialist on the issue now before the court. Marquis' Who's Who periodically updates the DIRECTORY OF MEDICAL SPECIALISTS. The directory lists all the experts certified in the recognized specialties and subspecialties. If the opposing expert is not certified, you should force them to admit the lack of certification. In addition, ask them to describe the standards for certification: the number of years of experience required for eligibility to sit for the certification test, the nature of the test itself, and the low passage rate on the test. Make it clear to the jury that a person cannot become certified merely by paying dues. If the opposing expert is honest and cooperative, you might even ask the expert whether a specialist would be "better equipped" to diagnose a particular illness. D. COHEN, ADMIT THE ACT AND WIN THE CRIMINAL CASE 710 (1979). Ideally, you have retained an expert who possesses the relevant certification.

§ 12.7 ATTACKING THE EXPERT'S TECHNIQUE OR THEORY

We shall assume for purposes of this section that the judge has already ruled that the scientific theory the expert is relying on can be a basis for courtroom testimony.

As we saw in Chapter 9, the proponent of scientific testimony must show that the underlying technique has been generally accepted (the *Frye* test) or has been empirically validated (the *Daubert* standard). Of course, even when the theory the expert relies on passes muster under the appropriate test in your jurisdiction, you can attack the weight of the testimony.

You can do so by forcing the witness to concede that other experts reject the theory. Typically, the cross-examiner confronts the opposing expert with passages from learned treatises rejecting the theory or technique the expert is using. The jurisdictions differ over the type of treatise you can use during this type of cross-examination. C. HIRSCH, R. MORRIS & A. MORITZ, HANDBOOK OF LEGAL MEDICINE 274 (5th ed. 1979). Some jurisdictions follow the "recognition" test; you can use the text only if the opposing expert acknowledges that the text is a standard authority in the field. Other jurisdictions permit you to employ only texts that the expert consulted in preparing to testify in the present case. Still other jurisdictions opt for the most liberal view and permit you to resort to any text in the field. R. HABUSH, CROSS EXAMINATION OF NON–MEDICAL EXPERTS 20–9–10 (1981).

To use this cross-examination technique, you must initially establish that the text satisfies whatever test your jurisdiction uses. To do so, you can use judicial notice, the testimony by one of your witnesses, or the opposing expert's admission on cross-examination. At the opposing witness's pretrial deposition, force him or her to identify the texts which they recognize as authorities in the field. Herman, *Going by the Book: Direct and Cross–Examination of Medical Experts,* 27 TRIAL 52, 58–59 (Aug. 1991). Sets out sample lines of questioning calculated to force the opposing expert to admit the authoritative status of a text or journal. For example, if the expert teaches at a medical school, the cross-examiner can elicit the expert's admission that she gives her students reading assignments in the text. To maximize the impact of the impeachment, have the opposing expert describe the credentials of the person who wrote the text. Those credentials often exceed those of the expert on the stand. Then confront the expert with the contradictory passage. You can simply read the passage to the expert. If you read the passage, you can be sure the passage is read loudly enough with proper emphasis. However, many experienced litigators believe that the impeachment is more dramatic if you hand the text to the opposing expert and force him to read the passage to the jury. Be selective in using this impeachment technique. You must "be sure the jury sees the point." S. HAMLIN, WHAT MAKES JURIES LISTEN 306 (1985). The attempted impeachment will be ineffective if the passage contains such technical language that the lay jurors cannot appreciate that the passage contradicts the witness's testimony. It is worth employing this technique only when the passage is written so clearly that the contradiction is evident to the jury. Conclude the impeachment with the quotation of the passage from the text; if you go further and challenge the opposing expert to explain away the apparent contradiction, an acute opposing expert may proceed to do precisely that.

Another method of attacking the expert's technique is to show that there are superior techniques the expert neglected to use. Suppose, for instance, that in the *Scott* case, a crime laboratory technician compared the hair strands found on Williams' clothing after the attack with hair strands obtained from Scott. At trial, the criminalist testifies that the two sets of strands were "indistinguishable" under an optical microscope. Most optical microscopes have an upper limit of magnification of 2,000 times. However, there are other types of microscopes. Many laboratories, including some crime laboratories, have or have access to a scanning electron microscope (SEM). An SEM can easily produce magnifications exceeding 200,000 times. As Scott's attorney, you could force the criminalist to admit that: She used a conventional optical microscope; there is another type of microscope, namely, the SEM; the SEM has much greater magnification power than the microscope she used; although she had access to an SEM, she did not use it to analyze these hair samples; and if she had, the jury would have heard "more facts" and "know more" about the hair strand evidence. The effectiveness of this impeachment technique explains why it is so important to stay abreast of advances in science. Especially when the other side has the burden of proof, it is critical to point out that the opposing expert used an inferior analytic technique; in effect, the expert has denied the jury information that the state of the scientific art would have permitted her to present to the jury. In a similar fashion, with a hostile medical witness in a civil case, you can ask about relevant diagnostic procedures that the witness neglected to perform.

§ 12.8 ATTACKING THE EXPERT'S MINOR PREMISE

The technique or theory serves as the opposing expert's major premise. The expert uses that technique or theory to analyze the data in the instant case, the physical evidence found at the scene or testimonial information about a patient's case history. That data is the minor premise in the expert's reasoning process. Under Federal Rule of Evidence 703, the expert can gain the data in one of three ways.

One is by personal knowledge. Williams' treating physician, for example, has firsthand knowledge of the nature and extent of the injuries he observed while examining Williams. If the opposing expert relies on personal knowledge of the minor premise, the best impeachment technique is often stressing the facts that the expert does not know. The expert's firsthand knowledge may be incomplete. Ask the expert "Do you know whether...." or "Did you notice whether...." This impeachment technique is particularly effective when your expert has more extensive, personal knowledge of the facts. During closing, you can make the common-sense argument that other things being equal, an opinion is likely to be more reliable when the expert has more relevant facts.

Rule 703 also allows the expert to opine on the basis of the assumed facts in a hypothetical question. When the expert does so on direct examination, you are entitled to vary the set of assumed facts during cross-examination; you can add, delete, or modify facts in the original hypothetical. R. CARLSON, SUCCESSFUL TECHNIQUES FOR CIVIL TRIALS §§ 4:42, 4:43 (2d ed. 1992). Some attorneys ask whether the variation "would change" the expert's opinion. However, "might affect" language is safer. I. YOUNGER, TRIAL TECHNIQUES 59 (R. Oliphant, ed. 1978). As long as the expert concedes that the variation is relevant, you have all the ammunition you need for closing argument.

Finally, Rule 703 permits the expert to rely on hearsay reports of the data in the instant case. The only express limitation in the rule is that the hearsay must be "of a type reasonably relied upon by experts in the particular field in forming opinions or inferences upon the subject. . . ." In most cases, the judge will find the expert's reliance to be reasonable if the expert gives foundational testimony that it is the customary practice in his specialty to consider that type of data. Again, though, while Rule 703 allows the admission of an opinion based on such hearsay reports, the weight of the testimony may be suspect. Tigar, *Handling the Expert Like an Expert: Back to Basics,* NAT'L L.J., Mar. 1, 1982, at p. 33.

For instance, suppose that in *Scott,* the defense claims insanity. To establish the insanity defense, the defense calls a psychiatrist. The prosecutor might cross-examine the psychiatrist in this fashion. Initially, the prosecutor could force the witness to admit that he has no personal knowledge of the facts in the case. Humphreys, *Cross-Examining the Expert,* 23 TRIAL 75, 76 (Oct. 1987) ("You weren't at the scene, were you, professor?" "You weren't in the operating room, were you, doctor?"). Then the prosecutor could compel the witness to make the related admission that "to a large extent, . . . you must rely upon the truthfulness of the" person who made the hearsay reports to him. Wolfstone, *Effective Deposition of Treating Doctor,* in EXAMINATION OF MEDICAL EXPERTS 168, 216 (1968). The prosecutor next presses the witness to concede that the hearsay declarant in question is "none other than the defendant" himself, Scott. The prosecutor then attempts to raise common sense doubts about the credibility of that person. For example, the prosecutor elicits the witness's admission that his interview with Scott occurred not only after charges had been filed but also after Scott had raised his insanity defense. The prosecutor concludes the impeachment by showing that the witness uncritically accepted everything Scott said at face value. Assume that during the interview, Scott referred to several incidents and made it clear that there were other witnesses to the incidents. The prosecutor would force the psychiatrist to admit that he never contacted the other witnesses to corroborate Scott's hearsay statements. J. DeMAY, THE PLAINTIFF'S PERSONAL INJURY CASE: ITS PREPARATION, TRIAL AND SETTLEMENT 217 (1977). Or Scott may claim that he wrote a letter evidencing his delusions. Force the psychiatrist to concede not only that he did not read the letter with his own two eyes; worse still, he made absolutely no effort to obtain access to the letter. In closing, the prosecutor will contend that the psychiatrist admitted that the value of his opinion depends upon the credibility of the source of the hearsay report. The prosecutor will point out that given the identity of that source and the timing of the interview, there is good reason to doubt the trustworthiness of the hearsay the expert relied on. Lastly, the prosecutor will assert that rather than verifying the hearsay reports, the expert naively accepted them at face value.

The preceding paragraphs discuss the substantive requirements under Federal Rule of Evidence 703. However, the opponent should not overlook a related procedural issue. Assume *arguendo* that although a hearsay report is independently inadmissible, the judge rules that the expert may rely on the report as part of the basis for his or her opinion. The only thing that Rule 703 says explicitly is that the expert may express an opinion premised on the inadmissible matter. Rule 703 does not state that the expert may recite the inadmissible matter in detail in the jury's presence. If the report is oral, may the expert quote it? If the report is written, may the proponent formally introduce it into evidence, hand it to the jurors, and have it sent to the jury in the deliberation room? Would a limiting instruction under Rule 105 be adequate protection against the jury's misuse of the material as substantive evidence? The courts are badly divided over this question. Carlson, *Policing the Modern Bases of Expert Testimony,* 39 VAND.L.REV. 577 (1986); Rice, *Inadmissible Evidence as a Basis for Expert Testimony: A Response to Professor Carlson,* 40 VAND.L.REV. 583 (1987). Kentucky and Minnesota amended their versions of Rule 703 to generally prohibit the proponent from exposing the jury to the inadmissible matter. Effective December 1, 2000, Federal Rule of Evidence 703 was revised to add the following concluding sentence:

> Facts or data that are otherwise inadmissible shall not be disclosed to the jury by the proponent of the opinion or inference unless the court determines that their probative value in assisting the jury to evaluate the expert's opinion substantially outweighs their prejudicial effect.

Under this amendment, in most cases the expert will be foreclosed from a detailed description of the technically inadmissible information. Carlson, *Is Revised Expert Witness Rule 703 a Critical Moderation for the New Century?,* 52 FLA.L.REV. 739 (2001).

§ 12.9   EXPOSING THE EXPERT'S MECHANICAL ERRORS

To generate an opinion, the expert must apply the major premise to the minor premise. When the technique is an instrumental one employing hardware such as a breathalyzer, the expert might commit a simple, mechanical error in maintaining or operating the equipment.

Before trial, you must learn the proper procedures for maintaining and operating the instrumentation. Research the statutes and administrative regulations to determine whether they prescribe maintenance or operational procedures. By way of example, many states have statutes or regulations governing the calibration and operation of breathalyzers. Subpoena any standing operating procedure used by the laboratory. Contact the manufacturer to obtain a copy of the operator's manual. The manual is often sitting in a corner of the laboratory, unread and collecting dust. Question your own expert about the correct steps to follow.

Next, find out whether the laboratory followed proper procedures in maintaining and operating the specific equipment used to test the physical evidence in your case. In some cases, the expert's report will contain information about the maintenance and operation of the equipment. In most cases, however, the report gives you little or no information on this subject. Subpoena the maintenance records for the equipment and the logs and diaries of the technicians who tested the evidence.

Suppose that you discover that in several respects, the opposing expert deviated from correct procedure in testing the evidence. How should you sequence the cross-examination? The initial temptation is to confront the expert with the statute, regulation, standing operating procedure, or manual at the outset of the cross. However, that sequence is ill-advised. By doing so, you refresh the witness's recollection of the required maintenance and operation procedures. If the witness is less than honest, the witness may shade the balance of his testimony to comply with the procedures. For that reason, it is usually best to begin by locking the expert into a version of the facts as to how he maintained or operated this equipment. After doing so, take the manual out of your briefcase and broach the subject of the correct procedures. You can then demonstrate to the jury that in several ways, the expert violated accepted protocol.

§ 12.10 EXPOSING THE EXPERT'S ERRORS IN REASONING

Even when the opposing expert has not committed a mechanical error in applying the major premise to the data in this case, the expert may be guilty of an error in reasoning.

The error could be a classic mistake in syllogistic reasoning. Again, assume that the *Scott* defense calls a psychiatrist to testify to Scott's insanity. On direct examination, the expert expresses the opinion that at the time of the actus reus, Scott was suffering from a particular mental disease that prevented him from appreciating the nature or quality of his conduct. That opinion may be a product of flawed syllogistic reasoning. The American Psychiatric Association has promulgated a DIAGNOSTIC AND STATISTICAL MANUAL. The manual is now in a revised fourth edition, DSM IV–TR. For many recognized mental illnesses, the manual lists inclusionary and exclusionary criteria. An inclusionary criterion is a symptom that must be present before the mental health professional can diagnose that illness. An exclusionary criterion is a symptom, the presence of which precludes a diagnosis of that illness. Suppose that the defense expert hastily prepares for trial without consulting the DSM. The DSM states an exclusionary criterion for the illness the defense expert is prepared to diagnose, and the defense expert will do so despite the fact that his report indicates that the exclusionary symptom is present in Scott's case history. At the beginning of the cross, the prosecutor should lock the defense expert into an admission that the symptom is present. Next, the prosecutor will force the expert to acknowledge the DSM's authoritative status. Finally, the prosecutor can confront the expert with the passage in the DSM indicating that the presence of that symptom rules out the diagnosis the expert has testified to.

In other cases, the error in reasoning occurs when the expert overlooks inconsistent facts. This error often happens when experts testify to the comparative analysis of toolmarks, bullets, fiber, and hair. Suppose that the criminalist testifies in *Scott* to establish that the hairs found on Williams' clothing came from Scott. During direct examination, the prosecutor might present photographic enlargements of the two sets of hair strands and have the criminalist mark the points of similarity. On cross-examination, you can force the expert to acknowledge apparent dissimilarities on the face of the enlargements. The dissimilarities are just as much "facts" as the similarities. In some disciplines such as fingerprint or bitemark analysis and questioned document examination, a single unexplained dissimilarity precludes a finding of identity. In closing argument, tell the jury that the ultimate test of the value of scientific testimony is the test of the facts, that is, whether it accounts for the facts which the jury can see with its own eyes. If the expert's opinion fails that test, dismiss the opinion as unscientific and unreliable.

§ 12.11 THE PHRASING OF THE EXPERT'S ULTIMATE OPINION

The final product of the expert's application of the major premise to the minor is an opinion relevant to the merits of the case. The opposing attorney should be cognizant of two restrictions on the phrasing of the ultimate opinion.

One limitation is that in most jurisdictions, the phrasing may not directly address either a pure question of law or a mixed question of law and fact. Federal Rule of Evidence 704(a) purports to abolish the traditional, ultimate issue prohibition, but most courts do not read Rule 704(a) literally. A 1977 Committee Comment to the Minnesota version of the Federal Rules states the still prevailing view:

> A distinction should be made between opinions as to factual matters, and opinions involving a legal analysis or mixed questions of law and fact. Opinions of the latter nature are not deemed to be of any use to the trier of fact.

It is true that the Texas courts have explicitly ruled that otherwise proper opinions may speak to mixed questions of law and fact. *Puente v. A.S.I. Signs,* 821 S.W.2d 400, 402 (Tex.App.1991); *Harvey v. Culpepper,*

801 S.W.2d 596, 601 (Tex.App.1990). However, the Texas position is a distinct minority view. Thus, most courts would preclude an accident reconstruction expert from opining either that a driver has a duty to yield the right of way (a pure question of law) or that a particular driver failed to yield the right of way (a mixed question of law and fact). *Terrell v. Reinecker,* 482 N.W.2d 428, 430 (Iowa 1992) (it was improper for the expert to testify that the plaintiff had "failed to yield the right-of-way;" the testimony stopped short of stating that negligence had occurred, but it extended "too far into the realm of legal conclusion"). The phrasing of the accident reconstruction witness's opinion would be limited to factual inferences based on the laws of physics such as conclusions as to velocity or point of impact.

A second common-law limitation on the phrasing of the opinion was that the expert had to vouch for any opinion to a reasonable degree of scientific probability or certainty. Joseph, *Less Than "Certain" Medical Testimony,* 1979 MED. TRIAL TECH. Q. 10 (1979). The Federal Rules of Evidence do not codify that view, and many jurisdictions no longer require that the expert vouch for the opinion in that fashion.

However, the abolition of the common-law view means only that the opinion is admissible; the opinion can still be subject to effective cross-examination. Suppose that the defense psychiatrist in *Scott* does not define the degree of the certitude of his opinion on direct examination. The prosecutor has obtained a copy of the psychiatrist's report and knows that the report uses the expression, "possibly." On cross-examination, the prosecutor can force the witness to admit that the opinion expressed during direct is merely a possibility, not a probability or a certainty. This line of impeachment is especially effective when the party calling the expert has the burden of proof on the issue. In our hypothetical, in some jurisdictions the defense may have both the initial burden of production and the ultimate burden of proof on the question of Scott's insanity. If so, the defense may win the battle but lose the war by relying on the psychiatrist's testimony. The judge may well admit the psychiatrist's opinion, but the prosecutor may be able to convince the jury that a speculative opinion about a possible mental illness does not satisfy the defense's burden of proof.

§ 12.12 SAMPLE IMPEACHMENT CROSS–EXAMINATION OF AN EXPERT

You are the prosecutor in *People v. Scott.* During its case-in-chief, the defense calls Professor Simon Pass. Professor Pass teaches in the Psychology Department of El Dorado State University. On direct examination, after describing his credentials, Professor Pass testifies to the general unreliability of eyewitness identification testimony. Pass then asserts that laypeople such as the jurors routinely overestimate the accuracy of eyewitness identification testimony. He adds that there is reason to doubt the trustworthiness of Williams' identification of Scott because of Williams' age and the traumatic nature of the attack. The cross-examination proceeds in this fashion:

(Attack on the Witness's Impartiality)

Q Professor, how many times have you testified as an expert in a court of law?

A As I said on direct, I believe the number is 41 times.

Q Those appearances occurred during a seven year period. Correct?

A Yes.

Q Isn't it true that each of those cases was a criminal prosecution?

A Right.

Q And in each case, you testified for the defense. Right?

A That's correct.

Q In a total of over 40 courtroom appearances, you've never testified in a civil case?

A Right.

Q And isn't also true that despite over 40 appearances, you've never testified for the prosecution?

A Yes.

Q Not once in seven years?

A Right.

(Attack on the Witness's Qualifications)

Q Let's go into a little more detail about those 41 courtroom appearances.

A All right.

Q Isn't it true that in each of those prior cases, you testified about psychological tests like the Minnesota Multiphasic Personality Index, the MMPI?

A Yes.

Q How many times have you testified as an expert on eyewitness identification testimony?

A I've never testified on that subject before.

Q Now on direct examination you also told us that you've published 15 articles in scientific journals. Is that the number?

A Correct.

Q All those articles discuss psychological tests like the MMPI. Right?

A Yes.

Q How many of the articles deal with the topic you're testifying about today, the topic of eyewitness identification?

A None of them.

Q Do any of those articles even include the expression, "eyewitness identification testimony"?

A Not to the best of my recollection.

(Attack on the Witness's Theory)

Q Let's talk about your articles for a moment. Five of them were published by the periodical, *American Psychologist.* Correct?

A Yes.

Q And that is a well known scientific journal in the field of psychology?

A Yes.

Q It's one of the most respected. Isn't it?

A Yes.

Q The *American Psychologist* is a peer-reviewed journal. Correct?

A Yes.

Q And doesn't that mean that before the journal publishes any article, several other experts check the article. Right?

A Yes.

Q American Psychologist is the official publication of the American Psychological Association. Isn't it?

A That's true.

Q And you're a member of that organization.

A Yes.

Q How long have you been a member?

A Over 15 years now.

Q Your Honor, I now request that this be marked People's Exhibit No. 9 for identification.

J It will be so marked.

Q Please let the record reflect that I am showing the exhibit to the defense counsel.

J The record will reflect that.

Q Permission to approach the witness?

J Granted.

Q Now, Professor Pass, I hand you what has been marked as People's Exhibit No. 9 for identification. What is it?

A It's an article from *American Psychologist.*

Q How do you recognize it?

A I know the format, and it just so happens that I'm familiar with this article.

Q Let's get the record straight. Which article are you looking at right now?

A It's an article entitled "Eyewitness Identification: What Can a Psychologist Tell a Jury." It appears to begin at page 550 of the May 1983 issue of *American Psychologist*.

Q Who wrote that article?

A Professors Michael McCloskey and Howard Egeth.

Q Who are they?

A They're two psychologists at Johns Hopkins University.

Q Is the Psychology Department at Johns Hopkins University a well respected one?

A I'd have to say that it's one of the best in the country, if not the world.

Q Are you familiar with Professors McCloskey and Egeth?

A Yes. They're quite well known in my field.

Q The article we're talking about now. It's the summary of a research project. Isn't it?

A Yes.

Q And the project was funded by the National Science Foundation. Wasn't it?

A Yes.

Q If I recall correctly, didn't you testify on direct examination that laypeople like the ladies and gentlemen of this jury generally are unaware of the various weaknesses of eyewitness testimony?

A Yes.

Q Let me direct your attention to page 551 of this article—the right-hand column. On that page, don't Professors McCloskey and Egeth write that there is "no reason to assume ... that people are not" aware of the weaknesses in eyewitness testimony?

A Yes.

Q Don't they also write that "there is virtually no empirical evidence that people are unaware of the problems with eyewitness testimony"?

A Yes. They say that on the same page.

(Attack on the Witness's Minor Premise)

Q Let's turn to the eyewitness identification in this case, the identification by Mr. Williams.

A O.K.

Q Were you there at the Senator Hotel on the morning of January 19, 19YR–1?

A Of course, not.

Q Then you have no personal knowledge at all of what happened that morning?

A I'd be the first to admit that.

Q So in testifying today, you're relying on what people told you about the events that morning?

A Sure.

Q Isn't it true that the only people you've discussed those events with have been the defense attorney and the defendant?

A Yes.

Q They're the ones who made all the statements about those events that you're relying on.

A Right.

Q When did you interview them?

A It was early this year—late January or very early February.

Q Were you aware that at that time, charges had already been filed against the defendant?

A Generally yes. I didn't know exactly when they were filed or what the precise charges were.

Q In addition to talking to the defendant and his attorney, did you talk to the investigating officer, Officer Taylor?

A No.

Q Did you make any attempt to reach her?

A No.

Q In addition to talking to the defendant and his attorney, did you talk to Mr. Williams?

A No.

Q Did you make any attempt to contact him?

A No.

Q When you spoke with the defendant, didn't he specifically mention a Ms. Joan Freeman?

A Yes.

Q After speaking with the defendant, did you contact Ms. Freeman?

A No.

Q Did you phone her?

A No.

Q Did you make any effort at all to contact her?

A No.

Q So in short, the only sources of information for your opinion were none other than the defendant and his attorney. Correct?

A Yeah.

(Attack on the Opinion Itself)

Q I just have a few more questions about your opinion in this case. Was it your testimony on direct examination that in this case, because of Mr. Williams' age and the surprising nature of the attack, there is "good reason" to question the reliability of his identification?

A I think you're being accurate; I believe that "good reason" were the words I used.

Q As a psychologist, can you testify under oath that it's 100% certain that Mr. Williams is wrong?

A No. Psychology's a soft science. I can't give you a number.

Q So you can't tell us for sure that there's even a 51% probability that Mr. Williams is wrong. Correct?

A Yes. It would be dishonest for me to quote a figure.

Q So all you can say for sure is that it's possible that Mr. Williams is mistaken. Would that be a fair summary of your testimony?

A Yes.

Q Thank you, professor. I have no further questions of the witness at this time, Your Honor.

§ 12.13 ETHICAL QUESTIONS

You are the prosecutor in *Scott.* You are convinced that Professor Pass is consciously biased and willing to stretch the truth to win over the jury. In particular, you sense that he is so arrogant and egotistical that he might even overstate his expertise and knowledge. In this situation, some texts suggest that you question the witness about his or her familiarity with a non-existent treatise. Messrs. Bailey and Rothblatt mention the tactic in CROSS–EXAMINATION IN CRIMINAL TRIALS 215 (1978). The hope is that a self-impressed witness will claim familiarity with the non-existent treatise rather than truthfully admit that he or she has never heard of the book. If the witness claims familiarity with the text, the cross-examiner then discloses that he made up the name of the treatise. Is this tactic ethical? Does the tactic necessarily involve a misrepresentation of fact? Would it make a difference if before beginning the cross-examination, the defense attorney disclosed his intent to the trial judge at sidebar? *See United States v. Sabater,* 830 F.2d 7 (2d Cir.1987); *United States v. Thoreen,* 653 F.2d 1332 (9th Cir.1981), *cert. denied,* 455 U.S. 938 (1982); *In re Metzger,* 31 Hawaii 929 (1931).

How likely is this tactic to succeed? *See* A. CUTLER, SUCCESSFUL TRIAL TACTICS 185 (1949). How will the jury respond if the witness denies familiarity with the text and adds that he doubts that there is such a text? How will the jury react if you are forced to admit that you fabricated the name of the text in order to trick the witness? In the light of your admission, how will the jury evaluate the witness's credibility? How will the jury evaluate you?

§ 12.14 TRIAL TECHNIQUE EXERCISES

You will conduct a cross-examination. Your instructor will announce any maximum or minimum length requirements for the cross. The designated opposing counsel may object and conduct any necessary voir dire to support the objection. The instructor may also indicate that the opposing counsel should be prepared to conduct a redirect examination, following up on the cross. In each case file, the witness to be cross-examined is the expert whose direct examination was conducted in the exercise at the end of Chapter 11. You should consult any technical references cited for your case file in § 11.12.

Figure 12-1

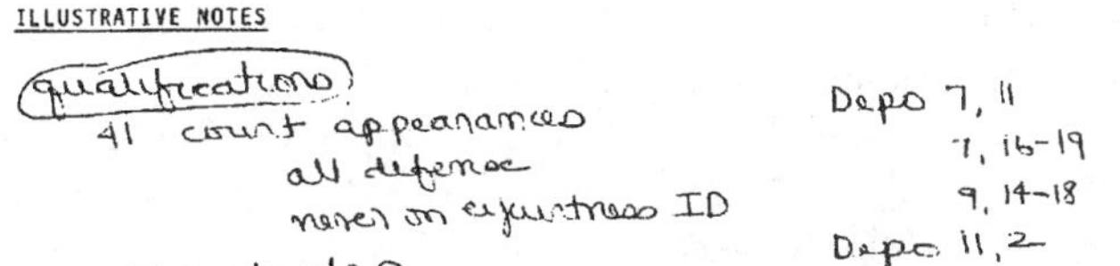
ILLUSTRATIVE NOTES

qualifications — Depo 7, 11
41 court appearances — 7, 16-19
all defense
never on eyewitness ID — 9, 14-18
15 articles — Depo 11, 2
none on ID — 12, 9-13

theory — Depo 14, 19-21
APA member 15 years
May 1983 AP 550 — 16, 1-7
Egeth, McCloskey — 16, 15-20
Johns Hopkins — article 550
NSF — 551
"no reason" — 551
"there is virtually no"

minor premise — Depo 20, 5-9
no personal knowledge — 20, 20
D, D's attorney — 23, 7-11
aware charges filed — 23, 15
contact Taylor — 23, 17
contact Williams

conclusion — Depo 29, 34
certainty — 33, 14
5% — 37, 7
possibility

Chapter 13

THE INSTRUCTIONS CONFERENCE—OBTAINING THE JUDICIAL IMPRIMATUR ON YOUR THEORY AND THEME

Table of Sections

§ 13.1 INTRODUCTION

In most jurisdictions, in major cases the judge and attorneys have an instructions conference between the close of the evidence, on the one hand, and the closing arguments and instructions, on the other hand. They frequently meet in the judge's chambers to discuss instructions and a number of other matters. This conference is critical for several reasons. To begin with, the conference is important because at the trial level, the conference determines what the judge tells the jury about the pertinent substantive and evidentiary rules. The jurors are usually skeptical of statements made by the attorneys as advocates, and they often perceive that witnesses have a financial or emotional "vested interest in the outcome of the case." Dombroff, *Jury Instructions Can Be Crucial in Trial Process*, LEGAL TIMES, Feb. 25, 1985, at p. 26. In contrast, jurors "typically listen more closely and weigh more heavily almost everything said to them by the judge, including the jury instructions." *Id.* Moreover, the instructions can be decisive in the event of an appeal. In some jurisdictions, over 60% of the alleged errors assigned on

320

appeal relate to the jury instructions. In a five-state study of criminal appeals conducted by the National Center for State Courts, 30% of the alleged errors related to jury instructions. Marcotte, *Few Reversible Errors,* 76 A.B.A.J. 30 (Sep. 1990). In short, the trial judge's rulings at the instructions conference can determine the outcome of the trial or the appeal.

§ 13.2 RAISING INSTRUCTIONAL ISSUES BEFORE TRIAL

In a given case, the verdict may turn on whether the juror appreciates a particular jury instruction. For example, there may be an instruction that directly supports your theme; and you believe that the case is so close that the outcome will depend on whether the jury concentrates on the precise wording of that instruction. Of course, you could wait until the instructions conference near the end of trial to request that instruction. However, if the instruction is that critical to your case, you may want to raise the issue before trial.

In the typical trial, after the jury has heard days, weeks, or months of testimony, the judge finally orally reads the instructions to the jury. Any dispassionate observer would probably conclude that that sequence is idiotic; since the jurors learn the relevant legal rules only after they hear the testimony, they do not even know what to listen for during the testimony.

However, in most jurisdictions, there is neither a statute nor court rule dictating that the judge read the instructions only once after the close of the evidence. The judge has discretion to vary the procedure to help the jurors understand the instructions. In a complex trial in which there will be myriad instructions or a case in which a particular instruction is vital to your case, before trial you may ask the judge to deviate from the typical procedure in several respects.

To begin with, you can ask the judge to preinstruct. Rather than reserving all the instructions until the end of the case, the judge could deliver some opening and midtrial instructions. For instance, before the plaintiff's or prosecutor's case-in-chief, the judge could deliver some of the key substantive law instructions on the cause of action or crime. Similarly, just prior to the defense case-in-chief, the judge could read some of the substantive law instructions governing the affirmative defense. Standard 5.c of the new A.B.A. Civil Trial Practice Standards deals with interim instructions. The standard states: "During the trial, the court may sua sponte, and should upon request of a party, consider giving instructions at any point at which they might be helpful to the jury." A field experiment conducted under the auspices of the Wisconsin Judicial Council indicates that preinstruction can help the jurors apply the rules of law in their decisionmaking. Heuer & Penrod, *Instructing Jurors: A Field Experiment with Written and Preliminary Instructions,* 13 LAW & HUM. BEH. 409 (1989). Other researchers have come to the same conclusion. SPEC. COMM. ON JURY COMPREHENSION, A.B.A. LITIGATION SECTION, JURY COMPREHENSION IN COMPLEX

CASES App. 10, pp. 15–16 (1990); Kassin & Wrightsman, *On the Requirements of Proof: The Timing of Judicial Instruction and Mock Juror Verdicts*, 37 J. PERSONALITY & SOC. PSYCHOLOGY 1877 (1979); Comment, *Memory, Magic, and Myth: The Timing of Jury Instructions*, 59 ORE.L.REV. 451 (1981).

Further, you can ask the judge to repeat an important instruction. You will often want the judge to reiterate the instruction supporting your theme. Suppose, for instance, that you are the prosecutor in the *Scott* case. From your perspective, the most important jury charge is the instruction telling the jurors that they may consider "how close" Williams was to his attackers and "how long" he had to view them during the attack. It would be ideal if the judge read that instruction both before your case-in-chief and during the final jury charge.

Customarily, the bulk of the instruction takes place at the end of the case. If the instructions will be quite lengthy, ask the judge to give the jury a break every half hour or so. Request that the judge allow the jurors at least to stand and stretch. Most jurors watch television, and they are accustomed to relaxing their concentration every half hour. In a complex case, reading the instructions may require several hours. When the judge reads the instructions without interruption, it is virtually certain that jury retention will fall off markedly after the initial half hour.

Finally, in the majority of jurisdictions, you may ask the judge to give the jury a written copy of all or some of the instructions. Some judges will even give the jury taped instructions. Pellham, *Judges Seek Ways to Ease Juries' Work*, LEGAL TIMES, May 15, 1989, at p. 1. There are only 10 states that flatly forbid the trial judge from submitting the instructions in writing to the jury. Standard 5.f of the A.B.A. Civil Trial Practice Standards states that "[f]inal instructions should be provided for the jurors' use during deliberations." It is true that even in the majority of states, many judges and trial attorneys are reluctant to give the jury written instructions; they fear that in the privacy of their deliberations, the jurors may focus on the wrong instruction. However, you must balance that risk against the potential gain that a written set of instructions may improve the jury's general comprehension of the instructions. You should not follow a categorical rule against ever requesting that written instructions be submitted to the jury. If the judge consents to giving the jury a written set of instructions, during closing you can point the jury to the critical instruction that supports your trial theme.

§ 13.3 THE DETERMINATION OF THE INSTRUCTIONS

The first item on the agenda of the instructions conference is usually the selection of the instructions which will guide the jury's deliberations. To prepare to argue this item, you must review several questions before the conference.

§ 13.3(A) Which Instructions Should You Request?

There are two instructions that you certainly must request at the conference. One is a substantive law instruction on your theory of the case. That instruction describes the law controlling your cause of action, crime, or affirmative defense. The second is an instruction supporting your theme. In many cases, this instruction relates to an evidentiary principle such as the factors the jury should consider in deciding whether to accept Williams' eyewitness identification of Scott.

There is a related question that you should resolve in your own mind before the conference: Do you want to take an "all or nothing" gamble during the jury charge? Initially, consider the question from the perspective of the plaintiff or prosecutor. When you filed your opening pleadings, you may have alleged four or 40 causes of action or crimes. If you have not as yet withdrawn any of those counts, the judge may instruct the jury on all counts. On the eve of trial, you presumably selected your best trial theory. If the judge instructs on all counts, there is a grave risk that the jury will become confused and lose sight of your best theory. When the trial has gone well and confirmed your pretrial evaluation that a particular theory is your strongest, at the conference you should consider asking the judge *not* to instruct on the other theories.

Now consider the problem from the defense point of view, especially the perspective of a criminal defense attorney. Your client is charged with a major felony that encompasses several lesser included offenses. For example, under the El Dorado law of crimes, there may be several degrees of battery; and the El Dorado procedural rule may permit the jury to return a verdict of guilty of any degree of battery so long as the charged offense against Scott is the highest degree. Assume that the judge does not have a sua sponte duty to instruct on the lesser included offenses (LIO). In some jurisdictions, the defendant has the sole right to decide whether to insist on an LIO instruction. *People v. Brocksmith,* 162 Ill.2d 224, 642 N.E.2d 1230, 205 Ill.Dec. 113 (1994). An LIO instruction can be particularly advantageous in a jurisdiction in which the judge must instruct on time-barred LIOs but may not inform the jury that the period of limitations has already passed on the LIO. *E.g., State v. Short,* 131 N.J. 47, 618 A.2d 316 (1993).

Should Scott's attorney ask the judge to instruct the jury on the LIO? The answer depends on your evaluation of the strength of the prosecution case. Suppose, for instance, that your assessment is that the prosecution case is strong and that there is a good possibility that the jurors may convict your client of the charged offense. You scored a few points against the prosecution, but on balance their evidence will probably seem persuasive to the jury. In this situation, it is advisable to request LIO instructions. If any of the jurors were impressed by your points, the jury might compromise on a lesser included crime. In contrast, assume that you believe that the prosecution case is weak. The best strategy may be waiving any request for an LIO charge. You may want the jury to think that their only alternatives are to find the defendant guilty of the charged offense or to altogether acquit your client. If you have correctly assessed the jury's perception of the prosecution case, faced with those alternatives, the jury is likely to acquit.

§ 13.3(B) Where Can You Find Instructions?

In many jurisdictions, there are officially approved, pattern instructions. Thus, California has official sets of instructions for civil and criminal cases. The civil set is contained in CALIFORNIA JURY INSTRUCTIONS—BOOK OF APPROVED JURY INSTRUCTIONS (8th rev. ed. 1994), and the criminal set is CALIFORNIA JURY INSTRUCTIONS CRIMINAL (6th rev. ed. 1996). Several of the federal Courts of Appeal have now promulgated pattern instructions for the district courts within their territorial jurisdiction.

There are also a number of commercially prepared sets of instructions in widespread use. The most popular set is O'MALLEY, GRENIG & LEE, FEDERAL JURY PRACTICE AND INSTRUCTIONS: CIVIL AND CRIMINAL (5th ed. 2000) (9 vols.). Until the promulgation of pattern instructions by the courts of appeal, this set was the primary source book for instructions in federal trials. Several new sets have been released within the past few years. Both J. POTUTO, S. SALTZBURG & H. PERLMAN, FEDERAL CRIMINAL JURY INSTRUCTIONS (2d ed. 1991) (3 vols.) and L. SAND, J. SIFFERT, W. LOUGHLIN & S. REISS, MODERN FEDERAL JURY INSTRUCTIONS (1984) (4 vols.) have been well received. In addition, the American Bar Association has released sets of recommended jury instructions for certain types of trials such as business tort cases and civil antitrust actions.

Unfortunately, in some cases, particularly in law reform litigation at the cutting edge, you will find neither a pattern instruction nor even a commercially prepared instruction stating the principle that you want the judge to charge the jury on. In that event, you must start from scratch and draft your own "special" instruction. To persuade a judge to give a special instruction, you must make a written submission including two things.

First, you should tender to the judge a proposed instruction. In most jurisdictions, if you merely request an instruction without tendering proposed language, you waive any issue for appeal. In addition, common sense suggests that when you want the judge to give a special instruction, you should make it as easy as possible for the judge to say Yes to your request; hand the proposed wording to the judge on a silver platter. Since 1970, social scientists have undertaken several studies of the effectiveness of the wording of jury instructions. *E.g.,* Burgins, *Jurors Ignore, Misunderstand Instructions,* 81 A.B.A.J. 30 (May 1995)(the Capital Jury Project studying the effectiveness of instructions in death penalty cases); Saks, *Judicial Nullification,* 68 IND.L.J. 1281, 1283–84 (1993); Charrow & Charrow, *Making Legal Language Understandable: A Psycholinguistic Study of Jury Instructions,* 79 COLUM.L.REV. 1306

(1979). One line of research led to the publication of A. ELWORK, B. SALES & J. ALFINI, MAKING JURY INSTRUCTIONS UNDERSTANDABLE (1982). That text and similar publications contain guidelines for drafting comprehensible instructions for lay jurors.[1] The guidelines can be of great help in writing a special instruction. Some of the guidelines include recommendations that the draftsman:

— avoid legalese (comprehensible to appellate courts but confusing to lay triers of fact),

— use concrete words,

— employ active voice sentences,

— eliminate dependent, embedded clauses within sentences, and

— tightly organize hierarchically,[2] associationally,[3] or algorithmically.[4]

In addition to submitting a proposed instruction, you ought to give the judge a memorandum of law. It is ideal if you can point out that an appellate court in your jurisdiction has approved a special instruction identical to your proposed language. Or other jurisdictions may have approved this language. At the bare minimum, you must convince the judge that the proposed wording correctly states a rule of law that your jurisdiction has adopted or should embrace. Your memorandum should recite the constitutional provisions, statutes, cases, or secondary authorities favoring the rule of law you have embodied in the proposed charge.

§ 13.3(C) What Objections Can You Make to Your Opponent's Proposed Instructions?

There are several possible objections to an instruction urged by your opponent:

There is no factual support in the record for the proposed instruction. The instructions should describe only the rules of law that are triggered

---

1. For a succinct overview of the research and the resulting guidelines, *see Guidelines for Drafting Understandable Jury Instructions: An Introduction to the Use of Psycholinguistics*, 23 CRIM.L.BULL. 135 (Mar.-Apr. 1987).

2. "In this scheme, the draftsman breaks high-level concepts down into lower-level concepts." The draftsman then integrates the components. Elwork gives the following example: "In defining an 'intent' to murder, we might explain that it has four components: willfulness, premeditation, deliberation, and malice. Each of these components may, in turn, have to be broken down further into its subcomponents." *Id.* at 146–47.

3. In associational organization, the draftsman groups connected topics together. The topics must share some conceptual commonality. For example, the draftsman can group evidentiary rules together if all the rules relate to how a particular item of evidence should be used. He may do so even when one rule prescribes the proper use of the evidence and another proscribes a particular use of the evidence. *Id.* at 147.

4. "Topics should be organized algorithmically when one flows from the other. One topic or concept builds on the other. Algorithmic structure is especially effective when there is a causal or temporal relationship between concepts. In the instruction, the sequence of the concepts should parallel the causal or temporal order. Thus, the instruction should mention an earlier event before a later event and a determination the jury must make before the consequences flowing from the determination." *Id.* at 148.

by the testimony in the case. If there is no testimony tending to prove a fact that is a necessary predicate of a rule of law, there should be no instruction on that rule. The instruction is not only irrelevant; worse still, the instruction can mislead the jury.

The proposed instruction misstates the testimony. The instruction could include a reference to the testimony in the case. If the reference is inaccurate, the instruction is objectionable.

The proposed instruction misstates the law. Just as the instruction can include an inaccurate description of the testimony, the instruction might describe the relevant law incorrectly. Like an instruction misstating the testimony, this type of instruction is objectionable.

The proposed instruction is argumentative. Suppose that in a contract action, the plaintiff requests an instruction on Uniform Commercial Code § 2–314 governing the implied warranty of merchantability. The initial part of the proposed instruction merely tracks the statute; that part is proper. However, the second half of the proposed charge includes language to the effect that the lack of a safety catch on the product is "a good indication" or "strong evidence" that the saw the defendant sold the plaintiff was unfit. That part of the proposed instruction goes well beyond describing the law; it comments on the evidence and tries to influence the jury to apply the law to the testimony in a particular case. An instruction doing that is objectionable as argumentative. *Slayton v. Wright,* 271 Cal.App.2d 219, 76 Cal.Rptr. 494 (1969). Under the rubric "argumentative," some cases prohibit instructions that single out particular items of evidence for special emphasis or highlighting. *Drake v. Dean,* 15 Cal.App.4th 915, 19 Cal.Rptr.2d 325 (1993).

The proposed instruction amounts to a comment on the credibility of a witness or the believability of an item of evidence. At early common law, the trial judge had the power to comment on the evidence; and federal judges still retain that power. *Quercia v. United States,* 289 U.S. 466, 469 (1933); *United States v. Jaynes,* 75 F.3d 1493, 1503 (10th Cir.1996). However, most states forbid such judicial comments. H. KALVEN & H. ZEISEL, THE AMERICAN JURY 420 (1966); Dorsaneo, *Broad-Form Submission of Jury Questions and the Standard of Review,* 46 S.M.U.L.REV. 601, 649–50 (1992).

The proposed instruction does not follow the state approved pattern instruction. If the jurisdiction has adopted model (or pattern) jury instructions, and the area addressed by the proposed instruction falls within the approved pattern, object on the ground that the adversary's instruction deviates from the model instruction.

The proposed instruction is cumulative. In some cases, to confuse the jury, the defense requests numerous instructions that are essentially repetitious. The plaintiff and prosecutor ordinarily stand to gain from short, clear instructions, and they should resist the inclusion of cumulative instructions in the jury charge. The lengthier the instructions, the greater is the risk of jury confusion; and confusion usually works to the detriment of the party with the ultimate burden of proof.

The proposed instruction would be confusing to the jurors. Suppose that the proposed charge includes undefined, technical terms or double negatives. That language could easily confuse the jury. You can object on that ground.[5]

These objections are especially important for the burdened party, typically the plaintiff or prosecutor. If you have the ultimate burden of proof, you want to minimize the risk that the instructions themselves will confuse the jury. You want a set of instructions that is as clear, short, and sweet as possible. Use the above objections to reduce the number and length of the instructions in the final jury charge.

§ 13.4   OTHER MATTERS THAT CAN BE DISPOSED OF AT THE CONFERENCE

Although the meeting between the judge and attorneys is usually called an "instructions" conference, at the conference the judge and attorneys can take up matters other than the jury instructions. The other matters include deciding which exhibits to send to the jury during deliberations, obtaining advance rulings on anticipated problems during summation, and renewing trial motions.

Assume, for example, that you introduced a number of exhibits during trial. In a few jurisdictions, all the exhibits are automatically sent to the jury during deliberation. However, the majority rule is that the judge has discretion to determine which exhibits to send to the jury. *United States v. Hofer,* 995 F.2d 746, 748–49 (7th Cir.1993); *Murray v. United States,* 130 F.2d 442 (App.D.C.1942); *First Nat'l Bank of Atlanta v. First Nat'l Bank of Tucker,* 158 Ga.App. 843, 282 S.E.2d 353 (1981). Standard 17.a of the A.B.A. Civil Trial Practice Standards states that "[e]xhibits admitted into evidence should ordinarily be provided to the jury for use during deliberations." Indeed, in some jurisdictions the jury has a right to ask for a written copy of the instructions. CAL.PENAL CODE § 1093(f). It may be particularly important for your case to ensure that the judge sends specific exhibits to the jury. As Chapter 14 will point out, during closing argument you want to stress the exhibits sponsored by your first and last witnesses (your best theory witness and your strongest theme witness). During closing you ought to attempt to associate those exhibits strongly with the sponsoring witnesses. You hope that the presence of the exhibits in the deliberation room will be a constant, visual reminder of the testimony by those two witnesses. If you want those exhibits to reach the jury, you should specifically request that the judge give those exhibits to the jury during their deliberation.

You can not only request that certain exhibits be sent to the jury room; you may also ask that they be sent in a particular form—for example, organized into exhibit binders or notebooks. *United States v. Rana,* 944 F.2d 123 (3d Cir.1991); *United States v. Best,* 939 F.2d 425

---

5. As to the timing of objections to the proposed jury charge, *see* Rule 51, F.R. Civ. P.

(7th Cir.1991). Understandably, the judge may have been reluctant to allow you to hand a binder to the jurors at the beginning of your case-in-chief; it might develop during trial that one or more of the exhibits included in the binder will prove to be inadmissible. However, at this late point in the trial, the judge can identify all the admissible exhibits. A binder with a table of contents may make it much easier for the jury to use the exhibits during deliberation.

Or you may anticipate problems during closing, perhaps based upon past experience. Because of your familiarity with your opponent, you fear that he is going to make a certain objectionable remark during closing. If so, tell the judge the basis for your fear; and request an advance ruling precluding that remark. Even if the judge does not rule on the merits of your request, you have put the opponent on notice that you object to that remark. If the opponent later makes that remark, you are in a better position to move for a mistrial; given your request at the conference, the opponent can hardly argue that the remark was inadvertent. Or the tables could be turned, and you may worry that a particular remark you would like to make might prompt a mistrial. If you think that the opponent is acute enough to object and move for the mistrial, it may be safer to request an advance ruling from the judge on the propriety of your contemplated remark.

Next, at the conference the judge may announce the time restrictions on closing argument. You need to know whether you have 15 minutes, half an hour, or an hour to deliver the summation.

In addition, you can request that the judge submit special interrogatories to the jury. *See* Cicero & Taylor, *Verdict Strategy,* 17 LITIGATION 41 (Sum. 1991). Although most jury trials result in a general verdict, in many jurisdictions the judge can submit special interrogatories to the jury either as well as or in lieu of a general verdict form. *See* FED.R.CIV.P. 49, 28 U.S.C.A. If you have a particularly sympathetic client and are relatively confident of victory, you will ordinarily prefer a general verdict. *Id.* at 43. However, if your client is unsympathetic and the case is a complicated one, the jury may err in answering the interrogatories. It may be a sound tactic to request that the judge submit special interrogatories; the jury's error may serve as ground for a new trial or appeal.

Finally, the conference gives you the opportunity to make or renew motions outside the jury's hearing. As Chapter 15 will point out, some motions must be renewed at the close of all the evidence to preserve the issue for appeal. The conference is a convenient time to make those motions outside the jury's hearing.

§ 13.5 MAKING A RECORD AT THE CONFERENCE

As § 13.1 stated, the conference often occurs in the judge's chambers. When the conference begins, the judge and attorneys may be the only persons present. Suppose that during the conference, the judge makes a ruling that you object to. The court reporter may not be in attendance. To preserve the issue for appeal, you should: (1) request that the judge instruct the court reporter to join the conference to make a record of the ruling, or (2) reflect the ruling at sidebar as soon as you go back into open court. *United States v. Nason,* 9 F.3d 155, 160–61 (1st Cir.1993). The judge may have changed the outcome of the trial by wrongfully denying you an instruction on your theory or theme, but you cannot appeal on that ground unless the record reflects the judge's ruling.

§ 13.6   SAMPLE JURY INSTRUCTIONS

The following is a set of instructions for the *Scott* prosecution. The initial section of the set discusses the respective roles of the judge and jury. The next section states the substantive Criminal Law rules that the jury must apply. The third section gives the jury guidance on the evaluation of the testimony about the facts. The set concludes by giving the jury deliberation and voting instructions. The instructions do not include any charge on self-defense or defense of others; the defense attorney's theory is mistaken identification, and at the instructions conference the defense attorney asked the judge to instruct on only that defensive theory.

"Ladies and gentlemen of the jury.

(The Respective Roles of the Judge and Jury)

"It is now my duty as judge to instruct you regarding the law that applies in this case. It is your duty as jurors to follow the law as I state it to you. You have the exclusive duty and power to determine the facts in this case and to consider and weigh the evidence for that purpose. However, this power is not arbitrary; you must exercise the power with sound discretion and in accord with the rules of law that I am about to state to you. At first, I am going to describe the rules of law concerning the crime that the People have charged against Mr. Scott.

(Substantive Law Instructions)

"The information against Mr. Scott alleges that on the morning of January 19, 19YR–1 at the Senator Hotel in downtown Morena, Mr. Scott committed the crime of battery against Peter Williams. Under the law of the State of El Dorado, any person who unlawfully uses force or violence against another person is guilty of the crime of battery. In order to prove the commission of the crime of battery, the prosecution must prove each of these elements:

    1.   That force or violence was used upon the person of Mr. Peter Williams;

    2.   That such use was unlawful. It is ordinarily unlawful for one person to apply force against another person without that second person's consent; and

    3.   That the defendant was the person or one of the persons who used the force or violence against Mr. Williams.

"If you are not satisfied beyond a reasonable doubt that all three elements have been proven, you must acquit the defendant.

"In our country, one of the most important rules of law is that the defendant in a criminal case is presumed to be innocent until the prosecution proves the contrary. If there is a reasonable doubt whether the defendant's guilt has been satisfactorily shown, he must be acquitted. The presumption of innocence places on the People the burden of proving the defendant guilty beyond any reasonable doubt. A reasonable doubt is not a mere possible doubt. Everything relating to human affairs is open to some possible or imaginary doubt. Proof beyond a reasonable doubt is that state of the case in which, after considering all the evidence, you have an abiding conviction to a moral certainty of the defendant's guilt.

(Guidance for Evaluating the Testimony About the Facts)

"You have to apply these rules of law to the facts of the case. Both the prosecution and the defense have offered evidence and testimony describing their versions of the facts. I am now going to give you some guidance for evaluating the testimony.

"To begin with, you must understand that you may not consider as evidence any statement by the attorneys during the trial. During this trial, I sustained several objections to questions asked of witnesses; and on other occasions I struck testimony from the record. As to any question to which an objection was sustained, you must not speculate about what the answer might have been. In addition, you must not consider for any purpose any testimony that I struck from the record. You must deliberate this case as if you never heard that matter.

"Now I am going to explain what you may consider during your deliberations. You are the sole judges of the credibility of the witnesses in this case. In evaluating a witness's credibility, you can consider: the witness's demeanor while testifying; the character of the testimony; the witness's opportunity and ability to observe, remember, and communicate; the witness's character for honesty or its opposite; the existence of any bias, interest, or motive in this case; and any statement by the witness inconsistent with his or her testimony.

"It is not necessary that the facts be proved by direct testimony or evidence. Direct testimony is evidence that directly proves a fact without an inference and which in itself, if true, establishes the fact. Circumstantial testimony is evidence that proves a fact from which an inference of another fact can be drawn. An inference is a deduction of fact that may logically and reasonably be drawn from another fact or group of facts established by the evidence. The facts may be proved by circumstantial evidence or a combination of direct and circumstantial evidence. There is no distinction between the weight to be ascribed to direct and circumstantial evidence as a means of proof. Neither is entitled to greater weight than the other.

"You are not bound to decide any issue of fact in conformity with the testimony of the larger number of witnesses. You should not decide a question of fact by the simple process of counting the number of witnesses who have testified on the opposing sides. Instead, you must decide which testimony appeals to your mind with more convincing force.

"In this case, you have heard the testimony of an alleged eyewitness, Mr. Williams himself. Mr. Williams has testified that the defendant was one of the men who attacked him on the morning of January 19, 19YR–1. The People have the burden of proving beyond a reasonable doubt that the defendant was one of the men who committed the alleged battery on Mr. Williams. You must be satisfied to a moral certainty of the accuracy of the identification of the defendant as one of the attackers. An identification is an expression of opinion by the witness. In deciding whether to accept the witness's opinion, you should consider these factors: How good is Mr. Williams' eyesight? How good was lighting during the alleged attack? How close was Mr. Williams to the alleged attackers? How long did Mr. Williams have to view the alleged attackers? At the time of the alleged attack, was there anything about Mr. Williams' state of mind that would make his later identification untrustworthy? I emphasize again that the People have the burden of proof on every element of the charged crime, and that burden specifically applies to proof of the defendant's identity as one of the alleged attackers. If after examining the testimony you have a reasonable doubt about the accuracy of Mr. Williams' identification, you must find the defendant not guilty.

(Deliberation and Voting Procedures)

"It is now your duty to deliberate and consult with each other with a view to reaching an agreement if you can do so without violence to your individual judgment. Each of you must decide for yourself, but you should do so only after considering the testimony with your fellow jurors. You should not hesitate to change your opinion if you become convinced that it is erroneous. You shall retire into the jury room and select one of your number to act as foreperson. The foreperson will preside over your deliberations. In order to reach a verdict, all of you must agree to that decision. As soon as all of you have agreed on a verdict, you will record it on the verdict form which will be dated and signed by your foreperson. You will then return with the verdict to this room. The bailiff will now escort you to the jury room."

§ 13.7　ETHICAL QUESTIONS

At the instructions conference stage, ethical problems can arise with respect to your relation to the judge, your client, or your adversary. You are the criminal defense attorney for Robert Scott. You are attending the instructions conference. You read the advance sheets, and you know that last week the El Dorado Supreme Court announced that El Dorado trial judges have a *sua sponte* duty to give the jury a cautionary instruction about eyewitness identification testimony. The court not only announced that rule; in a case strikingly similar to the *Scott* prosecution, the court held that the judge's failure to instruct was reversible error. During the conference, it becomes clear that neither the trial judge nor the prosecutor is aware of last week's decision; while the judge is listing the instructions she intends to give to the jury, the judge makes no mention of a cautionary instruction on eyewitness identification. May you remain silent—thinking to yourself that even if there is a conviction, you would have reversible error built into the trial record? Remember that A.B.A. Model Rule 3.3(a)(3) states that "[a] lawyer shall not knowingly ... fail to disclose to the tribunal legal authority in the controlling jurisdiction known to the lawyer to be directly adverse to the position of the client and not disclosed by opposing counsel...." Have you in any sense taken a "position" by merely remaining silent at the instructions conference?

Suppose alternatively that at the conference, the judge tells you that given the testimony, she is inclined to instruct on mistaken eyewitness identification and self-defense. You have already decided that your theory is mistaken eyewitness identification. Moreover, you have concluded that you do not want to make any "even if" arguments: Even if Mr. Scott participated in the fight, he acted in self-defense. You would like to ask the judge to forego any instruction on self-defense. In the following variations of the problem, would it be ethical for you to make that request to the judge?

— You discussed the question with Scott before trial, and he expressed his opinion that "the more defenses there are, the better off it seems to me I'd be." Scott tells you that he would "like" the judge to instruct on self-defense as well as mistaken eyewitness identification.

— Suppose that Scott used stronger language and told you that "I think it oughta be my choice, and my choice is that the judge instruct on self-defense too."

— Assume that you did not discuss the question with Scott before trial. In general terms, Scott told you that he trusts your judgment. Without consulting Scott, should you request that the judge forego the self-defense instruction?

— Suppose that for one reason or another, you felt obliged to request the judge to instruct on self-defense. Nevertheless, you are convinced that it would be a serious error to argue both self-defense and mistaken eyewitness identification. During your closing argument, may you ignore the self-defense instruction and argue only mistaken eyewitness identification?

In analyzing these questions, consider the materials included in § 3.5.

Now suppose you are the prosecutor. Also assume that Scott did not take the stand at trial. You feel that the Scott's refusal to testify went largely unnoticed by the jury. Your "jury sense" convinces you that Scott's silence is not uppermost in the jury's mind. May you attempt to change that by requesting a jury charge reminding the jurors that Scott did not testify, and advising them that Scott's silence "shall in no way be held against him"? What if the defendant objects to the instruction? Is it proper to place the matter firmly before the jury through an instruction designed to protect the defendant's right to silence? *See Lakeside v. Oregon,* 435 U.S. 333 (1978).

§ 13.8   TRIAL TECHNIQUE EXERCISES

Your professor will specify a source book for this exercise. It may be a set of official instructions in your jurisdictions, or it could be a commercially available set such as O'Malley, Grenig & Lee. For purposes of this exercise, assume that the specified set is the official set approved by the Supreme Court of the State of El Dorado. Prepare a written list of all the instructions within the set that you want the judge to charge the jury on.

In addition, draft one special instruction for your case—an instruction that is not included in the specified set. You must draft both the proposed instruction and a memorandum of law supporting the proposed instruction. Your professor will announce any minimum or maximum page lengths for the memorandum.

Finally, draft a verdict form, leaving appropriate blanks for completion by the jury.

Chapter 14

CLOSING ARGUMENT—USING THE THEORY AND THEME TO ANSWER THE "WHY" QUESTIONS

Reprinted by permission of Warner Books/New York from *The Law as Seen by Charles Bragg.* Copyright © 1983 by Charles Bragg.

Table of Sections

§ 14.1 INTRODUCTION

We have seen that you may not make argumentative statements during opening statement. We have also learned that you may not ask argumentative questions during cross-examination. We now turn to summation or closing argument. At this stage of the trial, you not only may but must argue. You must argue to answer the "Why" questions: why the jury should believe your witnesses, why they should draw the inferences in your favor, and why they should apply the legal standards in the manner you urge.

In most jurisdictions, there are three closing arguments at the close of all the evidence: an opening argument by the plaintiff or prosecutor, a defense summation, and then a rebuttal argument by the plaintiff or prosecutor. In some jurisdictions, the trial judge has discretion to permit interim argument midtrial. Buxton & Glover, *Managing a Big Case Down to Size,* 15 LITIGATION 22, 24 (Sum. 1989). Standard 13.a of the new A.B.A. Civil Trial Standards provides that "[i]n cases of appropriate complexity, the court should afford counsel the opportunity during trial to address the jury to comment on, or to place in context, the evidence that has been, or will be, presented." For example, interim summations were used in the *Westmoreland* trial. Sand, *Getting Through to Jurors,* 17 LITIGATION 3, 53 (Wint. 1991). However, in the vast majority of cases, the counsel will argue at the close of the case. The next section of this chapter discusses the general structure of a summation. This structure largely holds true for both the opening argument by the plaintiff or prosecutor and the following defense argument. Section 10.34 then discusses the specific tactical problems posed by the three different arguments.

§ 14.2 THE GENERAL STRUCTURE OF A CLOSING ARGU-MENT

Throughout this text, we have observed that your strategic, pretrial choice of theory and theme dictates virtually every word you utter at trial. That observation certainly applies to the closing argument. The concepts of theory and theme are the keys to effectively planning the closing argument.

§ 14.2(A) The Introduction

At the beginning of the argument, it is customary to thank the jurors for their attention and patience during the trial. Thank the jurors briefly and sincerely. Avoid being effusive or long-winded. If you are patronizing or spend too much time thanking the jurors, some of them will suspect you are being insincere.

§ 14.2(B) The Description of the Reasoning Process

At first blush, you might assume that most of the closing argument should be devoted to an emotional appeal. However, that assumption is erroneous:

> Psychological studies show that appeals to reason are better than appeals to emotion. They are ... more lasting. [V]ery strong emotions block out almost completely the ability to reason. [I]f a person is caught up in a storm of emotion, he will have ... little memory of what was said. He remembers his feelings about the subject matter, but he will not be in a position to defend those feelings in the jury room. [A]ppeals to emotion, while effective at the time they are given, are not lasting. Thus, if you give an argument which appeals strictly to emotion and if the jury could render its verdict immediately, you might win. But after the judge has charged the jury, and they have probably been to lunch, the appeal to emotion fades and they return to logic, looking for reasons to find in your favor. If your argument has given them no reasons to give you a verdict, you will certainly lose. The emotional appeal of your argument will have faded away.

L. SMITH, ART OF ADVOCACY: SUMMATION § 1.44, at 1–39 (1978).

As Mr. Smith indicates, a substantial amount of time is likely to elapse between the delivery of the closing argument and the beginning of the jury's deliberations. Moreover, studies indicate that jurors rarely reach a verdict on the very first ballot. They will have to discuss the case, and during that discussion the jurors favoring your position need an argument that they can use to persuade the other jurors. Finally, the jurors will feel more comfortable voting in your favor if they believe they reasoned to the conclusion on their own rather than having your conclusion jammed down their throats. R. WAICUKAUSKI, P. SANDLER & J. EPPS, THE WINNING ARGUMENT Ch. 4 (2001); McElhaney, *Linking*, 19 LITIGATION 59 (Spr. 1993). Consequently, the attorney must make a longlasting, reasoned appeal to the jurors.

Of course, your trial theory is a large part of the reasoning process that you want the jurors to use. To help them understand the process, initially describe the judge's substantive law instruction on your theory. If the judge permits, quote the instruction. To impress the jury that you are scrupulously describing the content of the instruction, pick up a sheet of paper stating the instruction; and read it to the jury. The substantive law instruction is critical. Since the instruction represents the judge's words, the jurors are likely to attach a good deal of significance to it. "[I]n some trials, a copy of the jury instructions is the only tangible thing that jurors take with them into their deliberations." Greene, *A Jury Researcher Joins the Jury,* 91 CASE & COMMENT 28, 34 (Jan.-Feb. 1986).

The difficulty is that the judge's instruction is usually couched in abstract, impersonal language. For that reason, immediately after describing or quoting the instruction, you should restate it in simple, factual language. You might tell the jury that the instruction "boils down to" a requirement that you prove a number of facts. Then list the facts for the jury. For example, in *Williams v. Scott,* you might list the facts that: Two men intentionally attacked Peter Williams; they did so without any provocation; Williams suffered injuries in the attack; and the defendant was one of the attackers. These, of course, are the elements of your theory. It is often effective to enumerate the elements on a chart in checklist fashion.

§ 14.2(C)   Simplification of the Issues

You must immediately simplify the case for the jury. Remind the jurors that you told them in opening that in the final analysis, this case would "come down to a single question."

Then review the elements of your theory that are formally or virtually conceded. If the opposition stipulated to an element or explicitly conceded an element during testimony, point that out. If an element is practically undisputed, make short shrift of the element. In an automobile case, you might tell the jury "It's true that the defendant did not expressly admit that there was a collision. However, five impartial eyewitnesses testified that there was a collision; and their testimony is absolutely uncontradicted."

If you used a chart to list the elements of the theory, at this point you can line through the undisputed elements or check them off. (Most attorneys use the check technique, since they fear that lining through the element might suggest to some jurors that the element is missing.) For example, in our hypothetical, you might put checkmarks next to the first three elements of the theory. Doing so graphically emphasizes that most of the elements of your theory have certainly been established.

§ 14.2(D)   Statement of the Pivotal Issue

In the prior phase of the closing, you affirmatively told the jury which elements of your theory are formally or virtually conceded. By process of elimination, you are singling out the central, controverted issue. This issue is the pivotal element of your theory., the one that your theme relates to.

There are three types of issues. To identify the three types, we must dissect the adjudicative process. Put yourself in the position of the decision-maker. What decisions do you have to make in order to adjudicate a case? The threshold question is always whether to believe a particular witness. When the evidence is circumstantial, after resolving that question, you must decide which inferences to draw from the witness's testimony. Finally, you must determine how to apply the legal rules to the testimony and the inferences.

This analysis of the adjudicative process suggests the three types of issues. One is a credibility issue. For example, *Williams v. Scott* turns on a credibility question. The eyewitness, Williams, has identified Scott as an attacker; but the defendant claims that he was in his room at the time of the attack. When both sides rely on direct testimony, the case becomes a swearing contest: Whom should the jury believe? Someone is lying or mistaken.

Other cases present historical inference issues. There may be little or no dispute over the believability of the two sides' witnesses. The key question is which inference to draw from the witnesses' testimony. Assume, for example, the following personal injury action. The plaintiffs were passengers in the defendant's car. They were sleeping in the backseat. The defendant's car ran off the road and struck a tree. Due to the collision, the defendant now suffers from retrograde amnesia. No direct testimony is available. The two sides will present primarily circumstantial evidence to the jury: physical evidence from the accident scene and accident reconstruction experts' evaluation of the physical evidence. The jury must decide which set of inferences from the circumstantial evidence is more plausible.

The final type of issue is a legal standard question. In some cases, there is little controversy over either the direct or circumstantial evidence. For instance, in a products liability action there may be no dispute over either the design of the product or its safety history. Or in a criminal case in which the defendant relies on entrapment, the transaction involving the defendant may be on videotape. The case will turn on the manner in which the jury decides to apply the legal instruction defining entrapment or an "unreasonably dangerous" product.

Characterizing the pivotal issue as a credibility, historical inference, or legal standard question helps you frame the issue for the jury. State the issue as bluntly as possible. If the issue is a credibility question, tell the jurors that the issue is "whether you are going to believe Mr. Williams' identification of the defendant as one of his attackers." When the issue is an historical inference question, tell the jurors that their task is to decide whether "to conclude that the collision happened in the northbound lane, as my client, Ms. Clark, claims." If the issue is a legal standard question, tell the jurors that they have to "decide whether the design of that gas tank was unreasonably dangerous."

§ 14.2(E) The Summation and Argument

The heart of the closing is the summation and argument dedicated to winning the pivotal issue. In part, this phase of the closing is a summation, a review of the testimony and evidence. As in the opening statement and on direct examination, you should make the closing visually appealing. If you have gone to the trouble to introduce exhibits during trial, exploit them now. In a murder case, the prosecutor should pick up the murder weapon holding it delicately to suggest that it is an evil, dangerous instrumentality. In a commercial lawsuit, pick up the pivotal documents. Walk up to the jury railing,[1] hold up the document, point to the key passage, and quote it. Tell the jurors that they will have the exhibit during deliberations and that they will be able to see for themselves how the language of the document proves your case. You Show the jury that you respect their intelligence and independence by telling them that you do not want the jurors to accept what you or opposing counsel say about the document; instead, you want the jurors to read the document themselves. It is critical to capitalize on any exhibits introduced during the testimony of your first and last witnesses—your best theory and theme witnesses. You want to associate those exhibits in the jurors' minds with the testimony of those two witnesses. If you do so, the presence of the exhibits during deliberation will be a constant visual reminder of the testimony of your two most important witnesses. You are not even restricted to the formally admitted exhibits. To highlight and summarize evidence, you can use charts specially prepared for closing argument. S. HAMLIN, WHAT MAKES JURIES LISTEN 360–66 (1985). You can even create a chart while you are speaking during closing argument. *United States v. Crockett,* 49 F.3d 1357, 1361 (8th Cir.1995). In civil cases, plaintiffs' attorneys often employ such charts to illustrate the damages computation. HAMLIN, *supra* at 365–66.

Although this phase of the closing is in part a summation, it must be more than that: It must also be an argument. You must argue for the inferences that you want the jury to draw. Focus on the question "Why": why should they believe Mr. Williams' identification of the defendant, why they should conclude that the accident occurred in the northbound lane, or why they should decide to characterize the design of the gastank as unreasonably dangerous. As Figure 14–1 indicates, depending on whether the pivotal issue in the case is a credibility, historical inference, or legal standard issue, there are different types of arguments to make; and there are three basic tools for strengthening the argument.

---

1. Even in courts where you are tied to a podium during the examination of witnesses, the judge will normally allow you to approach the jury box during summation.

Figure 14-1

THE IMPACT OF THE TYPE OF CASE ON THE CONTENT OF THE CLOSING ARGUMENT

	A CREDIBILITY CASE	AN HISTORICAL INFERENCE CASE	A LEGAL STANDARD CASE
FIRST, SUM UP YOUR CLIENT'S POSITION.	Restate your side's evidence. Be visually appealing	Restate your side's evidence and the inference your client favors	Restate your side's evidence and the manner in which your client favors applying the law to the facts.
NEXT, ARGUE FOR YOUR CLIENT'S POSITION.	WHY THE JURORS SHOULD BELIEVE YOUR WITNESSES —Describe your witnesses' positive demeanor —Highlight the corroborating testimony —Use the three tools: the theme, the instructions, and an analogy	WHY THE JURORS SHOULD DRAW THE FAVORABLE INFERENCE —Highlight the corroborating testimony, especially expert opinions on the propriety of the inference. —Use the three tools: the theme, the instructions and especially an analogy	WHY THE JURORS SHOULD APPLY THE LAW TO THE FACTS IN THE MANNER YOUR CLIENT FAVORS —Highlight corroborating testimony, especially expert opinions on the proper application —Use the three tools: the theme, an analogy, and especially the instructions.
FINALLY, ARGUE AGAINST YOUR OPPONENT'S POSITION.	WHY THE JURORS SHOULD DISBELIEVE THE OPPOSING WITNESSES —Review the impeaching evidence —Describe the witnesses' negative demeanor —Exploit failures of proof—promised or "missing" evidence	WHY THE JURORS SHOULD REJECT THE UNFAVORABLE INFERENCE —Emphasize the implausible aspects of the opposing theory; and assert that to accept the unfavorable inference, the jury would have to assume a "massive set of coincidences" —Exploit failures of proof	WHY THE JURORS SHOULD NOT APPLY THE LAW IN THE MANNER THE OPPOSITION FAVORS —Point to the undesirable social consequences of doing so —Exploit failures of proof

A Credibility Argument

In any type of argument, you should begin on a positive note to suggest to the jury that you are on the psychological offensive in the case. Simply stated, you should discuss the strength of your case before attacking the opposition's case.

The strength of your case. Initially, restate your client's testimony. Moreover, describe your client's demeanor. Walk over to the witness stand, rest your hand on the railing, and remind the jury of the manner in which your client testified: "He looked you straight in the eye. With no hesitancy, with certainty written on his face, he told you...." Point out that the opposition's cross-examination was unproductive; as hard as the opposing attorney tried, he could not shake the witness's testimony or composure. R. KLONOFF & P. COLBY, SPONSORSHIP STRATEGY: EVIDENTIARY TACTICS FOR WINNING JURY TRIALS 32, 258 (1990). Do not be defensive if your witness occasionally says that he or she is uncertain or simply does not know about a particular matter. Instead, turn the witness's candor to your advantage; argue that the witness's response is the best evidence of the witness's honesty. When the witness was uncertain, she said so; or when the witness did not know, he frankly conceded his ignorance.

Then highlight the corroboration for your testimony. When the trial has been lengthy and there have been numerous witnesses, as you mention each corroborating witness, give the jury a brief physical description of the witness or point to the person if she is still in the courtroom. Help the jury recall the witness. It is especially impressive to point out any corroborating testimony furnished by opposing witnesses. In *Williams v. Scott,* Williams' attorney should note that the defendant corroborated Williams' testimony about the chart of the second-floor hallway and that Ms. Freeman, a defense witness, said that the three men in the hallway were "right on top of each other."

In the process of presenting a credibility argument, you ought to develop your theme. By definition, your theme incorporates your best argument on the pivotal issue. Now is the time to elaborate on the theme. To do so, you have three tools. One is the theme itself: the label encapsulizing your best argument. At least once during this phase of the argument, Williams' attorney should use the expression, "so close for so long".

The second tool is a judge's instruction supporting the theme. As we saw in the last chapter, during the instructions conference Williams' attorney ought to seek an instruction charging the jury that they may consider "how close" Williams was to the attackers and "how long" he had to observe them. If the instruction is particularly favorable, you may want to write key words or phrases from it on the chalkboard, or mount the instruction on a chart. *See Boatmen's Nat. Bank v. Martin,* 223 Ill.App.3d 740, 585 N.E.2d 1328, 1332, 166 Ill.Dec. 306, 310 (1992) ("Nothing prohibits the use of poster-sized exhibits of jury instructions").

Finally, you should employ an analogy. McElhaney, *Analogies in Final Argument,* 6 LITIGATION 37 (Wint. 1980); Spangenberg, *Basic Values and the Techniques of Persuasion,* 3 LITIGATION 13 (Sum. 1977). For instance, consider the plaintiff's argument in our civil damage suit for assault. Early in the closing, Williams' attorney might point out that the attack lasted longer than she has been speaking during closing and that the attackers were closer to Williams than she is to the jurors at the moment. You may draw on literary allusions, fables, historical incidents, or Biblical references as sources of analogies. *See generally* R. MOSES, JURY ARGUMENT IN CRIMINAL CASES—A TRIAL LAW-

YER'S GUIDE (2nd ed. 1993).[2] The attorney may argue the sorts of matters of common knowledge which the judge can take judicial notice of. *Haynes by Haynes v. Green,* 748 S.W.2d 936, 939 (Mo.App.1988); *Beliveau v. John B. Varick Co.,* 81 N.H. 57, 120 A. 884, 885 (1923); *Harris v. Pacific Floor Mach. Mfg. Co.,* 856 F.2d 64 (8th Cir.1988) (the court approved counsel reading from an Ann Landers column during summation; "There is nothing improper in a civil case with a lawyer's citing widely recognized authorities during a closing argument (though Shakespeare and the Bible come more readily to mind than Ann Landers)....")

Note how the three tools interrelate. The label for the theme should be memorable. The label is a memory jogger, keeping the jury remember the theme during deliberations. The use of the judge's instruction signals the jury that the judge had placed his *imprimatur* on the theme; in effect, the judge has said that the law permits the jurors to embrace the argument embodied in the theme. The instruction legitimates the theme. Finally, the analogy should make it clear to the jury that the theme rests on common sense[3] nor substantial justice. As previously stated, the legendary New York trial attorney, Moe Levine, once remarked that your challenge at trial is to make the jurors proud to return a verdict in your client's favor. They can feel that pride if you convince them that your theme rests on substantial justice or common sense.

The weakness of the opposition case. After arguing the strength of your own case, shift to an attack on the opposition's case. To be sure, you should review any evidence that impeached the opposing witnesses: convictions, prior inconsistent statements, and the like. If you have effectively impeached one key part of a witness's testimony, resort to the *Falsi in uno, falsi in omnibus* pattern instruction: If the jury rejects one part of the witness's testimony, they have reason to be skeptical of the

---

2. In a trial advocacy seminar for defense attorneys in Milwaukee, Wisconsin on October 4, 1987, Mr. Joel Hirschorn, former president of the National Association of Criminal Defense Lawyers, discussed the importance of analogies in summation. He pointed out that he often tries cases in the South, a region in which many jurors have great respect for the Bible. In his experience, one of the most effective analogies is the story of Joseph and his coat of many colors. GENESIS 37:2–36. Joseph's father, Jacob, favored him; and for that reason, Joseph's brothers were envious. They beat Joseph and sold him into slavery. They took his coat, smeared it with a goat's blood, and told their father that they had seen Joseph killed by "an evil beast." Mr. Hirschorn noted that a defense attorney can use this analogy to good advantage in a case in which the prosecution has both eyewitness testimony and circumstantial evidence.

3. In a seminar in Kauai, Hawaii, on June 2, 1988, Ms. Juanita Brooks gave an example of a credibility analogy in a criminal case. She hypothesized a case in which the prosecution relied primarily on the testimony of two accomplices who have now "cut deals" with the prosecution. She began the analogy by quoting the jury instruction explaining to the jurors that a reasonable doubt is a doubt that would cause a person to pause in an important transaction. She then tells the jury that for most people, the purchase of a house is an important transaction. She next asks the jurors to imagine that the prosecution's accomplice witnesses are the salespersons for a realty company. The prospective buyer learns that one salesperson has been convicted of perjury, and the buyer catches the other salesperson in three different lies. Ms. Brooks concludes the analogy by asserting that common sense should lead the buyer to reject any offer to buy the land—just as she urges the jurors to refuse to "buy" the accomplices' testimony.

rest of the testimony.[4] When the opposing witnesses' stories are in complete agreement, characterize the testimony as a "contrived story which ... meshes" too perfectly. Williams, *Lawyer in the Jury Room,* 17 LITIGATION 8, 9 (Fall 1990). Moreover, you can exploit any demeanor by the opposing witnesses that indicated uncertainty or guilt. Describe the demeanor in vivid, concrete terms: There was a long silence before the witness answered, and when he finally answered he looked down at the ground;[5] the witness did not look even one member of the jury in the eye;[6] or the witness squirmed during cross-examination.[7] You can not only contrast the opposing witnesses' demeanor with that of your witnesses; you can also contrast the demeanor of the opposing witnesses on direct and cross-examination:

> Remember Mr. Ryan. He was the plaintiff's executive vice president who testified here about two weeks ago, the very tall man wearing horn-rim glasses and a blue suit. Remember how, when [plaintiff's counsel] questioned him and led him through his planned direct examination, Mr. Ryan confidently turned and looked at you after each question. Remember how he spoke at length in his deep resonant voice trying to ... convince you. Then remember what happened when I began to cross-examine him. He no longer spoke in those confident, resonant tones. His answers became short. They became clipped. They became sarcastic. They became evasive. In fact, you remember how his honor, the judge, had to tell him to be responsive and simply to answer the question.

Cicero, *Nondefensive Final Argument for the Defense,* 8 LITIGATION 45, 47 (Spr. 1982). Tell the jury that "they caught a glimpse of the real M. Clayton Ransom on cross-examination." McElhaney, *Prepping the CEO,* 82 A.B.A.J. 84 (Oct. 1996).

In addition, point out any failure of proof by the opposition. Remind the jurors that in opening statement, the opposing attorney promised them that he or she would present certain testimony. If the omission is critical, have the court reporter prepare a verbatim interim transcript of the opening and quote the opposing attorney's promise to the jury. A failure of proof can be decisive in a swearing contest. Why should the jury believe the opposition's witnesses when the opposition does not keep its word? Further, you may use a "missing witness" argument even when the opposing attorney has not promised to produce a particular

---

4. To explain the instruction to the jury, many attorneys use a restaurant analogy. Suppose, for example, that the waiter serves you a dish of stew. You choose a piece of beef for your initial bite and discover that that piece of meat is spoiled. At that point, you have the right to reject the entire dish and send it back to the kitchen. You do not need to dig through the bowl to find the good meat. Simon, *Closing Argument—Falsi in Uno,* THE CHAMPION, May 1995, at 46.

5. Mr. Randy Schaffer's Summation, Record of Jury Arguments at 27, State v. Stewart, No. _____ (209th Dist. Ct., Harris Cty., Tex. 1976).

6. Mr. Randy Schaffer's Summation, Record of Trial at 637, State v. Russell, No. 241461 (177th Dist. Ct., Harris Cty., Tex. 1977).

7. Mr. Randy Schaffer's Summation, Record of Jury Arguments at 315, State v. Carrillo, No. _____ (206th Dist. Ct., Hidalgo Cty., Tex. 1976).

witness to corroborate their version of the facts. Suppose that the testimony indicates that a particular person was in a position to observe relevant events and that the opposing party has a special personal or business relationship with that person. In those circumstances, the party's failure to call the person as a trial witness gives rise to an inference that the person's testimony would have been unfavorable to the opposing party. R. KLONOFF & P. COLBY, SPONSORSHIP STRATEGY: EVIDENTIARY TACTICS FOR WINNING JURY TRIALS 124–26 (1990). Assume, for instance, that in a personal injury action arising from a collision, the testimony indicates that there were two employees of the defendant drayage company in the truck at the time of the collision. At trial, the defendant calls only the driver as a witness and fails to call the second employee. Most judges would allow the plaintiff to argue during summation that the defendant's failure to call the second employee suggests that the second employee would have corroborated the plaintiff's testimony rather than the defendant's.

A "missing witness" argument can be a potent weapon. The celebrated Washington Post libel trial is illustrative. The president of Mobil Oil sued the Post over two articles suggesting that Mobil's president had "set up" his son in an oil tanker business serving Mobil. Brill, *Inside the Jury Room at the Washington Post Libel Trial,* American Lawyer 1 (Nov. 1982). In his summation, the plaintiff's attorney focused on the failure of the Post to call a key source of information to the stand, a witness who supplied the Post with early reports of the alleged "setup." The plaintiff's attorney repeatedly urged the jury to ask itself, "Where was [the witness]?" The six person jury deliberating on the case voted 4–2 in favor of Mobil's president. The swing vote later explained that she had switched to the pro-plaintiff majority because the defense had not called the absent witness to testify. Brill, *supra* at 94. Later, another pro-Post holdout apparently switched, again persuaded by the argument about the witness's absence. For a complete collection of authorities pro and con on the "where was this witness?" form of argument, *see* R. CARLSON, SUCCESSFUL TECHNIQUES FOR CIVIL TRIALS § 7:13 (2d ed. 1992).

There are three caveats, though. The first is that at least one court has questioned whether the "missing witness" doctrine survived the enactment of the Federal Rules of Evidence. *Herbert v. Wal–Mart Stores, Inc.,* 911 F.2d 1044 (5th Cir.1990). The court reasoned that a party's ability to subpoena any witness and impeach the party's own witness undercuts the rationale for the doctrine. Casenote, Herbert v. Wal–Mart Stores, Inc.: *The Death of the Uncalled–Witness Rule?,* 37 LOY.L.REV. 387 (1991). The second, procedural caveat is that in some jurisdictions, before arguing the inference during closing, you must obtain the trial judge's permission to do so. *United States v. Pitts,* 918 F.2d 197, 199 (D.C.Cir.1990). You could seek permission at the instructions conference. The third caveat is that in roughly half the states, you may not comment on the witness's absence if there is a privileged relationship between the party and the witness. 1 McCORMICK, EVIDENCE § 74.1 (5th ed.

1999). Thus, in those jurisdictions it would error to comment on a party's failure to call his or her spouse as a witness.

After highlighting the strength of your case and the weakness of the opposing testimony, bring your argument to a denouement. If you have the ultimate burden of proof in the case but it is a light burden such as a mere preponderance, at this point in the summation explain how lax your burden is. In summary fashion contrast the believability of your witnesses with the reasons to doubt the opposing witnesses' credibility. Argue that standing alone, the contrast shows that you have met your burden. Contrast your case with a hypothetically weak case:

> For example, assume a negligence case involving an automobile accident where the plaintiff's case is supported by two strong eyewitnesses and by a sobriety test revealing the defendant's intoxication. In such a case, the plaintiff should point out that the jury is not being asked to find liability based on a single witness of doubtful strength.

R. KLONOFF & P. COLBY, SPONSORSHIP STRATEGY: EVIDENTIARY TACTICS FOR WINNING JURY TRIALS 258 (1990). Conversely, remind the juror when the opposition has the burden of proof in the case. It is especially important to do so when the burden is a heavy one such as clear and convincing evidence or proof beyond a reasonable doubt. The jury's doubt about the credibility of a key opposing witness can be the key to persuading the jury that the opposition has not met its burden.

An Historical Inference Argument

The next type of argument that you will have occasion to make is an historical inference argument. Here too you want to begin on a positive note, emphasizing the strength of your case.

The strength of your case. Start by summing up your testimony and any supporting corroboration. The corroboration can take the form of an opposing witness's concession, physical evidence, or expert testimony. These types of corroboration sometimes dovetail. For instance, an opposing witness may concede a physical fact, such as the location of a gouge mark on the highway, that supports the inference you want the jurors to draw. In many cases, the thrust of your expert's testimony is an evaluation of the significance of physical evidence found at the relevant scene. Think back to Chapter 11. Argue your expert's superior credentials, her demeanor, the demonstrated validity of the theory she relied on, and the meticulous care with which she applied the theory to the facts in the instant case.

As in the case of a credibility argument, you must argue as well as sum up. You are entitled to argue for any rational, permissive inference from the witnesses' testimony. You can use the same three tools—the label for the theme, a jury instruction, and an analogy—to persuade the jurors that the inference you support is more plausible than the competing inference the opposing side urges. For example, assume that the location of the gouge mark is the single most important item of physical evidence in the case. Your theme might be that this trial is "the case of the telltale gouge mark." The very wording of the theme thus underscores the significance of that item of physical evidence. Admittedly, in this type of argument, you are usually forced to rely on circumstantial evidence. However, the judge will almost always give the jury an instruction that circumstantial evidence can be just as reliable as direct testimony. You ought to emphasize that instruction. Finally, you can use analogies to convince the jurors to draw the inference you desire. *See generally* R. MOSES, JURY ARGUMENT IN CRIMINAL CASES (2d ed. 1993). In a circumstantial evidence case, you could use such well-worn stories as Robinson Crusoe's discovery of the footprints in the sand. or snowmobile tracks in snow. Ring, *Effective Closing Arguments in Civil Trials,* 29 TRIAL 61, 62 (Oct. 1993); McElhaney, *Analogies in Final Argument,* 6 LITIGATION 37, 38 (Wint. 1980). However, it is usually better if the analogy is more tailored to the facts of your case. The closer the analogy is on the facts, the greater is the probability that the analogy will persuade the jury that your inference makes more common sense.

The weakness of the opposition case. After you argue the strength of your case, attack the inference the opposition favors. Tell the jury that they should test the inferences against their common, everyday experience: "Her Honor will tell you that you can take your common sense with you into the deliberation room and use it during deliberation to figure out which conclusion is more likely." Characterize the inference the opposition favors as "bizarre," "outrageous," "implausible," and "unlikely." Take the gloves off, and use blunt, forceful language such as "ridiculous." Point out that to draw that inference, the jury would have to assume "an incredible (or amazing) set of coincidences." Assert that "normal people simply don't act like that." S. HAMLIN, WHAT MAKES JURIES LISTEN 3 (1985). Explicitly invoke the general norms of human behavior. *Id.* at 316. This is the common—sense standard that the jurors will fall back on during deliberation, and you should argue the case in those terms. "[J]urors will sometimes refuse to accept something both sides agree is true when it doesn't fit with their personal experiences." McElhaney, *The Story Method,* 18 LITIGATION 49, 50 (Fall 1991). "One of the basic tenets involved in a jury's decision-making process is the so-called rule of probability. Under this [test], jurors test the evidence against what seems reasonable and likely given their own experiences." Salman, *Jury's Reactions: Post–Trial Interviews Revealing,* NAT'L L.J., Dec. 9, 1991, at p. 23; M. SAKS & R. HASTIE, SOCIAL PSYCHOLOGY IN COURT 93 (1986) ("the jury tests competing theories to see which holds the evidence most plausibly"). Stress the physical evidence at odds with the opposition's inference. Dant, *Gambling on the Truth: The Use of Purely Statistical Evidence As A Basis For Civil Liability,* 22 CO-LUM.J. LAW & SOC. PROBLEMS 31, 53 (1988). Tell the jury that just as a scientist would abandon an hypothesis contrary to observed phenomena, they should reject the opposition's hypothesis "because it just doesn't square with the hard, physical facts in this case."

As in the case of a credibility argument, point to any failures of proof by the opposition. If the opposition promised to present expert testimony supporting the inference and failed to do so, exploit that failure.

Again, if you have the burden of proof but it is a light burden such as a fair preponderance, at this juncture in the summation explain how slight the burden is. Contrast the common sense character of your inference with the implausibility of the inference the opposition is urging. Argue that the contrast shows that you have sustained your burden of proof. Conversely, when the opposition has the ultimate burden of proof in the case, remind the jury at this point in the summation. If a particular inference is essential to the opposition case and that inference is implausible, the opposition has not sustained its burden.

A Legal Standard Argument

The last type of argument is a legal standard argument. As in an appellate brief or oral argument, you make an express appeal to social policy. In his closing arguments, Clarence Darrow often made appeals to social conscience. Carlson, *Argument to the Jury: Passion, Persuasion, and Legal Controls,* 33 ST. LOUIS U.L.J. 787, 798 (1989). In this type of case, your task is to issue a Kantian call to duty to the jury to set the safety or law enforcement standards in the community. In ART OF ADVOCACY: SUMMATION (1978), Lawrence Smith describes a passage in a summation, illustrating a legal standard argument:

> Jurors, you are the conscience of the community. When you speak, the community speaks. You represent this community and its attitude toward safety and what ... (doctors, bus drivers, automobile drivers, manufacturers, etc.) ought to do with regard to safety, not only for this plaintiff but for everyone who lives in our community. It is for you to say whether the conduct of this defendant meets with the community's approval. By your verdict, you can set a new and better safety standard for this community.

Id. at 1–B.06.[8]

---

8. Westbrook v. General Tire and Rubber Co., 754 F.2d 1233, 1238–39 (5th Cir. 1985), can be read as generally prohibiting "conscience of the community" appeals. However, the case can be construed more narrowly. In *Westbrook,* the plaintiff's attorney tried to create the impression that the local community "expect[ed]" the jury to "return a large verdict ... against [the defendant] a nonresident corporation." *Id*. at 1238. As we shall see in § 14.4, the plaintiff's argument in *Westbrook* amounted to an improper appeal to geographic bias. If your trial judge seems inclined to read *Westbrook* broadly, you might consult § 15.06 and 1–B.08 of the Smith text. Those passages illustrate milder versions of the "conscience of the community" argument. In a criminal case, a court might treat a "conscience of the community" argument as a permissible plea for law enforcement. *United States v. Ferguson,* 935 F.2d 1518, 1530–31 (7th Cir.1991)("A prosecutor may stress to the jury the seriousness of drug charges and comment on the gravity of this country's drug problem"); *United States v. Smith,* 918 F.2d 1551, 1563 (11th Cir.1990); *United States v. Canales,* 744 F.2d 413 (5th Cir.1984); *Villegas v. State,* 791 S.W.2d 226 (Tex.App.1990) (the prosecutor could state that the jury was going to decide what conduct would be tolerated in the country; the statement was

The strength of your case. Here too you can use expert testimony corroborating your position. For example, legal and medical malpractice cases often resolve themselves into legal standard disputes; there may be little controversy over the historical facts, and the real issue is how the pertinent test for malpractice applies to the facts. In these cases, the plaintiff commonly calls another professional as an expert to testify that the defendant professional's conduct violated the governing standard of care. More broadly, expert opinion testimony is useful in legal standard cases when the trial judge permits the expert to express an opinion about the manner in which a scientific or expert standard applies to the specific facts of the case. Such testimony is especially available in jurisdictions such as Texas which allow experts to opine directly on mixed questions of law and fact. *Puente v. A.S.I. Signs,* 821 S.W.2d 400, 402 (Tex.App.1991); *Harvey v. Culpepper,* 801 S.W.2d 596, 601 (Tex.App. 1990).

As in the case of credibility and historical inference arguments, use the tools of the theme, instructions, and analogies to develop your affirmative position. Assume that the case is a wrongful death action arising from a worker's fall to her death at a construction site. The testimony indicates that an additional guard railing would have cost $30.00. The theme might be that "$30.00 is a small price to pay to save a human life." That theme should be stated during the argument.

Next, explicitly discuss the jury instruction charging the jurors that they can consider such factors as the cost of precautionary measures and the gravity of the injury to be avoided. Explain to them that the instruction means that they act as the voice of the community—they set the safety standards. Tell the jurors that the judge's instruction recognizes that this is a democracy in which citizens can judge safety standards for themselves. *Id.* at 1–B.01. Point out that the instruction explicitly permits them to weigh both factors mentioned in your theme, "$30.00" and "a human life." This instruction legitimates the "$30 is a small price" theme in the same way in which the pattern instruction on eyewitness identification legitimates the "so close for so long" theme in the *Scott* case.

Finally, give them an analogy illustrating the level of care that the community expects employers to exercise for their employees' safety. In a trial in Arizona, a British bank recovered a large judgment against Price Waterhouse on the theory that Price Waterhouse was negligent in failing to disclose unsafe investments by an American bank which the British bank purchased. During summation, the plaintiff's attorney analogized the defendant's conduct to the failure of the Titanic's crew to keep an adequate lookout and warn the passengers of danger. The trial judge permitted the attorney to show an 18–minute video during summation. The video included scenes from "A Night to Remember," the

tantamount to telling the jury that they were going to be the community's voice and was proper jury argument). *But see United States v. Solivan,* 937 F.2d 1146 (6th Cir. 1991) ("A prosecutor may not urge jurors to convict a criminal defendant in order to protect community values, preserve civil order, or deter future law-breaking").

1958 British movie about the sinking of the Titanic. The whole point of the video was to graphically emphasize the plaintiff's analogy. Sherman, *And Now, The Power of Tape,* NAT'L L.J., Feb. 8, 1993, at p. 1.

The weakness of the opposition case. Once you have affirmatively issued a call to duty to set the standards in a fashion favored by your client, negatively attack the opposition's position. When you represent the plaintiff, some judges will allow you to tell the jury that they can "send a message" to other companies "in our town that this sort of conduct is unacceptable and intolerable."[9] When you represent a defendant, explain to the jury that if they fix unrealistically high standards, they will "be driving honest, responsible business people out of this community." In general terms, you may discuss the social consequences of a particular verdict. (The defense attorney, however, must avoid referring to the impact of the jury's decision on insurance rates. References to that impact are not only objectionable; there is a significant risk that the judge will declare a mistrial based on such a reference.)

As in the case of credibility and historical inference arguments, you ought to exploit any failures of proof by the opposition. If the opposition did not present expert testimony promised during opening or the testimony turned out to be much less favorable than the opposing attorney forecast during opening, the jury should be reminded of the failure of proof. Similarly, you may be able to make a "missing witness's" argument."

§ 14.2(F) The Conclusion

Before ending your summation, you may want to pose a few rhetorical questions that the opposing attorney will find it difficult to answer. For instance, just before ending her closing, Mr. Williams' attorney might challenge the defense attorney to explain why Scott made up the story about lending his shoes to a friend. However, do not ask a large number of rhetorical questions—especially if you are the plaintiff or prosecutor. The jury expects you to know the truth. If you spend too

---

9. Some jurisdictions permit "send a message" arguments in civil cases only when punitive damages are in issue at trial. McCarter, *Closing Argument in Civil Cases,* 46 J.MO.BAR 31, 35–36 (Jan.-Feb. 1990). Such arguments can also be risky in criminal cases. *See Boatwright v. State,* 452 So.2d 666 (Fla.App.1984) (it was reversible error for the prosecution to ask the jury to "send these folks a message that we're not gonna put up with this kind of stuff"). Some jurisdictions allow such arguments in criminal cases but forbid them in civil actions. For a review of the conflicting views on the propriety of "send a message" arguments, *see Carlson & Carlson, "Over the Top" Final Arguments: How Far Is Too Far?,* 49 THE FEDERAL LAWYER 37 (Jan. 2002); Carlson, *Argument to the Jury: Passion, Persuasion, and Legal Controls,* 33 ST. LOUIS U.L.J. 787, 815–16 (1989). In McCormick, *The Permissibility of Consequentialist Closing Arguments,* 38 TRIAL LAWYER'S GUIDE 399 (1994), the author argues that the propriety of a consequentialist argument depends on the type of case. When the jury must resolve a credibility or historical inference dispute, the jury has no business considering the consequences of its decision. *Id.* at 405–07. In contrast, when the case is a legal standard dispute, the jurors must make a "normative judgment." *Id.* at 407–08. In this latter situation, the author contends that the courts ought to generally permit consequentialist arguments.

much time posing questions, you may create a doubt that results in a verdict for the opposition.

After posing any rhetorical questions that you think are appropriate, make a positive assertion of confidence in your own case: "The evidence has shown beyond any reasonable doubt that the defendant was one of the men who viciously and brutally attacked Mr. Williams." Incorporate the measure of the standard of proof—"beyond any reasonable doubt"—into the assertion.

There is one other thing to do before you conclude: tell the jury the precise verdict to return. The judge usually gives the jury a written verdict form to fill out. In a very complicated case, the judge may also submit special interrogatories to the jury. Make certain that the jury understands which lines or boxes to check to return a verdict for your client. Pick up the form, show it to the jury, and explain precisely the markings they should make on the form to return the verdict you desire. *See* Cicero & Taylor, *Verdict Strategy,* 17 LITIGATION 41, 44 (Sum. 1991). If you neglect to do so, you may win a hollow victory. The jury may orally announce a verdict in your favor; but if there are mistaken notations on the form or interrogatories, there may be ground for reversing the verdict on appeal.

§ 14.3 SPECIFIC TACTICAL PROBLEMS POSED BY THE THREE SUMMATIONS

Section 14.2 discusses a general format that is useful for planning the opening and defense summations. However, there are specific tactical problems peculiar to each of the three summations. This section broaches those problems. As previously stated, ordinarily as the party with the ultimate burden of proof, the plaintiff or prosecutor delivers an opening summation, the defense attorney then speaks, and lastly the plaintiff or prosecutor has an opportunity for rebuttal.[10]

§ 14.3(A) The Opening Summation by the Plaintiff or Prosecutor

What should be the tone of the opening summation? At one time, the style of closing argument was highly theatrical and flamboyant. Carlson, *Argument to the Jury: Passion, Persuasion, and Legal Controls,* 33 ST. LOUIS U.L.J. 787, 795–97 (1989). Modernly, the general consensus is that the tone ought to be relatively low-key. In most jurisdictions, you will have a second opportunity to address the jury in the form of the rebuttal summation. You should ordinarily save some of your emotional punch for the rebuttal. If you adopt a highly emotional tone in the opening summation, the jury may be drained by the time of the rebuttal:

---

10. In Minnesota, in criminal cases the defense counsel delivers the opening summation and has a right to rebut after the prosecutor's summation. In Georgia, if the defense puts on no evidence, the defense has the right to go first and last.

If you have ever watched the Billy Graham Crusade on television, you will note that the momentum begins at a very low key and progressively . . . increases. . . .

Love, *Persuasion in Closing Argument,* in Oct. 22–24, 1987 KY. ACAD. TR. ATTYS.

A significant substantive issue is the extent to which you should anticipate the defense summation. On the one hand, you can integrate the mention of some anticipated arguments into the discussion of your own affirmative case. By way of example, in *Williams v. Scott,* it is predictable that the defense attorney will attack the reliability of Williams' identification of Scott. As the plaintiff's attorney, you certainly ought to devote part of the opening summation to the evidence of the trustworthiness of the identification. On the other hand, if you explicitly concentrate on the defense in your summation, your summation can take on a defensive tone, suggesting that you have surrendered the psychological offensive in the case. Especially when the opposition relies on an affirmative defense unrelated to the merits of your case, you may want to reserve most of your attacks on that defense until rebuttal.

The most difficult problem for the plaintiff's or prosecutor's attorney is the question of "sandbagging." Suppose that the trial is unitary; the same trier of fact will simultaneously decide liability and damages or innocence and sentence. As the plaintiff or prosecutor, should you discuss damages as well as liability or sentence as well as innocence? The temptation is to "open on liability and close on damages." Some attorneys recommend doing so because that sequence effectively deprives the defense of an opportunity to rebut your arguments on damages or sentence. By sandbagging those issues and reserving them for rebuttal, the attorney attempts to insulate his arguments on these issues from defense rebuttal.

However, this practice is not only of questionable propriety; if you attempt to sandbag against an experienced opponent, the practice can backfire. Suppose that you are the first speaker and that you leave the subject of damages or sentence untouched in your speech. After your argument, the opposing counsel may approach the bench and point out to the judge that you neglected to discuss damages or sentence in your opening argument. The prevailing view is that during the rebuttal summation, the only thing you have a right to do is to meet the arguments advanced for the first time in the defense summation. The counsel might request an advance ruling by the trial judge that if she foregoes any argument on damages or sentence, the judge will forbid you from discussing those issues in your rebuttal. The judge well might grant that ruling. Once again, even if the jury finds the defendant liable or guilty, your victory could be a hollow one; denied the benefit of your argument on damages or sentence, the jury might return a wholly inadequate damages award or sentence. Even if the judge does not preclude you from arguing damages or sentence, in some jurisdictions the judge has discretion to give the defense a second argument when you discuss new issues during the rebuttal summation. If the judge does so, you will lose the opportunity to address the jury last.

Suppose that you have decided to argue damages. How do you do so? Distinguish between two situations.

In one situation, you are arguing a quantifiable element of damages such as travel expenses. In this situation, the argument can be straightforward. During summation, point to the evidence and document the damage. Hold up the receipts and invoices, and show the jury the precise passages which support your damage claim. When there are several such elements of damage, you probably want to list each amount on a chalkboard or easel and total the amounts.

However, in the other situation, you must argue an element of damage such as pain and suffering which defies quantification with any precision. This is a much more difficult argument to make; any reasonable juror will readily perceive that there is a large element of arbitrariness in assigning a dollar value to this element of damages. Attorneys differ over the question of the most effective method of arguing this kind of element of damage.

— Some attorneys approach the problem by giving the jury an analogy. The sample closing argument in § 14.5 illustrates this approach: "Ladies and gentlemen, it's obviously very difficult to place a dollar figure on something like pain and suffering. But think of it this way. How much do you pay your dentist for a shot of novocaine to give you relief from pain for the hour you're in the dentist chair? About $10.00? $10.00 for an hour of freedom from pain."

— Other attorneys use the technique of a "per diem" argument. Section 14.4 points out that many states permit you to suggest that the jury award a certain dollar figure for each day of pain and suffering. In truth, you pull the figure out of the air; but you can argue to the jury that the figure is a minimal amount to compensate the plaintiff for the hellish experience of constant pain. However, as § 14.4 adds, a large number of jurisdictions ban "per diem" arguments.

Quite apart from the legal propriety of a "per diem" argument (discussed in § 14.4(A)), there are doubts about the efficacy of this type of argument. Some experienced plaintiffs' attorneys no longer use such arguments. Booth, *Arguing Damages: The Power of Preparation,* 27 TRIAL 28, 32–33 (Mar. 1991). These attorneys believe that many lay jurors distrust "complicated" formulae for computing daily or hourly damages; the jurors may think that the attorney "picked [the number] out of the air." *Id.* at 33. These attorneys prefer to "pick a reasonable figure," frankly tell the jury that there is unavoidable imprecision in picking any figure, but confidently insist that the figure chosen is fair and reasonable. *Id.*

Greene, *On Juries and Damages Awards: The Process of Decision Making,* 52 LAW & CONTEMP. PROBLEMS 225 (1989) reviews the empirical studies of jury damages computations. The author cautions that there is only a "small body of literature" on this topic. *Id.* at 226. The author states that in relatively simple cases:

> [I]t is probably safe to assert that ... jurors will probably compartmentalize their discussion and consider evidence relevant to various damages discussed at trial (for example, medical expenses, lost wages) rather than use a single-sum approach.

Id. at 245. However, in more complex cases such as those involving conflicting expert testimony on damages, "jurors may agree on a [single-sum] amount suggested by one side or the other, rather than attempt to perform detailed and complicated calculations...." *Id.*

§ 14.3(B) The Defense Summation

At the very end of his or her summation, the plaintiff or prosecution might pose a number of questions and challenge the defense to respond. The temptation to respond immediately is understandably strong. However, "[d]o not allow your opponent to rewrite [your summation] for you at the last moment." Klieman, *Summation: The Criminal Defense Attorney's Perspective*, THE CHAMPION, June 1995, at 14, 15. As you planned, try to seize the offensive by talking about the strength of your case. Integrate responses to the challenges into your presentation, but do not abandon the basic outline that you have prepared for your summation.

In the last section, we noted that the plaintiff or prosecutor sometimes foregoes arguing damages or sentence in the hope of denying the defendant an opportunity to respond. To counter that tactic, the defense attorney might waive argument on damages or sentence to preclude the plaintiff or prosecutor from arguing on those topics during rebuttal. (To be on the safe side, though, before foregoing argument on damages or sentence, at the sidebar seek an advance ruling that if you do not mention damages or sentence, the judge will forbid the plaintiff or prosecutor from discussing that issue during rebuttal.)

There is, however, another reason why the defense might present little or no argument on damages or sentence. Suppose that the defense attorney believes that there is a good likelihood that he can win a complete acquittal or defense verdict—no damages or no sentence. On that supposition, should the defense attorney discuss damages as well as liability or sentence as well as innocence? Should the defense attorney take an "all or nothing" gamble? Paradoxically, not taking the gamble can be risky. If the defense attorney asserts that there is no liability or guilt but spends a good deal of time talking about damages or sentence, the jury may suspect that the defense attorney does not believe his own assertion. If he is so certain that there is no fault and, hence, no liability, why is he spending so much time talking about damages? As a practical matter, the jurors may perceive an inconsistency between the assertion and the content of the closing.

How should the defense attorney cope with this seeming dilemma? When they are firmly convinced that they can win a complete defense verdict, some attorneys entirely forego arguing damages or sentence. It takes a measure of courage and faith in yourself to follow this tack. Other attorneys handle the dilemma in this manner. To begin with, they try to give the jury the impression that the judge expects—and is virtually forcing—them to discuss damages or sentence: "In a few moments, her Honor will give your several instructions on damages. As I've said, I don't think that you need those instructions; you're never going to get to the issue of damages because I'm confident that you'll find that there is absolutely no liability on my client's part. However, since her Honor is going to give you those instructions about damages, I feel obliged to say a few words on that topic." In addition, they keep their attacks on damages as brief as possible—poking a few major holes in the testimony about damages. Some even make it a practice not to mention a specific dollar figure in their closing; they fear that if they do so, many, if not most, jurors would treat that mention as an implicit acknowledgment of some liability.

§ 14.3(C) The Rebuttal Summation

There are two guidelines for the rebuttal. One is to avoid a defensive tone. You should not begin every section of the rebuttal by stating, "The defense has contended ..., but...." Reaffirm your theory of the case, and then integrate the rebuttal of defense arguments into a restatement of your arguments.

Next, make an emotional appeal during the rebuttal—an appeal stressing the severity of the plaintiff's injuries or the enormity of the defendant's crime. As one author states, "After the defense has argued and you rise to rebut, you can show a little more emotion. This is what we call the 'rousements'...." Spangenberg, *Basic Values and Techniques of Persuasion,* 3 LITIGATION 13, 16, 17 (Sum. 1977). However, remember that an understated appeal can be the most powerful. The legendary New York trial attorney, Moe Levine, once delivered this closing at the end of a case:

> You know, ladies and gentlemen, prior to my giving this summation we all broke for lunch. His honor went to lunch with his clerk. I saw the defense counsel take the representative of his company and walk off to lunch. I knew the bailiff was taking you, the jurors, to lunch and so I decided that I did not want to eat alone. And so I went to lunch with my client. While you were having lunch served in the jury room, I was having lunch with Harold.... He has no arms! He eats like a dog! Thank you very much.

Levine, *Closing Argument (Child Dart Case),* 6 TRIAL DIPL. J. 10, 15 (Fall 1983).

In another case, after making a brief argument on liability, the plaintiff's attorney said:

> This little girl will never hear her mother say, "Run outside and play." This little girl will never hear anyone ask, "May I have the next dance?" This little girl will probably never have the thrill of

hearing anyone whisper, "Will you be my wife?" This little girl will never have the joy of confiding, "I'm going to have a baby."

Dempsey, *The Power of Understatement,* 2 TRIAL DIPL.J. 30, 35 (Fall 1979). Sometimes the most important words in a summation should be whispered. Lee, *Closing Argument in a Criminal Case,* 22 TRIAL 104 (Oct. 1986). In the last example, the closing argument "resulted in the largest verdict in New York in a single personal injury action to that date." Dempsey, *supra.* There is no necessary correlation between your emotional intensity and the volume of your voice.

§ 14.4 MOTIONS TO STRIKE STATEMENTS MADE DURING SUMMATION

The attorney might make objectionable statements during summation. If so, the opposing attorney can move to strike the statement and perhaps move for mistrial. What are grounds for moving to strike a statement made in a summation? When must the opposing attorney make the motion to preserve the issue for appeal? *See generally* Carlson & Carlson, *"Over the Top" Final Arguments: How Far Is Too Far?,* 49 THE FEDERAL LAWYER 37 (Jan. 2002); Conner, *What You May Not Say to the Jury,* 27 LITIGATION 36 (Spr. 2001).

§ 14.4(A) The Grounds for Motions to Strike

The attorney misstated the testimony. Perhaps the most common objection is that the attorney has misstated the testimony. The attorney could be mischaracterizing the evidence, or the attorney might be referring to facts outside the record. In some cases, when the judge clearly remembers the corresponding testimony, the judge rules on the merits of the motion. For example, the judge will grant the motion and give the jury a curative instruction to disregard the attorney's statement. In other cases, if the statement relates to a critical issue in the case, the judge will have the court reporter read back the testimony before the judge rules. However, in many cases, especially in courts of inferior jurisdiction, the judge simply reminds the jury that the attorney's statements are not evidence and that the jurors are to rely on their own recollection of the witnesses' testimony.

The subtler variation of this problem arises when the attorney misuses evidence admitted for a limited purpose. Suppose that a plaintiff's attorney was permitted to introduce evidence of a subsequent repair over a defense objection based on Federal Rule of Evidence 407. The judge might have overruled the objection on the theory that the evidence is admissible for the limited purpose of showing the defendant's control over the area where the tort occurred. However, during summation, the plaintiff's attorney might try to misuse the evidence as proof of the defendant's antecedent negligence in clear violation of Rule 407. Or assume that in a prosecution, the prosecutor is allowed to introduce evidence of a defendant's other crimes over a defense objection resting on Rule 404. The judge might have overruled the objection on the theory that the evidence is admissible for the limited, non-character purpose of showing the defendant's motive for the charged crime. However, during summation, the prosecutor might attempt to misuse the evidence as proof of the defendant's general, bad, law-breaking character in blatant violation of Rule 404. Just as when the attorney misstates the testimony, you can move to strike if the attorney misuses the testimony.

The attorney misstated the law or invited the jury to nullify the law. In most jurisdictions, the judge rules finally on legal issues that arise during the trial. The overwhelming majority of jurisdictions forbid the attorney from misstating the law or inviting the jury to disregard the law—"jury nullification." R. CARLSON, CRIMINAL JUSTICE PROCE-DURE 223 (6th ed. 1999). A misstatement of the law is subject to a motion to strike and a curative instruction to disregard. When the attorney invites the jury to nullify the law, the attorney can be subject to a contempt citation. If an opposing attorney invites jury nullification, you may want to request a contempt citation in the jury's hearing to emphasize for the jury's benefit that the opposing attorney's behavior is grave misconduct.

The attorney's statement exceeds the proper scope of the argument. This issue sometimes arises during the plaintiff's or prosecutor's rebut-tal. As previously stated, in most jurisdictions, the scope of the rebuttal is confined to rebutting new arguments raised for the first time during the defense summation. In § 14.3, we discussed the problem of "sand-bagging" by a plaintiff or prosecutor. If the defense omits any discussion of damages or sentencing, the trial judge could sustain a defense motion to strike based on scope when the plaintiff or prosecutor attempts to discuss damages or sentence later during the rebuttal.

The attorney's statement is inflammatory or prejudicial. In this setting, "prejudicial" has the same technical meaning that it has during the examination of the witnesses under Federal Rule of Evidence 403. Evidence is prejudicial in this sense when it tempts the jury to decide the case on an improper basis. Thus, it is objectionably prejudicial for an attorney to appeal to economic, political, racial, gender, or religious prejudice. *See* Bishop, *Name Calling: Defendant Nomenclature in Criminal Trials,* 4 OHIO NO. U.L. REV. 38 (1977); Vess, *Walking a Tightrope: A Survey of Limitations on the Prosecutor's Closing Argument,* 64 J. CRIM. L. & CRIMINOLOGY 22 (1973); Annot., Criminal Law—Prosecutor's negative characterization of defendant, 88 A.L.R.4th 8 (1991). It is similarly improper for a local attorney to appeal to geographic prejudice. For instance, if the case is being tried in a small, rural community and one party is a local resident while the other is "from the Big City," the attorney representing the local resident might urge the jury to side with her client simply because he lives "right here in our town." Of course, a passing reference to the parties' places of residence would be proper, but a more explicit appeal to geographic bias should draw a motion to strike.

The attorney's statement invites the jurors to adopt the attorney's client's perspective. This is the so-called "Golden Rule" followed in most jurisdictions. The original Golden Rule, of course, is that you should do unto others as you would have them do unto you. If the attorney were permitted to invoke that rule during closing, he could ask the jurors to do unto his client as they would have him do unto them if they were the party and he were the juror. Most jurisdictions forbid this argument because it is an implicit, objectionable appeal for sympathy. Sympathy is an improper basis for a jury verdict.

There is a related problem, which is actually governed by the prohibition of misstatements of the law rather than the Golden Rule. Suppose that in a tort action, the defendant has alleged that the plaintiff was guilty of contributory negligence. During summation, in discussing the reasonableness of the plaintiff's conduct, the plaintiff's attorney states: "Put yourself in the plaintiff's shoes turning that corner that fateful afternoon." Or assume that in a murder prosecution, the defense is claiming self-defense. During summation, the defense attorney says: "Put yourself in my client's shoes as that man walked into the room—as that man stepped into the room carrying a pistol in plain view. What would you have done?" Some judges would undoubtedly grant motions to strike on the ground that these statements violate the Golden Rule; many judges almost always grant the motion when they hear an attorney ask the jurors to adopt the client's perspective. It is arguable that these statements offend the Rule, since there is an implicit request that the jury empathize and sympathize with the attorney's client. However, completely apart from the Golden Rule,[11] these statements are objectionable because they misstate the legal standard. In both cases, the standard of reference is not the jurors' conduct but rather the conduct of the hypothetical, objectively reasonable person.

Distinguish cases, though, in which the issue is whether a witness could have seen what he or she testified to. When the question is whether it was physically possible the witness to have observed a certain fact or event from a particular position, it is permissible to ask the jurors "to put yourselves in the place that [the witness] was in." *United States v. Kirvan*, 997 F.2d 963, 964 (1st Cir.1993). You are not asking the jurors to sympathize with anyone or adopt anyone's beliefs. Rather, you are arguing the physical possibility of the observations the witness testified to.

The attorney is stating his personal opinion as to the credibility of witnesses, the proper inferences to draw from the testimony, or the merits of the case. We just saw that it can be improper for the attorney to use the pronoun, "you," in certain contexts during summation. It can also be dangerous for the attorney to use the personal pronoun, "I," too frequently during summation. Model Rule of Professional Conduct 3.4(e)

---

11. Some courts draw fine distinctions in applying the ban against Golden Rule arguments. A few indicate that the argument is improper when discussing damages but proper when counsel is discussing liability. In criminal cases, the rule is sometimes relaxed when self-defense is pled. The jury may be instructed that the evidence should be "viewed from the standpoint of the defendant at the time." R. CARLSON, SUCCESSFUL TECHNIQUES FOR CIVIL TRIALS § 7.2 (2nd ed. 1992).

provides that "[a] lawyer shall not ... in trial ... state a personal opinion as to the justness of a cause, the credibility of a witness, the culpability of a civil litigant or the guilt or innocence of an accused." There are several rationales for this provision. One is the fairness rationale that the opposing attorney has no opportunity to question the attorney making the statement about the basis for the statement. Further, the statement tempts the jury to decide the case on an improper basis. If one attorney strikes the jury as being honest and particularly fair, the jury may transfer its favorable impression from the attorney to his client. The jury is supposed to decide the case on its merits; the jury should not be enticed to rule in favor of a party because that party happens to have hired a attorney with an ingratiating personality. That temptation is always present in the case, but the attorney cannot heighten the danger by explicitly injecting her opinion during summation.

The attorney is inviting the jury to draw an adverse inference from the opposition's lawful invocation of a privilege. Suppose that during or before trial, one side invoked an evidentiary privilege to suppress information. During summation, the opposing attorney would love to make this argument: "I want you to think back, ladies and gentlemen, to our cross-examination of the defendant's wife. During that cross-examination, as you'll remember, I asked her whether the defendant had told her that he was at fault in this accident. At that point, the defense attorney stood up and objected on the ground of a privilege—the privilege for conversations between husbands and wives. Her Honor allowed the defense attorney to prevent me from getting an answer to that question. However, I want you to use your common sense. Why did they object? Why didn't they want you to hear the answer to that question? Obviously, the answer probably would have been that he did in fact admit his fault to her." There is a split of authority in the United States whether such comment is permissible. 1 McCORMICK, EVIDENCE § 74.1 (5th ed. 1999). Some jurisdictions recognize privileges but allow the opposing attorney to invite the trier to draw adverse inferences from the invocation of a common-law or statutory privilege. Other jurisdictions prohibit either the judge or the opposing attorney from inviting adverse inferences. California Evidence Code § 913 states that prohibition.

A particularly troublesome question arises when a prosecutor makes a statement during summation that expressly or implicitly refers to a defendant's silence at trial. *In Griffin v. California,* 380 U.S. 609 (1965), the Supreme Court announced that it violates the fifth amendment privilege against self-incrimination for a prosecutor to comment on a defendant's silence at trial. Silence implicitly invokes the fifth amendment privilege, and the comment would place an intolerable burden on the defendant's exercise of a constitutional right. The clear, easy case is a situation in which the prosecutor specifically notes that the defendant did not testify or sat silent. A tougher case is a situation in which the prosecutor notes that certain prosecution evidence is "uncontradicted." The prosecutor has not expressly mentioned the defendant; but when it is clear that only the defendant would be in a position to contradict that prosecution testimony, the courts tend to find a violation of *Griffin*. It is important, though, to remember that *Griffin* forbids comment only during a prosecution. Many jurisdictions permit adverse comment when a party invokes the fifth amendment in a civil action.

The attorney is making an improper "per diem" argument. One of the most difficult tasks facing a civil jury is attaching a dollar value to an element of damages such as pain and suffering. It is a common practice in many jurisdictions for the attorneys to suggest per diem dollar figures to the jury during summation. Thus, the attorney might say, "$50.00 a day would be a perfectly reasonable figure in this case, ladies and gentlemen." However, there is a division of authority over the propriety of per diem arguments. Tanford, *An Introduction to Trial Law,* 51 MO. L. REV. 624, 690–91 (1986). You should research your local law before including a per diem argument in your summation.

While in "per diem" arguments the attorney seeks monetary recovery on a daily basis, the attorney might request compensation on an hourly basis (and then multiply that figure by the roughly 5,000 waking hours in each year). Booth, *Arguing Damages: The Power of Preparation,* 27 TRIAL 28, 33 (Mar. 1991). One variation is the "want ad" argument. Lee, *Pain Analogies for Closing Argument,* 20 TRIAL LAW.Q. 60, 62 (Wint. 1990). The attorney tells the jurors that the following ad appears in a local paper:

> Wanted. For Hire: No education or previous experience necessary. [Here the attorney specifies an hourly rate of compensation.] Job requires applicant to undergo continuous pain. Note, however, that this is a lifetime job with no vacations, no time off, no coffee breaks, and no fringe benefits. Once accepted, applicant cannot quit.

Id. The attorney asks the jurors how they or a typical person would respond to such an advertisement. Still another variation is the so-called "job offer" argument. McCarter, *Closing Argument in Civil Cases,* 46 J.MO.BAR 31, 32–33 (Jan.-Feb. 1990). In this argument, "the jurors are asked to put themselves in the plaintiff's place, and given his 'job,' with the wages being based on a mathematical formula used to assess damages for pain and suffering." *Id.* The "job offer" argument is objectionable for many of the same reasons as a Golden Rule argument. *Id.* at 33.

§ 14.4(B) The Timing of the Motion to Strike

It is sometimes said that as a matter of etiquette, you should either move to strike only the most egregious misstatements by opposing counsel or hold all motions until the end of the opponent's summation. The proponents of this view point to two risks. One is that the jury may believe that it is rude for you to interrupt opposing counsel. The other is that a motion may serve only to highlight a damaging statement.

As in the case of evidentiary objections during the examination of witnesses, you certainly ought to consider the advisability of asserting your legal right to make an otherwise proper motion. When the trial has been lengthy and the jury has witnessed numerous objections interrupting witnesses' testimony, it is unlikely that a motion, if sustained, will strike the jury as merely a rude interruption. Of course, if the opposing counsel's objectionable statement relates to a relatively unimportant issue, you may decide to waive the motion. However, when the statement concerns the pivotal issue in the case—the issue which your theme relates to—you probably ought to move to strike.

Can you defer the motion until the end of the opponent's summation? A 1993 case addresses that question. Counsel for the injured plaintiffs in a products liability action against an auto manufacturer used his closing argument to deliver a "send the message" argument. The argument was improper. *Neal v. Toyota Motor Corp.*, 823 F.Supp. 939 (N.D.Ga.1993). However, no objection was lodged during the summation. Defendant's lawyers explained they did not want to object and risk irritating the jury. Despite that explanation, the defense counsel's failure was fatal and resulted in a waiver. While some arguments can so indelibly taint a verdict that even a timely motion and instruction could not cure the problem, they are rare. A timely motion to the closing argument is ordinarily necessary, and this rule applies even when the argument is found to be inflammatory ,and prejudicial and improper. The case of *Haygood v. Auto–Owners Ins. Co.*, 995 F.2d 1512 (11th Cir.1993) also underscores the need for an objection. On appeal the defense complained that plaintiff's closing argument misleadingly suggested that the insurer was hiding something. Reversible error was urged. However, "at no time during or after the closing arguments did [defendant] Auto–Owners object . . . nor did it ask for a limiting instruction, so the objection to the closing argument is waived." *Id.* at 1517.

§ 14.5 SAMPLE CLOSING ARGUMENT

You represent the plaintiff in *Williams v. Scott*. In this case, the judge followed the prevailing practice and chose to read the jury instructions after the closing arguments. The following is your closing argument:

(Introduction)

"May it please the court. Ladies and gentlemen of the jury, on behalf of my client, Mr. Williams, I want to thank you. We appreciate your attention during this trial. I'm going to ask for your patience for just a bit longer. I want to take a few moments now to review the case with you.

(Description of the Reasoning Process)[12]

"In about 30 minutes, her Honor is going to read you the instructions on the law in this case. She's going to give the following instruction. I want to quote it to be sure to be accurate (The attorney picks up a sheet of paper stating the instruction): 'A

---

12. In some jurisdictions, the customary phrasing is "I expect she's going to give you the following instruction." You must learn the local custom.

plaintiff who suffered any bodily injury as a proximate result of a battery committed upon him by a defendant is entitled to recover damages for such injury from that defendant. A battery is any intentional, unlawful, and harmful contact by one person with the person of another.' That instruction may sound a bit technical; but as you can see from this chart, what that instruction boils down to is this. Mr. Williams has to prove three things: Someone had intentional, unlawful contact with Mr. Williams; Mr. Williams suffered bodily harm because of that contact; and the defendant is one of the persons who made that contact with Mr. Williams.

(Simplification of the Issues)

"Let's review those elements one by one. There certainly was contact. No one denies that two men attacked Peter Williams in the Senator Hotel on January 19th, 19YR–1. In addition, we all agree that Mr. Williams suffered bodily harm. You heard testimony by Mr. Williams, Officer Taylor, and Doctor Morgan about Mr. Williams' injuries. That testimony is undisputed. (The attorney checks off those two elements on the chart.)

(Statement of the Pivotal Issues)

As I said in opening statement, there would be only one real issue in this case. (The attorney circles the remaining issue on the chart.) Richard Rogers was one of Mr. Williams' attackers. Who was the second attacker? Are you going to believe the defendant when he claims that he had nothing to do with the attack? Ladies and gentlemen, I submit to you that we've proven by a clear preponderance of the evidence that the defendant was the second attacker. I want to explain to you precisely why you should believe Mr. Williams' testimony and why you ought to reject the defendant's story.

(Summation on the Pivotal Issue)

"What was Mr. Williams' testimony? He is on duty at the desk. He hears a bottle crash outside. He steps outside to investigate. There is only one window lit. It was the window to the defendant's room. Mr. Williams takes the elevator up to confront the defendant. As soon as he steps off the elevator, two men grab him, beat him, and kick him until he's a bloody mess. Not content with that, they drag him into the restroom, try to strangle him with his own tie, and threaten to kill him. You all were here when sitting in that witness chair, Mr. Williams positively identified the defendant as the second attacker. He looked you straight in the eye. With no hesitation in his voice, with certainty on his face, he pointed to the defendant.

(Argument on the Pivotal Issue—the Strength of Your Case)

"The defense attorney has insinuated that Mr. Williams' testimony is too weak to be believed. After all, he's a 65 year old man trapped in a shocking, startling event. But I'd like to tell you some things about that man and that event. He may be 65 years old, but he's in good health and he has perfect eyesight. As Mr. Williams testified, he has 20–20 vision-never wore glasses a day in his life. And what do we know about the event? It may have been startling for Mr. Williams, but it was a close quarters battle that lasted at least four minutes in a narrow hallway and a well-lit restroom. Here is Plaintiff's Exhibit No. 2, the diagram of the second floor that her Honor admitted into evidence. It shows that the hallway is only six feet wide; it shows how many 60 watt lights there are in the hallway; and it also shows how many 100 watt lights there are in that small restroom. You'll have this chart with you during deliberation; you can see for yourself what a great opportunity for observation Mr. Williams had. And remember that the defense's own witnesses corroborate Mr. Williams. Mr. Williams was the witness who first testified about this diagram; but as you'll recall, at the beginning of his cross-examination, I showed the defendant this same diagram. He was forced to admit that it's correct. Moreover, the only other defense witness, Ms. Freeman, testified that when she looked into the hallway, she saw three men fighting 'right on top of each other other'. Those were her own words, 'right on top of each other.'

"Ladies and gentlemen, Mr. Williams was closer to his attackers than I am to you right now. That battle lasted as long as I've been speaking so far in this closing argument. Would you have any difficulty recognizing my face later today? You wouldn't, just as Mr. Williams doesn't have any difficulty recognizing the defendant sitting there as one of his attackers. In a few minutes, her Honor is going to give you an instruction on the way you should decide whether to accept Mr. Williams' eyewitness identification of the defendant. That instruction says that in making your decision, you should consider 'how close' Mr. Williams was to his attackers and 'how long' he had to look at them during the attack. I want to stress those words, 'how close' and 'how long.' Take a look at our exhibits number four, five, and six. These are photographs of Mr. Williams taken in the emergency room immediately after the attack. You can see the large number of injuries he suffered all over his body. Ladies and gentlemen, common sense tells you that those two men had to be right on top of Mr. Williams for a good, long time for him to sustain all these injuries. You'll have these photographs with you in the deliberation room. You can see for yourselves. In this case, there's only one sensible conclusion: Mr. Williams was so close to those two men for so long that his identification is reliable.

"It's true that Mr. Williams was a bit confused about the identification when he spoke with Officer Taylor right after the attack. But that's understandable. He had just been badly beaten; he was still bleeding from the attack. But his mind is clear now, and he's positive that the defendant was one of the attackers. You saw Mr. Williams on the stand. Two days ago, when we were choosing you as jurors, I asked you all whether you'd reject Mr. Williams' testimony simply because his identification of the attackers right after the beating was a bit hazy. You all assured me that you wouldn't; you all gave me your promise that you'd consider all the facts and circumstances surrounding the identification. When you do consider all the facts—Mr. Williams' condition immediately after the attack and his demeanor on the witness stand today—it's clear why you should believe him when he testifies that the defendant was one of the two attackers.

(Argument on the Pivotal Issue-the Weakness of the Opposition Case)

"What about the defendant's testimony? He testifies that he spent the early part of the evening with his friends, Joan Freeman and Dick Rogers. Joan Freeman, the friend who is the only other defense witness in this case. Joan Freeman, the friend who heard the defendant express his dislike for Mr. Williams several times. Joan Freeman, that great, public-spirited citizen. You heard her on cross-examination. She hears someone being brutally beaten in the hallway and then goes back into her room and goes to sleep. She admits that there's a phone in her room. But she doesn't call the desk. She doesn't call 911. She doesn't call the police. She goes back to sleep! And Dick Rogers, the friend whom both Mr. Williams and Ms. Freeman have identified as one attacker. According to the defendant's story, after his friends leave, he goes to bed. He hears some noise in the hallway and investigates. There's nothing there. He can't see or hear anything. So he goes back to sleep. Later a police officer arrives and 'unjustly' arrests him as one of the attackers. The officer seizes some of the defendant's shoes with bloodstains—stains he now says he picked up when he walked into the hallway to investigate.

"The defendant's story is ridiculous. The defendant testifies that although he quickly investigated the noise, he didn't see or hear anything in the hallway. We know that the attack started in the hallway and continued into the restroom. The defendant's room is closer to that restroom than Ms. Freeman's room is. His door is 15 feet—only 15 feet—from the door to the restroom. Remember our little experiment during my cross-examination of the defendant. I stood 15 feet away from him, and he admitted that he could hear me even though I was speaking softly. Yet he expects you to believe that he couldn't hear screams coming from only 15 feet away. When the same noise awoke Ms. Freeman and she looked into the hallway, she saw three men and heard their voices. The defendant's room is closer to the scene of the attack. Yet, when he looks out, there's nothing—nothing to see and nothing to hear, not even Mr. Williams' screams of pain from the restroom. The defendant's story isn't even consistent with the testimony of Ms. Freeman, his own friend and witness.

"The defendant's story is incredible for another reason. These are Plaintiff's Exhibit No. 7, the defendant's shoes. The defendant admits now that there was blood on these shoes that night. How did it get there? His story now is that he must have picked it up while he was investigating in the hallway. But what did he tell Officer Taylor? As he was forced to admit on cross-examination, he told her an entirely different story; his excuse then was that he must have lent the shoes to a friend. What friend? Ms. Freeman perhaps? Dick Rogers? And it's not just that he's given us two versions of the facts. Remember the way he acted when I questioned him about the story about lending the shoes to a friend. Did he look you in the eye the way Mr. Williams did during his testimony? No. The defendant turned away from you and looked down. Why? To try to hide the guilt written on his face. Ladies and gentlemen, we submit that the defendant was standing in his own shoes right next to Dick Rogers at the time of the attack and using those shoes to savagely kick the plaintiff in his stomach and face. The defendant's story is unbelievable because it's inconsistent with Ms. Freeman's testimony and with the defendant's own pretrial statement to the police.

(Satisfaction of the Burden of Proof)

"Ladies and gentlemen, in a short while her Honor will read you the instructions on the burden of proof in this case. She is going to tell that Mr. Williams has the burden of proof in this case and that he has to prove his case by a preponderance of the evidence. Remember that this is a civil case, not a criminal prosecution. We don't have to prove the defendant's guilt beyond any reasonable doubt. Since this is a civil case, we have to prove that the defendant was the attacker by only a preponderance of the evidence, anything greater than a 50% probability. If we tip the scales ever so slightly in favor of our case, we've established the defendant's liability. We've done more than that. When you consider all the corroboration for Mr. Williams' case—much of it supplied by the defense's own witnesses—and the inconsistencies in the defense story, there's only one reasonable conclusion in this case: The defendant *was* one of the attackers, and he is liable for Mr. Williams' damages.

(Damages)

"I'm going to discuss those damages with you in detail after the defense attorney has presented his closing argument. At this point, however, in fairness to the defense attorney, I want to give you a rough idea on this chalkboard of what the damages are. First, medical expenses. Mr. Williams testified that he had $1,500.00 in medical bills. You've seen the medical bills. Second, lost wages. Mr. Williams told you that he earned $700.00 a month and that his injuries kept him out of work for four months. Four months at $700.00 a month—for a total of $2,800.00. Third, past pain and suffering. Ladies and gentlemen, it's obviously very difficult to place a dollar figure on something like pain or suffering. But think of it this way. How much do you pay your dentist for a shot of novocaine to give you relief from pain for the hour you're in the dentist's chair? About $10.00? $10.00 for an hour of freedom from pain. We're going to ask for only $20.00 for each day of those four months of suffering. 120 days at $20.00 per day—$2,400.00 for past suffering. In addition, remember Doctor Walters' testimony. She testified that it's reasonably certain that Mr. Williams will regularly suffer from this level of pain for at least another two years. Another 730 days again at $20 a day—therefore $14,600 for future pain and suffering.

Finally, punitive damages. These are the damages the law imposes to punish intentional wrongdoers, the damages the law gives to deter such misconduct in the future. In this case, we're not talking about an accident or even a negligently inflicted injury. The defendant punched Mr. Williams. He kicked him. He dragged him. He choked him. They took this tie, Plaintiff's Exhibit No. 8, wrapped it all the way around his neck, and tried to strangle him. Then the defendant threatened to kill Mr. Williams. He threatened to kill him! It's never been truer that the facts speak for themselves, and the facts say that the defendant acted like a brutal savage. The facts say that $20,000.00 in punitive damages would be entirely reasonable here.

(Conclusion)

"Ladies and gentlemen, I'm going to sit down now. The defense attorney will have a chance to speak to you now. And while he's speaking and trying to defend their version of the facts, I want you to ask yourself some questions. Is Mr. Williams' identification likely to be mistaken if he was that close to his attackers for that long? If the defendant's room was so close to the restroom and Ms. Freeman saw and heard the attackers, why didn't the defendant see or hear anything? Finally, if the defendant was innocent, why did he come up with that flimsy story about lending his shoes to a friend? Think about those questions, and use your common sense. Those questions all point to the same answer. When you consider all the evidence in this case, we're certain you'll conclude that one attacker was Dick Rogers, and the other attacker was Dick Rogers' friend, the man Rogers had been with earlier in the evening, the man Rogers had been drinking with—and the man who together with Rogers beat and kicked Peter Williams until he was bloody and almost unconscious. He's the man Peter Williams pointed to today from this witness stand: the defendant. And the only just verdict in this case is one in favor of Mr. Williams against the defendant for at least $41,300."

§ 14.6   ETHICAL QUESTIONS

Suppose that before trial in a tort action for interference with advantageous, contractual relations between the plaintiff and a Mr. Newsome, the defense moved *in limine* to exclude certain memoranda exchanged between the defendant and her defense attorney. In one memorandum, the defendant acknowledged that when he initially contacted Mr. Newsome, Newsome told him that he, Newsome, already had a contract with the plaintiff. Newsome dies before trial. The defendant does not testify at trial; the defendant decides not to testify on his own behalf, and the plaintiff's attorney concludes that it would be too dangerous to call the defendant as a hostile witness. It is now time for summation. During closing, would it be ethical for the defense attorney to state that "there's been no evidence produced in this trial to show that my client even knew that Mr. Newsome had already entered into a contract with the plaintiff." In fact, there was no evidence to that effect, but is the statement nevertheless misleading? Would it be proper for the defense attorney to state that "all the sworn testimony shows that my client had no knowledge of the plaintiff's contract with Newsome"? What if the defense attorney asserted that "the only reasonable conclusion in this case is that my client had no knowledge whatsoever of the plaintiff's contract with Newsome"?

Now consider the use of analogies during summation. Sometimes the attorney uses personalized analogies. For example, one defense attorney often used "a story about his [own] boyhood on the farm." McElhaney, *Analogies in Final Argument,* 6 LITIGATION 37, 38–39 (Wint. 1980). A personalized analogy can be even more effective than a Biblical quotation or a reference to an historical incident. The personalized analogy not only helps sell the desired inference; at another level, the analogy can help humanize the attorney and sell his or her credibility to the jury. *Id.* at 39. If the jury likes the attorney, that may work to the advantage of the attorney's client. Should personalized analogies be allowed during closing? Little has been written about the limitations on the use of analogies during summation. However, one commentator argues that the courts ought to recognize a jury notice doctrine allowing the attorneys to use analogies illustrating matters of common knowledge that all or most of the jurors are presumably familiar with. Mansfield, *Jury Notice,* 74 GEO.L.J. 395 (1985). Given that doctrine, should personalized analogies be permitted? Model Rule of Professional Conduct 3.4(e) forbids the attorney from alluding during closing to "any matter that . . . will not be supported by admissible evidence. . . ." Whenever the attorney uses a personalized analogy, the attorney is referring to an extra-record fact that is not technically supported by any evidence. Should Rule 3.4(e) be construed as forbidding individualized analogies? *See Triplett v. Napier,* 286 S.W.2d 87 (Ky.App.1955) (an attorney's reference to his personal experience with a chiropractor).

§ 14.7 TRIAL TECHNIQUE EXERCISES

In the laboratory exercise this week, you will deliver a closing argument in your case. Plaintiffs and prosecutors will be permitted to reserve time for a rebuttal summation. Your instructor will announce any maximum or minimum length requirements for the summations.

Chapter 15

TRIAL MOTIONS

Reprinted by permission of Warner Books/New York from The Law as Seen by
Charles Bragg. Copyright © 1983 by Charles Bragg.

Table of Sections

§ 15.1 INTRODUCTION

Although many motions must be made before trial to be timely, other motions can be made during or after trial. For example, at trial the plaintiff's attorney could move for a continuance; or a criminal defense attorney might move for a psychiatric evaluation of a prosecution witness. However, the most common trial motions are motions for a directed verdict, mistrial, or new trial. This chapter discusses the substantive and procedural considerations governing these three types of motions.

§ 15.2 MOTION FOR A DIRECTED VERDICT

§ 15.2(A) Substance

The title of this motion varies from jurisdiction to jurisdiction; it may be called a motion for a directed verdict, judgment as a matter of law, nonsuit, or judgment of acquittal. F.R.Civ.P. 50 ("judgment as a matter of law"); F.R.Crim.P. 29 ("judgment of acquittal"). Whatever its local title, the motion is a challenge to the legal sufficiency of the opposition's evidence. When you make this motion, you in effect assert that even if the jury decides to believe all the opposing witnesses' testimony, the jury nevertheless could not rationally return a verdict in favor of the opposition. On its face, the opposing testimony does not have sufficient cumulative probative value to support a verdict in favor of the opposition.

In ruling on this motion, the trial judge must decide whether your opponent has sustained his or her initial burden of going forward or production. At this point, you may want to turn back to your Evidence casebook and refresh your recollection of the law governing the initial burden of production.[1] Suppose that you have the initial burden on a

---

1. *See* R. ALLEN, R. KUHNS & E. SWIFT, EVIDENCE: TEXT, PROBLEMS, AND CASES 814–20, 858–60 (3d ed. 2002); K. BROUN, R. MOSTELLER & P. GIANNELLI, EVIDENCE; CASES AND MATERIALS 109–29 (6th ed. 2002); R. CARLSON, E. IMWINKELRIED, E. KIONKA & K. STRACHAN, EVIDENCE: TEACHING MATERIALS FOR AN AGE OF SCIENCE AND STATUTES Ch. 30 (5th ed. 2002); S. FRIEDLAND, P. BERGMAN & A. TASLITZ, EVIDENCE LAW AND PRACTICE § 17.04 (2000); M. GRAHAM, EVIDENCE: AN INTRODUCTORY PROBLEM APPROACH CHAPTER 14 (2002); M. GRAHAM & E. OHLBAUM, COURTROOM EV-

factual issue and you fail to sustain the burden. If so, the judge makes a peremptory ruling against you. The plaintiff has the burden on the essential elements of the cause of action, and the prosecutor similarly has the burden on the elements of the charged crime. However, the defense can also have an initial burden. Suppose, for example, that in the *Scott* prosecution, you were the defense attorney attempting to establish the defendant's legal insanity as a defense. The judge would assign you the initial burden of production on the issue of Scott's insanity. Assume further that your only evidence supporting the defense was Joan Freeman's testimony that just before she left Scott's room, he was acting "a bit peculiar." Standing alone, that testimony has insufficient probative value to sustain a permissive inference of Scott's insanity; even if the jury accepted Freeman's testimony at face value, the jury could not rationally infer insanity from that testimony. Symbolically, the defense has presented evidence of only circumstance A; and the judge rules that even if the jurors believe the evidence A, they may not inter D, the fact in issue. Consequently, the judge would take the issue away from the jury; the judge would not even instruct the jury on the insanity defense. The defense could not mention, much less argue, insanity during summation.

Change the facts. Now assume that Freeman testified that she knew Scott quite well and that just before she left his room, he began acting in a bizarre fashion. Under Federal Rule of Evidence 701, the judge permits her to express the lay opinion that the defendant was acting in an "irrational, crazy sort of way." On this state of the record, the judge would instruct the jury on insanity. Freeman's testimony is sufficient to create a permissive inference of Scott's insanity. The judge rules that if the jurors believe Freeman's testimony, they could rationally infer the fact in issue. In this state of the record, the defense has presented credible evidence of circumstance B; and the judge rules that if the jury decides to believe the evidence of B, they may infer the evidence of D. Thus, the defense now has a submissible case and gets to the jury on the issue of insanity.

Vary the facts once again. Suppose that in another legal proceeding a few days before the attack on Williams, Scott had been adjudged mentally incompetent. In some jurisdictions, a recent adjudication of

IDENCE: A TEACHING COMMENTARY Ch. 18 (1997); E. GREEN & C. NESSON, PROBLEMS, CASES, AND MATERIALS ON EVIDENCE Ch. 10 (2d ed. 1994); R. LEMPERT, S. GROSS & J. LIEBMAN, A MODERN APPROACH TO EVIDENCE 1235–58 (3d ed. 2000); M. MENDEZ, EVIDENCE: THE CALIFORNIA CODE AND THE FEDERAL RULES—A PROBLEM APPROACH Ch. 18 (2d ed. 1999); D. PRATER, C. AGUELLO, D. CAPRA, M. MARTIN & S. SALTZBURG, EVIDENCE: THE OBJECTION METHOD 756–67 (1997); P. RICE, EVIDENCE: COMMON LAW AND THE FEDERAL RULES 24–31, 1309–27 (4th ed. 2000); P. ROTHSTEIN, M. RAEDER & D. CRUMP, EVIDENCE: CASES, MATERIALS, AND PROBLEMS Ch. 13 (2d ed. 1998); O. WELLBORN, CASES AND MATERIALS ON THE RULES OF EVIDENCE Ch. 9 (2000); J. WALTZ & R. PARK, EVIDENCE: CASES AND MATERIALS Ch. 11 (9th ed. 1999); J. WEINSTEIN, J. MANSFIELD, N. ABRAMS & M. BERGER, EVIDENCE: CASES AND MATERIALS Ch. 7 (9th ed. 1997); I. YOUNGER, M. GOLDSMITH & D. SONENSHEIN, PRINCIPLES OF EVIDENCE Ch. 7 (4th ed. 2000).

incompetency creates a presumption of insanity. A true presumption is a mandatory inference; if the jury believes that Scott was adjudged incompetent three days before the attack on Williams, they *must* infer insanity unless the prosecution proves the contrary. The defense not only gets to the jury on the issue of insanity. More importantly, if the presumption remains in the case, during the final jury charge the judge will give the jury an instruction that will be very helpful to the defense, namely, if you find that Scott was adjudged incompetent so shortly before the attack, you must find him insane unless the prosecution affirmatively proves his sanity. Here the defense has proffered credible evidence of circumstance C; and the judge rules that if the jurors believe that evidence, they must infer D unless the prosecution proves that D does not exist. This type of presumption not only gives you the benefit of an instruction couched as a mandatory inference; it also shifts the ultimate burden of proof to the opposition.

The preceding three paragraphs present a nutshell summary of the substantive law of the initial burden of production. However, our primary focus is the arguments that this body of law permits the attorneys to make in support of or in opposition to a directed verdict motion.

Possible arguments by the attorney resisting the motion. One argument is that you have presented "direct" evidence of the existence of the fact in dispute. In most cases, any witness's direct testimony to the existence of a fact or the occurrence of an event is legally sufficient to support a finding of the fact's existence or the event's occurrence. For example, California Evidence Code § 411 reads: "Except where additional evidence is required by statute, the direct evidence of one witness . . . is sufficient proof of any fact." Statutory and constitutional provisions sometimes require corroboration in perjury and treason prosecutions. Thus, Section 3[1] of Article III of the national constitution provides that "[n]o person shall be convicted of treason unless on the testimony of two witnesses to the same overt act. . . ." However, absent such a constitutional or statutory requirement, direct testimony automatically satisfies the initial burden. If you can persuade the judge to characterize your testimony on the issue as "direct," you have defeated the motion. The fact in issue is D, and the witness testifies directly to D.

Similarly, you can defeat the motion by convincing the judge that you have triggered a presumption of the existence of the key fact. Suppose that the defendant is charged with driving a vehicle while under the influence of intoxicating liquor. The only prosecution evidence is the arresting officer's testimony that he subjected the defendant to a breathalyzer test and that the reading was 0.15% alcohol. The prosecutor does not call a physician to give expert testimony that a reading of 0.15% alcohol indicates intoxication. However, in many jurisdictions, there is a statutory presumption that a person is intoxicated if his blood alcohol concentration (BAC) exceeds 0.08%. If the defense moved for a directed verdict at the close of the prosecution case-in-chief, the presumption would be operative; and the existence of the presumption would require that the judge deny the motion. Moreover, if under the law of the jurisdiction the presumption remains in the case at the close of all the evidence even when the defendant denies being intoxicated, the presumption will carry the prosecution to the jury.

Finally, when you do not have the advantage of direct testimony or a presumption, you can still argue that your circumstantial evidence creates at least a permissive inference of each fact on which you have the burden. In a civil case, a permissive inference suffices to barely sustain the burden. The permissibility of the inference is a matter of logic and experience. As you might expect, judges are reluctant to take cases away from the jury. When the rationality of the inference is a close call, the judge usually resolves the doubt in favor of submitting the case to the jury.

Possible arguments by the moving attorney. Suppose that the opposing attorney is relying on a presumption to carry the case to the jury. However, your witnesses flatly contradicted the presumed fact. For example, your client took the stand and denied being drunk. The traditional view is that once your witnesses contradict the presumed fact, the "bubble bursts" and the presumption disappears from the case. 2 C. McCORMICK, HANDBOOK OF THE LAW OF EVIDENCE § 344 (5th ed. 1999). Federal Rule of Evidence 301 follows the "bursting bubble" theory. *Texas Dept. Of Community Affairs v. Burdine,* 450 U.S. 248, 254–55(1981); *Usery v. Turner Elkhorn Mining Co.,* 428 U.S. 1 (1976). Point out that you presented evidence directly rebutting the existence of the presumed fact. In most jurisdictions, the mere presentation of your evidence destroys the presumption. Your opponent can no longer rely on the presumption as the means of satisfying the initial burden.

In other cases, you must ordinarily make a two-step argument. To begin with, isolate the weak link in the opposition's case, the element on which their evidence is flimsiest. Sometimes, an element slips between the cracks; a state prosecutor might neglect to offer admissible evidence of the ownership of the property in a larceny case, or a federal prosecutor might overlook proof of an interstate commerce connection. *E.g., United States v. Quigley,* 53 F.3d 909 (8th Cir.1995)(in a federal robbery prosecution, the government neglected to show the technical interstate commerce element). You should single out the element that the opposition has neglected, since judges are rarely persuaded by "shotgun" arguments.

Next, when appropriate, invoke an enhanced burden; and argue the opponent has not met it. As we have seen, in most cases the measure of the burden is a mere permissive inference; the opponent sustains the burden by creating a permissive inference of the existence of the fact or the occurrence of the event. However, in some cases there is a more rigorous burden. For example, some jurisdictions enforce a tighter standard in criminal cases when the prosecution's case consists entirely or primarily of circumstantial evidence. R. CARLSON, CRIMINAL LAW ADVOCACY—TRIAL PROOF ¶ 9.04, at 9–39–40 (1982). Further, a more rigorous standard is now a constitutional requirement in prosecutions. In *Jackson v. Virginia,* 443 U.S. 307 (1979), the Court passed on a challenge to the legal sufficiency of the evidence supporting a state court conviction. The challenge was made in a federal habeas corpus proceeding. Writing for the Court, Justice Stewart declared:

> We hold that in a challenge to a state criminal conviction brought under 28 U.S.C. section 2254 . . . the applicant is entitled to habeas corpus relief if it is found that upon the record evidence adduced at the trial, no rational trier of fact could have found proof of guilt beyond a reasonable doubt.

Id. at 324. Although the case arose under the habeas corpus statute, Justice Stewart's opinion is couched in terms of due process reasoning. All the commentators and lower courts which have considered the issue have concluded that the *Jackson* ruling is a constitutional mandate to toughen the initial burden in criminal cases. A bare permissive inference no longer suffices; the prosecution evidence must have sufficient probative value to permit the hypothetical juror to find each element of the crime beyond a reasonable doubt. Suppose, for instance, that under Federal Rule of Evidence 801(d)(1)(C), the judge admits a complainant's prior identification of the defendant as substantive evidence but the complainant cannot confirm the identification during his trial testimony—the complainant testifies that the offense occurred so long ago that he can no longer remember. On the one hand, the presence of the prior identification hearsay statement in the record probably supports a permissive inference that the defendant is the perpetrator. On the other hand, given the complainant's inability to repeat the identification on the witness stand, it is arguable that any rational juror would necessarily have a lingering doubt about the defendant's guilt. In this situation, the *Jackson* standard may mandate that the judge make a peremptory ruling in the defendant's favor. Goldman, *Guilt by Intuition: The Insufficiency of Prior Inconsistent Statements to Convict,* 65 N.C.L.REV. 1, 40 (1968).

If your trial is one of the rare cases in which the opponent must present corroborating evidence to make out a submissible case and the opponent neglected to do so, focus your argument on the corroboration requirement. Be prepared to cite the constitutional or statutory law imposing the requirement, and point out that the opponent altogether failed to present any independent corroboration.

§ 15.2(B) Procedure

If you decide to make a directed verdict motion, request permission to approach sidebar; make the motion there. The judge will ordinarily deny the motion, and you do not want the jury to hear the judge's denial. Admittedly, the judge could instruct the jury that in passing on the motion, she uses a different standard than the jury is to employ during deliberations. However, the jury may not appreciate the distinction between the two standards, and the fact remains that you will have lost a challenge to the sufficiency of the evidence in the jury's hearing.

In many jurisdictions, you must make the motion three different times—at the close of the opponent's case-in-chief, again at the close of all the evidence, and finally in any new trial motion you file. If you fail to make or renew the motion, you waive the issue for purposes of appeal.

Suppose your opponent moves to dismiss your client's case and that during the argument over the motion, it becomes apparent that the judge is leaning toward directing a verdict against you. It is also clear that the judge is inclined to do so because you inadvertently omitted calling witnesses to a particular element. You know that the witnesses are available. At that point, you can request permission to reopen your case. Confess your error; blaming someone else or citing a lame excuse can irritate the judge, and an irritated judge is more likely to grant the directed verdict motion. Then argue that especially since the witnesses are available to prove the fact in issue, granting the motion would be a miscarriage of substantial justice.

Some attorneys make directed verdict motions as a matter of course. The danger of foregoing the motion is underlined by cases denying appeals because of untimely motions, or the absence of them. *See Haygood v. Auto–Owners Ins. Co.*, 995 F.2d 1512 (11th Cir.1993). However, like evidentiary objections, a directed verdict motion can be counterproductive. Suppose, for example, that you know that the trial judge: (1) rarely grants such motions, and (2) routinely insists that the moving attorney specify the precise weakness in the plaintiff's or prosecutor's case. Assume further that although there is a gap in the opposition's case, the opposing attorney can easily cure the weakness by calling a readily available witness. On this set of assumptions, there is little to be gained by making the motion. Worse still, there may be much to be lost. After at the judge's insistence you specify the weakness in the opposition's case, the opposition may become conscious of that weakness, move to reopen, and then call the witnesses who can remedy the weakness. Hence, the net effect of making the motion is that the overall strength of the opposing case will be greater than it otherwise would have been. The jury may then find the opposing case even more persuasive.

§ 15.3 MISTRIAL MOTION

You may move for a mistrial as an end in itself, or under your jurisdiction's procedural rules you may need to make the motion in order to preserve certain types of error for appeal.

§ 15.3(A) Substance

When you move for a mistrial, it is ideal if you can show that there has been an important, indelible, and intentional error.

The error can take many forms: The judge may make an improper comment manifesting bias against your client, the bailiff escorting the jury might mention an accused's prior convictions that would be inadmissible during trial, a juror may contact a newspaper reporter writing a story about the case, the opposing attorney may make an inflammatory remark, or an opposing witness may make a gratuitous reference to inadmissible evidence. Any type of error can form the basis of a mistrial motion.

Understandably, before the judge will abort the trial on the ground of an error, the judge must be convinced that the error is an important one. When the error is the exposure of the jury to inadmissible evidence, the error ordinarily necessitates a mistrial only if the error relates to the pivotal issue in the case. For example, in the *Scott* case, during her testimony Officer Taylor might refer to an inadmissible hearsay statement that there was an attack or that Williams was injured in the attack. Those facts are virtually undisputed in the case, and an error relating to those issues would not warrant a mistrial. However, inadmissible evidence relating to Scott's identity as an attacker might require a mistrial; Scott's identity as an attacker is the real battleground at trial.

It is not enough to show that an important error has occurred; even when there has been a significant error, in most cases judges assume that a curative instruction to disregard is sufficient relief for the injured party. The judge strikes the inadmissible matter and instructs the jury to disregard the matter during deliberations. In some cases, however, even a strongly-worded curative instruction is an insufficient antidote for the error. Trial attorneys have long suspected that jurors have difficulty following curative instructions, and the empirical research indicates that that suspicion is well founded. Marcotte, *"The Jury Will Disregard ..."*, 73 A.B.A.J. 34 (Nov. 1, 1987) (an American Bar Foundation study).

On occasion, the Supreme Court itself has balked at naively assuming that the jury can follow the judge's instructions. There is a trilogy of cases. The first case is the Supreme Court's 1933 decision in *Shepard v. United States,* 290 U.S. 96 (1933). In that case, the defendant, Dr. Shepard, was charged with murdering his wife. One defense theory was that the wife had committed suicide. The issue on appeal was the admissibility of the wife's statement, "Dr. Shepard has poisoned me." Initially, the Court held that the statement did not fall within the dying declaration hearsay exception. The prosecutor argued alternatively on appeal that the statement was admissible as nonhearsay to show the wife's non-suicidal state of mind. The prosecution contended that the mere fact that the wife made the statement in question indicated that she lacked suicidal intent. The Court rejoined that even if the statement were logically relevant for that purpose, it was unrealistic to think that the jury could follow an instruction limiting the jury's use of the statement to that purpose. The Court declared that "discrimination so subtle is a feat beyond the compass of ordinary minds." *Id.* at 104. Thus, the Court rejected a limiting instruction as to purpose.

Jackson v. Denno, 378 U.S. 368 (1964), is another case in point. In that case, the Court ruled on the constitutionality of the procedure for determining the voluntariness of confessions. In some jurisdictions, the judge submitted the issue to the jury and further instructed the jury to disregard the confession if they found it involuntary. The Court held that procedure unconstitutional; even if the jury found the confession to be involuntary, there was realistically an intolerable risk that the content of the confession would subconsciously influence the jury. Here the Court rejected an instruction to disregard.

Similarly, in *Bruton v. United States,* 391 U.S. 123 (1968), the Court passed on the constitutionality of the procedure for admitting nontestifying defendant at joint trials. Suppose that after his arrest, defendant #2 confesses to his involvement in a conspiracy with defendant #1. Defendant #2 does not testify at trial. The confession is nevertheless admissible against defendant #2 as a personal admission. However, since defendant #2 confessed after arrest, the confession is inadmissible against defendant #1; the confession does not fall within the coconspirator hearsay doctrine codified in Federal Rule 801(d)(2)(E). Before *Bruton,* most jurisdictions admitted the confession at the joint trial; the judge gave the jury a limiting instruction as to party. The judge simply instructed the jury to disregard the confession while deciding the guilt or innocence of defendant #1. In *Bruton,* as in *Jackson,* the Court refused to presume that the jury could comply with the instruction. The Court reasoned that there was a grave risk that the jury would be influenced by defendant #2's confession. For that reason, functionally defendant #2 would be an accuser of defendant #1. Defendant #1 would therefore have a sixth amendment right to confront (cross-examine) defendant #2. However, since defendant #2 elects against testifying, there is a denial of confrontation; defendant #1 has no opportunity to cross-examine defendant #2. The options open to the prosecution are to sever the trials, forego using the confession, or redact the confession to avoid incriminating defendant #1.

In all these cases, the evidence was directly relevant to a critical issue in the case, and the source of the evidence was a declarant who presumably had personal knowledge of the facts. In these circumstances, it would be very difficult for a rational juror to disregard the probative worth of the evidence. When you are arguing a mistrial motion, have these three cases at your fingertips; it is sometimes useful to remind the judge that even the Supreme Court has expressed doubt in the efficacy of limiting and curative instructions.

When the alleged error is the exposure of the jury to inadmissible evidence such as a codefendant's confession, you should not only point out the prejudicial nature of the item of evidence; you should also stress the number of times the jury has been exposed to the evidence and the length of the exposure. The judge is more likely to declare a mistrial if the opposing attorney mentioned the inadmissible evidence during voir dire examination and opening statement. Likewise, the judge will be more inclined to grant a mistrial motion if a witness testified about the inadmissible matter for 15 minutes in the jury's presence before the judge finally ruled the evidence inadmissible. The more repeated the exposure and the lengthier the exposure, the greater is the probability that the error will make an indelible impression on the jury.

If you can show an important, indelible error, the judge should grant your mistrial motion. As a practical matter, though, you want to go further and, whenever possible, show that the error was intentional. Judges are far more likely to grant a mistrial when they believe that the error was bad faith misconduct on the part of the opposition. Some jurisdictions have formally recognized the trial judge's power to grant mistrials for prophylactic reasons to deter future, intentional misconduct.

§ 15.3(B) Procedure

Precisely because it is helpful to show that the error was intentional, you can use motions *in limine* to set up mistrial motions. Suppose that you know that the opposition has a prejudicial item of evidence which you believe is inadmissible. Assume, for example, that in the *Scott* case, when Scott gave his statement to the police, he mentioned that he had been arrested once before on rape charges. In your opinion, there is no legitimate, noncharacter theory for admitting that evidence under Federal Rule of Evidence 404(b). You could move before trial to bar any mention of that incident during voir dire, opening, or the examination of witnesses. You can also seek a court order that the prosecutor admonish her witnesses not to mention the incident. If the judge entertains and grants your motion and the prosecutor later elicits testimony about the rape charge, there will not only be error in the record, the prosecutor will be hard pressed to characterize the error as accidental. Even when the judge refuses to entertain the motion on the merits, you have put the opposition on notice that you strenuously object to the evidence in question. You have made it more difficult for the opposition to later claim inadvertence.

Assume that during trial, the opposition commits an act of misconduct which would otherwise justify a mistrial. Should you necessarily move for a mistrial? Before making the motion, consider three factors. First, can your client afford a second trial? In some cases, the cost of going to trial has exhausted your client's financial resources. In this situation, it would be foolish to exercise your legal right to move for mistrial. Second, read the jurors' faces. The jurors may be incensed at the misdeed. If they are, they may translate that anger into a verdict adverse to your opponent. In short, the misconduct may have backfired; the jurors' reaction to the misconduct may have greatly increased the likelihood that you can gain a favorable verdict in the case. An angry jury can return a huge award of punitive damages. Finally, will the judge allow you to refer to the misconduct during closing argument? At least when the opposing client was somehow personally involved in the misconduct, you arguably should be able to treat the misconduct as an admission by conduct, that is, as evidence of the opposition's consciousness of the weakness of their case. *A New Antidote for an Opponent's Pretrial Discovery Misconduct: Treating the Misconduct at Trial as an Admission by Conduct of the Weakness of the Opponent's Case,* 1993 B.Y.U.L.REV. 793. Analogously, Federal Rule of Civil Procedure 37(c)(1) authorizes the trial judge to inform the jury of the opposition's misconduct during pretrial discovery. Why else would the opposition have resorted to such an underhanded tactic? When the judge indicates that she will allow you to treat the misconduct in that fashion in summation, again it may be a mistake to move for a mistrial. A summation capitalizing on the opposition's misconduct may virtually ensure a verdict favorable to your client.

Assume, though, that after conducting a tactical cost/benefit analysis, you decide to move for mistrial. As in the case of directed verdict motions, when you decide to move for mistrial, initially ask to approach sidebar. Just as judges are reluctant to direct a verdict, they are anything but eager to declare a mistrial. To some extent they are even more reluctant to declare mistrials; a directed verdict often terminates the litigation while a mistrial sometimes necessitates a retrial, consuming more courtroom time. The judge will commonly deny the mistrial motion,[2] and you do not want to lose the motion in the jury's hearing.

In some cases, you will need to present extrinsic evidence in support of your mistrial motion. Suppose, for instance, that the basis of your motion is that a juror had unauthorized contact with a newspaper reporter writing an article about the case. The contact did not occur in the judge's presence, and you may need to schedule an evidentiary hearing and present either affidavits or live testimony to prove the improper contact.

Suppose that as a criminal defense attorney, you make the motion and the judge indicates that she is willing to grant it. In most cases, you have won your client only temporary respite. By moving for a mistrial, you ordinarily waive the protection of the fifth amendment double jeopardy prohibition. For that reason, the prosecution can retry your client. However, in some cases retrial is forbidden. In *Oregon v. Kennedy,* 456 U.S. 667 (1982), the Court stated that retrial is barred if the prosecution intentionally goaded the defense into moving for a mistrial. The prosecutor might do so, for instance, when the case has gone poorly and the prosecutor senses that the jury will acquit. In this situation, the prosecutor might deliberately engage in egregious misconduct in the hope that the defense will move for mistrial and prevent the case from ever reaching the jury. *Kennedy* establishes a minimal, national standard. Under its own constitution, a state court may adopt a more rigorous standard. For instance, in *Pool v. Superior Court,* 139 Ariz. 98, 677 P.2d 261 (1984), the Arizona Supreme Court held that retrial may be forbidden even when the prosecutor did not deliberately provoke a

---

2. Certain evidentiary violations increase the likelihood that a mistrial will be declared. In a criminal case, there is a good possibility of a mistrial if the prosecutor violates the rule forbidding comment on the defendant's invocation of the privilege against self-incrimination. *See Griffin v. California,* 380 U.S. 609 (1965). Likewise, references to inadmissible evidence of a defendant's uncharged crimes frequently prompt mistrials in criminal cases. *State v. Cook,* 673 S.W.2d 469, 472 (Mo.App.1984) ("uniformly warrant[s] the declaration of mistrial"). In civil cases, mention of liability insurance or a subsequent repair creates an above average probability of a mistrial declaration. Fed.R.Evid. 407, 411.

defense mistrial motion. The court announced that in its view, retrial should be precluded whenever the error prompting the mistrial "amounts to intentional conduct which the prosecutor knows to be improper and prejudicial. . . ." In this light, when the judge indicates to you that she is about to declare a mistrial, request that the judge make an additional special finding on the record that the error prompting the mistrial was intentional prosecutorial misconduct, calculated to goad you into a mistrial motion. If the judge makes that finding, your client's victory may become final and complete.

§ 15.4 NEW TRIAL MOTIONS

§ 15.4(A) Substance

In most jurisdictions, the scope of a new trial motion is identical to the scope of review on appeal; the only cognizable errors are errors that could be reviewed on appeal.[3] Under this view, as on appeal, you could allege that there was error in admitting evidence or in the wording of an instruction. Similarly, you could argue that as a matter of law, the opposition's evidence was insufficient to sustain the initial burden of production and support a verdict in their favor. However, under this view, just as most appellate courts will not redetermine credibility or reweigh the evidence, you cannot invite the judge to overturn findings supported by legally sufficient evidence.

In a significant minority of jurisdictions, though, the scope of a new trial motion exceeds the scope of appeal. These jurisdictions permit the trial judge to grant a new trial when the verdict is against the clear or great weight of the evidence. *Velazquez v. Figueroa–Gomez*, 996 F.2d 425 (1st Cir.), *cert. denied*, 510 U.S. 993 (1993). Under this view, the judge has a limited power to redetermine credibility and reweigh the evidence. *Commons v. Montgomery Ward & Co.*, 614 F.Supp. 443 (D.Kan.1985). Thus, the judge's power to grant a new trial is broader than her power to grant a directed verdict or judgment as a matter of law. *United States v. A. Lanoy Alston*, 974 F.2d 1206 (9th Cir.1992). The judge cannot order a new trial merely because she believes that she would have voted for a different verdict if she had been a juror, but she may grant a new trial when the jury has exercised exceptionally poor judgment in evaluating the testimony.

§ 15.4(B) Procedure

Typically, you must make a new trial motion shortly after the trial. Federal Rule of Civil Procedure 59(b) provides that the motion must "be

---

3. In rare cases, a new trial will be granted on the basis of after-discovered evidence. For a discussion of this ground for a new trial, see Carlson, *When Witnesses Recant: New Trials Based Upon After–Discovered Evidence,* 9 VERDICTS, SETTLEMENTS & TACTICS 404 (Dec. 1989). In most jurisdictions, the moving party must show that: The new information probably would have changed the outcome of the trial; and the late discovery of the information was not due to the party's negligence. A minority of states apply a more lenient standard; they permit new trials when the newly discovered evidence might have changed the outcome of the trial.

served not later than 10 days after the entry of the judgment." Criminal motions follow a similar pattern. Federal Rule of Criminal Procedure 33 states that after a guilty verdict, a new trial motion ordinarily "shall be made within 7 days after verdict." As *Carlisle v. United States,* 517 U.S. 416 (1996) illustrates, the courts tend to strictly enforce these filing deadlines.

Unlike directed verdict and mistrial motions, a new trial motion will ordinarily be in writing. Even if local procedure does not require a written motion, it is good practice to reduce the motion to writing. Doing so signals the trial judge that you are serious about the motion; you are not merely making a *pro forma* motion to insulate yourself from malpractice liability or an ineffective counsel claim. Submitting a written motion also makes a better record in the event of an appeal.

Suppose that you decide to challenge the legal sufficiency or weight of the evidence supporting the verdict. If you decide to move on that ground, you should seriously consider asking the court reporter to prepare a partial verbatim transcript of the key passages of testimony. You can then point to specific deficiencies in the opposing witnesses' testimony. Like reducing the motion to writing, going to the length of obtaining a partial transcript sends a message to the trial judge that you sincerely believe that your motion is meritorious.

When the new trial motion raises a question such as the legal sufficiency of the evidence to sustain the opposition's burden of going forward, it may be a simple matter to prepare for the hearing on the motion. The question is a purely legal one, and the only information the judge will need is a transcript of the key passages of testimony. However, the matter becomes more complex when the motion rests on a basis such as jury or attorney misconduct. To begin with, these bases raise factual questions; and you must be certain that you know the quantum of your burden on the factual issues. "The standard for granting a new trial based on improper conduct by counsel, including improper closing argument, is whether the conduct was such as to impair gravely the calm and dispassionate consideration of the case by the jury." *Neal v. Toyota Motor Corp.,* 823 F.Supp. 939, 944 (N.D.Ga.1993). As this quotation suggests, the moving party must persuade the trial judge both that an error occurred and that there is a good possibility that the error affected the verdict. In some instances, such as when the error takes the form of improper communication between a juror and an outside source of information about the case, the moving party may have the benefit of a presumption that the error was prejudicial. *E.g., United States v. Sanders,* 962 F.2d 660 (7th Cir.1992).

Moreover, you should give some thought to the admissibility of the evidence you intend to proffer to meet your burden. The admissibility of the evidence can be particularly problematic if you attempt to prove either jury misconduct or the effect of other misconduct on the jury. Federal Rule of Evidence 605(b) restricts the use of testimony by, or affidavits from, jurors; the subdivision reads:

(b) Inquiry into validity of verdict or indictment. Upon an inquiry into the validity of a verdict or indictment, a juror may not testify as to any matter or statement occurring during the course of the jury's deliberations or to the effect of anything upon that or any other juror's mind or emotions as influencing the juror to assent to or dissent from the verdict or indictment or concerning the juror's mental processes in connection therewith, except that a juror may testify on the question whether extraneous prejudicial information was improperly brought to the jury's attention or whether any outside influence was improperly brought to bear upon any juror. Nor may a juror's affidavit or evidence of any statement by the juror concerning a matter about which the juror would be precluded from testifying be received for these purposes.

Rule 606(b) codifies the traditional "Mansfield" view. Under this view, jurors are competent witnesses as to only: (1) "extraneous prejudicial information" such as the presence of a newspaper article about the case in the jury room; and (2) "outside influence" such as a phone threat to one of the jurors. The majority view precludes the jurors from testifying about either most juror statements during deliberation or the effect of any event upon the jurors' states of mind. There is a minority view. Timothy, *Demeanor Credibility,* 49 CATH.U.L.REV. 903 (2000); Carlson, *Impeaching Jury Verdicts,* LITIGATION 31 (Fall 1975). The minority view permits jurors to testify or supply affidavits about any "objective" fact or event, that is, information that can be corroborated by a third party. Under this view, one juror's statement, urging other jurors to agree to an improper quotient verdict, could be proven by another juror's affidavit; the statement is an objective event which still other jurors could corroborate. However, even under this view, jurors may not testify about the impact of any fact or event on their subjective decision-making process. The judge inquires whether the facts or event in question was likely to influence the hypothetical, rational juror. If your jurisdiction's exclusionary rule prevents you from using jurors as a source of information to establish the basis for your new trial motion, you must find an alternative source of information such as a bailiff who happened to overhear the improper statement as she walked by an open door or window to the deliberation room.

§ 15.5 SAMPLE MISTRIAL MOTION

In the *Scott* prosecution, assume that in his pretrial statement to the police, Scott mentioned that three years before he had been arrested on rape charges. You investigate the incident and research the case law applying Federal Rule of Evidence 404(b), and you correctly conclude that any reference to the arrest would be inadmissible at trial. You make a motion *in limine* to preclude any mention of the arrest. The trial judge grants the motion. The judge directs the prosecutor to instruct his witnesses to avoid any mention of the arrest. During his case-in-chief, the prosecutor calls Officer Taylor as a witness. She testifies about Scott's arrest and subsequent interrogation. The prosecutor then asks an open-ended question about Scott's admissions during the interrogation. In response Officer Taylor refers to Scott's admission that he had been arrested three years before on rape charges. The following ensues. In this sample, "D" represents defense counsel, "P" prosecutor, and "J" the judge.

D Your Honor, I move to strike the officer's reference to the arrest on the ground that it violates Evidence Rule 404(b).

J Granted. Ladies and gentlemen, I am striking from the record Officer Taylor's mention of the defendant's arrest on other charges. You are to completely disregard that remark. That remark has nothing to do with the facts in this case.

D Your Honor, may we approach the bench?

J Yes.

D Your Honor, I'm afraid that at this point, I'm also going to have to move for a mistrial. The reference to the rape charges was clearly inadmissible. Moreover, this error relates to a key issue in the case. The central dispute in this trial is the question of the identity of the men who attacked Mr. Williams. The jurors may be thinking that the earlier rape incident shows that the defendant is a violent person—precisely the type of person who would commit the attack alleged in this case. Its only possible relevance is on the key question of identity. Finally, realistically a curative instruction to disregard won't work here. Rape is a very serious charge. The witness on the stand is a police officer, whom the jurors are likely to have faith in; and we have a police officer saying that the defendant himself admitted the rape arrest. This is one of those rare cases in which a mistrial is warranted.

J Before I rule, Ms. Prosecutor, I'd like to know whether you carried out my order that you admonish your witnesses against referring to the rape charge.

P Your Honor, I've got to confess that things were so hectic after our pretrial conference that I forgot to do that. I'm sorry, but I still don't think that a mistrial is needed. After all, Taylor didn't say that the defendant admitted a rape; the only thing she testified to was that he admitted being arrested for rape. A curative instruction should suffice here.

D I think that the prosecutor is mischaracterizing the testimony. As I remember it, Taylor said that he admitted that "he'd been in trouble with the law before." That vague statement preceded the reference to the rape arrest.

J I think that the defense counsel's right. Moreover, I'm quite upset that the prosecution didn't take the time to carry out my instructions. I thought that I'd made my instructions sufficiently explicit. Consequently, I'm going to grant a mistrial here.

D Your Honor, we appreciate that. I'd ask for only one thing further. As you well know, under *Oregon v. Kennedy,* the prosecution can retry my client unless the prosecution intentionally goaded the defense into the mistrial motion. I'd like you to make a specific finding on the record of intentional prosecutorial misconduct calculated to do that.

J No. On the one hand, I think you're entitled to your mistrial. On the other hand, although there's negligence here—gross negligence in my opinion—there's an insufficient inference that the prosecutor was trying to goad you into a mistrial. Quite frankly, the case seemed to be going fairly well for the prosecution. This isn't the case of a desperate prosecutor trying to prevent a weak case from going to a jury that was almost sure to acquit. I'll grant the motion, but I won't make that finding.

D Very well, Your Honor.

§ 15.6 ETHICAL QUESTIONS

You are a civil defense attorney, and you have made a motion for a directed verdict. You are arguing the motion, and at one point the judge says, "Well, as I recall the testimony, the plaintiff didn't present any evidence that . . . ." When the judge says that, the plaintiff's attorney is distracted and does not hear the statement. As soon as you hear the statement, you realize that the judge is wrong; the plaintiff did present testimony, albeit brief, on that very issue. Do you have an obligation to correct the judge's misrecollection of the testimony? A.B.A. Model Rule 3.3(a) imposes an affirmative duty on attorneys to reveal facts when "disclosure is necessary to avoid assisting a criminal or fraudulent act by the client," but is that language applicable here? The plaintiff's attorney had ample opportunity to correct the judge's mistake, but the opportunity is being missed because the plaintiff's attorney was careless and inattentive. Suppose alternatively that during the oral argument on the motion, the judge says, "The plaintiff did present testimony that . . . , but I don't think that's legally sufficient under El Dorado law to support a verdict." The plaintiff's attorney says nothing to the contrary. During your pretrial legal research, you discovered a case in point by an intermediate appellate court in El Dorado. The case squarely holds that the type of testimony the plaintiff presented is legally sufficient to sustain a verdict. Think back to the discussion of Model Rule 3.3(a)(3) in § 6.7 of this text. Must you reveal the appellate decision to the judge if the judge asks you point blank whether you know of "any cases on this point"? Do you have a *sua sponte* duty to reveal the decision even if the judge does not ask you that question?

Compare the duty to reveal facts under Rule 3.3(a)(2) with the corresponding duty to reveal legal authorities under Rule 3.3(a)(3). Which duty of disclosure is more extensive? Is the differing extent of the two duties justifiable? If so, why?

An evidentiary hearing on a new trial motion is scheduled in *case file B–8*, the *Kidd* case set out in the appendix. Plaintiff's attorney will argue for a new trial, and defense counsel will oppose the motion. The plaintiff will call Harold Gunther as a witness at the hearing. Gunther was a juror at the trial of the *Kidd* case. The trial took four days, and the jury returned a defense verdict. On the third day of trial, Gunther was driving home with another juror, Ms. Paula Schmidt. Gunther and Schmidt began discussing the seeming inaccuracy of the accident scene measurements which the witnesses had testified to. Since the plant in question was on their way home, Gunther and Schmidt decided to swing by the plant. When they arrived at the plant, they entered the building and stepped off some measurements. They found that the plaintiff's testimony about the measurements was erroneous. In addition, while Gunther and Schmidt were at the plant, they met a Mr. Green, one of defendant's employees. Gunther and Schmidt told Green that they were "interested" in the incident. Green told Gunther and Schmidt that he remembered other employees saying that Kidd had had a few drinks on the day of the accident. At the outset of the jury deliberations, neither Gunther nor Schmidt made any mention of their visit to the plant. However, Ms. Schmidt was elected foreperson. After the jury had deliberated for over five hours, Gunther told the other jurors about the visit and described the measurements which he and Schmidt had made. Gunther circulated to the other jurors a sheet of paper on which he had written down the measurements. Even at that point, Schmidt made no mention of Green's statements; but she did state that Gunther had correctly described the measurements which they made at the plant. Green was not a witness at trial. Your jurisdiction has adopted Federal Rule of Evidence 606.

Chapter 16

CONCLUSION

If you decide to pursue a career in litigation, this course will be merely the beginning of your study of trial advocacy. That study should span your legal career. You should take steps to ensure that you receive continuing legal education in trial advocacy.

You can pursue that goal in several ways. To begin with, you should attend participatory trial technique courses designed for attorneys. The National Institute of Trial Advocacy (N.I.T.A.) conducts such courses throughout the country. The Institutes of Continuing Legal Education established in some states occasionally conduct short courses in trial advocacy. In addition, there are now Inns of Court in most major metropolitan areas. In these courses and programs, young attorneys refine their skills under the supervision of senior litigators and judges.

Moreover, you should read voir dires, openings, examinations, and closings by leading attorneys, past and present. F. WELLMAN, THE ART OF CROSS–EXAMINATION (4th ed. 1936) includes several brilliant cross-examinations. The late Professor Younger edited a transcript series entitled CLASSICS OF THE COURTROOM. The series includes summations by Clarence Darrow and cross-examinations by Max Steur and Edward Bennett Williams. F. HICKS, FAMOUS AMERICAN JURY SPEECHES (1925) contains some wonderful summations. You will often find excerpts from great lines of questions or jury speeches in biographies of famous attorneys. *E.g.,* K. TIERNEY, DARROW: A BIOGRAPHY (1979). You can learn a great deal by studying the art of eminent litigators.

You should not only read the old trial classics; you should also stay abreast of the new literature on trial psychology. The scientific analysis of the trial process is still a nascent enterprise. Vinson, *Litigation: An Introduction to the Application of Behavioral Science,* 15 CONN.L.REV. 767, 796 (1983). Compared to the hard, exact sciences, disciplines such as kinesics and proxemics are emerging fields; many of their findings are tentative at best. Willett, *A Matrix of Meaning,* 41 MO.B.J. 249, 253–54 (1985). However, it would be myopic for trial attorneys to ignore the insights that legal psychologists are giving us into jury behavior. Although a litigator's schedule can be hectic, you should make the time to read such texts as S. HAMLIN, WHAT MAKES JURIES LISTEN (1985), J. FREDERICK, THE PSYCHOLOGY OF THE AMERICAN JURY (1988), D. HERBERT & R. BARRETT, ATTORNEY'S MASTER GUIDE TO COURTROOM PSYCHOLOGY: HOW TO APPLY BEHAVIORAL SCIENCE TECHNIQUES FOR NEW TRIAL SUCCESS (1981), T. SAN-NITO & P. McGOVERN, COURTROOM PSYCHOLOGY FOR TRIAL LAWYERS (1985), K. TAYLOR, R. BUCHANAN & D. STRAWN, COM-MUNICATION STRATEGIES FOR TRIAL ATTORNEYS (1984), or D. VINSON, JURY TRIALS: THE PSYCHOLOGY OF WINNING STRATE-GY (1986). To be sure, these texts review the relevant psychological literature in a somewhat simplified fashion, since these texts are written for attorneys rather than psychologists. However, if these texts whet your appetite, you can then move on to the more sophisticated scientific literature itself. Many of the relevant scientific papers are cited in Tanford & Tanford, *Better Trials Through Science: A Defense of Psychol-ogist–Lawyer Collaboration*, 66 N.C.L.REV. 741 (1988).

Reading should not be the extent of your educational efforts. If you learn that an eminent attorney is going to be trying a case in a nearby court and your schedule permits, go down to court, sit in the spectator area, and watch the attorney in action. After your own trials, you may be able to obtain a critique from the judge. Some jurisdictions even allow you to interview your own jurors after the trial. Blum, *Federal Court Enjoins Hawaii Rule That Bars Contact with Jurors After Trial Ends*, NAT'L L.J., Feb. 26, 1996, at p. A6 (in *Rapp v. Disciplinary Board of the Hawaii Supreme Court*, 916 F.Supp. 1525 (D.Haw.1996), the court enjoined the enforcement of Rule 3.5 of the Hawaii Supreme Court Rules of Professional Conduct which had been interpreted as barring post-verdict contact with jurors); Fargo, *Make the Post–Trial Interview Work for You*, 3 CRIM.JUST. 2 (Sum. 1988); Salman, *Jury's Reactions: Post–Trial Interviews Revealing*, NAT'L L.J., Dec. 9, 1991, at p. 23; Goldberg, *Muzzled in Massachusetts: Lawyers Cannot Talk to Jurors After Trial Has Ended*, 28 TRIAL 81 (Jan. 1992) (five states "limit post-trial contact between jurors and lawyers. Of the 94 federal district courts, 18 forbid such contact"). Sadly, few trial attorneys avail themselves of this oppor-tunity to interview their jurors. Varinsky & Nomikos, *Post-Verdict Interviews: Understanding Jury Decision Making*, 26 TRIAL 64 (Feb. 1990). Feedback from judges and jurors you have appeared before can be highly educative.

You should attempt to learn something new about trial advocacy every day of your career as a litigator. If you do, you will achieve a sense of constant, personal professional growth. It is difficult for a busy litigator to find the time for continuing legal education, but doing so is the most important investment you can make in your career. Forcing yourself to learn more about trial work-by reading the classics, studying the new psychological literature, and observing great litigators—will not only make you a better trial attorney; more importantly, it will enable you to obtain satisfaction from your work.

Appendix A

All counsel have access to all the documents in these Case files. You may assume that each side obtained the other side's documents by a voluntary discovery exchange. By agreeing to the exchange, the parties have waived any evidentiary privileges, including the work product protection, that would otherwise attach to the documents themselves.

In evaluating your exercises based on their Case files, your instructor may use a copy of the enclosed Trial Techniques Evaluation Sheet. In any event, as you prepare for the exercises, you should be conscious of the stylistic considerations listed in the left-hand margin of the sheet.

TRIAL TECHNIQUES EVALUATION SHEET

CLASS DATE _____   EXERCISE _____

STUDENT _____   EVALUATOR _____

Overall Evaluation

(Superior)   (Satisfactory)   (Unsatisfactory)

Specific Weaknesses
PHYSICAL MANNERISMS   Comments

_____ Poor posture

_____ Too stiff

_____ Too many gestures

_____ Inappropriate gestures

_____ Distracting movement

_____ Fidgeting

_____ Grim facial expression

_____ Insufficient eye contact

VOICE AND SPEECH

_____ Poor sense imagery

_____ Formalistic diction

_____ Spoke too loudly

_____ Spoke too softly

_____ Spoke too fast

_____ Spoke too slow

_____ Lack of vocal variety

_____ Redundant sounds

_____ Disorganized

Case File A–1*

ALEXANDER v. MAPLES

Statement of Larry Alexander

I am a 25–year-old. I live in Morena with my wife and two-year-old son. On October 7, 19YR–3, I was working at Stephens Grain and Feed Co., in Auburn, a rural suburb of Morena. I was wearing the company overalls with a "Stephens Grain and Feed" label on them. My job was to load and unload trucks with 50–pound sacks of ground corn for feeding hogs. While lifting one of the sacks, I experienced a sort of twitch in my back. I paused for a moment but then seemed to feel all right. I started back to work. After loading a few more sacks, I felt a sharp pain in my lower back. It caused me to stumble backward against the truck and fall. I fell to the ground on top of the sack. No one was in the work area. I think I may have lost consciousness for a couple of minutes. When I regained my senses, I felt a dull pain in my lower back and a throbbing pain on the right side of my head. There was a small pool of blood which I soon realized was coming from the right side of my head. I got to my feet and somewhat shakily walked into the warehouse. I told my supervisor that I was "feeling poorly" and was going to see a doctor.

I went to my car, took the keys out of my pocket, got in, and started driving. Although my vision was a bit blurry and I felt a little dizzy, I was able to drive the ten miles to the office of my family physician, Dr. James Maples. Maples has been my family physician for over ten years; I started going to him while I was still in high school. Once in the office, I was taken immediately into an empty patient room. Dr. Maples came in alone, and I briefly explained what happened.

Dr. Maples examined me. He treated the wound and spent a few minutes talking to me about my symptoms. He seemed to be in a rush for some reason. I told him about the loss of consciousness, the dizzy feeling, and the throbbing headache. I'm pretty sure I told the doctor about the kind of work that I do. The doctor said that he did not think that it was a serious head injury but that I ought to take the rest of the day off to relax at home. The back injury, according to the doctor, was most likely a muscle strain which should clear up in a few days.

Dr. Maples told me to do some relaxation exercises. The doctor briefly demonstrated the exercises. He told me that if the pain in my back worsened, or if it did not get better in 10 days, I should come back and see him. Other than that, the doctor said only to do the exercises; the doctor told me that the injury did not appear serious and that if the pain was not severe the next day, I could go back to work.

The next day the pain was about the same in my back, and my head felt much better. I had gotten up a bit late that morning, and I did not

* Part of this case file was developed by Professor Roger Park of the Hastings College of Law.

have time to do the relaxing exercises. I went to work, began lifting the sacks, and did not feel that the pain was increasing. After about an hour and a half, however, the pain gradually began to worsen. For the first time, I noticed it shooting through my buttocks and all the way down my right leg.

I went to the emergency room where I was admitted to the hospital and placed in traction.

I have brought a malpractice action claiming that the advice—or lack of advice—that I received from Maples resulted in the serious back injury.

Dated: January 21, 19YR–1

/s/ Lawrence F. Alexander

_____

Lawrence F. Alexander

Declaration of Dr. James R. Maples

I have practiced in Auburn for the past 15 years. I graduated at the top of my class from the University of El Dorado Medical College, but I decided to practice in a rural area because I think that there are a lot of unmet medical needs in Rural America. I grew up on a farm in Iowa, and I feel a lot of ties to that part of the country. It's a simpler, better lifestyle than you can find in a big city.

Larry Alexander is one of my patients. I've known him for a long time. I'm not sure what kind of work he does. When he comes in, he usually doesn't say much about his work. He's fairly quiet. I do recall that Larry came in on October 7, 19YR–3. When I walked into the examination room, I first had him take off his overalls. He presented a head wound. I then examined the head wound and cleaned it with soap and water. I observed that it was approximately a 1/16–inch puncture wound which had closed up nicely. There was no need for any stitches. I applied a disinfectant to the wound and a gauze bandage affixed with four strips of tape. I shaved a small area around the wound to make certain the bandage would adhere.

I spent three or so minutes talking to Larry about his symptoms. I knew that I had to leave the office soon; I had an appointment at the local hospital in half an hour, and it takes 10 minutes to drive from my office to the hospital. Larry never mentioned anything about lifting heavy sacks. Larry told me about the loss of consciousness, the dizzy feeling, and the throbbing headache—but that was all that he said. I said that I did not think that it was a serious head injury but that Larry ought to take the rest of the day off to relax at home. The back injury, in my judgment, was most likely a muscle strain which should clear up in a few days.

I told Larry to do some relaxing exercises. The exercises were for diagnostic and therapeutic purposes. If there had been a serious problem and if Larry had done the exercises as I told him, he probably would have experienced a mild, but sharp, pain that would have alerted me. I demonstrated the exercises and told Larry that if the pain in his back worsened, or if it did not get better in 10 days, Larry should come back and see me.

Larry has brought a malpractice action against me. I deny any negligence. The written entry about Larry's visit on Larry's Patient Chart states that Larry injured his back at work and that he was advised to "return in 10 days if pain persists." (I can authenticate the entry because it is in my handwriting.) I acknowledge that I have little experience treating back injuries and that the relaxing exercises I prescribed for Larry would not have cured Larry's back problem. I also admit that a board-certified specialist in back injuries could probably have easily diagnosed the problem, but I do not know of any such specialists in this town.

I declare under penalty of perjury that the above statements are true and correct.

Dated: January 15, 19YR–1

/s/   James R. Maples
_____
James R. Maples

Statement of Dr. Elizabeth Jensen

I am a general practitioner in Winters, the suburb next to Auburn. My resume is attached at the end of the Case file. In 19YR–4, I sat for part of the certification examination of the American Board of Surgery, but I failed the examination. I have retaken the examination and am awaiting results.

I have practiced in Morena County since 19YR–9. I am familiar with the customary practices of and standards of care observed by physicians in the County. On the one hand, I believe that Morena physicians do not practice "defensive medicine" to the same extent as physicians in some of the more urbanized sections of El Dorado. Morena is a more rural county than most of the areas in El Dorado, and Morena physicians do not run up the bill for their patients by requiring unnecessary tests or making unnecessary referrals. We're not quite so hyper about malpractice suits as our brethren in the big cities. On the other hand, I believe that back injuries are so subtle to diagnose and potentially so dangerous that in almost all cases in which a general practitioner suspects a back problem, the doctor should refer the patient to a specialist. I am fairly certain that that is not only what I think but also the widespread practice in Morena. It's certainly the practice that I personally follow. I'm affiliated in a medical building with 10 other physicians, and my conversations with my colleagues convince me that they do the same thing. In my judgment, the general practitioner should refer whenever there's anything more than a remote possibility of a serious, disabling back problem.

In my opinion, Dr. Maples violated the standard of care. Some, equally experienced Morena physicians might disagree with me, but I am confident that the vast majority would concur. Unfortunately, I have not had the time to review any of the medical records in the case; I am relying solely on what the plaintiff's attorney has told me about the incident.

CHART

PATIENT: Larry Alexander

DATE: 10 / 7 / YR - 3

> Patient injured himself at work. Said he was experiencing back pain. Patient presented 1/16" head wound that was cleaned and bandaged. Rx Prescribed some relaxation exercises to release muscle strain. Told patient to return in 10 days if pain persists or immediately if it got worse.

JRM
[E8502]

I want to add that I do not take malpractice litigation lightly. I myself have been subject to two groundless malpractice actions, but I feel very strongly that it is our profession's responsibility to police itself. I've even volunteered to serve on the state medical disciplinary board.

Maples breached the required standard of care, and it is the responsibility of the medical profession to come forward to help prove that. I'm writing a guest editorial for the state medical journal about that responsibility.

Dated: February 14, 19YR–1

/s/   Elizabeth Jensen

_____

Elizabeth Jensen

RESUME—ELIZABETH JENSEN

Date of birth: May 3, 19YR–40.

Attended Tulane University as undergraduate, B.S. 19YR–22.

Attended Tulane University School of Medicine; received M.D. degree from Tulane 19YR–15.

Interned at University of Minnesota Hospitals 19YR–14.

Residency at University of Minnesota Hospitals 19YR–13.

Licensed to practice medicine in Louisiana in 19YR–14, in Minnesota in 19YR–11, and in El Dorado in 19YR–10.

Published an article in the Bulletin of the Tulane Medical Faculty in 19YR–14 and an article in the Journal of Pediatric Surgery in 19YR–9.

Dr. Jensen has testified as a medical expert in dozens of trials, including 10 malpractice actions. In each malpractice case, she testified for the plaintiff. She has testified several times in malpractice actions for this plaintiff's counsel.

Statement of Curtis Juenger

I am Larry Alexander's supervisor at Stephens Grain and Feed. I believe that Larry is a nice guy but hardly the most reliable or truthful employee. In particular, Larry takes more sick leave than any other employee. I think that that is suspicious; Larry is younger than and at least as apparently robust as any of the other employees. I suspect that at least half the time Larry takes off for sick leave, Larry just wants to take some time off and go fishing. He's always talking about how the trout are biting. On one occasion in particular in 19YR–5, Larry complained of back pain and took a week off. When Larry returned to work, I demanded that Larry furnish a letter from a doctor, certifying the back problem. When Larry failed to do so, I had the bookkeeper dock Larry's pay for a week. Larry never complained to me about the money missing from that month's paycheck. I thought that that was proof that Larry was malingering.

I was at work on October 7, 19YR–3, when Larry supposedly hurt himself while lifting sacks of ground corn. When Larry first reported the incident to me, I said, "Look, Alexander, not another one of your so-called injuries. We're short-handed today. We need as many people on this shift as we can have." However, after saying that. I noticed the blood on the right side of Larry's head. I immediately apologized, said that Larry should go straight to a doctor's office, and offered to drive him there. Larry declined and drove himself to Dr. Maples' office.

I was also on duty October 8, 19YR–3, when Larry returned to work. At the beginning of the shift, I asked Larry if he felt all right. Larry stated that "Doc Maples took real good care of me, and I'm feeling fine now." I asked what treatment Dr. Maples had prescribed. Larry answered that the doctor had recommended some back exercises and added, "And my back felt 200% better after doing those exercises this morning." I told Larry to "take it easy today" and walked back into the main office. As I began to walk away, I saw Larry beginning to lift sacks. About two hours later I noticed that Larry was gone. Another employee, Mutharika, told me that Larry had left to go to the emergency room at the local hospital in Auburn.

I have heard that Larry had to have surgery. I have seen Larry only once since October 8. Several months ago Larry stopped by to pick up his last paycheck. At the time, Larry told me that "my back is so sensitive now that I just can't do this line of work any more." He said that he was suing the doctor and that if he couldn't work any more, he wanted "a big judgment" to set him up "for life." I told Larry that I was sorry to lose him as an employee.

Dated: February 23, 19YR–1

/s/ Curtis Juenger

_____

Curtis Juenger

The parties have entered into the following stipulations of fact:

1. When Larry was placed in traction, he was suffering from a slipped disc in the lower vertebrae.

2. The subsequent surgery would probably have been unnecessary if Larry had not gone back to work immediately and begun lifting again.

In this trial, the parties are litigating only liability. The issue of damages has been severed.

Case File A–2*

PEOPLE OF THE STATE OF EL DORADO v. BARNES

The defendant is Sally Barnes. The crime of shoplifting is defined by El Dorado Penal Code § 1117 in the following manner:

Willfully taking possession of any merchandise with the intention of keeping it without paying for it.

El Dorado law also recognizes the common-law crime of larceny.

* This case file is based on a fact situation created by Professor Richard Gonzales of the University of New Mexico.

The prosecution can call two witnesses: (1) Terrence Swift, and (2) Officer Randy Martinez of the Morena Police Department. The defense likewise can call two witnesses: (1) Sally Barnes, and (2) Shawn Prentice.

Statement of Terry Swift

On December 18 of last year I was employed as a part-time security guard during the holidays at Gardenswartz at 4410 Menaul Boulevard, Morena. The store was crowded that day. On that date at about 3:15 p.m., I saw Sally Barnes in the ski department of the store. She seemed to be nervous-looking around and glancing back over her shoulder from time to time. Ms. Barnes was carrying a Gardenswartz paper bag. I saw her go over to a table on which the store had its ski gloves on display for sale. I saw her looking through the gloves. Her back was to me and I could not see exactly what she was doing; but it looked to me as if she put something into the bag.

Barnes then left the ski department and headed toward the front of the store. She did not stop at the checkout counter, but went directly out the door toward the parking lot. I followed her outside, stopped her, and asked her to come back into the store. She did so.

Once inside, I asked her what was in the bag. Barnes immediately handed the bag to me. She seemed to do so without any hesitation, but then she began to cry. I looked into the bag and saw a pair of ski gloves. The gloves were connected together with a plastic tab, and a Gardenswartz price tag was attached. I asked her if she had a sales slip for the gloves; Ms. Barnes just shook her head. There was guilt written on her face. I asked her to accompany me to the manager's office. She did. I called the city police. Officer Martinez arrived about ten minutes later.

I placed the gloves in a desk drawer in the manager's office where they have remained to date. I can recognize the gloves as the ones that Barnes took from the store.

I have given the same version of the facts to the defense attorney. I have also advised both the defense lawyer and the prosecutor that I am presently employed full-time by Gardenswartz as a salesperson supervisor; it was a promotion. I think the management thought I'd done a particularly good job stopping shoplifting. Shoplifting was down 27%, and we had not had any false arrest suits.

Last year, while I was still working as a security guard, I attended a short course at the F.B.I. Academy in Quantico, Virginia. The subject of the course was modus operandi analysis. I received an F.B.I. certificate that I completed the course. I am prepared to testify that the conduct I observed Barnes engaged in is "highly consistent" with a common shoplifting m.o. The way she positioned herself to block my view is especially characteristic.

Dated: January 2, 19YR

/s/   Terrence L. Swift

————————————————

Terrence L. Swift

Statement of Officer Randy Martinez

I have lived here all my life. I have been a police officer with the Morena Police Department for the past six years. I filed a police report on December 18 of last year in connection with this incident. The report was signed by me. I have given both prosecution and defense copies of the report.

Dated: January 3, 19YR

/s/   Randall Martinez

Randall Martinez

MORENA POLICE DEPARTMENT
SUPPLEMENTARY INVESTIGATION REPORT   YR-1-1266

EDPC 1117

4 LAST NAME, FIRST, MIDDLE (FIRM NAME IF CRIME AGAINST BUSINESS)
Gardenswartz

6 BUSINESS PHONE 753-7399

7 ADDRESS WHERE INCIDENT OCCURRED
324 Rodeo Drive, Morena

8 DATE INCIDENT REPORTED
12/18/YR-1

9 NARRATIVE SECTION

On December 18 I was dispatched by radio to Gardenswartz, 4410

Menaul Blvd. at appx. 3:25 p.m. suspected shoplifting. Arrived

appx. 3:35. I was directed by an employee to the mgr's office at

the rear of the store. At mgr's office encountered subject

Sally Barnes who was sitting in a chair. She was crying. Terry

Swift ID'd self as security guard, advised me that Barnes had

taken a pair of ski gloves out of the store without paying for

them; that gloves were worth $14.95. Swift gave me a pair of ski

gloves with price tag attached; I advised Swift to keep them in a

safe place and bring them with him if the matter went to court. I

advised Barnes that she was under arrest for petty theft

(shoplifting under $100) and read her her rights. I then asked

her if she had taken the gloves without paying for them. Her

response was, "Please don't arrest me. If you'll just let me go,

I'll pay for the gloves." I advised subject Barnes that I could

not do that. She then advised me that she didn't want to talk

about it any more, and refused to say anything further about the

matter. Subject then transported to booking.

REPORTING OFFICER
Randall Martinez   942 OUT 12/19/YR-1   APPROVED BY Marcia Christiansen

1800   231 12/19/YR-1   1830

SUPPLEMENTARY INVESTIGATION REPORT   PAGE 2 of 3

Statement of Sally Barnes

I am thirty years old and have been married for eight years to Norman Barnes, a public school teacher. We have two children, a boy aged six and a girl aged three. I have been a part-time nursing student at the El Dorado State University School of Nursing for the past three years. One week before I was arrested, I had bought the gloves at Gardenswartz for my nephew and had paid cash for them; I remember that they cost $14.95. Later, I decided to take them back and exchange them for a pair of ski mittens if I could find some I liked. I put them back in the bag; I thought that the receipt was still in the bag.

I returned to the store on December 18 and went to the ski department where I went through the gloves and mittens on sale. I did not see any mittens I liked, so I decided to keep the gloves. As I was leaving the store, I was stopped by Swift, the security guard. When Swift asked me what was in the bag, I voluntarily handed it to Swift so that Swift could see by the receipt that I had already paid for the gloves. Swift asked me if I had a receipt, and I said it was in the bag. Swift looked into the bag and said he couldn't find one. Swift let me look through the bag, but to my surprise I couldn't find the receipt either. I don't know whether I lost the receipt or whether Swift took it.

My attorney has reviewed Officer Martinez' report and Swift's story with me. I deny that I started to cry until Swift asked me to come to the manager's office. When Officer Martinez arrived, I tried to explain that I had bought the gloves a week earlier, but that I must have lost the receipt. Officer Martinez replied, "That's what they all say." I did tell Officer Martinez that I would pay for the gloves if he let me go, but I did so because I was scared and embarrassed—not because I had stolen the gloves. Unfortunately, I have been unable to locate the receipt. I keep receipts and stuff like that in a drawer in an organizer at home, but the kids sometimes get into the drawer.

Both the defense lawyer and the prosecutor also know that on June 13, 19YR–4, I pleaded *nolo contendere* in Municipal Court to another shoplifting in which I was charged with stealing a purse from Goldwater's. I was placed on probation on condition that I attend Petty Larceny School, which I successfully completed. I wasn't actually guilty of the charge, but I pleaded *nolo* because the D.A. had assured me at the time that he would recommend probation and that that would be the end of the matter.

In August, 19YR–3, I was also charged with shoplifting for stealing a blouse from Sanger–Harris, but the charge was dismissed when the store's security guard failed to appear for the trial.

Dated: January 1, 19YR

/s/ Sally Barnes
_____

Sally Barnes

Statement of Shawn Prentice

I am an Assistant Professor of Nursing at El Dorado State University. I am acquainted with Sally Barnes. She has been a student in two of my classes over the last three years. She also worked for me as a work/study student. Sally has a reputation for being a moral, honest and truthful person among the faculty and students at the school. (There are 15 faculty members and 200 students.) I am also of the firm opinion that she is an honest person. I sometimes give her the money to pay all the other work/study students, and I've never had one complaint about her handling of that money. I am aware that Barnes was placed on probation for some crime in 19YR–4.

While I was an undergraduate at The John Hopkins University, I was a Psychology major. During nursing training, I took several courses in psychiatric problems. After graduation, I worked for 15 years at the El Dorado Medical Correctional Facility; I was the head nurse for eight years. The facility housed prisoners with psychiatric problems. I assisted researchers studying "the criminal personality." Some of that research was published under the auspices of the National Institute of Justice. One of the articles even acknowledged my "contributions and insights." I am prepared to testify that Barnes exhibits none of the classic symptoms or signs of possessing such a personality. If she is found innocent, I'd accept her back to work for me in an instant.

Dated: January 4, 19YR

/s/   Shawn Prentice

————————————————————————

Shawn Prentice

Case File A–3

CROW v. PATTERSON

Statement of Barbara H. Crow

My name is Barbara H. Crow. I live at 7166 Waterman in Morena and teach in the City elementary school system. I am divorced. I don't know where my former husband is and I don't care. We had two children, both boys—Jack, Jr. and Jimmy. Jack, Jr. is 11 now. Jimmy just had his eighth birthday before he was killed in September 19YR–4. I remember the day well. It was really hot, and I had been drinking some ice tea with some neighbors. The kids had been playing outside around the house. Jack, Jr. was old enough and capable enough to cross the street with care, but Jimmy always wanted to go with him too. He was supposed to cross the street only at the corner and then only when holding his brother's hand.

We had dinner a little earlier than usual because of the heat; I cooked hamburgers out on the barbecue. That must have been about 5:00 p.m. After dinner the kids asked if they could have some money to get some ice cream bars. On weekends an ice cream vending truck usually drives around the neighborhood; and even when you can't find the truck, you can walk down to the B & R near Big Bend. I thought we would all have a treat, so I took the children across Kingsbury to wait for the truck on the northeast corner of Kingsbury and Williams. I thought we'd wait for five or so minutes; and if the truck didn't show, we'd walk down to the B & R.

We saw the truck a little ways down Williams. Jack, Jr. ran across Kingsbury to chase after it while I waited with Jimmy and talked with Mrs. Jameson, a friend of mine who lives in the 7100 block of Kingsbury. While I was talking Jimmy must have wandered off across Kingsbury because when I heard the ice cream truck I turned and found Jimmy gone. The truck had come up Williams toward me, pulled over to the sidewalk on the east side of the street, and there was Jimmy standing in the street near the back of the truck. I could barely make him out, however, because of the glare from the sun. It must have been 5:45 p.m. by now.

I started to run back across Kingsbury to get him when this blue convertible with a young man driving roared by me, made a sharp left turn onto Williams with his tires screeching, and seemed to accelerate down the street. I turned away from the sun and was looking to see if other traffic was coming up Kingsbury when I again heard some tires screeching, followed by a thump. My heart sank. I never did see the car hit Jimmy, but as I ran down the street I saw him lying in the street in front of the car. Mrs. Jameson had gone to call the police.

The driver of the blue car had gotten out and was standing over my boy. A man who looked like the driver of the ice cream truck was also there. All he said was "the kid looks like a goner, you better forget it lady. They never learn." Then he got back into the truck and drove off. The driver of the car said to me, "I never saw him. Don't worry. It was my fault, but I've got plenty of insurance. Everything will be O.K." Jimmy was alive but unconscious. There was not much I could do but wait for the police and an ambulance. I rode to the hospital with Jimmy. The doctors did all they could, but he died that evening. I don't care about myself, I just want to get something for Jimmy. He was such a bright, happy boy.

I have not heard from or seen the driver since the date of the accident. However, I was contacted by his insurance company. They wanted to know whether I was interested in settling the suit; you could tell from what the claims adjuster said that they realized the driver was at fault. I refused to settle out of court. I want that driver off the road; the public has to know about irresponsible persons like that.

Dated September 4, 19YR–1

/s/ Barbara H. Crow

_____

Barbara H. Crow

Statement of Robert L. Patterson

My name is Robert L. Patterson. I live at 7518 Cromwell, Apt. 6, in Morena. I am a student at El Dorado State U., majoring in Business Administration. My parents live in Chicago.

Late in the afternoon of September 23, 19YR–4, I left the apartment to pick up my girlfriend, Linda, for dinner and a rock concert at the Checkerdome. Linda lives at 7214 Pershing near where she goes to school. I hadn't been doing much that afternoon; just watching a football game on TV and going down to the Shaw Park pool for a dip to cool off. It was real hot.

I was supposed to pick Linda up at 5:30 p.m., but it was already late when I left, so I was in a hurry. However, I had to stop to pick up gas, and I think I did the windows at the same time. My car is a 1969 Mustang convertible—my Dad gave it to me as a graduation present. Since it was hot, I had the top down. I turned right off Big Bend onto Kingsbury and headed up the hill. As I approached Williams, I put on my left turn signal. This was 100 feet or so from the intersection, and I was going along about 25 miles an hour. I had to slow down to wait for another car coming down Kingsbury, and I was watching for other traffic. I glanced left and right before turning, but the traffic on Williams has stop signs so I didn't look long; besides, there isn't much traffic on Williams. I do remember seeing a blue pickup parked on the left side of Williams right near the corner where I was turning, and I could see the side of some kind of van just beyond that.

As I turned left on Williams, I got some sort of glare in my eye—maybe the sun—so I didn't speed right up. Suddenly this kid ran out from the left hand side of the street right in front of my car. He seemed to be looking at something across the street and was holding up one hand. He must have run out from behind what I later learned was an ice cream truck parked on the left (east) side of Williams. I tried to stop, but he was right in front of the car, and before I could even put my foot on the brake, I hit him. The impact knocked him into the air and some 20–30 feet down the street. I hit the brakes as hard as I could, but still almost ran over him as he was lying on the street. All I could think of was, "My God, where did he come from?"

After stopping the car, I jumped out to see what I could do for the kid. He was unconscious and there was blood on his head and chest—he was lying on his back. Some people from the neighborhood came out too. One man said he had already called the police. I think I was in shock, but I remember saying "Where did he come from; where did he come from? I hope he'll be O.K." Some woman came up; I guess she was his mother, and started crying and shouting and swearing at me. I don't remember what I said to her; I may have mentioned insurance, I just don't know. Dad made sure that I kept the car insured.

I must have driven down that street 20 or 30 times, and I never saw an ice cream truck before. There are some kids around, but I've never seen them playing in the street.

It seemed like forever before the police came and then the ambulance. After it left, I gave the policeman my version of the accident and all the information he asked for. My car was still driveable, so I went on to Linda's. I never did get to the concert. The next day I read in the paper that the kid had died at the hospital.

Dated: October 19, 19YR–1

/s/   Robert L. Patterson

_____

Robert L. Patterson

Statement of J.J. Jacobs

My name is J.J. "Jake" Jacobs. I'm 43 years old and self-employed. I've done a bunch of truck driving and odd jobs, mostly in Kansas, Illinois, and Missouri. I'm not married and never have been. I live in Overland, El Dorado.

For the last couple of years I've been driving an ice cream truck for the Yukon Ice Cream Company. It's a regular old Ford pick-up with a box-like refrigerator unit fixed up in the back. There are doors to the unit on all sides except where it's attached to the cab. It's maybe six and a half feet from the street level to the top of the unit. I lease the truck from Yukon and buy the ice cream products. I get to keep whatever I make selling them. During the fall of 19YR–4, my route was the Morena City College area. It's not a great route, but still there are some good days in terms of sales-especially when it gets real hot.

On the day the kid got it, it was real hot and business had been good. Instead of sticking absolutely to my planned route, I weaved in and out of some streets to pick up extra business. That must have been why I was driving on Williams rather than the main drags like Kingsbury and Pershing. It was near the end of the day, bright and sunny. I saw this kid coming down the sidewalk from the corner of Kingsbury and Williams; it looked like he wanted to buy something, so I pulled out of the traffic along the curb and went out to the back of the truck. The kid followed me. He couldn't have been more than 8 or 9 so I said, "Look kid if you haven't got any money, you're wasting my time" and started to get back into the truck. As I was getting back in the cab, I saw this sharp-lookin' blue convertible turn left onto Williams from Kingsbury. He drove right on by me going at least 25 or 30, and as I looked back he ran smack into the kid, sent him flying through the air and almost ran over him again. I got out of the truck, but I could see there was nothing I could do, so I took off to finish my route.

The next day I heard on the TV that the police were looking for an ice cream truck driver who witnessed an accident in the area near Morena City College where a kid was killed. I figured it was me, so I went down and talked to the police. I don't know what the kid was doing in the street, but it didn't look like he was running. Some kids never learn. But still, that guy shouldn't have hit him.

While I was living in Missouri seven years ago, I was convicted of manslaughter. I served three years in the state pen for it. I was lucky; I could have gotten up to 30 years for manslaughter. I got into a fight in a bar, I exchanged some words with the guy, and I ended up stabbing him. I pleaded not guilty and testified, but the jury found me guilty. I've paid my debt to society, and ever since my record's been absolutely clean. However, I concealed the fact of my conviction from Yukon when I hired on with them.

Dated: August 29, 19YR–1

/s/   J.J. Jacobs

_____

J.J. Jacobs

Statement of Officer Carlos Solis

I am a police officer employed by the Morena City Police Department. I have worked in the traffic division for the past two years as a traffic patrolman and accident investigator. I have had a basic, six-week training course in traffic accident investigation and two years of field experience. During the last two years, I have probably investigated nearly 200 traffic accidents. I have testified in court on roughly 25 occasions during this period. On several occasions, I qualified as an expert, and the judge permitted me to give a speed estimate based on my accident investigation.

On the early evening of September 23, 19YR–4, I was on duty in the city college area when I received a report of a vehicle/pedestrian collision on Williams between Kingsbury and Waterman, near Kingsbury. I proceeded to the scene immediately. I probably arrived at the scene about five minutes after the collision. I do not have any notes of my investigation other than the information I recorded on the accident report itself.

I cannot recall the driver's and witnesses' exact statements, but the information I obtained and recorded on the report was based either on my personal observation at the accident scene or the statements the driver and witnesses made to me. As far as I could determine, there were no other witnesses to the accident other than the ice cream truck driver who spoke to me two days later, on September 25, 19YR–4.

I asked the driver of the automobile involved, Mr. Patterson, what the speed of his car was at the moment of impact and noted his answer in the accident report. I vaguely recall that Mr. Patterson was very excited and overwrought; but based on my observations of his overall demeanor at the accident scene, I do not believe that his ability to operate a motor vehicle had been impaired by drugs or alcohol. I did not administer the field sobriety test or any chemical test to determine if he was intoxicated.

I also recall that the injured child's mother was extremely upset. She claimed Mr. Patterson was speeding down the street and had deliberately run over her child. No one else at the scene has seen the collision or the child in the street, although several persons volunteered that there was an ice cream truck nearby when the collision occurred. The driver came forward several days later following news and media publicity about the occurrence.

To my knowledge, Mr. Patterson's vehicle had not been moved from the position it was in after it came to a stop following the collision. At the most there was minor damage to the left front grille of the Mustang, just off the center. The child had sustained massive head and chest injuries and was given little chance of survival by the ambulance personnel who took him to the hospital.

I personally paced off the distances noted on my report and noted them down along with the visual observations. Cars were parked along both sides of Williams partially obscuring the vision of a driver westbound on Kingsbury turning left onto Williams. I also measured the skid marks left by the Patterson vehicle after impacting the child. However, I did not have time to determine the coefficient of friction of the road surface.

Based on my personal observation of the collision scene and the statements I elicited from the driver and witnesses, I am of the opinion that the Crow child ran into the street in front of the Patterson vehicle and thereby caused the collision which the driver was unable to avoid.

Dated: August 29, 19YR–1

/s/   Carlos Solis

Carlos Solis

FOR STATE FILES USE

ROUTED		No.	Type ____ Hwy. ____

UNIFORM ACCIDENT REPORT
METROPOLITAN POLICE DEPARTMENT

COMPLAINT NO. 78-4776

DISTRICT Morena City College

DATE Sep. 23, 19YR-4

No. of PERSONS issued M.U.T.T. ____

CARD	CODE	Hwy. ____ No. ____ Log. ____	INTERSECTION	NON-INTER.
		City ____ Pop. ____	X	
FAT. NO.	INJ. NO.	County ____	LOCATION CODE	
		ACC. Type ____		

1. ACCIDENT CLASSIFICATION   ☒ Property Damage   No. Killed 1   No. Injured 1   No. of Vehicles Involved 1

2. TIME   Date of Accident - Mo./Day/Yr. Sep. 23, 19YR-4   Day of Week Saturday   Hour 1750   ☒ A.M. ☐ P.M.   ☐ Standard Time ☐ Daylight Savings Time

☐ FEDERAL ROUTE   ☐ STATE ROUTE   ☐ COUNTY ROAD   ☐ MUNICIPAL   ☐ PRIVATE PROPERTY

3. LOCATION

In Morena County   Give Name of City, Village or Township   Morena   Log Point

Give Name of Road, Street or Route No.	Speed Limit		Intersecting Street or Highway Number	Speed Limit
On Williams	25	At Kingsbury		25

If not at intersection   175   ☐ N ☐ S ☐ E ☐ W   FEET OR MILES   of Kingsbury   Nearest Intersecting Street or Highway, Mile Post or Landmark

4. ACCIDENT INVOLVED

- A. ☒ Pedestrian
- E. ☐ Animal-Drawn Vehicle
- L. ☐ Overturned in Roadway
- B. ☐ Other Motor Vehicle
- F. ☐ Bicycle
- J. ☐ Ran Off Roadway
- G. ☐ Fixed Object
- C. ☐ R.R. Train
- H. ☐ Animal (Ridden, Unattended)
- K. ☐ Other Non-Collision (Fall From Veh., etc.)
- D. ☐ Street Car

5. VEHICLE NO. 1

Driver Robert L. Patterson   Phone No. 223-4455   Age 20

DRIVER INFORMATION

Date of Birth 8/28/YR-21   Mo. Day Yr.   Sex ☒ Male ☐ Female   Race Cau

Address 7518 Cromwell #6   City Morena   State El Dorado   Phone No.

Owner same as above

State of License ☐ Mo. State ☐ Other ☐ Unlicensed ☐ Learners ☐ Operators ☐ Chauffeurs

Driver's License Number 1138-5216-7627-7605

Address   City   State

Veh. Year 1969	Model Must	Make Ford	Color blue	Style (4dr, truck, etc.) convertible

Driver Education ☒ Yes ☐ No ☐ Unknown   Other Driver Tng. ☒ Yes ☐ No ☐ Unknown

Veh. Inspection No. G2179402   License Plate No. MCT 988   State El Dorado   Year YR-4   HEADED ☐ N ☒ S ☐ E ☐ W on Williams   (Street Name, Highway No., Alley, etc.)

Vehicle Damaged (Code)   Vehicle Towed Away? ☐ Yes ☒ No   By Whom?   Tow Slip #   Where To?   Ref. #

6. VEHICLE NO. 2

Driver   Phone No.   Age

DRIVER INFORMATION

Date of Birth __/__/__   Mo. Day Yr.   Sex ☐ Male ☐ Female   Race

Address   City   State

Owner   Phone No.

State of License ☐ Mo. State ☐ Other ☐ Unlicensed ☐ Learners ☐ Operators ☐ Chauffeurs

Driver's License Number

Address   City   State

Veh. Year	Model	Make	Color	Style (4dr, truck, etc.)

Driver Education ☐ Yes ☐ No ☐ Unknown   Other Driver Tng. ☐ Yes ☐ No ☐ Unknown

Veh. Inspection   License Plate No.   State   Year   HEADED ☐ N ☐ S ☐ E ☐ W on   (Street Name, Highway No., Alley, etc.)

Vehicle Damaged (Code)   Vehicle Towed Away? ☐ Yes ☐ No   By Whom?   Tow Slip #   Where To?   Ref. #

7. DAMAGE TO PROPERTY OTHER THAN VEHICLES   Name Object, Show Ownership, and State Nature and Amount of Damage

8. KILLED OR INJURED WITNESS OR PASSENGER INJURED D.

	Name	Address	Witness	Age	Sex	Car No.	Seat Loc.	Inj.	Ejection	Seat Belt	Phone
	James B. Crow	7166 Waterman		8	M						291-6481
	Barbara H. Crow	same as above		32	F						same
	ice cream truck driver	unknown									

9. CODES

SEAT LOCATION

XX - Not Known

FR	RR
FC	RC
FL	RL

SV - Occupant-Special Vehicle Bus, Truck, Motorcycle, Station Wagon
P - Pedestrian
B - Bicyclist

INJURY
- A. Fatal
- B. Disabling
- C. Evident (Not Disabling)
- D. Probable - Not Apparent
- E. None Apparent
- F. Unknown

SEAT BELT
- A. None
- B. Not Used
- C. Used
- D. Harness
- E. Use Unknown
- F. Belt-Failure

EJECTION
- A. No
- B. Partially
- C. Totally
- D. Unknown

Page ____ of ____ Pages

VEHICLE DAMAGE

R - Undercarriage   S - Windshield

MPD FORM 3 (R-3)

COLLISION SUMMARY

LOCATION: WILLIAMS BET. KINGSBURY AND WATERMAN DATE: SEPT. 23 YR-4 TIME: 1745

OFFICER'S CONCLUSIONS: (SUMMARIZE THE COLL. INV. WITH A WORD PICTURE. INCLUDE ALL EVIDENCE NECESSARY TO SUPPORT CHARGE).

WILLIAMS IS APPROX. 35 FT IN WIDTH WITH CARS, VANS AND PICKUPS PARKED ON BOTH SIDES OF THE ROADWAY (N+S THIS IS A RESIDENTIAL AREA WITH BOTH SMALL APARTMENT BUILDINGS AND SINGLE FAMILY TYPE HOMES. USUALLY THERE ARE SOME SMALL CHILDREN IN THE AREA, BUT NOT USUALLY PLAYING IN THE STREET. THE AREA IS HILLY. AT THE NORTH END OF BLOCK WILLIAMS INTERSECTS KINGSBURY WHICH RISES STEADILY FROM BIG·BEND TO WILLIAMS. KINGSBURY IS MODERATELY TRAVELED. Williams TRAFFIC HAS STOP SIGNS. WILLIAMS DEAD ENDS N OF KINGSBURY

     V-1 WAS ON KINGSBURY AND TURNED LEFT (SB) ONTO WILLIAMS V-1 WAS TRAVELING 10-15 MPH. AN ICE CREAM TRUCK WAS STOPPED ON WILLIAMS FACING NB   VICTIM (CRO- RAN TO REAR OF TRUCK AND THEN INTO ROADWAY   V-1 STRUCK THE PED. WITH LEFT-CENTER FRONT, OF VEHICLE AS CROW RAN IN FRONT OF HIM. CROW WAS KNOCKED INTO THE AIR AND DIRECTLY DOWN WILLIAMS SOME 20 FT. V-1 LEFT NO SKID MARKS PRIOR TO IMPACT. LEFT SKID MARKS APPROX. 21 FT. DOWN WILLIAMS V-1 CAME TO STOP APPROX. OVER CROW. V-1 SUSTAINED MINIMAL DAMAGE. CROW SUSTAINED SERIOUS INJURIES – HEAD AND BODY – AND WAS TAKEN TO BARNES HOSPITAL UNCONSCIOUS CROW DIED IN HOSPITAL APPROX. 1955 OF HEAD AND INTERNAL INJURIES

DATE AND TIME OF REPORT SEPT. 23 19YR-4 2030 OFFICER(S) C. SOUS #1139

[USE ANOTHER FORM 156 IF ADDITIONAL SPACE NEEDED FOR WITNESSES, CONCLUSIONS, ETC.]

PD-156 (REV. 7-79)

Traffic collision report form (partially completed by hand):

EXTENT OF INJURY / INJURED WAS

No. Injd	Witness Only	Age	Sex	Fatal Injury	Severe Wound/Bleeding	Other Visible Injuries	Complaint of Pain	Driver	Pass.	Ped.	Bicyclist	Other
1	☐	8	M	☒	☐	☐	☐	☐	☐	☒	☐	☐

Name: Crow, James Bruner   291-6481
Address: 7166 Waterman, Morena   Barnes Hosp?   AMR 179-H

| ☒ | 30 | F | ☐ | ☐ | ☐ | ☐ | ☐ | ☐ | ☐ | ☐ | ☐ |

Name: Crow, Barbara Harris   291-6481
Address: 7166 Waterman, Morena,

| ☒ | | | ☐ | ☐ | ☐ | ☐ | ☐ | ☐ | ☐ | ☐ | ☐ |

Name: Ice Cream Truck Driver – UKN.
Address: UNK.

| ☐ | | | ☐ | ☐ | ☐ | ☐ | ☐ | ☐ | ☐ | ☐ | ☐ |

SSP:

PRIMARY CAUSE
- ☒ Violated ped. right of way (unrelated pt. of way)

VEHICLE DEFECTS
- NONE

TYPE
- ☒ Collision of motor veh. with ped.

WEATHER
- ☒ Clear

ROAD CONDITION
- ☒ Dry

LIGHT CONDITION
- ☒ Daylight

OTHER ASSOCIATED FACTORS
- ☒ None apparent

VEHICLE ACTION
- ☒ Going straight ahead

SOBRIETY-DRUG
- ☒ Had not been drinking

PHYSICAL DEFECT
- ☒ Apparently normal

PED'S CONDITION
- ☒ Had not been drinking
- ☒ Apparently normal

PED'S ACTION
- ☒ Crossing into traffic / ice cream vendor

DRIVER'S VISION OF PEDESTRIAN LIMITED BY:
- ☒ Sun glare

WHERE WAS PED STRUCK
- ☒ In roadway not at intersection

WHAT WAS PED DOING?
- ☒ Coming to or from ice cream vendor

Reporting Officer	I.D. Number	Division	Date–Time	Approved
Carlos Solis	1139	T2	Sept. 23, 2030	R Puckett

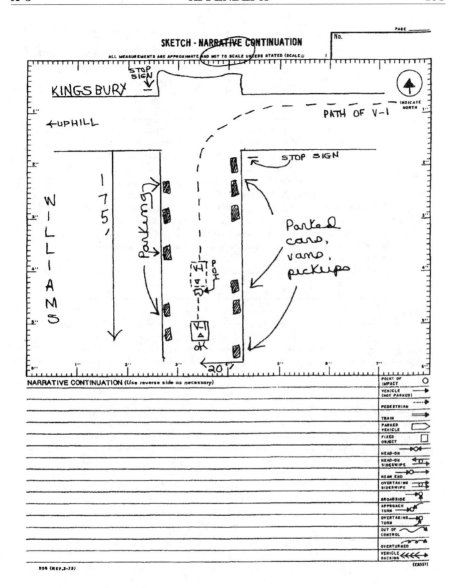

CHECK ONE	SUPPLEMENTAL	DATE OF ORIGINAL INCIDENT MO. 09 DAY 23 YR. 19YR–4	TIME (2400) 2030	PAGE ____ ORIGINAL NO. C11 NUMBER	OFFICER I.D.
	SUPPLEMENTS FORM 555 TRAFFIC COLLISION REPORT OTHER:	LOCATION/SUBJECT ICP 175 feet s of SCL Kingsbury, 20 feet w of ECL Williams			CITATION NO. BEAT
	FORM 555 NARRATIVE CONTINUATION ONLY	CITY	COUNTY	REPORTING DISTRICT	

    (ICP)
    POI determined by driver's statements and my investigation. POI was also confirmed
by initiation of skid marks which extended in straight SB direction down WILLIAMS to
position of V-1 upon my arrival ped. Crow. found lying in street under front bumper
of V-1.

    POI 175 FT S OF SCL KINGSBURY

       20 FT W OF ECL WMS. (Roughly middle of st.)

WILLIAMS rises slightly SB from KINGSBURY then begins moderate downgrade to WATERMAN

    The weather was hot and clear.

    Lighting was direct lighting from late afternoon (before dusk) sun.

    The roadway was of asphaltic concrete over concrete and concrete farther
WB. Condition - good to fair.

    All skids - RF, RR, LR, and LR - are 21.'

PREPARED BY NAME/RANK C. Solis	I.D. NUMBER	PREPARED MO. DAY YR. 09 23 19YR–4	REVIEWED - APPROVED BY NAME/RANK	I.D. NUMBER	DATE MO. DAY YR.

[E8550]

STOPPING DISTANCE CHART

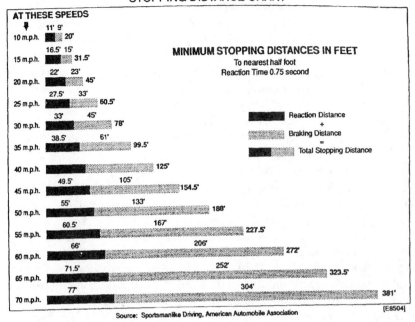

Source: Sportsmanlike Driving, American Automobile Association

[E8504]

Case File A–4*
LADD v. VALDEZ

This is a civil suit brought in Municipal Court by Marty Ladd against his former landlord Barbara Valdez to recover a security deposit.

Section 47–8–18 of the El Dorado Owner–Resident Relations Act states that a landlord may require a tenant to pay a deposit "to be applied by the owner to recover damages, if any, caused to the premises by the resident during his term of residency." The statute further provides that upon termination of the tenancy, the landlord may apply the deposit toward any damages to the premises caused by the tenant or toward the cost of restoring the premises to a clean condition. The statute also requires the landlord to provide the tenant with a written itemization of any deductions and to return the balance, if any, to the tenant within thirty days after the termination of the tenancy. If the landlord fails to comply with these provisions, the tenant may bring suit to recover the deposit.

Statement of Marty Ladd

On February 1 two years ago I entered a rental agreement (a copy of which is attached to these materials) with Barbara Valdez for the one-year lease of a furnished, two bedroom apartment located at 1821 Girard S.E. in Morena. At the time I was beginning graduate studies in the

---

* This case file is based on a fact situation created by Professor Richard Gonzalez of the University of New Mexico.

Theater Arts Department at El Dorado State University. According to the terms of the lease, rent was to be $400 per month with the first and last month's rent payable in advance and a $600 cleaning/damage deposit. I wrote a check to Valdez on February 1 and moved in on that date.

About two months after occupying the apartment, sometime in April, I found a roommate, an old childhood friend named Charles Thomas. I asked Valdez whether she had any objections to Thomas' moving in. Valdez had no objection if I would continue to be solely responsible for the lease. I said that was fine, and Thomas moved in about the middle of April.

Everything continued smoothly until May of last year when my school year ended. I decided to vacate the apartment and take a summer job at Yellowstone National Park. On May 1 I gave written notice to Valdez of my intent to terminate the tenancy, effective June 1. (A copy of the notice is attached.) I was rushing to get up to Yellowstone. During the last weekend of May, Thomas and I began cleaning the apartment in preparation for leaving. While we were cleaning the apartment we noticed a burn mark on the underside of one of the cushions on the couch in the living room. The burn mark appeared to be in the shape of an iron, and I assumed that a previous tenant had put a hot iron on the couch. In any case, neither I nor Thomas thought anything further about it.

On May 31 Thomas and I vacated the apartment. I telephoned Valdez to let her know we were leaving. I said something like, "It (meaning the apartment) may not be perfect, but I think it's in fairly good shape." I deny that she said anything more about the condition of the apartment. Valdez told me that she would inspect the apartment within the next few days and that the cleaning/damage deposit would be mailed to me within a week or so if everything was satisfactory. I gave Valdez my address at Yellowstone. I said that when I returned to school in the fall, I might contact Valdez again to rent the same or another apartment. We exchanged pleasantries and hung up.

I moved to Yellowstone on June 1. On June 15 I received a letter from Valdez enclosing a check for $185.00. (A copy of the letter is attached.) The letter explained that $415.00 was being deducted from my deposit because the apartment had not been properly cleaned and that a professional cleaning service had been employed to do the job (including some touch-up painting in the kitchen) at a cost of $350.00. In addition, Valdez had discovered the burn mark on the couch and had to have the cushion recovered at a cost of $65.00.

Upon returning to Morena toward the end of August last year, I consulted an attorney about getting back the balance of the deposit. Thomas and I had left the apartment spotless and had nothing to do with burning the cushion. The attorney advised me that in his opinion, the amount of money at stake does not justify the time needed to litigate this case, but I am so incensed at Valdez that I insist on taking the case to trial. My family isn't rich, but I can afford to take this case to trial. I understand that the matter is scheduled for a trial in Municipal Court.

Dated: December 1, 19YR–1

/s/ Marty Ladd
_____
Marty Ladd

Statement of Charles Thomas

I was Ladd's roommate from mid-April (I cannot recall the exact date) two years ago until the end of May this year. I did not sign the lease, but I contributed $200.00 per month toward the rent. I am a lifelong friend of Ladd's; we had gone to school together since fourth grade and considered ourselves "best friends." During the time we roomed together, I worked evenings at Dillard's as a salesperson while taking a few computer courses at Morena Business School.

During the final weekend in May last year, Ladd and I cleaned the apartment before vacating. Ladd cleaned the kitchen and bathroom while I vacuumed and dusted the living room and bedroom. While vacuuming the living room furniture, I turned over the seat cushion on the couch and discovered the burn mark. I called it to Ladd's attention and Ladd said something like, "That must have been there when we moved in." We discussed whether to bring it to Valdez's attention, but we decided against it because Valdez might think we had burned the couch. I do own an old steam iron which both Ladd and I used from time to time. We do not, however, have an ironing board. We usually did our ironing on one of the two twin beds in the bedroom. Ladd and I spent an hour on Saturday and two hours on Sunday cleaning the apartment. I believe that it was clean when we left.

I admit, however, that Ladd and I were not the best of housekeepers during the time we lived in the apartment. We never really worked out our mutual responsibilities for cleaning the apartment. In fact, other than the time we cleaned it when we moved out, the bathroom was cleaned only twice during our tenancy—both times by my mother who visited from Cleveland on two occasions. Nevertheless, we had the apartment in good shape when we vacated.

Five years ago I was arrested for shoplifting. The charge involved an incident at a Circle K store near the El Dorado State campus. The clerk accused me of taking a can of Coca Cola from the store without paying for it. I had stopped at the gas station nearby, and I walked over to the Circle K. I tried to swipe the Coke when the clerk wasn't looking. I don't know what came over me; I've never done anything like that before. The clerk stopped me and called the cops. I was so frightened that I lied to the cops and denied that I took the Coke. I told the same story to my mother. Fortunately, the charge was dismissed when the Circle K clerk never showed up for the hearing. I don't know what I would have said at the trial if the clerk had shown up. When I look back now, I feel real bad about the incident. I talked to an attorney a few months ago, and I know that the statute of limitations has run on the theft. I think it's best to be honest about the whole thing now.

Dated: May 2, 19YR–1

/s/   Charles Thomas

Charles Thomas

Statement of Barbara Valdez

I own eight apartments located at 1821 Girard S.E. Most of my tenants are E.D.S.U. students. All the apartments are furnished. The rent for each of the apartments is $400.00 per month, and I require all tenants to sign a written lease. The lease provides for prepayment of first and last months' rent plus a $600 security/damage deposit, refundable when the tenant vacates leaving the apartment in clean condition with no material damage.

Marty Ladd is a former tenant. Charles Thomas was a roommate, although not on the lease. Ladd was punctual in paying rent, and vacated at the end of May this year. I remember talking to Ladd by telephone shortly before he left and that Ladd asked about the deposit refund. I told Ladd that I would not be able to inspect the apartment until sometime the following week, but that I would forward any refund to Ladd by mail. Ladd told me "I've been pretty busy the last few days getting ready to leave for Yellowstone, and we haven't been able to clean the apartment the way we'd like." Ladd also said that if any further work needed to be done, I should take it out of the deposit and mail him the balance.

During the week following Ladd's and Thomas's leaving the apartment, I inspected the apartment. The place was positively filthy. Garbage was still in the garbage can. Cooking utensils, which had been furnished with the apartment, were stacked unwashed in the sink. Old, apparently discarded clothes were strewn about the bedroom and living room. A hungry cat was found cowering under the bed (despite a provision in the lease prohibiting pets). The bathroom was appalling. A tube of toothpaste had apparently fallen to the floor and been stepped on, staining some of the tiles under the sink. In the living room, the furniture had been totally rearranged; and I found that one of the cushions on the couch had been burned by an iron. I'm sure, however, that the burn occurred while Ladd and Thomas were living there. I can't remember whether I inspected it after the previous tenant, but I can say that it is my usual practice to turn all furniture cushions between tenants so that the furniture will last longer. I probably did so before Ladd moved in. If so, I would have noticed the burn.

The kitchen was in particularly bad shape. Grease was spattered on the walls around the stove. It appeared that a dartboard had been put up near the dinette table because hundreds of tiny holes appeared in a pattern around a circular space on the wall. The maple counter was left scarred by knife marks. In short, the place was a mess.

On June 5, I immediately called Gene Singer, owner of Imperial Building Maintenance, a local janitorial service, to have the apartment restored. Singer went to the apartment the next day with another worker, Bob Sullivan. Together they spent three hours cleaning and fixing the apartment. Sullivan vacuumed the apartment, cleaned the bathroom and kitchen, and washed the walls in the kitchen while Singer sanded the scars out of the kitchen counter and applied an oil stain to it. Singer also spackled the damaged dinnette and touched up the paint in the dinnette, kitchen, and a few other places. Singer gave me a bill for $350.00 (copy attached) which I paid by check. G. Singer also took the burned sofa cushion back to his shop and recovered it. He returned the cushion to me with a bill for $65.00 (copy attached), which Valdez also paid by check.

After the repairs had been made, I re-rented the apartment. I wrote to Ladd describing the damage, deducted $415.00 from the deposit, and enclosed a check for the balance, $185.00.

I have used the Imperial Building Maintenance many times in the past. In fact, it is my practice to have them clean every apartment when a tenant vacates, regardless of its condition. Normally, however, the cleaning charge runs between $25.00 and $50.00 which is always deducted from the previous tenant's deposit. Some (I can't remember how many or who—perhaps three or four) former tenants have complained about the deductions, but none has ever brought suit. I like to send business to Imperial because Singer is a good friend and tennis partner. Besides, he works as cheaply as any of the other companies I've dealt with.

Dated: December 3, 19YR–1

/s/   Barbara Valdez

Barbara Valdez

Statement of Gene Singer

I own Imperial Building Maintenance in Morena, a business I have had for the past eight years. In one way or another I've been in the maintenance business in Morena for 23 years. I furnish janitorial and other miscellaneous maintenance services for a variety of businesses, including several apartment complexes. In addition to routine cleaning, Imperial is prepared to do minor repairs, including painting, plumbing, electrical work and general fix up. I also have experience doing upholstery work and, on occasion, am called upon to repair furniture.

On June 5 of this year, I received a telephone call from Valdez requesting some clean-up work on one of Valdez's apartments on Girard. My employee, Bob Sullivan, and I went out to the apartment the next day and worked for three hours cleaning and fixing up. I gave Valdez a bill for $350.00 which I feel is a reasonable price for the services and Valdez paid by check on the spot. My recollection of the work done is substantially the same as Valdez' version.

Valdez also gave me a sofa cushion which has a burn mark on it, asking me to re-cover it. I took the cushion to my shop and made a new cover for it in a matching fabric. I returned it to Valdez with a bill for $65.00, which is a reasonable price for the service. Valdez paid the bill by check.

When I found out that there was going to be a suit, I wanted to make sure that we'd be able to prove the reasonableness of the $415.00 I had charged Barbara. For that reason, I made the rounds by phone of some of my competitors to ensure that I could truthfully testify that my charges were in line with the prevailing rates. I phoned seven other companies in my line of work, explained the situation, described the services I'd rendered to Ms. Valdez, and got their oral quotations. These were the quotations I received:

Excelsior Cleaning	$450.00.
Martin's Maintenance	$275.00.
Swenson Services	$400.00.
Giannelli Cleaning	$350.00.
Ace Maintenance	$425.00.
Mom's Maintenance	$370.00.
Ferguson's Maintenance	$300.00.

Before I made the calls, I thought that my charges would be at the high end. I like to think that we do better quality work than our competitors, and I consequently may charge a wee bit more. Now I realize that my charges are right in line with the prevailing practice. The people I called are all old friends, and I'm sure that they gave me honest estimates when I called them. The other basis for my opinion is some other, major cleaning projects that I've handled. When I found out we were going to court, I sat down and thought back to comparable jobs I've done in the past-like cleaning up one of the condos at The Willows complex a few months ago. To the best of my recollection, the job entailed roughly the same amount of work; and I think I billed that job out a little over $300.00. I have to admit that I'm relying on my memory; I'm not the best recordkeeper, and I didn't try to dive into my files to find any paperwork on that job. But I think that that job and another one at the Aurora Apartments required roughly the same amount of work and materials. I charged over $300.00 on all three jobs.

I regularly do work for Valdez and regard Valdez as one of my best customers, as well as a close friend and tennis partner. We occasionally go out to dinner.

Seven years ago I pleaded guilty to forging a check, a felony. I was sentenced to 18 months imprisonment; the prison sentence was suspended and I was placed on probation for two years. I completed the probation without incident. My business license was suspended during the probation, but the license has been reinstated now.

Dated: December 4, 19YR–1

/s/ Eugene Singer

_____

Eugene Singer

LEASE

I. Demise of Premises

A. Lessor and Lessee hereby enter the within lease agreement according to the terms and conditions set forth.

B. Lessor, in consideration of the agreements of the lessee herein contained, shall lease to lessee furnished *Apartment G,* beginning *February 1,* 19YR–2 and continuing thereafter from month to month until such time as may be mutually agreed upon in writing by the parties.

II. Terms and Conditions of Lease

A. Rent. Rent shall be $400.00 per month payable on the first of each month in advance. Said rent shall include the following utilities: electricity, gas, water and refuse disposal.

B. Maintenance of Premises. Lessee shall keep the premises and all of the contents and furnishings in good repair, reasonable wear and tear excepted. Upon termination of the lease, lessee shall leave the premises in a clean condition.

C. Deposits. Lessee shall, prior to occupancy, deposit with lessor the sum of $600.00 as a rent security deposit and the sum of $600.00 as a damage deposit. The rent security deposit shall be applied to the last months' rent upon termination of the lease. The damage deposit shall be applied to necessary cleaning and/or repair of the premises upon termination of the lease and any balance, if any, remaining thereafter shall be returned to lessee with a written account of all expenditures.

III. Termination of Lease

A. Either party hereto may terminate this lease upon giving 30 days notice in writing to the other.

B. In the event either party is in violation of the lease, the other party may give notice of the violation. If within three days of such notice, the violation has not been corrected, the party giving notice may terminate the lease forthwith.

IN WITNESS WHEREOF, lessor and lessee have executed this lease on the 1st day of Feb., 19YR–2.

Lessor: /s/ Barbara Valdez

_____

Barbara Valdez

Lessee: /s/   Marty Ladd

Marty Ladd

NOTICE

TO: B. Valdez

FROM: M. Ladd

RE: Termination of lease.

     I hereby give notice of my intention to vacate my apartment on May 31. I have enjoyed living here, and I will clean it up before I leave.

/s/   Marty Ladd

Marty Ladd

B.   Valdez
1821 Girard S.E.
Morena, El Dorado 12475
June 12

M.   Ladd
Yellowstone Lodge
Yellowstone National Park, Wyoming

Dear M. Ladd:

     Enclosed please find a partial refund of your cleaning/damage deposit in the amount of $185.00. I have had to do certain cleaning and make certain repairs to your apartment before I could rent it. The following amounts were deducted from your $600.00 deposit:

Imperial Building Maintenance
       (Cleaning apartment, repairing kitchen counter,
         spot painting and repairs to walls) $350.00

Imperial Building Maintenance
       (Repairs to burned sofa cushion) . . . . $ 65.00

Total $415.00

Thank you,

/s/   Barbara Valdez

Barbara Valdez

IMPERIAL BUILDING MAINTENANCE

INVOICE

Date June 6, 19YR–1

Name _Barb_

Address _1821 Girard_

Service	Amt.
Clean Apt G. Wash walls, Vacuum & clean carpets, sand kitchen counter, spot paint various places — 2 workers, 6 hours	350.00

Tax _Incl_

Total _350.00_

[E8505]

Paid by check
Singer
6/5/YR–1

IMPERIAL BUILDING MAINTENANCE

INVOICE

Date June 10, 19YR–1

Name _Barb V._

Address _1821 Girard_

Service	Amt.
Repair sofa cushion	
2 yards material	25.00
Labor 2 hrs	40.00

Tax _Incl_

Total _65.00_

[E8506]

Paid by check
Singer
6/10/YR–1

Case file A–5

PEOPLE OF THE STATE OF EL DORADO v. McIVER

Instructions

1. The law governing eyewitness testimony in this jurisdiction is stated in *People v. McDonald,* 37 Cal.3d 351, 690 P.2d 709, 208 Cal.Rptr. 236 (1984).

2. The defense will make no motions to suppress any evidence on the grounds of the fourth, fifth, or sixth amendments.

3. The attached Form 1332 is defendant's criminal history record. The defense may not object to the introduction of this record on authenticity, best evidence, or hearsay grounds.

4. It is stipulated that in each of the three robberies listed on the Form 1332, the robber used a small pistol; the establishment robbed was a liquor store; the robber was a male Caucasian; the robbery occurred between 8:00 and 9:00 p.m.; the robber used a brown Chevrolet getaway car; at the trial resulting in the acquittal, the victim of the robbery testified that the defendant "definitely was" the robber; lineups were held after the other two robberies; the defendant was in both lineups; and at both lineups, the victims stated that defendant's appearance was "similar" to that of the robber.

5. At trial, the prosecution may use facsimiles of the money and jacket seized from the defendant. It will be stipulated that they are the objects seized from the defendant's room. There is no stipulation that the bills are money taken in the robbery or that the robber wore the jacket found in the defendant's possession.

Statement of Marilyn F. Sandoval

My name is Marilyn Filomina Sandoval. I have lived in Morena all my life. I am an art student at El Dorado State. I work part-time as a clerk at Mory's Liquors in Morena.

I was on duty at the store the evening of February 7, 19YR–2. It was about 8:30 p.m. when I noticed a light-colored compact car come into the parking lot. Immediately thereafter a guy walked in as I was standing behind the cash register. He nodded at me as he walked and lit up a cigarette. He seemed to spend a lot of time walking between the shelves and then turned suddenly. The next thing I knew he was pointing a big gun at me. It seemed huge. He held it with both hands. It was a dark gun, maybe a revolver. Just looking at that gun scared the daylights out of me. I just don't know that much about guns.

He shoved a note in my direction. It read: "This is a stickup. Open the register." He put the note on the counter so I could read it and backed off a bit. He was standing maybe 5–6 feet away from me. I did as he asked and opened the register. I said, "Okay, but please don't shoot." He then motioned for me to get down. I crouched down behind the counter. He next reached over and cleaned out the cash register. I think he was wearing gloves. Anyway, the police couldn't find any fingerprints except mine and some other people's.

As I said, he cleaned out the register. We had a lot of money on hand because people like to cash checks on Friday night. I think we had about $1,500. We had a couple of hundreds in the stack. The whole incident took about 2–3 minutes. I was probably standing upright looking at him and the gun while he held the gun for about 30–45 seconds. It all happened so fast. I did get a look at him though. The counter and cash register area are well-lighted. I gave a description to the police who came. They put the description on the Crime Report. I also gave the officer a partly smoked cigarette—I remember it was a "Kool"—I found in the aisle where the robber had been walking. The robber never said anything the whole time he was in the store. He grabbed the money and ran out. I couldn't hear any car pulling away. I was really frightened; I had never been robbed before.

The next day Officer Krause, the investigator, asked me to come down to the station on Genesse. He showed me some photographs and said he was pretty sure that the robber was one of the men in the photographs. Four guys obviously weren't it; one guy didn't even have a moustache. The fifth guy sort of looked like the robber. As an art student, I pay attention to facial features; and some of the features were really close to what I remembered. It's just that the guy in the store looked much slimmer. The guy in the photo looked pretty heavy—maybe 180–190 pounds.

Later Officer Krause asked me to attend a hearing at the Courthouse downtown. They put me on the stand and asked me whether the robber was in the courtroom. This guy, McIver, was the spitting image of the robber. He didn't have a moustache, but he's the guy who held me up.

Some defense investigator named Bertram tried to interview me about the case. She tried to give me the third degree. However, the police told me that I don't have any legal obligation to talk to the defense outside the courtroom, and I just decided that I'm going through enough hassle as it is in this case. I didn't need another interview. I want to get this case over with and get this whole incident behind me. Besides, Bertram was real pushy; she acted as if she thought she was superior to me for some reason.

Dated: March 5, 19YR–1

/s/ Marilyn Sandoval
_____

Marilyn Sandoval

Statement of Officer Ronald J. Krause

My name is Ronald J. Krause. I am a member of the Morena Police Department. I have been a member of that department for 11 years. I spent four years in the Army, and I served as a Military Policeman. During the course of my police career I have undoubtedly investigated several hundred robberies.

On the evening of February 7, 19YR–2, we received a call from Mory's Liquors. The report was that they had just been robbed. I immediately drove to the crime scene. There I met the clerk, Marilyn Sandoval. She was quite upset; she said she was an art student and struck me as a sensitive, liberal artsy type person. However, I was able to calm her down enough to interview her. She gave me the information I originally recorded on the Crime Report. She gave me a general description of the robber and a pretty good, detailed description of the MO. She also gave me a cigarette butt she seemed to think was important. You can't get fingerprints off of a cigarette butt. I don't know what happened to it; probably I put it in an ashtray.

The next day I contacted Central Robbery Detail and gave them the information Ms. Sandoval had given me. I described the MO. Jessup told me that the MO matched that of a guy named McIver. It seems that they suspected McIver of three other robberies of liquor stores with the same routine of the type noted. He had been acquitted of one which occurred two years ago; and although he had been arrested for two others during the prior year, they were both dismissed for insufficient evidence. They gave me McIver's address.

Later that day I asked Ms. Sandoval to stop by the Genesse station. She did so, and I showed her some photographs, including McIver's. It was a two-year-old mug shot they'd made when they picked him up for the first robbery. I displayed five photographs to Ms. Sandoval. She definitely eliminated the other four, and she added that McIver's photograph looked a lot like the guy but the robber was much slimmer. She said she could not be sure but some of the facial features sort of resembled the robber.

Unfortunately, we have misplaced the photograph of the defendant which I used in the display.

I talked it over with the desk sergeant, and we decided to arrest McIver. I did so early the next afternoon. As we arrived at defendant's residence, I noticed a light-colored compact car parked next to the house as well as an old brown Chevy. When we arrested the defendant, we searched him and found some money, including two, one-hundred-dollar bills. I remembered Ms. Sandoval telling me that there were two, one-hundred-dollar bills in the register the night of the robbery. I noted the serial numbers in my notebook and marked my initials and the date on the bills. I will be able to identify the bills at trial. I remember the defendant said he needed a smoke and asked if I had any cigarettes on me. I think he asked if I had any Kools. Anyway, I told him that I didn't smoke. The defendant also became belligerent. I forgot to note this on the PD 100, but he made a wise remark like, "You guys are gonna blow it again. I'll walk this time like before.'' We searched McIver's apartment with his consent and found a dark-brown corduroy jacket. It was seized and tagged as evidence.

In preparation for trial, I went down to Central Robbery and logged onto their computer. I ran the modus operandi search myself and, again, came up with only three other robberies matching the precise MO used in this case. In each instance, the computer listed McIver as the suspect in the robbery. As far as I can tell, there's only one guy who does it just that way, and that guy is the defendant. I've never had occasion to personally access the Central Robbery computer before that time, but I've since done it for several cases and in retrospect I'm positive that I used the proper procedure. I kept the printout from the computer search.

Dated: March 5, 19YR–1

/s/   Ronald J. Krause
_____
Ronald J. Krause

DATA BASE: MODUS OPERANDI

SEARCH REQUEST:

    TYPE OF CRIME: ROBBERY

        TYPE OF ESTABLISHMENT VICTIMIZED: LIQUOR STORE

    PERPETRATOR:

        RACE: CAU

        SEX: M

        BUILD: MED

    GETAWAY CAR

        MAKE: CHEV

        COLOR: BR

    WEAPON USED: HANDG

        OTHER DETAILS: TYPED NOTE

    NUMBER OF ENTRIES IN FILE: THREE

    NAME OF SUSPECTS IN ENTRIES IN FILE:

        McIVER, JOHN D.

        McIVER, JOHN D.

        McIVER, JOHN D.

    Form 1332

FEDERAL BUREAU OF INVESTIGATION

IDENTIFICATION DIVISION

WASHINGTON, D.C. 20537

CRIMINAL HISTORY RECORD

JURISDICTION FBI CASE NUMBER	SUBJECT: NAME STATE NUMBER	ARRESTED OR RECEIVED	C–CHARGE D–DISPOSITION
MISSOULA, MONT. 80681	McIVER, JOHN 79–143	02/11/YR–8	C–SHOPLIFTING D–5 MOS. SUSP
WOODLAND, CAL. 94431	McIVER, JOHN	07/09/YR–4	C–ROBBERY D–ACQ
MORENA, E.D. 101123	McIVER, JOHN	01/14/YR–3	C–ROBBERY D–DISMD BY DA, INSUFF. EVID.
MORENA, E.D. 11221	McIVER, JOHN	09/23/YR–3	C–ROBBERY D–DISMD BY DA, INSUFF. EVID.

Statement of John D. McIver

My name is John D. McIver. I am 30 years old. My parents live in Wyoming where my father owns a car lot. I have been something of a drifter for the past 10 years. My parents send me money occasionally to help me out. I have lived in Morena for the past three years. I have had several brushes with the law in Morena; they've arrested me on false charges a couple of times. I have only one conviction: a 19YR–8 Montana conviction for shoplifting—a misdemeanor for which I spent some time in county jail.

On February 7, 19YR–2, I received a letter from my folks. They enclosed $300 because they knew I'd just lost my job as a car salesman. I was glad to get the money, but I really felt depressed. I was upset about losing the job and more upset that my folks had to keep helping me out. I just wanted to be alone and think. I went to a movie and spent some time at the Arizona Cafe that night. I was just pouring down a couple of shots and watching the news. I can't think of anyone I was with that night who could testify to give me an alibi.

On February 9, 19YR–2, I was home just taking it easy. This officer and a partner came by to arrest me. The officer, I think his name was Krause, really hassled me. He made some insulting remarks about my prior arrests. I cooperated fully, told him I was innocent, and accompanied him down to the station. When he finally got around to giving me the warnings, I told him that I did not want to talk to the police. As they were processing me, they found something over $200 in my pockets;

Krause made some markings on the bills. He said that it would be helpful as evidence against me. I didn't know what he was talking about at the time.

Later they took me to court for a prelim. It turned out that there had been a robbery of some liquor store. This lady took the stand and identified me as the robber! I couldn't have been more surprised. To the best of my recollection, I've never visited that store; and I've never seen her before.

I have been dieting for the past few years. I'm now about 25 pounds lighter than I was two years ago. I had a moustache until recently. In fact, I think I shaved it off on February 8th. I just got tired of it. As I recall, the lady at the prelim said something about the robber having a moustache.

I drive an old, beat-up, brown '68 Chevy. A couple of friends of mine drive white compact cars, but I wasn't with any of them on February 7. Yeah, I smoke—Salems mostly—and I "bum" cigarettes whenever I can—all brands. I don't smoke Kools; I take whatever's offered.

I don't own a gun, but I do have a dark-brown corduroy jacket I wear during cold weather. The officers took it out of my closet and down to the station with them.

Dated: March 3, 19YR–1

/s/   John D. McIver

_____

John D. McIver

Dear Johnny,

Your mother and I were sad to hear that you lost another job. We wish we could do more to help.

Things here in Rawlins are still pretty good despite the economy. We all figure the new President will get things going again. Your sister is doing fine at the University. She's been accepted to the law school there at Laramie.

You know I can always use another hand here at the car lot if you want to come home. It'd do you good to get away from all those El Dorado crazies. Anyway, keep in touch, and if you ever want to come back to God's country, you'll always be welcome here. Take care of yourself.

Johnny, please try to stay out of trouble. God be with you.

Love,
Dad and Mom

Statement of Dr. Janice Bertram

My name is Dr. Janice Bertram. I received my undergraduate Psychology degree from Stanford University and both my Master's and

Ph.D. from Washington University in St. Louis. I have appeared as an expert witness in cases, both civil and criminal, on 100 prior occasions. On 50 of those occasions, I was proposed as an expert witness on the unreliability of eyewitness identification. On 45 of those occasions I testified for the defense—on the rest for prosecution. I am being paid $2,000 for my testimony in this case by the defendant's parents. Over the past five years I have probably earned well over $150,000 in consulting fees in the cases in which I have appeared as an expert witness; I would estimate that figure represents maybe a third of my total income during that period.

My views on eyewitness identification are very consistent with the portion that a friend of mine, Bob Buckhout, took in his classic article in 231 SCIENTIFIC AMERICAN 23 (December 1974). As scientist, I try to maintain impartial objectivity on the subject; but I must frankly confess that I am personally strongly convinced of the inherent weakness of eyewitness identification. I am not a lawyer; but it is amazing to me that in light of the overpowering scientific case against eyewitness identification testimony, the American courts have not done more to limit the possibility of convictions based solely on uncorroborated eyewitness testimony. I know that the British courts have gone much further than the American courts to protect defendants in this regard.

I have not only studied the police reports and the statement of Marilyn Sandoval in this case. I also visited the crime scene and attempted unsuccessfully to interview Ms. Sandoval. However, based on the factors in this case—the obstructions to vision at the crime scene, the phenomenon of weapon fixation, the cross-racial identification element, her fear, and the suggestions by the police, I would testify that there is a reasonable degree of scientific probability of mistake here. If she had allowed me to interview her, I perhaps could refine my opinion; but she seemed very defensive. I do not know what the prosecutor or police told her about cooperating with the defense in this case.

Dated: June 10, 19YR–1

/s/   Janice Bertram

_____

Janice Bertram

morena **REGIONAL CRIME/INCIDENT REPORT** | PAGE 1 - 2 | CASE NUMBER 8-11819

CODE SECTION AND DESCRIPTION (ONE INCIDENT ONLY)

211 P.C. ARMED ROBBERY | MONTH 02 | DAY 07 | YEAR YR-2 | DAY OF WEEK FRI | TIME 2040

LOCATION OF INCIDENT (OR ADDRESS)

1715 GARNET AVE.   Morena   BEAT 694

VICTIM'S NAME (LAST, FIRST, MIDDLE /OR ORGANIZATION) | RESIDENCE ADDRESS | CITY | STATE | ZIP | RACE W | SEX F

SANDOVAL, MARILYN F. | 4370 CAMINO DEL RIO S. | | | | | V/P ASSIST

DATE OF BIRTH 6-30-YR-25 | ID TYPE AND NUMBER 565-38-2941 | RESIDENCE PHONE 291-6762 | DAYS OFF 06 | WORK HOURS S-M VARIES

EMPLOYER (RANK IF MILITARY) MORY'S LIQUOR | STATUS E | BUSINESS PHONE 272-2424 | BUSINESS OR MILITARY ADDRESS 1715 GARNET AVE. | CITY Morena

ADDITIONAL INFORMATION (VICTIM VEHICLE INFO, IF APPLICABLE)

TOTAL # OF WITNESSES 1

WEAPON: BLUE STEEL REVOLVER (POSS. 38 CAL.) TO EFFECT ROBBERY (SEE OVER)

ITEM NO. ARTICLE NAME | QTY | IDENTIFICATION NUMBERS | BRAND, MAKE, OR MANUFACTURER | MODEL NAME AND MODEL NUMBERS | MISCELLANEOUS DESCRIPTION | VALUE

ADDITIONAL PROPERTY LISTED | CASH MONIES $1500 | | | | | TOTAL $1500.00

REPORTING OFFICER KRAUSE R | I.D. # 1054 | DIVISION HQ | APPROVED BY Quigley

DATE AND TIME OF REPORT 2-7-YR-2 2100 | AGENCY P.D. | CRIME TYPE 211 P.C.

PAGE 2 of 2   **CASE #**

SUSPECT # 1 (LAST, FIRST, MIDDLE)
UNKNOWN

NICKNAME/AKA | **RACE** W | **SEX** M | **AGE** 25-30 | **DOB** | **HT.** | **WT.** | **BUILD** MED. SLENDER | **HAIR COLOR** BRN | **EYE COLOR**

CLOTHING DESCRIPTION
LONG DARK BROWN JACKET

SUSPECT'S ADDRESS | **CITY** | **STATE** | **ZIP** | **ARRESTED**

ADDITIONAL INFORMATION / FURTHER SUSPECT DESCRIPTION (I.R., GLASSES, TATTOOS, TEETH, BIRTHMARKS, JEWELRY, SCARS, MANNERISMS, ETC.)

SUSPECT # 2 (LAST, FIRST, MIDDLE)

CLOTHING DESCRIPTION

HAIR LGTH/TYPE	HAIR STYLE	FACIAL HAIR	COMPLEXION	GENERAL APPEARANCE	DEMEANOR	SPEECH	VOICE
1 SUSPECT 2	1 SUSPECT 2	1 SUSPECT 2	1 SUSPECT 2	1 SUSPECT 2	1 SUSPECT 2	1 SUSPECT 2	1 SUSPECT 2

SUSPECT VEHICLE(S) **YEAR** **MAKE** **MODEL** | **COLOR/COLOR** LIGHT COLORED | **TYPE** COMPACT | **LICENSE NO.** | **STATE**

ADDITIONAL VEHICLE IDENTIFIERS (SLOGAN, UNIQUE WHEELS, ETC.) | **VEHICLE IMPOUNDED** | **LOCATION**

EVIDENCE OBTAINED: FINGERPRINTS, WEAPON/TOOLS, OTHER PRINTS, VEHICLE, PHOTOS, STAINS, BLOOD/SEMEN, HAIR, OTHER | **DISPOSITION OF EVIDENCE** | **TAG NO.**

NARRATIVE: (INCLUDE ACTIONS AND CONVERSATION BY SUSPECT(S) AND VICTIM(S) AND OTHER EVENTS NOT PREVIOUSLY COVERED) | **ARE L PERSONS LISTED** | **WITNESS**

THE ABOVE-DESCRIBED SUSPECT ENTERED LIQUOR STORE 1775 GARNET AVE. APPROX. 2030, 2-7-YR-2 MAY HAVE DRIVEN IN LIGHT COLORED COMPACT CAR. ENTRY THROUGH FRONT DOOR. SUSPECT WALKED TO COUNTER WHERE CLERK SANDOVAL WAS STANDING. SUSPECT TURNED AROUND TO FACE SANDOVAL AT WHICH TIME SUSPECT WAS HOLDING BLUE STEEL REVOLVER, POSS. 38 CALIB IN BOTH HANDS. HE POINTED GUN AT SANDOVAL AND SHOWED HER TYPED NOTE, "THIS IS A HOLDUP. OPEN THE REGISTER." SANDOVAL COMPLIED. SUSPECT MOTIONED TO SANDOVAL TO GET ON FLOOR. SANDOVAL DID SO. SUSPECT REACHED OVER THE COUNTER AND REMOVED CASH (APPROX. $1500) FROM CASH DRAWER. SANDOVAL HEAR SUSPECT RUN OUT FRONT DOOR, BUT HEARD NO VEHICLE LEAVE. I RECEIVED A RADIO CALL TO INVESTIGATE POSSIBLE ARMED ROBBERY 1775 GARNET. ARRIVED 2045. INTERVIEWED SANDOVAL. SUSPECT EVIDENTLY USED GLOVES. NO PRINTS FOUND ON REGISTER OTHER THAN SANDOVAL'S.

ARSON TYPE: | **CONTENT LOSS $** | **STRUCT LOSS $** | **OCCUPIED** | **CONTINUED**

AR310-2 (REV. 1-00)

MORENA POLICE DEPARTMENT
ARREST/JUVENILE CONTACT REPORT

BOOKING NUMBER 744327

SAN DIEGO NUMBER

PAGE 1 OF 2

JUVENILE FILE NUMBER

REPORT	
[X] ARREST REPORT	
[ ] NOTIFY WARRANT	
[ ] JUVENILE CONTACT	

SUSPECT - CRIME

CHARGE(S): 211 P.C. (ARMED ROBBERY)

PERSON ARRESTED (LAST, FIRST, MIDDLE): McIVER, JOHN D.   NICKNAME/AKA

RACE/SEX: CAU/M AGE: 30 HT: 5'9" WT: 160 BUILD: MED. HAIR: BR. EYES: BR. DATE OF BIRTH: 8/31/YR-30

ADDRESS: 1270 SAN LUIS REY   CITY: MORENA   STATE   RESIDENT: [X] YES [ ] NO   TIME: 3

CLOTHING DESCRIPTION: BLUE + GRAY T-SHIRT, BLU JEANS + TENNIS SHOES

OCCUPATION: SALESMAN   EMPLOYER/DATE

MILITARY SERVICE NO./SSN: N/A   DRIVERS LIC. NUMBER: WYO. 27543   TELEPHONE NUMBER: 453-2876

IS SUBJECT A SUSPECTED USER OF NARCOTICS/DRUGS: YES [ ] NO [X]   INTERPRETER REQUIRED: YES [ ] NO [X]   ILLEGAL ALIEN: YES [ ] NO [X]   SUSPECT'S RELATION TO VICTIM(S)   RELATIVE [ ] ACQUAINTANCE [ ] STRANGER [X]

LOCATION OF ARREST: SUSPECT'S RESIDENCE   DATE: 2/8/YR-2 TIME: 1340   LOCATION OF OCCURRENCE: 1775 GARNET AVE.   DATE: 2/1/1 TIME: 2030   DIVISION/BEAT NO: 694   DISTRICT

CITIZEN ARRESTED: YES [ ] NO [X]   ARRESTED BY: R. KRAUSE #1054 YES [X] NO [ ]   BOOKED BY: KRAUSE   MARRIED YES [ ] NO [X] STATEMENT YES [ ] NO [X]   ADDRESS   HOME PHONE   BUS. PHONE   RES. BEAT

JUVENILE ONLY

LIVES WITH

FATHER/STEPFATHER'S NAME   ADDRESS   EMPLOYER   HOME PHONE   BUS. PHONE

MOTHER/STEPMOTHER'S NAME   ADDRESS   EMPLOYER   HOME PHONE   BUS. PHONE

SCHOOL   GRADE   PARENTS NOTIFIED BY: WHOM, AND HOW   DATE   TIME

DISPOSITION OF JUVENILE   JUVENILE UNIT DISPOSITION (INVESTIGATOR ONLY): INF [ ] DIV [ ] PB [ ] JH [ ] PARENT [ ] RTN [ ] CLEARED [ ]

SUSPECT DESCRIPTION

LGTH/TYPE	HAIR STYLE	FACIAL HAIR	COMPLEXION	GENERAL APPEARANCE	SPEECH	VOICE	DEFENSE MEASURES
UNKNOWN	UNKNOWN	UNKNOWN	UNKNOWN	UNKNOWN	UNKNOWN	UNKNOWN	NA
BALD	AFRO/NAT.	CLEAN SHAVE	ACNE	CASUAL	ACCENT	DISGUISED	CAME ALONG
(COLLAR)	BRAIDED	FULL BEARD	DARK	DIRTY	LISPS	HIGH PITCH	SLEEPER
LONG	BUSHY	FU MANCHU	FRECKLED	BIGUISE	MUMBLES	LOUD	MACE
SHORT	GREASY	GOATEE	(LIGHT)	FLASHY	OFFENSIVE	LOW PITCH	BATON
(SHOULDER)	MILITARY	LOWER LIP	MEDIUM	GOOD-LOOKING	(QUIET)	(MEDIUM)	FIREARM
(SOURCE)	PONYTAIL	MUSTACHE	PALE	MILITARY	RAPID	MONOTONE	OTHER:
FINE	PROCESSED	NONE/FIXED	POCKED	UNKEMPT	SLOW	NASAL	
(THICK)	STRAIGHT	SIDEBURNS	RUDDY	UNUSUAL ODOR	STUTTERS	PLEASANT	
THINNING	WAVY/CURLED	UNSHAVEN	SALLOW	WELL GROOMED	TALKATIVE	RASPY	
WIRY	(YES)	VAN DYKE	TANNED	OTHER:	OTHER:	SOFT	
OTHER:	OTHER:	OTHER:	OTHER:		BELLIGERENT	OTHER:	BY OFFICER I.D. 1054

FURTHER SUSPECT DESCRIPTION (I.E., GLASSES, TATTOOS, TEETH, BIRTHMARKS, JEWELRY, SCARS, MANNERISMS, ETC.)

VEHICLE

YEAR: 1968 MAKE: CHEV. MODEL: IMPALA COLOR/COLOR: DARK BROWN BODY STYLE: 2-DR HD TOP LICENSE NO.: RAW-790 STATE: WYO

ADDITIONAL VEHICLE IDENTIFIERS (DAMAGE, CHROME WHEELS, ETC.)   VEHICLE IMPOUNDED: YES [X] NO [ ]   DISPOSITION

EVIDENCE

EVIDENCE OR PROPERTY IMPOUNDED: YES [X] NO [ ]   PROPERTY TAG NOS.: B-514-515   COMPLAINT OF ILLNESS OR INJURY: YES [ ] NO [X] EXPLAIN IF YES   EVIDENCE OF ILLNESS OR INJURY: YES [ ] NO [X]   TREATED BY:

EVIDENCE (ITEMS): WHERE FOUND, DISPOSITION:
SUSPECT HAD $211 ON HIM, INCLUDING TWO ONE HUNDRED DOLLAR BILLS.
IMPOUNDED AT ROOM #70. DK. BRN. CORDUROY JACKET FOUND IN CLOSET - SUS. RES.

VIC./WIT.

[O/F] MARILYN SANDOVAL   ADDRESS: 4370 CAMINO D. RIOS   CITY: MORENA STATE   RESIDENCE PHONE: 291-6763   BUS. PHONE: 272-2424   EXT.   ADDRESS   CITY STATE

COMPANIONS

COMPANIONS		INVESTIGATOR INFORMATION	
#1 NAME	ARRESTED [ ] YES [ ] NO, A [ ] BOB / /	DETECTIVE ASSIGNED	DEPUTY DISTRICT ATTORNEY
#2 NAME	ARRESTED [ ] YES [ ] NO, A [ ] / /	CRIME REPORT OFFICER	REVIEWING DEP. DIST. ATTORNEY
#3 NAME	ARRESTED [ ] YES [ ] NO, A [ ] / /	ARRESTING OFFICER	DEFENSE ATTORNEY
#4 NAME	ARRESTED [ ] YES [ ] NO, A [ ] BOB / /	CASE NUMBER	PROSECUTOR'S INFORMATION

REPORTING OFFICER: R. KRAUSE   I.D.: 1054   RANK   DIVISION: HQ   DAYS OFF: T-W   RELATED REPORTS: [X] YES [ ] NO — ARJIS-2   LIST TYPE: Stan Ernest   REPORT APPROVED: K. Moller   BOOKING APPROVED

PD-100 (REV. 6-80)

	POLICE DEPARTMENT SUPPLEMENTARY INVESTIGATION REPORT	

9 NARRATIVE SECTION

Following investigation of P.C. 211 armed robbery 2-7-YR-2, 1775 Garnet,

as per ARJIS-2, Case No. 81-11819, this officer spoke with Central

Robbery. Central Robbery informed this officer that M.O. matched that

of suspect McIver. Following probable ID by victim Sandoval from photo

line-up, arrest warrant for suspect McIver obtained. Arrested suspect

McIver at his residence. Suspect McIver was unarmed, offered no physical

resistence, but was a bit belligerent in demeanor. Search at McIver

residence as per consent of suspect revealed no viable evidence except

corduroy jacket as noted above.

Case File A–6

PAPPAS v. WHEELOCK

The parties have entered into the following stipulations of fact:

1. The defendant, Merle Wheelock, is the owner and sole proprietor of B.M.E., Building Materials and Equipment, a company located in Villa Peak, a suburb of Morena, El Dorado.

2. The principal place of business of B.M.E. is located at 1422 Lakeside Drive in Villa Peak.

3. At 1422 Lakeside Drive, B.M.E. maintains two facilities, one large brick building and a 60 by 100 tin building with a concrete floor.

The tin building houses some of the equipment which B.M.E. rents and lends to local contractors and businesspeople.

4. B.M.E. also owns a 4½ foot tall orchard heater. During the winter, the heater is moved inside the tin building to furnish heat for persons using the building during cold weather. The heater is designed to use exclusively diesel fuel. The attached photograph accurately depicts the heater in question.

5. At all relevant times Steven Havens was an employee of the defendant and was acting within the course and scope of his employment.

6. On February 2, 19YR–2, the plaintiff sustained second and third degree burns on his body while he was inside the defendant's tin building.

7. When the plaintiff was admitted to the Gold Country Memorial Hospital at 11:00 a.m. on February 3, 19YR–2, he had a blood alcohol concentration of 0.175. At the time of his admission, the plaintiff displayed merely moderate clinical symptoms of intoxication.

8. El Dorado Vehicle Code § 23417 makes it a per se offense for a person to operate a motor vehicle when the person has a BAC exceeding 0.10.

9. At the first hearing in this case, the parties will litigate only the issue of liability. The issue of damages has been severed for trial.

Statement of Kenneth Pappas

I'm 30 years old and weigh about 160 pounds. I run a grading business in the vicinity of Villa Peak. I do most of the work myself, and I occasionally hire other guys to help me out with big projects. I've lived in the Villa Peak area my entire life. I went to grammar school, high school, and community college here. I'm married, but we don't have any kids yet.

I often rent equipment from B.M.E. They run a pretty informal ship. I know the owner, Merle Wheelock, real well, since we went to high school together. Even when no one's around, I can just pick up the stuff I need, bring it back, and pay Merle later. A lot of the bigger equipment is kept in a large tin shed near the brick building where Merle has the cash register and such. If Merle knows you the way he knows me, he doesn't mind if you just go right in and take what you need. There's a clipboard with a signout sheet on it.

That tin building can get pretty damn cold during the winter. Villa Peak's up near the mountains; and although we don't get much snow, you can really feel it in your bones when winter rolls around. To keep the tin building warm, Merle moves an orchard heater into the building. They're sometimes called smudge pots. Since I'm not a farmer, I don't know much about that sort of heater; but I'd seen other guys light it while I'd been at B.M.E. before. When it's dying down and you need to refuel, you open the fuel port and pour the fuel into the reservoir at the bottom. You have to be sure to let the old fire die all the way down. Then you can light it with burning paper or an acetylene torch. You remove the lid while the thing was operating. When you want to shut it down, you cut off the air intake and put the lid on top of the stack.

On February 2, 19YR–2, I had stopped by late in the afternoon to pick up a "come-along"—you use it to help get stranded equipment out of the mud. I'd been working on a grading job for a local developer, and there was lots of mud because of all the rain we'd been having. I got a dozer stuck in the mud, and B.M.E. was the closest place to get the "come-along" I needed to free the bulldozer. I'd spent a little time getting the dozer out, and then I headed back to B.M.E. to return the "come-along."

When I got to B.M.E., it was already past the normal closing time. It must have been about 6:00 or 6:15 p.m. already. Merle had shut the brick building down and headed home. When I saw that there were no lights there, I drove over to the tin shed. There are often people there well after closing. When I pulled up by the shed, I could see that the lights were on. Merle's helper, Steve Havens, was there. I told Steve that I was returning a "come-along," and he helped me drag it inside the shed.

I was just about to head home when Steve offered me a Bud. I was in no particular rush, since my wife was out of town; and I said that that would be more than O.K. Steve handed me a beer, and we just stood and talked for awhile. It felt real cold even though we were standing near the heater. Steve said something like, "The old heater must be gettin low on fuel. Time to crank her up again." I just stood there while he went outside to get some fuel. After a minute or two he came back in with a red can. I could hear something sloshing inside, so I figured it was the fuel for the heater. To tell you the truth, I wasn't paying all that much attention to what Steve was doing. It had been a long day. I was just enjoying the beer and sort of chatting with him while he was tending to the heater. I like an occasional beer, and it was great to relax at the end of a frustrating day. It had been tough working in all that mud, and that was the only drink I'd had all day.

I can't be sure, but I would guess I was standing about ten feet away from the heater at the time. I remember Steve opened the fuel port and started pouring. The next thing I hear this terrible sound like an explosion, and a fireball comes blasting out of the heater. It comes right at me! It hit my pants first. I think I was wearing nylon pants, and they just burst into flame. The fireball hit the floor, and it seemed to ignite the sawdust right there. I ran a couple of steps and threw myself down where there wasn't any fire. Steve came over right away and helped me put the flames out.

I could tell that Steve felt bad about what had happened. Rather than sending me to a hospital, he took me straight to his trailer. He parks the trailer next to the brick building, and he lives there most of the time. He helped me get into his bed. Then he went to the nearby

Food and Liquor and got me some Vaseline and some booze. As I recall, he brought a bottle of Southern Comfort back to the trailer.

I'm not clear on the times, but it was probably past midnight when I finally left Steve's. I told him I felt better—but I was saying that just to make him feel better. When I got back to my house, the burns hurt like hell. I took out a bottle and had a good, strong shot to help kill the pain. When morning came around, I was in so much pain that I couldn't go to work. I drank a lot then to try to kill the pain. I waited a little while that morning, and then I drove to the nearest hospital. It was painful just to hold onto the steering wheel. They told me that I had second degree burns on my legs and third degree burns on my arms.

The constant pain has gone away, but there's still a lot of scar tissue and my skin is very sensitive. It's hard for me to do my old work now. I hate to have a falling out with an old friend like Merle, but my injuries are so bad that I have no choice but to sue.

Dated: July 2, 19YR–1

/s/ Kenneth Pappas

_____

Kenneth Pappas

Statement of Maureen Marcus

I am an employee of and shareholder in Accident Analysis, a company specializing in reconstructing accidents for litigation. Our office is in Morena. I have an Associate's degree from the Marshall Institute in Chicago, and I received both a B.S. and a Master's degree in mechanical engineering from Rennselaer Polytechnic in New York. I have worked for Accident Analysis for the past nine years. During that time I have probably testified as an expert witness on over 100 occasions. I have also served as a member of the committee on fatigue analysis of ASTM, the American Society for Testing and Materials.

On March 15, 19YR–1, I got a phone call from the plaintiff's attorney. She asked me to go to the premises of a company called B.M.E. in Villa Peak and take a look at an orchard heater. I was glad to help; I've never worked with her before, but my company has consulted with her law firm several times, and we've always had good experiences working with them—and I think we've gotten some good results for our clients. I drove out there the next day. I was met by the plaintiff's attorney and the owner, a Mr. Merle Wheelock. Wheelock was very cooperative; he gave me access to the heater and answered some questions I had. At the time the heater was located outside a tin building on the premises. It's the type of heater that orchards use to ward off frost during the cold seasons.

I carefully inspected both the interior and exterior of the heater. I took some notes on the dimensions of the heater and some other measurements I made. I attached some of the notes to this statement. I understand that this accident occurred in 19YR–2. It's a shame that no one thought to call in an expert earlier. That heater had just been standing outside during the rainy season, and the rain may have washed away valuable physical evidence. For example, it would have been an important clue if the day after the accident, there had been blistering in the stack. In any event, I did the best I could under the circumstances. In the pot where the fire actually burns, there was a lot of dirt. I measured the sludge, and it was more than an inch deep. The sludge consists of burnt or partially burnt fuel oil. The stack was also filthy; it was layered with soot, tar, and coke. This was not new sludge; it was caked on as if it had been there a good long time.

Since I came on the accident scene so late, I can't be absolutely certain as to the cause of the accident. I have to confess that there are several plausible scenarios as to how this accident occurred. I want to list them and then explain why I think one is the most likely.

To begin with, you can rule out defective design of the heater itself. There was absolutely nothing wrong with that heater. The cause had to be the way the heater was maintained or operated.

One possible cause is that whoever filled the heater overfilled it. If they did, that would cause fuel and flames to spill out onto the floor. The flames would spread in the sawdust and well might injure someone standing near the heater. The problem is that this scenario doesn't account for the fact that both eyewitnesses saw there was a fireball and a loud noise that sounded like an explosion. You wouldn't get the fire and that noise if you just overfilled the fuel port. The fire would spread but not in the precise way the eyewitnesses describe.

Another good possibility is that whoever filled the heater was careless, didn't let the active flames die out before refueling, and poured fuel on a hot heater. If you did something stupid like that, you well might get a lot of flame—a general conflagration-pouring out of the heater. But the thing that troubles me is that again this theory alone doesn't account for what the eyewitnesses said. I know the plaintiff said he saw a fireball that shot at least 10 feet. I think that the other eyewitness said something similar. You couldn't get that effect unless there was some denser matter being propelled through the air.

That's why I think that the last possibility is the best. I think that they mixed different types of fuels. This heater is designed to operate on diesel fuel. I had our patent attorney track down the patent on this heater, and it specifically says that it operates safely only on diesel. I gather that that night someone might have mixed gasoline with diesel fuel. If they did, the fuels could have agitated each other and created a pressurization. As I said, when I inspected the heater, it was filthy. Suppose that it was also in that condition on the night in question. From what I've read, these heaters tend to build up residue in the neck of the stack. It's sort of a carbon buildup. Suppose that the person who was filling the heater didn't shut it down properly for refueling. That residue might keep burning—a little glowing, incandescent ring of debris like a piece of charcoal. When the pressure was created by mixing the fuels, it was a wave that blew the residue buildup out of the louvers-almost like napalm. That atomized debris would still be dense enough to travel a good distance.

I wish I could be more definite, but that would have required an opportunity to inspect the heater immediately after the incident-and certainly before it was dragged outside to sit exposed to the elements during the rainy season. However, even with this limited information, I think it's pretty clear that the defendant's improper maintenance of the heater was at least one of the primary causes of the plaintiff's injuries. It's a clear-cut case of negligence.

Dated: April 29, 19YR–1

/s/ Maureen Marcus

Maureen Marcus

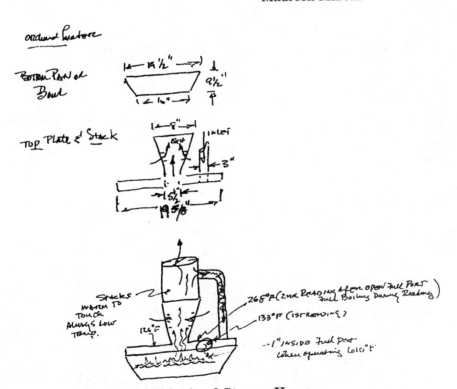

Affidavit of Steven Havens

My name is Steve Havens. I'm pretty much of a drifter. I grew up in Georgia and then headed north after high school. I've moved around a lot, but in 19YR–2 I tried to set down some roots in Villa Peak. It's the sort of small, rural community where I think I can be happy.

Anyway, early in 19YR–2 I began working for Merle Wheelock. Merle's a real good guy. He always treats me well, and he treats his customers the same way. He's real informal. He lets guys like Pappas come in, sign stuff out on their own, and pay him on an honor system. You don't find many guys like Merle any more.

Pappas is one of Merle's longtime customers. A few days after I started working for Merle, he introduced me to Pappas. He said, "This here is Ken, and I want you to take special good care of Ken. He gives us almost all his business, and I appreciate that." I got to know Pappas fairly well over the next couple of weeks. Just like Merle said, Pappas rented a lot of stuff from us, but he always brought the stuff back in good condition and paid his bill on time. Besides, Pappas is a friendly guy; I liked dealing with him.

During the afternoon of February 2, 19YR–2, Pappas stopped by to borrow a "come-along." He said he was doing some grading in a muddy area, and he got a dozer stuck. I told him to take the one in the corner of the tin shed. I noticed at the time that he had a six-pack with an open beer can in his truck. It seemed to me that it was a little early in the day to start hitting the beer, but that was his business.

The next time I saw Pappas was about 6:30 p.m. that night. Merle had already shut the main office down, but I was tidying up in the shed. Pappas pulls up and tells me that he's returning the "come-along." Pappas looked tired. He said, "Before I drag that sucker back in here, I'm gonna help myself to one of those beers I know you keep in the frig over there." I told him to help himself. I was puttering around for the next half hour or so, and he must have killed at least two beers. He appeared to be able to hold it, though.

It was getting cold, and I was just about to refuel the heater because I had about another hour's work left. When I said that I was going to do that, Pappas said, "Hey, I'll do that for you if you'll drag the 'come-along' in. I'm so sick of mud today that if I even look at that thing covered with mud, it'll turn my stomach." I said that that was all right by me. As I started to head out toward his truck, I told him to be absolutely sure that the fire had died out before he refueled. I also told him to use only diesel fuel. I pointed to some empty gas cans over in another corner. I said, "Be sure there's no gas in those babies before you put diesel in." I walked outside to get the "come-along." I climbed into the back of his pickup, and there were a lot of relatively new, empty beer cans in the back; and I didn't see the six-pack any more. A couple of minutes later Pappas came out with a red five-gallon can to siphon diesel from a rig parked near the shed.

I got the "come-along" inside, and I saw Pappas kneeling by the heater to refuel it. The next thing I knew there was this big noise, and I saw flames or something just shooting out of the heater—they must have gone five, maybe ten, feet—I just can't be sure, I was so scared. Pappas screams in pain and throws himself down to put out the flames. I ran over to him to help. We got the flames out right quick, but I could see that he was hurt.

He said that he didn't need to go to the doc, but I didn't want to turn him out like that. So I helped him over to my trailer. It's about 200 yards from the shed. It's over by our main building. I made him as comfortable as I could, and then I went to Rick's Food and Liquor down the road to get some Vaseline and liquor for him. When I got back, I put the Vaseline on as delicately as I could; he didn't seem to be in all that much pain. I asked him whether he wanted some liquor, and he said, "No. I've already had too much today. That's for damn sure." I asked him what he meant by that, but he just shook his head and mumbled. In the wee hours he insisted on going home. I offered to drive him, but he said No. I gave him some handkerchiefs to wrap around his hands to make it easier to grip the steering wheel. That's the last I saw of Pappas until this lawsuit started.

I'm the guy who works regularly in the shed. I had been on the job only a few weeks before Pappas' accident occurred. I have to admit that I didn't clean out the heater during the few weeks I was there, and it did look pretty dirty when I started work. I didn't have occasion to clean it after the accident. Right after the accident Merle told me to haul the thing outside the shed and not to use it again. Someone else could have used it outside, but I know that I haven't. It's just been sitting there.

I still work for Merle. He knows that I wasn't at fault in causing this accident, and I respect him for sticking with me. This is the absolute truth. So help me God.

Dated: September 19, 19YR–1

/s/   Steven R. Havens
_____
Steven R. Havens

Sworn to before me.

/s/   Constance Swail
_____
Constance Swail
Notary Public

[seal]

Statement of Robin Felice

I am a graduate of Case Western Reserve University. I attained my B.S. magna cum laude. After graduation, I went to work as a toxicologist for the Dade County Medical Examiner's Office in Florida. After a few years there, I went back to school, specifically to the University of Florida, to get my Master's and Ph.D. For the past seven years I've headed the Toxicology Department of the University of El Dorado Medical College. Three years ago I chaired the Toxicology Section of the American Academy of Forensic Science. I occasionally consult in meritorious private cases. A few months ago I received a telephone call from Mr. Wheelock's liability insurer. They asked me to evaluate the facts in this case and submit a report to the defense attorney they had retained to represent Wheelock. I agreed to do so.

At the outset, I want to make my factual assumptions clear. I understand that the parties have stipulated that at the time of the plaintiff's admission to the hospital at 11:00 a.m. the day following the incident, his BAC was 0.175. There evidently is a further agreement that at that time, the level of the plaintiff's clinical symptoms of intoxication (staggering gait, slurred speech, etc.) was only "moderate." In addition to reviewing the stipulation, I got hold of the records from the hospital. Those records state that the patient told the staff that he "had been drinking." However, the only other reference to intoxication in the admission record is that "patient's speech is a bit slow and somewhat difficult to understand." Finally, I read the statements submitted by Messrs. Pappas and Havens.

There is a good deal of interperson variability in elimination rates, but you can use the rule of thumb that a person is going to eliminate alcohol from his or her system at the rate of about 0.02 per hour. The BAC is one of the factors that will affect the intensity of clinical symptoms that a person manifests. The other factor is the speed with which the person consumed the alcohol. Once again you can't treat these as hard-and-fast rules, but they're guidelines. You expect a more marked level of clinical symptoms when the intoxication results from rapid consumption of alcohol—it's more of a shock to the person's system. In contrast, the level can be less severe at the same BAC when the level results from drinking over an extended period of time. It is ideal if you can test the person in question and attempt to measure their personal elimination rate and alcohol tolerance, but none of that data is available to me.

Based on the data I have, I'd have to say that Mr. Havens' version of the plaintiff's drinking is much more consistent with the stipulated and proven facts. 0.175 is a rather elevated BAC. In El Dorado, the limit for the per se statute is only 0.10. Hence, we're talking about a BAC almost twice the legal limit. A person is much more likely to attain that high a BAC if they've been drinking over a several hour period. According to the plaintiff, the only time he drank seriously was just before reporting to the hospital. I don't think that that would do the trick. In addition, I'm impressed by the fact that at the time he walked in the door at the hospital, the plaintiff's level of clinical symptoms was low. If he had ingested most of the liquor just before going to the hospital, you could reasonably expect more marked symptoms.

I hate to say it, but this is just another case illustrating the tragic consequences of drinking. Over half the caseload of my laboratory consists of intoxication analysis; I see this on a daily basis—how people ruin their lives with drinking. This is an issue of intense professional and personal concern to me. I consulted with the El Dorado Attorney General's Office when they were drafting the new, stiff laws on drunk driving. My husband is one of the founders of the local RID chapter, and

I'm proud to say that both of my kids are active in SADD. The truth is that whether you're driving or handling dangerous equipment like Pappas was, you've got to lay off the booze.

Dated: July 19, 19YR–2

/s/ Robin Felice

_____

Robin Felice

BLOOD ALCOHOL CONCENTRATION (BAC) CHARTS
DRINKING UNDER 21 YEARS OF AGE IS ILLEGAL.
(Drivers under 18 years old with a BAC of .05–.09 can be cited for violation of Section 23140 VC.)
IF YOU DRINK, DON'T DRIVE!

There is no safe way to drive after drinking. These charts show that a few drinks can make you an unsafe driver. They show that drinking affects your **BLOOD ALCOHOL CONCENTRATION (BAC)**. The BAC zones for various numbers of drinks and time periods are printed in white, grey, and black.

HOW TO USE THESE CHARTS: First, find the chart that includes your weight. For example, if you weigh 160 lbs., use the "150 to 169" chart. Then look under "Total Drinks" at the "2" on this "150 to 169" chart. Now look below the "2" drinks, in the row for 1 hour. You'll see your BAC is in the grey shaded zone. This means that if you drive after 2 drinks in 1 hour, you could be arrested. In the grey zone, your chances of having an accident are 5 times higher than if you had no drinks. But, if you had 4 drinks in 1 hour, your BAC would be in the black shaded area. . .and your chances of having an accident 25 times higher. What's more, it is ILLEGAL to drive at this BAC (.10% or greater). After 3 drinks in 1 hour, the chart shows you would need 3 more hours—with no more drinks—to reach the white BAC zone again.

REMEMBER: "One drink" is a 12-ounce beer, or a 4-ounce glass of wine, or 1¼-ounce shot of 80-proof liquor (even if it's mixed with non-alcoholic drinks). If you have larger or stronger drinks, or drink on an empty stomach, or if you are tired, sick, upset, or have taken medicines or drugs, you can be **UNSAFE WITH FEWER DRINKS**.

TECHNICAL NOTE: These charts are intended to be guides and are not legal evidence of the actual blood alcohol concentration. Although it is possible for anyone to exceed the designated limits, the charts have been constructed so that fewer than 5 persons in 100 will exceed these limits when drinking the stated amounts on an empty stomach. Actual values can vary by bodytype, sex, health status, and other factors.

Dl. 606 (REV. 3/88)

BAC Zones:	90 to 109 lbs.	110 to 129 lbs.	130 to 149 lbs.	150 to 169 lbs.
TIME FROM 1st DRINK	TOTAL DRINKS 1 2 3 4 5 6 7 8	TOTAL DRINKS 1 2 3 4 5 6 7 8	TOTAL DRINKS 1 2 3 4 5 6 7 8	TOTAL DRINKS 1 2 3 4 5 6 7 8
1 hr				
2 hrs				
3 hrs				
4 hrs				

BAC Zones:	170 to 189 lbs.	190 to 209 lbs.	210 to 229 lbs.	230 lbs. & Up
TIME FROM 1st DRINK	TOTAL DRINKS 1 2 3 4 5 6 7 8	TOTAL DRINKS 1 2 3 4 5 6 7 8	TOTAL DRINKS 1 2 3 4 5 6 7 8	TOTAL DRINKS 1 2 3 4 5 6 7 8
1 hr				
2 hrs				
3 hrs				
4 hrs				

SHADINGS IN THE CHARTS ABOVE MEAN:
☐ (.01%–.04%) Seldom illegal   ☐ (.05%–.09%) May be illegal   ■ (.10% Up) Definitely illegal
     ▦ (.05%–.09%) Illegal if under 18 yrs. old

[E85101]

Case File A–7*
UNITED STATES v. WILLIAMS
Following his indictment by a federal grand jury in Morena on
December 8, 19YR–1, Charles Williams was arrested pursuant to a bench

* This case file is based on a fact situation
created by Professor Leonard Packel of Villanova University.

warrant by Special Agent McNally on December 9, 19YR–1. On December 18, 19YR–1 Williams was arraigned and entered a not guilty plea.

File #3800   21 U.S.C. § 841(a)(1)

IN THE UNITED STATES DISTRICT COURT
FOR THE DISTRICT OF MORENA

UNITED STATES OF AMERICA)	Criminal No. 7–200
)	21 U.S.C. § 841(a)(1)
v.)	(Distribution of controlled
)	substance)
CHARLES WILLIAMS)	Filed: 12–8–19YR–1

INDICTMENT

Count I

THE GRAND JURY CHARGES:

That on or about December 1, 19YR–1, at Morena, in the Southern District of El Dorado, CHARLES WILLIAMS did knowingly, intentionally and unlawfully distribute approximately 10.07 grams of cocaine, a Schedule II narcotic drug controlled substance.

In violation of Title 21, United States Code, Section 841(a)(1).

A TRUE BILL:

/s/   Jane Doe

_____

Jane Doe
FOREPERSON

/s/   John Q. James

_____

John Q. James
United States Attorney

Statement of Charles Williams

Address:	280 S. 29th Street
	Morena, El Dorado
Age:	31
Occupation:	Part time bartender
	Alice's Tavern
	388 S. 34th Street
	Morena, El Dorado

Education:	Southern Senior High, Graduated
Military Service:	U.S. Navy, 4 years, Honorable Discharge as Machinist.

Sometime around the middle of November, 19YR–1 it started. I was clean. I wasn't involved in anything. Then Snake, that's Waldo Seymour, starts coming around. We call him Snake because he has a "forked tongue;" I mean he is a liar. Anyway, Snake used to be related to my girlfriend, Mary Green, and he knows I did time for a drug bust. About two years after I got out of the Navy, I was tending bar at Ernie's Cave, on 20th Street. This guy, Max Smith, comes in, and we start talking. Next thing I know I'm messing around with some cocaine, delivering it for Smith over the bar. So, I got busted and did a year. I was sentenced on May 12, 19YR–4. The jury got me on April 8, 19YR–4. I'll never forget that because it's my mother's birthday. When I got out, I promised my Mom I'd never break the law again, and I haven't 'til now. The cops never let you forget though, and I've been picked up twice on suspicion of possession by the narcs. They never found anything, and I was let go.

Anyway, in November Snake comes around and tells me that he is in big trouble. He doesn't look too good at the time. I hear he is a heroin user; and when he comes around, he looks like he needs help in a big way. So he tells me that he is in terrible trouble. He says that some guy he knows is going to finish him, and he needs my help. He says he stole a couple of cars in September and October and sold them to this guy. Now, this guy wants some cocaine from Snake. Snake says this guy got busted at the beginning of November for possession of cocaine, and the coke wasn't his. Snake then says this guy has since been given the word that either he replaces the coke or he's dead. The guy then turns on Snake and tells him to find some coke, or he will turn him in to the cops on the two cars. Snake tells me that this guy has borrowed some money, but no one will deal with him because they know he just got busted and think he is working for the narcs. Snake then begs me to help him.

I tell Snake no! Snake hangs around some more and pleads, but I won't change my mind. After that Snake is over at Mary's house every day trying to get me to help. He even cried a couple of times and says he will kill himself before he goes back to jail. Finally, I tell Snake that I would like to help him, but I don't know where there is any coke for sale. Snake then asks me about the guy Smith I got into trouble with before. I reply that I know he's around town, but I haven't seen him. This is like November 25 or 26.

Next day I'm working at Alice's Tavern, and Snake comes in and gives me a phone number of Max Smith. The number is for Chubby's Pool Palace because that's how the phone is answered when I call. I talk to Smith, and he says he has some coke for sale. I tell him it's a one time thing to help a friend who's in a world of hurt. I also tell him I haven't got any cash, but will pay him as soon as the deal goes down. Max doesn't trust me, and he says that he will come with me for the deal.

On the last day of November, I telephone Snake and tell him that I got him some coke. We arrange for him to come early afternoon on the next day. I then call Max back and tell him. On December 1, 19YR–1, the next day, Max comes over to Mary's place (a stone row house in the middle of the block) with a package of what he says is coke. He wants $1,000.00 but says he will take $800.00. He then goes upstairs.

I am watching T.V. in a back room Mary calls the den. It is a small room with a shaggy rug and posters on the wall. The T.V. is in there, but I forget what I was watching on that day. Anyway, I hear Mary talking and then Snake and some guy he calls Jim walk in. We talk about price, and I sell him the package for $900.00. Jim unwraps the stuff and tastes it, and then he asks if I can get more. I say no because I will be out of town. I say this because I don't want to ever do this again. Snake and Jim leave. I give Max $800.00 and he leaves. I kept $100.00 from Max to buy something nice to surprise Mary. Next thing I know, I'm under arrest. I never got a chance to buy her anything. I am sorry I did it. I feel Snake set me up, you know, trapped me or whatever lawyers call it. I'll bet he set it all up with Max too.

My girlfriend, Mary Green, is not involved. She asked me a couple of times why Snake was around so often, but I only told her that I was trying to help Snake. On December 1, 19YR–1 we got into a little argument after Smith went upstairs, and she demanded to know what was happening. I told her only that Snake was coming with a man who had threatened him, and that Smith and I were going to help. It was because of this that I wanted to surprise her with a gift. I have known Mary for almost three years. She is a fine person and knows nothing about drugs.

If you want a character witness, Rev. Albert Maxwell has promised that he will testify for me. He is at the Holy Redeemer Baptist Church, 12th and Montgomery Streets, in Morena. I have gone there for a year and a half. He does not know about my police record.

Mary will also testify for me, but I think you better know something. Mary and I live together at her house. We aren't married, but I love her and her two children, Louise Carol (Age 3) and Timothy Charles (Age 1).

Dated: January 1, 19YR

/s/ Charles Williams

_____

Charles Williams

Statement of Mrs. Mary Green

Address:	280 S. 29th Street Morena, El Dorado
Age:	25
Occupation:	Secretary

AJS, Inc.
8th and Walnut Streets
Morena, El Dorado

Marital Status: Divorced from Harvey Seymour

Children: Louise Carol—Age 3
Timothy Charles—Age 1

Education: Southern Senior High Graduate

I rent a brick row house which is in the middle of a block. The address is 280 S. 29th Street, Morena, El Dorado. I live there with my two children. I am divorced, and the children are by my former husband, Harvey Seymour. I support myself as a secretary at AJS, a book publisher. I earn $195.00 a week. My mother cares for the children while I am at work. I also receive support payments from Harvey pursuant to a settlement agreement.

My boyfriend is Charles Williams. He lives with me, and I am hopeful that we will get married. He is a part-time bartender at Alice's Tavern on 34th Street in Morena. If he can solve his present problem, I am going to suggest that he go to Electronics school on the Veterans Plan. I haven't told him this. Williams has been living with me since January 19YR–1.

In the middle of November, 19YR–1 my former brother-in-law, Clarence Seymour, started coming around almost every day. He would go into a room alone with Charles, and they would talk. I couldn't hear what they were talking about, but whatever it was, it really upset Charles. After Clarence started coming, Charles had trouble sleeping, and he would often get up and go downstairs to the den. I came down a couple of times and found him pacing around.

Finally, near the end of November Charles told me that Clarence (he called him Snake but I don't know why) was in serious trouble and that he was going to help him. He said that he didn't want to get involved because it might be trouble, but that someone had to help Clarence. He then left for work.

On the morning of December 1, 19YR–1, Charles told me that today was the day he was going to have to help Clarence. I was worried and called in sick to work. Charles wouldn't talk about what was going to happen, but at approximately 1:30 p.m. a man named Max come to the house. He said something to Charles, and he gave Charles a package of something wrapped in cellophane. Charles then sent him, Max, upstairs. My children were taking a nap upstairs, and I blew up and demanded to know what was going on.

Charles told me that Clarence was bringing a man who had threatened Clarence. This man, he said, needed badly to make a deal with Max. That was all he would say.

At about 2:30 p.m. there was a knock at the door. I answered it, and Clarence and a man I had never seen were there. I told them that Charles was in the den, which he was, and I pointed the way. The den is a room about 12 x 12 with white walls. I have some travel posters on the wall. There are two easy chairs, a coffee table, and a TV console in the room. There is a blue shag rug on the floor. After Clarence and the man arrived, I went upstairs and stayed there by myself with the children until everyone was gone. After everyone left, Charles seemed very relieved. I have known Charles and many of his friends for three years. He is a good and honest man. I know he was in jail, although I don't know if his friends know, but that doesn't change my mind.

Clarence has always been in trouble. He is no good at all. Besides, he used to be a junkie.

Dated: January 2, 19YR

/s/ Mary Y. Green
_____

Mary Y. Green

Statement of Clarence Waldo Seymour

Drug Enforcement Administration Informant SDI–007

Age: 25

Residence: Various places in Gary, Ames, presently
The Ace-in-the-Hole Motel, Room 4,
8th and Race Streets
Morena, El Dorado

Education: 8th Grade, Eastern Junior High
12th and Rapp Streets
Morena, El Dorado

Occupation: Unemployed, on welfare

Around the middle of November of 19YR–1, I was shooting pool at Chubby's Pool Palace, 10th and Diamond Streets, in Morena and I heard that Charles Williams was dealing cocaine. I know Williams because he is going with my former sister-in-law, Mary Green. Mary was married to my brother Harvey; but they got a divorce three years ago. They had two kids, a girl and a boy. Their names are Louise and Timmy. I don't know their ages but they are very young, probably less than four. Timmy is younger.

On November 18, 19YR–1 at approximately 8:00 p.m. I went over to Mary Green's house at 280 S. 29th Street, Morena, a brick row house in the middle of the block, and Charles Williams was there. After some casual talk, I told Charles that the word on the street was that he was dealing cocaine. Charles said that might be the situation for the right price. I told him that I had a connection who might be interested in buying. Charles said he'd like to meet my connection but only if my man had plenty of cash. I promised Charles that this friend had a good supply of cash because he was a soldier for the mob, mainly enforcing for loan sharks. I then left after telling Charles that I would try to set up a meet.

On November 20, 19YR–1, I called DEA Agent James J. McNally and told him that I knew a man who had some cocaine to deal. McNally told me to set up a meeting in which he, McNally, would pose as a drug dealer. I tried to contact Charles Williams, but I couldn't get him until November 29, 19YR–1, when I finally got him on the phone. On the phone we set up a meeting for December 1, 19YR–1 at 2:30 p.m. at Mary's house. I called McNally on November 30, 19YR–1 to tell him about the set-up, and he instructed me to meet him in the parking lot of the Blue Mariner Motel, 20th and Market Streets, on December 1, 19YR–1 at 1:00 p.m.

On December 1, 19YR–1 at approximately 1:15 p.m., I met McNally at the Blue Mariner in the parking lot. I told McNally my set-up, namely, that he was a drug dealer named "Jimmy" who also was a loan shark enforcer for the mob. After we were there for about a half an hour, Smart and Watson, two DEA Agents, arrived in a dark van, and we then all left for Mary Green's house. I rode with McNally in a V.W. Beetle. When we got to the house, McNally and I went in and talked to Mary Green. She told us Charles Williams was in the back and disappeared after pointing out a room. I don't remember what her exact words were. We went into the room, a small dark place with a T.V. which was tuned into a game show, and talked to Charles Williams. I introduced McNally as "Jimmy" and after Williams and McNally talked, the deal went down. Williams first wanted $1,000.00, and McNally offered him $900.00, which Williams finally accepted. McNally gave Williams $900.00, and Williams gave McNally a package wrapped in a plastic bag with the words "shower cap" on it and a picture of a Playboy bunny. We then left, and McNally and I returned to DEA Headquarters. McNally did some kind of test on the package which contained the "coke" and said that it was positive. He then paid me $150.00, and I left.

I have three prior convictions, all involving drugs. In 19YR–1 I plead guilty in federal court to possession with intent to distribute heroin. I was looking at some heavy time if I didn't deal, so I agreed to be an informant and work with DEA. I got 5 years probation. On July 9, 19YR–2, I plead guilty to possession of cocaine (15 grams) in the Superior Court of Morena. I received a sentence of 11 to 23 months and served 11 months. In January of 19YR–3 I plead guilty to possession of 2 grams of heroin (two bundles) in the Municipal Court of Morena. I received a sentence of 3 years probation.

I understand what entrapment is. DEA Agent McNally and some other Agents talked about it. It means that you can't threaten or force anyone to break the law. The agents told me never to entrap anyone.

My nickname is Snake because when I was a boy in grade school I had three pet garden snakes.

I have used heroin in the past and was addicted. I am over that now and don't need it anymore, although I occasionally take a taste now and then.

I have worked with Agent McNally on seven different occasions in the past. I began working with DEA on September 5, 19YR–1, the date of my plea bargain, which required me to work for DEA in return for the government's acceptance of a sentence of probation. At the DEA's request, I took and passed a polygraph test about this incident. The plea bargain requires that I testify truthfully in this case.

I was released from state jail in June of 19YR–1, and committed the federal offense on August 12, 19YR–1. I have also worked on two occasions with DEA Agents Leon Black and Buddy Johns. They paid me $300.00 for one heroin bust. The other occasion did not result in an arrest.

Dated: January 2, 19YR

/s/   Clarence Seymour
_____
Clarence Seymour

Statement of James J. McNally

Occupation:	Special Agent, Drug Enforcement Administration
Address:	Regional Office 6th and Arch Streets Morena, El Dorado
Age:	28
Years an Agent:	4 Years
Education:	Gary High School, Morena, 19YR–10 University of Southern California, B.S., Business Administration, 19YR–6
Home Address:	2120 S. 8th Street Morena, El Dorado

On November 20, 19YR–1, SDI–007 (Clarence Waldo Seymour) called me at DEA Headquarters and told me that a man he knew, Charles Williams, was dealing cocaine. I told him to set up a meeting with me in which I would work undercover as a drug dealer. SDI–007 called me again at DEA Headquarters on November 30, 19YR–1, and said that a meeting was set for December 1, 19YR–1, at 2:30 p.m. in the home of Mary Green, Williams' girlfriend.

On December 1, 19YR–1, at 1:40 p.m. SDI–007 and I met with DEA Agents Jack Smart and Telly Watson in the parking lot of the Blue

Mariner Motel, 20th and Market Streets, Morena, and we proceeded in official vehicles to the home of Mary Green, 280 S. 29th Street, a two story brick row house, located in the middle of the block. I drove Official Vehicle No. 124, a white 19YR–20 V.W. Beetle. SDI–007 rode with me. Agents Smart and Watson drove in Official Vehicle No. 98, a black 19YR–4 Dodge van. We all arrived at approximately 2:15 p.m. Agents Smart and Watson established a surveillance in the van. The van has observation ports in the rear section through which Agents Smart and Watson were able to see the front of Mrs. Green's home.

At approximately 2:20 p.m. the surveillance was established. SDI–007 and I walked to the front door of Mrs. Green's home. SDI–007 knocked, and a female, approximately age 24, answered and greeted SDI–007. I learned later that this was Mrs. Green. Mrs. Green said to SDI–007, "Hi Snake, is this the one?" SDI–007 replied that I was. Mrs. Green also greeted me and told me not to worry that Charles was here. She directed SDI–007 and me to a room she referred to as the den and left us. The defendant, Charles Williams, was sitting in a chair watching a daytime TV game show when we entered. The den is on the first floor of the house in the rear. It measures approximately 10 x 14 and contains 2 chairs, a sofa and a TV console.

SDI–007 introduced me to the defendant as "Jimmy" and told the defendant I was the one who wanted to buy some stuff. The defendant said he thought he could take care of me and produced Exhibit No. 1 from under his chair. I asked him how much, and he replied, "it will cost you one G." I responded that all I could handle was $900, and the defendant paused and said, "O.K. I'll go for it this time." I gave the defendant $900 in official funds, and he gave me Exhibit No. 1. I opened the package, stuck my finger in it, removed it with some white powder on it and then lightly licked the powder on my finger. I told the defendant it was "cool" and then asked if I could call him for more. He said that he wasn't sure because he was going to be out of town for a while.

SDI–007 and I left at approximately 2:35 P.M. and returned to DEA Headquarters, 6th and Arch Streets, Morena. A field test I performed for cocaine hydrochloride was positive. (A field test consists of putting a very small portion of the powder in a vial and adding acid. If the mixture turns dark, the test is positive.) I paid SDI–007 $150.00 for his assistance in the buy.

On December 9, 19YR–1, the defendant was arrested by me and Agent Smart. The defendant declined to make any statement.

SDI–007 and I have worked together in the past on seven different cases. On each occasion in which a successful purchase of narcotics was made, which was in five of our cases, he was paid. The amount he was paid depends on the size of the buy, the danger involved, and the importance of the defendant as a drug dealer. He has received a total of $2,850.00 from me and other DEA agents in 18 months. If a buy is not made, he is not paid.

SDI–007 was convicted in Morena Superior Court on September 5, 19YR–2, of possession with intent to distribute heroin. Because of an agreement to cooperate and assist DEA, he was sentenced to five years probation on a plea bargain. I believe that he has two prior convictions in state court for use and possession of heroin. He is unemployed, and has no permanent residence. When I need him, I look for him at Chubby's Pool Palace, 10th and Diamond Streets, Morena.

As standard procedure with all informants, I instructed SDI–007 on the law of entrapment, i.e., that he could ask someone if they had drugs for sale but that he couldn't talk or force them into it.

On December 21, 19YR–1, I traveled to New York by automobile with Exhibit No. 1, and I delivered it to the DEA Laboratory. I gave it to James Winslaw. It was in a sealed envelope, and the seal was unbroken. After the buy on December 1, 19YR–1, I had placed Exhibit No. 1 in the sealed envelope and personally sealed it. I then placed it in the DEA evidence vault where it remained until December 21, 19YR–1. The seal was unbroken when I removed it from the vault, and the vault log showed that the vault had not been opened in the interim. The log is a book we keep in the vault. If it is opened, office regulations require that an entry must be made. Only two people know the evidence vault combination, DEA Supervisor David Broom and Regional Director Robert Bond. Broom opened the vault for me each time, and I personally looked at the log and saw no entries. Both have told me that the vault was not opened in the interim.

On December 29, 19YR–1, I returned to New York by automobile and went to the DEA Laboratory. James Winslaw returned Exhibit No. 1 to me from the DEA Laboratory vault. He told me that he had maintained custody of it at all times except to give it to a DEA chemist for analysis (see DEA Form 7). After analysis, he said that it was returned to him, and he maintained it under his personal supervision in the laboratory vault. Only Mr. Winslaw and Laboratory Director Philip V. Pinto know the vault combination, and both told me that their vault log showed that Exhibit No. 1 had only been removed once on December 28, 19YR–1, for analysis. Chemist Maria Carrubba told me that she had maintained continuous personal custody of Exhibit No. 1 after it was given to her by Mr. Winslaw. It never left her possession until she returned it to him.

After accepting delivery of Exhibit No. 1, I returned it directly to DEA Headquarters in Morena, where Mr. Broom and I put it in the evidence vault. It has remained there since December 29, 19YR–1. I will deliver it to Government counsel on the day of trial.

Charles Williams has a prior conviction for possession of cocaine. Specifically, on April 8, 19YR–2, he was convicted by a jury in Morena. He was sentenced on May 12, 19YR–2 to 18 months, and served one year. The word on the street has been that he is dealing cocaine, and the narcotics squad has picked him up twice since he got out. Both times, unfortunately, he was clean.

I have spoken to Agents Smart and Watson. They told me that they saw SDI–007 and me enter Mary Green's house on December 1, 19YR–1 at 2:22 p.m. They saw us leave at 2:36 p.m. and return to the V.W. and drive away.

My entire report consists of Documents 1, 2 and 3. The time, 3:40 p.m., in my statements must be a typographical error.

SDI–007 has worked with me since September 5, 19YR–1, the date of his plea agreement. His cooperation is part of the plea agreement, but it is not a condition of probation.

Dated: January 2, 19YR

/s/   James J. McNally

James J. McNally

DEA Special Agent's Report: Statement of James J. McNally

On December 1, 19YR–1, at approximately 3:40 p.m. I purchased a quantity of purported cocaine hydrochloride from one Charles Williams at 280 S. 29th Street, Morena, for $900.00 in official funds. I made the purchase in an undercover capacity as a man named "Jimmy," and was accompanied by SDI–007.

On December 9, 19YR–1, at approximately 7:00 a.m. I arrested Charles Williams at 280 S. 29th Street, Morena. He made no statements.

DEA Special Agent's Report: Statement of SDI–007

On December 1, 19YR–1, I went to the home of Mrs. Mary Green, 280 S. 29th Street, Morena, with Special Agent James J. McNally of the DEA. While there, Agent McNally, posing as a man named "Jimmy" purchased a package of purported cocaine from Charles Williams, the boyfriend of Mary Green. Agent McNally paid Williams $900.00 for the purported cocaine. Agent McNally paid me $150.00 for my assistance.

1. NAME OF SUBJECT OR ESTABLISHMENT	2. IDENTIFIER	3. FILE NO.
Charles Williams	UC-228-45	54213

| 4. HOW OBTAINED (Check) ☒Purchase ☐Seizure ☐Free Sample ☐Lab. Seizure ☐Money Flashed ☐Compliance Sample (Non-Criminal) ☐Unknown ☐Other (Specify) | 5. WHERE OBTAINED (City, State/Country) Morena, El Dorado | 6. DATE 12/1/YR-1 |

7. Exhibit No.	8. ALLEGED DRUGS	9. MARKS OR LABELS (Describe fully)	APPROX. GROSS QUANTITY		12. Purcha Cost
			10. Seized	11. Submitted	
1	Cocaine	A clear cellophane bag containing a white powder with a yellowish tint. Further wrapped with a ripped plastic bag with the words shower cap on it and the picture of a Playboy bunny on it.		35.9 grams	$900 O.R Expen

13. WAS ORIGINAL CONTAINER SUBMITTED SEPARATE FROM DRUG ? ☒ NO (Included above) ☐ YES (If Yes, enter exhibit no. and describe original container fully)

REMARKS:

Exhibit #1 was purchased by Agent McNally from defendant Williams in Morena at approximately 2:30 PM on 12/1/-1 for $900.00.

| 14. SUBMITTED BY *(signature)* John J. McNally | 15. APPROVED BY (Signature & Title) DEA Supervisor David Broom |

LABORATORY EVIDENCE RECEIPT REPORT

16. NO. PACKAGES	17. RECEIVED FROM (Signature & Date) 1/99 82	18. TITLE
19. SEAL ☐Broken ☒Unbroken	20. RECEIVED BY (Signature & Title) James Winslow	21. TITLE 12/21/YR-1

LABORATORY ANALYSIS / COMPARISON REPORT   12/29/YR-1

22. ANALYSIS SUMMARY AND REMARKS   Drug Code 9042

Ex. #1 - was found to contain cocaine hydrochloride, starch and magnesium sulfate.

Gross weight 36.46 gms.   Net weight 10.07 gms.   Qualitative analysis by GC, quantitative assay by UV.

23. Exhibit No.	24. Lab. No.	25. ACTIVE DRUG INGREDIENT (Established or Common Name)	WEIGHT PER UNIT ANALYZED			29. TOTAL NET	30. RESERVE
			26. Strength	27. Measure	28. Unit		
1	2730	Cocaine Hydrochloride	73.2	percent		7.37 gms	9.53 gms.

31. ANALYST (Signature) Maria Carrubba	32. TITLE Maria Carrubba, Chemist	33. DATE COMPLETED 12/28/YR-1
34. APPROVED BY Philip V. Pinto	35. TITLE Laboratory Director	36. LAB. LOCATION New York

DEA Form (Jan. 1979) - 7   Previous editions are Obsolete.

RESUME OF PHILIP V. PINTO

Address: DEA Regional Laboratory
1414 New York Plaza
New York, NY 10004

Present Position: Director

Education: Bachelor of Sciences, 19YR–17
Washington University
St. Louis, Missouri

Additional coursework in Chemistry
New York University
New York, NY

Forensic Chemistry Short Course
F.B.I. Academy
Quantico, Virginia

Publications: "Forensic Chemistry for the F.B.I. Agent," F.B.I. Law Enforcement Bulletin, p. 125 (Dec. 19YR–8)

"The Analysis of Marijuana by Gas Chromatography/Mass Spectrometry," Identification Digest p. 477 (June 19YR–6)

"Quantitative Analysis of Suspected Cocaine Samples," The Practical Prosecutor p. 23 (Sep. 19YR–2)

Courtroom Experience: I have testified for the prosecution as an expert on drug identification in over 200 cases. I have also testified as an expert for the government in civil forfeiture actions in over 30 cases.

Case file A–8

GREEN v. ANDREWS

This is a civil action. The defendant, Mr. Andrews, is a 42–year-old lawyer. He is a general practitioner, and lives in the state of El Dorado.

Mr. Andrews drew up a will for Ms. Theress, a wealthy widow. Ms. Theress has died, and the will has been found ineffective because it was *improperly executed*. The intended beneficiary of the will, Mr. Green, sues Mr. Andrews for legal malpractice. Mr. Green claims that Mr. Andrews was negligent, especially in his supervision of his law clerk, Ms. Lunda, to whom Mr. Andrews assigned the execution of the will. Mr. Andrews denies any liability.

During the trial, the plaintiff will call an expert, the law clerk who conducted the will execution, and the beneficiary. The defendant will testify as well as an expert for the defense. It is stipulated that when she worked on Ms. Theress' will, Ms. Lunda was a law clerk certified under the relevant provisions of the El Dorado Business and Professions Code. Under the El Dorado Business and Professions Code, an attorney may be held legally liable for malpractice by a certified clerk in his or her employ only if the attorney is guilty of some personal negligence, including incompetent supervision of the clerk.

WITNESS FOR PLAINTIFF: EXPERT

WITNESS STATEMENT OF PLAINTIFF'S EXPERT—ELISE VON HECKMANN

I have long had a private practice in estate planning, wills and trusts, and related tax matters in El Dorado. I also teach a trust/wills course at El Dorado State University. Due to my expertise in the area I am often called as an expert witness. In the past ten to fifteen years I have testified approximately 30–40 times. My current fee is approximately $3,000.00 plus travel expenses.

A few months ago Mr. Green contacted me and asked me to consult and testify in his malpractice suit against Mr. Andrews. Initially, when I interviewed Mr. Green, he told me that he was asked by Ms. Lunda, Mr. Andrews' student intern, to sign as a witness on Ms. Theress' will. Ms. Theress is the decedent. Immediately I knew there was a problem, since Mr. Green was the sole beneficiary under this will.

Mr. Green told me that he arrived at the law office of Mr. Andrews on April 16, 19YR–1. Mr. Andrews was on vacation. Ms. Lunda asked him to sign the will as a witness. Things happened quickly and were somewhat confused. Mr. Green doesn't recall if Ms. Theress had signed her will when he signed it. He believes that Ms. Theress had already signed by the time he arrived. He doesn't recall seeing her sign anything.

I briefly spoke with Ms. Lunda. She doesn't clearly recall the sequence of events when the will was executed. Ms. Lunda told me that she observed Ms. Theress sign her will and believes that she signed the will herself as a witness in Ms. Theress' presence. Then, Mr. Green arrived at the office and signed the will.

After speaking with Mr. Green and Ms. Lunda, I reviewed a copy of the will. It appears to be a straight-forward, simple will.

The El Dorado Probate Code section 6112(b) requires two witnesses for a valid will. The code states that if a beneficiary under a will is one of the two necessary witnesses, there is a rebuttable presumption of undue influence. If the beneficiary cannot rebut the presumption, he or she will take only a intestate share. In this case, since Mr. Green is not a blood relative of Ms. Theress, he would receive nothing under the will via intestate succession if the will were improperly executed.

The Probate Court has found the will to be invalid due to improper execution. A valid execution requires two witnesses who witness the testator signing her will after she has acknowledged the document as her will. Both witnesses must see the testator sign the will. From the facts, it is clear that Ms. Theress signed her will in front of Ms. Lunda, who then signed. However, Mr. Green apparently never saw Ms. Theress sign the will. Since only one of the two witnesses actually witnessed the execution, and the El Dorado Probate Code requires two witnesses, the will is patently invalid.

As stated above, a validly executed will requires two witnesses. At common law both witnesses must be disinterested, i.e. they must not be beneficiaries under the will. If one or both witnesses are beneficiaries, then the will is invalid. However, modernly, interested witnesses do not invalidate the will itself. The only issue that arises from an interested witness signing is whether the beneficiary will take over the will.

Mr. Andrews has committed several acts which constitute malpractice. First and foremost, he improperly delegated too much authority and responsibility to his student intern, Ms. Lunda; after all she was only a law student and had little knowledge of wills. Mr. Andrews wasn't present to supervise her, since he was on vacation. He never even took the time to instruct her on the basics of executing a valid will. Furthermore, he allowed a sole beneficiary to be a necessary witness. Finally, he failed to ensure the proper execution of Ms. Theress' will having two witnesses sign the will in the presence of the testator.

In my opinion, if Mr. Andrews had competently handled Ms. Theress' will, Mr. Green would have inherited the estate as the testatrix wished. Presently the will is invalid and Mr. Green will receive nothing unless he can somehow rebut the presumption of undue influence.

ELISE VON HECKMANN

Work History:	Private Practice in estate planning, wills and trusts, and tax matters.
	Expert Witness in 30–40 wills related cases; 19YR–16–19YR–1.
	Law Professor at El Dorado State University Law School teaching wills and trusts course; 19YR–5–19YR–1.
	Lecturer for El Dorado Continuing Education of the Bar for estate planning and wills; 19YR–7–19YR–1.
	Chairperson of State Bar Planning Commission, Estate Planning Division working on revising the Probate Code; 19YR–3–19YR–1.
Educational Background:	University of California at Los Angeles, California Juris Doctorate, 19YR–20, magna cum laude
	Certified Public Accountant, 19YR–22
	Claremont McKenna College, Claremont, California B.A. 19YR–25 in Business and Accounting
Recent Publications:	Numerous small publications for CEB
	Discount Attorneys: Are You Buying a Malpractice Suit?, *Business Week,* 19YR–3.
	Taking Title in Community Property vs. Joint Tenancy: Step-up Basis for Capital Gains Tax Upon Sale of Property, *El Dorado Law Journal,* 19YR–4.

Married Womens' Presumption: Evening the Score a Little, *Women Lawyer's Journal of Reform,* 19YR–6.

Other Publications upon request.

WITNESS FOR PLAINTIFF; ADVERSE WITNESS
STATEMENT OF LAW CLERK, MS. LUNDA

My name is Kathryn Lunda. I have just started my third year of law school at Marathon Law School. I am twenty-three years old and divorced. I began to look for work in a law office after completing my second year classes. Mr. Andrews (an alumni of Marathon) placed a notice on the daily board at school advertising for a law clerk. I knew immediately that this was the job for me. It paid $9.00 per hour and I could do much of the work at home or in the school library. I removed the notice and saved it. It is attached to this statement.

I was in desperate need of job when Mr. Andrews' notice appeared. My husband had just left me; he cleaned out our bank accounts and disappeared. He took everything but a few pieces of furniture and the two dogs. We were married for three years. Things were pretty good at first; but after I started law school, the marriage went down hill fast. My husband reappeared two months after I started work with Mr. Andrews to serve me with divorce papers and tell me that he had a new girl friend.

The day I saw Mr. Andrews' notice, I called his office and arranged an interview for the following day. When I went for my interview, the first person I met was Stella, Mr. Andrews' secretary. Stella told me about the office and treated me really well. She told me that Mr. Andrews was also going through a divorce and this common ground between us would help me land the job.

Soon Mr. Andrews asked me into his office. He asked me numerous questions about wills. I frankly told him that this was a subject which I had little interest. Although I had taken the class, I did poorly-just barely passing with a D+. I did not tell Mr. Andrews what my grade was. I assumed that if he had wanted to know, he would have asked. I really needed that job. Although usually I would not talk about my personal life in an interview, I decided to take Stella's advice and bring up my marital problems in the conversation. After mentioning that I was going through a divorce, that is all that Mr. Andrews talked about. Thirty minutes later, the job was mine. He never asked me what my grade in Trust, Wills was. He did insist that I take the examination for certification as a law clerk under the Business and Professions Code. I passed the examination the next week.

Initially, the job was great. Soon, though, Mr. Andrews began to depend on me more than I expected. One day, just before Mr. Andrews was going on vacation, he asked me to handle the execution of Ms.

Theress' will. He hurriedly gave me a few instructions which I jotted down, and told me that Stella was always available to help.

On the day before the execution, I was nervous. I couldn't remember whether a will required one or two witnesses. Since Stella didn't know either, I faxed a memo to Mr. Andrews. The memo is attached to this statement. Mr. Andrews answered the memo by telling me to look it up in a text in his office. He did say that witnesses were important. I really meant to look it up; but just as I received the fax, Ms. Theress arrived at the office. Ms. Theress was impatient and did not want to wait around. Under the circumstances, I believe I did the best that I could.

I could not remember whether some states required one witness and other states two witnesses or whether all states required two witnesses and some states three. Anyway when Ms. Theress arrived, Stella was out of the office. Consequently, I was the only available witness. I executed the will and signed as a witness. I read Mr. Andrews' fax again and noticed that it said that witnesses are important. From that I decided that at least two must be required. I asked Ms. Theress if she knew anyone who could be a witness. She said that her fiancee Mr. Green would be glad to come down and sign. I phoned Mr. Green and told him my problem. He was sympathetic and came right down. I had Mr. Green sign the will as the second witness.

I meant to tell Mr. Andrews about my decision; but by the time he returned, Ms. Theress had already died.

WITNESS FOR PLAINTIFF

STATEMENT OF ROBERT GREEN

I'm a successful lawyer and businessman in El Dorado. I travel around a lot. That's how I met Elise Theress. We intended to marry (my sixth time, her second), but she passed on before we could.

I should have known that something would go wrong with the will when I found out that Andrews was in charge of drawing the will. He's hated me ever since I stole his girlfriend in college. I swear he's been trying to get back at me ever since. In my opinion, Andrews is incompetent, and has been ever since I've known him.

I also know that Kathy Lunda, the intern to whom Andrews assigned the execution of the will, was having some stressful personal problems. I know her personally, and sometimes we talk. Kathy's a sweet girl. I wouldn't even have known there was a new will, by the way, unless she'd mentioned it to me. She didn't know what to do about it . . . something about an execution. I guess she wasn't getting much guidance from Andrews. I told her I'd help her in any way I could. On 4/16/YR–1 she called me to ask me to be a witness. I was happy to help out.

In my opinion, Andrews gave Ms. Lunda scant instruction on how to handle a will. He probably gave her far too much responsibility for someone still in law school. I wouldn't put it past Andrews to have intentionally botched this will just to ruin my life. He's like that.

Ten years ago I was disciplined by the El Dorado State Bar. I pled guilty to a disciplinary charge of depositing clients' funds in my personal account. I was placed on probation for a year, successfully completed the probation, and was then permitted to resume the active practice of law. When I joined the firm I currently work with, the hiring partner asked me some vague questions about my record with the bar; and as I seem to recall, I neglected to mention the disciplinary incident.

WITNESS FOR DEFENDANT

STATEMENT OF DEFENDANT

I am a hardworking, general practitioner. I have worked in El Dorado for the past 15 years, after my graduation from Marathon Law School, an unaccredited law school. I've had no complaints from any clients until now; people seem to like me and they can tell I work hard. I'm financially comfortable. My home life, however, is less than perfect. I've just gone through a divorce. I was in the midst of it when Ms. Theress came to me to draw up her will.

I advertise low rates for writing wills. My rates are substantially lower than any other lawyer's in the area. I do this in the hope of encouraging additional business.

I was surprised when Ms. Theress came to me. I knew she had lots of money; she's got a fortune from her deceased parents, and her late husband did pretty well, too. I assumed that, having so much money, Ms. Theress would already have a satisfactory will, and I told her so. I admit I was curious about why she would want to change her will at her age (about 70 yrs., I'd guess). She told me that she wanted a brand new, and very simple, will. She said she had met a wonderful young man, and she wanted to leave everything she owned to him. When she told me who this "wonderful young man" was, I almost had a heart attack: Bob Green. I know Bob from college. We had many of the same classes there. He was always competing with me. You could say that we were old rivals. He always struck me as dishonest and greedy. I was the presiding judge in a college Honor Court proceeding which found Green guilty of cheating on an examination. He always said that he would eventually get even with me. I suspected that he was taking advantage of Ms. Theress. Since Ms. Theress seemed to be madly in love with him, I decided against voicing my suspicion to her.

Ms. Theress insisted on changing her will, however, and I agreed to draw her a new will. I told Ms. Theress that my extremely low rates meant that a less complex will would be available, and that I wouldn't be able to devote my full time and attention to any will I did draw for her. She told me that didn't bother her. She added that she imagined it would be a simple will, as she was leaving everything she owned to Mr. Green.

Bob Green had done a little legal work for her-odds and ends, nothing substantial. The reason she didn't have Green do the will, she explained, is that while he was a lawyer, she knew he did mostly bankruptcy work, not wills and estates.

She told me that she was confident that I'd do just fine. Since she didn't look too healthy, even though I was going on vacation soon, I immediately drafted her will. I assigned the execution of the will to Ms. Lunda, my law clerk. Ms. Lunda is in her second year at the local law school, and she seemed to me to be a competent, well-adjusted clerk. (I hired her only after she passed the B & P Code certification examination. When I phoned the State Bar to check on the results of the examination, they told me that she had attained one of the highest scores ever in the four-year history of the examination. Needless to say, I had a lot of faith in Ms. Lunda.) I was in a bit of a rush, but she seemed to understand what I needed her to do. I told my secretary to make herself available to Ms. Lunda should she need any help.

While I was on vacation, Ms. Lunda faxed me a note on 4/15/YR–1. The note stated that she wasn't quite sure how to proceed with the execution. The next day I faxed her back a note telling her to do some legal research, but that it was important that she get witnesses to Ms. Theress' signing the will. I have the note with me, if you want to see it. While I was on vacation, I got a lovely note from Ms. Theress, thanking me for being so kind and competent. Well, she didn't exactly use those words, but that was the gist of the note. I also have that note with me.

When I returned from vacation, I found that Ms. Theress had passed on. Evidently she'd had some sort of cancer. Only then did I discover that Ms. Lunda had asked Mr. Green to witness the signing of the will. I also discovered that Mr. Green, that money-grubbing con man, had sued me. He's got a lot of nerve. He's an attorney. I half-suspect that he witnessed the will with full knowledge that his witnessing would invalidate the will. He's that sick.

DEFENSE WITNESS: EXPERT

TRANSCRIPT OF TESTIMONY

[All parties must stipulate that this is an accurate transcript of the testimony given by J. Kenneth "Ken" Henderson, an expert witness for the defendant, in a sworn deposition and that at the time of trial, the deponent is unavailable]

Attorney (A): Now that you've been sworn, Mr. Henderson, would you please state your full name for the record, and spell your last name?

Witness (W): My name is Jaques Kenneth Henderson H-e-n-d-e-r-s-o-n.

A: What is your occupation, sir?

W: Primarily, I am an associate dean and a professor of law at the Franklin School of Law. I teach courses in Marital Property, Real Estate Law, and Estate Planning.

A: You said you were "primarily" a law professor. What else do you do for a living?

W: I make self-help home videos. "Ken Henderson's Do–Your–Own Will," "Ken Henderson's Do–Your–Own Trust." Also, I've written three articles for various legal journals, and I co-authored the wills outline for the Bar Winners bar review course.

A: Could you elaborate a little bit about those articles?

W: I've written articles for various publications, including one for the Stanford, Tulane, and University of Chicago Law Reviews.

A: Please tell us about your educational background.

W: I graduated with a B.S. in Egyptology from Harvard University in 19YR–20. I got my J.D. from Duke in 19YR–16, and an MBA from the University of Michigan in 19YR–10.

A: Please tell us about your professional background.

W: I worked for a law firm as an estate planner from 19YR–16 until 19YR–11. I was working on my MBA from 19YR–11 to 19YR–10. I then worked for a consulting firm from 19YR–10 until 19YR–6. I was a professor at Marathon Law School from 19YR–6 until 19YR–1. In 19YR–1, I was hired as a professor by Franklin.

A: What, if any, honors or awards have you earned in your profession?

W: Well, in 19YR–4, I was a semi-finalist for the Gulliver Honorarium, which is a research fellowship grant given by the university to one professor each year. Unfortunately, I did not win.

A: Have you ever testified as an expert witness?

W: Yes. Four times before. Each of those cases involved an attorney accused of malpractice in the drafting of a will.

A: How much were you paid to testify in those cases?

W: My fee varied somewhat with the complexity of the specific issues involved. The lowest fee I have received was $2500. The highest was $4000.

A: How much are you being paid to serve as an expert in this particular case?

W: $3850.

A: Do you have any specific knowledge or training in the area of malpractice in the making of a will?

W: I have done research and have written one article regarding that subject. I would say that based on my education, my experience as a lawyer myself and as a professor, and my academic research, I have specific knowledge concerning malpractice in the preparation of a will. The answer to your question concerning special training, I suppose, is no-no more than any other law school graduate.

A: Now, I'd like to ask you some questions about this case. Have you seen the instrument in question?

W: Yes, I have. I have had a copy in my possession for some months now. I examined the original briefly—for a few minutes—last week. I think what you really want to know is how well acquainted I am with the contents of that instrument; and on that matter, I would say that I am extremely well acquainted with the contents. It helps that I have a virtually photographic memory.

A: That's O.K. A simple description will be fine.

W: It was a fairly standard will. It complied with the local wills statute in terms of both its structure and its dispositions in almost every respect. In a typical situation such as this, in order to be valid, the will must be signed by the testator. The signing of the will must take place in the presence of at least two witnesses who understand what it is they are witnessing. Those witnesses must be legally competent in terms of age and mental fitness, and they must be disinterested, which is to say that they are not named as beneficiaries in the will. Really, the only problem with the will in this case was the fact that it was witnessed by one of its beneficiaries. To use the vernacular, that's a definite no-no.

A: Would you please explain what you mean by a "no-no?"

W: Well, El Dorado law requires that a valid will must be witnessed by at least two disinterested persons. Interested witnesses are simply legally nonexistent. Therefore, this will was, in the eyes of the law, witnessed by only one person. Ergo, the will is invalid. If a third person had witnessed the will who was not designated to receive something pursuant to the will, it would still be valid. Unfortunately, this Ms. Lunda apparently lacked the requisite experience to add a "safety witness." An attorney with some expertise would have known better than to let Mr. Green serve as a witness. The most cautious attorneys use three or four witnesses instead of only two-just to be safe. It's unfortunate that Mr. Andrews was not personally on hand when this will was executed. All of this mess would have been avoided.

A: So are you saying that for a lawyer to allow a will to be witnessed by one of the beneficiaries amounts to malpractice?

W: Well, you're asking me to draw a pretty quick conclusion, there, but I would say that when the person is explicitly named as a beneficiary like this, and the will is signed right in front of the lawyer, it probably would be, yes. That would fall below the standard of reasonable practices in the legal community. A competent lawyer would either know the law, seek the advice of a lawyer who did, or tell the client to go somewhere else. But, but, but—Mr. Andrews was not even at the office when this will was executed! It was his assistant who failed to uphold the minimum standards of competent lawyering.

A: So it was Ms. Lunda who committed malpractice—not Mr. Andrews?

W: Yes. That is true. Now, Mr. Andrews could—theoretically—be held liable for negligence in allowing the relatively inexperienced Ms. Lunda to handle this will. He was not, however, negligent in doing so.

Ms. Lunda was a certified clerk. The state bar association has declared her fit to perform such tasks. This error was so fundamental that it was unforeseeable to Mr. Andrews. He should not be held accountable here.

A: What is your basis for that opinion?

W: My general sense of what would be reasonable conduct for an attorney under circumstances such as these. I believe that Mr. Andrews did perform his duties in a reasonable manner. That's really the only way to determine whether someone is liable for malpractice or not. He did not commit malpractice in my opinion.

A: But that's only your opinion, Professor?

W: True. But, dear sir, under circumstances such as these, nothing more is required to preclude any actions against Mr. Andrews.

NOTICE MS. LUNDA FOUND ON MARATHON
COLLEGE OF LAW DAILY BOARD

LAW CLERK WANTED

Independent third-year student wanted to work in small active practice.

Interest in general practice a must.

Much work can be done at home or here in your library.

Twenty hours per week; $9.00 per hour.

Call: Mr. Andrews: 555–1212

FAX FROM MS. INTERN

Mr. Andrews:

I expect that Ms. Theress will be here in the morning. I am pretty confused about the witness requirements for the execution of the will. Please advise. Stella says hi.

    Kathy Lunda

LAST WILL AND TESTAMENT OF ELISE THERESS

I, Elise Theress, a resident of El Dorado, declare that this is my last will and testament.

FIRST: I do hereby revoke all Wills and Codicils I have previously made.

SECOND: I am a widow. I have no close relatives. I have no servants or pets of any sort. I do, however, have one very dear friend, Robert Green.

THIRD: Therefore, I do hereby leave my entire estate, including all of my property, both real and personal, to Robert Green.

FOURTH: If Robert Green fails to survive me, I leave my entire estate to the sitting vice-president of the United States at the time of my death, whoever that may be.

FIFTH: I nominate the SECOND BANK OF EL DORADO to serve as the executor of this will.

I subscribe my name to this Will on this, the 16th day of April, 19YR–1, in El Dorado.

_____ Date: _____
Elise Theress

On the date hereinbelow stated, the undersigned witnessed Elise Theress sign this document, at which time Ms. Theress advised the undersigned that this was her last will and testament.

_____ Date: _____
Kathryn Lunda

_____ Date: _____
Robert Green

FAX

April 16, 19YR–1

Dear Kathy:

Do research before having Ms. Theress sign the will. Look up proper execution procedures in El Dorado Continuing Education of the Bar Wills volume sitting on my desk. Remember witnesses are important. Good Luck.

Mr. Andrews

April 20, 19YR–1

Dear Mr. Andrews:

Thank you for squeezing me into your busy schedule. That was very nice of you. I really appreciated your inexpensive rates and handling my case so quickly.

Sincerely,

Ms. Theress

Case File A–9

BURSON v. AUSSIE TRANSCONTINENTAL

Table of Contents

CASE SUMMARY:

Plaintiff, Ted Burson is bringing a civil action for conspiracy to interfere with parental custody and negligent infliction of emotional distress against Defendant Aussie Transcontinental. Plaintiff is suing for $500,000. Plaintiff was married to Susan Dave Burson, who died two years ago in a car accident. They had two children together, Tabatha, who is presently eight, and Robbie who is six. Susan's parents, Hazel and Philip Davis are Australian, but have lived in El Dorado for many years.

Defendant is Aussie Transcontinental, a sole proprietorship owned by Greg Trundale. It is a small airline company that is controlled by Greg Trundale and his family. Greg Trundale has been a close family friend of Hazel and Philip Davis for many years. He has often provided the Davis family with free airfare and tickets to Australia.

Hazel and Philip Davis have been seeking custody of their grandchildren, Tabatha and Robbie. On May 10, 19YR–1, they attempted to kidnap Ted Burson's children by taking them to Australia on Aussie Transcontinental. Ted Burson believes that the abduction of his children could have been successful only if Aussie Transcontinental knew about it and assisted his in-laws. Aussie Transcontinental denies any part in the Davis' abduction of Ted Burson's children.

STIPULATIONS

1. Following Susan's death, Hazel and Philip have attempted to get custody of Tabatha and Robbie. The Court has ordered that pending determination of the custody suit, the children were to remain with their father but that the grandparents could have custody every other weekend.

2. In violation of this custody order, Hazel and Philip attempted to take the two children to Australia on May 10. They have been found guilty of kidnapping in violation of El Dorado Penal Code section 207 and 208. They flew on Aussie Transcontinental flight 410 from Morena to Jackson and then made a connecting flight from Jackson to Sydney on flight 1076 on the same airline. They have stated on the record during the sentencing phase of their criminal trial that they never would have tried to take Tabatha and Robbie without the advice of their good friend, Greg Trundale.

3. The parties have stipulated as to the value of Aussie Transcontinental, which is approximately 11 million dollars. However, Aussie Transcontinental recently purchased three new planes with borrowed money and consequently has debt to the amount of 9 million dollars. Thus, the net value of Aussies Transcontinental is 2 million dollars.

4. Carol Johnson is unavailable to provide testimony during trial. She recently suffered a severe stroke and is currently hospitalized.

5. The parties have agreed to bifurcate the issues of liability and damages.

SUMMARY OF LAW

1. El Dorado Civil Code Section 49 states that "the rights of personal relations forbid (a) the abduction or enticement of a child from a parent, or from a guardian entitled to its custody . . ."

2. Family Code Section 3010 states that "(a) the mother or an unemancipated minor child and the father . . . are equally entitled to the custody of the child. (b) if one parent is dead, is unable or refuses to take custody, or has abandoned the child, the other parent is entitled to custody of the child."

3. The El Dorado Supreme Court follows *Rosefield v. Rosefield* 221 Cal.App.2d 431, 34 Cal.Rptr. 479 (1963).

JURY INSTRUCTIONS:

1. PATTERN EL DORADO 13.95—Conspiracy

A conspiracy is an agreement entered into between two or more persons with the intent to agree or conspire and the intent to commit [a] wrongful act[s], namely _____. Membership or participation in a conspiracy to commit a wrongful act is by itself not a basis for liability. Conspirators have no liability unless a wrongful act is committed by one or more of the conspirators in furtherance of the conspiracy causing another party to sustain injury, damage, loss or harm. The liability of any alleged conspirator to plaintiff shall be determined by you in accordance with the following instructions:

2.   13.86—Conspiracy—Joint Responsibility

Each member of a conspiracy is liable for each act and bound by each declaration of every other member of the conspiracy if such act or such declaration is in furtherance of the object of the conspiracy. The act of one conspirator pursuant to or in furtherance of the common design of the conspiracy is the act of all conspirators.

A member of a conspiracy is not only liable for the particular wrongful act that he knows his confederates agreed to and did commit. But he is also liable for the natural and probable consequences of any wrongful act of a co-conspirator to further the object of the conspiracy, even though such act was not intended as a part of the agreed upon objective and even though he was not present at the time of the commission of such act.

3.   13.87—Proof of Express Agreement Not Necessary

The formation and existence of a conspiracy may be inferred from all circumstances tending to show the common intent and may be proved in the same way as any other fact may be proved, either by direct testimony of the fact or by circumstantial evidence, or by both direct and circumstantial evidence. It is not necessary to show a meeting of the alleged conspirators or the making of an express or formal agreement.

4.   13.88—Association Alone Does Not Prove Membership in Conspiracy

Evidence that a person was in the company of or associated with one or more other persons alleged or proved to have been members of a conspiracy is not, in itself, sufficient to prove that such person was a member of the alleged conspiracy.

5.   13.91—Conspirators not bound by act or declaration of non-conspirators

The act or declaration of a person who is not a member of a conspiracy is not binding upon the members of the conspiracy, even if the act or declaration tended to promote the object of the conspiracy.

6.   13.92—Commission of Act in Furtherance of a conspiracy does not itself prove membership in conspiracy

Evidence of the commission of an act which furthered the purpose of an alleged conspiracy is not, in itself, sufficient to prove that the person committing the act was a member of such a conspiracy.

7.   13.93—Joining the conspiracy after its formation

Every person, who joins a conspiracy after its formation, is liable for and bound by the acts done and declarations made by other members in pursuance and furtherance of the conspiracy, before and during the time that he is a member of the conspiracy.

8. 13.97—Determination of Admissibility of Co–Conspirator's Statements

Evidence of a statement made by one alleged conspirator other than at this trial shall not be considered by you as against another alleged conspirator unless you find by preponderance of the evidence that:

1. other evidence independent of the statement has established the existence of a conspiracy to commit a wrongful act at the time such statement was made;

2. the statement was made while the person making the statement was participating in the conspiracy and that the person against whom it was offered was participating in the conspiracy before and during that time; and

3. such statement was made in furtherance of the objective of the conspiracy.

The word "statement" as used in this instruction includes any oral or written verbal expression of the nonverbal conduct of a person intended by that person as a substitute for oral or written verbal expression.

9. 12.80—Negligent Infliction of Emotional Distress

The plaintiff also seeks to recover damages based upon a claim of (negligent infliction of emotional distress) (willful violation of statutory standards). The elements of such a claim are:

1. The defendant engaged in (negligent conduct) (a willful violation of a statutory standard);

2. The plaintiff suffered serious emotional distress;

3. The defendant's (negligent conduct) (willful violation of statutory standards) was a cause of the serious emotional distress.

Serious emotional distress is an emotional reaction which is not an abnormal response to the circumstances. It is found where a reasonable person would be unable to cope with the mental distress caused by the circumstances.

10. 12.72—Emotional Distress—Defined

The term "emotional distress" means mental distress, mental suffering or mental anguish. It includes all highly unpleasant mental reactions, such as fright, nervousness, grief, anxiety, worry, mortification, shock, humiliation and indignity, as well as physical pain.

11. 12.88—Damages—Emotional Distress

If you find that plaintiff is entitled to a verdict against defendant, you must then award plaintiff damages in an amount that will reasonably compensate plaintiff for all loss or harm, provided that you find it was (or will be) suffered by plaintiff and was caused by the defendant's conduct.

STATEMENT OF PLAINTIFF, TED BURSON

My name is Ted Burson, and I am 32 years old. I currently live at 55 Pamela Drive, Morena, El Dorado. I grew up in San Francisco; that's where my foster parents live. I lived in their home from the time I was placed in their care by Child Protective Services. I have not seen my natural parents since I was five. My foster parents are good people but are very "traditional." When I was young, we didn't really get along; they felt it was important for kids—teenagers even—to have lots of structure. They were always very watchful about where I went. We used to fight a lot about how late I could come home and who I could hang out with. With all that goes on in a city like San Francisco, that can be a real drag.

Once I graduated from high school, I moved out because I wanted to be free to party. I had some trouble every now and then with the law. Once, I was convicted for possession of drugs when I was at some party. During this time I worked off and on. I worked on the docks for a while and bussed tables. Once I even worked as a used car salesman. I was really good at that, I guess all that practice talking my way out of trouble paid off. I tried college for awhile, but didn't like it so I quit. However, while I was there, I really got into writing. I worked some on the school newspaper. Since then, I have been able to support myself by writing human interest stories for newspapers. I also wrote a book about seven years ago. It's titled *One of the Fosters*. It's about what a child experiences in the foster care system. On occasion, I have been asked to be a guest lecturer in various schools to share my experiences.

About nine years ago, I met Susan. Man, she was great. She worked in advertising at this newspaper I was doing some work for. She was really quiet, but so sweet. I think that was what drew me to her in the first place. She had grown up on a farm near Woodland. She had a pretty strict upbringing as well. We used to joke around and compare "war stories" about how uptight our parents were. I think that's why she liked me initially, I was full of surprises and spontaneity. Well, we got married pretty quick. I met her parents, Hazel and Philip, a month or two before the wedding. Her parents never really liked me much. They thought I was the wrong kind of man; and, though they never said anything to Susan, I could tell that she felt that they were disappointed. Once Susan and I had Tabatha and Robbie, Hazel, Phil and I would often argue because they did not like my views on parenting. Susan and I agreed that kids should be allowed to explore the world at their own speed. Hazel and Phil felt that our kids were out of control as they would do or say anything they wanted whenever they wanted. To my outrage, Susan's parents told me on various occasions that they felt that I bullied Susan into agreeing with my methods.

Two years ago, Susan and I moved to Morena. One night Susan was riding her bike over the Richards Blvd. Overcrossing when she was hit by a drunk driver. She died two days later. At that time my children were 6 and 4, and I just couldn't deal with raising them on my own on top of losing my Susan. So I left them with Susan's parents ,since they lived nearby in Woodland. I would be the first to admit that they took pretty good care of my kids. They enrolled Tabatha in kindergarten and Robbie in preschool. My kids did always love the farm, with all the animals and such. Since Susan's death, things have been hard. For example, I have been struggling to make the mortgage payments on my house.

After about a year, I had gotten my feet on the ground financially and wanted to get my kids back. Hazel and Phil told me that they were suing for custody, and of course I contested. The Court ordered that Tabatha and Robbie stay with me until the whole matter was settled. However, the Court also held that since my kids had lived with their grandparents for a year, they could have visitation for two weekends a month. We usually worked it out to be the first and third weekend of every month. Sometimes, if they wanted to take my kids on a trip for a week, I would let Hazel and Phil take them then instead of letting them have the weekend visit. In February last year (19YR–1), Susan's parents didn't bring back my kids one Sunday afternoon. I was frantic. They told me that they thought I had given them permission to keep my kids for a week. I don't know why they thought I had agreed to that. After that experience, I told them in no uncertain terms that they could not have any more week long visits.

Hazel and Phil were from Australia originally, and still have family there. My kids have gone to Australia with them many times before, usually once a year, during the summer. Prior to when they stole my kids, I had heard from Tabatha that they were thinking of taking my kids on a trip to Australia in late May. Once I heard this, I promptly called Susan's parent and said "No!" I know that Hazel and Phil are good friends with the president of an Australian airline, Greg Trundale. In fact, every time my kids had gone to Australia, they had flown free on that same airline, Aussie Transcontinental. Tabatha had told me that reservations had been made for them with "Uncle" Greg. Tabatha often calls Mr. Trundale "Uncle Greg." So I called up the defendant and told him in no uncertain terms that Hazel and Phil were not allowed to take the kids to Australia by Court order. I also told him that my kids could not fly at any time without my written authorization. I told him that I was mailing him a copy of my handwriting so that there would be no confusion. (Unfortunately, I forgot to send the copy.) In any event, Turndale said that he didn't know anything about reservations being made for Tabatha and Robbie. He also said that I should speak with the reservations desk if I had any questions at that time and that he would talk to me later because he was in a big rush. He never called back.

On May 10 Hazel and Phil took my kids without my consent to Australia. After all the smoke cleared and Hazel and Phil were found guilty of kidnapping, I discovered that they were able to get the kids on the plane because they had changed the kids' names on the passenger list. Obviously, I never gave any written consent. I think that defendant had to have known and played a part in it or else. How could it get by that the kids' names on the passports and passenger list didn't match? I can't see any other explanation.

STATEMENT OF PLAINTIFF'S WITNESS, BONNIE BLAIR

My name is Bonnie Blair and I live at 3231 G Street in Morena. I am 28 years old. I work as a reporter for the Morena Bee. I am unmarried.

I first met the plaintiff while working at the Morena Bee, we both were writing articles for the paper at that time. I have known the plaintiff for about three years, though in the last year we have gotten pretty close. We're not romantic or anything like that any more, but we have spent quite a lot of time together and have recently gone out a few times. I really adore his kids. Ted sure does have some pretty different ideas about parenting. He believes that kids should pretty much do what they want. For example, if the kids stay out late, then so be it, they will learn what is best for them in their own time. Sometimes this means that he doesn't even know where his kids are all the time. Even though it's a very different philosophy, it seems to work. I think his kids are very well adjusted and mature for their age. They sure seem to be happier than most kids that age I know.

Last May, on the tenth, Ted called me and told me that his kids were missing. He was so worried and frantic that I must admit, it was hard to understand him. I understood that he was sure that Hazel and Phil had taken them away. He kept screaming that he was sure that "That bastard Greg must have helped them out somehow. I was worried. I had never seen Ted so distraught."

After the story broke, I decided to help Ted out and investigate. I mean, what else are friends for? The next morning I went to Aussie Transcontinental. I could tell that this story was "big" because there were peace officers around and lots of press. In fact, only the press and officers were allowed into the inner offices of Aussie at the airport. Even though I wasn't assigned the story, I still used my press badge to get in. The airport security guard didn't specifically ask whether I was working on a story, and I certainly didn't volunteer the information. I might have bent the truth a little, but it was in a good cause. I figured that if I got any leads, my boss would appreciate them. So I went in and asked to speak with Greg Trundale. I was told by the public relations representative that he was not in. I asked when he was last in and was told that he had unexpectedly left town and wasn't due back for a few days. I overheard one of the reporters mention a "Carol Johnson" so I poked around until I discovered where she was working that day. She turned out to be a flight attendant for Aussie Transcontinental.

When I approached her, I noticed that she was reading clippings from the newspaper about the kidnapping. She seemed real nervous.

When she noticed me, she tried to compose herself. I asked her if she had ever heard of Tabatha or Robbie Burson. She said that she knew the names, but only because the police had asked her about them already. She said that she had been shown a picture of the two kids and remembered seeing and talking to them on a flight leaving America for Australia a few days earlier. She said that she was one of the attendants on that flight. She stated that she had spoken with the grandparents on occasion throughout the flight. She thought that they had seemed like really nice people.

We spoke for quite awhile. We discovered that we had attended the same high school and had some mutual friends. She seemed to trust me for some reason, and I sensed that I could take advantage of that. I made up that we were also sorority sisters. I figured that I'd hit her up for some sensitive info once she settled down a bit. At one point she got sort of quiet and was looking around suspiciously. She let out a big sign. When she was convinced that we were alone, she remarked that she wanted to speak "off the record" because she could lose her job if she "spilled the beans." I told her I'd keep our conversation confidential. She said that she had been standing next to the fellow flight attendant and noticed that the other attendant had not compared the names on the passports with the passenger list. She thought that the other flight attendant must have been ordered to do that because it was a "firm" company policy to ensure that passenger identification match the names on the airline passenger list. She explained that this rule was even more demanding than the FAA's regulations. In fact, when she was at Aussie's flight attendant academy, the instructors had repeatedly stressed this rule. She further explained that in her entire ten years with Transcontinental, she had never seen a flight attendant mix up that rule.

STATEMENT OF DEFENDANT, GREG TRUNDALE

My name is Greg Trudale and I am 62 years old. I live at 656 Glen Drive, in Jackson, El Dorado. I am the President and owner of Aussie Transcontinental where "Kuala-ty is everything!" I pride myself on the quality of my airline. I started Aussie Transcontinental from scratch when I was a young man. I am planning to retire in a few years and my two children are going to take the reins. They have been working for me for since they left college. My company wouldn't be where it is today without their ideas and hard work. We are a smaller airline, with about 100 employees, and we have quite a family atmosphere. Since we are such a small company, it is easy for information and gossip to get around. One of the effects of being a small airline is that one big accident, or lawsuit even, could wipe us out financially. I self-insure for a lot of risk. As such, I am extremely careful about compliance with federal regulations. We dot every *i* and cross every *t*. I have developed a reputation for excellence in the business community. I am known for being an upstanding businessman. I have won various awards honoring my integrity in my profession.

My company scrupulously adheres to the regulations of the FAA. Because of the rising concern regarding the abduction of children, we have strict safeguards regarding the transportation of children. Children, or the adults that accompany them, must prove their identity before getting on any plane. We usually use passports for international flights, but domestic flights are a bit more difficult as children do not generally have photo identification. We require that children have adult supervision. If they are traveling alone, then our highly trained flight attendants are to provide supervision. We also like to see that the children are related to their adult companions in some way, but of course this is not the law. However, I have an informal rule that if the adults are not related to the kids, I ask that the flight attendants keep an eye on the kids. It is absolutely mandatory that the passenger names on the passenger manifests perfectly match the names on the passports. There are absolutely no exceptions—period, end of sentence.

I first met Phil and Hazel Davis when Phil and I were in the MBA program at Sydney University. I have been good friends with them both ever since. I know they consider me to be part of their family, especially since my wife died about ten years ago. Our families often get together on holidays and vacations. Because of our close relationship, and as Phil and Hazel still have family ties in Australia, I have often given them free tickets on their trips to Australia. It's just my way of saying thank you for all that they have done for me over the years.

Because of our close relationship, I know all about Ted—especially how he just dumped his kids with Susan's parents after she died, and how little contact he had with them. I couldn't believe that. People suffer loss, I certainly did when my wife passed away, but that didn't mean I flaked out on my kids. His decision meant that his kids essentially lost two parents instead of one. I have seen, at family gatherings, how little control and guidance he provides his kids. Half of the time, he doesn't even know where his kids are. He just says "they'll find their way home." He seems to be a dad only when he wants to be one. He is just so irresponsible. He's clueless as a parent. He sometimes forgets to pick up his kids or remember when they have games or sporting activities. I do believe in parents getting second chances and that they should be the ones to raise their own kids, but I also support Hazel and Phil's attempt at custody. They are very loving and would provide a stable environment for Tabatha and Robbie. As far as I'm concerned, Ted is a worthless hippie. Frankly, he disgusts me.

I have had discussions with Hazel and Phil regarding their desire to obtain custody of Tabatha and Robbie. I knew that they were allowed to have custody of the kids every other weekend. I also knew that on occasion, Ted would let Hazel and Phil have custody for a week so that Tabatha and Robbie could go on vacation with their grandparents. Once, I think there was some sort of misunderstanding where Hazel and Phil took the kids on vacation for a week when Ted didn't want his kids to go anywhere. Hazel and Phil told me that Ted wasn't going to let them take their grandkids on trips anymore. They said later that Ted was simply really angry and was just blowing hot air.

In April of last year Phil and Hazel told me how they wanted to take the kids to Australia to visit their relatives. They mentioned that they were going to talk to Ted about it. They were hoping to get his permission but were worried that Ted wouldn't allow it. In fact they were nearly positive he wouldn't allow it. I reassured them that Ted would certainly let the kids visit their relatives as he had done so every year. They then asked me if I could help them make the travel arrangements. I said sure. I asked them when they were planning to go. They said sometime in late May. I told them to leave the dates that they wanted to depart on with my secretary and that I would take care of everything.

I didn't think anymore about it until a few days later when Ted called me. He asked me if any reservations had been made for his children. I said no, and as far as I knew at that time, that was true. He then said that he didn't want his kids flying anywhere on my airline without his written authorization. He said something about sending me a sample of his handwriting. As far as I know, he never bothered to follow up. That's just so typical of Ted. I then told him to talk to my secretary because I was in a big rush to get to a board meeting.

A few days later Phil and Hazel called me and told me that there was a sudden change in plans and that they wanted to fly out on May 10. I mentioned Ted's comment regarding written authorization. Phil told me that he would "handle" it if I would "take care" of things on my end. I told them that I was going on vacation myself around that time, but I gave him my cell phone number so that if there were any problems, he could get hold of me directly. I then directed his call to my secretary and instructed her to "pull out all the stops and do whatever was necessary to help Phil and Hazel out."

I did not know that they didn't have Ted's permission. If I had known, I never would have allowed them to fly on one of my planes. After all, it's against the law. They're my friends, but I'm not crazy enough to risk my whole business over this. I wouldn't have anything left for my own kids. I'm not that stupid.

STATEMENT OF DEFENDANT'S WITNESS, MARGE BROWN

My name is Marge Brown and I live at 219 Washington Drive, in Fairfield. I have my B.S. degree *cum laude* from Michigan State. I chose MSU because it has a number of degree programs directly related to the airline industry. I am 42 years old and am married. I have three children. My husband works as a electrician. We have been married for 17 years. We are very active in our church and believe that the success of our marriage is due in part to our faith. I formerly worked for United Airlines. I have worked for Aussie Transcontinental for 15 years as a flight attendant. A couple of years ago, I was promoted to Supervising Flight Attendant. Now on all flights, I am in charge of all the attendants on the flight. I have a clean record; I have never had any problems with the law, not even a speeding ticket.

Flight 410 was a flight that went from Morena to Jackson. One of my duties as a flight attendant is to check in passengers. On such domestic flights, children do not need identification. Identification is required only on international flights. However, if a passenger has an ultimate destination that is out of the country, then usually when they initially check in, we request to see their passports. This is not required however, so long as passengers show their identification before they board the plane that will take them to their international destination. Checking identification is a voluntary company policy that is tougher than both industry and F.A.A. standards.

My duties also include ensuring passenger safety. It is important, in the event of an emergency, that I help passengers remain calm at all times on the flight. If any passengers are upset, I am to try to help calm them down so that the comfort of other passengers is maintained.

I was Supervising Flight Attendant on flight 410, the flight in question. Before the flight departure, Hazel and Phil Davis were introduced to me by Mr. Trundale's secretary. She then whispered in my ear that I was under "direct orders from the top" to make sure that Mr. and Mrs. Davis and their grandchildren reached their destination. The fact that the secretary walked down to tell me to keep watch over the Davises meant that Mr. Trundale was personally involved. I struck up some small talk with the Davises and found out that they were old friends of Mr. Trundale.

Prior to departure, I noticed that the younger boy was crying, but it is not unusual for children to cry before a flight. I bent down to talk to the young boy and asked him what was wrong. He kept saying "I want my daddy." I asked him what his name was and he said "Robbie." I thought that was odd because the passenger list said it was Steven. When Mrs. Davis heard this, she said that Robert was his middle name. She seemed just a bit nervous when she said it. After she spoke with me, she seemed pretty stern with the child.

Mr. Davis gave me a handwritten note purportedly from the children's father that stated 'I authorize Phil and Hazel Davis to take my children Steven and Angie Burson to Australia.' It was signed "Ted Burson." I asked Mr. and Mrs. Davis to produce the children's passports and they said that they would do that when they checked onto the plane that was actually taking them to Australia. I asked them what flight number that was and they said flight 1076. When I pulled up the flight manifest for 1076, I didn't immediately see the names Steven Burson or Angie Burson. I must admit I wasn't looking very closely because right then I was in a bit of a rush. At the same time that one of the other flight attendants, I think it was Ms. Johnson, had started to board passengers, some safety equipment had malfunctioned, and I had to look into the problem right away.

The bottom line is that while it is conceivable that we could have done more, our airline's procedures exceed both the industry and F.A.A. requirements. If someone is determined to circumvent safety and check procedures, they can often find a way—no matter how rigorous the procedures are. We're only human, but we do just about the best job in this respect in the whole industry.

Memorandum

To: Aussie Transcontinental
Employees
From: Greg Trundale, CEO

Date: February 7, 19YR–2
Rr: The Transportation of
Children

AUSSIE TRANSCONTINENTAL

GUIDELINES

Regarding the Transportation of Minors (Effective immediately)

In addition to the regulations promulgated by the Federal Aviation Administration, it is the policy of Aussie Transcontinental that all employees actively follow these guidelines.

1.   Identification is required for all minors traveling on international flights. Proper identification includes passports, student identification cards, driver's licenses, state identification cards, and any other form of photo identification.

2.   Identification is to be requested for all minors traveling on domestic flights. Proper identification includes passports, student identification cards, driver's licenses, state identification cards, and any other form of official photo identification.

Signed:

Case File A–10

WINTERS v. OCEANSIDE COLLEGE

Factual Background:

Rebecca Winters is a 19 year old female who is currently attending Oceanside College as a freshman. She was the star of her high school volleyball team. She currently participates on an intramural volleyball team organized around residence dormitories at Oceanside College. In the intramural league there are several other females who excelled in volleyball in high school. She is the plaintiff and has brought suit in state court alleging discrimination on the basis of sex with respect to intercollegiate athletics in violation of the state's Equal Athletic Opportunity Act. Specifically, she alleges that the Defendant, Oceanside College, discriminated against her by sanctioning fewer sports for females than for males and by refusing to sanction an official collegiate female volleyball team. Plaintiff claims that the refusal to sanction female volleyball denies her access to athletic scholarship funds and to showcase her talent for later opportunities in the field of athletics.

Applicable Law: (Evidence and Civil Procedure will be governed by federal law.)

The jurisdiction (the State of El Dorado) has recently enacted the Equal Athletic Opportunity Act which is similar to federal Title IX. Its provisions are as follows:

1. No person shall, on the basis of sex, be excluded from participating in, be denied the benefits of, or be subjected to discrimination under any education program or activity at any educational institution.

2. An educational institution must effectively accommodate the interest of both sexes in both the selection of sports and the level of competition, to the extent necessary to provide equal athletic opportunity.

3. If a particular sex is statistically underrepresented in athletics at an educational institution, the interest of the underrepresented sex must be fully accommodated unless the institution in question can demonstrate a history and continuing practice of program expansion.

4. "Effective accommodation" means that if an institution sponsors a team for members of one sex in a non-contact sport, it must do so for members of the other sex under the following circumstances:

    a. The opportunities for members of the excluded sex have historically been limited;

    b. There is sufficient interest and ability among the excluded sex to sustain a viable team and a reasonable expectation of intercollegiate competition for the team; and

    c. Members of the excluded sex do not possess sufficient skill to be selected for a single integrated team or to compete actively on such a team if selected.

5. "Educational institution" means all schools including, but not limited to, kindergartens, preschools, elementary and secondary schools, junior and community colleges, four-year colleges, universities and graduate and professional schools.

Plaintiff witnesses:

Rebecca Winters—plaintiff, freshman at Oceanside College

Huey Short—Athletic Director at UED San Marino

Defense witnesses:

Patricia Vasquez—Dean of Students at Oceanside College

Richard Maxwell—Athletic Director at Oceanside College

Documents:

- Witness Statements
- Letter to the editor of the Oceanside College Student Newspaper, written by Plaintiff
- Informal sign-up sheet for females interested in forming a collegiate volleyball team
- Letter written by Patricia Vasquez to Board of Director of Oceanside College providing update on developments regarding women's sports offerings
- Athletic Department Budget for Oceanside College's men's and women's teams
- Letter from attorney for the estate of an Oceanside College alumni announcing gift left to Oceanside College for athletic purposes

Witness Statement of Plaintiff, Rebecca Winters:

My name is Rebecca Winters, and I am a freshman at Oceanside College. I am 19 years old. I live in Oceanside in the dorms now, but my family is from San Diego. I was born in San Diego and have lived there until I left for college.

Except for one problem, I am very happy at Oceanside College. When I was considering colleges, it was very important to me to choose a school which was not only strong academically, but which also had good placement into graduate physical therapy programs. Oceanside has a good pre-med type program and has a great record of getting graduates into physical therapy school. Today, admission to physical therapy school is just as competitive as medical school. So far, I've received very good grades, maintaining better than a "B" average. I'm proud of my grades, and I study hard to maintain them. If I can keep my grades up, I'll have a very good chance of getting into a physical therapy graduate program. Next to being a physical therapist, my other great passion is volleyball.

The only problem is that Oceanside College does not have an official collegiate women's volleyball team. Oceanside does have intramural volleyball, but I can't receive scholarship funds from participating on an intramural team. A scholarship would really help my family, because my parents do not have much extra money for my education and they do not want me to work during school. Further, if I can't play on a competitive team, no one in the volleyball world will ever see my talent.

I was the star of my high school volleyball team, and I know that I would have a real shot in the professional volleyball arena if scouts could only see me play. I was on the all-star team my senior year of high school and was an honorable mention to the All–American team. Even if I don't make it as a professional player, I would at least have the opportunity to make contacts and meet people in the industry. Perhaps I could connect with a professional team that would be interested in me as the team's physical therapist.

The attitude of certain administrators at Oceanside with regard to a women's volleyball team has made me really mad. When I first started asking questions about it, I was told that there just wasn't any way that the school was going to put any more money toward women's sports. That's ridiculous to me. I bet a women's volleyball team would draw in more people that some of the men's sports on campus like the old golf team and probably swimming too. Volleyball is also one of the least expensive teams for a school to maintain. I tried to talk to Mr. Maxwell, but it took me weeks to get an appointment with him. I told him that there was some real interest on our campus for a women's volleyball team, and he basically told me that he didn't think volleyball was a real sport, "especially a women's team". If fact, I remember exactly what he said because it infuriated me. I was so mad I couldn't see straight. He told me, "Listen, honey, there is no way I am going to sponsor a team where women just hit a ball over a net."

It was right after this meeting that I wrote a letter to the editor of the Oceanside College newspaper. Maybe it wasn't the smartest thing to do; the wording might have been intemperate. But at least it got people's attention. Right before writing the letter, I read an article about how women's athletics are on the rise. I read the article on the subject, "Prime Time Players" in the February 10, 1997 issue of *Newsweek*. If Oceanside gave me a chance to showcase my talent, I could have some of the opportunities that the women in the article have. I don't like to brag, but I am certainly the best female player in our intramural league, although there are some girls in it who give me a run for my money. I am leading the league in both kills and service aces. Our team is undefeated. I organize all of our practices, and I am constantly explaining various serving and spiking techniques to my teammates. We don't have formal coaches for the intramural teams, but most of the guys who coach men's basketball played volleyball in college and they've helped out by holding informal clinics for our intramural teams. One of them expressed interest in coaching the women's team if I can get one established. I know some of the other girls on the team would be interested in playing on a sponsored collegiate team. Many of them played in high school as well.

Except for the administration, most people have been very supportive of what I've been trying to do. Nationwide that's true. A lot of students can't understand why Oceanside invests so much money into our mediocre basketball team and football team, but won't give us any money for volleyball. Some people have asked me why I came to Oceanside if I knew there was no women's volleyball team here. A few schools in the area recruited me pretty heavily, but their academic records were not impressive. I really don't think I should have to pick a school with lesser academic credentials just to have access to a volleyball team. School and sports both are important to me, and men certainly don't have to make a choice between the two, because every good school has plenty of athletic opportunities for men. Why should I expect less?

Rebecca Winters

Dated: July 1, 19YR–1

Witness Statement of Plaintiff's Witness, Huey Short:

I am Huey Short, Athletic Director at University of El Dorado at San Marino. I am 45 years old. I have a bachelor's degree in physical education and a masters degree in sports management. I attended undergraduate school on an athletic scholarship in men's water sports at University of El Dorado at Merced. I am married. My wife's name is Eleanor, and I have one daughter, Ariel, seven years old.

University of El Dorado at San Marino is in the same conference as Oceanside College. I actually started out at Oceanside College twenty years ago in 19Yr–21. I taught English at Oceanside College and coached the club teams for men's volleyball and water polo for five years. Shortly before I left in 19YR–11, those club teams were elevated to official intercollegiate varsity status. The formation of club teams is often the first step in creating new sports programs. Unfortunately, schools with established varsity teams consider these teams to be good for only one thing: warm-up. I left Oceanside College ten years ago to take a position as Assistant Athletic Director at University of El Dorado at San Marino.

Since coming to University of El Dorado at San Marino, I have been active in adding female competitive sports to our varsity program. The Chancellor has made it a priority here. After arriving, I started and coached women's volleyball and water polo from club team to official varsity status. I was promoted to Director of the Athletic Department three years ago. I'm glad to be working at a major university like University of El Dorado, San Marino, which enrolls 45,000 undergraduate students. Since we were established in 1920, we have graduated many successful alumni and alumnae who continue to donate substantially to our academic and athletic endeavors. We are well known regionally and nationally for our fine men's football and basketball teams.

I am aware of the fact that some of the schools in the conference have been slow in adding new sports to the roster, especially women's sports. Most of these schools claim a lack of funding. Though it is true that bigger schools attract more alumni funding for sports, the flip side is that the sports like water polo, volleyball, soccer and golf do not cost very much to maintain. For instance, last year we spent approximately $35,000 each on women's and men's volleyball; $60,000 each on women's and men's soccer; $12,000 each on women's and men's water polo; and $40,000 on men's golf. These figures include coaching, facilities, travel and office support. At the University of El Dorado, San Marino, women's and men's volleyball has shown a profit in each of the last five years, while the men's golf team has shown a net loss. Further, the men's football team pretty much breaks even, and that's even after we upped the concession prices by 25% two seasons ago.

The truth is a lot of the coaches in the conference are chauvinists from the old days when females just wore skirts and held pom poms. It's hard for them to take female demands for equal access to competitive athletics seriously. They think females are here to pay tuition and look pretty. This is especially true of some of the smaller, private schools that have a more traditional or elite alumni roster. I never actually heard anything said while I was at Oceanside because I was not really considered one of the "old boys inner circle." But every one knows that they consider themselves keepers of the status quo. At Oceanside, you constantly heard references to "traditional values." Every year we sponsor a regional conference on women's athletic programs. Representatives from public and private colleges and universities from across the nation are in attendance. Not once has Oceanside sent a representative, even just to sit and listen to the growth and success stories. Last year I even personally phoned Rich Maxwell, the Athletic Director at Oceanside, to invite him to attend. I can't remember his exact words, but he said something about not having the funds and that what money they did get was not going to be wasted on making girls more competitive. Rich alumni are always leaving that school money, so I know that the real reason for their lack of interest is tradition. The old school just doesn't think girls should be competing in certain "non-traditional" sports.

One of the reasons I left Oceanside College was because I wanted to be in an environment that fostered change. I am into adding new sports programs for women and non-traditional sports for men as well. Like I said, most of these programs do not cost much relative to men's football and basketball, and the change in these young ladies is evident from their increased confidence on the field and in the classroom. As I see it, women of today have to compete in a world very different from the one that allowed them only to be mothers. I have a daughter. Athletic competition is just as crucial to her development as the three R's.

Huey Short

Dated: July 2, 19YR–1

Witness Statement of Defense Witness, Richard Maxwell:

My name is Richard Maxwell. I am 48 years old, and I'm the Athletic Director at Oceanside College. Oceanside College is a private four-year university with a student body of 20,000. Prior to my promotion to A.D. in 19YR–3, I was the head coach of the Oceanside football team for ten years. I have two daughters, Corrine who is 17 and Marcia who is 14. Corrine plays soccer for her high school team. Marcia runs track. They both played soccer when they were younger, and I coached their teams for a while.

The number of men on our collegiate teams is slightly more than double the number of women on such teams. I realize there is a statistical disparity between men's and women's sports at Oceanside, but there simply is not enough money in the athletic budget to support an additional team right now. Creating a women's volleyball team would place the football program in serious jeopardy. Because football is very popular and draws more alumni support and ticket revenues than all other sports, as a practical matter my hands are tied.

We recently received $45,000 from the will of alumnus, Ray Allen. Allen was probably the greatest wide receiver Oceanside ever had. He regularly attended football, baseball, and basketball games. He knew the football program was experiencing some financial difficulties these last four years. Ray expressed a desire to help the football program and other men's teams, but held a very firm, old-fashioned view with regard to women playing competitive sports. He told me that he was leaving money to the athletic program, and I promised that it would be used as he "wished." However, the actual language of the will designated simply "the Oceanside athletic program" as the beneficiary.

Mr. Allen's views about women in sports are outdated, but typical of many, if not most, of our alumni. I tried to explain to Miss Winters when she came to my office, but the young woman has a real chip on her shoulder and didn't seem to understand that I'd like to help, but my hands are tied because of our dependence on alumni donations. I told her that "... many of the alumni do not think of you young women as athletes." Our financial situation is really tight right now, and we simply do not have the money to establish another team—for men or women. Even putting Allen's wishes for the money aside, his gift is not even enough to cover our most dire needs for the existing teams.

Our football team desperately needs new uniforms and we hope to also replace some of our most worn-out helmets and other equipment. Our university attorneys told us point blank that we could be held liable if the boys sustained any injuries due to the defective equipment. Uniforms alone will cost approximately $370 per player and we have 100 players. Below is a rough estimate of the cost of our most needed items:

Helmets	$125	each
Pants	$60	each (need both home and away colors)
Jerseys	$60	each (need both home and away colors)
Socks	$12	per pair
Shoes	$30	per pair
Training Supplies	$20,000	

Oceanside College has a skeleton football staff. We want to hire another assistant coach (even then we'd still have one less coach than any of our competitor schools in the league). All of our competitors enjoy a bigger budget and average two more coaches per team. Money is tight here. We recently had to drop men's golf. Investing our money in football is our best chance to increase the revenues to the athletic department. Perhaps when our football program is up to speed with its competitors in a few years, it will generate enough to support a volleyball team.

Richard Maxwell

Dated: July 1, 19YR–1

Witness Statement of Defense Witness, Patricia Vasquez:

My name is Patricia Vasquez. I am the Dean of Students at Oceanside College. I have a Masters Degree in Education from Stanmore University and I received my undergraduate degree in Political Science from Nills Women's College. I headed the NOW chapter at Nills. I have maintained my NOW membership since then. I am 45 years old, and divorced with a 14 year old daughter, Maribel. I live at 444 Pembrook Road in Carmel, El Dorado.

I grew up with two older brothers, one younger brother, and my mother and father. Although I was the only girl, my dad taught me that with a good education and effort, I could be anything that I wanted to be. My family is one of the premier wine growers in the central valley, so I learned early how to be organized and effective through sweat and hard work. Having three athletic brothers, I incorporated athletics as a part of my life structure. I was a gold and bronze medalist in the 100 meter and 200 meter relays on the swim team in college. I have instilled these same ideals in my daughter, and this year, as a freshman in high school, she made the girl's swim team.

My father and grandfather both attended Oceanside College. It was established in 19YR–68 as a men's college for academic excellence. Initially, the only sports we offered were men's swimming, an equestrian team, and rugby. In 19YR–43, we began admitting women. Today 47.5% of our student body is female. We rely heavily on alumni support for our programs, both academic and athletic. Though tuition at our school is higher than at state schools, we pride ourselves on drawing a special class of young people who believe in the traditional values that America and Oceanside College were built upon. We try to serve as a guardian of those values.

I am fortunate enough to get to know much of our student body through my duties as Dean of Students. I have heard some of the students grumbling about the lack of a women's volleyball team. I understand their desire to play volleyball, but it simply isn't possible to support a women's team at this time due to financial constraints. There are a number of other opportunities available to women at Oceanside and quite frankly I believe their accusations are unwarranted. If we want to build up athletic programs, we must first bolster the ones that are already established by attracting talented athletes. We can't tear down the programs we already have. We've made progress. We recently added women's water polo. Once we increase our alumni support, we can try to create still more new programs. We receive only limited federal funding through grants. To a much greater extent than at state schools, it is our alumni support that keeps us going. Many of our esteemed alumni have earmarked their contributions for the programs in effect now and Oceanside could not risk losing these or additional funds by transferring them to new programs. It is hard enough to continually get the alumni support that we need now, without trying to create whole new programs that would require additional support.

While I realize that girls today want to compete in all sorts of sports programs, they have options available at Oceanside. Although Oceanside does not have a women's volleyball program now, the Board of Directors is considering it. I sent a memo to the Board to voice the concerns of some of the students who came to my office. As a matter of fact I know it was reported that after the Board's last meeting, the local paper quoted me as saying, "If girls want to engage in non-traditional sports, they should go to a state school." This was a misquote. I would never say something like that. I believe that I was speaking about the fact that women usually have more athletic opportunities at one of the larger public universities. For better or worse, the Board has delayed taking final action on this issue pending the outcome of this lawsuit.

Patricia Vasquez

Dated: July 2, 19YR–1

Letter to the Editor of Oceanside College Student News

Remember the old saying, "If you can't say anything nice, don't say anything at all"? Well, I think there must be some exceptions to this rule and after what I just went through with Athletic Director Maxwell, I am sure this is one of those occasions. I can't believe his sexist attitude and the students of this school have a right to know about it.

As many of you know, I've been pushing to get the school to recognize a women's volleyball team. Everyone I've talked to supports me in this. After he avoided me for weeks, I finally got an opportunity to speak to Athletic Director Maxwell; it was a raving waste of my time. I had to sit and listen to a school director telling me that he thought women's sports were a joke. In fact, he said that we were "quite fortunate" that Oceanside had four school-sanctioned women's teams.

The student body should be outraged to attend a school where a Neanderthal like Athletic Director Maxwell is in any position of power. What is so ironic is that Mr. Maxwell's true baby, the football team, isn't worth the Astroturf they play on. He is just interested in making sure money isn't taken away from the team that he used to coach. But no one even goes to the football games anymore because we always lose. Money isn't the problem with that team; it's the lack of talent.

Talent is something that we can promise with a women's volleyball team. Anyone who attends the intramural volleyball games knows that Oceanside has plenty of talented, spirited female volleyball players. If Oceanside gave us a chance, we could be one of the most competitive volleyball teams on the West Coast. But, the only way we'll ever have a volleyball team is if Athletic Director Maxwell realizes that his precious football team just isn't as popular as he thinks. In his dreams!

What I propose is that every student do one of two things. For those of you who actually attend the football games, stop going in a show of support for women's athletics. Maybe Maxwell will get the message when his precious men's athletic program goes belly up. For those of you who don't go to the football games, go to Mr. Maxwell's office and tell him you support women's volleyball. Thanks for your help.

An irritated female athlete.

Rebecca Winters

MEMORANDUM

TO: Oceanside College Board of Directors

FROM: Patricia Vasquez, Dean of Students

DATE: March 1, 19YR–1

RE: Women's Sports at Oceanside College

CC: Rebecca Winters

     Richard Maxwell

Recently a number of students came to me expressing the concern that there are limited resources and opportunities for women in sports at Oceanside. Several students voiced their desire to create additional sports teams for women. It seems as though a number of them especially want to make the women's intramural volleyball team a full fledged varsity sport. I explained that forming new varsity sports teams costs a lot of money, and that there are other opportunities for them to join teams or enjoy other athletic endeavors at Oceanside. Furthermore, I told them about how some of the funding is currently set aside for specific programs, and that raising additional money is a lengthy and difficult endeavor. I have attached a copy of the 19YR–2—19YR–1 budget. Nonetheless, I promised the students that I would bring their concerns to your attention since I feel there is some merit to their argument (as well as it being commensurate with my responsibility to the student body).

In addition to these meetings, I kept track of student comments via an informal survey that I conducted. Most of the women I talked to were lukewarm at the prospect of creating a volleyball team; the vast majority of them were far more concerned about investing more funds in the academic program. I assumed that the more information you had available to you, the easier your decision would be as to what course of action you will pursue. Thank you for your time and attention to this matter. I will be happy to forward your response on to the student body. Please feel free to contact me if you have any additional questions or concerns.

Sincerely,

Patricia Vasquez
Dean of Students

OCEANSIDE ATHLETIC DEPARTMENT
TEAMS BUDGET 19YR–2—19YR–1

MEN'S TEAMS:		**WOMEN'S TEAMS**	
Football	$270,000	Soccer	$ 50,000
Baseball	$150,000	Swimming	$ 25,500
Basketball	$100,000	Water Polo	$ 10,500
Swimming	$ 25,000	Slow Pitch Baseball	$ 85,000
Totals	**$545,000**		**$171,000**

All Team Total: **$716,000**

PICKFORD AND WOODBRIDGE

400 Ivy Towers

Sacramento, El Dorado 95400

916–222–3300

January 10, 19YR–1

Ms. Beane Countberg

Department of Finance and Accounting

Oceanside College

Oceanside, El Dorado 95600

Dear Ms. Countberg:

We regret to inform you that Mr. Ray Allen passed away in March of this year. Mr. Allen was a 19YR–58 graduate of Oceanside College. Our law firm has been retained to represent the probate estate of the late Mr. Ray Allen.

As you know, Mr. Allen was a proud alumnus of Oceanside College having graduated as one of the greatest wide receivers Oceanside ever had. We are informed that some of his all-time records still stand. Mr. Allen was a big contributor to Oceanside's football program throughout his professional career as a wide receiver for the Saint Louis Reds and later as part owner of that franchise. His philosophy was that to make a good professional football team, the best talent must be developed at the high school and college levels. For that reason, his last will and testament bequeaths $45,000 each to the athletic departments of the high school and college he attended.

The process of probating Mr. Allen's estate is a complex matter. However, the will has been accepted into probate. You will receive notification prior to the time disbursements to donees are to be made. In the interim, if you have any questions, please do not hesitate to phone our office directly.

Sincerely,
Ivana Pickford, Esq.

STIPULATIONS

It is stipulated for purposes of this Mock Trial, that the following facts have been properly introduced into evidence and may be relied upon by both parties in the presentation of their case:

1. Oceanside College has a student body of 20,000 students; 47.5% of the students are female. Oceanside College was founded in 1930 as a men's college. In 1955 the college began accepting women under an equal opportunity policy.

2. Oceanside College is a private four-year educational institution and receives federal and state funding.

3. University of El Dorado at San Marino has a student body of 45,000 students; 50% of the students are female. University of El Dorado at San Marino is a state school and receives federal and state funding.

4. Oceanside College and University of El Dorado at San Marino are in the same athletic conference. Oceanside is a division C school; University of El Dorado at San Marino is a division B school. Of the ten schools in the conference, five sanction an official women's volleyball team and two schools sponsor club teams. Three schools, including Oceanside College, do not sanction or sponsor a women's volleyball team.

5. After a diligent search, Ms. Vasquez cannot locate the survey referred to in the final paragraph of her memo to the Board of Directors.

6. The letter from Ms. Pickford is authentic and is an original. Mr. Maxwell read the letter in February 19YR–1.

7. The determination of whether there has been an "effective accommodation" within the meaning of that expression in the Equal Athletic Opportunity Act is a jury question.

Appendix B

As in the case of the files in Appendix A, all counsel have access to all the documents in these Case files. The parties have waived any evidentiary privileges that would otherwise attach to the documents.

A good faith rule applies to the trials of these Case files. Counsel and witnesses may draw reasonable inferences from the facts and even add facts to fill in obvious gaps in the fact situation. However, please do not add facts that would materially change the balance of the fact situation. If you are in doubt whether it is proper to add a particular fact, ask your instructor.

The instructor will announce the time allowances for the various stages of the trial. As a general proposition, any time consumed in making and answering objections will be charged against the side questioning the witnesses at the time. However, if the other side believes that the opposition's objections were frivolous, the questioning side may move the judge for an extension of time.

If the instructor decides to team you with a partner to try your Case file, attempt to divide the responsibility as evenly as possible. One team member should make the opening while the other should deliver the summation. Each team member will conduct examination of one witness on that side and the cross-examination of an opposing witness. The team member responsible for examining or cross-examining a witness will have sole responsibility for objecting to the opposition's questions to that witness.

Case File B–1*

BLOCK v. EL DORADO INSURANCE COMPANY

This case involves a claim for benefits under a life insurance policy. Patrolman Dill will be a defense witness.

The witnesses are:

1. George L. Block, Jr., approximately 26 years old;

2. Patrolman Melvin Dill, approximately 30 years old;

3. Wayne Norman, approximately 25 years old; and

4. Susan Montgomery, approximately 32 years old.

---

* This case file is based on a fact situation created by Professor Leonard Packel of Villanova University.

The defendant concedes its liability for $100,000, but it disputes the recoverability of the double indemnity.

Statement of George L. Block, Jr.

Date of Birth:	December 11, 19YR–26
Address:	2220 Spruce Street, Apt. 4G, Morena
Employment:	Morena Art Museum, Curator's Assistant. Salary, $27,000 per year.
Education:	B.A. in Fine Arts, University of El Dorado. Majored in Art History.

I am the only child of George L. Block, Sr., and Helen Master Block. My mother died on June 3, 19YR–3, quite suddenly of a heart attack at the age of 54. My father died exactly one year later on June 3, 19YR–2, when he drowned after falling from the Falls Bridge. My father was 58 years old at the time.

My mother's death was quite hard on my father. They had been married for over 30 years. It came at a difficult time for him because he had just sold his business and had not really settled on what he intended to do next. He had been in the retail wall coverings business for many years on the 1900 block of Chestnut Street in Morena. He had begun in that business with his father who passed away a number of years ago. My father enjoyed the business because he loved color and design, and he could take advantage of that love in a business in which he could also make quite a good living. He always said that, if he could do anything he wanted, he would paint but no one could make a living from that. He satisfied his artistic bent by helping people decorate their homes. The business was not as good, however, in the years right before he sold it. As is the case in so many businesses, the discounters are making it difficult for the conventional retail businesses. My father refused to discount. He believed in giving service and satisfying customers' needs. He didn't want to sell shoddy merchandise and seconds. Eventually, he just sold out. On the other hand, he did quite well when he sold out. With what he got for the business and the building, which he owned, I think he netted out with $600,000 or $700,000. I was surprised to find that his estate was over $900,000. I am the executor and the sole beneficiary.

My father and I have always been close. We shared an interest in art and he encouraged me to further that interest. When I became interested in art history, he was delighted. From a very young age, he had taken me to art museums and exhibitions like some fathers take their sons to ball games. He, of course, supported me financially through college, and made it clear that he would help me should I seek an advanced degree. In fact, I do intend to enter a Ph.D. program in the near future.

After my mother's death, my father sold their house at 118 Gladwyne Avenue, and moved into the Park City West Apartments at 3900 Ford Road. I thought that he had made a mistake moving into those apartments. Most of the people in there are quite a bit older than my father, and I think that was depressing to him. But we spent quite a bit of time together, and he seemed to be coming around. He began to talk about taking a trip; and when he told me that he had made arrangements with a travel agency for a Caribbean cruise in late June, I thought that would be good for him. He also began to talk about going into business again or getting a job, but he had nothing definite in mind so far as I know.

He even began to take an interest in bike riding, of all things. My father had never been athletic or even interested in sports, but he told me that he bought a second-hand bike and had taken up riding. He said that he liked to take his bike down to the East and West River Drives early in the morning so he could watch runners and other bikers. I borrowed a bike on a couple of occasions and went for a ride with him. I was surprised at how well he was doing on the bike. In fact, I teased him, that he was becoming a "jock." I said that because I have always had an interest in sports which my mother encouraged and dad never understood. I still play basketball and tennis when I get a chance. The bike rides, his planned trip, and his overall attitude all had convinced me by June that had was doing fine. I certainly saw no inclination that dad would or could commit suicide. By June, I was pretty sure that my father was going to be allright.

On June 3, about 11:00 a.m., I was at work when I got a call from the police that a man they thought was my father had drowned. I remember saying, "My father doesn't swim; he wouldn't go in the pool," and the police told me that it was the result of a fall from the bridge. I went down to the Medical Examiner's Office on University Avenue. I talked with a Dr. Briskman and identified the body. I then went to the 5th District at 449 Cinnaminson Street with Officer Dill, where the police had my father's wallet and the bike. It was a Schwinn, I think, with a basket on the handlebars. I didn't want the bike. I didn't even take it from the station. Officer Dill did give me my father's wallet. There was no money in it; and that was unusual. My father always had $200 or $300 in cash in his wallet. He liked to pay for things with cash. Officer Dill told me that the wallet had been found in the street with no money in it. He said that was consistent with my father's being mugged and pushed off the bridge. Frankly, that's harder for me to think about than suicide. I also found in the wallet the $300 check from Ardmore Travel Agency. There was no letter or explanation with the check so I called and spoke with a woman there. She told me that my father had cancelled his trip and that the check was a return of the deposit. She told me to cash the check, and I did.

I never knew anything about my father's insurance until I was going through his papers after his death. Then I found the policy (copy attached).

I notified the insurance company of my father's death; and they declined payment, claiming that his death was suicide.

Dated: March 3, 19YR–1

/s/ George L. Block, Jr.

George L. Block, Jr.

PERTINENT CLAUSES IN LIFE INSURANCE POLICY ISSUED BY EL DORADO INSURANCE COMPANY

1. Named Insured: George L. Block, Sr.

2. Date of Issue: October 11, 19YR–5

3. "Whereas, upon receipt at the home office of due proof of the death of the insured, the Company will pay to the named beneficiary $100,000.00."

4. "Further, upon receipt at the Home Office of due proof that the insured death resulted, directly and independently of all other causes, from accidental bodily injury, the Company will pay the amount of the Accidental Death Benefit specified in the Schedule of Supplemental Benefits in lieu of the payment provided in paragraph three (3) hereof."

. . .

"The double indemnity provision of this contract shall apply to any accidental death whether resulting from violent or non-violent means. It shall not apply to death resulting from any disease or physical condition."

5. "Provided, HOWEVER, that death from suicide within two (2) years from the effective date of this policy, then the benefits of this policy shall not be paid and all obligations of the above-named company shall be discharged."

6. "Exceptions. No Accidental Death Benefit shall be payable if the injury or death results from (1) suicide or any attempt thereat, whether the insured is insane or sane."

7. Named Beneficiary: George L. Block, Jr., (son).

Statement of Melvin Dill

Date of Birth:	July 2, 19YR–30
Address:	7618 Brockton Road, Morena
Employment:	Patrolman, Morena Police Department, Since 9/1/19YR–15. Attached to 5th District at 449 Cinnaminson Street.
Education:	Morena public schools—Frankford High School, Morena Community College, Associate Degrees in Psychology and Criminology, May 19, 19YR–15.

Marital Status: Married to Angela Conti Dill, 6/18/19YR–13. Two children, Paula 5, Gregory 3.

My report (attached) is accurate. When I first stopped by Mr. Norman's, I was reluctant to call for assistance because it seemed likely that subject had just taken a walk. I was trying to calm Norman as we walked off the bridge onto the drive. Mr. Norman pointed to the bike which was laying on the sidewalk right at the beginning of the bridge, but I thought it had just slipped off its kick stand. Then when we walked about 100 feet south on the drive, I found the wallet at the curb. When Norman identified the picture on the license as the man he had seen, I knew we had a potential problem. I called the district and they called the Harbor Patrol. The Patrol came and found Mr. Block in the river about 30 yards south of the bridge.

Of course, I would just be speculating if I guessed about the cause of Mr. Block's death. I know that it would be very unlikely that he would fall. Either he jumped or he was pushed. I think it is possible that someone attempted to take his wallet and had to assault him to take it. This is consistent with the fact that there was no money in the wallet, since Mr. Block, Jr., told me that his father usually carried a good bit of cash. Also, I cannot understand how Mr. Block's bike got from where Mr. Norman saw him, which I understand was 60 or 70 feet onto the bridge, to the end of the bridge.

Norman told me—and I confirmed—that the bridge is an old, cast iron bridge, painted light blue/green. Aside from the color, it is a beautiful, Victorian-style bridge. There are three lanes for auto traffic, but they are very narrow so as a practical matter, there is one lane in each direction. There is a sidewalk for pedestrians, about four feet wide on each side. There is a railing on the sidewalks to prevent people from falling into the river. It's about four feet high. You could climb over pretty easily, but it's hard to imagine falling over accidentally. I've noticed that just below the deck level, there are braces or supports which extend out about one and one-half feet beyond the deck. If someone fell, he would probably hit those supports or braces and could probably hold on if he tried. As you turn off the bridge onto the West River Drive, there are a number of trees and shrubs which block your view of the bridge and which would prevent someone on the bridge from seeing you. It's almost like turning the corner of a building. There is a lot of foliage in this area.

One of my Associate degrees is in the field of Psychology. While I was an undergraduate, I became particularly fascinated with the writings of Dr. Otto Bendheim on the psychiatric autopsy technique. I even visited the Los Angeles Suicide Prevention Center (SPC) which routinely uses the technique in its investigations. The technique is particularly useful in cases in which the manner of death may have been suicidal. It is true that a live, face-to-face interview is usually the preferable method of evaluating a subject, but it's now generally believed that you can often reliably diagnose the mental condition of a decedent before death by reconstructing the events of the person's life—like an autopsy conducted by a forensic pathologist. The mental health expert reviews the person's life history, psychiatric and psychological data, communications, and other relevant information to retroactively determine a decedent's state of mind. I have personally reviewed all the data in the file on Mr. Block's death. I am convinced that given the loss of his beloved wife and his objective conduct shortly before his death, he was in a suicidal frame of mind.

Dated: April 17, 19YR–1

/s/   Melvin Dill

_____

Melvin Dill

MORENA POLICE DEPARTMENT

SUPPLEMENTARY INVESTIGATION REPORT

Crime Classification or Type of Incident: Drowning

VICTIM OR COMPLAINANT

4 LAST NAME, FIRST, MIDDLE: Block, George L, Sr.

RESIDENCE PHONE: 223-7499   BUSINESS PHONE: N/A

7 ADDRESS WHERE INCIDENT OCCURRED: 3900 Ford Road, Morena, El Dorado

DATE INCIDENT REPORTED: 6/3/19YR-2

NARRATIVE SECTION

At approximately 7:00 a.m., 6/3/19YR-2, I was on routine patrol in the vicinity of the East River Drive and Falls Bridge. I was called to a halt by a male in running attire who identified himself as Wayne Norman, age 25, of Park Town West Building, Park Town Apartments, 22nd and Parkway. He stated his belief that an unknown, elderly man had jumped from the bridge. Search of the bridge and surrounding area revealed a Schwinn bicycle which Norman identified as belonging to the elderly male. Additional search revealed one man's wallet laying by curb approximately 100 feet from bridge on East River Drive. Wallet contained credit cards in the name of George L. Block. License in the name of George L. Block and check in the amount of $300 payable to George L. Block and other miscellaneous papers; no money. Norman identified man shown in picture on the license as individual suspected of jumping.

I contacted 5th District which notified Harbor Patrol Unit. The Harbor Patrol Unit located body at point approximately 30 yards south of bridge.

The body was taken to Medical Examiner's Office. I contacted George L. Block, Jr., at phone number contained in wallet. I met George L. Block, Jr., at Medical Examiner's Office where he identified body. I returned to the 5th District where I turned over the wallet and contents to George L. Block, Jr. Bicycle was not returned but was left for disposal.

Medical Examiner reported cause of death drowning. Notified Wayne NOrman at approximately 11:45 a.m. of the death and cause of death. Confirmed facts contained in report with Norman.

Further action - none.

REPORTING OFFICER: Melvin Dill   BADGE: 5117   DATE: 6/3/-2

ASSISTING OFFICER: TIME: 2100hrs   BADGE: 213   DATE: 6/4/YR-2   ZONE: 0830

I, the undersigned, certify that I am the deputy Records Custodian of the Morena Police Department and that the attached page is a true and accurate copy of an original official report in my custody.

[*seal*]

/s/   Marcia Hirsch

Marcia Hirsch
Morena P.D.
Badge 4333

Statement of Susan Wilks Montgomery

Date of Birth:	April 7, 19YR–32
Address:	Broomall, El Dorado
Marital Status:	Married June 17, 19YR–10, to John Montgomery. One child, John Jr., born 5/3/19YR–8.
Education:	Public schools in Haverford Township. Graduated May, 19YR–11, from El Dorado State University. Major in English Literature.
Employment:	Ardmore Travel Agency, Lancaster Avenue, Ardmore, El Dorado.

I have worked at Ardmore Travel Agency ever since I graduated from EDSU. I had originally planned to look for a teaching job but there wasn't much available. I had a friend who worked for Ardmore and told me there was an opening. I've enjoyed the work and have stayed with it. John and I enjoy travelling and this job gives me the opportunity to do a lot of travelling at prices we can afford. Since the birth of our son, I've been able to adjust my hours so that I have continued in my job close to full time.

I first met Mr. Block in February of 19YR–2. He came in to talk about a cruise. He told me that his wife had passed away recently and that he wanted some kind of trip which a single man of his age (somewhere in his middle 50's) would be able to enjoy. I showed him a few things, and he said he would think it over and come back. He did. In fact, he came in at least once a week. It was apparent that he was quite lonesome and that he came in as much for someone to talk with as to find a trip. I didn't mind because he was such a nice and interesting man.

Finally, he did decide to book a ten-day cruise on the Fairwind to the Carribean on June 27, 19YR–2. He was really very excited about it, and he continued to call me every once in a while to ask about clothing or meal arrangements and things like that. I was very happy for him because I knew he would enjoy the cruise and I was sure that he would meet people on the cruise. He was actually quite a charming man; and I felt that once he got over the initial shock from the loss of his wife, he would find a lot of women who would be interested in him.

Mr. Block sent me a deposit of $300 in late April. I was disappointed in May when he called me and asked if I could get a refund on the deposit. He explained that he was not going to be able to take the trip because he was going into a new business. It was still early, and I was able to get a full refund and I sent Mr. Block a check on May 25. Then, on June 4, I read in the paper that Mr. Block had passed away. It was very upsetting, almost like losing a friend.

Attached is the carbon copy of the letter which I sent to Mr. Block with the return of his deposit.

The attached brochure has information on the cruise.

Several weeks after Mr. Block's death, his son called about the check which had not yet been cashed. I told him to endorse it and deposit it since that would save the time and effort of issuing a new check.

Dated: March 11, 19YR–1

/s/ Susan Montgomery
_____

Susan Montgomery

May 26, 19YR–2

Mr. George L. Block
Park City West Apartments
3900 Ford Road
Morena, El Dorado

Dear Mr. Block:

I enclose a refund of your deposit for the June 27, 19YR–2, cruise on the Fairwind. I'm sorry that your new business venture will not permit you to take the trip. Of course, we wish you the greatest success in the new venture and look forward to serving you in the future.

Sincerely,
Susan Wilks Montgomery

Enclosure

Statement of Wayne Norman

Date of Birth: 19YR–25

Address: Park Town West, Park Town Place Apartments
                    22nd and Parkway, Morena, El Dorado

Employment: CIGNA Corp., 1600 Arch Street, Morena.
                 Product management—Designing insurance products and policies.
                 Salary, $35,000 per year.

Education: Public schools of Susquehanna Township—just outside Harrisburg, P.A. B.S., Villanova University, College of Commerce and Finance, 19YR–5. Majored in Management.

Marital Status: Single.

After I graduated from Villanova, relocated to Morena, and took my job with CIGNA Corp., I moved into the Park Town West Building of the Park Town Place Apartments. I am single and live alone. I live in the Park Town Place Apartments because they are close to my job and I can walk to work.

About a year and a half ago, I decided that I was starting to get heavier than I wanted to be, so I began running. Four or five mornings a week, I get up early and run. I usually run on the East and West River Drives. On my ambitious days, I run on the East River Drive to the Falls Bridge, cross on the bridge and come back on the West River Drive. That's about eight and one-half miles.

I usually leave my apartment to run about 6:30 a.m. You see a pretty regular crew of people on the drives at that time in the morning. That's how I first became aware of Mr. Block. About seven or eight months before his death, I began to see Mr. Block riding his bike on the drives when I was running, I never knew his name until he died, and I never spoke with him; but I said hello or nodded to him or waved when I saw him. He did the same. The regulars all do that to one another.

There was nothing unusual about Mr. Block. He was an ordinary looking man in his fifties. He wasn't a serious bike rider like some that you see. His bike was an old one with upright handle bars, and a basket on the front. It wasn't a racing bike, and he never rode fast or like he was looking for serious exercise. He seemed much more like someone who went riding for the scenery and fresh air. He certainly was pleasant whenever I saw him and I sort of looked forward to seeing him like I do all of the regulars.

On June 3, 19YR–2, I was doing one of my long runs. When I turned from the East River Drive onto the Falls Bridge, I saw Mr. Block standing on the sidewalk on the bridge looking over the rail at the river. He was about sixty or seventy feet from the East River Drive. His bike was standing next to him. I don't think that I had ever seen him do that before but it was a beautiful morning, and I didn't think there was anything unusual about his behavior. It was the kind of morning when a lot of people might just stop and look at the river and the rest of the scenery. But I did notice that he didn't turn toward me and even when I said "Good morning," he kept looking at the water. He didn't respond. I remember thinking that he must have something on his mind.

Just as I got off the bridge on the West River Drive, I noticed that my lace was untied and I stopped to tie it. That's when I heard a loud splash, and I looked up to see what had happened. I saw ripples in the water like something large had fallen in and I noticed that Mr. Block was no longer standing at the rail. I went back onto the bridge and sidewalk and saw his bike was laying down where he had been standing. I went back to where his bike was and he wasn't there. I became very concerned, and I began looking for him; and of course, I didn't find him. I stood there for ten minutes or so trying to figure out what to do.

At first I didn't believe that the splash was Mr. Block; but when he didn't reappear, I thought I had better notify the police. I saw a patrol car coming, and I waved. He stopped, and I explained what had happened. The officer, his name was Dill, asked me to wait with him. While we were there, he asked me for my name; and I explained what I knew about the situation. We walked a little bit on the East River Drive looking for some sign of Mr. Block. Then Officer Dill picked up a wallet which was laying in the street next to the curb about seventy feet from the bridge. He looked in the wallet and found a driver's license with Mr. Block's name and his photo. He asked me if I recognized the photo. I told him I wasn't sure, but I thought that was the man on the bike.

At that point, the officer got into his car and called for assistance. He told me that I could leave and that he would call me if I were needed. I went home, showered, and went to work. I was pretty upset, but I didn't know what else to do. At about 11:30 a.m., I got a call at work from Officer Dill. He told me that they had found Mr. Block's body in the river. He read his notes to me about what I had told him, and they sounded right. He asked if I had anything to add, and I didn't. He told me that he would contact me if there was anything further, but I guess there wasn't because he never did contact me. I read the obituary in the paper, and that was the last I heard about it.

There certainly were other people out that morning, but I didn't notice anyone in particular, and I didn't see anyone else on the bridge at the time of this incident.

The bridge is an old, cast iron bridge, painted light blue/green. Aside from the color it is a beautiful, Victorian-style bridge. There are three lanes for auto traffic, but they are very narrow so as a particular matter, there is one lane in each direction. There is a sidewalk for pedestrians, about four feet wide on each side. There is a railing on the sidewalks to prevent people from falling into the river. It's about four feet high. You could climb over pretty easily, but it's hard to imagine falling over accidentally. I've noticed that just below the deck level, there are braces or supports which extend out about one and one-half feet beyond the deck. If someone fell, he would probably hit those supports or braces and could probably hold on if he tried. As you turn off the bridge on the West River Drive, there are a number of trees and shrubs which block your view of the bridge and which would prevent someone on the bridge from seeing you. It's almost like turning the corner of a building. That's why I couldn't see what happened or even whether Mr. Block was on the bridge until I walked back onto the bridge.

Dated: March 7, 19YR–1

/s/   Wayne Norman

Wayne Norman

STATE OF EL DORADO
DEPARTMENT OF HEALTH
VITAL STATISTICS
CERTIFICATE OF DEATH
(Physician)

PRIMARY DIST. NO.　　　　　　　STATE FILE NO.

DECEDENT

Name of deceased — George L. Block — Sex: M — Date of death: 6/3/19YR-2

Race: White — Age last birthday: 58 — Date of birth: 3/28/YR-60 — Country of birth: E.D. Morena — City, Boro, or Twp. of birth: Morena

Country of death: Morena — Hospital or Institution: — Marital Status: Widower — Surviving Spouse: Mildred

Military Address: 3900 Ford Rd. Morena, E.D. — Usual Occupation: Business — Kind of business or industry: Retail Sales

Citizen of what country: U.S. — State E.D. — County Morena — Social Security Number: 173-66-0131 — Mother's maiden name: Morena Mildred Dean

PARENTS

Father's name: Harrison Block — Mother's name: Morena

DISPOSITION

Informant's name: George Block, Jr. — Informant's Mailing address: 2220 Spruce Street, Morena, E.D.

Date of burial: UNK — Name of cemetery or crematory: UNK — Location: UNK

Signature of Funeral director and license number: 20A. John Morrisey

FD — [1][7][1][1] [0][6][1][6] - [3]

CERTIFIER

To the best of my knowledge, death occurred at the time, date and place and due to the cause(s) stated.

Signature: [signature] Asst. Medical Examiner — M.D.
Date Signed: 6/3/82 — Hour of Death: 7:00 A.M.

John Briskman, Medical Examiner's Office

CAUSE OF DEATH

PART I

Immediate Cause (a): Drowning
Due to (b): Fall from Falls Bridge
Due to (c):

PART II — Other Significant Conditions: Injuries to head and shoulder

Date of Injury: 6/3/82 — Hour of Injury: 2:00 A.M.
Describe How Injury Occurred: Undetermined
Location: Falls Bridge — Schuylkill River — Morena E.D.

Autopsy: ☒ Yes ☐ No
Was Case referred to Medical Examiner or Coroner? ☐ Yes ☒ No

IS THIS CERTIFICATE A RECIPROCAL? ☐ YES ☐ NO

H 108.143　REV. 8/79

(E8560)

I, the undersigned, certify that I am the Records Custodian of the Morena office of the El Dorado Department of Health (Vital Statistics) and that the attached page is a true and accurate copy of an original death certificate in my custody.

[seal]

/s/　Glenn Bailey

_____

Glenn Bailey

The Sitmar Experience

The three Sitmar ships are Fairsky, Fairsea and Fairwind.

Each is a spectacular example of the ship-building art. Each reflects old world craftsmanship.

Fairsky is a magnificent 46,000-ton vessel so perfectly designed you're hardly aware of her movement through the water.

The twin ships, Fairsea and Fairwind, are also included among the world's great luxury cruise ships. They're so beautifully crafted that Fielding's has given each of them an exclusive 5-Star rating.

The three ships have a great deal in common.

An Italian ambience. The warm hospitality of an Italian and Portuguese crew.

Elegant styling. Teakwood decks and polished railings and rich wood paneling. Plush carpets and soft lighting and tasteful artwork. And, of course, superb service, splendid dining and an endless variety of recreational and social activities.

All the things that add up to Sitmar Class.

AIRFARE INCLUDED FROM THESE 150 CITIES

ZONE 1	ZONE 2		ZONE 3	
ALBUQUERQUE, N.M.	ANCHORAGE, ALASKA[2]	LUBBOCK, TEX.	AKRON, OHIO	PHILADELPHIA, PA.
BAKERSFIELD, CALIF.[1]	AMARILLO, TEX.	MADISON, WIS.	ALBANY, N.Y.	PITTSBURGH, PA.
BURBANK, CALIF.[1]	AUSTIN, TEX.	McALLEN, TEX.	ALLENTOWN, PA.	PORTLAND, ME.[5]
EUGENE, ORE.	BATON ROUGE, LA.	MEMPHIS, TENN.	ATLANTA, GA.	PROVIDENCE, R.I.
EUREKA, CALIF.	BILLINGS, MONT.	MEXICO CITY, MEX.	AUGUSTA, GA.	RALEIGH, N.C.
FRESNO, CALIF.	BIRMINGHAM, ALA.	MIDLAND/ODESSA, TEX.	BALTIMORE, MD.	RICHMOND, VA.
HONOLULU, HAWAII[2]	BISMARCK, N.D.	MILWAUKEE, WIS.	BANGOR, ME.[5]	ROANOKE, VA.
LAS VEGAS, NEV.	BOISE, IDAHO	MINNEAPOLIS, MINN.	BOSTON, MASS.	ROCHESTER, N.Y.
LOS ANGELES, CALIF.	BOZEMAN, MONT.	MOBILE, ALA.	BUFFALO, N.Y.	SAN JUAN, P.R.[2]
MEDFORD, ORE.	CHICAGO, ILL.	MOLINE, ILL.	CHARLESTON, S.C.	SAVANNAH, GA.
MONTEREY, CALIF.[3]	COLORADO SPRINGS, COLO.	MONTGOMERY, ALA.	CHARLESTON, W.VA.	SYRACUSE, N.Y.
OAKLAND, CALIF.[4]	CORPUS CHRISTI, TEX.	NASHVILLE, TENN.	CHARLOTTE, N.C.	TALLAHASSEE, FLA.
ONTARIO, CALIF.[6]	DALLAS/FT. WORTH, TEX.	NEW ORLEANS, LA.	CINCINNATI, OHIO	TAMPA, FLA.
PALM SPRINGS, CALIF.[1]	DAVENPORT, IOWA	OKLAHOMA CITY, OKLA.	CLEVELAND, OHIO	TOLEDO, OHIO
PHOENIX, ARIZ.	DENVER, COLO.	OMAHA, NEB.	COLUMBUS, OHIO	WASHINGTON, D.C.
PORTLAND, ORE.	DES MOINES, IOWA	RAPID CITY, S.D.	DAYTON, OHIO	WEST PALM BEACH, FLA.[7]
RENO, NEV.	DETROIT, MICH.	ROCHESTER, MINN.	DAYTONA BEACH, FLA.	WILKES-BARRE, PA.
SACRAMENTO, CALIF.	EL PASO, TEX.	SAGINAW, MICH.	ERIE, PA.	
SAN DIEGO, CALIF.	EVANSVILLE, IND.	ST. LOUIS, MO.	FT. LAUDERDALE, FLA.[7]	
SAN FRANCISCO, CALIF.	FT. WAYNE, IND.	SALT LAKE CITY, UTAH	FT. MYERS, FLA.[7]	
SAN JOSE, CALIF.	GRAND FORKS, N.D.	SAN ANTONIO, TEX.	GREENSBORO, N.C.	
SANTA ANA, CALIF.[3]	GRAND JUNCTION, COLO.	SHREVEPORT, LA.	GREENVILLE, S.C.	
SANTA BARBARA, CALIF.[1]	GRAND RAPIDS, MICH.	SIOUX FALLS, S.D.	HARRISBURG, PA.	
SEATTLE/TACOMA, WASH.	GREAT FALLS, MONT.	SPRINGFIELD, ILL.	HARTFORD, CONN.	
SPOKANE, WASH.	GUADALAJARA, MEX.	SPRINGFIELD, MO.	JACKSONVILLE, FLA.	
STOCKTON, CALIF.[3]	HOUSTON, TEX.	TULSA, OKLA.	LEXINGTON, KY.	
TUCSON, ARIZ.	HUNTSVILLE, ALA.	WICHITA, KAN.	LOUISVILLE, KY.	
	INDIANAPOLIS, IND.		MERIDA, MEX.	
	JACKSON, MISS.		MIAMI, FLA.	
CANADA	JOPLIN, MO.		NEW YORK, N.Y.	
CALGARY, ALTA.	KANSAS CITY, MO.	**CANADA**	NEWARK, N.J.	**CANADA**
EDMONTON, ALTA.	KNOXVILLE, TENN.	REGINA, SASK.[9]	NORFOLK, VA.	OTTAWA, ONT.
PRINCE GEORGE, B.C.[8]	LINCOLN, NEB.	SASKATOON, SASK.[9]	ORLANDO, FLA.	MONTREAL, QUE.
VANCOUVER, B.C.	LITTLE ROCK, ARK.	TORONTO, ONT.	PENSACOLA, FLA.	QUEBEC CITY, QUE.
VICTORIA, B.C.[8]		WINNIPEG, MANITOBA		

SOUTH PACIFIC AIR ADD-ONS

ZONE 1	ZONE 2	ZONE 3
Oct. 12 San Francisco to Tahiti Cruise—$200	Oct. 12 San Francisco to Tahiti Cruise—$300	Oct. 12 San Francisco to Tahiti Cruise—$400
All other South Pacific Cruises—$600	All other South Pacific Cruises—$700	All other South Pacific Cruises—$800

Air add-on is a supplemental charge (per person) for air transportation which is added to the cruise fare.

[1] Air program applies to all Mexico and San Francisco Alaska sailings. For all other destinations, air program applies from Los Angeles airport. Transportation to/from Los Angeles airport not included.

[2] Passengers flying from these cities must add the following amounts to the airfare table above:

Honolulu: Caribbean, Amazon and Canada/New England—$300
Trans-Panama—$200

Anchorage: Trans-Panama, Amazon, Caribbean and Canada/New England—$200

San Juan: Mexico and Alaska—$200

[3] Air program applies to all Mexico, South Pacific, and San Francisco Alaska sailings. For all other destinations, air program applies from San Francisco airport. Transportation to/from San Francisco airport not included.

[4] Air program applies to all Mexico, Canada/New England, and South Pacific sailings. For all other destinations, air program applies from San Francisco airport. Transportation to/from San Francisco airport not included.

[5] Air program applies to all Caribbean, Amazon, Canada/New England, Mexico and Alaska sailings. For all other destinations, air program applies from Los Angeles airport. Transportation to/from Los Angeles airport not included.

[6] Air program applies to all Caribbean, Amazon, Canada/New England, and South Pacific sailings. For all other destinations, air program applies from Boston. Transportation to/from Boston not included.

[7] Air program applies to all Caribbean, Mexico, Canada/New England, Alaska, and South Pacific sailings. For Amazon and Trans-Panama sailings, air program applies from Miami. Transportation to/from Miami not included.

[8] Air program applies to all Mexico, Alaska and South Pacific sailings. For all other destinations, air program applies from Vancouver airport. Transportation to/from Vancouver not included.

[9] Air program applies to all Mexico, San Francisco Alaska, Caribbean, Amazon, and South Pacific sailings. For Trans-Panama cruises, air program applies from Calgary airport. For Canada/New England and Seattle Alaska sailings, Regina passengers fly from Saskatoon airport. Transportation to/from Calgary or Saskatoon airports not included.

CRUISE PLUS PROGRAM

ORLANDO/DISNEY WORLD & EPCOT

Extend your vacation to enjoy one of the world's largest entertainment parks —Disney World. Your tour package includes 3 nights at the Hyatt Orlando Hotel with a one-day admission to Disney World and a one-day admission to EPCOT Center.

The windmills in St. Croix turn back the clock to the 18th century.

FT. LAUDERDALE

Explore this lovely city with its luxurious waterfront homes, splendid yachts and broad beaches. Your stay includes 2 or 3 nights at the Embassy Suites Hotel, a Voyager City Tour and a Jungle Queen Cruise.

10 DAYS/6 PORTS   **WESTERN**

This exciting itinerary combines the best of the Western Caribbean with the most popular U.S. Virgin Islands. You'll also enjoy 3 relaxing days at sea.

ITINERARY DAY PORT	FAIRSKY or FAIRWIND ♦ ARRIVE	DEPART
1 FT. LAUDERDALE		7:00 PM
2 NASSAU, BAHAMAS	7:00 AM	12:00 N
3 AT SEA		
4 ST. CROIX, U.S.V.I.	12:00 N	12:00 M
5 ST. THOMAS, U.S.V.I.	7:00 AM	6:00 PM
6 AT SEA		
7 MONTEGO BAY, JAMAICA	1:00 PM	6:00 PM
8 GRAND CAYMAN, CAYMAN ISLANDS	8:00 AM	1:00 PM
9 PLAYA DEL CARMEN/ COZUMEL, MEXICO†	8:00 AM	9:00 PM
10 AT SEA		
11 FT. LAUDERDALE	9:00 AM	

DEPARTURE DATES	RETURN DATES
JAN 26, TUE	FEB 5, FRI
FEB 25, THU	MAR 6, SUN
MAR 26, SAT	APR 5, TUE
APR 25, MON	MAY 5, THU
JUL 24, SUN ♦	AUG 3, WED
OCT 11, TUE	OCT 21, FRI
NOV 10, THU	NOV 20, SUN
DEC 20, TUE	DEC 30, FRI

1988 CRUISE PLUS RATE CHART

CITY	HOTEL PROPERTY	2 NIGHTS PER PERSON/ DOUBLE	1 EXTRA NIGHT	EFFECTIVE DATES
FT. LAUDERDALE	EMBASSY SUITES	$145	$55	JAN 1-APR 15; DEC 16-31
		$110	$40	APR 16-DEC 15
ORLANDO	HYATT ORLANDO	$285 (3 nights)	N/A	JAN-DEC

N/A–Not Applicable

1988 EARLYBIRD RATE CHART

CITY	HOTEL PROPERTY	PER PERSON/ DOUBLE	EFFECTIVE DATES
FT. LAUDERDALE	MARRIOTT MARINA	$65	JAN 1-APR 15; DEC 16-31
		$45	APR 16-DEC 15

CHRONOLOGICAL SCHEDULE

	JANUARY	FEBRUARY	MARCH	APRIL	MAY	JUNE
Caribbean	6 Wed 10 Days Fairsky (E)	5 Fri 10 Days Fairsky (E)	6 Sun 10 Days Fairsky (E)	5 Tue 10 Days Fairsky (E)	5 Thu 10 Days Fairsky (E)	4 Sat 10 Days Fairwind (E)
	16 Sat 10 Days Fairsky (E)	15 Mon 10 Days Fairsky (E)	16 Wed 10 Days Fairsky (E)	15 Fri 10 Days Fairsky (E)	15 Sun 10 Days Fairsky (E)	14 Tue 10 Days Fairwind (E)
	26 Tue 10 Days Fairsky (W)	25 Thu 10 Days Fairsky (W)	26 Sat 10 Days Fairsky (W)	25 Mon 10 Days Fairsky (W)		24 Fri 10 Days Fairwind (W)
Trans–Panama	6 Wed 10 Days Fairwind	13 Sat 14 Days Fairsea	6 Sun 10 Days Fairwind	2 Sat 14 Days Fairsea	5 Thu 10 Days Fairwind	
	16 Sat 10 Days Fairwind	25 Thu 10 Days Fairwind	16 Wed 10 Days Fairwind	16 Sat 14 Days Fairsea	15 Sun 10 Days Fairwind	
	26 Tue 10 Days Fairwind		26 Sat 10 Days Fairwind	25 Mon 10 Days Fairwind	25 Wed 10 Days Fairwind	
	30 Sat 14 Days Fairsea				25 Wed 14 Days Fairsky	
Amazon Caribbean		5 Fri 10 Days Fairwind		5 Tue 10 Days Fairwind		
		15 Mon 10 Days Fairwind		15 Fri 10 Days Fairwind		
South Pacific						
Mexico	6 Wed 10 Days Fairsea	27 Sat 7 Days Fairsea	5 Sat 7 Days Fairsea	30 Sat 7 Days Fairsea	7 Sat 7 Days Fairsea	
	16 Sat 7 Days Fairsea		12 Sat 7 Days Fairsea		14 Sat 7 Days Fairsea	
	23 Sat 7 Days Fairsea		19 Sat 7 Days Fairsea		21 Sat 7 Days Fairsea	
			26 Sat 7 Days Fairsea			
Canada & New England						
Canada & Alaska					31 Tue 10 Days Fairsea	8 Wed 12 Days Fairsky
						10 Fri 10 Days Fairsea
						20 Mon 10 Days Fairsea
						20 Mon 12 Days Fairsky
						30 Thu 10 Days Fairsea

JULY

4 Mon 10 Days Fairwind (E)
14 Thu 10 Days Fairwind (E)
24 Sun 10 Days Fairwind (W)

2 Sat 12 Days Fairsky
10 Sun 10 Days Fairsea
14 Thu 12 Days Fairsky
20 Wed 10 Days Fairsea
26 Tue 12 Days Fairsky
30 Sat 10 Days Fairsea

AUGUST

3 Wed 10 Days Fairwind (E)
13 Sat 10 Days Fairwind (E)

7 Sun 12 Days Fairsky
9 Tue 10 Days Fairsea
19 Fri 10 Days Fairsea
19 Fri 12 Days Fairsky
29 Mon 10 Days Fairsea
31 Mon 10 Days Fairsky

SEPTEMBER

27 Tue 14 Days Fairsky

7 Wed 9 Days Fairwind
16 Fri 9 Days Fairwind
25 Sun 9 Days Fairwind

8 Thu 10 Days Fairsea
12 Mon 12 Days Fairsky
18 Sun 10 Days Fairsea

OCTOBER

11 Tue 10 Days Fairsky (W)
21 Fri 10 Days Fairsky (E)
31 Mon 10 Days Fairsky (E)
13 Thu 14 Days Fairwind
27 Thu 10 Days Fairwind

12 Wed 14 Days Fairsea
26 Wed 14 Days Fairsea

4 Tue 9 Days Fairwind

NOVEMBER

10 Thu 10 Days Fairsky (W)
20 Sun 10 Days Fairsky (E)
30 Wed 10 Days Fairsky (E)
6 Sun 10 Days Fairwind
16 Wed 10 Days Fairwind
26 Sat 10 Days Fairwind

10 Thu 14 Days Fairsea
23 Wed 14 Days Fairsea

DECEMBER

10 Sat 10 Days Fairsky (E)
20 Tue 10 Days Fairsky (W)
30 Fri 10 Days Fairsky (E)
6 Tue 10 Days Fairwind
16 Fri 10 Days Fairwind
26 Mon 10 Days Fairwind

8 Thu 13 Days Fairsea
21 Wed 12 Days Fairsea

Caribbean

Save $200 per person with our Early Booking Discount.

Trans-Panama

Save $300–400 per person with our Early Booking Discount

Amazon Caribbean

Save $200 per person with our Early Booking Discount.

South Pacific

Save $200–300 per person with our Early Booking Discount

Mexico

Save $200–300 per person with our Early Booking Discount

Canada & New England

Save $200 per person with our Early Booking Discount.

Canada & Alaska

Save $300 per person with our Early Booking Discount.

(E)–Eastern Caribbean
(W)–Western Caribbean

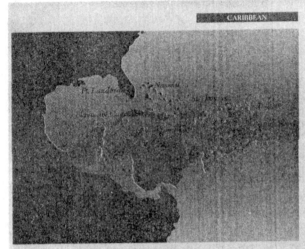

CABIN CATEGORIES AND
FARES—1988. *INCLUDES AIRFARE.*

CABIN CODES *See pages 66-67*		10-DAY	
		TARIFF	EBD FARE
A	O/S	$3,540	$3,340
B	O/S	2,790	2,590
C	O/S	2,440	2,240
D	O/S	2,365	2,165
E	O/S	2,315	2,115
F	O/S	2,250	2,050
G	O/S	2,215†	2,015†
H	I/S	2,145	1,945
	I/S	2,085	1,885
	I/S	2,045	1,845
K	O/S	SGL 2,480†	2,280†
		DBL 1,985†	1,785†
	I/S	1,970	1,770
N	I/S	1,895	1,695
	I/S	SGL 2,280†	2,080†
		DBL 1,825†	1,625†
P	I/S	SGL 2,180†	1,980†
		DBL 1,745†	1,545†
3RD AND 4TH BERTHS	ADULT	945	945
	CHILD	755	755

*SAVE $200 WITH OUR EARLY
BOOKING DISCOUNT*

---

10 DAYS/6 PORTS — WESTERN

*This one-time sailing includes the
same 6 ports as our 10-day western
itinerary, with ports in reverse order.*

ITINERARY		FAIRWIND	
DAY	PORT	ARRIVE	DEPART
1	FT. LAUDERDALE		7:00 PM
2	AT SEA		
3	PLAYA DEL CARMEN/ COZUMEL, MEXICO†	7:00 AM	6:00 PM
4	GRAND CAYMAN, CAYMAN ISLANDS	1:00 PM	6:00 PM
5	MONTEGO BAY, JAMAICA	8:00 AM	4:00 PM
6	AT SEA		
7	ST. THOMAS, U.S.V.I.	11:00 AM	12:00 M
8	ST. CROIX, U.S.V.I.	7:00 AM	2:00 PM
9	AT SEA		
10	NASSAU, BAHAMAS	1:00 PM	7:30 PM
11	FT. LAUDERDALE	9:00 AM	

DEPARTURE DATE	RETURN DATE
JUN 24, FRI	JUL 4, MON

---

10 DAYS/6 PORTS — EASTERN

*This popular itinerary makes the
most of the Caribbean's international
flavor. You'll sample islands of Danish,
British and French influences.*

ITINERARY		FAIRSKY or FAIRWIND♦	
DAY	PORT	ARRIVE	DEPART
1	FT. LAUDERDALE		7:00 PM
2	NASSAU, BAHAMAS	7:00 AM	12:00 N
3	AT SEA		
4	ST. CROIX, U.S.V.I.	12:00 N	7:00 PM
5	ST. JOHN'S, ANTIGUA	8:00 AM	3:00 PM
6	BRIDGETOWN, BARBADOS	9:00 AM	8:00 PM
7	FORT-DE-FRANCE, MARTINIQUE	7:00 AM	2:00 PM
8	ST. THOMAS, U.S.V.I.	9:00 AM	11:00 PM
9	AT SEA		
10	AT SEA		
11	FT. LAUDERDALE	9:00 AM	

DEPARTURE DATES	RETURN DATES
JAN 6, WED	JAN 16, SAT
JAN 16, SAT	JAN 26, TUE
FEB 15, MON	FEB 25, THU
MAR 16, WED	MAR 26, SAT
APR 5, TUE	APR 15, FRI
MAY 5, THU	MAY 15, SUN
JUN 4, SAT ♦	JUN 14, TUE
JUN 14, TUE ♦	JUN 24, FRI
JUL 4, MON ♦	JUL 14, THU
JUL 14, THU ♦	JUL 24, SUN
AUG 3, WED ♦	AUG 13, SAT
AUG 13, SAT ♦	AUG 23, TUE
OCT 31, MON	NOV 10, THU
NOV 30, WED	DEC 10, SAT
DEC 10, SAT	DEC 20, TUE

---

10 DAYS/6 PORTS — EASTERN

*This itinerary features the same 6
ports as our 10-day eastern cruise,
with ports in different order.*

ITINERARY		FAIRSKY	
DAY	PORT	ARRIVE	DEPART
1	FT. LAUDERDALE		7:00 PM
2	AT SEA		
3	AT SEA		
4	ST. THOMAS, U.S.V.I.	8:00 AM	3:00 PM
5	ST. JOHN'S, ANTIGUA	8:00 AM	4:00 PM
6	BRIDGETOWN, BARBADOS	9:00 AM	8:00 PM
7	FORT-DE-FRANCE, MARTINIQUE	7:00 AM	2:00 PM
8	ST. CROIX, U.S.V.I.	7:00 AM	2:00 PM
9	AT SEA		
10	NASSAU, BAHAMAS	1:00 PM	7:30 PM
11	FT. LAUDERDALE	9:00 AM	

DEPARTURE DATES	RETURN DATES
FEB 5, FRI	FEB 15, MON
MAR 6, SUN	MAR 16, WED
APR 15, FRI	APR 25, MON
MAY 15, SUN	MAY 25, WED
OCT 21, FRI	OCT 31, MON
NOV 20, SUN	NOV 30, WED
DEC 30, FRI	JAN 9, MON

EBD Fare—Early Booking
Discount Fare. Available
when booking 3 months in
advance of sailing date.

O/S = Outside Cabin
I/S = Inside Cabin

3rd and 4th berth fares
(sharing cabin with 2 full-
fare adult passengers).
Air/Sea Program or Travel
Allowance applicable.

Adult, 12 and over; child,
under 12 on day of sailing.

Single occupancy fares for
cabin categories other than
K, N & P available on
request.

†This cabin category not
available on Fairsky.

• Cruise fares are for each
adult in U.S. dollars, based
on double occupancy
except where otherwise
noted.

• Cruise fares include
roundtrip air transporta-
tion. Passengers not using
Sitmar's Air/Sea Program
can deduct $250 per
person.

• Passenger port charges
are additional and not
included in the cruise fare.
At time of printing, pas-
senger port charges range
from $40 to a maximum of
$50 per person, per cruise,
depending on the ship's
itinerary.

†Passengers may disembark in Playa
del Carmen for optional shore tours to
Chichen Itza or Tulum.

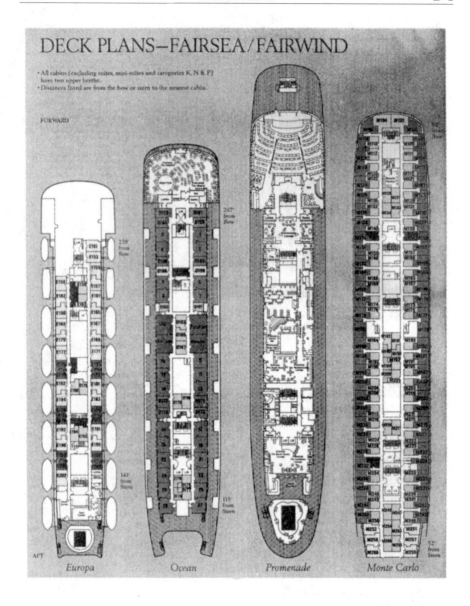

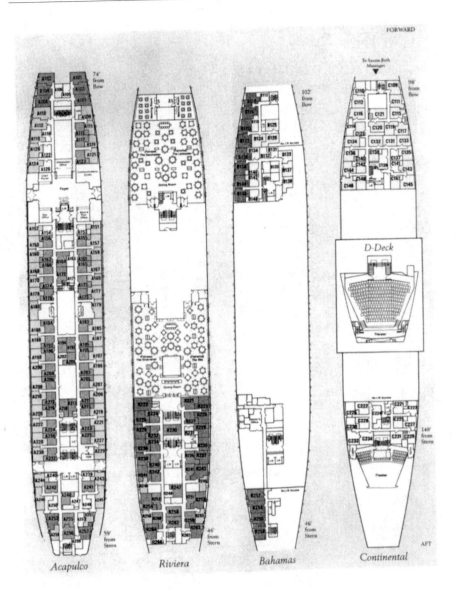

Acapulco   *Riviera*   *Bahamas*   *Continental*

FAIRSEA/FAIRWIND CABINS

CABIN	DECK	CABIN DESCRIPTION
A	OCEAN	OUTSIDE SUITE
B	OCEAN	OUTSIDE MINI-SUITE
C	OCEAN/MONTE CARLO	OUTSIDE–TWO LOWER BEDS
D	EUROPA/MONTE CARLO/ACAPULCO	OUTSIDE–TWO LOWER BEDS
E	ACAPULCO/RIVIERA	OUTSIDE–TWO LOWER BEDS
F	EUROPA/OCEAN/MONTE CARLO	OUTSIDE–TWO LOWER BEDS (Views obstructed)
G	BAHAMAS	OUTSIDE–TWO LOWER BEDS
H	EUROPA/OCEAN/MONTE CARLO	INSIDE–TWO LOWER BEDS
I	ACAPULCO	INSIDE–TWO LOWER BEDS
J	RIVIERA	INSIDE–TWO LOWER BEDS
K	EUROPA/MONTE CARLO/ACAPULCO/RIVIERA	OUTSIDE–ONE LOWER BED AND ONE UPPER BERTH (Views on Europa deck obstructed)
L	BAHAMAS/CONTINENTAL	INSIDE–TWO LOWER BEDS
M	CONTINENTAL	INSIDE–TWO LOWER BEDS
N	EUROPA/OCEAN/MONTE CARLO/ACAPULCO	INSIDE–ONE LOWER BED AND ONE UPPER BERTH
P	OCEAN/MONTE CARLO/ACAPULCO/RIVIERA/BAHAMAS/CONTINENTAL	INSIDE–ONE LOWER BED AND ONE UPPER BERTH

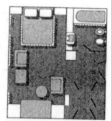

A

Suite Private bedroom with double beds. Capri and Portofino suites have twin beds. Sitting room area for entertaining. TV. Refrigerator. Private bath with tub.

B

Mini-Suite Private bedroom with sitting room area for entertaining. TV. Extra-large wardrobe closets. Private bath.

 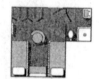

C D
E F
I J
L M

Outside or Inside Double Outside cabins have a sea view. Two lower beds with two upper berths. Private bath.

K N P

Outside or Inside Single/Double Typical lower-priced cabin. Outside cabins have a sea view. One lower bed. One upper berth. Private bath.

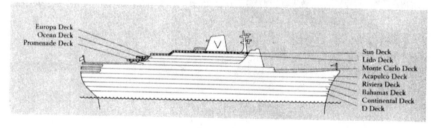

Europa Deck
Ocean Deck
Promenade Deck

Sun Deck
Lido Deck
Monte Carlo Deck
Acapulco Deck
Riviera Deck
Bahamas Deck
Continental Deck
D Deck

Case file B–2

PEOPLE OF THE STATE OF EL DORADO v. HARPER

Wallace Harper was indicted for murder and manslaughter in the killing of Emille Rankin on Nov. 29, 19YR–2 in Morena, El Dorado. Harper claims self-defense.

Statement of Odell Jones

On the evening of November 29, I was playing gin rummy with Emille Rankin in his apartment at the Northgate Apartments in Morena. Rankin and I were buddies from a long way back. We had been together in the Marines in Nam in 1971, and we both happened to end up working in Morena. We both had had about five glasses of vodka and orange juice.

At approximately 9:30 p.m. the defendant Wallace Harper came in the screen door (the main door was open). Harper introduced himself and asked Rankin why he had not paid back the $250.00 gambling debt that he owed Harper's boss. Rankin said he did not have the money and further that Harper had no right to barge into his apartment for any reason. While Harper was still standing in the door about six feet from where we were sitting at a coffee table, Harper pulled a Mauser automatic pistol from his pocket and said, "If you don't pay the money by tomorrow at six o'clock, I'm personally going to blow you away." With that, Harper turned and started to open the screen door to leave. All of a sudden, Rankin grabbed a small glass ash tray and got to his feet. Rankin said, "instead of the money, you can take this back to Green." Rankin then threw the ash tray at Harper. The ash tray just grazed him on the back of the head. Harper turned and fired three or four quick shots. The pistol sounded like a cannon-it was so loud. Rankin slumped to the floor. Harper then turned and ran out the door. The whole thing happened in a couple of seconds. I called the 911 number and told whoever answered to send an ambulance and the police right away.

Dated: January 13, 19YR–1

/s/ Odell Jones

─────────────────────

Odell Jones

Statement of Officer Judd Wortham

While on duty as a Morena police officer on November 29, I received a call at 9:41 p.m. about a possible homicide at the Northgate Apartments. I proceeded to the scene and entered the apartment listed to an Emille Rankin. I entered through the screen door and observed a man lying on the ground near the door. There was blood on the outside of his clothes around the chest area. Another man, who identified himself as Odell Jones, told me that the victim was Emille Rankin and that he had been shot by Wallace Harper. I attended to the victim and saw that he was already dead. There were three holes which looked to me like bullet holes around a three inch area on the victim's chest. The three holes were tightly bunched-as if somebody had been using his chest for target practice! I can't bunch shots that close together at the Police Academy firing range, and I have a marksman rating!

Witness Jones also stated that Harper may have been injured by a glass ash tray which the victim had thrown at the back of Harper's head.

I found the broken pieces of a large, heavy glass ash tray near the doorway. There were traces of blood and hair on some of the pieces.

I checked the area hospitals and learned that Harper was being treated in the Emergency Room at Mercy Hospital. I proceeded there and placed Harper under arrest. After advising him of his rights, Harper declined to make any statement.

Dated: February 13, 19YR–1

/s/ Judd Wortham
_____
Judd Wortham

Statement of Mr. Wallace Harper

I work for a debt collection agency in Morena. I carry a gun because some of those deadbeat debtors get pretty rough (I couldn't get a license for it, since I had some court-martial problems while I was on active duty in the Marine Corps years ago). My agency does a lot of work for Mr. Hector Green who is some kind of business investor. If you ask me, Mr. Green has some strange "business associates"; but I guess that's none of my business. On November 29, Hector asked me to pick up some money that was owed him by Emille Rankin. I've attached the memo Hector gave me. I arrived at the Northgate Apartments that evening and knocked on the frame of the screen door. There was no answer. Since I heard voices inside, I assumed that they could not hear the knock. I opened the door and entered. There were two men seated at a table. They looked like they were playing cards. The larger of the two men said, "What the fuck do you want, asshole?"

I said, "Are you Emille Rankin?"

He said, "What's it to you?"

I said, "Hector sent me over to pick up the money you owe him."

The man said, "Tell Mr. Green that if you live to see him again, I'll kill any mother-fucker he sends after me for his juice." The man started to get to his feet and move towards me. I saw him reach for something on the table. I turned as fast as I could to go out the door; and as I was midway through the door, I felt a terrible jolt to the back of my head. I didn't know whether I had been shot or stabbed or hit with a club or what. I felt myself falling. As I stumbled, I reached into my pocket and pulled out my pistol. I fired at the man standing about three feet from me. I don't remember how many shots I fired. I ran away because I was hurt and scared. The other guy made some motion in my direction and said something like, "You can't do that to a buddy of mine." I wanted out of there fast. I went to a hospital downtown where I had thirteen stitches put into the back of my head. The police came to the hospital and arrested me there. I had intended to call the cops as soon as I left the hospital, but the cops walked in while I was literally still being stitched up.

I've since learned that Rankin threw an ashtray at me. I've drawn the ashtray I remember sitting on the table in Rankin's apartment. I've tried to make the drawing the size of the actual ashtray.

Dated: November 3, 19YR–1

/s/   Wallace Harper

Wallace Harper

MEMO

FROM: H. Green

TO: Wally H.

Wally, I understand that the boss is assigning you this case. Here's the IOU. Rankin is unlucky-and a welsher. You may have to pressure him to get the juice. I understand he lives at the Northgate Apartments.

11:30 p.m.
Feb. 27, 19YR-2

I O U

I, Emelle Rankin, admit that I owe M. Hector Green $250. I promise to pay $250 to Hector Green.

Emelle Rankin

SIDE VIEW

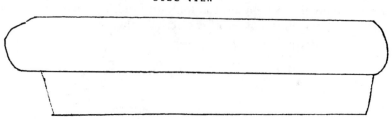

OVERHEAD VIEW

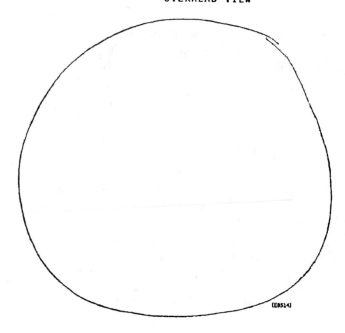

[E8514]

WH   11/3/YR–1

Statement of Dr. Kathleen Schultz

I am a licensed physician in the State of El Dorado. I work at the Emergency Room of Mercy Hospital, located in downtown Morena. Mercy Hospital is privately owned. I was on duty the evening of November 29, 19YR–2 when the defendant, Wallace Harper, presented himself for treatment. He had a gash on the side of his head. The gash was not particularly deep, but it was long and had produced a lot of bleeding. I'm not a forensic pathologist, but even I can tell that someone had to hurl an object with considerable force at Harper to produce that type of wound. As I recall after checking the emergency room log, I had to make 13 stitches. Harper was cooperative, but he seemed visibly upset by something; his speech was a bit garbled, and I was frankly surprised that he'd been able to drive himself any distance to our hospital. While I was getting Harper's case history, he said something to the effect that someone had thrown something at him and that he "didn't know what was coming next." He didn't explain any further. To treat Harper, I had him strip to his underwear. When he did so, I noticed that he had several scars—scars that appeared to be old bullet and knife wounds. I asked Harper about them. He didn't answer at first. When I told him that I needed his prior history to make sure that I gave him the right treatment, he said that the wounds were the result of "some old, close scrapes—unfortunately, they go with the territory." Again, he didn't explain any further.

I had just finished the stitching and was about to prescribe some pain killer when a police officer burst into the emergency room. I believe that the officer's name was Worthy or Wortham or something like that. The officer interrupted my conversation with Harper and arrested Harper right there in the emergency room. I protested that I hadn't yet completed my conversation with my patient, but the officer—rather rudely, in my opinion—told me to shut up and not to interfere with "official police business." He slapped handcuffs on Harper, forced him to his feet, and took him from the emergency room.

Dated: June 30, 19YR–1

/s/   Kathleen Schultz, M.D.

Kathleen Schultz, M.D.

Mercy Hospital
1433 Grant Street
Morena, El Dorado
December 10, 19YR–1

Chief
Morena Police Department
777 McAllister Avenue
Morena, El Dorado

Dear Sir:

I am a licensed physician in this state and a taxpayer. On the evening of November 29th of this year, I was on duty in the emergency room of Mercy Hospital. I was working on a patient named Walter Harper. I was in the process of completing the 10 stitches he needed. Just as I was finishing my treatment of this seriously injured patient, one of your officers—I believe his name was Wortham—burst into the room. I told Wortham to get out until I was finished with my patient, but he insisted on remaining. He not only stayed; he arrested my patient right in the room. When I protested, your officer told me to be quiet. He made some vague threat that I was obstructing the administration of justice. He treated me rudely and my patient roughly.

You cannot expect hospitals to operate when police officers interfere in this fashion. This is the most shameless display of police brutality I have ever witnessed. It seems to me that something is very wrong with your personnel policies if you hire and retain officers like this fellow Wortham. I expect both a full apology and the initiation of departmental charges against Wortham.

Very truly yours,
Kathleen Schultz, M.D.

Case File B–3

LARGENT V. CITY OF VILLA PEAK

Villa Peak is a suburb of Morena.

IN THE UNITED STATES DISTRICT COURT FOR THE NORTHERN DISTRICT OF EL DORADO MORENA DIVISION

MARY LARGENT, individually and as next friend of RONALD FRANKLIN LARGENT,	)))	
Plaintiff	)	CIVIL ACTION
v.	)	FILE NO. CYR–2902A
CITY OF VILLA PEAK and Chief C.L. Flowers,	))	
Defendants	)	

CASE STATEMENT

1.

GENERAL NATURE OF THE LITIGATION

Ronald Franklin Largent's mother brings this action pursuant to 42 U.S.C.A. § 1983 against the City of Villa Peak for deprivation of the decedent's constitutional rights. Largent was found hanged in the City of Villa Peak's jail on December 7, 19YR–2. The Plaintiff alleges that Largent's death was the result of the acts that indicated gross negligence and a complete disregard for the consequences or rights of the deceased. Further, Plaintiff alleges excessive use of force and cruel and unusual punishment.

2.

PLAINTIFF'S CONTENTIONS

The Plaintiff contends that on December 6, 19YR–2, the deceased Ronald Largent was arrested by police officers for the City of Villa Peak

Police Department. From the time of his arrest until the time of his death on December 7, 19YR-2, the deceased was in the custody of the Villa Peak Police Department and confined to the medical personnel at Morena General Hospital. He received a laceration over his right eye for which stitches were required.

While incarcerated, the deceased refused to sign the forms necessary to secure his release on bond from the Villa Peak jail. On December 7, 19YR-2, the deceased was found dead from hanging in his cell in the City jail.

Defendants contend that the deceased was afforded all civil and constitutional rights and due process of law. They urge the deceased's injuries and death were the result of his own actions and that no action, inaction or policy, practice, custom or procedure of the Villa Peak Police Department or any of its employees proximately contributed to such injury or death. Defendants maintain a defense of good faith conduct on the part of all members of the Villa Peak Police Department.

3.

RELATED LITIGATION

At this time, the Plaintiff states that there are no pendent state claims or related federal litigation.

4.

JURISDICTIONAL ISSUES

This Honorable Court has the exclusive original jurisdiction of this controversy pursuant to 28 U.S.C.A. § 1983, and the Plaintiff anticipates no jurisdictional or venue problems.

_____

Attorney for Plaintiff

_____

Attorney for Defendants

IN THE UNITED STATES DISTRICT COURT FOR THE NORTHERN DISTRICT OF EL DORADO MORENA DIVISION

MARY LARGENT, individually and as next friend of RONALD FRANKLIN LARGENT,	)))	
Plaintiff	)	CIVIL ACTION
v.	)	FILE NO. CYR-2902A
CITY OF VILLA PEAK and Chief C.L. Flowers,	))	
Defendants	)	

COMPLAINT

Comes now the Plaintiff in the above styled case and respectfully presents her complaint as follows:

COUNT ONE

1.

This Honorable Court has exclusive original jurisdiction of Count One of this complaint under 42 U.S.C.A. § 1983, § 1985, 28 U.S.C.A. § 1343 and 28 U.S.C.A. § 1331.

2.

The Defendant City of Villa Peak is a municipal corporation chartered under the laws of the State of El Dorado and is subject to this Court's jurisdiction. Service may be perfected upon this Defendant through the corporation's principal office, namely, the office of the Mayor of the City of Villa Peak located at 8667 Civic Drive, Villa Peak, State of El Dorado 80837.

3.

The Defendant C.L. Flowers, is the Chief of Police for the City of Villa Peak and is subject to this Court's jurisdiction. Personal service may be perfected upon this Defendant at the office of the Chief of Police for the City of Villa Peak, 8667 Civic Drive, Villa Peak, El Dorado.

4.

The Plaintiff, Mary Largent, is the natural parent of Ronald Franklin Largent. Until his death, she was married to Clarence Largent.

5.

Clarence Largent, the father of Ronald Largent, died before the date of this complaint.

6.

Ronald Franklin Largent died on or about December 7, 19YR–2.

7.

At the time of his death Ronald Franklin Largent was unmarried and had no minor children.

8.

On or about December 6, 19YR–2, the deceased Ronald Franklin Largent was arrested by police officers for the City of Villa Peak Police Department.

9.

From the time of his arrest on or about December 6, 19YR–2, until the time of his death on December 7, 19YR–2, Ronald Franklin Largent was in the custody of the Villa Peak Police Department and confined to the Villa Peak jail.

10.

Police Chief C.L. Flowers and police officers of Villa Peak, while acting under color of law, conspired to deprive the Plaintiff of his civil rights.

11.

The Defendants conspired to deprive the deceased Ronald Largent of his constitutional rights in several ways, including deprivation of his right to due process of law. Ronald Largent was deprived of his rights by means which included, but were not limited to:

    (a) Use of excessive force;

    (b) Intentional infliction of cruel and unusual punishment in contravention of the Constitution of the United States;

    (c) False imprisonment through the denial of bond; and

    (d) Refusing to provide prompt medical attention for injuries and inattention to proper medical treatment.

12.

As a direct and proximate result of the conspiracy to deny the deceased his civil rights, the deceased was deprived of his rights guaranteed under the Constitution of the United States and suffered not only physical injury and pain and suffering, but also loss of life.

COUNT TWO

13.

The Plaintiff realleges and incorporates into Count Two all the numbered paragraphs of Count One, that is, paragraphs one (1) through twelve (12).

14.

This Honorable Court, having exclusive original jurisdiction of Count One of this complaint, therefore has exclusive original jurisdiction of Count Two and all subsequent counts of this complaint under 42 U.S.C.A. § 1983, § 1985 and 28 U.S.C.A. § 1343.

15.

While the deceased was in the custody and control of the police officers of the City of Villa Peak, those officers deprived the Plaintiff of his civil rights guaranteed under the Constitution of the United States.

16.

The acts constituting deprivation of civil rights by police officers for the City of Villa Peak included but were not limited to the following:

(a) Cruel and unusual punishment prohibited by the Constitution of the United States;

(b) Willful infliction of excessive force;

(c) Denying the deceased prompt medical treatment while in the custody and control of the police officers for the City of Villa Peak;

(d) Unprovoked and unwarranted physical attacks upon the deceased; and

(e) Gross negligence exhibiting a complete indifference to consequences and to the rights of the deceased.

17.

As a direct and proximate result of the acts of the employees of the Defendant herein, the deceased suffered:

(a) Physical injury;

(b) Extreme mental anguish, pain and suffering;

(c) Loss of life; and

(d) Deprivation of civil rights.

18.

The City of Villa Peak Police Department has established a policy through custom and usage which results in deprivation of civil rights of not only the deceased but of other citizens.

COUNT THREE

19.

The Plaintiff realleges and incorporates into Count Three the numbered paragraphs of Count One, that is, paragraphs one (1) through twelve (12) and the numbered paragraphs of Count Two, that is, paragraphs thirteen (13) through eighteen (18).

20.

At all relevant times referred to in this complaint, Defendant C.L. Flowers served as the Chief of Police for the City of Villa Peak.

21.

The Defendant C.L. Flowers had a legal duty to establish correct policies, procedures, and training and to exercise supervision of the police officers to insure that the citizens of Villa Peak and all people incarcerated in police care and custody were not deprived of their civil rights.

22.

The Defendant C.L. Flowers failed to perform his legal duties to establish adequate policies and safeguards to protect the civil rights of the citizens.

23.

The Defendant C.L. Flowers failed in his legal duties to adequately train and supervise the police personnel to insure the health, safety and well being of citizens and to protect their civil rights.

24.

The Defendant C.L. Flowers knew or should have known of the conduct of his employees who were engaged in the deprivation of the civil rights of citizens.

WHEREFORE, Plaintiff prays:

(a) That she recover a joint and several judgment against the Defendants;

(b) That she recover consequential damages in such amount as the jury may determine, but not less than one million ($1,000,-000.00) dollars;

(c) That she recover punitive damages in such amount as the jury may determine, but not less than one million ($1,000,000.00) dollars;

(d) That she recover reasonable attorney's fees as well as the costs of prosecuting this action; and

(e) That she have such other and further relief as this Court deems appropriate.

_____

Attorney for Plaintiff

IN THE UNITED STATES DISTRICT COURT FOR THE NORTHERN DISTRICT OF EL DORADO MORENA DIVISION

MARY LARGENT, individually and as next friend of RONALD FRANKLIN LARGENT,	)))	
Plaintiff	)	CIVIL ACTION
v.	)	FILE NO. CYR–2902A
CITY OF VILLA PEAK and Chief C.L. Flowers,	))	
Defendants	)	

ANSWER

COME NOW the Defendants and answer Plaintiff's complaint as follows:

1.

Defendants admit the allegations of Plaintiff's paragraphs 1–3.

2.

The Defendants can neither deny nor admit that the Plaintiff is the mother of the deceased.

3.

The Defendants do not have sufficient information to either admit or deny the allegation set forth in paragraph 5 of Plaintiff's complaint.

4.

Defendants admit the allegations of Plaintiff's paragraphs 6, 8, and 9.

5.

The Defendants do not have sufficient information to either admit or deny the allegations of Plaintiff's paragraph number 7.

6.

The Defendants deny the allegations of Plaintiff's paragraphs 10, 11, 12, 13, 15, 16, 17, 18, 19, 22, 23 and 24.

7.

The Defendants admit the allegations of Plaintiff's paragraphs 14, 20 and 21.

8.

Any allegations not specifically admitted are hereby denied.

9.

The Plaintiff has filed this suit with the knowledge that the claims stated in her complaint are frivolous.

WHEREFORE, the Defendants pray that Plaintiff's complaint be dismissed with costs cast upon the Plaintiff and that the Defendants be awarded attorney's fees for the defense of this action.

Respectfully submitted,
City Attorney
City of Villa Peak

_____
Attorney for Defendants

STATEMENT OF MATERIAL FACTS AS TO WHICH THERE IS NO ISSUE

Pursuant to local District Court Rule 91, the defendants propose statements of fact as to which there is no genuine issue to be tried:

1. Ronald Franklin Largent was a nineteen-year-old white male who died on December 7, 19YR–2.

2. Plaintiff Mary Largent is the mother of the deceased Ronald F. Largent.

3. Ronald Largent died leaving no dependents and was never married.

4. Ronald Largent was arrested for criminal damage to property and burglary in the City of Villa Peak on December 6, 19YR–2.

5. Warrants were obtained for Ronald Largent for the offenses of burglary and criminal damage to property, and bond was set by the Magistrate at $1,000.00 and $500.00 respectively.

6. Ronald Largent was struck once in the head while being arrested by Officer C.A. Cleetz.

7. Officer Cleetz thinks Largent probably had on a belt when he was arrested. Cleetz does not remember if the belt was taken from Largent while Largent was detained in jail.

8. At no time during his life before this arrest had Largent ever exhibited suicidal behavior or been treated for mental illness.

9. At no time did Largent exhibit to the arresting officers or jail employees any signs of suicidal behavior.

10. At approximately 6:45 p.m. on December 6, 19YR–2, Largent was found sitting in his cell, bleeding from a cut above his right eye.

11. At 8:00 p.m. Largent received help for the cut. He was given medical attention by an emergency medical technician, Steven Spurlock, from the Villa Peak Fire Department; Spurlock advised that Largent should be transported to a hospital emergency room for treatment of the cut above his eye.

12. Largent stated to Spurlock that he had fallen out of his bunk and hit his head, thereby cutting his head.

13. Largent was transported to the Morena General Hospital and received 19 stitches. While at the hospital, Doctor Cox allowed Largent to call his sister. Largent informed her that after he had been arrested and taken to jail, he was hit by a police officer, inflicting the cut. He also told her that he described the incident differently around jail, because he would not get into further trouble. His last words were "Tell Mom not to worry." This was the extent of the conversation.

14. Largent was returned to Villa Peak jail at 9:45 p.m.

15. Sometime during the night, Largent told a jail trustee (Albert Rollo Buckingham) that Largent had cut his head while attempting to commit suicide but would not try to kill himself again if the trustee would not tell anyone that he had tried to kill himself.

On the evening of December 6, Mary Largent attempted to post bond for Ronald Largent, but Ronald refused to sign the bond papers. Mary came to the jail at about 8:45 p.m.; she had money for Ronald's bail. When she was informed that Ronald was in the hospital and the police did not know when he would return, she departed, leaving the bail cash in the custody of the desk sergeant. When Ronald came back, he refused to sign the bond papers.

16.   At about 5:30 a.m. on December 7, jail trustee Buckingham found Largent hanging in his cell and informed desk sergeant G.A. Crockett. Largent was pronounced dead by the Morena County Medical Examiner, who determined that Largent died of self-inflicted hanging.

17.   No jailer was on duty at the time of Largent's death. The jailer's duties were performed by the desk sergeant, assisted by the arresting officer. Jailer duties normally included dispensing food to prisoners, periodic checks on prisoners, and summoning medical assistance for emergencies. No written policies for jailers were in existence, and jailers hired by the city received only in-service training.

18.   The Villa Peak jail is used to hold prisoners charged with state offenses until a preliminary hearing is conducted. When defendants are bound over, they are transferred to Morena County Jail. Villa Peak jail is also used to jail persons serving their sentences under city ordinance or state misdemeanor violations.

19.   At the time of Largent's death there were four prisoners in the jail, which is capable of housing up to 32 prisoners. Two of the other prisoners were charged with felony assault; one, Mr. Buckingham, was serving out a 30–day misdemeanor.

20.   Burglary is a felony under El Dorado law.

RESPONSE OF PLAINTIFF TO STATEMENT OF MATERIAL FACTS

Plaintiff, subject to the following exceptions, agrees that the above facts are accurate and may be received into evidence by stipulation at trial. However, plaintiff disagrees with points 7 and 15 and the conclusion of suicide referred to in point 16.

REPORT OF MEDICAL EXAMINER

Morena

Case No. YR-2-2051

Name   Ronald Largent

Name of Deceased: Ronald Franklin Largent

Age: 19

Sex: M

Race: Cau.

Height: 67"

Weight: 147

Notification Date: 12/7/YR-2

Hour: 5:35 a.m.

By: Sgt. G. A. Crockett

From: Villa Peak Jail

Autopsy: Yes

Cause of Death: Asphyxia due to hanging

Manner of Death: Suicide

Method of Injury (if violent):   Hanged self with belt

Autopsy Findings Attached

[Certification with Seal Affixed]
[E8515]

REPORT OF MEDICAL EXAMINER

Morena County   Case No. YR-2-2051
                                                           Name Ronald Largent

---

Page 2

INFORMATION AVAILABLE AT TIME OF AUTOPSY:

This 19-year-old white male was found hanging by a belt by personnel of
the Villa Peak Jail. The belt was untied, but was left about his neck when
he was identified being dead at the scene. An investigator from this
office observed the body at the jail. He was then brought to Morena
General Hospital where he was pronounced dead and then transferred to the
Morena County Medical Examiner's Officer for the purpose of this autopsy and
examination.

When received, the body is noted to be wearing jockey shorts, white
pullover shirt, blue jeans pants, and black socks. These articles of
clothing are marked for identification YR-2051 JF and placed in a labeled
grocery bag in order to be transported to the El Dorado State Crime
Laboratory for possible further study. The loop of belt with buckle is
still about the neck, the other end having been untied by an investigator
from this office. This belt measures approximately 40 inches from leather
end to leather end and approximately 35 inches from far edge of buckle to
used belt hole. On the underside of the belt, the number 38 is impressed.

The belt was removed and placed in a properly labeled plastic bag for
transmission to the State Crime Laboratory.
[E8516]

REPORT OF MEDICAL EXAMINER

Morena County   Case No. YR-2-2051
                                       Name Ronald Largent

Page 3

EXTERNAL EXAMINATION OF THE BODY:

This is the unembalmed, well developed, well nourished body of a white

male appearing approximately the stated age of 19. This body is 67 inches

in length. The weight is 147 pounds. The head is covered with somewhat

bushy black hair. The scalp is unremarkable externally. There is, however,

a 1-inch laceration in the lateral 1/3 of the right eyebrow. This

laceration is oriented vertically and has been previously sutured. Also

noted on the right side of the face is a 1/4-inch area of bruise similar to

those seen on the right angle of the jaw and immediately below that on the

upper portion of the neck or underside of chin. These are red brown in

color and seem somewhat older than the incident of the hanging.
                                                        [E0517]

REPORT OF MEDICAL EXAMINER

Morena County

Case No. YR-2-2051
Name Ronald Largent

Page 4

They are, however, consistent in appearance with the laceration of the right eyebrow and also with a horizontally oriented 4-inch area of contusion and light abrasion overlaying the mass of the left breast and left upper chest. The face is otherwise unremarkable. There is a well trimmed mustache and a slight stubble of beard. The tongue protrudes from the mouth and has dried on the tip. The face is somewhat congested as is the neck. About the neck there is the belt described above. It has caused an indentation of the neck across the cartilage of the Adam's apple and thereafter coursing upward and backward bilaterally.

The chest is robust and shows a 4-inch area of contusion and light abrasion horizontally oriented overlaying the left upper chest above the nipple. There is congestion of the right upper shoulder region, but no bruising is seen. The abdomen is flat. The external genitalia are those of a circumcised male. The lower extremities show marked livor mortis with tardieau spots seen prominently on the anterior thighs and on the anterior areas of the legs and on the dorsa of the feet. The back of the legs are unremarkable.

The hands show a similar degree of livor mortis but no tardieau spots. The back is unremarkable. There is livor mortis in the back.
(E8510)

REPORT OF MEDICAL EXAMINER

Morena County

Case No. <u>YR-2-2051</u>
Name <u>Ronald Largent</u>

Page 5

INTERNAL EXAMINATION OF THE BODY:

The body is opened in the usual "Y" shaped incision exposing approximately 1 cm. of yellow subcutaneous adipose tissue and a thick red brown musculature. The bony rib cage is intact. There are no abnormal fluid collections in any body cavity.

Heart:

The heart is contained within a glistening pericardial sac. The heart weighs 290 grams. The epicardium, myocardium, and endocardium are unremarkable. The valve leaflets are thin and delicate. The coronary arteries are free of arteriosclerosis. The aorta and great vessels are intact throughout.
[E8519]

REPORT OF MEDICAL EXAMINER

Morena County

Case No. YR-2-2051
Name Ronald Largent

Page 6:

Lungs:

The lungs are bilaterally congested and edematous. Pleural surfaces are smooth and free of petechiae. They weigh 650 grams each. The airway is patent except where it has been compressed in the area of the laryngeal cartilage. The neck dissection is described below. The lungs show no antecedent parenchymal disease. A small amount of pink tinged edema fluid exudes from the cut surface. The pulmonary vessels are free of thrombo emboli.

Liver:

The liver is in a normal anatomical position. It weights 1550 grams. Its capsule is smooth. The hepatic parenchyma is red brown, firm, and free of pathological pattern. The biliary tract is patent to the duodenum.

Pancreas:

The pancreas is pink tinged, coarsely lobular, and unremarkable.
[E8520]

REPORT OF MEDICAL EXAMINER

Morena County

Case No. YR-2-2051
Name Ronald Largent

Page 7

Spleen:

The spleen is in normal position. It weighs 160 grams. Its capsule is smooth; and, on sectioning, the splenic parenchyma is red brown, firm, and unremarkable.

Adrenals:

The adrenal glands bilaterally are unremarkable. The cortices are tan. The medullae are gray.

Kidneys:

The kidneys are in normal positions bilaterally. The capsules strip with ease. The surfaces are smooth. On sectioning the cortices are of normal sizes, thicknesses, proportions, and colors. The urinary outflow tract is unremarkable. No urine is recovered from the bladder.

The perianal region is soiled with feces, some of which was recovered within the underwear and thereafter discarded. No abnormalities of the perianal region are seen.

G.I. Tract:

The esophagus is intact. The stomach contains approximately 8 ounces of partially digested food, some of which is recognized as small fragments of white meat, rice, and small well-chewed pieces of green vegetable. No abnormal colors or odors are noted when the stomach is opened. The gastric mucosa is gray, wrinkled, and unremarkable. Multiple loops of small and large bowel are dissected in situ. There is no internal gastrointestinal hemorrhage. Feces in the distal colon is described elsewhere. [E8521]

REPORT OF MEDICAL EXAMINER

Morena County

Case No. __YR-2-2051__
Name __Ronald Largent__

Page 8

Neck:

The neck is dissected in situ. There are no strap muscle hemorrhages although there is marked compression of the laryngeal cartilages upward and backward. This compression is also noted on the prominence of the thyroid lobe somewhat more marked on the left. No local hemorrhages within the mucosa of the upper airway are seen. The anterior cervical spine is white and unremarkable.

Head:

The head is opened in the usual manner. Upon inspection of the scalp there is a circular area of bruising, red brown in color measuring 1 inch in greatest diameter. This is not visible externally. It lies on the right frontal parietal area, above the elsewhere described previous laceration of the lateral right eyebrow. The underlying calvarium is otherwise intact. The dura and meninges are unremarkable. The brain weighs 1250 grams and appears acutely congested. Scattered small petechiae are seen within the white matter. On multiple frontal sectioning of the cerebrum, mid brain, pons, cerebellum, medulla, and upper spinal cord, no hemorrhaging is seen above or below the dura. There is no fracturing of the skull.

Other procedures:

Blood is withdrawn from the heart and submitted to El Dorado State Crime Laboratory for possible drug studies and alcohol.

[E8522]

REPORT OF MEDICAL EXAMINER

Morena County

Case No.   <u>YR-2-2051</u>
Name   <u>Ronald Largent</u>

Page 9

Diagnoses:

1.   Asphyxia due to hanging.

2.   Pulmonary congestion secondary to above.

3.   Laceration of right eyebrow and contusions of face.

4.   Status post suturing, laceration right eyebrow.

CAUSE OF DEATH:

Asphyxia due to hanging.

Date: <u>12/7/YR-2</u>

Signed: <u>/s/ J.R. Fulton</u>

J.R. Fulton, M.D.

[Certification with Seal Affixed]
<small>[E8523]</small>

Statement of C.A. Cleetz

On December 6, 19YR–2, Ronald Largent was arrested by me for the offense of criminal damage to property and burglary. During the arrest I struck Mr. Largent over the head with a flashlight. At the time Mr. Largent was placed in Villa Peak jail, I apparently forgot to remove his belt and shoelaces. I am not the regular jailer, and the jailer's practices are not routine to me; we have to perform these duties only one night per week. The jailer did tell me to take the belt and shoelaces; but with reports and other police matters to take care of, it is sometimes hard to remember things you do not do all the time.

My shift on December 6 was 4:00 p.m. to 12:00 a.m. Shortly after I began work that day, I received a call to go to the Fenton Laundromat on Villa Avenue in Villa Peak. Apparently Largent, who is a nineteen-year-old unmarried male, entered the laundromat and washed his clothes. When the coin-operated dryer malfunctioned by taking his money and not drying his clothes, Mr. Largent summoned Mr. Owens, the attendant, who later called in the complaint to our department. Owens refused to reimburse Largent. Largent then forced his way into the manager's office and grabbed a can of red spray paint, went back into the laundry machine area, and painted "Bitch" on the dryer which took his money. Then he broke out the glass window of the dryer.

Largent was in the process of this criminal destruction of property when I pulled up. He saw me through the front window and apparently took off through the back door. I came through the laundromat and saw the broken machine. Mr. Owens, who had come back into the laundromat, yelled and pointed: "He went that way!"

I caught up with Largent about a block away, in the alley near the back of the old Goodyear Tire Warehouse. I struck him on the top of the head with my 3–cell steel flashlight as I was chasing him. It was a glancing blow, not real hard. He fell down on some rubble. I did not hit him again, across the chest or anywhere. He was face down when I cuffed him, and we went back to the laundromat.

Owens was waiting out in back and he said: "Oh, I should have given him his money back. Look what happened now." I told him to calm down, but he went on reiterating what had happened and how he felt he should have handled it differently. Officer Alex Thomas pulled up and came inside the laundromat. He took Largent to the station, and I followed.

In the squad room I told Largent to empty his pockets, which he did. After booking procedures Thomas took the subject's statement. Largent confessed to the offense of criminal damage to property, as well as burglary of the paint can when he broke open the door of the laundromat office. He stated that he had become angry, lost his temper, and tore up the dryer. He offered to make restitution for the damage. After the interview I asked him if he wanted to call his family, and he responded in the negative. He gave the same answer when I asked him if he wanted a paramedic to look at his head.

After Largent gave his statement he was placed in the southwest cell, the one closest to the main locked entry door. You can use any cell for your prisoners. They are selected at random unless the jail is pretty full. I guess Sergeant Easley called Largent's home, because later that night he told me the perpetrator's mother came by about 8:45 p.m.

After I locked Largent up, I went back on patrol. I remember another officer called me and said: "Hey, I heard you got you another burglar!" I saw Largent again for about 5 minutes at about 6:30 p.m. Since we are to help out when no jailer is there, we sometimes have to check on our own prisoners. I came in off patrol and took a look at him. I needed to take a break at the station anyway. He looked O.K. to me. He still was angry, and the exchange wasn't what you would call friendly. At one point he asked: "Why the hell did you have to hit me so hard?" He clenched his fist like he might hit me. I shoved him back from the cell door (I was outside), but I didn't hit him. Nor did he fall down.

The last time I saw him was right at the end of my shift. I walked through the cell area and out the locked back fire door. I have a key. I turned off the alarm momentarily when I left so it would not wake people. Albert Buckingham saw me out. I know Albert Buckingham. I arrested him once for public drunkenness—the sentence he was serving at the time of the Largent incident. He is not a bad guy, and from time to time gives helpful information to the police. He pretty much has the run of the jail; and when he is in there for drunk driving or stealing a bottle of wine, he helps serve the food, clean the cells, fix some of the plumbing if it gets fouled up, things of that sort. When I walked past Largent, he was on the top bunk with his head near the wall and his feet near me. When I went in and checked him, he was asleep. I am pretty sure I locked that cell on my way out. It locks automatically when you pull the cell door tight shut. I talked to Albert for a few minutes, and then left. Albert and I talked very quietly, since most of the prisoners seemed to be asleep. It was just small talk. My car was parked in the back (north end lot) of the jail.

Largent's other arrest by me was almost three months before the December incident. He was painting graffiti on a cement wall here in town with a yellow spray paint can when I caught him. I arrested him for damage to property, and two days later he was back on the street. They told me the judge gave him a suspended sentence. It is unfortunate that they try the police department in a case like this civil rights suit, then let criminals go.

I am 25 years old. I have been on the Villa Peak force for three years. Before that, I delivered construction supplies and hardware to job sites around town. Right after high school I took two years at Morena Junior College in police science. I always wanted to get on with a department and was real glad when Chief Flowers decided to hire me. Every year I get two weeks schooling at El Dorado State Police Academy, including firearms training, crowd control, traffic, treatment of prisoners, criminal law, and the like.

I have never shot anyone in the line of duty or otherwise. A few months before the Largent deal, I arrested two minors in possession of beer. One tried to hit me with his fist. I busted the two of them up pretty good with my flashlight. The one who was swinging at me got a broken jaw. I would like to point out that it was a two on one confrontation, and one of the men had a beer bottle, although not the one who was swinging at me. There was no reprimand of me by the chief or anyone else, and that is really the only time I ever got complaints about my handling of a perpetrator up until this situation.

I live at 16 Piedmont Place, Villa Peak, married, child age 3.

Dated: June 2, 19YR-1

/s/　C.A. Cleetz

_____

C.A. Cleetz

Statement of A.R. Buckingham

I am Albert R. Buckingham, but I like my friends to call me by my middle name, Rollo. Years ago I played football, junior college and semipro (defensive backfield), but that was before the drugs and the booze took over. After a couple of years where I got my share of injuries, I was out of a job. My dad had been a plumber, and he taught me the trade. I worked for contractors in Villa Peak and around this area, but pretty soon I started losing jobs because I missed work. After I started getting arrested I couldn't hold a job, it seemed. I have been in the Villa Peak jail before the night they brought in Ronnie Largent. At the time of his death, I was serving my 20th day of a 30–day sentence for public intox. That is the kind of criminal charge which I know well.

The night he died, I first met Ronnie a little after 5:00 p.m. when the police put him in his cell. I served him his dinner. We had chicken that night. As a trustee I am not locked up. I was occupying the far northeast cell, and there were two male prisoners directly across from me. Both are gone now on detainers from Kansas. They were fairly good-sized men. These two fellows were in Villa Peak jail for criminal assault. I heard a local loan shark brought them in to collect on some bad debts, and they kicked one guy silly, choked another one until he came up with the cash, and they konked somebody with a bottle. They seemed like pretty mean characters, and I didn't have too much to do with them, except to bring their food. They were interviewed after Ronnie did himself in, but neither one heard anything that night. I couldn't say if either one was wearing a belt. I just didn't notice. But probably not. I had on a belt, and I still have it. They don't take everything like that away from a trustee like they do the other prisoners. That's why they trust me with the cell keys sometimes, to do work around the jail.

Ronnie was a nice kid; but he was talking crazy. He told me how he disappointed his mother and how he didn't want her to see him like this. She had gotten him out of another scrape a few months before, and he couldn't face her again. I told him he would feel better when he got out of jail, and he said: "That won't happen because I'm not leaving, at least not on my own two feet." Later, sometime after 6:00 p.m., I heard the main door open and somebody came in. I was taking a nap. There was some shouting, and a voice said: "You son of a bitch, you are getting what you deserve." I didn't hear much else. I couldn't tell whose voice it was. A little later I got up and went to the south end. Ronnie was sitting on a bottom bunk with a cut over his eye. He was crying, and there was blood coming down his face. I said "What happened?" and he said: "I tried to kill myself by jumping off the top bunk, but don't tell anybody." Then he looks at me kind of funny and says: "Rollo, can I have a belt?" I told him no, I needed it for my pants, and he says: "Are there other guys down at your end?" Then he said: "Look, I'm kidding. I won't try anything again if you just don't tell anybody. O.K.?" That's when I told Sergeant Easley about him being cut. I didn't tell the other part until the next day. I could tell the Sergeant was real busy when I reported Ronnie's cut. I didn't tell the Sergeant that Ronnie was going to bleed to death or anything like that, just that the kid had a nasty cut and it would be good for him to see a doc.

When Ronnie came back from the hospital, I was out by the desk getting the printed sheet for breakfast. Sergeant Easley told Ronnie he could sign the bond papers and go, but Ronnie said he didn't want his mom to lose any money. Then he looked down, and wouldn't sign the papers. I saw him for a few minutes in the cell-block. He said he wasn't going to make his mom embarrassed about him any more and that he had made a decision. I asked him what he meant, and he said, "Don't worry, I'll make it look like something else. After that I went to sleep until midnight when Officer Cleetz came by. I sleep real deep; back when I was married, my wife said I could sleep through a hurricane. Anyway, Cleetz told me everything was O.K. with Ronnie, not to bother him. I didn't hear anything until that time Cleetz woke me up. Then I went back to sleep. The two guys in the cell directly across from me didn't wake up, as far as I could tell. Nobody else was brought in that night. There wasn't any noise. The only thing I heard as I was falling asleep— or was it after I slept a little—was a metal sound. Like a door creaking open, or steel scraping on concrete. Then I nodded off.

I always wake up early, since I am supposed to do a head count of prisoners for breakfast. I knew how many there were, but out of habit I walked by all the cells. I saw Ronnie hanging. He was in the middle of the cell, strung up from a pipe that runs along the top of the cells. The pipe is about a foot down from the ceiling, and runs a little closer to the front of the cells than the back. It is a water pipe, I think, real securely anchored. The cells are 9 feet high, each is 12 feet wide, and there are two bunks on each side in a cell, an upper and a lower. The bunks in Ronnie's cell were in their regular place. The top bunk is about 5 1/2 to 6 feet off the ground. The bunks are 3 feet wide and 7 feet long. They are assembled with a metal frame, like bunk beds; and there is about 2 1/2 or 3 feet from the end of the bunk to the bars at the front of the cell. The bunks aren't attached to the walls or floor. The front of the cells are bars, including the doors, but the walls on the sides are solid. The bars on the front of the cells run top to bottom with no horizontal supports or braces in the middle, but they are real solid anyway. As you look into the cell the doors are on the left, about 3 feet wide. After 10:00 p.m. all the lights are turned off in the cells except for the row of lights that runs down the center of the walkway between cells.

I know Officer Cleetz. He has never treated me badly, except he won't ever bend the law or let you go. Everybody says he goes by the book.

There's one other thing I know. Ronnie killed himself. If someone else had done it, I would have heard it. I know of guys who do suicide, and try to make it look like something else. When I was on construction, there was an iron worker named Floyd Welken who jumped off a building we were working on, but he tried to make it look like a fall.

My home is now at 42 Castaway House, Apartment 16, in Villa Peak. It is a place that helps runaways, homeless, and street people."

Dated: June 10, 19YR–1

/s/ Albert R. Buckingham
_____

Albert R. Buckingham

POLICE RECORDS

[Certified under Seal as Correct by El Dorado State Bureau of Criminal Investigation]

Albert R. Buckingham

Time of Arrest (preceding Largent's death)	Offense	Disposition
3 years preceding	cocaine possession	convicted; sentenced to 2 years in state pen.; served 1 1/2 years
1 year preceding	drunk and disorderly	state code misdemeanor; pled guilty; 10 days in Villa Peak jail
6 months preceding	drunk driving	convicted; 20 days in Atlantic City jail
1 1/2 months preceding	petty theft (wine)	state code misdemeanor; charge dismissed; held 2 days for investigation in Villa Peak jail
20 days preceding	public intoxication	state code misdemeanor; pled guilty; 30 days in Villa Peak jail

Ronald Largent

2 years preceding	burglary (television sets from warehouse)	convicted; 18 months probation
3 months preceding	criminal damage to property	charge dismissed by Villa Peak magistrate

Mary Largent

6 years preceding	speeding	pled guilty; $35 fine, plus costs

C.A. Cleetz

None

C.L. FLOWERS

State of El Dorado   )
)   Affidavit

County of Morena   )

Personally appeared before me C.L. Flowers, who, after being duly sworn, made this statement:

1. I am employed by the City of Villa Peak as the Chief of the Villa Peak Police Department. I work days, except when I am alerted to an emergency situation, in which event I respond either day or night.

2. I was not personally involved in either the arrest or the incarceration of Ronald Largent.

3. The rules and regulations of the Villa Peak Police Department enforced in December, 19YR–2, prohibited the use of excessive force in either making an arrest of a person or in incarcerating any prisoner.

4. No custom existed within the Villa Peak Police Department in December, 19YR–2 which either condoned or encouraged the use of excessive force in the arrest or incarceration of any individual.

5. The Villa Peak Police Department routinely, as a matter of policy and procedure, disciplines officers found to have violated any policy, custom, practice or procedure of the Villa Peak Police Department.

6. The Villa Peak jail has the capacity to house 32 prisoners. Our highest population during the past year was 22 prisoners, down to a low of 2.

7. To the best of my knowledge, there were four prisoners in the Villa Peak jail at the time of Ronald Largent's death.

8. The Villa Peak jail is utilized for the purpose of holding persons charged with state offenses only until a preliminary hearing is held and they are then transferred to the appropriate County facility.

9. At the time of Ronald Largent's death, there was no jailer on duty. It was the desk sergeant's responsibility to perform the duties of jailer, assisted by the officers on duty. Further assistance may be provided by a trustee, a particularly trustworthy prisoner who has proven reliable in performing duties such as passing out food and clean-up.

10. On the night of December 6, Mr. Buckingham apparently reported the cut on Largent's forehead promptly. Apparently the delay in securing medical help was due to the fact that Sergeant Easley was very heavily tied up during that period. A number of traffic and other arrests had come up during that part of the evening; and while they did not require incarceration of the arrestees, these matters did entail a good deal of processing and paper work, such as taking collateral for potential

future forfeiture upon nonappearance of auto drivers, and preparing papers for release of offenders on their own recognizance.

11. My conversations with Sergeant Easley, as well as Officers Cleetz, and Thomas and the medical personnel who attended Mr. Largent, indicated that during the time he was in custody, Largent never exhibited any erratic behavior. Nor did he complain to me or any member of the police department that he had been abused by Officer Cleetz.

12. Jailer Wallace Mootry covers the jail six nights per week. He works a 12–hour shift, 5:00 p.m. to 5:00 a.m. He gets one night off, which occurred on December 6. I would like to have a full-time jailer every night, but budgetary and manpower limitations are such that this is impossible. It would mean pulling an officer off the street, and the safety of the community requires every man and woman we have to be out in cars on patrol. Furthermore, until this incident we have not had a prior hanging or fatality in the jail, at least in the last 10 years.

13. Officer Tara Dixon was discharged from this department because of an uncooperative attitude, as well as her casual approach to procedure. Sometimes she would not call in, and we had to send a car out to find her.

14. Officers in our department are issued plastic flashlights. However, many (if not most of them) purchase and substitute metal Kell lights for their plastic flashlights, as was the case with Officer Cleetz here.

15. Some states have a statute requiring a full-time jailer on duty at a detention facility at all times. El Dorado does not.

16. After Largent's death, I interviewed the officers who had contact with Largent, and concluded there was no reason to disagree with the written report of the medical examiner. I am knowledgeable about penitentiary incidents and jail deaths generally. It is not unknown for a prisoner, intent upon killing himself, to attempt to make the death look like something else. Individuals can be very clever about this.

17. The day jailer has talked at length to the desk sergeants and the officers about treatment of prisoners when he is not on duty. As a matter of fact, every year we have him do a couple of in-service training lectures on the topic, and his subjects include the need for the officer to effect removal of certain items of clothing and locking the cells. Until this incident, we have not had reports of deficiencies in these regards.

18. I understand that Officer Cleetz checked on Largent a couple of times during the night, once after 6:00 p.m. and another time at the end of the shift, which would be about midnight.

19. At the end of a shift, many officers use the washroom in the jail before going home, or some of the midnight to 8:00 a.m. crew may use it before they go out. The solid door into the interview and washroom area is usually locked, but the officers have keys. Sergeant Easley does not notice who goes in and out. Nor is he required to. It should be pointed

out that he is at the end of his shift at the time also, and busy with other things. The door into the cell block is also a solid door, with a large shatterproof window in it. At no time during the night, either before or after midnight, did a desk sergeant report hearing a scuffle or argument within the jail.

20.   Largent's body was found at a midpoint between the bunks.

21.   We had an officer here three years ago who regularly used excessive force on arrestees in his squad car after he made a custody arrest. I investigated and discharged him. He is no longer on the force. When a prior complaint was made against Officer Cleetz concerning the force he used in a minor-in-possession case, I concluded that no excessive force was involved. A husky teenager had threatened the officer. With our other officers, I can recall only about 3 or 4 such incidents over the past 3 years. In each case, the complaint was groundless. We have 24 patrol officers on the force, plus detectives.

22.   Because it is essentially a short-term or a holding facility, we do not furnish the cells, outside of the bunks and necessary bedding. Prisoners can have reading materials.

23.   We have not changed policies since this incident, and no further difficulties have occurred.

Dated: June 11, 19YR–1

/s/   C.L. Flowers

_____

C.L. Flowers

Sworn to before me.

/s/   Raymond Fontenot

_____

Raymond Fontenot
Notary Public

[*seal*]

Statement of Mary Largent

Ronnie had some trouble a few years ago. Some older boys in the neighborhood took him to a warehouse where they took some T.V. sets. They went in an unlocked door at night. Ronnie has just turned 17, old enough to be tried as an adult. He had always been a good boy, never in trouble before. He was trying to find himself and had decided to be a carpenter like his older brother, Joe. In addition to Joe, I have one other son, Michael, a West Point graduate who is a Captain in the U.S. Army. My daughter, Ilene, is a dental assistant. My husband died 10 years ago, killed in a car wreck. I did my best to raise the children. Ronnie got angry sometimes. I think he resented it that other kids had their dads around to play ball and do other things with them but his was taken from him in a freak accident. However, Ronnie's anger was disappearing, and he was maturing. Every once in awhile he would strike out, but in recent years this was only a passing emotional feature. His girl friend, Mary Jo Ebert, was finishing cosmetology school. She and a friend were going to open a hairstyling and beauty salon in a building here in town, and Ronnie was going to do the renovating for them. They were planning to be married in May, and were trying to pick a date.

A few months ago Ronnie was seeing off his best friend, who was joining the Navy. They had some drinks and then painted on a wall in Magnus Town, a deserted section of Villa Peak across the railroad tracks. While I don't approve of such pranks, Ronnie explained that Bud had some paint in his car. When they stopped at the old wall to relieve themselves, Bud brought out the paint can and painted "Bye, bye Bud" on the wall. An officer arrested them, and Ronnie told me the policeman "blew his stack." The boys apparently went along quietly, but there was some shouting and profanity by the officer who called Ronnie a son of a bitch. Two days later, Bud Belmont went away with the Navy. He's somewhere in the Sea of Japan now serving his country. Before he did anything with the boys, I got to talk to the judge and explained about Ronnie's dad being killed years before. Since Bud was going away, the judge let both the boys off with a stern lecture. It was a good lesson for them. Bud wrote me a letter after somebody sent him a clipping about Ronnie in the paper. He told me how sorry he was.

When Ilene called me on December 6, I took my purse and went straight to the police station. The desk sergeant said that I could post 10% of the bail in cash, or $150. But he said Ronnie would have to sign the releases and bond papers, so I left because the sergeant said Ronnie might not be back until midnight or later. I left the cash and got a receipt. I didn't go to the hospital because I thought I might miss Ronnie coming back the other way. I asked the desk sergeant to call me when Ronnie came in. I sat up in my living room chair until midnight or so, I guess, when I fell asleep. I might have dozed, off and on, a little before then.

Ronnie never talked about suicide. He always had a good outlook on life. He had finally started to make something of himself and was working for Williams Construction Company at the time of his death. He lived at home, and I know how he dressed. Not only was he without a belt that afternoon, he never wore one. He would buy his blue jeans tight, then he would wash them good to get them real snug. His pants never fell down.

He came home from work at 3:30 p.m. on December 6 with his work clothes real dirty. Since our washing machine at home was broken, he went to Fenton on Villa Avenue. It is about 10 blocks away. I live at 6245 Belmont Avenue. He slipped on a fresh pair of jeans and a T-shirt and said he would shower later. I never saw him alive again. He wasn't "high" on drugs or liquor that afternoon. Like I said, he had come straight home from work. There weren't any cuts or bruises on his head or chest. He was a healthy young man.

Ronnie finished high school (Villa High) and was an apprentice carpenter at the time of his death. He never went to a doctor except for strep throat and routine shots and immunizations as a child. He promised me he wouldn't get into trouble again after the incident with the yellow paint. I know he wouldn't do this to me, or his family, or himself.

Dated: June 7, 19YR–1

/s/ Mary Largent
_____
Mary Largent

Statement of Dr. Paul

It is my understanding that paramedics were immediately summoned by the desk sergeant when Mr. Largent was discovered hanging in his cell. Upon the paramedics' arrival Mr. Largent was examined and found to have been dead for a considerable period of time since the body showed signs of rigor mortis and all of his extremities had cooled considerably. Mr. Largent was taken down, and the Morena County Medical Examiner was notified. An autopsy was performed, and Dr. J.R. Fulton determined that Ronald Franklin Largent committed suicide by hanging himself. I disagree with this conclusion.

Largent had a deep bruise on his head, a deep laceration above the eye, which was bandaged, and other bruises. There were minor lacerations to the face. There was a long bruise across the chest. These wounds are consistent with being struck by a hard slender object such as a Kell light or nightstick; they are not consistent with a fall on a floor from a bunk. The chest bruise is quite significant. Its pattern is identical with being struck by a Kell light.

I have reviewed the autopsy report, as well as photographs taken during the autopsy, inspected the jail, and had the location of where the body was found hanging pinpointed by jail personnel. I have reached this conclusion. It is my opinion that this is not a self-inflicted hanging, but rather a hanging by a party or parties unknown. I base this on the presence of four different areas of force application to the body:

1. Right frontal parietal area.

2. Laceration of right eyebrow and associated abrasion of the right zygomatic area.

3. Small abrasion on the right cheek.

4. A patterned abrasion and contusion at the junction of the left anterior thoracic wall with the left shoulder-arm area. This is patterned and has a pattern that would be expected from the application of force with a Kell light.

I also note from the dimensions of the cell that the hanging was almost exactly at the midpoint between the bunks on either side. It would be my opinion that had a suicidal hanging taken place, the point of suspension would be much closer to the side of the cell which was used as a take-off point for applying the belt. That is, the individual would have stood, in my opinion, on the lower or upper bunk; and the point of suspension would be much closer to the side that he used for support.

Furthermore, I note that the individual did not wear a belt and had no belt and that the belt that was used for suspension was not his.

In brief, it is my opinion that this is a homicidal hanging.

I have reviewed the other witness statements in this file, and they in no way alter my opinion.

I am a graduate of Duke Medical School, with internship and residency in pathology at Massachusetts General Hospital. I am the Director of Consolidated Pathology Laboratories in Dallas, Texas. I employ 3 other specialists in this office. I have practiced pathology for 7 years and am on the staff of two Texas hospitals. My article, "Homicides and Suicides in Mental Hospitals and Jails," appeared in the International Quarterly of Pathology and Toxicology. I have testified in 5 or 6 prior cases, a couple of times for the state, some criminal and some civil cases.

Mary Largent's attorney contacted me several weeks ago. I studied the records in the case and visited the jail, which is in the same condition as when the Largent death occurred. With the assistance of an Officer Dixon, I was able to inspect the sort of Kell light customarily used by Villa Peak police. It is typical of this kind of heavy flashlight. I received $2,000 for my pretrial work, and will get $550 in connection with my courtroom appearance.

Dated: June 17, 19YR–1

/s/   Daniel Wm. Paul

_____

Daniel Wm. Paul

TARA DIXON

State of Clanton   )
)   Affidavit
County of Clanton   )

Personally appeared before me Tara Dixon who, after being duly sworn, made this statement:

1. I was employed on December 6 by the Villa Peak Police Department as a patrol officer, a position I had occupied for about 2 years. As a result of my disagreement with Chief Flowers over shift, manpower and personnel resource allocations, as well as disciplinary policy, I am now an officer with High Point Police Department and have been so employed for a little less than two months.

2. On the night of December 6, Sergeant Easley asked me to take Ronald Largent to Morena Hospital. He had a severe cut in the front of

his head. On the ride over I asked him what had happened. He did not say anything. Then I asked him if either of the officers struck him while interrogating him and he said "no."

He added that one of the officers was nice. He did state that he was hit on the top of the head when arrested and he did not understand why, since he was already on the ground and handcuffed. Then I asked him if he had been hit while inside the jail, and he looked down. Then I asked: "What's this about falling off a bunk?" Ronald said that that was what one of the officers had told him to say. I explained to him that we all were police officers, and if any police officer did something out of line it reflected on us all. I explained that he would not be in trouble if he told me what took place. He said nothing further for a time.

As we neared the hospital, I asked: "Ronald, are you afraid to go back to the jail when we get done here?" He dropped his head and in a low tone after a long pause said: "No ma'am."

3. In the emergency room, I was seated some distance from where Dr. Cox was examining Ronald. Shortly after we arrived, Dr. Cox asked if Largent could make a call. I approved, and I saw them bring Largent a phone, which he used in the presence of Dr. Cox.

4. I took Ronald back to the jail. He had a bandage on his forehead. The thought of Largent harming himself came to mind because a young man his age hanged himself in the Morena City jail approximately one month previously. I talked to Largent, and he appeared to be a stronger person than that. He did not seem depressed. Nor did he speak of suicide. It is my opinion that he was not the type to cause injury to himself. About the laundromat incident, he said he was glad he had been caught, so he could get such incidents out of his system and go on from here.

5. After Ronald's death, Chief Flowers made only a cursory investigation and quickly "closed the books." He talked to a couple of police, but no family members or medical doctors.

6. Rollo has been around the jail on several occasions. I do not think he would say things that would displease the department; he would want to curry favor in anticipation of his next visit.

7. I saw the youngster that Officer Cleetz worked over before in the minor-in-possession case. The young man looked like he had gone through a war. Mr. Cleetz arrested two teenage boys and confiscated their beer. When one of the two threatened to hit the officer, Cleetz first hit him on the side of the head and then broke his jaw with the Kell light. I was surprised when the Chief exonerated Cleetz so quickly, because I know he threw somebody off the force a few years ago for doing the same thing. In this case I saw the parents come out of the Chief's office with the boy. His jaw was wired shut. A few minutes later the Chief came out with his arm around Cleetz's shoulder. They were laughing.

Dated: June 13, 19YR–1

/s/ Tara Dixon

Tara Dixon

Sworn to before me.

/s/ Carrie Kingman

_____

Carrie Kingman

Notary Public

[*seal*]

STIPULATIONS AND RULINGS

1. If Doctor Jonas Cox were called, he would testify consistently with point 13 in the Statement of Material Facts, but his surgery schedule does not permit his appearance at this trial. It is agreed that if Doctor Cox or Ilene were called, they would confirm the conversation mentioned in point 13. Formal proof is dispensed with and the jury may be informed of the fact of the conversation without further proof, as is the case with all facts appearing on the Statement as to which there is no disagreement. Any party wishing to submit such fact at trial may, but is not required to, do so in this fashion.

2. If Sergeant Easley were called, he would state that he called Mary Largent's home at about 10:30 p.m. and the phone rang several times, but there was no answer.

3. Any point in the affidavits of Chief Flowers and Officer Dixon may be read into evidence without the need to call the author as a trial witness. While points in these two affidavits may be subject to a relevancy objection, objections which go to the form or authentication of evidence are not allowed. Nor may hearsay or opinion objections be used to block the admission of passages in either affidavit.

4. Mary Largent has standing to bring this action.

5. The oral report of the paramedics supports the understanding contained in Dr. Paul's statement; the statement correctly states the findings of the paramedics. At trial the doctor may refer to what they found without further foundation.

6. Laboratory tests at El Dorado State Crime Laboratory added nothing new to the record, except they confirmed that the deceased tested negative for drugs and alcohol. This fact is stipulated to be correct.

7. The report of the El Dorado medical examiner is an official record required to be prepared pursuant to statute, and an appropriate certificate is attached to the copy in this file.

8. The following witnesses will be called to the stand upon trial of this case:

Mary Largent

Dr. Paul

Officer Cleetz

A.R. Buckingham

9.   As a result of pretrial rulings, the court will submit the case to the jury for a determination of liability under counts two and three of the complaint. The amount of damages will be addressed, if necessary, in a separate proceeding.

If you feel you need additional background in civil rights litigation, you might browse through these cases.

AUTHORITIES

Pembaur v. City of Cincinnati, 475 U.S. 469 (1986) (while single occasion of misconduct does not usually justify recovery, that rule is subject to exception where decision by municipal policymakers denies plaintiff constitutional rights as result of act that municipality has officially sanctioned or ordered).

City of Oklahoma City v. Tuttle, 471 U.S. 808 (1985) (proof of custom or city policy).

Rizzo v. Goode, 423 U.S. 362 (1976) (liability of supervisory official; plaintiff must establish affirmative link between actions of supervisor and injury).

Colburn v. Upper Darby Tp., 838 F.2d 663 (3d Cir.1988) (liability for suicide).

Spell v. McDaniel, 824 F.2d 1380 (4th Cir.1987).

Rymer v. Davis, 775 F.2d 756 (6th Cir.1985) (city's failure to train officers in arrest procedures was proper basis for liability).

McLaughlin v. City of LaGrange, 662 F.2d 1385, 1388 (11th Cir. 1981) (city police must be shown to be involved; no liability for isolated incident, because acts which inflict injury must result from official policy).

Turpin v. Mailet, 619 F.2d 196 (2d Cir.), cert. denied, 449 U.S. 1016 (1980) (liability for informal acts and omissions; inadequate training or supervision can amount to deliberate indifference; liability for single incident).

Martinez v. Rosado, 614 F.2d 829 (2d Cir.1980) (force by prison officials).

Hampton v. Hanrahan, 600 F.2d 600 (7th Cir.1979) (civil conspiracy defined).

Richardson v. City of Conroe, 582 F.2d 19 (5th Cir.1978) (excessive force).

Harris v. Chanclor, 537 F.2d 203 (5th Cir.1976) (right of incarcerated persons to be protected from attacks by other inmates).

Martinez v. Mancusi, 443 F.2d 921 (2d Cir.1970) (medical care rights).

Holly v. Rapone, 476 F.Supp. 226 (D.C.Pa.1979) (deliberate indifference required to prove actionable denial of adequate medical treatment).

Case file B–4
MOORE v. TAYLOR

Moore has filed a tort action against Taylor for a stabbing on November 10, 19YR–4. The complaint alleges that on that date, without any justification the defendant attacked and intentionally injured the plaintiff. The complaint alleges that the attack occurred at 11:55 p.m. at the Biltmore Hotel in downtown Morena. The Morena District Attorney filed criminal battery and attempted murder charges, but the prosecution resulted in two hung juries and mistrials. The District Attorney has decided against filing charges a third time. In the present trial, you are litigating only the issue of liability. The plaintiff has three potential witnesses: Mr. Moore, Officer Wilson, and Mr. Greene. At trial, the plaintiff may call only two of these witnesses.

Statement of William Moore

Two friends and I were talking in Room 406 of the Biltmore Hotel at 316 Turk Street—part of what you might call the "low rent district" in downtown Morena. One friend was Amy Christopher, who was also an "old girl friend" of the defendant, Jack Taylor. I had won Christopher away from Taylor about a year before by having some of my good friends tell Christopher lies about Taylor; I had them tell her that while Christopher and Taylor were going together, Taylor was fooling around with other women. At the time, I knew that that was untrue, but I just wanted her real bad. The second person present was Jerry Greene, a good friend of mine.

I heard a knock at the door, answered it, and was met at the doorway by the defendant. He began yelling and waving a pocket knife at me. Jerry Greene left immediately. I asked Taylor to step outside into the hallway. Taylor and I then walked into the hall. After a brief conversation, I tried to get the knife away from Taylor; but Taylor was angry and thrashing it around. Taylor attacked and stabbed me before I wrestled it away. The wounds in my hands came from the struggle over the knife after I was stabbed. I then went down to the lobby and asked Greene to call the police. When the police came, I was placed in an ambulance and taken to the hospital. At the time I refused to talk to the police other than to identify Taylor as the guy who had stabbed me. I do not remember what I did with the knife after I wrestled it away from Taylor. Taylor may have been drunk. Christopher and I were drinking, and I was "pretty tight." Taylor and I at least used to be good friends, and nothing like this ever happened before.

A few years ago I got into a fight in the Buena Vista Bar in Morena. I have always maintained that the other guy started the fight in the bar, but I did pay the other party $400.00 when the party hired an attorney and threatened to sue me.

I testified at both of the trials in Taylor's criminal prosecution. So did Jerry. I just can't believe that the jury refused to convict Taylor. Taylor didn't even testify at the second trial. Yet, when the judge asked the foreperson for the vote at the second trial, the woman said that they were hung 11 to 1 in favor of acquittal!

Dated: September 10, 19YR–1

/s/   William Moore
_____
William Moore

Statement of Officer Dave Wilson

I made the police report on this incident. My partner Officer Brown and I arrived at 316 Turk Street at about 12:10 a.m., November 10, following a midnight call about a stabbing. Upon our arrival we met the plaintiff, Bill Moore, and witness, Jerry Greene, in the hotel lobby. Both Moore and Greene informed us that Moore had just been stabbed by a man named Taylor. They added that Taylor lived in Room 201, but was currently upstairs in Room 406. Otherwise, Moore was relatively uncooperative. However, Moore's attitude was understandable, since Moore was disheveled, was bleeding profusely from both hands, and appeared intoxicated.

My partner and I next responded to Room 406 and were told by someone in the hallway that Taylor had gone back to his own room. I noted that there was blood on the walls, floor, and stair railing on the fourth floor around Room 406. We went to Room 201. We knocked on the door, identified ourselves as police officers, and announced that we wanted to enter. After a long pause, we were let in by Taylor. He matched the description given us by Greene and Moore. Taylor had blood on his face and in his hair, a cut over one eye, and several cuts on his hands. Taylor had no shirt on. Taylor was holding a face towel, as if he had just come from the bathroom. His forearms seemed to be wet. I could not detect any alcohol on Taylor's breath. Taylor was arrested for assault.

I later searched for the knife supposedly used in the fight, but neither Officer Brown nor I could find it. The next day Greene gave me a knife he claims to have found in the hallway. Moore later identified it as the knife Taylor used.

Dated: October 24, 19YR–1

/s/   David Wilson
_____
David Wilson

Statement of Jerald Greene

I was talking upstairs with Moore and Amy Christopher. Taylor came in stinking of booze. He took a knife out of his right pocket and was waving it around wildly. I left immediately. I went downstairs and struck up a conversation about baseball with the desk clerk. I was in the lobby later when Moore staggered down the stairs and asked me to call the police. I vaguely recall that Moore said something like, "I just had it out with Jack. I could of taken him, but he had that damn knife." I could see Moore had been stabbed; he was bloody and had cuts on his hands and body. I called the police and then waited with Moore until they came. I am a friend of Moore's, and I know Taylor and Christopher, too. We all drink heavily.

The day after the fight, I found a knife in the hallway near Bill's room. It looked like the knife Taylor had used during the fight. I guess the police just overlooked it. I picked it up and brought it down to the police station. The investigating officer, Wilson, happened to be on duty; and I hand delivered the knife to him. Bill tells me that Wilson had since shown the knife to Bill, and Bill says he can recognize it as the knife Taylor used to cut Bill up. I wanted to help the cops any way I could.

Dated: June 6, 19YR–1

/s/   Jerald L. Greene

Jerald L. Greene

Statement of Jack Taylor

I am a carpenter. I've been in that line of work ever since graduating from high school. Amy Christopher and I were high school sweethearts. After I broke up with Amy, I got a new girlfriend. On the evening of November 10th, I came home, changed, and phoned my new girlfriend-only to discover that she had stood me up for a date. I was angry; I had a right to be. When I found out that my new girlfriend was not going to be able to keep our date, I blew my stack at her and read her the riot act. Then I tried to reach Christopher; but she was out.

I then walked upstairs to Room 406, where I knew Moore was staying. I was carrying a pocket knife. The knife was handy in my line of work. Moore and I began to argue and went out into the hallway. I took out the knife but did not attack Moore. Moore tried to grab the knife and use it against me, and a struggle over the knife ensued. During the fight Moore was stabbed, and we both were cut. I had the knife in my left hand. Moore was facing me; he lunged at me and grabbed at the knife with his right hand. Then Moore twisted around; we were standing side by side-Moore was to my left, still struggling, and the knife was between us. The two of us fell backwards, still almost side by side. The knife was underneath Moore when we fell. The knife just happened to stab Moore in the back.

When we made it to our feet again, the fight continued. We both grabbed at the knife, and I got it. I was holding it in front of me protectively as Moore came at me. He grabbed at me, and the knife hit him in the chest. Even though I was holding it out in front of me in plain view, Moore virtually lunged into the knife. We continued hand-to-hand fighting, during which our hands were cut up.

Moore finally succeeded in getting the knife away from me and ran downstairs. I do not know what happened to the weapon. I cooperated fully with the police when they came to my room after the incident.

The cops have shown me the knife they say I used in the fight with Moore. It's not mine. The knife they have is a big stiletto. My knife is a small pocket knife; everyone at the mill knows I always carry a pocket knife. What use would a carpenter have for a stiletto?

I understand that that guy Greene claims that I was drunk. If he says that, he's a liar. I'll admit that I once was an alcoholic. But I've been off the bottle for four years. In fact, I'm the vice–president of the Morena chapter of Alcoholics Anonymous.

Until this incident, my record has been absolutely clean. I've never been arrested for or convicted of anything. Thanks to Moore and Greene, the local D.A. twice tried to convict me for the fight. Both times the juries had the sense to see through all the lies by Moore and Greene. The last time the jury voted 11—1 in favor of innocence. After that, the D.A. saw the light and gave up. Now it's only Moore who's suing me.

Dated: April 7, 19YR–1

/s/   Jack Taylor

_____

Jack Taylor

POLICE RECORDS

[Certified under Seal as Correct by El Dorado Bureau of Criminal Investigation]

Jack V. Taylor

Time of Arrest	Offense	Disposition
None	None	None

Statement of Vernon Hilton

I know Bill Moore. Moore works as a salesperson at a used car lot, and I am the assistant manager of the lot. I originally hired Moore—that was a big mistake on my part.

In my opinion, Moore is a violent person. I used to go out drinking on Saturday nights with Moore, but on several occasions Moore got into fights after he had had too many drinks. On one occasion in particular,

Moore was with Amy Christopher, me, and my wife at a disco. Moore almost started a fight with a guy simply because the guy had asked Ms. Christopher for a dance.

I also think that Moore is a liar. On several occasions customers have complained to me that Moore had misrepresented the condition of cars they had purchased from the lot. There are all sorts of complaint letters in his personnel file. I've enclosed a Xerox copy of one. I have told several of the other salespersons at the lot that Moore is the sort of jerk who gives all us used car salespeople a bad name. I had recommended to Ms. Falco, the general manager, that she fire Moore; but Ms. Falco always said that she would not do that until I could "get the goods" on Moore. I think that Ms. Falco won't fire Moore primarily because Moore is so slick and handsome.

When Moore returned to work after the hospitalization resulting from the fight with Taylor, Moore discussed the fight with me. In that conversation, Moore insisted that Taylor had started the fight. However, I distinctly remember Moore saying "But I almost finished the fight and that bastard Taylor once and for all."

Dated: November 1, 19YR-1

/s/   Vernon Hilton

Vernon Hilton

Bernstein Used Cars
442 Magellan
Morena, El Dorado

Dear Sir or Madam:

Two months ago I bought a used, 19YR-8 Ford station wagon from your lot. The salesman who sold it to me was named Moore. Before I bought the car, Moore made all sorts of representations to me. He told me that the car had undergone "a complete overhaul." He assured me that the brakes were good, the fuel line had been replaced, and there were only 45,000 miles on the car. Because of those assurances, I bought the car.

About a month later the car started falling apart on me. It stopped dead in its tracks on an offramp of the freeway-my family could have been killed! I took the car to the nearest mechanic. I understand you guys know the mechanic-Roy Foster at Mel's Chevron on Third Street. Mr. Foster tells me that the brakes are shot, the fuel line-which is in terrible condition-must be the original, and the odometer has been turned back.

Last week I went to your lot and confronted Moore. At first, he just pulled the contract and pointed out the "as is" clause to me. When I wasn't satisfied, he insulted me, called me a "jerk," and told me to "sue" if I wanted to.

The truth is that I don't have the money to sue. I spent my last cash to get some good, reliable transportation for my family. Because of you and your salesman Moore, now I have neither the money nor the transportation. I demand restitution.

Very truly yours,
Gary Anderson

STIPULATIONS

1. There is a stipulation of the expected testimony of Doctor Samuel Merit about the knife wounds to Moore. If present, Dr. Merit would testify that: He is on the staff of Good Samaritan Hospital in Morena; he was the physician who treated William Moore; there were two near-fatal wounds caused by a mediumsized knife, one in the back necessitating removal of the spleen and one in the chest near Moore's heart; Moore was hospitalized in serious condition for one week; and Moore remained in the hospital in fair condition for two weeks before his release.

2. Dr. Merit is a board-certified forensic pathologist.

3. Amy Christopher cannot be located and will not testify.

Plaintiff's Attorney

/s/   William N. Moore

William N. Moore
Plaintiff

Defense Attorney

/s/   Jack V. Taylor

Jack V. Taylor
Defendant

Case File B–5[1]

PEOPLE OF THE STATE OF EL DORADO
v. CORREY RAUSCH

SUMMARY OF FACTS: (The purpose of this summary is merely to acquaint you with the case; the summary itself is not evidence.)

On June 15 last year, several patrons were in the Red Apple, a neighborhood tavern located at 3300 North Clark Street in Morena.

1. This case file is based in large part on a fact situation developed by Professor Thomas A. Mauet of the University of Arizona and the Hon. Warren Wolfson. The

Among those present were Correy Rausch, the defendant, and William Jones, the alleged victim. Both Rausch and Jones were regular patrons of the tavern and, like the others, had a few drinks from about 9:00 p.m. until 11:00 p.m.

At approximately 11:00 p.m., Rausch and Jones got into an argument. A few minutes later Rausch left, telling people he was going to walk home. About two minutes later, Jones followed him out. They argued again, and Rausch shot and killed Jones.

The People have filed murder and manslaughter charges against Rausch. He has entered a plea of not guilty. The case is being tried in El Dorado Superior Court. The Prosecution may call the following witnesses: Fred Martin and Edna Felton. The Defense may call the following witnesses: Correy Rausch and George Garner.

The parties have entered into the following stipulations of fact: On the day of the shooting, Rausch was 35 years old, 5N6O tall, and weighed 150 pounds; Jones was 22 years old, 6N2O tall, and weighed 200 pounds; Rausch was adjudicated a juvenile delinquent because of several theft incidents while he was in high school; as an adult, Rausch was convicted of aggravated battery eight years ago and placed on five years' probation; at the preliminary hearing, the defendant was represented by Albert Hewitt, Esq.; but Mr. Hewitt did not conduct any cross-examination.

There are also stipulations of law that the photographs of the gun and casings may be admitted in evidence and that Officer Connor complied with Miranda in questioning the defendant.

There is a stipulation of expected testimony that if present, Police Officer Thomas Connor would testify to the facts stated in the "narrative" section of police report.

TRANSCRIPT OF PRELIMINARY HEARING

Report of Proceedings, held before the Honorable Roberta Collins, on June 30, 19YR–1.

EDNA FELTON, having been first duly sworn, testified as follows:

p. 7

Q. (By the prosecutor). How long were you in the Red Apple tavern before the trouble broke out?

A. About two hours. I'm a regular patron, and I usually spend a couple of hours there each weeknight.

Q. Who came in first that evening—Rausch or Jones?

A. Jones.

Q. What happened when Jones arrived?

original fact situation appears in T. MAUET & W. WOLFSON, MATERIALS IN TRIAL ADVOCACY 859–83 (5th ed. 2002). Reprinted with the kind permission of Aspen Law Publishing and the authors.

A. He started mouthing off that Rausch had "ripped off" some of his money. He said that Rausch was either going to make good on it or "get the point" that night.

Q. Was Rausch there when Jones made that statement?

A. No.

Q. When Rausch and Jones started arguing, could you hear what they said?

A. No, I wasn't really paying attention.

Q. What happened next?

A. Well, they left—first Rausch and then Jones. Maybe a minute later I heard a loud bang. We all ran outside, and I saw Rausch standing over Jones. Rausch was holding a gun. He looked at us, dropped the gun, and started running up the street. A few of the guys shouted at him to stop, chased him, and brought him back.

Q. Did Rausch do anything then?

A. No, he just stood there until the police arrived. He never said anything other than "I didn't want to fight him."

FRED MARTIN, having been first duly sworn, testified as follows:

p. 13

Q. (By the prosecutor). What were you doing at approximately 11:00 p.m.?

A. I was on my porch reading the paper.

Q. Did anything happen at that time?

A. Yes, I heard two men at the end of the block. It sounded like they were arguing. Both of them were talking loudly, but I couldn't make out the actual words.

Q. What happened next?

A. The short man was backing up, and the other one was following. They appeared to be keeping the same distance apart.

Q. How far apart were they?

A. I'd estimate about fifteen feet.

Q. Then what happened?

A. They were still arguing in loud voices, then a shot rang out, and the tall man fell. The short one just stood there.

Q. How far apart were the two men then?

A. Probably about ten feet. They were simply standing there-facing each other just before the shot.

Q. Then what happened?

A. Some people came out of the Red Apple and started shouting.

p. 14

The short man dropped the gun and ran up the street towards me, but some of the people from the Red Apple caught him and held him until the police arrived.

Q. How far were you from where the shooting took place?

A. I'd say around 100 feet or so.

Q. Did anything obstruct your view?

A. There may have been a garbage can here or there on the street, but I really can't remember. There might have been a car or van parked somewhere along the street. But I still had a real good view.

Q. (To the defendant) At this point, with Her Honor's permission, I would ask the defendant to rise.

J. Granted. The defendant will stand.

Q. Now, Mr. Martin, I want you to think very carefully before you answer my next question.

A. I will.

Q. Look around this courtroom, and tell us whether you see the man who did the shooting that night.

A. I do.

Q. Where is he?

A. He's the last man at the table to my right.

Q. How is he dressed?

A. In a blue suit with a green tie.

Q. Your Honor, please let the record reflect that the witness has identified the defendant.

J. It shall.

Q. Mr. Martin, how positive are you that the defendant is the man who did the shooting?

A. Absolutely, 100% certain, sir!

p. 15

I, the undersigned, certify under my seal that: I am an official court reporter for the Superior Court of the State of El Dorado; my state court reporter license expires on June 30, 19YR + 4; I attended the preliminary hearing of the defendant Correy Rausch held on June 30, 19YR–1, at the Morena County Courthouse; and the attached document is a true and correct copy of the proceedings of that preliminary hearing.

Dated: July 19, 19YR–1

/s/ Vera Shultz

_____

Vera Shultz

[seal]

POLICE REPORT

Date: 6/15/YR–1

Time: 2310 hrs.

Location: approx. 3309 N. Clark, on sidewalk

Arrested: Correy Rausch, M/W, 35, 5N6O, 150 lbs.

Victim: William Jones (deceased)

Witnesses: Fred Martin, 333 N. Clark
Edna Felton, 3140 N. Kenmore

Charges: murder, manslaughter

R/O: Thomas Connor, patrolman

Narrative: On 6/15/YR–1 at 2310 hrs. R/O on routine patrol received radio message of "man shot" at Clark and Elm. Proceeded to location, observed several persons holding a man, arrestee Rausch, and another man, William Jones, lying on the sidewalk, with apparent through-and-through wound to chest-back. Ambulance called, took victim to St. Mary's Hospital. Searched area, .38 cal. revolver, Smith & Wesson, 2O barrel, found approx. 3N from Jones' head, containing 5 unspent, 1 spent shells, and smelled of fresh gunpowder. No other weapons found in area. Jones' body laying on sidewalk approx. in front of 3309 N. Clark, about 40N from Elm, parallel to street, feet toward Elm. Revolver marked and inventoried.

Investigation:

Following persons interviewed:

1. Edna Felton stated she was in the Red Apple tavern, 3300 N. Clark, since about 9:00 p.m. Rausch and Jones were there, as well as several other persons. Everyone was drinking socially. Around 11:00 p.m. Rausch and Jones got into an argument. Other patrons broke it up and things returned to normal. A few minutes later Rausch left, followed shortly by Jones. A minute or two later Felton heard a shot from outside the tavern. She and the other patrons went outside, saw Rausch across the street standing near Jones, who was lying on the sidewalk. Rausch looked at them, dropped a gun, and started to run up the street. Several patrons chased Rausch, caught him and returned him to the scene of the shooting. Rausch said nothing from that time until police arrived.

2. Fred Martin stated he was sitting on his porch at 3333 N. Clark, and noticed two men talking loudly at the end of the block near Elm. They were approx. across from the Red Apple at the time. The short man (Rausch) was backing away from the tall man (Jones). The short man was backing up towards Martin. The taller man was following. Because

of the light and distance, he wasn't too sure how far apart they were, although it didn't seem very far. They seemed to be keeping the same distance, still talking loudly, when a shot rang out, and the tall man slumped to the sidewalk. The short man just stood there. People came out of the Red Apple and crossed the street. The short man threw what appeared to be a gun down and started to run up the sidewalk towards Martin. The people from the tavern caught him and returned him back to where the tall man had fallen, and held him until police arrived.

3.   Rausch was handcuffed, advised of his *Miranda* rights, and put in the rear of the squad car. R/O asked Rausch what happened, and he stated that he and Jones got into an argument in the Red Apple. According to Rausch there was an ongoing dispute between the two over whose money was used to buy some drinks at the Red Apple the previous week. Rausch stated that the previous week both he and Jones had been in the Red Apple, and Jones had accused him of using Jones' money, which was on the bar counter, to buy some drinks. Rausch denied the accusation, but Jones kept "hassling" him about it that night and was threatening to beat him up, and again the night of the shooting. On the night of the shooting, Jones wanted to go outside and fight. Rausch said he didn't want to, so the whole thing died down. He then left the tavern and crossed the street, when he noticed Jones following him. Jones kept saying, "You want to fight?" and kept following. Rausch said he kept backing up, and Jones kept coming closer until he was only about 3 feet away, then lunged at him. Rausch said he reached for a gun in his jacket pocket and fired it at Jones, who fell down. According to Rausch, Jones is known to carry a knife on him. Rausch says he has personally seen Jones with a knife several times in the past. On the night of the shooting, Rausch believed Jones was carrying his knife as usual, and was afraid that Jones was going to stab him with it on the street. Rausch said that after he fired, he panicked and ran, but was caught by the people from the tavern.

/s/   Thomas Connor

Thomas Connor, patrolman
Morena P.D.

I, the undersigned, certify that I am the records custodian for the Morena Police Department and that the attached document is a true copy of an original police report in my custody.

/s/   Kenneth So

Kenneth So
Morena P.D.

[seal]

Statement of Correy Rausch

I grew up in the Midwest on a small farm. However, these are hard times for small farms, and I could see that my home town was just drying up and dying. So a couple of months ago I decided to move to El Dorado. I arrived in Morena in early April last year. I didn't have much money, and consequently, I had to rent a flat in pretty rough part of town. There are lots of muggings and burglaries in that area, and I was glad that I had remembered to pack my revolver in my bags when I moved here. Back home I used it on small varmints, but here I needed it for protection. This flat was just a couple of blocks away from the Red Apple Tavern.

There isn't a lot to do in this part of town at night, so I started hanging out at the Red Apple at night. I figured that I'd get to know some locals, and maybe they could give me a lead on a good job. Most of the people at the bar were friendly enough. There was one dude, though, a guy named Jones, who seemed to be the bully. He was always bragging about how tough he was and how many guys he'd beaten up. Just to impress people, he'd pull out a knife and flash a couple of moves. I'd seen him pull that stunt a couple of times.

However, one night—maybe June 8 or 9 last year—I ended up standing near him at the counter. The place was packed that night, and there wasn't any other place I could find to get close enough to the bartender to get a drink. I was buying a drink, and I guess Jones was paying for some drinks at about the same time. All of a sudden he whirls on me and claims that I used some money he put on the bar to pay for my drink. I told him that I was sorry there'd been a misunderstanding, but I was absolutely certain that I hadn't touched his dough. I turned to the bartender and the other guys standing around and asked them whether anyone of them had seen me take any of Jones' money. They all said they hadn't, and the bartender told Jones to chill out. Jones kept on hasslin' me for about another hour. He referred to me as a "chicken shit thief" and threatened to "beat the shit" out of me. I just let it roll off. When I thought he was getting drunker and maybe a little more dangerous, I just left. I didn't want a fight. I'm a peaceful sort of person. I said goodnight to Marla, the bartender, and went back to the flat.

I stayed away from the Red Apple for a couple of days. I was tired at night because I'd been hitting the pavement to find a job, and I guess I also wanted to let Jones cool down. However, when the night of June 15 rolled around, I figured I needed some entertainment and a drink. So I headed down to the bar. I hoped that Jones had mellowed out by now, but I remembered his knife and decided to take my revolver along just to be on the safe side. You can use a gun to put some sense into some pretty stubborn heads. I brought it along only for self-defense; I wanted to be able to pull it out and frighten him off if he started anything.

When I got to the Red Apple, at first I didn't notice Jones. I walked up to the counter and ordered a shot from Marla. Then from behind me I heard Jones. He said something like, "Well, look who's here. Gonna steal anybody's money tonight? Huh?'' I told him again that I didn't take his money and that I didn't want any trouble. He bugged me for a couple more minutes, and then I guess he got more interested in other things and let me alone. I spent a while at the bar. As I walked to the door, I thought I heard him make some crack about beating me up, but I can't be sure. There was a lot of noise in the bar.

I got outside and decided to have a smoke. I lit up, took a couple of drags, and then started walking back toward my flat. I got to the other side of the street when I heard the door to the bar open. I looked back over my shoulder and saw Jones. He screamed, "Hey, chicken shit, you man enough to fight tonight?" I didn't even answer him. I just kept walking away from him.

I took another couple of steps, but I could hear footsteps behind me. I looked back again, and it was clear Jones was following me. By this time he was in the middle of the street and moving toward me. He kept saying, "You want to fight?" I kept backing up away from him. I was shaking my head to let him know that I didn't want any fight that night. I tried to walk away at a quicker pace, but then he started moving faster. I was really getting worried. Before I knew it, he was almost on top of me. He was maybe three to five feet away, and he had this vicious look on his face. I figured he was ready to whip out his knife and start carving on me. I wasn't going to give him that chance. He made a move as if to lunge at me. I didn't have any choice. I reached into my pocket, grabbed my gun, and fired at him while he was in midair coming at me. He fell-dead, I guess.

Obviously, the whole thing shook me up. I just stood there over him with the gun in my hand. Then some guys came out of the bar. I knew that Jones had a lot of friends, and it raced through my mind that some of them might try to finish what he had started. So I turned and ran away. However, a bunch of the people from the bar caught up with me and brought me back to the bar to wait for the police. I settled down as soon as I realized that they just wanted to hold me for the cops.

I never, never wanted to fight him. Killing him was the last thing I wanted to do that night. So help me God.

Dated: August 3, 19YR-1

/s/ Correy Rausch

Correy Rausch

Statement of Dr. George Garner

My name is George Garner. I am a licensed physician in the State of El Dorado. My specialty is pathology, but I am not a certified forensic pathologist. However, I had training in forensic pathology when I studied at St. Louis University Medical School. I have a contract with the County of Morena to conduct autopsies for the county. I was the physician who autopsied the body of William Jones. I determined that the cause of death was a bullet which entered the victim's chest at the left nipple level and exited the back near the spine at the third lumbar vertebra level and perforated the victim's heart, left lung, and diaphragm. Although both the Jones' body and clothing displayed bullet holes, there was no singeing, soot, or stippling on either the body or the clothing. Experts differ, but I use these guidelines: You'll get singeing or scorching of the skin with a contact wound. A close-range shot-up to half a foot from the skin surface-can result in a soot deposit. However, you get peppering or stippling with intermediate range shots. The effect is produced by the particles of powder; since they have greater mass, they carry farther than soot. An intermediate range shot is potentially from $3\frac{1}{2}$ or 4 feet from the skin surface.

I have agreed to appear as a defense witness in this case. I have testified in over 200 prior cases—in the overwhelming majority of instances for the prosecution. I understand that the defendant is indigent and I consequently agreed to testify on a contingent fee in this case; I'd get my regular $200 an hour fee only if Rausch is acquitted.[1] I realize that if he's imprisoned, he won't be able to earn any money to pay my fee.

Dated: September 3, 19YR–1

/s/   George Garner

————————————————

George Garner

1. Neither the rules of the El Dorado Bar nor the rules of the El Dorado Medical Association expressly forbid compensating experts on a contingent fee basis.

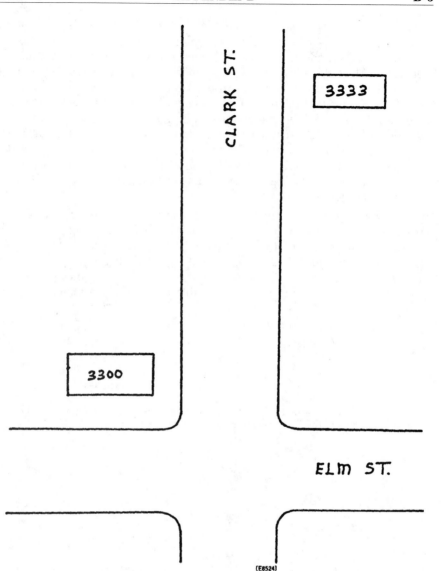

6/15/YR-1   off. T. Connor

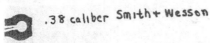

.38 caliber Smith + Wesson

3333 N. Clark / RAUSCH

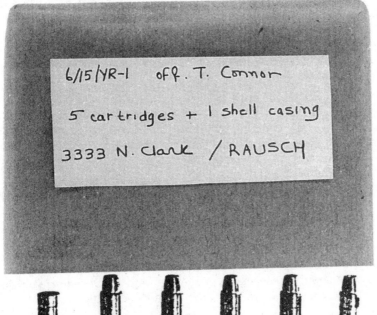

6/15/YR-1   off. T. Connor

5 cartridges + 1 shell casing

3333 N. Clark / RAUSCH

Case file B–6
STRIPLING v. AHRENS

The defense may not invoke a statute of limitations defense.

Statement of Jeffrey L. Stripling

My name is Jeffrey L. Stripling. Until recently, I resided in Silver Springs, Maryland. I own a chain of retail sporting goods stores in Maryland. In 19YR–7, I purchased a house in Morena near Dixon. I purchased the house as an investment and rented it through a local rental agency, Haney Rentals. In January 19YR–3, the defendant George Ahrens moved into my house as tenant.

I first met Ahrens in February 19YR–3. One of the major suppliers for my sporting goods stores is a Dixon manufacturer, and I decided that I might as well meet my tenant. I stopped by the house one day and introduced myself. We immediately took a liking to each other, and Ahrens invited me over for drinks and dinner that evening. My date, Maureen Tissier, and I visited Ahrens and his wife that evening. We had a pleasant time. I gathered that Ahrens was a real estate broker, involved in various commercial developments throughout El Dorado and Nevada. He briefly described some business opportunities in the area, but I didn't give the topic any serious thought at the time.

Ahrens was a pretty good tenant. He and his wife kept the house in good repair. They were occasionally late on rent payments, but an occasional late payment is to be expected.

I flew out to Morena on business again in April 19YR–3. On that visit, I phoned Ahrens to let him know that I was in town. He said he was glad I called. He explained that he had found a site suitable for development as a tennis club and wanted me to go along. As I recall, Maureen went with us. As we were driving up, Ahrens explained that he had given tennis developments a lot of thought and had invested a lot of time running down prospective sites. We drove west on the main highway, toward Dixon I think, and then pulled off on a road leading to the east. Ahrens stopped his car at the fence surrounding the property. I was quite impressed by the site. Ahrens pointed out that old house on the property and explained how we could renovate it into the clubhouse. I told him that I had just read somewhere that tennis clubs were becoming very popular, especially in Florida, and El Dorado. I told him that I'd definitely be interested in going in on the development.

While we were driving back, we reached agreement on an interim partnership. Ultimately, we wanted a corporate entity, but we figured that that would pose S.E.C. problems if we formed the corporation while I was still a permanent resident of Maryland. To avoid federal headaches, we decided on a partnership. It was to be an equal partnership; I would contribute $10,000, and Ahrens would put in the same amount. At the time, we did not discuss the topic of compensation he or I would receive for work for the firm. As Ahrens pulled up to drop me off at my hotel, we shook hands and I guaranteed him that I'd be sending him my $10,000 as soon as possible. He said he'd stick it in an account and get right to work on the project.

When I returned to Maryland in mid-April, I immediately contacted my local banker. I arranged for a $10,000 cashier's check. The bank issued the check, and I sent it to Ahrens. I enclosed the check with a letter. In the letter, I asked him to be sure to keep me apprised of the progress of the tennis club project.

In early May, I received a letter from Ahrens (by this time, I was familiar with his handwriting style, and I recognized his handwriting). In the letter, Ahrens acknowledged receipt of the $10,000 check. The letter added that he would begin pressing for the necessary permits. I guessed that he meant building permits, any environmental stuff, and the like. Finally, the letter assured me that the project was coming along nicely.

I flew out again in July 19YR–3. I had a brief dinner meeting with Ahrens. I think Mo was with me. We had dinner at China Camp. Ahrens told me once again that although there were some problems with permanent financing, the project was almost ready to fly. He told me that he heard a rumor from a reliable source that a local sporting goods company was on the verge of bankruptcy and might want to sell all of its tennis equipment for a song. We talked about the advisability of getting the equipment for the tennis club. We agreed that it would be a good idea. In passing, Ahrens also mentioned that our initial capital was running out. I then volunteered to send him a $5,000 check from Maryland. Ahrens said he thought that he could bargain the club down to around $5,000.

I flew back to Maryland that weekend. I made immediate arrangements for the second cashier's check. As soon as the check was ready, I mailed it to Ahrens.

Between July and October, I had only one letter from Ahrens. The letter acknowledged the $5,000 check and said that the project was perking along. I was pretty busy with my sporting goods stores in Maryland at the time, and I let things slide a bit. I occasionally phoned Ahrens at the realty firm where he worked, but I was rarely able to reach him. I left messages, but he didn't return my calls.

Finally, in November, I again had occasion to visit Morena. I figured it was time for a showdown. As soon as I got into town, I phoned Ahrens and demanded that he meet me. We met at the Port Morena restaurant that evening. I asked him point blank where the project stood and whether he was still interested in proceeding. Ahrens said that financing had proved to be too much of a problem and he thought that he couldn't get financing at a reasonable rate. I asked him for an accounting. He then admitted that he had spent a lot of the $15,000 for personal expenses, even rent payments on the house he was renting from me! He told me that he felt a moral obligation to me and would give me a promissory note for the whole $15,000. I told him that he'd damn better come up with the money. I think he could sense that I was ready to blow up. He assured me that he would give me the note the next day and could raise at least half the money immediately.

Ahrens delivered the note to me the next day. He also gave me his file on the tennis club project. For a while I used the file to pursue the project on my own, but I think I eventually dumped the file; all the junk Ahrens had put in it was worthless. Ahrens has never paid me a red cent on the note. He comes up with one excuse after another. One time he said the I.R.S. had impounded his accounts. Another time he said he had prepared a check but his secretary mislaid it. My patience with the man has run out. I am now convinced that Ahrens embezzled the $15,000, and I want him prosecuted to protect other honest investors from con men like Ahrens.

I moved to Morena this month. I am now a permanent resident of El Dorado.

On my attorney's advice, I am suing Ahrens for fraud and seeking punitive damages.

Dated: January 14, 19YR–2

/s/   Jeffrey L. Stripling
_____
Jeffrey L. Stripling

Statement of Maureen E. Tissier

My name is Maureen E. Tissier. I live in Morena. I work for Haney Rentals in downtown Morena. Mr. Jeffrey Stripling is one of our customers. Jeff lives in Maryland, but he occasionally comes to Morena on business trips. Whenever Jeff is in town, we usually get together for dinner or a few drinks.

The first time I met the defendant was in March 19YR–3. Jeff had flown into town on business, and he said that his tenant had invited him over for dinner and drinks. He asked whether I wanted to come along. I said that that would be great. Jeff picked me up, and we drove over to Ahrens' house. We had a nice evening, but at the end Jeff and Ahrens were into a heavy conversation about local investment opportunities. Even though I work for a realty company, I'm not into that sort of thing; and I'm afraid that I didn't listen too carefully. I do remember that Ahrens seemed to know a lot about the local realty market.

The second time I met the defendant was in April 19YR–3. Jeff was out here again on business, and he said that Ahrens was going to drive him out to Dixon, one of the nearby suburbs. I hadn't spent much time in Dixon, but I'd liked what I'd seen; and I thought it would be nice to take another look around in that area. So the three of us drove up there in Ahrens' Lincoln. I remember Ahrens going through a big routine about how much time he'd spent researching tennis club developments. It struck me as a bunch of hype, but Jeff certainly seemed to believe Ahrens.

I turned out that Ahrens wanted to show Jeff the proposed site for a tennis club. It was a nice enough location. While we were at the site, Jeff told Ahrens that he would contribute $10,000. I'm not certain whether Ahrens said he'd put in any money at first. Ahrens said something along the lines that he'd get to work using the money as soon as Jeff mailed the check; I can't remember quite what Ahrens said. I do know that Ahrens said he would be Jeff's partner in the tennis club. When we drove back, Jeff assured Ahrens that he, Jeff, would send him a check soon.

I met Ahrens one last time. It was in late June or early July. Jeff flew out on business. Jeff and I had dinner with Ahrens and his wife at Min's Cafe. Jeff asked some straight questions about how the project was coming; but as far as I was concerned, he didn't get any straight answers out of Ahrens. As usual, Ahrens said that things were going great but he gave Jeff some jive about "financing." I really wasn't interested enough to pay close attention. Ahrens said that some local sporting equipment manufacturer wanted to get rid of all its tennis gear. He hinted around that it would be great if Jeff came up with some more dough to buy the gear. Jeff did just that; he offered to send Ahrens another $5,000.

As we were driving back to my place after dinner that evening, I told Jeff that I was beginning to worry about the project. I told him that Ahrens' answers didn't ring true to me and that Jeff might be pouring good money after bad by giving Ahrens another $5,000. I guess I was right. I'm certainly willing to testify against Ahrens. Jeff is a good friend, and I hated to see Ahrens take him for all that money.

Dated: January 20, 19YR–2

/s/   Maureen E. Tissier

——————————————————

Maureen E. Tissier

Statement of George R. Ahrens

My name is George R. Ahrens. I have lived in Morena for seven years. I work part-time as a real estate salesman for Amerson Realty. I live with my wife in a house I rent from Mr. Jeffrey L. Stripling. I met Jeff for the first time in March 19YR–3. He had flown out from Maryland and wanted to introduce himself while he was in town. He seemed like an awfully nice fellow, and I invited him over for drinks that night. He and his date, a Maureen Tissier, dropped by that evening. We talked about a lot of things, the East Coast, sports, but the conversation eventually turned to local investment opportunities. I told Jeff that I was a real estate salesman and was generally familiar with development opportunities in the area. That's as far as our conversation went that night.

I didn't see Jeff again until a while later. In the meantime, I had become rather interested in tennis club developments. I read an article about tennis clubs in FORTUNE or BUSINESS WEEK, and it seemed like a perfect project for a place like Dixon or Woodland. I found a particularly favorable site in Dixon. I stumbled across the site just a few days before Jeff flew into town. When he got in, he happened to phone me. I remembered that he was interested in local investment opportunities, and I knew I would need additional capital for the tennis club; I hadn't been making many sales, and I was even late on some of my rent payments. I thought that Jeff might be the source of capital I needed. I told him about the site I'd found and invited him to drive up there with me.

He accepted my invitation and brought Ms. Tissier along. As we were driving up, I described all the time, effort, and expense I'd already put into the tennis club concept. I explained that I had invested maybe $10,000 or $20,000 in time and money. When we got up there, I showed him around. I pointed out the large, old house on the property and indicated how we might renovate it. He seemed impressed by the layout. I said I'd conservatively value my time and expenses at $10,000, and we'd be equal partners, each having a 50% interest. I made it clear to him that he would have to put in working capital later; he was paying the $10,000 just to get in on the ground level. We also agreed that I'd eventually be reimbursed 50% for any additional money I had to put out of pocket for the project. We shook hands, and Jeff promised that he would send me a check from Maryland.

Jeff kept his word. About a week later I received a cashier's check for $10,000 in the mail. I took the check and deposited it in my personal checking account at First National Bank of El Dorado. I didn't put the money in a trust account simply because I considered the money mine. I used the money to pay my expenses, airline tickets, rent, groceries, etc. Of course, some of the expenditures were related to the project. For example, I paid an attorney $200 to do a draft of the partnership agreement.

Between April and July, I kept working on the project. I naturally had to spend most of my time on the job for Amerson Realty. However, I'd say I spent at least 20% of my business time on the project. I contacted the owners of the site I'd shown Jeff to see what they wanted for the property. I checked on the requirements for building permits, and that sort of thing. I researched the zoning. I even checked on the operating procedures of some established tennis clubs in Morena. As time passed, though, it became increasingly apparent that the Morena money market was getting pretty tight. I began to worry whether we'd be able to get the permanent financing we needed at a reasonable interest rate.

Jeff flew out in late June. I told him that while prospects were still good, I was having trouble with the financing. He said that he was sorry he didn't know anybody in the local money market; all his contacts were on the East Coast. He said he had faith in me. I mentioned in passing that I'd heard that a sporting goods company might want to unload its tennis gear. He said that we should try to pick it up at a bargain price. He then volunteered to send me another $5,000, I guess to be used basically for that purpose. Besides, I had told him that I was getting low on funds and needed some working capital to proceed. I had gone through most of the $10,000, hadn't hit any sizeable commissions lately, and was running out of money.

Once again, Jeff kept his word. A couple of weeks later I received the $5,000 check. I deposited it in the same checking account. I checked with the sporting goods store, but they were holding out for $7,500. I had to let that opportunity pass. I continued to work on financing. Things came to a head in early November. I had one last chance, a loan officer at Heart Federal who had worked over the details of the project. She quoted me an interest figure that in my opinion, was way out of line.

A few days later, Jeff flew into town. I told him that his timing was right because I had just about run out of luck and needed help. We met, and I explained that financing was practically unavailable. At first, he just seemed disappointed. Then he became very angry and started making all sorts of threats, suing me, filing criminal charges, everything he could think of. I told him to cool down. I said I felt a moral obligation to him because I had handled the project and if anyone had failed, it was me. I offered to execute a promissory note for the $15,000. I said I would stand good for the money.

The next day I gave him a promissory note for $15,000 and turned over all the files on the tennis club project. I had hoped that a trailer park project I'd been working on would go through just about then; that would have given me an $8,000 commission. Unfortunately, through no fault of mine, the deal fell through. I haven't been able to make any payments on the note.

I am sufficiently familiar with Jeff's handwriting style to recognize his signature.

I have had my real estate license since 19YR–12. In 19YR–9 one of my former customers filed a complaint against me with the state board. She claimed that I stole $1,000 of $7,000 she had given me to make a down payment on a condo. It was just an innocent misunderstanding, like my dispute with Jeff. After the hearing the board found me not guilty, and the District Attorney agreed not to file charges after I paid my former client $400 to settle her claim against me. I would never cheat anyone. I am active in my church, and cheating would be against my religious beliefs. It's also un-American; I fought for this country in Vietnam, and I would be the last person to stoop to something as despicable as lying or cheating.

I have given Jeff the file containing almost all my material on the development project. The file contains some photographs of the site we visited, copies of Dixon ordinances on permit procedures, and xerox copies of some real estate ads for other possible sites. I understand that Jeff is going to continue the project on his own. All the material in the file should give him more than a good head start.

Dated: January 22, 19YR–2

/s/   George R. Ahrens
_____
George R. Ahrens

Statement of Andrew E. Amerson

My name is Andrew E. Amerson. I have lived in Morena my entire life. I have my B.A. and an M.B.A. from El Dorado State University. I graduated at the head of my M.B.A. class. In 19YR–20, I founded Amerson Realty. I did so immediately after obtaining my broker's license. It is now the largest—and most successful—realty firm in northern El Dorado. I have 60 sales people working for me. My firm has been so successful, I honestly think, because I'm a great judge of character and I keep real close tabs on the sales people I hire.

In 19YR–7, I hired George Ahrens as a part-time salesman. Over the years, I've come to know George real well. In my judgment, he's a straight shooter. He's as honest as the day is long. George may not be the sharpest real estate agent around, but he's just about the most honest. You could ask anybody in our business in Morena about him, and they'd say exactly the same thing.

I understand that this fellow Stripling is suing George over some contract claim. I can't bring myself to believe that George would ever swindle anyone. Quite to the contrary, it sounds to me as if Stripling has only himself to blame. Morena's not a small, hick town, but we're not a New York or Chicago. In this town, when you're talking about a sum of money like $5,000, you take the time to reduce the agreement to writing. At least that's the almost invariable practice in real estate deals in northern El Dorado. If I was investing $5,000 in any real estate transaction in this community, you had better believe that I would have the deal reduced to writing; and I don't know of any responsible, competent business person in Morena who would just hand $5,000 to someone without getting the terms of the deal hammered out in some sort of document. I am willing to bet that this is a simple case of innocent misunderstanding, and the root cause of the misunderstanding was Stripling's informal approach to the whole transaction. I'm not just giving you my opinion; I've served two terms as president of the Greater Morena Chamber of Commerce, and I'd be willing to say under oath that I'm describing the almost universal practice in this part of the country.

Dated: February 9, 19YR–2

/s/   Andrew E. Amerson

Andrew E. Amerson

May 15, 19YR–3

Mr. Jeffrey L. Stripling
3420 Albany Lane
Silver Springs, Maryland

Dear Jeff:

Jeff, you are a man of your word. I have the $10,000 check. I immediately deposited it in my checking account. Now I can begin pressing for the permits. I'll be meeting with the attorney representing the owners of the land in Dixon pretty soon. I'll get an attorney for us to start working on the partnership papers.

Hope this letter finds you well. Get out to Morena again when you have a chance. In the meantime, I'll be looking after our interests.

> Very truly yours,
> /s/ George Ahrens
> _____
> George Ahrens

PROMISSORY NOTE

> November 17, 19YR–3

I, George R. Ahrens, hereby acknowledge that I am indebted to Jeffrey L. Stripling in the amount of $15,000.00. I promise to pay him that sum of money.

> /s/ George R. Ahrens
> _____
> George R. Ahrens

> September 19, 19YR–3

Mr. Jeffrey L. Stripling
3420 Albany Lane
Silver Springs, Maryland

Dear Jeff:

Wow, you are a great partner; you come through in the clutch again. I've got the $5,000 check. I'm making inquiries about the liquor license.

The project is coming along. I'm having some difficulty with the financing. The money market is tightening up around here. I still hope to pull it off.

It was great to see you again. You ought to get out here more often. I don't know; after living on the East Coast for so long, maybe you couldn't cope with all this great weather out here.

That's about all from here. Drop me a line if you get a chance.

> Very truly yours,
> /s/ George Ahrens
> _____
> George Ahrens

SUPERIOR COURT OF EL DORADO COUNTY OF MORENA

JEFFREY L. STRIPLING,	)	
Plaintiff	)	
vs.	)	**STIPULATION**
GEORGE R. AHRENS,	)	
Defendant	)	

It is hereby stipulated and agreed by and between the parties hereto, and by their respective counsel that:

1. At all relevant times, the defendant had a personal checking account with First National Bank of El Dorado, account #5105524.

2. As of March 31, 19YR–3, the balance in the account was $100.

3. On April 16, the defendant deposited a $10,000 cashier's check in the account. The defendant received the check from Mr. Jeffrey L. Stripling. The deposit brought the account balance to $10,100.

4. Between April 16, 19YR–3 and June 30, 19YR–3, the defendant did not make any additional deposits in the account. In the same time period, he drew the following checks on the account for the following purposes.

NO.	DATE	AMOUNT	PAYEE	PURPOSE
77	Apr 17	$300	Haney Rentals	Rent on house
78	Apr 18	$400	Standard Oil	Gasoline credit card pymt.
79	Apr 21	$1,000	I.R.S.	Federal Income Tax
80	Apr 21	$20	Pacific Bell	Telephone bill
81	Apr 21	$30	P.G. & E.	Electricity bill
82	Apr 21	$350	Weinstocks	Payment on credit amount
83	Apr 23	$100	Air El Dorado	Ticket for flight to Reno related to Amerson Realty business
84	Apr 25	$50	Harvey's	Hotel bill in Reno
85	Apr 28	$20	Sports Illustrated	Magazine subscription
86	Apr 28	$100	Grant Lincoln–Merc.	Car payment
87	Apr 29	$50	Bishops' Relief Fund	Charitable contribution
88	Apr 30	$700	Grant Kirwan	Payment to attorney for work on realty trans. with third party

NO.	DATE	AMOUNT	PAYEE	PURPOSE
89	May 2	$60	United	Ticket for flight to San Francisco City to check on possibility of financing for tennis club
90	May 7	$150	Holiday Inn	Hotel bill in San Francisco
91	May 8	$200	Ace Auto Repairs	Repair work on auto
92	May 12	$25	Pacific Bell	Telephone bill
93	May 12	$25	P.G. & E.	Electricity bill
94	May 12	$10	Better Homes & Gardens	Magazine subscription
95	May 14	$300	Haney Rentals	House rent
96	May 15	$2,000	Heart Federal	Repayment of personal loan
97	May 16	$400	Grant Kirwan	Same as above
98	May 20	$100	Grant Lincoln–Merc.	Car payment
99	May 23	$600	El Dorado Franchise Tax Board	State income tax
100	May 29	$100	George Turner	Club membership
101	June 2	$150	Sears	Payment on credit acct.
102	June 4	$250	Frontier	Airline ticket for trip related to Amerson Realty business
103	June 8	$100	Marriott Hotels	Hotel bill on trip
104	June 11	$500	Thomas Summers	Architect's fees for plans for renovating tennis clubhouse
105	June 12	$30	Pacific Bell	Same as above

NO.	DATE	AMOUNT	PAYEE	PURPOSE
106	June 12	$10	P.G. & E.	Electricity bill
107	June 12	$300	Haney Rentals	House rental
108	June 17	$400	Emporium	Payment on credit acct.
109	June 20	$100	Grant Lincoln–Merc.	Car payment
110	June 25	$75	Boy Scouts of America	Charitable contribution

5. On July 16, after the above checks cleared, the account balance was $1,085. On that date, the defendant deposited a second cashier's check from Mr. Stripling. That deposit brought the account balance to $6,085.

6. Between July 16, 19YR–3 and October 31, 19YR–3 the defendant did not make any additional deposits in the account. In the same time period, the defendant drew the following checks on the account for the following purposes.

NO.	DATE	AMOUNT	PAYEE	PURPOSE
111	Jul 18	$100	Grant Lincoln–Merc.	Same as above
112	Jul 21	$20	Pacific Bell	Same as above
113	Jul 21	$30	P.G. & E.	Same as above
114	Jul 23	$300	Haney Rentals	Same as above
115	Jul 24	$100	American Realty Assoc.	Short course on tennis development projects
116	Jul 28	$25	United Way Campaign	Charitable contribution
117	Jul 30	$60	Cash	Misc. personal expense
118	Aug 1	$200	American Airlines	Airline ticket on trip related to Amerson Realty business
119	Aug 5	$70	Marina Hotel	Hotel bill on trip

NO.	DATE	AMOUNT	PAYEE	PURPOSE
120	Aug 7	$32	Pacific Bell	Same as above
121	Aug 7	$18	P.G. & E.	Same as above
122	Aug 11	$300	Haney Rentals	Same as above
123	Aug 14	$100	Grant Lincoln–Merc.	Same as above
124	Aug 25	$450	Continental Airlines	Pleasure trip for husband and wife to Hawaii
125	Aug 31	$160	Honolulu Hyatt	Hotel bill on trip
126	Sep 2	$100	Grant Lincoln–Merc.	Same as above
127	Sep 5	$20	Pacific Bell	Same as above
128	Sep 5	$30	P.G. & E.	Same as above
129	Sep 8	$1,000	Aetna Finance	Repayment of personal loan
130	Sep 15	$300	Haney Rentals	Same as above
131	Sep 18	$50	Cash	Misc. personal expense
132	Sep 24	$250	Flip's Stereo	Purchase of receiver and speakers
133	Oct 3	$40	Heart Fund	Charitable contribution
134	Oct 7	$100	Grant Lincoln–Merc.	Same as above
135	Oct 9	$10	Pacific Bell	Same as above
136	Oct 9	$47	P.G. & E.	Same as above
137	Oct 14	$300	Haney Rentals	Same as above

Plaintiff's Attorney

/s/   Jeffrey L. Stripling

_____

Jeffrey L. Stripling
Plaintiff

_____

Defense Attorney

/s/   George R. Ahrens

_____

George R. Ahrens
Defendant

Case file B–7

PEOPLE OF THE STATE OF EL DORADO v. SWEENEY

Arthur Sweeney, 68, is charged with the murder and manslaughter of Jimmy Hill, a 16–year-old boy from his neighborhood in Morena. The indictment alleges that the killing occurred on July 17, 19YR–1. The enclosed statements were voluntarily given to the police. Assume that there is no fifth or sixth amendment objection to the admission of the defendant's statement.

Statement of Tom Brunner

I am 16 years old. I was a good friend of Jimmy Hill. For the last three years, before and after school, a bunch of us would always hang out across the street from the school on the corner where Mr. Sweeney now lives at Jackson and Green Streets. The house has a three-foot-high brick wall around it. We'd sit on the wall and talk, have a smoke, and drink some pop. Then about a year ago, Mr. Sweeney and his wife moved into the house. The first day they were there, we did our usual thing after school—we went across the street and sat on the brick wall. He came running out of the house; he was waving a rake and yelling at us to get off his property. It really bugged us. He never asked us friendly—like once—he just came running out with his rake and calling us good for nothing kids and stuff like that. So over the next few weeks it became a game we'd play—go sit on old man Sweeney's fence and watch him run out waving his rake like a maniac. Once in a while we'd even run up to his door, ring the bell, and then run back to the wall—just to see him come out madder. We were just having some innocent fun. We never hurt his property or anything.

Then one night about midnight we had nothing to do, so we decided to go have some fun with the old man and his wife. There were four of us—me, Jimmy, Mark Miller, and Todd Seaver. We went to his house and stood on the sidewalk. We called to him to come out and chase us with his rake. After a long time—about 10 minutes, or so, he came out; but he was carrying a rifle, not his rake. He came right down to the sidewalk and pointed the rifle at us. He was holding the rifle level and pointed right at us. He told us to go away. But we were on the sidewalk, not his property, so we figured he couldn't make us leave. Some of us, including Jimmy, had big rocks in our hands. We'd been thinking of tossing them at the house—just to wake up Sweeney if we needed to. But we never threw any—although Jimmy did run up once and ring the bell. So Sweeney was telling us to leave and we were teasing him a little— telling him the sidewalk's not his property and he can't make us leave. Then Jimmy took a step forward, and Sweeney just blew him away. When he shot Jimmy, Jimmy had his back to me. Sweeney shot him down in cold blood. Jimmy didn't make any threatening gestures toward Sweeney.

Dated: October 26, 19YR–1

/s/   Thomas Brunner

_____

Thomas Brunner

Statement of Officer John Garcia

I am a member of the Morena Police Department; I patrol the neighborhood where the defendant lives. I investigated the shooting of Jimmy Hill. I knew Hill before the incident; I didn't know the kid well, but he always impressed me as a nice, truthful kid. Hill had never given me any problems in my entire time on that beat, and I had never heard any bad reports about him. During the investigation of the incident, I attempted to question Tom Brunner, but Brunner invoked his privilege against self-incrimination.

When I attempted to question the defendant, he said he was more than willing to talk about the shooting. The defendant told me that just before going outside, he heard a loud crash against his house. I inspected that area around the defendant's bedroom window. I discovered a dent in the woodwork around the window. I couldn't tell whether the wood was freshly damaged. There was a rock laying about a foot and a half from the other window; the rock was big enough to have made the dent. There was another rock near the decedent's feet, but that one was much smaller than the rock near the window.

The defendant's wife was in the area while I was conducting the investigation. She seemed very upset and shaken even though more than two hours had passed since the shooting. At one point, she said, "The noise was so loud. I thought the hooligans were breaking into the house. What they tried to do to my poor husband! They could have killed him."

I checked the area and notice that there are no street lamps in front of the Sweeney house.

Unfortunately, at the time it didn't occur to me to pick up or preserve the rocks I saw at the scene of the shooting. The Deputy D.A. has since made the importance of the rocks—specifically their size—in this case very clear to me. In the process of preparing this statement, I therefore have prepared drawings of the rocks I saw. Drawing #1 is the rock I found near the Sweeney's house—the rock that might have made the dent in the side of the house. Drawing #2 is the rock I found near the dead boy's feet. I made the drawings to scale to the best of my ability and memory.

Dated: October 1, 19YR–1

            /s/   John Garcia
                 _____
                 John Garcia

DRAWING #1

This rock was fairly round.

JRG
10/1/YR–1
[E8525]

DRAWING #2

View from the Side

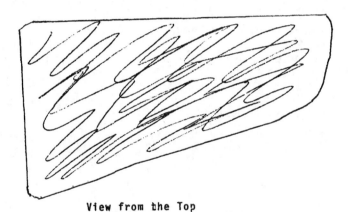

View from the Top

Statement of Arthur Sweeney

My wife and I moved into the neighborhood about a year ago. We left our old neighborhood downtown because there had been too many attacks on elderly people. With all the young hoodlums, an elderly person just wasn't safe on the street anymore. Initially, the new neighborhood looked much quieter. However, about 3 o'clock the very first afternoon we were there, the kids got out of school; and about six or seven of them came across the street and sat on our brick wall. They were smoking, drinking beer, and throwing cans on my lawn. I went out to tell them to leave—I took a rake with me just to show them I meant business. They started calling me all kinds of obscene names. The only way I could get them off my wall was to wave the rake at them. Then they were back the next day anyway. The same thing happened when I called the police. They'd come talk to them—the police were too soft on the kids—the kids would leave, but they'd be back the next day teasing me more for calling the police. Sometimes they'd run up my path, ring the doorbell, and run back to the sidewalk.

Then one night around midnight my wife and I were in bed, and I woke up hearing yelling outside. Those same kids were shouting for me to come out and chase them with my rake. Then I heard the doorbell ring and I heard a thud against the house like something hit it. I thought that maybe they had broken a window and were going to climb in to get at us and shoot us or stab us. I looked out the bedroom window, and they all were standing out on the sidewalk. I could see clearly that they were holding big rocks. I was scared they'd break the window and come in. I took off my pajamas, quickly got into street clothes, and grabbed my rifle downstairs. After loading the rifle, I stepped outside, went straight to the sidewalk, and told them to leave. They just taunted me—asking if I owned the sidewalk, etc. Then the leader, Jimmy, asked me if I was afraid they were going to throw the rocks at what they called my "precious house" or if I was afraid they were going to go in and rape my "precious wife." They just kept taunting me like this without making any move to leave. Then finally Jimmy started coming towards me. He was holding a huge rock in his hands. He stopped for a second. He made a threatening gesture with one hand; and then when he was almost on top of me, he acted as if he was going to throw the rock right at me. What was running through my mind was a jumble of fear and anger. I had no choice; I just shot.

My wife and I have decided that she won't testify. She shouldn't have to go through that ordeal.

To help you understand the facts, I've drawn a diagram of my house and the nearby area. I'm sorry I'm no artist, and the drawing is pretty rough.

Dated: December 19, 19YR–1

/s/   Arthur Sweeney

_____

Arthur Sweeney

Statement of Gertrude Marshall

My house is right next to the Sweeney residence. I am a retiree and a widow; I've lived in the same house across the street from the school for the last 30 years. Although they have lived in their house only a short time, the Sweeneys are good neighbors; I sometimes go out to dinner or a movie with them. Arthur and Sheila are wonderful, peace-loving people. I know that kid Tom Brunner. In my opinion, he is just another young punk. I've seen him sitting on the Sweeney wall and talking back to poor Mr. Sweeney. Brunner also has given me back talk. He'll be walking by my house and throw trash on my lawn; if I complain to him, all I get is smart talk. There are times when I'll see him throw junk in my yard and complain; and even though I just saw him do it with my own two eyes, he'll out-and-out lie and say he never did it. He'll say something like, "You old folks can't even see straight."

I don't know that much about Jimmy Hill. He was always hanging around with Brunner—I do know that. I guess that says a lot about Hill. I sometimes saw Hill sitting on the Sweeney fence with Brunner, but Hill never said anything bad to me. He was just another one of that gang.

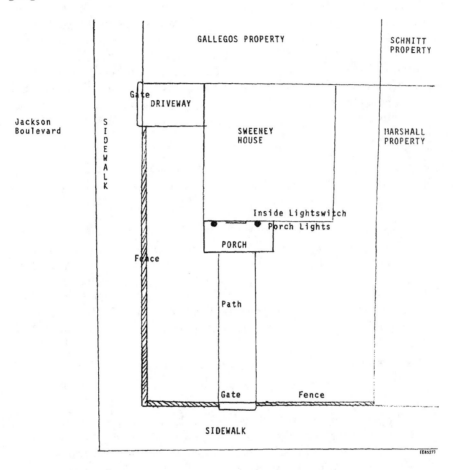

Grant Street

I was home the night of July 17, 19YR–1. I am certain that I heard the gunshot. I also think that I heard some noise a little bit before that. The problem is that my hearing isn't so good any more; I use a hearing aid. Even if there had been a lot of screaming or shouting before the gunshot, I might not have heard it; I was in bed with the hearing aid off. When I heard the gunshot, I ran to my window. I could see a body on the ground. Mr. Sweeney was just standing there as if he were dazed. I called the police right away, and they arrived a few minutes later. After they arrived, I thought it was safe to come outside. Poor Mr. Sweeney was just pale as a ghost; and his wife, Sheila, was just coming apart at the seams. Those kids just pushed Arthur too far; no one should have to put up with what they were doing to the elderly people in our neighborhood.

I am not sure how much time the boys spent outside the Sweeney house that night. It seemed that there was a good deal of time between the first noise and the gunshot; I am sure that it was at least several minutes. After the noise woke me up, I went downstairs to the kitchen to have a glass of warm milk. Then I went back to bed. When I heard the first noise, it crossed my mind to call the police. However, like Arthur, I've often called the police to complain about the local hooligans without getting any satisfaction. I can see why Arthur might think that he had to do something about the problem himself. We shouldn't have to put up with delinquents who are constantly abusing our property.

Dated: September 3, 19YR–1

/s/   Gertrude Marshall

_____

Gertrude Marshall

STIPULATIONS

1. The parties have agreed to a stipulation of expected testimony. The parties stipulate that if Dr. Hugh Overholt were present in court, he would testify that: The decedent died from one rifle bullet in the forehead; the muzzle of the rifle was at least 30 inches from the decedent's forehead when the rifle was fired; and the bullet took a slightly upward path (front to back) as it traveled through the decedent's body.

2. The parties have agreed to the following stipulations of fact:

    a. Dr. Hugh Overholt is a licensed, board certified forensic pathologist.

    b. Two years before the incident in question, Jimmy Hall and Tom Brunner together defaced a neighborhood store by spray painting obscenities on the store's windows. They were represented by the same public defender, tried jointly at their request, and adjudicated delinquents by the local juvenile court in Morena.

_____

Deputy District Attorney

_____

Defense Attorney

/s/   Arthur Sweeney

_____

Arthur Sweeney
Defendant

Case File B–8

KIDD v. WILLIS CONTRACTING SUPPLY COMPANY INC.

Synopsis of File

Summary of Case

Bureau of Workers' Compensation Report, with Witness Statements, Kendall Willis' Affidavit and Diagrams

Additional Witness Statements

    Alan Ellis

    Ken Fletcher

Stipulations

OSHA Report of April 25

OSHA Report of May 1

OSHA Citation of May 4

Instructions to Defense Attorneys

Summary of Case

Gary Kidd was injured in an accident when he was painting while standing on a high platform. The platform is motorized and on wheels, and can move around construction jobs for the painters to reach high places such as girders, ceilings, and pipes. Another worker was operating the platform, and this operator was painting when he was not driving. When the platform ran into a shallow trench in the floor the platform fell over. Kidd was thrown and seriously injured.

Kidd has collected worker's compensation for his occupational injury, and that case is not before the court. However, witnesses in this trial will testify in accord with the manner in which they described the facts to the worker's compensation investigator. Kidd is now bringing a negligence suit against a company which supplies motorized and heavy equipment to construction companies. Willis Contracting Supply Company leased painting platforms to Kidd's employer. The leases do not contain any exculpatory clauses cutting off Willis' liability or guaranteeing Willis' indemnification or exoneration, in the event someone is injured by reason of Willis supplying faulty equipment.

The conduct of Willis was negligent in two ways, according to Kidd. They supplied a painting platform which was "inherently unstable" in the words of witness Kenneth Fletcher. He stated that "the lack of a fourth wheel on the Workwell [platform] makes all the difference in the world.'" A less important but still noteworthy aspect of Willis' alleged negligence was its failure to provide contracting parties with posted written directives advising that outriggers stabilizing the platform are to be extended when workers use the platform.

Willis denies the platform which they leased to Kidd's employer was unstable. Although Willis has not invoked any third-party procedural options to formally name others as defendants, Willis claims that the accident was the fault of Kidd's co-worker, his employer, Ferguson Construction Co., and Kidd himself. Willis argued that the negligence of these parties concurred to cause this accident, relieving Willis of liability. There was no negligence in supplying an unsafe and unsteady platform to the building contractor; rather, the accident is attributable to the negligence of others, and Willis contends there is no primary negligence on its part.

The attorneys trying this case will litigate only the issue of liability; the issue of damages has been severed.

KIDD v. WILLIS CONTRACTING SUPPLY COMPANY INC.

INSTRUCTIONS TO PLAINTIFF'S ATTORNEYS:

This is a civil action. You represent Gary Kidd. Mr. Kidd suffered injuries from a work-related accident while he was an employee of Ferguson Contracting Co. Mr. Kidd claims that the accident resulted from Ferguson's negligence.

You are to interview your client and other designated witnesses. After receiving the defendant's answer, you should conduct appropriate discovery, including depositions, interrogatories, production requests, and requests for admissions. You will try only the issue of liability; the issue of damages has been severed. Plaintiff's theory of liability in this action does not include products liability.

Client: Gary Kidd

Witnesses: Gary Kidd

                 Kenneth Fletcher

KIDD v. WILLIS CONTRACTING SUPPLY COMPANY INC.

INSTRUCTIONS TO DEFENDANT'S ATTORNEYS:

This is a civil action. You represent Willis Supply Co. Mr. Kidd suffered injuries from a work-related accident while he was an employee of Ferguson Contracting Co. Mr. Kidd claims that the accident resulted from Willis Company's negligence in providing unsafe equipment.

You are to interview your client and other designated witnesses. After receiving the plaintiff's complaint, you should file a timely answer, and then conduct appropriate discovery, including depositions, interrogatories, production requests, and request for admissions. You will try only the issue of liability; the issue of damages has been severed.

Client: Willis Supply Company

Witnesses: David Schonk

                     Alan Ellis

BUREAU OF WORKERS' COMPENSATION INDUSTRIAL COMMISSION DEPARTMENT OF INVESTIGATIONS MORENA, EL DORADO

CONTENTS OF DEPARTMENT'S FILE

1. Investigation Report
2. Statement of Gary L. Kidd
3. Statement of David Schonk
4. Affidavit of Kendall Willis
5. Diagram of A.P. Technoglass Plant

BUREAU OF WORKERS' COMPENSATION INDUSTRIAL COMMISSION DEPARTMENT OF INVESTIGATIONS MORENA, EL DORADO

REPORT OF INVESTIGATION

CLAIM NO: 9883

CASE OF: Gary L. Kidd
1717 Market Street
Vacaville, El Dorado

RISK NUMBER: 623781

EMPLOYER: Ferguson
Contracting Co.
2850 Dryden Road
Vacaville, El Dorado

Date transcribed: 10/3/ YR–4

Initials: lj

To the Industrial Commission,

Pursuant to instructions, the above numbered claim has been made the subject of an investigation, and the following report relative to the same is herewith submitted.

Investigation covered the following matters: *To determine whether the injury of the claimant was caused by the employer's violation of a specific safety requirement.*

HISTORY:

The investigation revealed that on April 24, 19YR–4 the claimant sustained his injury of record while engaged in his duties in the position of "Painter" for the employer.

The claimant sustained his injury while painting the piping installed in the ceiling area. The painting was being done from an aerial work platform. The platform was a Workwell scissors lift similar to those shown in exhibit A except that the outriggers on the model used were manually operated.

See affidavits and exhibits for more information.

AFFIDAVITS:

GARY L. KIDD

Gary L. Kidd upon his oath deposes and states that he is of legal age and resides at 1717 Market Street, Vacaville, El Dorado and that he is the claimant.

CLAIMANT–GARY L. KIDD

CLAIM NO.–9883

EMPLOYER–FERGUSON CONTRACTING CO.

Claimant further states that he was employed by the employer in the position of "Painter." He had held that position for about one (1) year at the time of the accident.

Claimant further states that the accident occurred while in the process of painting the piping that was suspended from the ceiling of A.P. Technoglass plant in Winters, El Dorado.

Claimant further states that at the time of his accident, the claimant was working from a self-propelled scissors platform along with a co-worker (Alan Ellis). The scissors lift was raised to about twenty (20) feet. The co-worker was operating the controls from the raised platform attempting to move to another location when one of the wheels rolled into an open trench drain in the concrete floor. The manually operated outriggers had not been extended thus allowing the scissors lift to tip over. As it tipped, the claimant struck his head on the piping and then fell to the concrete floor as the lift fell over thus causing the injuries of record.

Claimant further states that in his opinion, the co-worker had very little, if any, experience operating this type of lift.

Claimant further states that the painters had asked the employer to cover or place guards around the trench drains several times prior to the accident. Nothing was done; however, immediately following the claimant's accident, the trench drains were covered or guarded with posts and plastic "caution" tape.

DAVID SCHONK

David Schonk upon his oath deposes and states that he is of legal age and resides at 973 North Texas Street, Fairfield, El Dorado and that he is not a witness to the claimant's accident.

Affiant further states that he is employed by the employer in the position of "Field Superintendent" and has held this position for about four and one half years. Affiant further states that prior to claimant's accident, the affiant had advised the claimant and his co-worker, Alan Ellis, directly to "be sure and use the 'outriggers.'"

Affiant further states that the scaffold used by the claimant was a Workwell self-propelled scaffold. The wheel of the scaffold rolled into a floor trench drain that was uncovered.

Affiant further states that after the claimant's accident Ferguson Contractors did cover and put yellow caution tape around the open trench drains.

Affiant further states that the proper name for the equipment is a "scissors lift."

CLAIMANT–GARY L. KIDD

CLAIM NO.–9883

EMPLOYER–FERGUSON CONTRACTING CO.

Affiant further states that when he advised the claimant and his co-worker to use the outriggers, they just shrugged their shoulders and continued their work.

Further that after the accident the affiant visited the claimant in the hospital. The affiant asked why the claimant did not use the outriggers and he (claimant) stated to the effect that it was just stupidity.

EXHIBITS:

    A.   Statement of Gary L. Kidd, dated July 20, 19YR–4.

    B.   Statement of David Schonk, dated July 13, 19YR–4.

    C.   Affidavit of Kendall Willis.

    D.   Diagram of A.P. Technoglass Plant prepared by Special Investigator.

DISCUSSION:

Conversation between the investigator and the claimant as well as the claimant's attorney indicated that a named witness, Alan Ellis, would not cooperate and had not cooperated in the past. No further effort was made to contact this witness.

Further, the investigator was unable to make contact with named witness Kenneth Fletcher (several attempts to contact were unsuccessful.)

Respectfully submitted,

Russell H. Creager

Special Investigator

Statement of Gary Kidd

My name is Gary Kidd. My address is 1717 Market Street in Vacaville, El Dorado. Currently, I am unemployed. I am married to Theresa Kidd, and we have two children: a son, Kenneth, age 7, and a daughter, Amy, age 10. I was born in 19YR–34. This is my second marriage. My first wife and I divorced in 19YR–12, and she is now deceased. Theresa, my present wife, and I have been married for nine years.

I graduated from Park Hills High School in Vacaville in 19YR–17. Immediately after high school, I went to work for Howard Farrell Painting out of Fairfield, El Dorado. I worked there about a year and a half, from mid–19YR–17 to the end of 19YR–16, doing exclusively brush and roller painting walls, doors, things like that. I left Howard Farrell to go and work for Clyde Beatty Company. I was a painter for them also. They are a subcontractor, and I worked on housing projects in Vacaville and Fairfield. I worked for Clyde Beatty for a little over a year.

After Clyde Beatty, I went to work for Solano Metropolitan Housing doing low-income residential maintenance and painting. They are a county agency. I worked for them for about four and a half years. I then decided I wanted to go into industrial painting. My brother-in-law told me to go into industrial painting because I could make a lot more money than in residential painting. I left Solano Metropolitan about 19YR–10.

I got a job in industrial painting with R and R Painting in Vacaville. I worked at R and R for a little over a year. Then I got fired because the foreman and I got into it over my work habits. He thought I was lazy and wouldn't follow safety instructions, which wasn't true.

This was in 19YR–5. I drew unemployment for a couple of months, and then applied for a job at Ferguson. They hired me. Ferguson is a general contractor. I was a general painter for them. I had been working for Ferguson for about 11 months when I had my accident on April 24, 19YR–4. I no longer work for Ferguson. They didn't fire me, and I didn't quit. The Industrial Commission won't let me go back to work because of injuries I got from the accident. My doctor is Doctor Vice in Vacaville, and he says I cannot go back to painting because of the climbing. I'm not allowed to do a lot of walking and stair climbing. Doctor Vice is an orthopedic surgeon. He has been treating me since the accident.

While I was at Ferguson, I did general industrial painting and ran the sprayer rig. Industrial painting involves a lot of high work, painting pipes and running spray rigs. 75% of industrial painting work is probably spray work.

When my accident occurred, we were working on the A.P. Technoglass building in Winters. This wasn't the first job I'd been on. We had already completed another building in Vacaville. Ferguson employed about 10 painters.

Ferguson never gave me any training as an industrial painter-just on-the-job instruction. What I learned at R and R was the same type of thing we did at Ferguson. My supervisor at Ferguson was Mike Cohorn; he was the foreman for the painters. Mike was killed in a car accident about a month ago.

Ferguson was a good company to work for, and I never had any problems with them aside from a couple of written warnings. One was for being late to work a couple of times; the other was because I told a small fib to Mike Cohorn to cover for another employee. Although I had seen OSHA inspectors at the previous job site, I don't recall ever seeing any at the A.P. Technoglass site.

Like I said, my accident occurred on April 24, 19YR–4. I started work that morning at 7:30. Each morning, we got job assignments for that day. That day I was working with Alan Ellis. Cohorn usually told us what to do; but he was out, so Dave Schonk was there telling the painters what they would be doing that day. Schonk was the superintendent for the job site. He's OK, I guess. We've had our differences in the past, but never anything serious.

Schonk told me that Ellis and I would be working together in a lift painting pipes. Other guys were working when Schonk told us this, but there wasn't any one within 50 or 60 feet.

Alan and I were working in a lift. The lift had a front and a back. The front of the lift was facing southward. I was in the back of the lift, and Alan was operating the thing. There were several trenches in the floor. This place was going to be a glass plant of some kind, and the trenches were for water drainage from the machines. The trenches were probably about 20 inches wide and maybe 8 to 10 inches deep. Basically, Alan was driving the lift, one of the wheels went into a trench, the lift toppled over, and I was injured. The accident was as simple as that.

We were painting the pipes in the ceiling. We weren't using a sprayer that day. We were doing it brush and roller. There were a bunch of different pipes-probably five or six-and they were color coded. Each pipe had to be a different color. We were painting the white ones. At this point in the building, the pipes run north and south.

The lift we were working in had a bed about six feet long and three and a half feet wide. Most of the bed was solid, but there were some see-through grate areas so we could watch the floor. There was a railing all the way around the lift. The railing was about three feet high. We could reach about nine or ten feet of pipe before we had to move the lift. We would reach out each end of the lift probably about two feet. The ceiling in this building was 15–20 feet high. We were up there a ways, and didn't want to stretch beyond the bed of the lift too much. Although the bed of the lift was pretty high up, the lift wasn't fully extended.

We were on a scissors lift. I had never been on a scissors lift before, although I had been on and operated a JLG, a different kind of lift. A scissors lift has smaller wheels. The JLG has bigger wheels and is meant for higher work. It's better equipped to get in different places. It has a bucket at the end of a boom—like you might see the phone company using on telephone lines. The scissors lift is more straightforward; it just goes up and down. Ferguson used both JLGs and scissors lifts.

I had been trained on the JLG a little bit by Ken Fletcher, another Ferguson painter, but as I said, I had never been on a scissors lift before. The JLG has hand controls—toggle switches—to go left, right, forward, reverse, up, and down. It's pretty self-explanatory. The controls are located in the bucket; you can operate the thing while the boom is still extended. The scissors lift was the same way in that you could operate and move it while the bed was extended up in the air. The JLGs do not have outriggers, stabilizer bars that come out from the sides from some of the lifts to balance them, but the scissors lifts did, I think.

Alan was running the thing. I guess the scissors lift we were using that day did have outriggers. I don't know how they worked. I think there were two of them. They sure weren't extended when my accident happened.

This day, we were painting pipes in the vicinity of one of the trenches. The trenches were open because the job wasn't complete yet, and the metal covers weren't in place. There is supposed to be bright six inch yellow caution tape around open trenches and hazards.

Anyway, this tape that I saw was attached to 2 X 4s stuck in a cement thing, so they could be moved around. But on the day of my accident, I don't remember seeing any of this tape anywhere. I wasn't really looking for it; but as I walked through the plant, I noticed that it wasn't there any more. I didn't say anything to anybody, though.

I never moved any of the tape. I have seen other guys do it if it was in their way. Guys do that especially on the JLGs—their wheels are so big that they can just roll right over an open ditch.

I don't know how long Alan had been working for Ferguson, or whether he ever had any training in operating the scissors lift or any other lift. I don't remember ever seeing him up in a lift before. We had been in the lift since 7:30 without a break. Alan was operating the lift. Nobody had ever shown me how. I hadn't ever asked anyone how to operate a scissors lift because I never planned to go up in one. I always thought they were dangerous. I remember watching other guys in them. When they were extended to the max, they would sway back and forth even with the slightest movement. I've seen them tip over before. I didn't even know I was going to be up in one until I got to work that morning. Schonk told me we were going to use a scissors lift because we didn't have to go as high or get in tough places that required a JLG. I told him I didn't know anything about running one, and he said that's OK. He assured me that Alan knew how to run them; according to Schonk, Alan had been running them ever since he's been here. I thought that was kind of funny because I had never seen Ellis in a scissors lift before. Alan was over by the lift during this conversation. I just assumed Schonk was telling the truth.

We had painted 50 or 60 feet of pipe that morning. It took us about 30 minutes to paint a section of pipe before we had to move the lift.

I didn't pay real close attention to the lift because I wasn't operating it. I do know that it was called a Workwell. I assumed that Alan knew how to operate it because he took the controls when we got there. The scissors lifts only go forward and backward; they don't go sideways like the JLGs can. The engine is electric, and the only time it runs is when you turn the controls to engage it. As soon as you take your hands off the controls, the lift stops immediately. I don't really know anything about the controls other than that. I don't know if the thing had a brake.

Alan operated the thing from the front, and I was standing in the back right-hand corner on the opposite side of the pipes from Alan. The controls are in the middle of the front. Alan was operating them from the left hand side of the bed, and we would each paint our own side of a section of pipe. When it came time to move the lift, I would continue to paint; I painted as we moved along.

Right before my accident, I was painting a pipe while the lift was moving. We were nowhere near any walls. I was using a roller. I could paint while the lift was moving because the thing just barely moves along.

I had seen the trench earlier in the day. There were several trenches throughout the building; but as far as I remember, this was the only one in this area. The trench ran perpendicular to the pipes and the direction we were moving. But it ended right under the pipes. It didn't run all the way across the building; it didn't extend out to my side of the lift. It went far enough for one of the wheels to run into it, which is what happened. I didn't think to point the trench out to Alan before we started to be sure he saw it. We were moving straight for the trench—not at an angle or anything—and one of the wheels fell in. I never even saw us go into the trench because I was busy painting. Alan had said that he was going to try and get as close to the trench as possible, so I guess he saw it. I don't know why he said that, but I told him O.K. This was right before the accident. I assumed he thought we could reach across the trench; and when we were done, we would go around the other side of the trench and pick up where we left off. I wasn't giving him directions or trying to keep any special lookout.

As far as I know, Alan could see the trench while he was moving the lift. I never looked down myself, though. The next thing I knew, the lift was starting to tilt. I tried to duck, but a pipe caught me in the face as we started to fall. I ended up on the ground. The impact broke my nose. I never heard Alan yell or say anything. The lift fell towards the left—towards the trench. I landed smack on the floor. The fall broke my hip. I got several lacerations and busted up my knee. I've had several knee operations. The fall did not knock me out, though. An ambulance was called, and it took us to the hospital. I don't think Alan was hurt. He was able to jump as the lift started to fall. He just sprained an ankle a little bit. We were taken to Sutter Hospital. I was later transferred to Solano County Hospital in Vacaville, where Dr. Vice worked on me. I ended up spending six days in the hospital.

I had not been drinking that day. Nor had I taken any drugs. I do drink a few beers from time to time, after work. I have never been treated for alcoholism, and have never been convicted of a felony. I was convicted of petty theft several years ago. The state sent me to see a psychiatrist as a result of this accident. It was just one visit. I don't remember her name, although I do remember she was located in Fairfield. I have never talked to anyone about this accident, except slightly in passing with Alan. I told my family what happened, but I never filled out an accident report. I did talk with Russ Creager from the Workers Compensation Bureau last week to try and get some money. I don't know what Ferguson filled out. I think Ken Fletcher saw the whole thing; he was working in another lift about 50 feet away.

I think this accident could have been avoided if a more stable lift had been sent over from the leasing company, or the trenches had been covered, or maybe if the caution tape had been in place like it was supposed to be. I do know that Ferguson went around and covered up all the trenches right after the accident. Even if those outriggers were out, I think the lift would still have tipped. I base this opinion on two things. First, a guy was running the same lift about two weeks before my accident and he made a sharp turn on a level floor and the lift tipped over. The outriggers were out. I saw it. Also, in my case they would not have worked because of the depth of the trench. And I sure don't remember Schonk or anyone else telling us that day to put the outriggers out.

I went back to work for Ferguson about four months after the accident. I worked for ten days on a trial basis. At the end of that time, I went back to see Dr. Vice. I could hardly walk because of the pain. Then the Doctor told me I shouldn't be working. I didn't return to the A.P. Technoglass building because it was finished at this time. Instead, we were working on another restaurant job in Vacaville. I didn't go up in any lifts. I haven't been able to work since then.

Date: October 2, 19YR–1.

/s/ Gary Kidd
_____
Gary Kidd

Attachment to Gary Kidd's Statement

Attached is a picture of the Workwell that I drew. The view is from the top looking down, and shows where Alan Ellis and I were located just prior to the accident. You can't tell it, but the lift is extended. The drawing is upside-down in that north is really towards the bottom, and south towards the top.

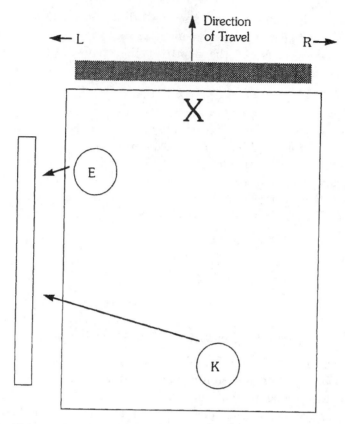

The E is where Ellis was located, and the K indicates where I was located. The X inside the bed of the lift is where the controls were. The long shaded area towards the top (south) of the drawing shows where the trench would have been. The two arrows coming out of the bed to the left show the direction of our fall. The long, unshaded box shows the lift after it fell.

Statement of David Schonk

My name is David Schonk. I live at 973 North Texas Street in Fairfield. I have lived at that address since 19YR–14. I am 35 years old. I graduated from Rio Vista High School in 19YR–18. I attended one year of college at the State University where I took some prerequisite courses in Engineering. I'm married and have one child, a teenager. I began working for Ferguson Contracting in the summer of 19YR–17 and have worked there ever since.

I started out at Ferguson as a construction worker, and did that for about two and a half years. After that they made me a foreman, which I was until 19YR–6, when they made me a superintendent. I was the superintendent at the A.P. Technoglass job site. My job was to oversee the overall operation of the job. Ferguson doesn't contract out; we have our own plumbers, construction workers, electricians, and painters. My job is a little easier than some because I don't have to coordinate all the subcontractors. But I still have to coordinate my own people.

I was on the job site every day. I had foremen working under me-a foreman for the plumbers, one for the electricians, and so on. One foreman, Mike Cohorn, had direct control over the painters, but he was out on the day of Gary Kidd's accident. On a normal day, we probably had about 30 people at the job site.

One of the requirements of the A.P. job was to color code the overhead pipes. This meant painting them all a different color. On the day of Kidd's accident, the pipes were one of the projects the painters were working on.

Painters come into work and receive job assignments every day. Painters have to work around the other workers, so their jobs can change daily. Since Cohorn was out that day, I gave assignments to the painters. Basically, I just asked them what they had been doing the day before. If it didn't conflict with what other workers were doing, I told them to continue what they were doing.

Kidd told me he had been painting walls with a sprayer the day before and that he was sick of it. I really didn't want to get into it with him. He's got an attitude and a temper. For that reason, I told him he could paint the pipes. He grumbled a little bit about having to do such tedious work, but finally agreed. I told him he would have to use the Workwell, and he said that was fine. I asked him if he had ever operated one. He said something like, "No problem. I know how to use the Workwell. Anybody can operate one of those." I told him he would be working with Alan Ellis. I also told him to be certain to use the outriggers on the Workwell, and that was the last I saw of him that day until the accident. Ellis was late that day. For that reason, I couldn't pair them immediately.

Ferguson has a number of different types of lifts that we use in our work. We have JLGs, which are boom lifts like you might see utility companies using. The JLG has a bucket at the end of a long arm. We also have scissors lifts. The lifts have outriggers on them; the JLGs don't. I don't remember how many scissors lifts we had, but there was more than one, different sizes and models. Same thing with the JLGs.

Our workers were supposed to get instruction on how to use the lifts before they could operate them. Ken Fletcher was in charge of training people because he knew about them and had attended courses which Ferguson sent him to.

I remember seeing painters and others using the scissors lifts on a number of occasions. However, I never saw them using the outriggers-neither before nor after Kidd's accident. Whenever I saw outriggers not being used, I would order the foreman to tell their people to use the outriggers. I distinctly recall that on the day before the accident, I told Mike that the painters on the lifts needed to use the outriggers. I remember because I was taking a tour through the building with a state safety inspector. I noticed that outriggers weren't being used, and I told Mike that they had to be used. The gentleman from OSHA told me that the outriggers needed to be out, and I relayed the message to Mike right there. At that time we saw only one lift, but I have no idea who was in it. He put his outriggers out. I didn't see anyone else in lifts right then, so I can't tell you if anyone else put out their outriggers, but like I said, I did tell Kidd to use outriggers on the day of his accident.

On the accident two weeks before the Kidd fiasco, neither Ellis nor Kidd were involved. The guy driving had one side on the level and the other wheel traveling along an incline. Then he hit top speed, so naturally it turned over.

I know Gary Kidd. He had been working for Ferguson for about 11 months before the accident. He's not a bad worker if the moon is in the right phase, but he likes to make his own rules and can be real hard to get along with. He likes to work on his own. If he doesn't feel like working, he either just won't show up; or he'll try and pair up with someone else and let them do the work. We gave him a few oral and written warnings for slacking off or breaking safety rules. But we tolerated him because when he painted, he painted well-and fast. I'd heard on the grapevine that he'd gotten into trouble with earlier employers, but I don't know anything specific.

I didn't see the accident occur, but I arrived no more than a minute after it happened. Kidd and this other person, Alan Ellis, were the ones in the lift. Kidd was lying on the ground. Ellis was standing, but something seemed to be wrong with his leg or ankle. The lift was laying nearby. One of its wheels had gone into a drainage trench. We didn't photograph the accident because we didn't have a camera.

There was no cover on the trench at the time of the accident. There were a number of trenches through the building. Some were for drainage, some were electrical raceways, and some were plumbing. This trench was for waste water discharge from the glass manufacturing machines. For that reason it was a little wider and a little deeper than the others. I suppose it was about 20 inches across and six inches deep. All the trenches were completed before January 15th, 19YR-4.

We had metal plates to cover the trenches, but I don't recall when they arrived. I do remember that at the time of Kidd's accident the building was just one big open room. The plates were stored somewhere in the middle of the building. I don't know if any of the plates were in place when Kidd's accident occurred. We tried to keep all the trenches well marked with yellow caution tape-six inch wide construction tape. However, different people would remove the tape sometimes. I seem to recall that Mike had to caution Gary Kidd about removing the tape one time. Actually, they wouldn't completely remove the tape, but just lay it on the floor out of the way. The tape was supported by moveable standards–2 X 4s in small concrete blocks. We wrapped the tape around the 2 X 4s. Workers would move the standards a little, and the tape would fall to the floor. We periodically went around and made sure all the trenches were properly marked if they weren't covered. However, there was no tape around the trench in question on the day of the accident. I don't know how long it had been missing.

We refrained from putting the plates on the drainage ditches because we didn't want the JLGs to drive over them. The plates for the electrical and plumbing conduits were solid, and they could withstand the weight of the JLGs. But the plates for the drainage trenches were a grate, so water could get into the trench. If a JLG ran over one of the grates, it would bend the grate because of the weight of the JLG. They are bigger than the scissors lifts and much heavier. I don't recall if we put on all the plates right after the accident, but they all were certainly in place by the time we finished the job. We replaced the tape right after the accident.

The guy from OSHA didn't say anything about the caution tape not being in place, but he stated that what we had was sufficient. The tape must have been in place at least the day before the accident. I have no idea who removed the tape.

An accident report was filled out by Ken Fletcher. Ken claimed to be an eyewitness to the accident. I don't know of anyone else who saw the accident. Since Kidd's accident, we have had no problems with lifts toppling over. The OSHA guy didn't say anything about putting the plates in place because the caution tape was there, and that was adequate.

OSHA stopped by the day after the accident, but I didn't really talk with them. However, we did receive a citation about a week later.

Dated: October 2, 19YR–1

/s/   David Schonk

David Schonk

THE INDUSTRIAL COMMISSION OF CALIFORNIA
BUREAU OF WORKERS' COMPENSATION

In the Matter of the Claim of

     Gary Kidd

No. <u>9883</u>

_____

Affidavit

State of El Dorado

ss.:

County of <u>Vacaville</u>

My name is Kendall Willis, and I am Vice–President of Willis Contracting Supply Company. Construction companies rely on us to recommend and supply equipment for big construction jobs like assembly plant construction, warehouses, new office buildings, and the like. I handled arrangements with Ferguson Company. We had done business with them once before, and never had any trouble. For their high painting work, it was clear that the Workwell would be ideal. I understood there might be some rough spots along the floor, so I told them to use the outriggers. A man named David Schonk was superintendent of the Technoglass job, and I informed him of that when we dropped off the first of the Workwells.

I am in regular contact with the people at Workwell as well as with others in the industrial safety field, and stay informed by reading government reports on equipment safety. I have never heard of nor seen any report of the Workwell platform being unsafe. We have leased this product for three or four years, and have received no reports of accidents except the two at Technoglass. Sometimes we have as many as eight Workwells leased at one time.

As far as the injury to Mr. Kidd, this appears to be negligence by a co-worker as well as a failure of his employer to cover the trenches, as opposed to an unsafe product. The operations manual is inside the glove box of each unit, on the platform. It is true that we do not place a sticker warning about the outriggers on the machine itself, nor do we post written instructions on the machine. Our clear advice to a job supervisor would be sufficient, however.

_____
(Signature of Affiant)

Sworn before me and subscribed in my presence this 3d day of October, 19YR–4

R.   Creager
_____

BWC–1228 (Rev. 3B80)

C–105–R

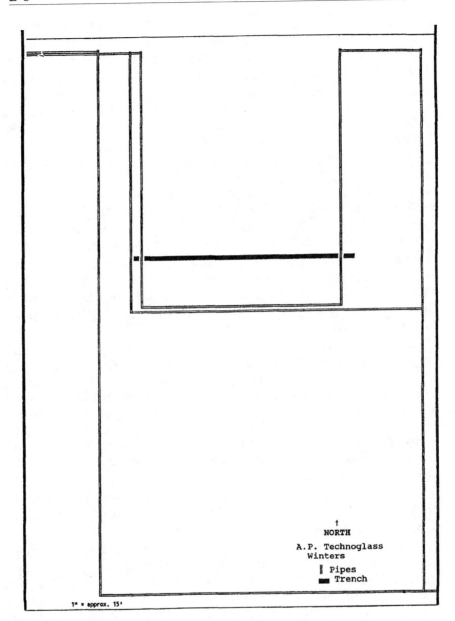

↑
NORTH

A.P. Technoglass
Winters

‖ Pipes
▬ Trench

1" = approx. 15'

Statement of Alan Ellis

My name is Alan Ellis. I live at 8 Cottonwood Avenue in Vacaville. I'm 32 years old and married to Katherine Ellis. We've been together for the past eight years. We have four children, and have lived at our present address for about 2 1/2 years.

I graduated from Lee High School in Fairfield in 19YR–8 and then joined the Navy. After a few years in the Navy I attended ITT Technical Center where I got an associate's degree in electronic engineering.

I am currently employed by Real Properties, Inc., and handle maintenance for the King's Hall Apartment Complex where I used to live. I work there full-time, and have been there for only about a month and a half. Before that, I worked for Quality Decorating, Inc. in Fairfield. Before that, I was at Ferguson Contractors.

Ferguson laid me off about a year ago, and I was out of work for about five months before I got the job at Quality. I have no desire to go back to Ferguson. My wife does not work. I've never been able to use my degree from ITT because I would have to start at a little over minimum wage, and I have a wife and four kids to think about. To support us the way we are used to, I would have to go back and get a masters degree.

I know Gary Kidd through Ferguson. We hung around together at work, and occasionally had a beer with him at a local bar. I was working with him the day of his accident. I have talked to people at Ferguson about it, but I don't remember who. I have never given a written statement to anyone. Nor has anyone ever recorded what I have to say.

I started working for Ferguson in February, 19YR–4. At that time Ferguson was involved in the A.P. Technoglass job. That was the site I started at. I began doing clean up stuff, and started painting about a month after I started. I suppose it was about mid-March 19YR–4. Since I had had some past experience painting with other contractors, it was easy for me to pick it up. But with my other jobs, I had never used lifts before. The day of the accident was the first day I had been up in a lift of any kind for painting. I had been working a little over a month when the accident occurred.

The painters didn't have regular partners, but we switched around. Before the time of the accident, I had never painted with Gary Kidd, although I had assisted him a couple of other times.

The accident occurred in the morning-probably around 10:00 or 10:30. We're not unionized, and we typically worked the whole morning without a break. I had not taken any medication or drugs that day. Nor had I been drinking. I have never been treated for alcoholism. I didn't see Kidd taking anything, either, although I had seen him drinking at lunch on several occasions.

When I got to work that day, Dave Schonk was telling painters what to do since Mike Cohorn, the painter's foreman, wasn't there. Schonk is Ferguson's supervisor. As far as I know, he is still with Ferguson. Cohorn was killed in a car wreck a little while ago, though. I got to work a little late—probably 20 minutes before 8:00. When I got there, Schonk told me that I was going to be on a scissors lift painting pipes. I told him I had never been on one before, and I didn't know how to operate it. I was concerned because the scissors lift seemed obviously a bit unstable to me. Also, I had heard about the accident a couple of weeks earlier, although I guess nobody got hurt when that Workwell tipped over. Schonk understood and said OK, but added he would put me with someone who did know how to operate it. That's when he put me with Kidd. Gary was already over by the Workwell. I joined him, and we started working.

Schonk didn't give me instructions on how to use the lift. He told me that Kidd knew how to operate the thing. When I got over to where Gary was, I told Gary we were going to be working together. He said fine. He said that I was going to run the machine. I told him that I had never used one, and he told me he would tell me how. Gary just told me to look at a little instruction plate on the controls, which I did. Then we drove it back and forth a couple of times. That was the extent of my training. Although the instructions were on the machine, at no time did I see the outriggers. Nor did Kidd ever point them out to me, or even mention them. We started working. Kidd drove the thing a couple of times, but mostly he was either standing there pretending to work or sometimes painting. I guess I handled the controls 90% of the time on that day. I was handling them at the time of the accident. I probably did 90% of the painting, too. Gary was in one of his moods where he was pretending to work, but not doing any actual work.

We were working primarily at the north end of the building painting pipes. They are probably 15 or 20 feet off the ground. The pipes are spaced probably six inches apart, and were color coded. We had to paint each one a different color. We would paint only one color of pipe at a time. That way we didn't have to worry about getting the colors mixed up. That day we were painting just the white pipes. It's pretty difficult work because the pipes are so close together.

We were working on the pipes and approaching this drainage trench in the floor. The pipes were directly over our head as we approached the trench. The trench was uncovered. We got as close to the trench as we could and then stopped. The pipes went directly over the trench.

I was driving the lift. The control panel is in the center in the front. The lift was controlled by an arm that you swing back and forth to indicate your direction of travel. We were running the lift with the bed extended, and it was impossible for me to see where we were in relation to the trench. I couldn't hold my hand out to the side and look over the edge because I wouldn't have been able to steer it that way.

Kidd was standing on the left hand side of the lift about half-way back. There was a rail around the lift about three or four feet high. He was looking over the edge and directing me how far to travel to ensure that we wouldn't have any problem with the trench. He would instruct me to pull up farther and farther as we painted. When we got close to the trench, he was directing me how far we could get without actually going into it. When we got close enough, he said: "That is just about far." Before he finished his sentence, we tipped over. I was able to jump clear, but Kidd went down with the lift.

This particular model of lift had three main wheels, like a tricycle. I now know that this model also had four outriggers-two on each side. You can run the lift while the lift is in the air, but you can't put the outriggers in and out because you have to get out and do that by hand. They weren't hydraulic.

The Workwell is battery powered. At top speed it probably goes about five miles an hour. The machine was an older model. The newer ones have four wheels because they are more stable. The machine had a little plate on it next to the controls to tell you the basics of how to operate it (but I don't recall seeing any plates or labels telling you about the outriggers). There was only one speed, and there was a button you pushed to make it go. When you took your finger off the button, the machine stopped. You steered it with a lever which moved from side to side. The single front wheel steered the thing. The bed was probably four feet wide and eight feet long.

We had never used the outriggers at any time that day. I didn't see anyone else using them that day. Before the accident, no one ever gave me instruction on how to use this lift, except the two-minute exercise I got from Kidd right before we started work.

The trench ran right under the pipes. The trench was probably about 20 inches wide and maybe a foot deep. I think it continued on both sides of the pipe. But that wasn't a problem because some of the metal plates which were supposed to cover the trench were in place just beyond where the pipes crossed the trench. However, under the pipes, the plates weren't in place, and the trench was open.

There were several trenches throughout the floor of the building, but this was the only one in this area. A few of them had covers on-maybe 5 or 10%. The rest of the covers were there, but Ferguson hadn't put them in place yet. They were stacked in piles in various locations throughout the building. I don't know how long they had been there. When I returned to work the next day, Ferguson was putting all the plates in place. The plates that went over this particular trench were grates to permit water to flow into the trench. Other plates for other trenches were solid. I don't know what the other trenches were for.

After the accident, I noticed a skid mark that was a foot and a half, maybe two feet, long. It ran from where we were sitting to the trench where it drug the main drive wheel into the trench. I couldn't really see the trench from where I was in the lift because I was at the controls. The floor of the bed was solid plywood, and you couldn't see through it. Kidd could see the trench, since he was looking right down on the trench giving me directions. We were trying to get as close to the trench as we could to maximize the area we could paint; we tried to paint as much of the pipe above the trench as we could before we had to move around to the other side.

Gary and I developed this plan together. He would guide me, and I would maneuver the lift as close to the trench as he told me. He was looking over the side and giving me directions, and I was at the controls.

I remember he would tell me to get so close, and then back up and try it again from a slightly different angle. We went through this probably three times. Then I started to get frustrated because I didn't see what a couple of inches mattered. The trench wasn't so wide that it was that big a problem. I told Gary we should just stop this game of seeing how close we could get to the trench and get back to work. But like I said, he wasn't really in a working mood that day. At the time of the accident, neither one of us was doing any painting.

I was taken to the hospital with Gary. He was pretty banged up. I guess he did something to his hip and knee, and busted his nose. Since I was able to jump clear when the thing started to go, I came off with a slightly sprained ankle. The accident was on a Thursday. I missed Friday, but was back at work on Monday.

Gary and I never talked about the accident that day. I did talk with him about six months later when he called me up to see how I was doing. But at that time we just talked about the accident in passing.

I don't remember any kind of barricades or caution tape around the trench on the day of the accident. I recall seeing it in the building around trenches, but I don't remember when and where. I had been working there only a month or so. I thought Gary knew what he was doing, so I wasn't really thinking about it at the time of the accident.

I believe Ken Fletcher, who also is a painter for Ferguson, saw the whole thing. He was painting on another lift maybe 30 feet away. Right after the accident he told me that he had heard me yelling "Oh, shit" or something like that. When he looked over to see what the yelling was about, the lift started to fall. He said he heard me yell as we began to fall.

After the accident, I got formal training on lifts from Fletcher. He was the one who trained people on use of the lifts. Maybe they figured that since I had firsthand knowledge of the importance of the outriggers, I would use the lift safely. The truth is that a lot of times guys, painters as well as other workers, didn't use the outriggers. But for the next three weeks or so I worked almost exclusively from the scissors lift, the Workwell.

I have to admit that I was mad as hell when I got the subpoena. If Gary hadn't been screwing around, none of this would have happened in the first place.

Dated: November 30, 19YR–1

/s/ Alan Ellis

_____

Alan Ellis

Statement of Kenneth Fletcher

My name is Kenneth D. Fletcher. I am single and live at 843 Powell Street in Dixon, El Dorado. I am currently employed by Ferguson

Contractors, and have worked for them for a total time of four years off and on. I don't know why I stay with them. I really don't like the work or the people at Ferguson. I was working for Ferguson at the time Gary Kidd was injured. I know Gary from his working with Ferguson, but we aren't close friends. We didn't socialize outside work much except for having a few beers from time to time.

I am a painter for Ferguson. At the time of Gary's accident, I was working for Ferguson at the A.P. Technoglass building. I had started work at 7:30 that morning like everyone else. I was working on a lift painting pipes at the time of the accident, and saw Gary's lift topple over. I was probably 20 or 25 feet away from their lift. I was on a scissors lift, but it was larger than the one Gary was working on. I was working on the lift with a guy named Chuck, but I don't remember his last name. I think that Chuck saw the whole thing, too. I have no idea where Chuck is now; Ferguson fired him a couple of weeks after the accident for being too slow.

When the accident occurred, I was in front of their lift and on their right (they were in front of my lift and on my right). There was a wall about 15 feet to my left. We were moving in opposite directions; I was moving north as they were moving south. We were operating our lift in reverse-it's just as easy to move it forward as in reverse. I was in the back of the lift-the front of the lift as we were moving-so that I was at that end closest to their lift. I noticed the trench they were near before they went in. The trench was about 15 inches wide and maybe nine inches deep. It was a drainage trench for water.

Gary's lift had outriggers that were supposed to be out when the lift was extended. I know about outriggers because I have had a lot of experience with several different kinds of lifts, including the Workwell, Gary was on at the time of his accident. Dave Schonk had shown me the lifts when I first started at Ferguson, and had given me some instruction on using them. Early on, Schonk appointed me to train people to operate the different lifts. Ferguson pays me a little extra for this, and sends me to different classes. I received certification from OSHA in 19YR-4 to permit me to teach other guys how to use the lifts. I attend additional classes yearly to get recertified. I have also attended several worker safety seminars on elevated platforms sponsored by OSHA. Each time Ferguson purchases or leases a different type of lift, they send me to classes sponsored by the manufacturer on the use and operation of the lift. I have attended manufacturer training for all models of JLGs and scissors lifts, including the Workwell. I'm generally familiar with the various manuals. Most of my time at Ferguson was spent in lifts; and I had trained several people, painters and other workers, including Chuck. Ferguson had about ten painters at the time of the accident. I suppose I had trained about four of the painters on operating the scissors lift.

The outriggers on Gary's lift were not out at the time of the accident. Gary's lift was the type that had only three wheels-one in the front and two in the rear, like a tricycle. The front wheel is made of rubber, and is larger than the rear wheels. The front wheel ran into the ditch causing the lift to fall. The front wheel steered the thing. The wheel went into the ditch about a foot from the end of the ditch. I was looking right at the lift as it went into the ditch, but I never called out. I assumed they knew where they were.

Alan Ellis was driving the lift at the time. He was standing next to the controls in the middle of the front. Since the platform was extended at the time, they were maybe 15 or 20 feet in the air. Gary was in the back of the lift, and he was facing the opposite direction painting a pipe. He was looking in the opposite direction that the lift was travelling, and he was painting while the lift was moving. Gary didn't seem to be talking to Alan or giving him any directions about how to position the lift. At the time of the accident, our lift was extended like theirs; we were up about the same height to paint pipes. After the accident, we lowered our lift and went over to see if they were all right. I tried to talk to Gary, but he was only semi-conscious. I told him that an ambulance was on the way. I didn't speak to Ellis at all. He seemed OK; he was just limping a little bit. He jumped when the lift went down. Dave Shonk, the job supervisor, came over. He asked me what happened, and I told him that the lift went into the ditch. I filled out an accident report for Ferguson about three weeks after the accident, but I don't know what happened to it. Besides that, I have never given a statement to anyone.

I've worked for Ferguson for a total of four years, but not continuously. I got laid off in February 19YR–2, and went to work for Governor's Square Apartments in Dixon doing general maintenance. I just got rehired at Ferguson about two weeks ago. I received my subpoena to appear at this trial about two days before I was rehired at Ferguson. I tried to get back on about two months before the subpoena arrived. At that time they said that things were slow, and that they didn't need me. After I got the subpoena, I went back in to reapply. I mentioned the subpoena to someone, and they hired me back on that day.

I used a lift almost every day I was on the job at A.P. Like I said, I have a lot of experience and teach others how to operate them. I don't need permission to use a lift, although other painters are supposed to get it from a foreman or supervisor. I suppose they do this to make sure that only trained people operate the lifts. I had used the one Gary was on quite a few times before, and didn't like it. I don't know how Gary and Ellis got permission to use the lift.

The outriggers on Gary's lift were not extended like they should have been. I am absolutely sure about this. Not having the outriggers out on a machine like that is something I would notice. Because the machine has only three wheels, it's not that stable. The outriggers stick way out-probably 10 feet or so on each side. There are two on each side. The outriggers are designed to keep the lift from falling over on its side. The lift I was on had four wheels, and therefore was much more stable. We could get by without extending the outriggers, although we should use them. But we don't all the time, at least not on the 4–wheeler. They were extended some of the time on the day of the accident, but not at the time of the accident because we weren't near a ditch or anything. If I had been near a ditch, I would have used the outriggers, even on the 4–wheeler.

As I recall, I had seen Gary operate that same scissors lift about three days before the accident. At least I thought it might be Gary. He wasn't just on the lift; he was working the controls. I don't know how he got permission to use it that time either. I just assumed that Schonk gave him permission, and some kind of instruction on how to use it. He was the supervisor, and I figured he knew what was going on. Schonk had given me part of my training.

When Schonk trained me, he never told me anything about the outriggers. I don't even know if he knew about them. When Ferguson leased the Workwell, I told Schonk that the 3–wheelers were a bad idea because they were inherently unstable.

On the day of the accident, Alan was operating the lift. I had never seen him operate the Workwell lift. However, I had given him some training on the type of lift that I was using the day of the accident. In general he was familiar with the use of a scissors lift and outriggers.

Alan was facing the ditch when they went into it. I saw him looking down at the ditch, evidently trying to inch his way towards it to reach the pipes over the trench. He must have seen it.

The lack of a fourth wheel on the Workwell makes all the difference in the world. Three wheels makes the lift inherently unstable, and the outriggers should be extended. The outriggers are supposed to be out any time the bed of the lift is raised. The lift should not be moved while the lift is raised; if the outriggers are out, the lift operates pretty awkwardly, although it will still move. It's kind of a bother to lower your lift, bring in the outriggers, move only about 10 or 15 feet, extend the outriggers, and then go back up in your lift. The outriggers are extended and put back in by hand. You had to get out of the lift and pull them out, and then get out and push them back in. It's not hard, or all that time-consuming, but it is a bother. But on that thing you had to do it because of its instability. Every time I trained on the Workwell, I stressed the importance of the outriggers.

Another thing. The floor in this area was slightly slanted. Water would flow into the trench and not just stand on the floor. The purpose of the trench was to channel waste water discharged from the machinery that was going in the building when it was finished. The slant was steep enough to spill a soda if you tried to set it on the floor. The floor was slick with a concrete sealer. It's a clear sealer and hard to see. The whole floor at that end of the building was covered with sealer. As Alan got too close to the ditch, the wheel probably slid into the trench because of the slant and the sealer. I don't know how the sealer got there, but I noticed it as I walked through the area about a week before. Before the accident I didn't have any trouble with the sealer on my lift, though.

There were no warnings around the trenches. At an earlier point in time there had been some wide yellow construction tape around the ditches, but I don't know what happened to it. Maybe they took it away when they put down the sealer and didn't put it back up. I just don't know. We were never warned to stay away from the trenches in our lifts, or warned about the sealer. We were simply told by Schonk to paint the pipes. I never moved any tape myself. However, I had seen other guys-both painters and others-move it when they're in a JLG. They just went right over the trench instead of going around it.

The trenches were supposed to be covered by metal plates. Ferguson had the plates at the building at the time of the accident, but didn't have them in place. They had been there for quite awhile. I had noticed them at least a month before the accident. In fact, there were four piles right in the middle of the floor. OSHA had come out a couple of days before the accident, and told someone from Ferguson to put the plates on the trenches. I can't remember who from Ferguson he told this to. It might have been Schonk. But they didn't say anything about the operation of the lifts. Ferguson didn't do anything about the plates at the time; but by the day after the accident, all the plates were in place and all the trenches covered. They stayed there until the job was finished.

After the accident, I continued to work for Ferguson until the A.P. Technoglass job was finished. I've talked to Gary only a couple of times since the accident, but we didn't talk about the accident other than my asking how he was doing.

Dated: November 27, 19YR-1

/s/   Kenneth D. Fletcher

Kenneth D. Fletcher

Attachment to Ken Fletcher's Statement

Attached are figures of the Workwell that were drawn by hand. Figure #1 shows a side view of the lift when the bed is all the way down. The little squares just above the wheels show where the outriggers would be. Figure #2 is a view of the Workwell from the top.

Figure #3 again shows the lift from the top, but this time without the bed or the base platform. The three larger squares represent the three main wheels on the lift. The one large wheel is at the front of the lift. Figure #4 is the same view as figure #3. Only figure #4 shows the location of the outriggers by the dark circles with the "Xs" next to them.

Finally, figure #5 is a side view of the lift with the bed extended. The little box on the base platform is the drive box for the lift, and is located at the lift's rear.

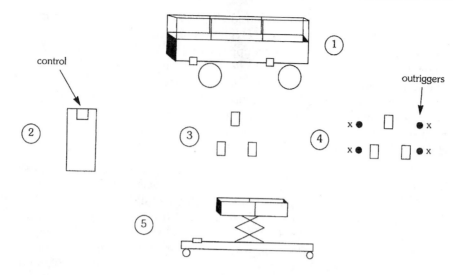

The parties have entered into the following stipulations:

1. At all relevant times, Willis Contracting Supply Co. was a corporation with its principal place of business in the State of El Dorado. At all relevant times the corporation had at least 70 full-time employees.

2. On the day of April 24, 19YR–4, Gary Kidd was an employee of Ferguson Construction. At all relevant times he was working within the scope of his employment. Kidd has received worker's compensation for his injuries.

3. All machinery and equipment at issue were owned by Willis Contracting Supply Co. Ferguson regularly leases specialty equipment from Willis, and had done so for the high painting work at Technoglass. Ferguson was the only contractor present at the A.P. Technoglass plant and had sole and exclusive control of the premises at the time of the accident.

4. If Russell H. Creager were present at trial, he would testify to the facts stated in his report to the El Dorado Bureau of Workers' Compensation.

5. The Bureau of Workers' Compensation investigated this accident and filed a final report. El Dorado law permits introduction of such reports as a business record, subject to relevancy and opinion objections. El Dorado's substantive tort law is identical to your state's law.

6. Although the attached diagram of the A. P. Technoglass site is not to scale, it is substantially true and accurate.

7. The attached photograph of a Workwell scissors lift is true and accurate.

8. The attached Occupational Safety and Health reports and Citation are authentic and duplicate originals under the El Dorado best evidence rule. The reports are official records, properly prepared by the government officials who personally conducted the investigations described in the reports.

9. At the time of the accident, the El Dorado Department of Industrial Relations had issued a valid General Safety Order 36838(a) requiring all El Dorado businesses with ten or more full-time employees to comply with the American National Standards for Self–Propelled Elevating Work Platforms.

10. The American National Standards Institute of New York had issued a standard for Self–Propelled Elevating Work Platforms. The group which prepared the standard included all major platform manufacturers, testing laboratories, underwriting laboratories, government safety agencies, and the American Societies of Civil and Mechanical Engineers. Standard 14.2 provided that work platforms "shall be

used only in accordance with the manufacturer's operating instructions." The Workwell scissors lift involved in this case was an elevating work platform subject to the ANSI standard.

11. Page 3 of the Operating, Service, and Maintenance Manual for the model of Workwell lift involved in this case stated "usually extend and lock outriggers during operation of unit." All the quoted language appeared in capitalized, bold print.

OCCUPATIONAL SAFETY AND HEALTH REPORT

DEPARTMENT OF INDUSTRIAL RELATIONS
DIVISION OF OCCUPATIONAL SAFETY AND HEALTH

1. INSPECTION IDENTIFICATION

IDENT NUMBER: 3 7 2 6 4   REPORT NO: 0 0 4   FISCAL YEAR: YR-4   TYPE: B

DATE INSPECTION WAS STARTED — MO DAY YR: 0 4 2 5   REGION: 9   DISTRICT: 4

2. PRIMARY SIC (S=STATE, L=LOCAL, X=PVT. INDUST.): 6 4 0 0 X   COMPLAINT LOG NUMBER: R-7 2 6 3 3

3. ESTABLISHMENT NAME: FERGUSON CONTRACTORS

4. STREET NUMBER: 3 3 6 3

5. STREET NAME: MERCHANT ST

6. CITY: VACAVILLE

7. COUNTY CODE: 4 6

8. ZIP CODE: 9 5 6 8 8   9. TELEPHONE NUMBER: (916) 447-2100

10. TYPE OF LEGAL ENTITY: GENERAL CONTRACTORS

11. TYPE OF BUSINESS: CONTRACTING – CONSTRUCTION

12. ADDRESS OF PRINCIPAL OFFICE (Mailing Address): 3363 MERCHANT ST
(City): VACAVILLE   (State): El Dorado   (Zip Code): 95688

13. ADVANCE NOTICE — GIVEN: N (Y/N)

14. FOLLOW-UP INSPECTION — IDENT NUMBER: REPORT NO: FISCAL YEAR: YR-4

15. NUMBER OF EMPLOYEES
A. EMPLOYED IN COMPANY (ALL BRANCHES): 30
B. EMPLOYED IN ESTABLISHMENT (OR SITE): 30
C. AFFECTED BY INSPECTION: 30

16. REASON FOR INSPECTION (Check one):
ACCIDENT: ✓ (A)   ACCIDENT INITIATED (B)   COMPLAINT (C)   COMPLAINT INITIATED (D)   FOLLOW-UP (E)
FDB (F)   PERMIT (G)   OTHER SCHEDULED (H)   REFERRAL (R)

17. DIS REQUESTED TECHNICAL ASSISTANCE FROM OR ENFORCEMENT ASSISTANCE WAS REQUESTED BY HEALTH
(For DIS use only) TECHNICAL ASSISTANCE REQUESTED BY DIS: Y
(For OHB use only) ENFORCEMENT ASSISTANCE REQUESTED BY HEALTH: Y

18. EMPLOYER EVALUATION
GOOD FAITH: G 30%, F ✓ 15%, P 0%
SIZE: 1-10 40%, 11-25 30%, 26-40 ✓ 20%, 51-100 10%, 101 & up 0%
HISTORY: G ✓ 10%, F 5%, P 0%

19. EMPLOYEE REPRESENTATIVE EXERCISED WALKAROUND PRIVILEGES DURING THIS INSPECTION: N (Y/N/X)

20. EMPLOYEE(S) INTERVIEWED ONLY: Y (Y/N/X)

21. RECORDKEEPING INJURIES/ILLNESSES
LOG (Form 200): Y (Y/N/X)   SUPPLEMENT (5020-101-Ins.): X (Y/N/X)

22. REQUIRED POSTING
POSTER: Y (Y/N)   CITATION: N (Y/N/X)   INJURY/ILLNESS SUMMARY (Form 200): Y (Y/N/X)

23. INSPECTION
WALL-TO-WALL: (C)   PARTIAL: P   NO INSPECTION: (N)

24. EMPLOYER FOUND TO BE IN COMPLIANCE — DIS: Y (Y/N/X, For DIS use only)   OHB: (Y/N/X, For OHB use only)

25. DATE INSPECTION WAS COMPLETED — MO DAY YR: 0 4 2 5 YR-4

26.   26A. OSHA 4: Y (Y/N)

ENGINEER SIGNATURE: [signature]   DATE: 4/25 YR-4
DISTRICT MANAGER SIGNATURE: [signature]   DATE: 4/25 YR-4

27. MANAGEMENT OFFICIALS CONTACTED:

NAME	TITLE	PRESENT AT: OPENING	INSPECTION	CLOSING
David Schonk	Site Supervisor	☑	☐	☐
		☐	☐	☐
		☐	☐	☐

28. EMPLOYEES CONTACTED

NAME	ORGANIZATION AND TITLE	HOME ADDRESS		TELEPHONE
Kenneth Fletcher	Painter	843 Powell St. Dixon/El Dorado 95820	✓	916-678-3280

29. OPENING AND CLOSING CONFERENCE SUMMARY AND ADDITIONAL COMMENTS

Accident at job site 9/24. Employee Gary Kidd injured when scissors lift fell over. Contacted Schonk. Not very helpful. Told me to talk to eyewitness Fletcher. According to Fletcher, Alan Ellis operating lift. Ellis attempted to move lift w/ bed extended 15'-20'. Kidd painting overhead pipes at the time. Ellis tried to position lift next to drainage trench. Front wheel of lift entered trench, causing it to fall, and injuries. No contact w/ Ellis, who was out for the day. According to Fletcher, Ellis had no training operating this type of lift. Floor around trench slightly graded. Skid mark 17" long at point of entry. Trench not covered at time of accident, and no barricades in place. Since lift was being moved with bed extended, outriggers could not have been in place as required. On date of inspection, noted outriggers being used, and employees putting metal grates over trenches.

No citation issued. Employer sent copy of report.

30. CHECK LIST

YES	CAL/OSHA
☑	Program
☐	Employee Rights
☐	Variances
☑	Inspection Procedure
☐	Security Clearance
☐	Violations
☐	Citation Procedure
☐	Penalty Calculation
☐	Right to Access
☐	Right to Informal Conference
☐	Follow up Procedure
☐	Invite Questions
☐	Offer Help Summarize
☐	Employee Conference
☐	Distribution

31. IN YOUR OPINION IS A FOLLOW UP NECESSARY? ☑ YES ☐ NO

32. EVALUATION OF SAFETY AND HEALTH PROGRAM

	EFFECTIVE	AVERAGE	INEFFECTIVE		EFFECTIVE	AVERAGE	INEFFECTIVE
SAFETY RESPONSIBILITY -	☐	☑	☐	PROTECTIVE EQUIPMENT -	☐	☑	☐
EMPLOYEE PARTICIPATION -	☐	☑	☐	HOUSEKEEPING -	☐	☑	☐
TRAINING -	☐	☑	☐	FIRST AID -	☐	☐	☐

33. Region _9_ District _4_ Ident. No. _37264_　　OSHA 1 Rep. No. _11_ Fiscal Yr. _YR-4_

OCCUPATIONAL SAFETY AND HEALTH REPORT

DEPARTMENT OF INDUSTRIAL RELATIONS
DIVISION OF OCCUPATIONAL SAFETY AND HEALTH

1. INSPECTION IDENTIFICATION

IDENT NUMBER: 3 7 2 6 4
REPORT NO: 0 3 7
FISCAL YEAR: YR-4
TYPE: B

DATE INSPECTION WAS STARTED
MO 0 5 DAY 0 1 YR

REGION: 9
DISTRICT: 4

2. PRIMARY SIC B=STATE L=LOCAL X=PVT. INDUST.
0 4 0 0 X

COMPLAINT LOG NUMBER: R - 7 2 6 8 7

3. ESTABLISHMENT NAME
F E R G U S O N
C O N T R A C T O R S

4. STREET NUMBER
3 3 6 3

5. STREET NAME
M E R C H A N T S T.

6. CITY
V A C A V I L L E

7. COUNTY CODE
4 1

8. ZIP CODE
9 5 6 8 8

9. TELEPHONE NUMBER
(94) 447-2100

10. TYPE OF LEGAL ENTITY
General Contractors

11. TYPE OF BUSINESS
Contracting

12. ADDRESS OF PRINCIPAL OFFICE (Mailing Address)
3363 Merchant St.
(City) Vacaville (State) El Dorado (Zip Code) 95688

13. ADVANCE NOTICE
GIVEN: N
Y/N

14. FOLLOW-UP INSPECTION
A. IDENT NUMBER: 3 7 2 6 4
REPORT NO: 0 0 4
FISCAL YEAR: YR-4

15. NUMBER OF EMPLOYEES
A. EMPLOYED IN COMPANY (ALL BRANCHES): 30
B. EMPLOYED IN ESTABLISHMENT (OR SITE): 30
C. AFFECTED BY INSPECTION: 30

ENGINEER SIGNATURE: George McKinney DATE 5/1 YR-4

16. REASON FOR INSPECTION (Check one)
ACCIDENT □
ACCIDENT INITIATED □ B
COMPLAINT □
COMPLAINT INITIATED □
FOLLOW-UP ☑
SOB □
PERMIT □
OTHER SCHEDULED □
REFERRAL □ R

17. DIS REQUESTED TECHNICAL ASSISTANCE FROM OR ENFORCEMENT ASSISTANCE WAS REQUESTED BY HEALTH
(For DIS use only) TECHNICAL ASSISTANCE REQUESTED BY DIS
Y □
(For OHS use only) ENFORCEMENT ASSISTANCE REQUESTED BY HEALTH
Y □

18. EMPLOYER EVALUATION
GOOD FAITH:
G 30% □
F ☑ 15%
P 0% □
SIZE:
1-10 60% □
11-25 30% □
26-50 ☑ 20%
HISTORY:
G ☑ 10%
61-100 10% □
F 5% □
101 & up 0% □
P 0% □

19. EMPLOYEE REPRESENTATIVE EXERCISED WALKAROUND PRIVILEGES DURING THIS INSPECTION N Y/N/X

20. EMPLOYEE(S) INTERVIEWED ONLY N Y/N/X

21. RECORDKEEPING INJURIES/ILLNESSES
Log (Form 200): X Y/N/X
SUPPLEMENT (5020-101-Ins.): X Y/N/X

22. REQUIRED POSTING
POSTER: Y Y/N
CITATION: Y Y/N
INJURY/ILLNESS SUMMARY (Form 200): □ Y/N/X

23. INSPECTION
WALL-TO-WALL: □ C
PARTIAL: ☑ P
NO INSPECTION: □ N

24. EMPLOYER FOUND TO BE IN COMPLIANCE
DIS: N Y/N/X (For DIS use only)
OHS: Y/N/X (For OHS use only)

25. DATE INSPECTION WAS COMPLETED
MO 0 5 DAY 0 1 YR YR-4

26.
26A. OSHA 4: Y Y/N

DISTRICT MANAGER SIGNATURE: Hailey Robinson DATE 5/1 YR-4

27. MANAGEMENT OFFICIALS CONTACTED:

NAME — David Schonk   TITLE — Supervisor

PRESENT AT: OPENING ☑   INSPECTION ☐   CLOSING ☑

28. EMPLOYEES CONTACTED

NAME | ORGANIZATION AND TITLE | HOME ADDRESS | | | | TELEPHONE

29. OPENING AND CLOSING CONFERENCE SUMMARY AND ADDITIONAL COMMENTS

FOLLOW UP TO POST-ACCIDENT INSPECTION. (RPT #004). OUTRIGGERS ON LIFTS NOT IN USE. THREE DAYS BEFORE ACCIDENT, NOTED OUTRIGGERS NOT PROPERLY BEING USED. OUTRIGGERS MAY HAVE PREVENTED 4/24 ACCIDENT. HOWEVER, OUTRIGGERS NOT BEING PROPERLY USED ON DATE OF POST ACCIDENT INSPECTION.

METAL PLATES OR METAL GRATES IN PLACE. NO EXPOSED TRENCHES.

CITATION ISSUED.

EMPLOYER SENT COPY OF REPORT

GM

30. CHECK LIST

	YES
CAL/OSHA Program	☑
Employee Rights	☐
Variances	☐
Inspection Procedure	☑
Security Clearance	☐
Violations	☐
Citation Procedure	☑
Penalty Calculation	☐
Right to Appeal	☐
Right to Informal Conference	☐
Follow up Procedure	☑
Invite Questions	☐
Offer Help Summarize	☐
Employee Conference	☐
Discrimination	☐

31. IN YOUR OPINION IS A FOLLOW UP NECESSARY? ☐ YES ☐ NO

32. EVALUATION OF SAFETY AND HEALTH PROGRAM

	EFFECTIVE	AVERAGE	INEFFECTIVE		EFFECTIVE	AVERAGE	INEFFECTIVE
SAFETY RESPONSIBILITY –	☐	☐	☑	PROTECTIVE EQUIPMENT –	☐	☑	☐
EMPLOYEE PARTICIPATION –	☐	☑	☐	HOUSEKEEPING –	☐	☑	☐
TRAINING –	☐	☑	☐	FIRST-AID –	☐	☑	☐

33. Region 9 **District** 4 **Ident. No.** 37264   **OSHA 1 Rep. No.** 11   **Fiscal Yr.** YR–4

DEPARTMENT OF INDUSTRIAL RELATIONS
DIVISION OF OCCUPATIONAL SAFETY AND HEALTH

CITATION

2. ⌐ Ferguson Contractors
    c/o A.P. Tachnoglass Building Site
    3363 Merchant St.
    Vacaville, El Dorado   95688 ⌐

3. Page ___1___ of ___1___

4. Type of alleged violation(s):
    Mechanical lifts-safety

5. Citation number S2387

6. An inspection/investigation of a place of employment located at __12378 County Road 31 Winters, El Dorado__
was conducted by __George McKinney__ on __01MayYR-4__.

7a. Item No.	7b. No. of Instances	8. Standard, rule, order, or regulation allegedly violated	9. Description of alleged violation	10. Date by which alleged violation must be corrected
1	1	3646/3645	outriggers not properly being used; units being moved without lowering platforms	07MayYR-4

11. Signature _George McKinney_
                        Safety, Engineer/Industrial Hygienist

12. Signature _Thomas Robinson_
                    District Manager/Senior Industrial Hygienist   13. __04MayYR-4__
                                                  Date of Issuance

---

Declaration of Service
by Safety Engineer/Industrial Hygienist

On __04May__, 19 __YR-4__, I served a true and correct copy of the Citation upon __David Schonk__ _____ who was identified as the (Title) __site supervisor__ _____
of the employer.

I declare under penalty of perjury that the above statement is true and correct of my own knowledge except as to any allegations made on the basis of information and belief and as to those I believe it to be true.

George McKinney
Safety Engineer/Industrial Hygienist

                                    04MayYR-4
                                      Date

Case file B–9

PADDY'S PLUMBING & SUPPLY, INC. v. SANDRA R. ERTEL

A Case of Adverse Possession

The plaintiff brings an action against a neighboring homeowner to recover possession of a small parcel of land. The defendant claims acquisition of title under the doctrine of adverse possession. The materials present a range of issues typically encountered in adverse possession litigation: whether the claimant's use of the disputed land amounts to possession that is actual, continuous, open and notorious, and under a claim of right for the time period specified by the statute of limitations.

Prepared by
James C. Smith
University of Georgia School of
Law

IN THE SUPERIOR COURT OF MORENA
COUNTY STATE OF EL DORADO

PADDY'S PLUMBING   )
SUPPLY, INC.,   )
             Plaintiff,   )
)   CIVIL ACTION
            vs.   )
)   FILE NO. 124578
SANDRA R. ERTEL,   )
            Defendant.)

CONSOLIDATED PRETRIAL ORDER

The following constitutes a pretrial order entered in the above-styled case after conference with counsel for the parties.

1.

The following is Plaintiff's brief and succinct outline of the case and contentions:

This case involves title to approximately .131 acres of real property located in Morena County, El Dorado (hereinafter the "Subject Property"). Plaintiff is the record title owner in fee simple of the "Subject Property." Defendant Ertel claims to have obtained title by adverse possession to the Subject Property. Plaintiff contends that Defendant has not obtained adverse possession title to the Subject Property, but rather is a trespasser and squatter subject to ejectment and is liable to Plaintiff for damages resulting from Defendant's trespass.

2.

The following is Defendant's brief and succinct outline of the case and contentions:

In September YR–26 Defendant Ertel's husband, Barry Ertel, purchased certain real property known as 1873 Wildwood Place, Morena, El Dorado, upon which they constructed their family home. They additionally caused the Subject Property (which is adjacent to their home) to be bulldozed, cleared and included as a part of the backyard of their home. Barry Ertel later conveyed the residence to Defendant in June YR–18.

Defendant and her family have possessed the Subject Property for over 20 years and said possession has been adverse, continuous, exclusive, uninterrupted, open, peaceable, and under claim of right. Defendant acquired adverse possession title to the Subject Property as early as September YR–6, 20 years following the initial possession of the Subject Property by Defendant and her family.

3.

The names of the parties as shown in the caption to this order are correct and complete. There is no question by any party as to misjoinder or non-joinder of any party. There is no question as to jurisdiction or venue.

4.

The issue for determination by the jury is whether Defendant has obtained adverse possession title to the Subject Property. If Defendant has not obtained adverse possession title to the Subject Property, the amount of damages sustained by Plaintiff will be determined in a separate proceeding. The assessment of damages is not before the jury at this time.

5.

It is stipulated that Plaintiff has record title to the Subject Property under a regular chain of transfers originating in the sovereign. It is stipulated that Defendant has record title to Lot 8 of the Wildwood Place (North Extension) Subdivision under a regular chain of transfers originating in the sovereign.

6.

It is stipulated that Exhibit A to the Complaint and Exhibit A to the Answer and Counterclaim are true and correct plats of surveys made on the ground during the year preceding the filing of the Complaint, and that such Exhibits accurately describe the parties' ownership of record and the Subject Property. Either party may introduce such Exhibits into evidence.

7.

Discovery has been completed. The following witnesses will be called to the stand at trial:

Paddington W. Roberts, Jr.
Sandra R. Ertel
James Ertel
Barney Toro
Mary Tucker

8.

The verdict will be rendered through special interrogatories listed on the Verdict Form.

Judge, Superior Court

IN THE SUPERIOR COURT OF MORENA
COUNTY STATE OF EL DORADO

PADDY'S PLUMBING &
SUPPLY, INC.,   )
)
                    Plaintiff,   )
)   CIVIL ACTION
          vs.   )
)   FILE NO. 124578
SANDRA R. ERTEL,   )
)
                    Defendant.   )

COMPLAINT

NOW COMES Paddy's Plumbing & Supply, Inc. and files this its Complaint and shows the Court the following:

1.

This action involves title respecting real property located in Morena County, State of El Dorado.

2.

Plaintiff, Paddy's Plumbing & Supply, Inc. (hereinafter "Paddy's"), is a company incorporated in the State of El Dorado whose principal place of business is located at 2211 Longstreet, Morena, El Dorado 10001.

3.

Defendant Sandra R. Ertel (hereinafter "Ertel") is an individual who resides at 1873 Wildwood Place, Morena, El Dorado 10001.

4.

Defendant Ertel is subject to the jurisdiction and venue of this Court.

5.

For the past 22 years Paddy's has held record title in fee simple absolute to certain real property in the City of Morena, County of Morena, State of El Dorado, containing 9.05 acres, more or less, located at 2211 Longstreet, and being more particularly described in Exhibit A attached to this complaint and incorporated herein by reference.

6.

A smaller tract of real property, believed by Plaintiff to be owned by Defendant Ertel, is one of many smaller tracts of real property adjoining the real property described in the paragraph above.

7.

On or about February 18, YR-1, Paddy's entered into a contract for the sale of realty whereby Paddy's agreed to sell to Republic Homes

Corporation 8.30 acres of vacant land out of the property described in paragraph 5 for $275,000.00, being more particularly described as Tract 2 in Exhibit A attached hereto.

8.

On or about February 25, YR–1, the land described in paragraph 7 was surveyed by the engineering survey firm of Brown & Jones. At the time the survey was performed, clearly visible wooden survey stakes were placed along the boundary of said 8.30 acre tract owned by Paddy's. Several of these stakes were placed, in an open and obvious fashion, immediately adjacent to the property now believed to be owned by Defendant Ertel.

9.

The survey described above revealed a cleared area on Plaintiff's property adjoining the property at 1873 Wildwood Place now believed to be owned by Defendant Ertel. Plaintiff requested that Defendant execute a Quitclaim Deed, to Paddy's as grantee, covering said cleared area. On or about April 23, YR–1, Paddy's received correspondence from Amy Bailey, an attorney representing Defendant Ertel, stating that "for approximately the last twenty-six (26) years Mrs. Sandra R. Ertel has claimed all right, title and interest in and to that certain tract or parcel of land measuring approximately 70 feet by 70 feet located adjoining that certain property known as 1873 Wildwood Place, Morena, El Dorado 10001 (hereinafter the 'Subject Property'). The correspondence further alleged that 'title to said 70 foot by 70 foot tract is vested in and owned by Mrs. Sandra R. Ertel.' "

10.

The Subject Property described in the April 23, YR–1 correspondence lies within the bounds of the property owned by Paddy's as described in paragraph 5. Defendant Ertel later claimed that she had cleared, grassed, planted, mowed and continually maintained the Subject Property.

11.

Because of the claim of ownership by Defendant Ertel to the Subject Property, a cloud has been placed on Plaintiff's title to the real estate described in paragraph 5. Plaintiff is unable to transfer clear and insurable title to the Subject Property to the purchaser of the property who is identified in paragraph 7. In addition, the purchaser of the property is unwilling to pay to Plaintiff the total agreed purchase price for the property.

12.

Paddy's has never conveyed, leased, licensed, deeded, quitclaimed or transferred in any way whatsoever any right, title, or interest in the Subject Property to Defendant Ertel or to anyone else.

13.

Before April 23, YR–1, neither Paddy's nor any of its officers, agents, representatives or employees received any claim, orally or in writing, from Defendant Ertel or anyone on her behalf concerning the Subject Property.

14.

Paddy's has never permitted Defendant Ertel to possess, squat upon, mow, clear, seed, cut, cultivate or maintain in any fashion the Subject Property.

COUNT 1

EJECTMENT

15.

Plaintiff realleges and incorporates by reference herein the allegations set forth in paragraphs 1 through 14, above.

16.

Paddy's has at all times relevant hereto been the rightful, true and sole record title owner in fee simple of the Subject Property.

17.

Defendant Ertel, who claims to be in possession of the Subject Property, has no right, title or interest in said property and, therefore, occupies the position of a mere squatter.

18.

Paddy's is entitled to an ejectment of Defendant Ertel, a writ of possession and a judgment whereby Defendant Ertel is deemed to have no right, title or interest in the Subject Property.

COUNT II

TRESPASS

19.

Plaintiff realleges and incorporates by reference herein the allegations set forth in paragraphs 1 through 18, above.

20.

Defendant Ertel has interfered with the Plaintiff's rights of ownership and possession of Plaintiff's property by trespassing thereon.

21.

Defendant Ertel's trespass has caused considerable financial loss to Plaintiff for which Defendant Ertel is liable.

COUNT III

MESNE PROFITS

22.

Plaintiff realleges and incorporates by reference herein the allegations set forth in paragraphs 1 through 21, above.

23.

Defendant Ertel has unlawfully benefitted from the trespass upon Plaintiff's property and is therefore liable to Plaintiff for mesne profits in an amount to be determined at the trial of this action.

WHEREFORE, Plaintiff demands as follows:

(a) that a writ of possession be issued and that Defendant Ertel be ejected from the Subject Property;

(b) that the Court declare that Plaintiff has all right, title and interest in and to the Subject Property and that Defendant Ertel has no right, title or interest in such property;

(c) that Plaintiff have judgment in its favor for compensatory damages in an amount exceeding $50,000.00;

(d) that Plaintiff recover its reasonable attorney's fees and the costs of prosecuting this action;

(e) that Plaintiff be granted a jury trial on all issues so triable; and

(f) that Plaintiff be granted such other further relief as the Court deems just and proper.

_____

Attorneys for Plaintiff

IN THE SUPERIOR COURT OF MORENA
COUNTY STATE OF EL DORADO

PADDY'S PLUMBING   )
SUPPLY, INC.,   )
           Plaintiff,   )
)   CIVIL ACTION
         vs.   )   FILE NO. 124578
SANDRA R. ERTEL,   )
          Defendant.   )

ANSWER AND COUNTERCLAIM

NOW COMES Defendant Sandra R. Ertel (hereinafter "Ertel") and files this her Answer and Counterclaim as follows:

1.

Ertel admits the allegations of Paragraphs 1, 3 and 4 of Plaintiff's Complaint.

2.

For want of sufficient information, Ertel can neither admit nor deny the allegations of Paragraphs 2, 7, 8, and 13 of Plaintiff's Complaint.

3.

For want of sufficient information, Ertel can neither admit nor deny the allegations of Paragraph 5 of Plaintiff's Complaint, except that Ertel denies that Plaintiff is the owner of certain real property determined by survey to be 79.89N x 74.75N x 72.26N x 74.91N containing approximately .131 acres as is more fully described in Exhibit A attached hereto and incorporated herein by reference (said .131 acre parcel hereinafter called the "Subject Property"). Further, Ertel shows that she is the owner of the Subject Property.

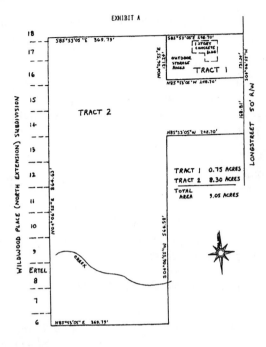

EXHIBIT A

4.

For want of sufficient information, Ertel can neither admit nor deny the allegations of Paragraph 6 of Plaintiff's Complaint, except that Ertel admits that Ertel's residence and real property is adjacent to the Subject Property.

5.

Ertel admits the allegations of Paragraph 9 of Plaintiff's Complaint and further shows that after a survey was conducted on Ertel's behalf, the Subject Property was determined to be 79.89N x 74.75N x 72.26N x 74.91N containing .131 acres as is more fully described in Exhibit A attached hereto and incorporated herein by reference.

6.

Answering Paragraph 10 of Plaintiff's Complaint, Ertel denies the allegations of the first sentence of said Paragraph except that Ertel admits that three sides of the Subject Property are bounded by property owned, at one time, by Plaintiff; Ertel admits the allegations of the second sentence of said Paragraph.

7.

Answering Paragraph 11 of Plaintiff's Complaint, Ertel denies that a cloud has been placed on Plaintiff's title to the Subject Property; Ertel admits that Plaintiff is unable to transfer clear and insurable title to the Subject Property for the reason that Ertel has acquired complete title to the Subject Property by adverse possession; and for want of sufficient information, Ertel can neither admit nor deny the remaining allegations of said Paragraph.

8.

Answering Paragraph 12 of Plaintiff's Complaint, Ertel admits the allegations of said Paragraph as applied to Ertel; and for want of sufficient information, Ertel can neither admit nor deny the allegations of said Paragraph regarding "anyone else."

9.

Ertel admits the allegations of Paragraph 14 of Plaintiff's Complaint.

10.

Ertel denies the allegations of Paragraphs 15, 16, 17, 18, 19, 20, 21, 22, and 23 of Plaintiff's Complaint.

COUNTERCLAIM

1.

Defendant Sandra R. Ertel's husband, Barry Ertel, purchased certain real property known as 1873 Wildwood Place, Morena, El Dorado in September YR–26 upon which he and Defendant Ertel had a house constructed to be used as their family residence.

2.

At the time of said construction, Barry and Sandra Ertel caused a certain parcel of real property determined by survey to be 79.89N x 74.75N x 72.26N x 74.91N containing approximately .131 acres as is more fully described in Exhibit A attached hereto and incorporated herein by reference (hereinafter the "Subject Property") to be bulldozed, cleared and included as a part of the backyard of their residence.

3.

Barry Ertel conveyed the real property known as 1873 Wildwood Place, Morena, El Dorado to Defendant Ertel in June YR–18. (Said conveyance evidenced by Warranty Deed attached hereto as Exhibit B and incorporated herein by reference.)

4.

Ertel has treated the Subject Property as her own by, *inter alia,* planting grass, flowers, shrubbery and trees and by cultivating and maintaining the Subject Property beginning in or about September YR–26 and continuing uninterrupted to the present.

5.

Ertel has possessed the Subject Property for over 20 years and said possession has been adverse, continuous, exclusive, uninterrupted, open, peaceable, accompanied by a claim or right, and not permissive.

6.

Ertel has acquired title by adverse possession to the Subject Property and is the owner of the Subject Property.

7.

Plaintiff claims ownership of the Subject Property as evidenced by the allegations contained within Plaintiff's Complaint and which claims are expressly disputed by Ertel.

WHEREFORE, Defendant prays as follows:

(a) that Plaintiff's Complaint be dismissed with costs cast upon Plaintiff and that Defendant be awarded attorney's fees for this litigation; and

(b) that this Court declare that Defendant has acquired title in fee simple to the Subject Property by adverse possession and that Plaintiff has no right, title or interest in the Subject Property.

—————————————————

Attorney for Defendant

EXHIBIT B

WARRANTY DEED

THIS DEED made and entered into on June 1, YR-18, between BARRY ERTEL of the County of Morena, State of El Dorado (hereinafter called "Grantor"), and MRS. SANDRA R. ERTEL, of the County of Morena, State of El Dorado (hereinafter called "Grantee").

WITNESSETH, that Grantor, for and in consideration of the sum of Ten Dollars ($10.00) and Love and Affection in hand paid, at and before the sealing and delivery of these presents, the receipt whereof is hereby acknowledged, has granted, bargained, sold, aliened, conveyed and confirmed, and by these presents does grant, bargain, sell, alien, convey and confirm unto the said Grantee, her heirs and assigns, the following described property, to wit:

All of Lot 8, Wildwood Place (North Extension) Subdivision, situate in the City of Morena, Morena County, El Dorado, as shown on subdivision plat recorded on April 7, YR-29, in Plat Book, Volume 107, Page 21 of the Morena County Plat Records.

EXHIBIT A

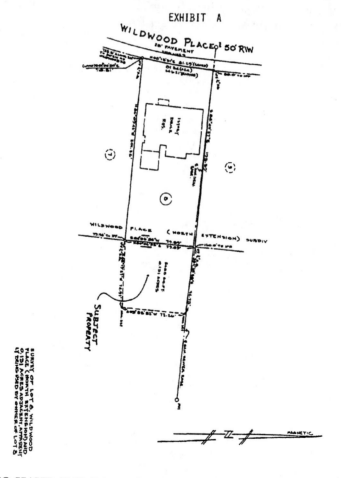

TO HAVE AND TO HOLD the said described property, with all and singular, the rights, members and appurtenances thereunto appertaining, to the only proper use, benefit and behoof of the said Grantee, her heirs, executors, administrators and assigns, in Fee Simple.

And the said Grantor warrants and will forever defend the right and title to the above described property unto the said Grantee, her heirs and assigns, against the lawful claims of all persons whomsoever.

IN WITNESS WHEREOF, Grantor has hereunto set his hand, affixed his seal, and delivered these presents the day and year first above written.

Signed, sealed and delivered in the presence of

/s/_____
Barry Ertel

/s/_____
Notary Public, State of El Dorado

SWORN STATEMENT OF PADDINGTON W. ROBERTS, JR.

I am Vice–President of Paddy's Plumbing & Supply, Inc., a corporation chartered under the laws of the State of El Dorado. We are a family-owned small business, selling plumbing fixtures, tools, and supplies, mainly to contractors and retailers. My father, Paddington W. Roberts, Sr., founded the company in YR–34. He is still President, but he retired in YR–4. I am now responsible for day-to-day management and operation of our plumbing supply business.

Our business is located at 2211 Longstreet Road and has been since YR–22. My father bought this land for the company in YR–22, paying $10,000 to James Franklin for about 9 acres of land. The location on a busy street was ideal for us. Though it was far more land than we needed, Dad thought it'd be a good investment. Maybe our plumbing business would grow and grow, and we'd need more buildings. Or else sooner or later developers would want to buy it. In the meantime, we'd just keep it as a long-term investment. We did not have a survey done when we bought the land.

At the time there was a small concrete block building on Longstreet, but the rest of the land was heavily wooded. In YR–20 we added on to the building for more room to keep our inventory. Over the years, we cleared trees and brush near the building for more parking and space for outside storage.

We never paid much attention to the woods. When Dad bought the land I was a teenager, and right before the purchase we walked through the woods. We tried to get as close to the property lines as we could, but this was hard with all the trees, brush, and briars. It was not very dense near our building on Longstreet, but further back towards Wildwood it was very heavily grown up. And there was a creek that went through the center of the property that was very hard to get across. We didn't see any encroachment by the Ertels or anyone else.

In YR–9 a residential developer showed a little interest in buying our vacant land. Then I again walked the property lines of our land and again saw no use or occupation by the Ertels. However, I did discover during this inspection that a child's tree house had been built on our land by one homeowner a few doors up the street from the Ertels. This was on part of our land maybe 100 yards up the ravine from the Ertels' backyard. We were mainly worried about liability. We told the people responsible for this tree house to remove it. And they did move it pretty quick.

The back boundary of our land is a straight line, but when you're going through the woods it's difficult to pick up a property line. For example, on the Wildwood side the homeowner lots do not end in a straight line. It jogs in and out and you just have to approximate where the line is there. Some of the lots are not developed fully to our lot line, so you have to approximate where they are. I'd like to be able to swear that I set foot on the disputed property, which I can't do. But to the best of my knowledge, I walked where I felt were our boundary lines.

Since we bought the 9 acres, we've paid all the property taxes on the land. No delinquencies, city, county, and state property taxes.

The Ertels never came to me or to anyone else in our family to ask permission to use the disputed property. They never offered to buy it or rent it from us. They never told us they were encroaching on our land. We never knew they were on it until the surveyor was hired last year in connection with our sale to Republic Homes Corporation.

In YR–1 Republic Homes came to us and asked to buy all of our vacant property to build single-family homes. We signed a contract to sell our vacant land, about 8 acres, to them for $275,000. Before closing they got their surveyor to check the land. When he found the Ertels' use, that clouded our title. We asked Mrs. Ertel to get off our land and give us a quitclaim deed to give up her claim, but she contacted an attorney and they said no. So we couldn't give Republic clear title to that part. Subsequently, we worked with them to jiggle the lot lines around so all the disputed property fell on only one lot, one of the lots they had platted for the subdivision, and we excluded that one lot from the sale. We amended the sales contract and sold Republic the rest of the property with the exception of the one lot, which we kept. This problem, the Ertels' claim, reduced the sales price we got by $35,700. Now Republic has put in a street down the center and they're currently building houses.

Paddington W. Roberts, Jr.

DEPOSITION OF SANDRA R. ERTEL

Q: Let me start by getting some background information such as your name and current address, full name.

A: Sandra R. Ertel. I live at 1873 Wildwood Place.

Q: Is your husband alive?

A: No, he died in YR–15.

Q: How long have you lived at that address on Wildwood?

A: A little over 26 years.

Q: Where did you live before that?

A: We lived in a house we built on Johnson Road in Morena.

Q: What was the reason for moving out of that home?

A: The traffic on the street and the home was not big enough.

Q: Did you have any kids at the time?

A: Yes, four and I was pregnant with Carol.

Q: And where did you go from the Johnson Road house?

A: To Wildwood Place.

Q: Was it an existing home?

A: No, my husband contracted to have it built. We did the purchasing. It was cost plus.

Q: You say "we." Were you involved in any of that?

A: Well, helping to design the house, the rooms.

Q: What was the area like before you started construction? Were there many homes there?

A: We were the last home on the street. All of the other homes were completed when we started.

Q: What did the property at 1873 Wildwood Place look like before you started construction, do you remember?

A: Just woods, a lot.

Q: Who was the owner?

A: His name was Grafman, I believe. Grafman sold my husband the land.

Q: Did you ever walk the property before construction began?

A: I didn't.

Q: Your husband did?

A: I don't know.

Q: Did you see the property in its various construction stages? Did you go out to watch the house go up?

A: Yes.

Q: Was it cleared to begin with? First thing that was done, did they clear all the trees?

A: Yes.

Q: Do you remember how much of the land they cleared?

A: All the way back to the present, where it is now.

Q: Why was it done that far?

A: So that I could have a playground for the children.

Q: Who made the decision to extend the property back that far?

A: My husband.

Q: Did he consult with you on it?

A: No.

Q: He decided to do it without asking you?

A: Well, he knew that he had five children that had to have a place to play.

Q: And this clearing was done at your husband's instructions to the grading subcontractor; is that your understanding?

A: Yes.

Q: Do you know why he designated this much property? Did he tell the grading subcontractor just to add an extra square back there, 75 by 75 foot parcel, or why was this amount determined to be the amount that the grader would go out and grade?

A: It was the level area, I would imagine.

Q: You say you would imagine. Do you know anything about that?

A: No.

Q: You hadn't gone out with your husband and said, "I'd like to have this much property" or anything?

A: No.

Q: At the time that was done, the areas to the side of this disputed land were wooded, weren't they?

A: Yes.

Q: Were you aware at the time that the grading included land that was not part of the property your husband purchased from Mr. Grafman?

A: No.

Q: Did your husband know at the time that the grading went past the boundary line, onto someone else's land?

A: I think so. Later he said he had tried to purchase it. I didn't know this at the time, when we moved in, but he told me several years later that he had tried to buy it when he bought the land from Grafman.

Q: Who did he try to purchase it from?

A: I don't know who the owner was, but he did try to purchase it.

Q: Obviously, the owner wouldn't sell it?

A: Right.

Q: Do you know whether he told the owner that he was going to be clearing out that parcel anyway?

A: I don't know.

Q: Did your husband feel that he was entitled to that property in any way?

A: I don't know.

Q: Was the sole purpose of extending the property for your kids to play?

A: Absolutely.

Q: What else was done with the property when it was cleared?

A: It was planted. It was completely cleared. We planted grass on it.

Q: Any trees?

A: Not at that time.

Q: When were trees planted on it?

A: When Carol went off to college.

Q: Was anything else planted on that property? When I say "that property," I'm talking about the portion that we claim Paddy's Plumbing & Supply, Inc. owns.

A: Bushes, garden, a vegetable garden, flowers.

Q: When were bushes planted on the property?

A: Throughout the years. I don't know what year it was.

Q: When was the vegetable garden there?

A: Every year for a while. But I stopped with the vegetable garden 8 or 9 years ago.

Q: Did you maintain it; was it your garden?

A: Yes, yes.

Q: Did you ever fence the property?

A: No.

Q: Did you ever put up any kind of barrier to designate what part you considered your property?

A: No.

Q: Did you ever put up any signs on the property that said anything to the effect that this is Ertel property?

A: No.

Q: Did you ever put up any no trespassing signs?

A: No.

Q: Do you remember talking to any of your neighbors about the property, generally about your backyard?

A: No.

Q: You admit, don't you, that your property looks very different from the other pieces of property on your street in that you have a section that goes back further than everybody else's?

A: Yes.

Q: Did any of your neighbors ever ask you about that; about why your property goes back further?

A: No.

Q: Have you ever moved out of your house for any period of time after it was built?

A: No.

Q: How often have you and your family taken vacations? Can you describe your vacations?

A: Typical family vacations. While the kids were growing up, two weeks every summer. The longest vacation we ever took was 6 weeks to Europe, the summer before Carol left for college.

Q: I believe earlier you stated that some bushes had been planted and a garden. Had anything else been done on this property since you all moved into your house?

A: No.

Q: Did you ever place any buildings out there?

A: No.

Q: Storage sheds or anything like that?

A: No.

Q: Swing set ever been put back there?

A: Not back there.

Q: Did the kids, in fact, use the property?

A: Yes.

Q: What did they use it for?

A: Football, baseball.

Q: Did you use the property for anything other than your garden?

A: No.

Q: Ever have a swimming pool out there?

A: No.

Q: Do you know approximately how much money you've spent on that piece of property; that is, the cost of trees or bushes or seeds or anything like that?

A: No.

Q: Can you give me a general idea?

A: I had the yardman cut it every week. It added up.

Q: Have you ever had your property appraised?

A: No.

Q: Ever tried to sell your property since you've lived there?

A: No.

Q: One of the attachments to your Answer is the warranty deed between Barry Ertel and Sandra Ertel. Can you identify that document, Mrs. Ertel?

A: Yes. That is a warranty deed from my husband to me. It appears to be dated in YR–18.

Q: Do you remember at that time your husband conveying the property to you for $10 and love and affection?

A: He said it was in my name.

Q: Do you know why it happened?

A: No. He just said it was in my name.

Q: Can you tell me what else you have done with the property? Let me identify them now. You say it's been cut, mowed, by your yardman. Your kids played on it. You have a garden on it. You've planted some trees since Carol went off to school. The kids played football, baseball. What else has been done with this property by you or your family?

A: Nothing else.

Q: Was grass planted there originally with the rest of the property?

A: Yes.

Q: How big was your garden?

A: About 12 feet by 4 feet.

Q: Do you ever sell anything out of your garden?

A: No.

Q: Did you ever make any money off this property back here by selling anything off of it?

A: No.

Q: What was grown in the garden?

A: Corn, carrots, vegetables. Standard vegetable garden.

Q: Do you remember anybody ever walking across the property back there other than your family?

A: No.

Q: You never had to run anybody off?

A: No.

SWORN STATEMENT OF JAMES ERTEL

Sandra Ertel is my mother. I was 11 years old when we moved into the house at 1873 Wildwood Place, and I lived there for the next 7 years until I went away to college. At first, the backyard was just a big cleared field. We grew up in a wonderful neighborhood. There were lots of kids on the street, basically in all age groups, and we had the best backyard for playing ball. So I used it along with other children from the neighborhood and my brothers and sisters as our ball field and playground. We did all sorts of things there. For two consecutive summers, we had carnivals that involved the basement and the backyard. And twice we had a haunted house for Halloween. Dad took home movies of us back there. When we played, we used the entire backyard, all the way to the trees.

The size of the cleared area in our backyard was always the same. We had a patio area near the carport, and a swing set in one part of our backyard. One portion way in the back we allowed Mom to have a garden and agreed not to play ball in that particular section. Our football and baseball field were in the middle of the backyard, all the way up to the back tree line. Also, we have a pet cemetery way back there. Our dog Ginger, a couple of cats, a rabbit, a bird in a shoe box that's buried back there. Later Mom and Dad planted trees in the middle of our backyard, after we no longer played out there.

As we got older we had fewer softball games in the backyard. Home plate was at the back of the woods, and we'd play toward the house. One of the big kids in the neighborhood broke one of the windows at our house, and my parents said it was not such a good idea to keep playing softball there.

As much time as we spent playing in the backyard, we also played in the woods. The guys in the neighborhood would play war games in the woods occasionally. There was a creek back there, at its largest a few feet wide. Behind our next door neighbor's house there was a pond where two streams came together. It had a lot of sand there, so on occasions we would feverishly dam it up and it would get about 6 or 7 feet wide, maybe 2 feet deep. And we had a plastic boat we would get in and go down the rapids.

SWORN STATEMENT OF BARNEY TORO

I am an attorney and I lived on Wildwood Place for 25 years, from YR–26 until we moved about a year ago. We've been family friends with the Ertels ever since we were first neighbors. I have been at the Ertels' home many times, and the grass part of their backyard has always looked about the same. The grass extended all the way back to the tree line.

A long time ago Mr. Ertel and I had a conversation about the extent of his property. Sometime during the first few years after the Ertels built their home they had a big party. They had set out tables and chairs in the backyard to entertain guests, and I was one of them. We were at a table, drinking and eating, and I remarked that this was a very pleasant place to have a party, with room for all these tables. I asked him how far was his property—did it go that far to the trees? And he said "yes" and gestured that his land went all the way back to the tree line.

SWORN STATEMENT OF MARY TUCKER

I have lived at 1929 Wildwood Place for almost 10 years. We live 5 or 6 houses away from the Ertels. We've been neighbors and friends for about 28, 29 years, something like that. We belong to the same garden club. We formed the garden club when our street was new, with about 30 houses, and we were all fairly young people with young children.

Over the years, we've visited the Ertels' home. On many occasions, we've seen their backyard. Basically, the grass area in the backyard always has been the same size since the Ertels moved in. This grass area is where children played. Boys played a lot of ball, there was always a crowd of children playing in that yard. The Ertels have 4 boys and one girl. Our garden club had several parties in the Ertels' backyard. One function I specifically recall because the neighbors of the adjoining street called the police about the noise. We had a record player out there for some square dancing. We had a caller who brought his own equipment. Of course it was amplified and really did travel. We were young people and the police just asked us to tone it down.

From my personal observation, the Ertels always used all of the grassy area as their backyard. Their activities and uses covered it all.

STATUTE OF LIMITATIONS

The El Dorado Civil Practice and Remedies Code provides:

§ 6.01 Definitions

In this subchapter:

(1) "Adverse possession" means an actual and visible appropriation of real property, commenced and continued under a claim of right that is inconsistent with and is hostile to the claim of another person.

(2) "Peaceable possession" means possession of real property that is continuous and is not interrupted by an adverse suit to recover the property.

§ 6.02. Tacking of Successive Interests

To satisfy a limitations period, peaceable and adverse possession does not need to continue in the same person, but there must be privity of estate between each holder and his successor.

§ 6.03. Adverse Possession. 20–year Limitations Period

A person must bring suit not later than 20 years after the day the cause of action accrues to recover real property held in peaceable and adverse possession by another who cultivates, uses, or enjoys the property.

AUTHORITIES

I. Cases

1. Aud–War Realty Co. v. Ellis, 557 A.2d 69 (R.I.1989) (minor encroachment).

2. Cuthbertson v. Tate, 544 So.2d 1236 (La.Ct.App.1989) (visible boundary).

3. Davis v. Sponhauer, 574 N.E.2d 292 (Ind.Ct.App.1991) (notorious possession).

4. Dorner v. Wishon, 809 S.W.2d 866 (Mo.Ct.App.1991) (actual possession).

5. Gurwit v. Kannatzer, 788 S.W.2d 293 (Mo.Ct.App.1990) (continuous possession).

6. Hermes v. Fischer, 226 Ill.App.3d 820, 589 N.E.2d 1005 (1992) (privity of estate for tacking; visible boundary).

7. Maggio v. Pruzansky, 222 N.J.Super. 567, 537 A.2d 756 (App. Div.1988) (minor encroachment on strip of neighbor's lot).

8. Walker v. Hubbard, 31 Ark.App. 43, 787 S.W.2d 251 (1990) (planting trees and grass).

II. Secondary Materials

Roger A. Cunningham, William B. Stoebuck & Dale A. Whitman, The Law of Property § 11.7 (2d ed. 1993)

Jacqueline P. Hand & James C. Smith, Neighboring Property Owners §§ 6.01–6.08 (1988 & Supp. 1993).

PROPOSED JURY INSTRUCTIONS

Plaintiff has the burden of proof, which means that he must prove whatever it takes to make out his case, except for any admissions by Defendant. Facts may be proven by indirect or circumstantial evidence. The comparative weight of indirect or circumstantial evidence on any given issue is a question of fact for you to decide.

A trespasser is a person who enters the real property of another person without permission, invitation, or other right. If the trespasser remains wrongfully upon the real property of another person, a landowner holding legal title to real property may maintain an action for ejectment. This action for ejectment is proper even though the landowner is not in actual possession of the property.

Adverse possession of real property in conformance with the requirements of the law for a period of 20 years shall confer good title to the possessor against everyone. There are four requirements for title by adverse possession. (1) First, it must involve actual possession by the claimant. Fencing by the occupant is not required. Actual possession may be evidenced by enclosure, cultivation, or any use or occupation of the lands which is sufficient to prevent actual possession by another person. When the occupant locates boundaries by visible marks such as crops, blazes, setting up stones, or some other visible marks and uses the land within them, this constitutes possession. In other words, such possession is established whenever the boundaries of the occupied property can be clearly determined in any way.

(2) Second, the claimant's possession must be continuous and uninterrupted. This means that the occupant's possession must remain intact for not less than the required period of 20 years. A break in the possession of a person claiming adverse possession defeats the requisite continuity. However, short intervals of temporary absence do not break the continuity of adverse possession.

The same claimant does not need to be in continuous possession for the entire 20 year period. Successive occupants who are in "privity of estate" may add together their periods of possession to come up with 20 years. Privity of estate exists when the earlier occupants' possession and claim passed or was transferred to the latter occupants by sale, deed of gift, agreement, devise, or inheritance.

(3) Third, the claimant's possession must be open and notorious. This means that the occupier's acts must provide some form of visible evidence that the land is being adversely used. Actual knowledge by the real owner of the adverse possession is not required. However, the acts of dominion must be of such a nature that the real owner is presumed to have known that there was a possession adverse to his title.

(4) Fourth, the occupant's possession must be accompanied by a claim of right. This means that the occupant has asserted a claim of exclusive ownership since the commencement of the 20 year period. You may presume a person had a claim of right if you find that he or she exercised dominion over the disputed property. This presumption may be rebutted if you were to find from other evidence that this person did not claim to own or hold title to the disputed land at the commencement of the running of the 20 year period or thereafter.

When you get to the jury room, you should select one of your members to be foreperson and then begin your deliberations. Your verdict should be unanimous and in writing. Your verdict should be entered on the verdict form provided to you and signed by the foreperson. When you reach a verdict, please notify the deputy. You may now retire to the jury room.

SPECIAL VERDICT FORM

1. Do you the jury find that Defendant has been in actual possession of the disputed property for a period of at least 20 years? (answer yes or no) _____

2. If the answer to the preceding question is Yes, was Defendant's possession of the disputed property:

    a. Continuous and uninterrupted? (answer yes or no) _____

    b. Open and notorious? (answer yes or no) _____

    c. Under a claim of right? (answer yes or no) _____

    _____
    Foreperson

Case file B-10
BOXER v. CAMPBELL

This is a civil case alleging sexual harassment under El Dorado Fair Employment and Housing Act (FEHA), Gov't Code § 12940(f, h). Plaintiff Diane Boxer alleges that Kevin Schmidt sexually harassed her while they both were employed at the law firm of Campbell, Stoneman, Bettran & Cole. The law firm is the defendant in the case for its alleged failure to adequately provide Ms. Boxer with a harassment-free environment.

The plaintiff alleges a chronology of unwanted sexual attention from defendant Schmidt, including notes, cards, comments and physical contact. The plaintiff further alleges that the law firm defendant failed to respond to her complaints and request for help. The law firm, through its office manager Christine Moore, asserts that it took appropriate actions.

Exhibits and statements are to be distributed as set out below. Attorneys are to interview their own witnesses and depose witnesses to be presented by the other side.

Plaintiff attorneys: complaint
                       stipulations
                       memo entry

Plaintiff witnesses: *Diane Boxer,* plaintiff.
                       William Hepworth, former secretary to Ms. Boxer

Defense attorneys: answer
                       stipulations
                       Christmas card from Boxer
                       law firm's sexual harassment policy

Defense witnesses: *Kevin Schmidt*
                       Christine Moore, office manager for defendant law firm

Boxer v. Campbell

Instructions:

To Plaintiff Attorneys:

The law firm of Campbell, Stoneman, Bettran & Cole, has been accused in a civil complaint of sexual harassment. You have been provided with a copy of the complaint, which has been filed with the clerk of the court. You also received various facts and stipulations and exhibits.

You are to interview the plaintiff as well as witness Hepworth. If you wish to file any documents, they must be filed with the clerk of the court and served on opposing counsel. You should attempt to discover any evidence held by the defense. At the appropriate time, you can arrange with opposing counsel for interviews and/or depositions of Schmidt and witness Moore.

Witness: Ms. Diane Boxer

Witness: Mr. William Hepworth

Boxer v. Campbell

Instructions:

To Defense Attorneys:

Your clients, the law firm of Campbell, Stoneman, Bettran & Cole, has been accused in a civil complaint of sexual harassment. You have been provided with a copy of the answer, which has been filed with the clerk of the court after you have been properly served with the complaint. You also received various facts and stipulations and exhibits.

You are to interview Schmidt as well as Moore. If you wish to file any documents, they must be filed with the clerk of the court and served on opposing counsel. You should attempt to discover any evidence held by the plaintiff. At the appropriate time, you can arrange with opposing counsel for interviews and/or depositions of plaintiff Boxer as well as witness Hepworth.

Witness: Mr. Kevin Schmidt

Witness: Ms. Christine Moore

IN THE SUPERIOR COURT OF MORENA
COUNTY STATE OF EL DORADO

DIANE BOXER,
 	
        Plaintiff
 	
      v.
 	
CAMPBELL, STONEMAN, BET-
TRAN & COLE, AND
DOES 1 THROUGH 50
        Defendants
	))
	))
	))
	))
	))
	))
	))
	))
		Case No. 51110
		
		COMPLAINT FOR SEXUAL
		HARASSMENT

Plaintiff Diane Boxer alleges as follows:

GENERAL ALLEGATIONS

1. Defendant is, and at all times herein mentioned, was a law corporation organized under the law of the State of El Dorado and having its principal place of business in the City and County of Morena, El Dorado.

2. At all times herein mentioned the plaintiff was an agent and employee of the defendant corporation.

3. At all times herein mentioned Mr. Kevin Schmidt was an agent and employee of the defendant corporation. Mr. Schmidt was an associate of the defendant corporation.

4. At all times herein mentioned Ms. Christine Moore was an agent and employee of the defendant corporation. Ms. Moore was the office manager of the defendant corporation. As office manager, she was the person designated to receive complaints of sexual harassment by one employee against another.

5. At all times herein mentioned Mr. Fred Norton was an agent and employee of the defendant corporation. Mr. Norton was a partner at the defendant corporation with supervisory responsibility over both the plaintiff and Mr. Schmidt.

6. The true names and capacities of defendants named as DOES 1B50, inclusive, are unknown to plaintiff who therefore sues such defendants by fictitious names. Plaintiff will amend this complaint to show the true names and capacities when they have been determined.

7. The plaintiff is informed and believes and thereon alleges that at all times mentioned herein, each of the defendants sued as DOES 1B50, inclusive, as an agent or employee of the defendant corporation and were at all times acting within the course and scope of their agency and employment.

8. The plaintiff began work for the defendant corporation on September 10, 19YR–3 at the defendant corporation's Morena office. The plaintiff worked for the defendant corporation until December 16, 19YR–2.

9. On January 4, 19YR–1, the plaintiff filed a complaint of sex discrimination with the Department of Fair Employment and Housing (DFEH). Plaintiff has received a right to sue letter from the DEFH dated January 29, 19YR–1. On March 15, 19YR–1, the plaintiff filed a charge of sex discrimination with the federal Equal Employment Opportunity Commission (EEOC) and received a right to sue letter from the EEOC on May 1, 19YR–1.

First Cause of Action for Sexual Harassment and Retaliation in Violation of Title VII of the Civil Rights Act of 1964 (42 U.S.C. §§ 2000 et seq.)

10. Plaintiff incorporates by references paragraphs 1 through 9, inclusive, of the General Allegations, as if fully set forth herein.

11. From approximately December 19YR–3 until on or about December 19YR–2, Kevin Schmidt subjected the plaintiff to offensive and despicable sexual conduct.

12. Said sexual conduct on the part of Kevin Schmidt constituted sexual harassment and created a hostile, abusive, and intolerable work environment. This conduct as pervasive, ongoing, and included specific acts too numerous to count. All of the sexual harassment about which plaintiff complains occurred during the time period set forth in paragraph 10 herein. The sexually harassing conduct included, but was not limited to, the following:

a. At the defendant corporation's December 19YR–3 Christmas party, sitting so close to plaintiff that she was made to feel ill at ease and telling the plaintiff that she had "a great body" and should dress less modestly;

b. At the party mentioned in subparagraph 12a herein, after the plaintiff objected to the harassing conduct described in that subparagraph, staring at plaintiff constantly and intently for the rest of the party;

c. On Valentine's Day 19YR–2, giving the plaintiff a hug and a kiss without the plaintiff's express or implied invitation or permission;

d. In late March 19YR–2, while the plaintiff was recuperating from back surgery, hugging the plaintiff again without the plaintiff's express or implied invitation or permission and doing so so hard that he broke two of the stitches still in the plaintiff's back;

e. On April 21, 19YR–2, at the plaintiff's birthday party at work attended by many of the plaintiff's co-workers, severely embarrassing the plaintiff by giving her a gift of skimpy lingerie from Frederick's of Hollywood;

f. On April 21, 19YR–2, after the plaintiff objected to the sexually harassing conduct described in subparagraph 12e herein, telling the plaintiff that he and she were having an "office romance;"

g. During August 19YR–2, constantly forcing his presence upon the plaintiff on the pretext of needing to consult her about work-related legal projects when there was absolutely no need for him to consult the plaintiff;

h. In September 19YR–2, accusing the plaintiff of having an affair with another attorney at the defendant corporation and making his, Schmidt's, life, miserable;

i. On December 13, 19YR–2, on a flight between Los Angeles and Minneapolis, Minnesota, sitting so close to the plaintiff that she was made to feel ill at ease;

j. During the flight described in subparagraph 12i herein, telling the plaintiff that he and the plaintiff would "get real close again;"

k. During December 19YR–2, while working on a project with the plaintiff in Minneapolis, frequently leaving embarrassing and sexually suggestive notes in the plaintiff's briefcase; and

l. During December 19YR–2, while working on the project described in subparagraph 12k herein, frequently leaving embarrassing and sexually suggestive telephone messages for the plaintiff.

13. Plaintiff formally complained about the sexually harassing conduct described in paragraph 12 herein to both Ms. Moore, the office manager responsible for investigating sexual harassment complaints, and Mr. Norton, the partner with supervisory responsibility over the plaintiff as well as Mr. Schmidt.

14. The plaintiff is informed and believes and thereon alleges that despite her complaints, none of the defendant's corporation's employees took any action to punish Mr. Schmidt for his sexual harassment of the plaintiff. The plaintiff is informed and believes and thereon alleges that defendant corporation has failed: to adequately supervise Mr. Schmidt; to implement reasonable and necessary procedures and precautions to ensure a work environment free from sexual harassment; and to take immediate and appropriate corrective action when it knew or should have known of the sexual harassment by Mr. Schmidt. Mr. Schmidt is still in the employ of the defendant corporation. The defendant corporation has not taken any disciplinary action against Mr. Schmidt on the basis of the sexually harassing conduct described in paragraph 12 herein.

15. In performing the actions and omissions alleged herein, the defendants, and each of them, violated Title VII of the Civil Rights Act of 1964, 42 U.S.C. §§ 2000e et seq., and the regulations pertaining thereto."

16. The defendants, and each of them, by and through their wrongful conduct alleged herein, humiliated and harassed plaintiff. The defendants' conduct caused her to suffer real and legitimate fear of harm to her job and livelihood.

17. The defendants, and each of them, by and through their wrongful conduct alleged herein, caused the plaintiff to quit her job with the defendant corporation on December 16, 19YR–2.

18. The plaintiff is informed and believes and thereon alleges that defendants, and each of them, knowingly and willfully conspired and agreed to perpetrate, perpetuate, condone, allow, and ignore some or all of the harassment alleged herein and that in so conspiring, the defendants committed the wrongful acts alleged herein and caused the plaintiff actual damage.

19. As a proximate result of defendants' conduct alleged herein, the plaintiff has suffered and will continue to suffer special damages in excess of this court's jurisdictional minimum, including, but not limited to, back and front pay, lost benefits, and costs for medical services and drugs, in amounts to be proven at trial.

20. As a further proximate result of defendants' conduct, the plaintiff has suffered and will continue to suffer general damages in excess of this court's jurisdictional minimum, including, but not limited to, mental and emotional distress, pain and suffering, loss of reputation, humiliation, and degradation, in amounts to be proven at trial.

21. The plaintiff is informed and believes and thereon alleges that the defendants engaged in these discriminatory practices with malice and/or with reckless indifference to plaintiff's federally protected rights, entitling plaintiff to punitive damages under 42 U.S.C. § 1981A.

22. As another proximate result of defendants' conduct, the plaintiff has incurred attorneys' fees and costs for which she is entitled to receive an award under Title VII.

Second Cause of Action for Sexual Harassment and Retaliation in Violation of El Dorado Fair Employment and Housing Act (Govt. Code §§ 12900 et seq.)

23. The plaintiff incorporates by reference paragraphs 1 through 22, inclusive, as if fully set forth herein.

24. In performing the acts and omissions alleged herein constituting sexual harassment and retaliation, the defendants have violated the El Dorado Fair Employment and Housing Act (FEHA), Government Code sections 12900 et seq. and the regulations pertaining thereto.

25. Defendants and each of them, by and through their wrongful conduct alleged herein, humiliated and intimidated plaintiff and caused her to suffer real and legitimate fear of harm to her job and livelihood.

26. Defendants and each of them, by and through their wrongful conduct alleged herein, caused the plaintiff to quit her job with the defendant corporation on December 16, 19YR–2.

27. Plaintiff is informed and believes and thereon alleges that defendants, and each of them, knowingly and willfully conspired and agreed to perpetrate, perpetuate, condone, allow, and ignore some or all of the harassment and retaliation alleged herein and that in so conspiring, the defendants engaged in wrongful acts which caused actual damage to the plaintiff as alleged herein.

28. As a proximate result of defendants' conduct alleged herein, the plaintiff has suffered and will continue to suffer special damages in excess of this court's jurisdictional minimum, including, but not limited to, back and front pay, lost benefits, and costs for medical services and drugs, in amounts to be proven at trial.

29. As a further proximate result of defendants' conduct, plaintiff has suffered and will continue to suffer general damages in excess of this court's jurisdictional minimum, including but not limited to, mental and emotional distress, pain and suffering, loss of reputation, humiliation, and degradation, in amounts to be proven at trial.

30. The plaintiff is informed and believes and thereon alleges that the defendants acted despicably and intentionally subjected the plaintiff to malicious, oppressive, and unjust treatment, and/or consciously disregarded her rights, entitling the plaintiff to an award of exemplary and punitive damages.

31. As a further proximate result of defendant's conduct, the plaintiff has incurred attorneys' fees and costs for which she is entitled to receive an award under FEHA.

WHEREFORE, plaintiff prays for judgment as follows:

1. For special damages, as alleged, according to proof;

2. For general damages, as alleged, according to proof;

3. For exemplary and punitive damage;

4. For prejudgment interest;

5. For attorneys' fees and costs, according to proof; and

6. For any other relief which the court deems proper.

PLAINTIFFS HEREBY DEMAND JURY TRIAL.

Dated: May 15, 19YR–1

By: _____

Attorney for Plaintiff
DIANE BOXER

STIPULATIONS

1. El Dorado law will govern all issues in this case, including the legality of relevant conduct occurring outside the State of El Dorado.

2. The defendants will not file a motion to dismiss or motion to strike to challenge the legal sufficiency of the allegations in plaintiff's complaint.

3. The issues of liability and damages have been severed for purposes of trial. The first trial in this case will be limited to the issue of liability.

4. At all pertinent times, El Dorado Government Code § 12940 read:

§ 12940. Employers, labor organizations, employment agencies and other persons; unlawful employment practice; exceptions

It shall be an unlawful employment practice, unless based upon a bona fide occupational qualification, or, except where based upon applicable security regulations established by the United States or the State of El Dorado:

(f) For any employer, labor organization, employment agency, or person to discharge, expel, or otherwise discriminate against any person because the person has opposed any practices forbidden under this part or because the person has filed a complaint, testified, or assisted in any proceeding under this part.

(h) For an employer, labor organization, employment agency, apprenticeship training program or any training program leading to employment, or any other person, because of race, religious creed, color, national origin, ancestry, physical handicap, medical condition, marital status, sex, or age, to harass an employee or applicant. Harassment of an employee or applicant by an employee other than an agent or supervisor shall be unlawful if the entity, or its agents or supervisors, knows or should have known of this conduct and fails to take immediate and appropriate corrective action. An entity shall take all reasonable steps to prevent harassment from occurring. Loss of tangible job benefits shall not be necessary in order to establish harassment. The provisions of this subdivision are declaratory of existing law, except for the new duties imposed on employers with regard to harassment. For purposes of this subdivision only, "employer" means any person regularly employing one or more persons, or any person acting as an agent of an employer, directly or indirectly, the state, or any political or civil subdivision thereof, and cities.

5. The El Dorado Supreme Court has authoritatively construed Government Code § 12940 as creating an implied private cause of action.

IN THE SUPERIOR COURT OF MORENA
COUNTY STATE OF EL DORADO

DIANE BOXER,	)	
Plaintiff	)	Case No. 51110
v.	)	**ANSWER**
	)	
CAMPBELL, STONEMAN, BET-	)	
TRAN & COLE, AND	)	
DOES 1 THROUGH 50,	)	
Defendants	)	

Come now the defendant CAMPBELL, STONEMAN, BETTRAN & COLE and, severing itself from its co-defendants, admits, denies, and avers as follows:

1. This answering defendant admits the allegations contained in paragraphs 1 through 5 of the plaintiff's Complaint.

2. This defendant has no information or belief sufficient to enable it to answer the allegations in paragraphs 6 through 30 of the plaintiff's Complaint and, basing its denial on that ground, denies the allegations.

3. This defendant specifically denies that it injured the plaintiff in any way.

WHEREFORE, the defendant prays that the suit be dismissed as against it and for costs of suit incurred.

Dated: May 27, 19YR–1

By: _____

Attorney for Defendant
CAMPBELL, STONEMAN,
BETTRAN & COLE

Plaintiff's Witness Statements

Witness Statement of Plaintiff Diane Boxer

My name is Diane Boxer. I am 28 years old. I graduated from Cornell University Law School in May, 19YR–3. The following September I started work in Morena with the firm Campbell, Stoneman, Bettran & Cole. I had not worked there the previous summer; all the faces there were new. Living in Southern El Dorado was also a new experience for me. I grew up in a small New England town. All of my family, immediate and extended, live in the Northeast. Accepting this job and moving to Morena was a bold move for me. Frankly, I was a bit intimidated. I started my new life free of any romantic encumbrances.

I met Kevin Schmidt at the firm's introductory social mixer on September 21, 19YR–3. Kevin told me that he had also just graduated from law school and was starting with the firm. He also said that he had worked with the firm the previous two summers and was a long-time family friend of one of the senior partners. Kevin was quite friendly and offered to introduce me to Morena. Naturally, I accepted. Over the next few weeks we went out several times for dinner or bike rides. At all times Kevin was a gentleman. There were no romantic interludes.

By mid-October we were both so busy at work that our free time evaporated. I saw little of him at the office since we were working in different departments. Outside of work, I helped him do some Xmas shopping. Naturally, we exchanged Xmas gifts. We both attended the firm's Xmas party at the Century Plaza Hotel. This is where the problems began. I was seated at a full table of associates, not including Kevin. He walked up and started a conversation, saying how nice I looked and asking where my "date" was. After I told him I came without a date, he pulled up a chair to our already full table and sat next to me. He volunteered that I must be a great dancer, but that I was dressed far too modestly given my "great body." I don't know if he was drunk or not, but I told him that his comments were "out of line" and that he should be careful not to spoil our professional relationship. He left the table and did not approach me for the balance of the evening. However, he watched my every step. I felt very uncomfortable.

Kevin left me alone after the Xmas party, at least for a while. We continued to work in separate areas of the firm. Through mid-February, I saw him a few times in the elevator, but that was the extent of our interaction. He seemed apologetic, although he didn't speak a word to me. I tried to put that episode behind me and continue on with my new career. In February, however, I received a Valentine's Day card from him. The pre-printed message of the "Garfield" card wished me a "purr-fect Valentine's Day" and was signed "Love, Kevin." I thanked him for the card; he gave me a brief hug and kiss which I did not return.

This episode seemed really odd and inappropriate, although I wasn't offended.

Shortly thereafter, I hurt my back very badly while skiing. I was out of work for the entire month of March. Much to my discomfort, Kevin visited me often in the hospital. After I returned home to recuperate, he continued his visits. It seemed as though he was trying to mend our friendship. Since he was trying so hard and now behaving himself, I didn't have the heart to tell him to get lost, but I think he sensed my coolness. I could have killed him one day when he surprised me with a great big hug. He broke out the stitches in my back, but the doctor said no other damage was done. Perhaps it was accidental, but I suspect it was done out of anger.

Some co-workers gave me a lunch-time birthday party in April. Several gifts were given; all but one accompanied by a card. After lunch I was urged by my friends to open them all. I opened the anonymous gift last. It contained lingerie from Frederick's of Hollywood. I was terribly embarrassed in front of my co-workers and friends. Some of them thought it was funny, but most were offended. I knew right away who the culprit was. I went to Kevin's office straight away after lunch. He immediately asked me how my party was and asked if I received any "interesting" gifts. I told him that I had. I asked him if he sent the lingerie, and he said that he had. He told me the gift was anonymous because "office romances should not be public." I agreed with the rule, but told him that it was inapplicable on these facts; there was no romance to be kept private! I told him that he deeply embarrassed me, that I was ashamed to face my co-workers, and that I was the butt of much office gossip.

I hardly saw Kevin all spring. In June and July he sent me notes asking for some help on a legal issue he was researching. He should have asked his supervising partner, but as a new associate I understand that it is easier to ask another associate than a partner; you don't want to look stupid. This was especially true at that time because rumors were circulating that two or three associates would be losing their jobs. No associate wanted to appear incompetent, either in their profession or their interpersonal life.

In August the notes became transparently gratuitous. It became clear to me that these requests for help were mere pretexts for interactions with me. I began to suggest that he ask his supervising partner next time. The notes continued. I asked him to stop asking for help; I was too busy. The notes continued. Finally, when he asked me how to formulate a basic query on LEXIS, a skill he had learned and practiced in law school, I sent his request for help to his supervising partner. Apparently he was chastised for seeking help for such an elementary task. I also spoke to Christine Moore, the firm's office manager. I briefed her on the past episodes and asked her for help in restoring an appropriate work environment. She said she would help.

Apparently Kevin didn't appreciate my calls for relief. He stormed into my office and accused me of having an affair with another attorney in the office. He was making my life miserable. I asked my secretary to talk with him. I hoped that he might listen to a third-party. He told my secretary that he would "cool it." At the same time, I spoke to my supervising partner about the problem. She was sympathetic, and offered to insure that Kevin's path didn't cross mine at the firm.

In November I was assigned to a new litigation project. The senior partner specifically asked that I be made a member of the team. Much travel to the Midwest would be required, but this didn't bother me. The atmosphere at work was becoming increasingly poisoned and I welcomed the opportunity to get away. I made several short trips to the client's offices in Minneapolis in November. An extended trip was scheduled for mid-December. In early December I learned that Kevin had been assigned to the same project. Worse yet, he was going to Minneapolis as well. While the other firm members on the trip were to leave after two days, Kevin and I were to remain a full week. I briefly spoke with him and made it clear that his behavior must be appropriate at all times. With a smirk, he answered, "no problem." I also spoke to the senior partner, telling him that Kevin and I had a poor working relationship and that I preferred a minimum of contact. He asked for particulars. In a diplomatic way I told him that Kevin couldn't seem to take "no" for an answer. He chuckled and remarked that Kevin was quite a determined fellow.

On Sunday night, December 13, 19YR–2, the team left for Minneapolis. The senior partner wanted to discuss the case with us on the flight and arranged that the three of us sit together. I was in the middle in cramped three-across coach seating. The partner asked how we were getting along. I told him "OK." I wanted to give Kevin one last chance to mend his ways. Later in the flight, while the partner was absent, Kevin told me that this trip would give us time alone and "a chance to get real close again." I tried to say something to the partner, but he was much too busy talking to other members of the firm during the balance of the flight. Once we got to the client's office, we all worked at a frenzied pace. I didn't have time to speak to anyone.

Kevin had some time on his hands, however. He left me notes in my briefcase and left embarrassing telephone messages with the hotel clerk. There was no way anyone could get me to remain alone with him the rest of the week. Tuesday at lunch I discovered a note from Kevin which alluded to the events which were to follow after the others' departure. I couldn't think of my work after that. I insisted that the senior partner listen to my complaints, but he couldn't break away from meetings with the client. I decided then that I would have to leave town with the others. I boarded the plane with the senior partner, unable to get his ear until he realized I wasn't staying in Minneapolis. He was furious. I explained the problem and he blamed me for my "inability to separate my personal life from [my] work." I quit on the spot.

One week after I got back the personnel manager wrote me an apologetic letter offering me another position with the firm. Despite the terrible job market (I still haven't found new work), there is no way I could go back to the firm while Kevin Schmidt still works there. The firm isn't big enough for the both of us. It's so unfair, I'm without a job while Kevin still works there.

Time Line

May, 19YR–3	Graduate from Law School.
Sept., 19YR–3	Start work with Campbell, Stoneman, Bettran & Cole. Meet Schmidt at firm mixer for new associates.
Dec., 19YR–3	Schmidt made advances at Xmas party (was drunk?).
Feb., 19YR–2	Schmidt sent Valentine's Day card, inappropriate, but not offensive.
March, 19YR–2	Boxer hurts back and receives attention from Schmidt.
April, 19YR–2	Schmidt gives lingerie as birthday gift. Boxer has talk with Schmidt.
Aug./Sept. 19YR–2	After calm period, comments and acts escalate. No formal complaints made since layoffs were rumored.
Oct., 19YR–2	Secretary William Hepworth has talk with Schmidt, asking him to "cool it." Balance of month is quiet.
Nov., 19YR–2	Boxer's efforts to avoid Schmidt are stymied when they are assigned to same case. Boxer speaks to partner, who is lead on case. Advised to "deal with it yourself, we're all adults." Option to make formal complaint raised.
Dec., 19YR–2	Boxer and Schmidt assigned to travel to Minneapolis for week-long meetings with client. They will be alone last three days.
12/13/YR–2	Firm members depart in the evening. Partner arranges for self, Boxer and Schmidt to sit three across, putting the parties here in close proximity. Partner asks how they are getting along. "OK" is response. During flight, while partner is absent, Schmidt makes offensive comments to Boxer.

12/14 & 15YR–2	Boxer avoids Schmidt, who leaves notes and embarrassing telephone messages with hotel.
12/16/YR–2	Boxer leaves town with others rather than remaining in town alone with Schmidt. On plane partner confronts her. They engage in heated discussion. Boxer quits.
12/21/YR–2	Firm sends letter to Boxer, offering her job back and suggesting that Schmidt would be reassigned.
May, 19YR–1	Boxer brings suit.

Witness Statement of William Hepworth

My name is William Hepworth. I am 43 years old. I have been employed as a legal secretary at Campbell, Stoneman, Bettran & Cole for more than ten years. Because of my experience at the firm I am usually assigned to work with new associates in order to help them learn the ropes. After a year or two, I take two new associates under my wings. In the fall of 19YR–2 I started working with Diane Boxer. She was new to the area and spent a fair amount of time with Kevin Schmidt, another new associate. Kevin worked on a different floor in the building so I rarely saw him, although we frequently talked on the phone. He would call for Diane several times a day.

Although Diane was new to the area, she quickly developed an outside social life. Not infrequently she received outside calls which were clearly not professional in nature. I don't know if she had a serious relationship or not, but I do know that Kevin Schmidt was not in the running. Diane told me that he was a real nice guy, but not her type. Besides, Kevin was recently divorced and probably not ready for anything serious.

I first noticed a problem with Kevin at the firm's Christmas party. He appeared unhappy and perhaps disturbed. He stared at Diane constantly, like he was fixated. Diane was enjoying herself tremendously for most of the evening. I saw the two of them speak briefly. After that Diane looked worried; she left soon thereafter. I spoke with her when we returned to work. She told me Kevin "had flipped." Diane wouldn't elaborate, but I could tell that the episode bothered her. Diane maintained a frenetic pace inside the office. Schmidt didn't call or come by her office, although Diane left a standing order to tell him that she was "out of the office," if he should ask.

We lost Diane for much of March. She was in the hospital for back surgery. I spoke with her daily as she tried to maintain some control of her docket. She would also tell me who came to visit and what they brought her. Much to her chagrin, Kevin Schmidt was making daily appearances. This annoyed her, it seemed. She put up with this attention without much complaint, though. After she went home to recuperate he left her alone, I guess, because she stopped mentioning his visits. I know he stopped by at least once because they had some altercation and Diane broke some stitches. Diane refused to talk to me about it.

In April I organized a birthday party for Diane. It was a pleasant, festive occasion. She received some nice gifts and some gag gifts, including some sexy underwear from some anonymous admirer. I thought it was sort of funny, but I could tell that some office women were visibly upset. Afterwards, Diane was really upset. She said she knew who sent the gift and was tired of the hassles. I didn't immediately think of Schmidt because he seemed to be leaving Diane alone. Diane stormed off "to fix his clock."

Schmidt was invisible for awhile. He would send some notes to Diane, but she didn't seem perturbed. I don't know if the notes were strictly business or not. Maybe Diane was getting accustomed to the attention. Diane seemed to be noticed by many of the male attorneys in the firm, although none seemed as persistent as Kevin Schmidt.

All hell broke loose in August. Diane and I had a "heart-to-heart" talk about Schmidt. She told me that she was trying her best, but that he was making work unbearable. She couldn't understand how he was getting away with this behavior. I offered to talk to Schmidt, kind of man-to-man, since Diane seemed to be at the end of her rope.

I do remember that on one occasion, I heard a loud argument between Diane and Schmidt in her office; I happened to be walking by the office at the time. I couldn't make out what they were saying. However, a few minutes later Diane stopped by to see me. She was obviously upset. She told me that she had just "read Kevin the riot act" about his sexual overtures. She seemed very emotional, and I just sat there and let her talk for a couple of minutes. She seemed relieved to have been able to tell me about it, and then she went back to work.

One day I stopped in to see Schmidt in his office. I asked him why he was making Diane's life miserable. His demeanor was sort of arrogant. He said he didn't know what I was talking about. He claimed that Diane welcomed his advances and complained only to preserve her image in the firm. Schmidt claimed that Diane was "sleeping around" with other members of the firm and that I had listened to too many of her lies. He agreed to mellow out, but I seriously doubt the truth of his wild claims. Everyone knows that secretaries know all the good gossip in the firm. If there was any truth to his claims, I would have heard about it long ago.

After that, Diane seemed on edge much of the time. She got a break when she was assigned to the Atlas project, which involved steady travel. She really deserved this breath of fresh air. She left in December for a visit to the client's offices, but she never came back to the firm. She quit or was fired when she was back there. I was flabbergasted when I heard. She had the potential to be a fine attorney. She had an excellent legal mind and good writing and research skills to boot. When I learned Schmidt was back there at the same time, I wondered if he had anything to do with this.

Plaintiff's Exhibits

Also says that I
have to get a grip
on my emotions
because I was
crying when I told
him that I didn't
appreciate all the
dirty jokes, sexual
innuendos and that
I wasn't raised
like that he said

"THATS EVIDENT"

Defendant's Witness Statements

STATEMENT OF KEVIN SCHMIDT

My name is Kevin Schmidt. I am 30 years old. I received my B.A. in Political Science from Clemson in 1988. I graduated from U.C.L.A. Law School in May, 19YR-3. I began working for Campbell, Stoneman, Bettran, & Cole in September, 19YR-3. I had interned with the firm for the previous two summers. Diane Boxer also began with the firm about the same time. Since we started at the same time we had a lot to discuss. We often would go for a drink after work and discuss the perils of working for a large firm as a first year associate.

She became a trusted friend and I often discussed my personal problems with her. She helped me get over a tough divorce and gave me advice on dealing with my ex-wife. To thank her for her help, I gave Diane a cross pen with her name engraved on it. At Christmas I gave her a crystal vase which we had seen when shopping together. She seemed to like it and she gave me an executive desk set with a thank you note.

At the firm Christmas party for some reason Diane was very unfriendly. I drank two or three glasses of egg nog and was having a good time. Diane spoiled the fun by saying I was out of line for giving her a compliment about the way she was dressed! I left her table and did not go near her for the rest of the evening.

After the Christmas party, I was afraid to go near her. I didn't even talk to her in the elevator. Well, gradually things got better. We started having more conversations and even went to lunch in early February. My next contact with her was a Valentine's Day card I sent her. She had previously told me that she liked Garfield so I sent her a Garfield Valentine. I then gave her a hug which she returned. I was glad we were friends again.

In March, Diane was hospitalized for a slipped disk. I visited her often and brought her books to read, flowers and get well cards. When she returned home I often took lunch to her at her house. On one occasion, which I deeply regret, I hugged her very hard. I was so relieved she was recovering so well and the doctor had just told her she was going to be fine. Well I guess I got a little too excited because two of the stitches in her back came out prematurely.

After Diane returned to work, our friendship continued to improve. As we became better friends, we became more affectionate with each other. For example, she gave me a back rub in my office when I was really tense one day.

In April, a birthday party was given for Diane. I was very busy that day so I didn't attend. I did send a gift. A friend of mine, a senior associate at the firm, decided we should send risque gifts. He picked out the gift and showed it to me before he had it wrapped. It seemed like it could be pretty funny. Everyone deserves to be embarrassed on their birthday. Anyway, when I didn't show up at the party my friend took his gift out of the pile. I couldn't believe how upset Diane was. It was just a joke. She came running into my office acting like a mad woman. Trying to make light of the situation, in an obviously joking tone I told her my name wasn't on the package because office romances shouldn't be public. She informed me there was no romance, as if it wasn't painfully obvious. I apologized sincerely, but she was not listening, she just ranted and raved about office gossip and her precious reputation. The conclusion I reached from this situation was that Diane is too uptight and cannot take a joke.

After Diane's birthday party, I again decided to avoid her for awhile. Frankly, I would rather not spend time with someone who is that uptight. For Pete's sake, I've got better things to do with my time. In June or July, I did ask Diane for some help researching an issue she knew more about. After helping me two or three times she decided she was too busy. This was just like Diane, she helps you only as long as it's convenient for her. She is just not a team player.

I was called in to speak with the Office Manager, Christine Moore. She told me that some of my acts were coming very close to sexual harassment. I couldn't believe what I was hearing. Diane, my friend, was accusing me of sexual harassment! Needless to say, I was upset. I went directly to her office. I tried to convince Diane that I never intended to harass anybody. I explained that she was being overly friendly with numerous guys in the office. I know how guys are and I know that they often misconstrue a woman's friendship for sexual advances. I was trying to get across the point that it was not me she had to worry about but the other guys she flirted with. She didn't listen to my warning. In fact she just became irrational with me and yelled some foolishness about how I was trying to get even with her.

Again I tried to avoid Diane so there would be no more problems. Diane's secretary told me to stay away from her for awhile which I did. Then we were assigned to the same case. We were scheduled to go to Minneapolis together. I made sure all contact I had with Diane was on a purely professional level.

When we were in Minneapolis, I tried to lighten things up a bit. I left Diane one or two innocuous notes and maybe one phone message to break up the boredom of working out of town. Diane was supposed to stay in Minneapolis with me for the entire week. She instead left after two days with the senior partner. This caused enormous problems on the case. I was left alone to handle all of the work simply because Diane overreacts to everything. She cannot handle herself in a professional environment and unfortunately, I must say it is for the best that she is no longer with the firm.

WITNESS STATEMENT OF CHRISTINE MOORE

My name is Christine Moore. I am 30 years old and have lived in El Dorado my entire life. I graduated at Stanford University with a degree in human resource management in 19YR–10. I then took a position as Office Manager for Campbell, Stoneman, Bettran & Cole. I have held that position for the past 7 years.

My principal duties as Office Manager are to handle personnel, recruiting, and employee benefits. I have two assistants to help me in these tasks. One of the reasons the firm created my position was so someone who was outside of the partnership structure could handle employee complaints. If an associate has a problem with a partner, the associate is told s/he should come to me for guidance.

Two of our new associates in 19YR–3 were Kevin Schmidt and Diane Boxer. I knew Kevin fairly well. He had interned for the firm for the previous two summers and he worked out pretty well. All of his reviews ranged from good to excellent so I recommended that he be hired. The partners, who had the final decision, decided to hire Kevin.

Kevin and Diane both started in September, 19YR–3. I heard gossip that they were seeing each other. I had very little other exposure to them until Diane came to see me the next August. She came into my office demanding appropriate action be taken. I asked Diane to go over all the instances in which Kevin had caused her problems.

Diane went through several instances of what she considered inappropriate behavior. I took notes on the instances she described. She admitted they had been dating and she had given him an executive desk set for Christmas. The only ones that seemed even questionable to me were his supposed compliment that she has a "great body" (she does) at the Christmas party and a gift of lingerie at her birthday party. I wrote down a detailed account and placed them in Kevin Schmidt's file with Diane's complaint.

After Diane left I took out a copy of the firm regulations to determine whether Kevin's behavior rose to the level of sexual harassment. I of course had not heard Kevin's side of the story yet but I decided that if Diane's description of the behavior was not sexual harassment then the problem was solved. In my professional judgment, however, Kevin's behavior did not rise to the level of sexual harassment. There seemed to be equal initiation and participation including their dating, being personal friends, visits, and exchanging gifts.

Even though Kevin's behavior did not violate our policy prohibiting sexual harassment, I still chose to call him into my office. I informed Kevin of Diane's complaint and warned him about future contact with Diane. He was visibly upset. He assured me he had never harassed anyone at the firm, and I found him believable. He seemed most disturbed by the fact that he was being accused of sexual harassment when he was merely Diane's friend when other guys in the firm were even closer to Diane.

When Kevin and Diane were assigned to the same case, I said nothing because our complaint resolution process is confidential. Since Kevin had not been disciplined, I had no reason to speak to the senior partner assigned to the case. I did not want to get Kevin in trouble when, in my judgment, he had done absolutely nothing to violate any firm regulation. The only instance that could possibly have risen to the level of sexual harassment was the gift at the birthday party. However, this was only one instance and according to Regulation 7.4(d), in order to rise to the level of sexual harassment, verbal or physical conduct of a sexual nature must occur on more than one occasion.

After Kevin got back from Minneapolis I learned that Diane had quit the firm. I was sorry to hear she would no longer be with us. I am afraid she has not learned to work in an office environment and needs to (a) become a team player, and (b) not take herself so seriously to be an effective member of a firm.

Defendant's Exhibits

CAMPBELL, STONEMAN, BETTRAN & COLE SEXUAL HARASSMENT REGULATIONS

7.4 SEXUAL HARASSMENT.

(a) Sexual harassment is a form of sexual discrimination that involves unwelcomed sexual advances, requests for sexual favors, and other verbal or physical conduct of a sexual nature when:

(1) Submission to or rejection of such conduct is made either explicitly or implicitly a term or condition of a person's job, pay or career or

(2) Submission to or rejection of such conduct by a person is used as a basis for career or employment decisions affecting that person, or

(3) Such conduct interferes with an individual's performance or creates an intimidating, hostile or offensive environment.

(b) Any person in a supervisory position who uses or condones implicit or explicit sexual behavior to control, influence, or affect the career, pay or job is engaging in sexual harassment. Any employee who makes deliberate or repeated unwelcome verbal comments, gestures or physical contact of a sexual nature is also engaging in sexual harassment.

(c) Examples of behavior that constitutes verbal or physical conduct of a sexual nature includes but is not limited to: sexual jokes or innuendoes, sexual touching, requests for sexual activity and unwanted repeated requests for dates.

(d) In order for sexual harassment to exist, the individual accused must have knowledge that another person finds their actions offensive. Furthermore, verbal or physical conduct of a sexual nature must be directed at one person and must occur on more than one occasion in order to be sexual harassment.

(e) The firm takes this issue seriously and will not tolerate sexual harassment of or by anyone in or from the office.

HAPPY HOLIDAYS
And may this
be the start of a
bright and wonderful
New Year

Dearest Kevin,
Thanks for all your
kind support.
Yours,
Diane

Name: Kevin Schmidt
Working Since: September 19YR-3

DATE 8/12/YR-2   **REPORT** Christine Moore

Today, I received an oral complaint from Diane Boyer about Kevin Schmidt. The complaint regards Kevin's allegedly inappropriate behavior towards Diane.

Specifically, Kevin has been approaching her at the firm to consult her on legal problems, visited her at the hospital after her back surgery, and has hugged her on a few occasions.

Also, Diane thinks Kevin has been "hitting" on her on a regular basis. In the past they have gone out together, chatted and exchanged gifts. During the firm's christmas party Kevin told her she had a "great body." He gave her some lingerie from Frederick's of Hollywood on her birthday.

Diane asked that I "do something" to change Kevin's behavior.

Also, Diane thinks Kevin has been "hitting" on her on a regular basis. In the past they have gone out together, chatted and exchanged gifts. During the firm Christmas party Kevin told her she had a "great body." He gave her some lingerie from Frederick's of Hollywood on her birthday.

Diane asked that I "do something" to change Kevin's behavior.

Case file B–11

PEOPLE OF THE STATE OF EL DORADO V. JODY CRAY

TABLE OF CONTENTS

Felony Child Endangerment: El Dorado Penal Code § 273a

Jury Instructions: El Dorado 9.37—Child Abuse/Neglect/Endangerment Felony

Judicially Noticed Facts & Law

Stipulation of Facts

Sworn Statement of Prosecution Witness, Regina Blackwell

Sworn Statement of Prosecution Witness, Dr. John Garner

Sworn Statement of Defendant, Jody Cray

Sworn Statement of Defense Witness, Dr. Herb Tenent

Stipulation of Expected Testimony of Dr. Harold Newsome

Patient Visit Record from Dr. Newsome's Office

Patient Visit Record from Dr. Newsome's Office

Stipulation of Expected testimony of Harold Beringer

Stipulation of Expected Testimony of Dr. Robert Summers

Stipulation of Expected Testimony of Dr. Gary Snyder

Stipulation of Expected Testimony of Harold Beringer

Billing Statement from San Francisco General Hospital

JUDICIALLY NOTICED FACTS & LAW

The court hereby takes notice of—and the parties, with defendant's express consent agree to—the following judicially noticed facts and points of law.

1. On March 17, 19YR–1 Dr. Harold Newsome filed a report of suspected child abuse with Morena County's Child Welfare Services agency. CWS' records indicate that Dr. Newsome suspected Jody Cray of seeking unnecessary medical treatment and procedures for, and administering prescription medications without a prescription to, her then ten-year old daughter, Sarah Beringer.

2. On September 6, 19YR–1, the Morena County District Attorney, on information provided by Morena County CWS, filed criminal charges of felony child endangerment against Ms. Cray. The District Attorney's charges allege that Ms. Cray, over a ten month period, subjected her daughter Sarah to numerous invasive medical tests and procedures, including exposure to x-rays, a radioactive barium enema, and an appendectomy.

3. The American Association of Psychiatrists is the officially recognized national association of psychiatric doctors. The Association publishes a monthly journal, *The Journal of American Psychology*. The Association's journal is generally recognized by psychiatrists as the leading professional publication on modern psychiatric studies, diagnoses and treatments.

4. Munchausen Syndrome by Proxy was originally described and identified as a discrete psychological disorder by Pediatrician Alex V. Levin, M.D. in 1977.[1] Munchausen Syndrome proper is a disorder recognized in 1951 that causes a medical patient to persistently fabricate or induce his or her own symptoms and then seek medical treatment.[2] In Munchausen Syndrome by Proxy, the symptoms of illness are induced, either physically or psychologically, in another—generally a child. A parent suffering from Munchausen Syndrome by Proxy convinces the child that the child is ill, or induces hard-to-trace symptoms (*e.g.*, withholding prescribed medication, administering toxins and poisons, etc.). The parent then seeks gratification and recognition by presenting the child repeatedly for medical treatment. "[T]he label of [Munchausen Syndrome by

---

1. *See* ALEX V. LEVIN & MARY S. SHERIDAN, MUNCHAUSEN SYNDROME BY PROXY: ISSUES IN DIAGNOSIS AND TREATMENT 3 (1995).

2. *See id.* at 4 n. 7.

Proxy] might" be applied to anyone who persistently fabricates symptoms on behalf of another, so causing that person to be regarded as ill "...."[3]

5. Munchausen Syndrome by Proxy has been sufficiently studied and documented by the scientific community for this court to take judicial notice that Munchausen Syndrome by Proxy is a medically recognized and valid diagnosis for purposes of satisfying the *Frye* evidentiary standard for expert testimony. (Assume that the *Frye* general acceptance standard governs in El Dorado). The scientific community agrees that the average practitioner of psychiatry has the requisite skill to diagnose Munchausen Syndrome by Proxy.

6. This proceeding is not for the purpose of determining whether the defendant, Jody Cray, in fact suffers from Munchausen Syndrome by Proxy. Rather, the sole purpose of this criminal trial is to determine whether Ms. Cray is guilty of felony or misdemeanor child endangerment. The jury may consider expert testimony regarding Munchausen Syndrome by Proxy for purposes of determining whether Ms. Cray is guilty of the charged crime. Whether Ms. Cray does, or does not, suffer from Munchausen Syndrome by Proxy is not, in itself, determinative of guilt or innocence. However, the jurors may consider evidence of Munchausen Syndrome by Proxy in determining whether the prosecution has met its burden of proving guilt beyond a reasonable doubt.

7. Without more, a diagnosis of Munchausen Syndrome by Proxy does not support a defense of not guilty by reason of insanity. A person affected by Munchausen Syndrome by Proxy is able to discern right from wrong, but is unable to control his or her actions. Defendant insists that she is not afflicted with Munchausen Syndrome by Proxy. Defendant has conceded, after full disclosure and advice by her attorney, that an insanity defense is not available and will not be advanced in this trial.

8. The sworn statements, stipulations and physical evidence that are on record in this proceeding and currently in possession of the prosecution and the defendant are the sole and entire extent of the evidence and testimony to be offered in this case. The parties may not attempt to introduce or refer to facts that do not appear in this record. Either side may point out any inconsistencies in the record, or that certain facts are absent from the record, without penalty.

STIPULATION OF FACTS

It is hereby stipulated between the People and the defense, with the defendant's express consent, that the following facts are to be accepted as true by the trier of fact:

---

3. *See id.* at 4.

1. A review of Dr. Newsome's office records show that Sarah's first visit for abdominal pains was on April 13, 19YR–2. Sarah visited Dr. Newsome's office fourteen times over the next year, each time claiming symptoms of abdominal pain. The following is a list of the dates of the visits: April 21, 19YR–2; May 2, 19YR–2; May 24, 19YR–2; June 22, 19YR–2; June 30, 19YR–2; July 11, 19YR–2; July 19, 19YR–2; August 17, 19YR–2; September 1, 19YR–2; October 3, 19YR–2; November 7, 19YR–2; December 18, 19YR–2; January 9, 19YR–1; and February 16, 19YR–1.

2. A review of Sutter Morena Hospital's records show that Sarah visited the Sutter Morena Emergency room nineteen times between April 15, 19YR–2 and February 10, 19YR–1. Each time, Sarah reported general abdominal pain to the physician on duty. The following is a list of the dates of the evening visits: April 15, 19YR–2; April 20, 19YR–2; May 1, 19YR–2; May 23, 19YR–2; June 21, 19YR–2; June 29, 19YR–2; July 1, 19YR–2; July 11, 19YR–2; August 17, 19YR–2; September 1, 19YR–2; September 19, 19YR–2; October 3, 19YR–2; November 7, 19YR–2; November 8, 19YR–2; November 27, 19YR–2; December 18, 19YR–2; December 25, 19YR–2; January 1, 19YR–1; and February 10, 19YR–1.

3. One of Sarah's visits to Sutter Morena Hospital was at 5:30 a.m. on November 27, 19YR–2. Another was at 11:30 p.m., December 25, 19YR–2.

4. Sutter Morena's records show consecutive emergency room visit on July 1, 19YR–2, and July 11, 19YR–2. Dr. Newsome's records show no visits between June 22, 19YR–2, and July 21, 19YR–2.

5. On February 17, 19YR–1 Dr. Newsome signed forms admitting Sarah Beringer to Sutter Morena Hospital and reserving a surgery unit for the following morning to perform an appendectomy on Sarah. On the same day Ms. Cray signed release forms for the procedure. On February 18, 19YR–1 at 10 a.m., a hospital surgeon, aided by Dr, Newsome, placed removed Sarah under general anesthetic and removed her appendix.

6. Post-operative tests on Sarah's removed appendix conducted at Sutter Morena Hospital's laboratory indicated that Sarah's appendix was normal at the time it was removed. No signs of appendicitis were found.

7. A March 18, 19YR–1 CWS intake record indicates that Dr. Newsome called CWS' "child abuse hotline" to report that he suspected Jody Cray of abusing her daughter, Sarah Beringer. CWS' records state that Dr. Newsome said he felt that Jody Cray was suffering from some mental imbalance. The matter was referred to CWS Chief Psychiatrist Dr. John Garner for follow up evaluation.

8. Dr. Garner is licensed to practice psychiatric medicine in the state of El Dorado. Dr. Garner holds a medical degree with

emphasis in psychiatric medicine from the University of California, San Francisco. Dr. Garner graduated *summa cum laude* from UCSF in 19YR–22, and has practiced general psychiatric medicine in a variety of settings since that time. CWS hired Dr. Garner in July of 19YR–13. Dr. Garner has been CWS' Chief Psychiatrist since November of 19YR–5.

9. Dr. Herb Tenet is licensed to practice psychiatric medicine in the state of El Dorado. Dr. Tenet earned a degree in psychiatric medicine from the Johns Hopkins University in 19YR–29. Dr. Tenet has practiced psychiatric medicine in a variety of settings since that time. Dr. Tenet started his solo practice in 19YR–15. Dr. Tenet's solo practice specializes in psychiatric evaluation and treatment of child and family disorders.

10. Ms. Cray's phone records for March 19YR–1 indicate that two phone calls were made from Ms. Cray's house to the Fairfield office of Dr. Gary Snyder, pediatrician. The first phone call was placed at 9 a.m. on March 2, 19YR–1. The second phone call was placed at 2 p.m. the same day.

11. Dr. Gary Snyder's records indicate that a 1 p.m. appointment was made for Sarah Beringer, and later canceled. The appointment was made by computer entry which cannot be traced to any particular member of Dr. Snyder's staff.

12. Ms. Cray has tendered, as Defense Exhibit A, a copy of a billing statement from Jackson General Hospital's emergency room for services rendered to Sarah Beringer on Sunday, February 14. The exhibit is authentic, satisfies the best evidence rule, and falls within the business entry exception to the hearsay rule. It appears from examining Jackson General's files that any more specific documentation of Sarah's treatment or diagnosis that day has been lost or simply was never filed.

SWORN STATEMENT OF PROSECUTION WITNESS, REGINA BLACKWELL

I, Regina Blackwell, having been duly sworn under oath, hereby declare:

1. My name is Regina Lee Blackwell. I live at 745 B Street, in Morena, El Dorado. I am 25 years old. I have been married for six years, and I have two children—a four-year old, Samantha, and a two-year old, Dillan. I work as a part-time accountant for Borders Books in Morena, El Dorado. My husband, Mike Blackwell, is a security guard with Golden One Credit Union in Morena, El Dorado.

2. My mother is Jody Lynn Cray. My father is Jeffery Lee Jones. I have one full-sister, Theresa Esther Jones, age twenty-two. My mother and my father divorced about twenty years ago, shortly after the birth of my sister, Theresa.

3. I also have one half-sister, Sarah Nicole Beringer, age eleven. Harold Beringer is Sarah's father, and was my step-father for four years—between the time I was twelve and sixteen years of age. Harold Beringer was a model stepfather and never physically or verbally abused me. To the best of my knowledge, he also never physically or verbally abused my sisters. Although I do remember Mr. Beringer and my mother mutually exchanging harsh words on occasion—leading to their break-up—to my knowledge, he never physically abused my mother.

4. During my childhood and early adolescence, my mother verbally and physically abused both me and my sisters. On one occasion, when I was thirteen years old, I remember that my mother called me a "stupid little bitch," and slapped me twice for "talking back" to her. When I was nine years old, I observed my mother pull my sister, Theresa—who was seven at the time—by the hair into the bathroom to scold her for making a mess.

5. When I was fifteen years old, I observed my mother slap Sarah. Sarah—only about five months old at the time—was nursing and had apparently bitten my mother's nipple. My mother cried out, slapped Sarah's face, and said, "That will teach you not to bite!" My mother then put Sarah—who was hungry and crying—into a crib, turned out the lights, left Sarah in the room alone, and closed the door.

6. Just before my sixteenth birthday, I stole a blouse from a clothing store at the Woodland mall while shopping with my friend, Amy Daniels. Later than evening, Amy's mother called my mother. Amy had told her mother that I had stolen the blouse. When my mother learned of this, she told me that she was going to call the police. I cried and begged my mother to just let me return the blouse, or to give her the money so that she could go to the store and pay for it. My mother refused. She called the police, who then came to our house, took the blouse, and issued me a citation and notice to appear in juvenile court. At juvenile court, my mother stated to the judge that I should have to accept full responsibility for what I had done. The judge ordered me to perform fifty hours of community service, which I completed during the next year. I was horribly embarrassed and frightened by the whole ordeal. For many years I insisted that I would never forgive my mother for what she had done. However, now having children of my own, I understand that my mother—in her own misguided way—was just trying to teach me a lesson. Still, I believe that this incident provides just one more example of my mother's poor parenting skills and her inability to make decisions that properly recognize her children's best interests.

7. Shortly after I turned sixteen, I ran away from home to live with my then-boyfriend, Mike Blackwell. My mother, who had no husband and no job at the time, insisted that I return home to support her and my sisters through my part-time job at Alberston's supermarket. When I refused to return home, my mother threatened to report me as a delinquent to the authorities. My mother never took any formal action. Two years later, when I turned 18, I married Mike.

8. A few years later, I began speaking with my mother again. We do not have a close relationship, but I do permit her to have occasional, supervised visits with my children—primarily at holiday events such as Thanksgiving and Christmas. I do not allow my mother to have unsupervised visits with her grandchildren because I am afraid that she may subject them to physical abuse.

9. In July of 19YR–2, I learned from my sister that my mother had taken Sarah—who was nine-years old at the time—to Dr. Henry Newsome and the Sutter Morena emergency room on several occasions. My sister informed me that Sarah was having stomach pains and that the doctors, so far, were unable to diagnose the cause.

10. A few weeks later, on Saturday, July 4, 19YR–2, my mother allowed Sarah to spend the day and night with my family. I picked Sarah up at 10 a.m. on July 4. We went shopping, and then to an afternoon barbecue hosted by my husband's employer. That evening, Sarah ate dinner with me and my family, watched the fireworks with us, and then slept with my children in their room. The next morning I returned Sarah to my mother's house at 9 a.m. At no time during her visit did Sarah complain of any stomach pain or any other symptoms. She ate full, regular meals at the barbecue, at dinner and the next morning at breakfast. She played with my daughter (who was two-and-one-half years old at the time). I did tell my daughter to "play gentle" with Sarah, because Sarah seemed a little bit weak and tired after the barbecue. On returning Sarah home, my mother immediately asked me if Sarah had experienced any stomach pain. I told my mother that she had not. My mother immediately knelt down to Sarah, took her by the shoulders, and said, "Honey, are you okay? Didn't your stomach hurt yesterday" It's okay, you can tell me the truth. Sarah looked up at me, then down at the ground, and glumly agreed that her stomach had hurt the day before.

11. On two other occasions in 19YR–2, Sarah and my mother visited my family at my house: once on Thanksgiving day, Thursday, November 26th, and once on Christmas day, Friday, December 25th. On each occasion, my mother and Sarah spent most of the day at my house.

12. During her 19YR–2 Thanksgiving visit, Sarah spent a fair amount of time alone with me and my daughter in the kitchen preparing food while my mother watched television with my husband. During our time alone, I shared food with Sarah and we talked. I never asked Sarah how her stomach felt. Sarah ate bits of the food we were preparing with me, talked with me, and laughed at jokes that we shared. Sarah never mentioned any stomach pain or acted as if she were in any physical discomfort or distress. When we sat down for our Thanksgiving meal, I prepared a regular plate of food for Sarah and set it in front of her. Almost immediately my mother objected, stating that Sarah could have only milk and some mashed potatoes without butter because anything else would "make her tummy bad." When I stated that Sarah had spent several hours with me in the kitchen and had already sampled just about

everything at the table without the slightest ill effect, my mother shot me a very angry stare. She then turned to Sarah and asked if it that was true. Sarah looked at her lap and nodded yes. My mother took Sarah from the table, retrieved their coats, and left the house. As she was leaving, my mother scolded me for not having more concern for the fragile health of my little sister. During the entire visit, Sarah never complained at all of any stomach pain or other discomfort.

13. During their 19YR–2 Christmas visit, my mother was careful to keep her eye on Sarah in the kitchen. While we all were in the kitchen together, my mother reminded me of the experience at Thanksgiving, and informed me that Sarah had become very ill after they went home. She looked down at Sarah and asked, "Isn't that right, honey Sarah looked at me, and then at her shoes and slowly nodded yes. Later, I had to send my husband on an errand to the store to pick up milk to go with dinner. My mother and I stayed at the house. My husband took Sarah with him for the ride to the store. When they returned, we had dinner. My mother insisted on serving Sarah, and allowed her to have only a very small helping of stuffing, some mashed potatoes and a glass of milk. She mentioned several times during the meal that it was a terrible shame that Sarah was so ill, and that she could have only bland foods. After my mother and Sarah left, my husband confided to me that he had bought Sarah a coke and a hot-dog with mustard and relish at the store on Sarah's promise of strict secrecy. I never received any report from my mother that Sarah felt stomach pain or any other symptoms as a result of her visit—and her clandestine snack—on Christmas day."

14. On the evening of Wednesday, February 17, 19YR–1, my mother called me in tears. She informed me that Sarah had been hospitalized with appendicitis. My mother told me that the doctors were going to operate on Sarah the following morning. Surprised, I asked my mother if the doctors were sure of the diagnosis. She told me, "Yes. I can't believe that they were so incompetent that it took them this long to realize what was going on. But, after I threatened to take Sarah to Jackson for emergency surgery by real doctors, they finally figured out what was wrong." My mother sounded genuinely upset. I know my mother well enough to be able to tell when something's really bothering her. I became worried for her as well as Sarah.

15. On the morning of Friday, February 19, 19YR–1, I went to Sutter Morena Hospital to visit Sarah. When I got there, my mother and Dr. Newsome were in an angry discussion in the hallway. As I approached, I heard Dr. Newsome tell my mother, "I told you before the operation, and you wouldn't listen. And now, I'm telling you again— because we know *for sure* from the post-operative tests—your daughter does not have, nor did she *ever* have appendicitis." Seeing me approaching, my mother and Dr. Newsome broke off their conversation. I went inside the room to visit Sarah, who was recovering from her surgery. My mother and Dr. Newsome resumed a heated discussion in low tones outside the door. I did not hear any more details of what was said. When my mother entered the room, she glared at me and said, "I cannot

believe the incompetence of the doctors in this town." After I left the room, I tried to speak with Dr. Newsome. However, when I asked him about his conversation with my mother, a strange look came over his face, and he stated evasively that "professional medical ethics" prevented him from discussing the matter with me. After saying that, he abruptly turned and rushed away.

16. On March 11, 19YR–1,—about three weeks after Sarah's surgery—I called my mother's house to make tentative plans for Easter Sunday. My mother informed me that she didn't know if she and Sarah would be able to visit, because Sarah had developed fainting spells, seizures, and asthma since her recovery. When I expressed alarm at the situation, my mother informed me that she had taken Sarah to see Dr. Newsome, and that he had, somewhat reluctantly, agreed to run some tests to determine the cause of Sarah's most recent problems. I asked my mother if she was sure that Sarah really had asthma. My mother responded in an exasperated tone, "I'm tired of everybody questioning me about this. Sarah is very sick. I should know, I'm her mother. And, I'm a good mother. Look at how much I care for her. Why does everybody treat me like I'm just making this all up?!"

17. One week later, on Thursday, March 18, my mother called me. She was angry and crying. She explained that Dr. Newsome had reported her to Child Welfare Services for investigation of child endangerment. She told me that Dr. Newsome was "unfit to be a veterinarian, let alone a doctor ...," and that he was "a horrible man, who is determined to undermine my relationship with Sarah." She further explained that Dr. Newsome's incompetence had caused him to overlook the fact that Sarah had developed an allergy to amoxycillin. My mother stated that she personally had taken Sarah off the amoxycillin on Monday (March 15th), and that Sarah had immediately improved and had not had a fainting spell or seizure since that time.

18. Sarah was temporarily placed in the custody of her father, Harold Beringer, two weeks later, on about the beginning of April 19YR–1. Since that time I have visited with Sarah and her father several times. I have never seen Sarah experience any fainting spell, dizziness, asthma attack, or any related symptoms. In her father's care, to the best of my knowledge, Sarah has had absolutely no health problems.

19. I am of the opinion that my half-sister, Sarah Beringer, never had appendicitis or any other illness requiring extensive medical testing, surgery or other invasive procedures. I suspect that my crazy mother coached and mentally intimidated Sarah into agreeing that she had abdominal pains and other medical symptoms. I also believe that my mother intimidated local doctors into performing unnecessary invasive tests and surgery on Sarah, and then later manufactured a new set of symptoms when it was factually shown that Sarah's prior "illness" never actually existed. I am afraid that if my mother regains custody of Sarah, she will subject Sarah to more psychological and physical abuse that will seriously threaten the physical and mental health and well

being of my half-sister. I was my mother's first victim, and I don't want Sarah to suffer the same fate.

I declare under penalty of perjury under the laws of the State of El Dorado that the foregoing is true and correct to the best of my knowledge.

Executed in Morena, El Dorado this 30th day of December, 19YR–1.

_____

Regina Lee Blackwell

SWORN STATEMENT OF PROSECUTION WITNESS, DR. JOHN GARNER

I, John Garner, having been duly sworn under oath, hereby declare:

1. My name is John Garner. I live at 925 Harris Street, in Grant, El Dorado. I am 46 years old. I have been married to my wife, Sandra Garner, for eighteen years. We have one sixteen-year old child, Josie.

2. I hold a medical degree, with emphasis in psychiatric medicine, from UCSF. I have practiced psychiatric medicine since my graduation from UCSF in 19YR–22. Until I was hired by Child Welfare Service of Yolo County in 19YR–13, I practiced general psychiatric medicine in several different settings including hospitals, out-patient clinics and private partnerships. Since 19YR–13, my specific area of practice within CWS has been limited to evaluation and treatment of parent-child disorders.

3. I have been Chief Psychiatrist at CWS for nearly five years. Since becoming Chief Psychiatrist, my psychiatric case load has decreased significantly due to my administrative duties. I currently spend only about ten percent of my time at CWS handling psychiatric case-work. Usually, the cases that I personally handle are simply overflow that no other staff psychiatrist has time to handle. However, in some situations—such as potential Munchausen Syndrome by Proxy diagnoses—I assume control over a case because I feel that I have particular expertise as compared to other CWS staff psychiatrists.

4. In 19YR–7, I attended a three-day, national convention sponsored by the American Association of Psychiatrists—the professionally recognized national association of psychiatrists—on family related psychiatric disorders. The theme for the convention was a parent-child disorder known as Munchausen Syndrome by Proxy. At that seminar, I learned about the warning signs of Munchausen Syndrome by Proxy, methods of diagnosing the disease, and methods of treatment. I had only casual familiarity with the disease before that time.

5. At the 19YR–7 seminar, one point of contention among the psychiatrists at the panel on diagnosis was whether a parent must knowingly intend to submit a child to needless medical procedures in order to diagnose the disease. Out of five psychiatrists on the panel, four maintained that the only intent required was to actually seek medical

treatment. The fifth panelist vehemently insisted that just seeking medical treatment was not enough, but rather that the affected parent must have some actual understanding and knowledge that the treatments are unnecessary. Articles in the Journal of American Psychology—the magazine published by the American Association of Psychiatrists—have consistently declared that only a finding of intent to seek treatment is required to make a proper diagnosis of Munchausen Syndrome by Proxy.

6. Since the 19YR–7 seminar, I have had a continuing interest in Munchausen Syndrome by Proxy. Although I have had no additional formal training on this disease, I read and save any articles about Munchausen Syndrome by Proxy that I run across in professional psychiatric journals, or in generally circulated newspapers and magazines. I am planning to write an article on case studies of Munchausen Syndrome by Proxy for the Journal of American Psychiatry next year. The cases that I will draw upon are those that I have come across in my work with Morena County CWS since 19YR–7. It will be the first article I have published in quite a while—my administrative duties have taken their toll.

7. Since my 19YR–7 training, I have diagnosed eleven cases of Munchausen Syndrome by Proxy in Morena County. Prior to 19YR–7, this specific diagnosis had never been made by any Morena County CWS psychiatrist. Within the past four years, other psychiatrists at CWS have also started to recognize and diagnose cases involving Munchausen Syndrome by Proxy. Since 19YR–4 a total of five additional cases of the disease have been diagnosed and treated by three other CWS staff psychiatrists. In each case I consulted with the staff psychiatrist to verify their diagnosis. In each case I concurred with the diagnosing psychiatrist's determination.

8. To my knowledge, most other El Dorado county CWS agencies in their entire history never have diagnosed Munchausen Syndrome by Proxy. As far as I know, only thirteen county CWS agencies have documented a handful—anywhere from one to five per county—cases of the disease, most within the past five years. While the number of cases in Morena County may seem disproportionate to the number found in other counties, I attribute this difference to a lack of training and familiarity in these agencies with diagnosis and treatment of the disease. I would like to think that I have pretty much singlehandedly raised the consciousness of this problem in our county.

9. It is my considered, professional opinion that Ms. Cray suffers from Munchausen Syndrome by Proxy. My diagnosis is based on the following considerations:

– Sarah's Vague and Ill–Defined Symptoms: On reviewing all the available medical records from April 19YR–2 to present, Sarah's singular complaint to doctors was of vague and generalized stomach pains. Until the supposed diagnosis of appendicitis by an unidentified JGH emergency room doctor, no doctor was able to identify any source of Sarah's pain, and Sarah herself could never pinpoint the location of the pain for the doctors.

– Sarah's Vanishing Symptoms in her Mother's Absence: As part of my investigation of this case, I spoke with Sarah's sister, Regina Blackwell. Ms. Blackwell discussed with me a number of instances where she and Sarah spent extended periods of time together without Ms. Cray being present—including the July 4th Holiday, Thanksgiving and Christmas of 19YR–2. In each instance Ms. Blackwell told me that Sarah ate normally, behaved normally, and indicated no stomach pain while her mother was absent. However, each time when Ms. Cray returned, Sarah would agree that she was suddenly having stomach pain upon prompting by her mother.

– Lack of Any Proof of Illness: In reviewing Sarah's medical records, two facts stand out: 1) the sheer number of tests and procedures ordered to diagnose Sarah's supposed stomach pain, and 2) the absolute absence of any hard evidence of actual illness. Sarah endured multiple blood and body fluid tests, x-rays and other invasive diagnostic procedures during more than thirty visits to physicians over a ten-month period. Ms. Cray demanded a barium enema and x-ray series and an appendectomy be performed on her daughter. Each of these tests and procedures was performed—less-and-less willingly—by Sarah's physicians. In every case, including the pathology report on Sarah's excised appendix, the exact same conclusion was reached: Sarah is a physically normal, healthy child.

– Ms. Cray's Persistent and Unreasonable Demands for Medical Procedures: Even after doctors repeatedly assured Ms. Cray, that nothing was physically wrong with Sarah, Ms. Cray continued to demand increasingly invasive and dangerous medical procedures to be performed on Sarah, including surgery under general anesthetic and repeated exposure to x-rays and radioactive materials (barium). Other than the fact that doctors acknowledged that they *could* perform such procedures, Ms. Cray had absolutely no reason to believe that such procedures were really necessary, or to demand that doctors perform such procedures against their best professional judgment.

– Ms. Cray's Denial of Scientific Fact: During my investigations, Dr. Newsome—Sarah's treating physician—told me that he had confronted Ms. Cray with direct, pathological evidence that Sarah's appendix was completely normal and should not have been removed. Dr. Newsome informed me that Ms. Cray "refused to accept reality" by insisting that Dr. Newsome had fabricated the test results to "cover up" for his failure to diagnose appendicitis in the first instance.

– Sarah's "New" Symptoms Following Her Appendectomy: Ms. Cray claims that Sarah began suffering asthma and fainting spells shortly after Sarah's unnecessary surgery. Nobody, other than Ms. Cray, ever observed any of these "attacks" or symptoms. I believe that—because of her confrontation with Dr. Newsome following Sarah's appendectomy—it must have been clear to Ms. Cray that further feigned symptoms of abdominal pain would receive no more attention. So, she shifted to another ploy and manufactured a new set of symptoms in an attempt to justify a whole new series of tests and invasive procedures.

- Sarah's Absolute Lack of Symptoms Since CWS' Investigation Commenced: Finally and perhaps most telling, Sarah has had absolutely no medical complaints or symptoms since Dr. Newsome notified Ms. Cray that he was reporting her actions to CWS for investigation. During the CWS investigation and Sarah's custody hearing, Sarah has been examined by at least three psychiatrists: Dr. Robert Summers, Dr. Herb Tenet and myself. Through conversations with these doctors, I have learned that Sarah has manifested absolutely no physical symptoms requiring invasive medical treatment since the CWS investigation began. While Dr. Tenet and I disagree on Ms. Cray's diagnosis and the source of Sarah's earlier complaints, Dr. Tenet has clarified for me, in informal conversations, that he has recommended only psychological therapy for Sarah and Ms. Cray, nothing more.

10. Based on Ms. Cray's disorder of Munchausen Syndrome by Proxy, and the related facts upon which my diagnosis is based, it is also my considered opinion that Ms. Cray, with full knowledge of her actions, placed Sarah in situations that endangered Sarah's mental and physical well-being. During my investigation, Dr. Newsome informed me that Ms. Cray's demeanor and repeated demands that unnecessary invasive procedures be performed made clear to him that he had no real choice but to comply with her demands. There was no question in his mind that if he did not perform the procedures, Ms. Cray would not stop until she found a doctor who would.

11. I never previously have referred a diagnosed case of Munchausen Syndrome by Proxy to the District Attorney for criminal prosecution. All of the earlier cases that I have handled have either been resolved through medication and therapy, or alternate placement of the child, or both. I decided to refer Ms. Cray's case to the D.A. because of the extreme and persistent nature of Ms. Cray's actions in demanding numerous, invasive medical procedures to be performed on Sarah, and because of Ms. Cray's absolute refusal to accept or seek help with her mental problems until well after the CWS investigation of Sarah's case was under way. This is a truly exceptional case, and I will treat it that way in my forthcoming article.

I declare under penalty of perjury under the laws of the State of El Dorado that the foregoing is true and correct to the best of my knowledge.

Executed in Morena, El Dorado this 20th day of December, 19YR–1.

_____

John Garner, M.D.

SWORN STATEMENT OF DEFENDANT, JODY CRAY

I, Jody Cray, having been duly sworn under oath, hereby declare:

1. My name is Jody Lynn Cray. I live at 1965 Pole Line Road, in Morena, El Dorado. I am 43 years old. I am currently unmarried and have been twice divorced. I have two children by my first marriage— Regina Lee Blackwell, age twenty-five, and Theresa Esther Jones, age twenty-two. I have one child by my second marriage, Sarah Nicole Beringer, age eleven. I have a baccalaureate degree from El Dorado A & M in pre-medical studies, and I am trained as a physician's assistant. Between 19YR–25 and 19YR–18 I worked as a physician's assistant at Sutter Morena Hospital. In November of 19YR–18 I was injured in a slip-and-fall accident at work. Since that time I have since been on disability, and I remain unemployed.

2. My relationship with my oldest daughters, Regina and Theresa, is strained although we see each other on occasion at holidays. My relationship with Regina and Theresa's father was tumultuous. We argued a lot because he never paid enough attention to me or the children. The constant arguments had negative impacts on both Regina and Theresa. Because of the strain that I was under during my marriage, there were occasions when I verbally scolded and chastised Regina and Theresa for their behavior. I regret these incidents and have apologized to each of them since then. I never spanked or otherwise physically abused Regina. On one occasion I did pull my daughter Theresa by the hair when she made a mess in the bathroom. I have since apologized to Theresa, and she has accepted my apology.

3. My relationship with my youngest daughter, Sarah, is very close and loving. Sarah was born several years after my first two daughters, and is the "baby" of the family. I love Sarah dearly, and would do anything to protect her safety and health. I do not recall any instance in which I have either physically or verbally abused Sarah, either as an infant, or in more recent times.

4. On April 8, 19YR–2, Sarah woke up very early in the morning, at about 4 a.m., with terrible pains in her stomach. She was crying, and begged me to make the pain stop. I gave her some alkaseltzer. When that didn't help, I tried some pepto-bismol. Nothing seemed to help. We waited until 8 a.m., and then I took her to Dr. Harold Newsome's office in Morena, El Dorado.

5. On his initial examination, Dr. Newsome said that he could not find any trace of physical illness. I asked Sarah if her stomach still hurt, and she said, "Yes." Dr. Newsome suggested that he could perform some blood and stool sample tests that might give more definite answers. I thanked him and authorized the tests. Dr. Newsome suggested that the next time Sarah had an attack, I should take her straight to the Sutter

Morena Hospital emergency room, so that they could try to diagnose her at the onset of the attack.

6. During the next week, Sarah had nighttime attacks on three separate occasions. Each time I bundled her up and immediately took her to the Sutter Morena emergency room. Each time she was examined, but the doctors were unable to determine the cause. I became very concerned about the quality of health care being offered by the hospital because they were evidently unable to properly diagnose my daughter's illness, or offer any rational explanation for her pain. One doctor even pulled me aside and asked if Sarah might just be faking her symptoms. I informed him that Sarah's pain was genuine.

7. On April, 23, 19YR–2, Sarah and I returned to Dr. Newsome's office to go over her test results. Dr. Newsome informed us that no cause had been discovered for Sarah's sudden attacks of abdominal pain. I informed Dr. Newsome that there had been three more episodes since I had brought Sarah to see him. Dr. Newsome again examined Sarah, and still could find nothing wrong. He asked me to bring her back to see him if she had any attacks during the day, and advised me to continue visiting the emergency room for nighttime attacks.

8. Over the next ten months, I visited Dr. Newsome's office and the local emergency room on approximately thirty different occasions. Each time, the doctors were unable to find anything physically wrong with Sarah. On one visit I asked Dr. Newsome if there were any other tests that he could run. Dr. Newsome suggested that he could draw fluid samples directly from Sarah's abdomen and perform x-rays by using a radioactive barium enema. Although these tests concerned me, I authorized them because I was concerned about my daughter's ongoing, acute attacks. I did not relish the thought of having my daughter subjected to such invasive procedures and radioactive materials, but I did not know what else to do. They were the only options Dr. Newsome gave me. I consented to Dr. Newsome's advice. All tests eventually yielded negative results, according to Dr. Newsome.

9. By September of 19YR–2, I had figured out that I could at least minimize the severity of Sarah's attacks by keeping her on a strict diet of very small portions of bland foods and milk. It pained me to deny my child all the foods she loved so much, but her health was of paramount concern to me. Although the doctors disagreed that the diet I had put her on would make any difference, I could see for myself that the diet did reduce the frequency and severity of Sarah's attacks.

10. By December of 19YR–2, Sarah's attacks were becoming more frequent, even on her special diet. At the same time, the doctors were still unable to provide any diagnosis for Sarah's pain. On one visit to the emergency room the day after Christmas of 19YR–2, a physician took me aside and told me, "Look, Ms. Cray, you've been in and out of here like we have a revolving door. I'm telling you if anything is wrong with your daughter, it's in her head—or maybe yours. We have done all we can do here, and there is nothing more to be done. If you or Sarah comes up

with more than these mystery abdominal pains, feel free to come back; but otherwise I doubt there is anything that can be done for you." I informed the doctor that he was out of line for suggesting that either Sarah or I were making up Sarah's illness. I gathered up Sarah and left.

11. On Sunday, February 14, 19YR–1, I was visiting Jackson, El Dorado with Sarah. She had another severe attack, and we immediately rushed to Jackson General Hospital's emergency room. By the time we got to the emergency room, Sarah's pain had subsided, but the physician on duty performed a routine examination. In fifteen minutes, he noted that Sarah's appendix felt "odd." He placed my hand on Sarah's stomach and had me feel a small lump. I asked him if it was life threatening. He said that it did not require immediate action, but that Sarah would probably need an appendectomy within the next two weeks if her attacks continued. I thanked the doctor for finally discovering my daughter's underlying problem. Unfortunately, I have forgotten the name of the doctor who treated Sarah that day in Jackson. I have formally requested, in writing, that Jackson General Hospital provide any records related to the visit. Jackson General replied that they appear to have misplaced Sarah's intake sheet. They insist that they have no other documents verifying that Sarah was treated that day or any other day. The only document that I have showing that Sarah was seen at Jackson General that day is a billing statement sent to me by the hospital about three months after Sarah's visit. I paid the bill immediately. I had not received any bills prior to that time.

12. The following week, on the morning of Tuesday, February 16th, 19YR–1, I went back to Dr. Newsome to inform him of Sarah's actual illness as diagnosed by the Jackson emergency room physician. Dr. Newsome appeared embarrassed when I asked him *why* all the doctors in Morena, including himself, had been unable to make a simple diagnosis of appendicitis in a year of prodding, poking and testing my daughter. He immediately performed a quick examination himself, and stated that he felt only a small bump which seemed "normal" to him, and that it "was not in the right place" to indicate appendicitis. Dr. Newsome then asked me if I had *really* taken Sarah to any doctor in Jackson. I became extremely angry with Dr. Newsome for his incompetence and arrogance at that point. I told him that either he was going to authorize the appendectomy, or I was going to take Sarah to Jackson to have the procedure done. I added that I was then going to sue him for malpractice for failing to diagnose—for nearly a year—such a readily recognizable and dangerous textbook disease.

13. It is my belief that Dr. Newsome was not telling the truth when he said that the lump was not appendicitis. I believe this because Dr. Newsome immediately authorized Sarah's surgery, even though he had insisted no disease existed. Sarah was admitted to Sutter Morena General Hospital for her appendectomy to be performed the very next day. On February 18, 19YR–1 Sarah's appendix was removed. Since that day, to my knowledge, Sarah has not experienced any abdominal pains comparable or similar to those that she had before her surgery.

14. On February 19, 19YR–1, Dr. Newsome approached me outside Sarah's hospital room and stated that he had ordered a test of Sarah's appendix after it had been removed, and that the test indicated there was no sign of appendicitis. I informed Dr. Newsome that I knew that he was simply trying to cover up his own incompetence and that of the other doctors at the hospital, in failing to diagnose my daughter's true illness. Nevertheless, I informed him that I was satisfied that the proper procedure had been performed, and that I bore no continued ill will toward Dr. Newsome or the other doctors for the "unfortunate oversights." I also told him that I had decided not to sue for malpractice. Dr. Newsome seemed very relieved by this statement, and left me with my recovering daughter.

15. About two weeks after Sarah's surgery, Sarah contracted a raspy cough. Sarah told me that her stitches hurt when she coughed. I became afraid that she would rip open her stitches or injure herself if the cough was not brought under control. I considered taking Sarah to the Sutter Morena Emergency Room or Dr. Newsome, but, due to their past hostility, I decided that it would be best to go outside the area to obtain unbiased treatment. I called a private practitioner in Fairfield, Dr. Gary Snyder, to explain my situation. Dr. Snyder took my call, and asked for a description of Sarah's symptoms. After a brief conversation about her situation, he set up an appointment for later that afternoon. When I inquired what procedures would be performed, he stated that he would run some simple tests, and that he would probably prescribe an antibiotic such as amoxycillin. After hanging up, I remembered that my doctor had prescribed a different brand of amoxycillin for me several months ago for a different illness, and that I still had a large number of pills on standby. I decided to spare Sarah the discomfort of a road trip to Fairfield, and just started to administer the amoxycillin to her. I called Dr. Snyder's office a couple of hours later, explained that I had some amoxycillin, and canceled Sarah's appointment. They didn't seem to have any problem with that.

16. On Wednesday, March 10, 19YR–1, Sarah suddenly fainted and fell down while walking from her bedroom to the bathroom. I helped her up and asked what had happened. She said that she had suddenly felt dizzy and fallen down. Also, even though I had been treating her with the amoxycillin, her cough had only gotten worse—it had developed a "whooping" sound, like asthma. Terribly frightened, I felt that I needed medical advice right away, and—against my better judgment—called Dr. Newsome's office to tell them I was bringing Sarah in for an emergency examination.

17. When I arrived at Dr. Newsome's office, we were ushered into an examination room. Dr. Newsome, obviously displeased to see me, asked, "So, what problems do you *think* your daughter has today, Ms. Cray?" I told him about the fainting spell and Sarah's worsening cough. I informed Dr. Newsome that I had been giving Sarah amoxycillin, and how I had come to the decision to administer the antibiotic. Dr. Newsome listened to Sarah's chest, verified that she did have some wheezing

in her lungs, but denied that she had asthma. He informed me that it was improper for me to dispense prescription medication to my daughter with first having a physician's advice and approval. He agreed to run some tests however, and to report back to me within a week. I felt a week was too long to wait, but I did not want to argue with Dr. Newsome further. I took Sarah home.

18. Sarah's fainting spells continued for another four days. I was very scared for her health. Then, I remembered that Sarah's fainting spells had not started until I had started her on the amoxycillin. I immediately stopped giving her the antibiotics. Within a day, Sarah's cough had markedly improved, and she had no more fainting spells. As best I can explain it, it seems clear that Sarah was having some sort of allergic reaction to the amoxycillin. Her symptoms vastly improved once she was off of the drug. I decided that I would not notify Dr. Newsome of Sarah's improvement right away, because our relationship was obviously so terribly strained.

19. On the morning of March 18, Dr. Newsome called my house. He would not address me by my first name and would call me only "Ms. Cray." First, he stated that "as usual" there was nothing indicated by the tests, and that Sarah's cough was merely a minor respiratory infection requiring nothing more than time to heal. Then, he told me that he and the other physicians who had worked on Sarah's case over the past year had met and decided that it was "unfortunately necessary" to request Child Welfare Services to initiate an investigation into my fitness as Sarah's custodial parent. I was angry and devastated. I informed Dr. Newsome that he and his "cronies" were "incompetent in the practice of medicine," and that they were looking to take their lack of professional ability out on the only person who was really able to provide proper care for Sarah: me. I then informed Dr. Newsome that I had discovered Sarah's actual problem: her allergic reaction to amoxycillin. Dr. Newsome seemed stunned for a moment that I had discovered the real problem. Then he once again tried to cover up his incompetence. He insisted that even if somebody was allergic to amoxycillin, they would not get dizzy and faint from it. Then, he insisted that since he himself had prescribed amoxycillin for Sarah several months ago, and no problems had occurred at that time, it was clear that Sarah couldn't have an allergic reaction to the antibiotic. After another short silence, Dr. Newsome then told me that he felt I needed psychological counseling and offered me a psychologist's name. I was so angry that I called him a "self-serving quack" and hung up the phone.

20. On April 5, 19YR–1 the Superior Court of Morena County entered an order, giving my ex-husband, Harold Beringer, temporary custody of Sarah, pending the results of CWS's investigation and any resulting proceeding. I have now been deprived of my daughter's companionship for over a year. I have never coached my daughter to fake any illness or symptom. I have never made up any illness or symptom to seek improper medical diagnosis or treatment for my daughter. It is my firm belief that Dr. Newsome, the Sutter Morena Emergency Room

physicians, and the investigators from Child Welfare Service have engaged in an elaborate attempt to hide their own incompetence and failure to render proper treatment for my daughter, by claiming that I have manufactured her illnesses to gain attention for myself.

I declare under penalty of perjury under the laws of the State of El Dorado that the foregoing is true and correct to the best of my knowledge.

Executed in Morena, El Dorado this 19th day of December, 19YR–1.

Jody Lynn Cray

SWORN STATEMENT OF DEFENSE
WITNESS, DR. HERB TENET

I, Herbert F. Tenet, having been duly sworn under oath, hereby declare:

1. My name is Herbert ("Herb") Tenet. I live at 622 Hetfield Circle, in Rancho Cordova, El Dorado. I am 55 years old. I am recently divorced—my wife, Judy, and I had been married for thirty years. I have three full-grown children—two boys, David and Michael, and a girl, Jennifer.

2. I hold a medical degree in psychiatric medicine, from the Johns Hopkins University. I have practiced psychiatric medicine since my graduation from Johns Hopkins in 19YR–29. I have practiced psychiatry in various private partnerships and as a solo practitioner since that time.

3. In 19YR–15, I opened my solo practice, specializing in diagnosing and treating child and family related psychiatric disorders. My practice is strictly limited to these practice areas.

4. On average, about one-quarter of my business involves divorced or separated parents who are seeking to retain custody of their children in proceedings initiated by the other parent or by the State—typically through a county CWS agency. Since 19YR–15, I have testified as an expert witness in over fifty civil trials and CWS agency proceedings on behalf of my clients. I charge sliding-scale fees for my expert testimony, depending on the difficulty of the case and the amount of time involved. My average fee for testifying in a case is $150 per hour for reviewing documents and interviewing involved persons. For courtroom testimony, I normally charge $200 per hour, with a four hour minimum, plus expenses.

5. I am testifying on behalf of Jody Cray in this case in exchange for monetary compensation. Due to Sarah's voluminous medical records and the complexity of this case, I have asked Ms. Cray to pay me at a rate of $250 per hour for all my services. However, knowing that the trial would be held in Morena, which is not far from my office in Rancho Cordova, I have agreed to waive my four hour minimum for testimony, and to cover my own expenses, which are minimal.

6. Although I have no formal training in the particular disease, I am familiar with, and recognize, the symptoms of so-called "Munchausen Syndrome by Proxy." While Munchausen Syndrome by Proxy is recognized as a scientifically valid diagnosis, as a professional I have reservations about the standards used to diagnose this somewhat recently "discovered" disease. Some of the standards strike me as frightfully vague and subjective. In particular, I agree with a minority of psychiatrists who have studied the disease who insist that Munchausen by Proxy should be diagnosed only where the parent exhibits clear intent to subject the child to unnecessary treatment. In contrast, the current majority position is that seeking treatment for non-existent illnesses is enough in itself to support a diagnosis of Munchausen Syndrome by Proxy. I have never seen a patient yet whom I would diagnose as suffering from Munchausens Syndrome by Proxy as I understand the etiology of the disease—that is, requiring intent.

7. I have testified on behalf of parents in eight custody proceedings in the Morena County Courts based on a diagnosis rendered by Dr. John Garner or his staff at CWS of Munchausens Syndrome by Proxy. In each case I testified as a paid expert witness on behalf of the parent who supposedly suffered from the disease. In five of the cases, the court found insufficient evidence of threat to the child to require alternate placement. My analysis was certainly vindicated in those cases. In three other cases, including Sarah's custody case, the child was removed from my client's care and placed in alternate custody.

8. To my knowledge, no other El Dorado county CWS agency has diagnosed a number of Munchausen Syndrome by Proxy cases even approaching the large number of cases identified by Morena County CWS. There is no good reason for such an "epidemic" to be breaking out in Morena County. I have raised my concern with Dr. John Garner that Morena County CWS psychiatrists may be searching for parents to fit a popular diagnosis. Dr. Garner has explained to me that he believes that Munchausen Syndrome by Proxy goes too often unrecognized by other county CWS agencies due to a lack of familiarity with the disease. Dr. Garner's explanation seems implausible to me because any competent psychiatrist should be able to recognize typical symptoms of the disease. It takes no specialized training or certification to recognize Munchausen Syndrome by Proxy. You don't need to be a rocket scientist—only a competent mental health professional.

9. It is my considered, expert opinion that Ms. Cray does not suffer from Munchausen Syndrome by Proxy. In my professional opinion, Sarah either actually suffered actual symptoms as she complained of them, or she made them up on her own. My diagnosis is based on the following considerations:

– Sarah's Lack of Specificity in Describing Her Symptoms: Sarah's only complaints to doctors were extremely vague and generalized. The fact is that Ms. Cray is a licensed physician's assistant. If Ms. Cray had been "fabricating" or "coercing" Sarah's symptoms, surely she would have coached more specific responses to doctors' questions to indicate a specific illness or illnesses.

- The Consistency of Sarah's Attacks: As part of my study of Sarah's case I interviewed Sarah's sister, Regina Blackwell. Ms. Blackwell noted several dates, including Thanksgiving and Christmas 19YR–2, where she had been alone with Sarah, and aware that Sarah had not complained of symptoms in her mother's absence. Ms. Blackwell was particularly agitated about these visits because, according to her, "Sarah had no problems until my mother found out she had eaten food she wasn't supposed to have." Particularly notable were Ms. Blackwell's comments about the Christmas incident. According to Ms. Blackwell, nobody told Ms. Cray that Sarah had eaten a hot dog and some other "bad" food, and Sarah never complained of any symptoms. Yet, my review of Sarah's medical records indicate that Ms. Cray took Sarah to the Sutter Morena Emergency Room at 11:30 pm on December 25, 19YR–2. In other words, Sarah developed symptoms requiring treatment that very same evening, *even though Ms. Cray had no idea* that Ms. Blackwell's husband had given Sarah food that was "off limits."

- Lack of Any Demonstrated Intent by Ms. Cray to Subject Sarah to Unnecessary Medical Procedures: On my review of Sarah's medical records, and discussing her case with Dr. Newsome and the treating Sutter Morena Hospital physicians, I can find no compelling evidence that Ms. Cray ever intended to subject her daughter to unnecessary invasive medical procedures. To the contrary, the records I have examined show that the doctors were always the final decision-makers as to what procedures would be performed, and when. Dr. Newsome made much of the fact that Ms. Cray "insisted" on drawing Sarah's blood, performing a barium enema, and an appendectomy. Yet, on reviewing the contemporaneous records from Dr. Newsome's office, all I can conclude is that Ms. Cray inquired into the usefulness of such procedures, and then—following advice and consultation by Dr. Newsome—provided consent for Dr. Newsome to go forward with the procedures. In each case the doctor had to independently determine that the procedure was warranted. Doctors don't take order like that from patients—or at least that's what I learned in medical school.

- Evidence Supporting Ms. Cray's Claims That Other Doctors Diagnosed Sarah's Illness: Ms. Cray stated that a Jackson General Hospital physician suggested to her that Sarah may have had appendicitis. I have personally seen a billing statement from that visit. Ms. Cray has also made it clear that a Fairfield pediatrician, Dr. Gary Snyder, diagnosed Sarah's asthma and suggested amoxycillin to treat the underlying lung infection. I personally called and spoke with Dr. Snyder at his office. Although Dr. Snyder stated that he does not specifically remember his conversation with Ms. Cray, he agreed that he usually would use amoxycillin to treat a typical asthma case. He said that he could easily have forgotten the conversation. Although the other experts who have studied this case have unreasonably assumed that Ms. Cray has fabricated these stories, it is my opinion that she did not. Ms. Cray was only following up on professional medical advice, not "making up" non-existent office visits and diseases.

   – Sarah's Improvement After Ms. Cray's Actions: Sarah has had no medical problems since Ms. Cray discovered Sarah's allergy to amoxycillin. Sarah's medical records demonstrate that Sarah has had no stomach pains since her appendectomy. From these facts, other experts suggest a rather unlikely theory: that Ms. Cray somehow "controlled" Sarah's medical complaints and actual physical symptoms. I suggest a simpler, more plausible, alternative theory. Ms. Cray was right. Ms. Cray was told Sarah had appendicitis. An appendectomy was performed. Sarah never had another stomach pain. Sarah began fainting after Dr. Snyder recommended treatment with amoxycillin. Ms. Cray—realizing the chronology of these events—decided to try taking Sarah off the amoxycillin. Sarah never fainted again. It seems strange to prosecute a mother for acting on sound medical advice and deductive skills, especially where those actions led to resolution of the child's pain and symptoms.

   10. My professional opinion is rendered based on an extensive review of Sarah's medical records. I have also discussed Sarah's case with each physician who treated or examined Sarah including Dr. Newsome, Dr. Summers, the Sutter Morena Emergency Room physicians, and Dr. Snyder. The only treating physician whom I did not interview was the unidentified doctor from Jackson General Hospital who diagnosed Sarah's appendicitis.

   11. I also discussed the facts of Sarah's case with Ms. Regina Blackwell, Ms. Cray's oldest daughter. Ms. Blackwell was extremely hostile toward any suggestion that her mother may actually have been acting in Sarah's best interest. At one point, Ms. Blackwell went so far as to say, "My mother wouldn't know what it means to act in her children's best interest. All she cares about is herself. Believe me, I should know." She described herself as a "victim" of her mother. I asked Ms. Blackwell to elaborate on her comment, but she refused. It is apparent to me that Ms. Blackwell must have had some personal disappointment with her mother at some point in the past that has colored Ms. Blackwell's ability to objectively evaluate Ms. Cray's actions with regard to Sarah.

   12. Ms. Cray has been my patient since shortly after these proceedings were initiated by CWS. The first time I saw Ms. Cray was on September 8, 19YR–1. I have been treating Ms. Cray ever since on a bi-weekly basis. When Ms. Cray came to see, me I diagnosed her as having

moderate depression due to Sarah's placement with her father. After several months of therapy and discussion with Ms. Cray, I believe that the worst that can be said of her actions is that she paid attention to Sarah's repeated complaints of stomach pain, took them largely at face value, and sought in good faith to have the cause diagnosed and treated.

13.   Based on the above facts, I am quite certain that Ms. Cray does not suffer from Munchausen Syndrome by Proxy. It is my professional opinion that either Sarah was in fact ill with the appendicitis and asthma as diagnosed by licensed, practicing physicians, or that Sarah may have possibly made up her symptoms to gain attention from her mother and the doctors who treated her. There simply is not sufficient, credible scientific evidence to support CWS' and Dr. Summers' conclusion that Ms. Cray intended to subject her daughter to unnecessary medical treatments. If there is any victim in these proceedings it is not Sarah, it is her mother.

I declare under penalty of perjury under the laws of the State of El Dorado that the foregoing is true and correct to the best of my knowledge.

Executed in Morena, El Dorado this 21st day of December, 19YR–1.

_____

Herbert F. Tenet, M.D.

STIPULATION OF EXPECTED TESTIMONY OF DR. HAROLD NEWSOME

It is hereby stipulated between the People and the defense, with the defendant's express consent, that if Dr. Harry Newsome, M.D., 2121 F St., Morena, El Dorado, was present in court and sworn as witness, he would give the following testimony:

1.   My name is Harold Newsome. I am licensed to practice pediatric medicine by the State of El Dorado. My office is located at 2121 F St., in Morena, El Dordo. I received my medical degree from Stanford School of Medicine in 19YR–26. On completion of my residency requirements, I worked as an emergency room physician at Sutter Morena Hospital until 19YR–15. In 19YR–15 I opened my private practice, specializing in pediatric medicine. Since 19YR–17 I have been continuously certified in pediatric medicine by the El Dorado Medical Association.

2.   I have examined the original of the copied Patient Visit Records from my office that are offered by both sides in this litigation dated February 16, 19YR–1 and August 17, 19YR–2. The original records are in my personal handwriting, and are in the same condition as the day that I wrote them. I verify that, other than the fact that the exhibits are photocopies, they are true and accurate representations of my notes from Sarah's visits on the specified dates.

3. On April 8, 19YR–2, Jody Cray brought her daughter, Sarah Beringer, to my office. Ms. Cray claimed that Sarah was suffering from intense and sharp stomach pains. On examination, Sarah was not directly responsive to my questions and would only nod "yes" or "no." As I manipulated Sarah's abdomen, I asked whether Sarah felt any pain. She did not respond. Ms. Cray knelt down to Sarah, and said, "Sarah, honey, you don't have to be scared. Now tell Dr. Newsome the truth. Your stomach hurts, doesn't it." Sara nodded affirmatively while looking at the ground. The results of that examination, as with many to follow, were indeterminate. Other than Sarah's generalized indication of stomach pains, there was no evidence of actual illness. I prescribed mild sedatives for Sarah. I advised Ms. Cray to keep an eye on Sarah and her eating habits to identify any foods that might trigger Sarah's apparent illness.

4. By August 17, 19YR–2 Sarah had visited my office six times. She had visited the Sutter Morena Hospital Emergency Room a comparable number of times. Over this four month period, Sarah's complaints were remarkably consistent—generalized abdominal pain with no apparent physical cause. On August 17, Ms. Cray asked whether there were further diagnostic tests that might determine the source of Sarah's pain. Half thinking out loud to myself, I mentioned that a barium enema and x-ray series might shed some light on Sarah's condition, but that her present symptoms were not typical of ailments that could be diagnosed through this process. Ms. Cray immediately requested that I perform the procedure, because no other tests had diagnosed her daughter's problems. I advised Ms. Cray that there were dangers associated with the procedure, including exposure to radioactive materials, and that the likelihood of successful diagnosis was low. Ms. Cray nevertheless pressed me to authorize the x-ray procedure. I set up the enema and x-rays for early the next week. As expected, the procedure yielded no new information about Sarah's condition.

5. Over the next 6 months, Ms. Cray brought Sarah to my office and the Sutter Morena Emergency room on multiple occasions. By February of 19YR–1 Sarah had visited my office thirteen times. Each time Sarah complained of generalized stomach pains, but could not provide any more specific information. At one visit I took Ms. Cray aside and suggested that Sarah's pain might be psychologically, not physically, based. Ms. Cray became deeply offended, and insisted that Sarah's pain must have some physical basis. Rather than argue, I apologized to Ms. Cray, and promised to continue my efforts to diagnose Sarah's illness.

6. In December of 19YR–2, I attended a Morena County Medical Society luncheon where Dr. John Garner, with Child Welfare Service, was giving a talk on Munchausen Syndrome by Proxy. Dr. Garner explained that a parent suffering from Munchausen Syndrome by Proxy might encourage their child to feign illness or even go so far as to induce symptoms in a child, in order to seek

gratification through presenting the child to medical professionals for treatment. Sarah's case came to mind as Dr. Garner described Munchausen Syndrome by Proxy. The more he said, the more it seemed to fit. After the meeting, I approached Dr. Garner to ask some general questions about identifying cases of Munchausen Syndrome by Proxy. At that time, I kept my questions general, and did not mention the specific details of Sarah's case. Dr. Garner eagerly answered my questions. He also told me to be on the outlook for any such cases. He asked that I contact him if I identified any cases.

7.　By early February, I was all but convinced that Jody Cray suffered from Munchausen Syndrome by Proxy, and that Sarah was at genuine risk in Ms. Cray's care. On February 16, 19YR–2, Ms. Cray brought Sarah to me one more time, again complaining of generalized stomach pain. When Ms. Cray arrived at my office, she was angry and upset. In the examination room, Ms. Cray informed me that Sarah was suffering from appendicitis, even before I began my customary examination. Already doubting that Sarah was actually ill, I asked Ms. Cray how she could possibly know that Sarah had appendicitis. Ms. Cray informed me that she had taken Sarah to the Jackson General Hospital Emergency Room on February 14, and that the doctors there had diagnosed Sarah with appendicitis. Surprised, I excused myself and called Jackson General Hospital to obtain whatever information I could. The staff at JGH stated that at the moment, she couldn't locate any record of Sarah's visit.

8.　On learning that JGH had no record of Sarah's visit, I confronted Ms. Cray and told her that I suspected her of coaching Sarah's symptoms. Ms. Cray was visibly shaken by my assertion, but quickly regained her composure and went on the offensive by calling me a "quack." I proceeded to examine Sarah, and explained to Ms. Cray that I could find no evidence of appendicitis or any other illness—although I did feel a small lump in Sarah's abdomen that Ms. Cray pointed out. The lump appeared to be normal organs, and did not seem to indicate any particular illness. Yet Ms. Cray insisted that I perform an appendectomy on Sarah. When I informed Ms. Cray that there was no rational reason to perform an appendectomy, she became very angry, and told me that she would go back to JGH so that Sarah could be treated by real doctors. I could tell that Ms. Cray was not kidding, and that she would take every step necessary to have surgery performed on Sarah. Reluctantly, I agreed to consult with a surgeon on Sarah's case to perform exploratory surgery to try to determine the source of Sarah's pain.

9.　On February 18, I assisted Sutter Morena Surgeon David Cox, in performing exploratory surgery and an appendectomy on Sarah Beringer. Both Dr. Cox and I were skeptical about the likelihood of success, but I knew that if Dr. Cox and I refused to operate, she would find a doctor who would. Dr. Cox and I informed Ms. Cray that any surgery, especially when putting a child under general anesthesia, is a risky undertaking that could possibly result in additional trauma or, in extreme instances, death. Ms. Cray acted oblivious to the risk. Ms. Cray stated, "I don't care what you think. We both know that Sarah has appendicitis, and you are too stuck-up to admit that a Jackson emergency room doctor found the disease that you couldn't find for the past year. If you don't perform this surgery, I will not stop until I find a doctor who will." I reluctantly agreed to authorize the surgery and assist Dr. Cox with the procedure. I agreed only because I knew that Ms. Cray would simply go to a physician with little or no familiarity of Sarah's case to have the surgery done. I didn't think that I had any alternative.

10. As soon as Dr. Cox and I removed Sarah's appendix, we ordered laboratory tests on the tissues. By the next morning, February 19, the lab results were in. As I had suspected all along, Sarah's appendix was normal. Later that day, I approached Ms. Cray in the hospital, and delivered the news that Sarah's appendix was normal. Ms. Cray became nearly hysterical, and accused me of fabricating the test results to cover my earlier failure to diagnose appendicitis. I then tried to show Ms. Cray the test results, but she refused to even look at the lab reports—going so far as to accuse me of forging the documents. I told Ms. Cray that I was concerned about her and Sarah's mental health, and I offered Ms. Cray a referral to see Dr. Garner with Child Welfare Services. Ms. Cray refused to take the referral, and stated that I was the one who needed counseling.

11. About an hour later, Ms. Blackwell, Jody Cray's oldest daughter, approached me in the hospital hallway. Ms. Blackwell stated that she had overheard some of my conversation with Ms. Cray, and wanted to know the details of Sarah's condition. I very much wanted to warn Ms. Blackwell that her mother was the likely cause of Sarah's poor health. However, I was afraid that if I was wrong, and word got back to Ms. Cray, I would be sued for a breach of physician-patient confidence or malpractice. I politely informed Ms. Blackwell that I could not discuss Sarah's case without Ms. Cray's consent as a matter of professional ethics. We engaged in some small talk, and then she left to go to Sarah.

12. On March 10, about three weeks after Sarah's surgery, Ms. Cray called my office to report that Sarah had developed a new set of symptoms including a "whooping" cough and fainting spells. My first inclination was to refuse treatment, but for Sarah's sake I decided to examine Sarah for myself. We made an appointment for later that same day.

13. When Ms. Cray arrived, she informed me that she had started administering amoxycillin to Sarah several days before. I was shocked. I asked Ms. Cray where she obtained the amoxycillin. She informed me that a doctor in Fairfield had prescribed the medication for Sarah's cough. I told Ms. Cray that I doubted the truth of her story, and that it was illegal for her to administer prescription drugs to Sarah without proper prescriptions. I per-

formed a series of tests on Sarah for her supposed cough and fainting.

14. One week later, I called Ms. Cray with Sarah's test results. As expected, all tests were negative. I then informed Ms. Cray that I had consulted with several Sutter Morena Hospital Emergency Room physicians about Sarah's case. I explained that after some discussion, the doctors and I had reluctantly reached a consensus that Child Welfare Service should investigate Sarah's supposed illness, and that we would be filing a report with CWS outlining Sarah's case. Ms. Cray got very angry. She informed me that she had taken Sarah off the amoxycillin three days before, and that Sarah had improved significantly since that time. Ms. Cray insisted that Sarah's latest symptoms were an allergic reaction to the antibiotic. I explained as best I could to Ms. Cray that Sarah had no known allergy to amoxycillin and, that even if she did, fainting and a raspy cough would not be typical symptoms for such an allergy. I again offered to refer Ms. Cray to Dr. Garner. Ms. Cray angrily stated that I was "too incompetent to practice medicine" and hung up on me.

Based on my experience with Ms. Cray and Sarah, it is my personal and professional opinion that Sarah never actually had appendicitis. Under normal circumstances, I would never have authorized Sarah's surgery. However, I felt that Ms. Cray would not relent until a physician agreed to perform the surgery that Ms. Cray had unilaterally decided was necessary for her daughter. Having been Sarah's personal physician, I am concerned for her health and well being. I believe that Ms. Cray poses a continuing threat to her daughter's health through her ability to manipulate Sarah and to convince Sarah that she has non-existent symptoms. Ms. Cray suffers from Munchausen Syndrome by Proxy-she is a classic case. As a result of her disease, Ms. Cray has caused her daughter unjustified mental suffering and physical pain. Ms. Cray has insisted that physicians carry out unnecessary, invasive testing and surgical procedures on Sarah with no justifiable reason.

Offices of Dr. Harold Newsome, M.D.

2121 F. St., Morena, El Dorado 95616   Phone: (530) 555-9872   Fax: (530) 555-9873

Patient Visit Record

Date of Visit	February 16, 19YR-1 2:15 p.m.
Patient Name / Guardian (if applicable)	Sarah Beringer / Jody Cray
Social Security No.	655-98-9872 / 549-34-4997
General Complaint / Symptoms/ Diagnosis	General stomach cramp / abdominal pain.
Observations on Examination	Continued, ongoing non-localized pain in abdominal region. Same as multiple previous episodes. Child mildly unresponsive to questions about location and nature of pain. All vital s appear normal, child appears otherwise healthy.
Prescriptions Ordered	Mild sedative
Other Procedures Ordered	Surgery consultation scheduled: Dr. Cox, 2/17/YR-1. Possible exploratory surgery for appendicitis(*)
Additional Comments	Patient has been in and out of office and E. Room at least 30 times in past year. Mother insists appendicitis diagnosed at JGH. No traditional indicators. Mother demands exploratory surgery, may be correct. Tentative surgery date February 18,

Physician: H. Newsome   Date: 8/17/19yr-2

Physician: <u>H. Newsome</u>   Date:<u>2/16/19yr-1</u>
Offices of Dr. Harold Newsome, M.D.
2121 F. St., Morena, El Dorado 95616   ?   Phone: (530) 555-9872   ?   Fax: (530)
555-9873

Patient Visit Record

Date of Visit	2:15 p.m. **August 17, 19yr-2**
Patient Name / Guardian (if applicable)	Sarah Beringer / Jody Cray
Social Security No.	655-98-9872 / 549-34-4997
General Complaint / Symptoms/ Diagnosis	non-localized stomach pain.

Physician: <u>H. Newsome</u>   Date: <u>8/17/19yr-2</u>

Observations on Examination	Persistent non-localized pain in abdominal region. Several months running. Non-responsive to standard treatments. Cause difficult to pinpoint, child not responsive to specific inquiry on nature or source of pain without mother's assistance.
Prescriptions Ordered	Mild sedative
Other Procedures Ordered	Enema - Barium / full series x-ray / Aspiration by Injection - Pancreatic Fluids

Additional Comments	Patient has been seen six times at this office in the past four months. Mother reports eight other trips to JH E. Room. Patient appears to have no response to traditional, non-invasive treatments. Mother inquired about possible radiological exam. Discussed barium enema / work up on pancreatic fluids, mother consents. Set up next week.
Date of Next Visit	T.B.D. - Schedule radiological exam - barium, aspiration by injection - pancreatic fluids.

STIPULATION OF EXPECTED TESTIMONY
OF HAROLD BERINGER

It is hereby stipulated between the People and the defense, with the defendant's express consent, that if Harold Thomas Beringer, 758 Glacier Valley Drive, Coos Bay, Oregon, was present in court and sworn as witness, he would give the following testimony:

1. My name is Harold Thomas Beringer. I am forty-eight years old. I am the Day Operations Supervisor at Fresh–Pac. Ltd., a sea-food processing and canning plant located in Coos Bay. I am divorced. My ex-wife, Jody Lynn Cray, and I have one biological child, Sarah Nicole Beringer. Jody and I were married in June of 19YR–14. Sarah was born in 19YR–11.

2. Shortly after Sarah was born, I began to suspect that Jody was having an affair—she seemed distant, and refused to engage in intimate relations with me. When I confronted Jody with my suspicions, she became very angry with me and denied everything. From that time on, it seemed like all we did was argue—about everything. Although I never had any proof of my suspicions, I am sure that I must have been right because of Jody's exaggerated and continuous denials. As our arguments became more heated, our marriage soured rapidly.

3. Jody filed for divorce in 19YR–9. I contested nothing in the divorce settlement except for Jody's demand that she retain primary custody of Sarah. Jody insisted that I should agree to have visitation with Sarah for only one week at Christmas and three weeks during the summer. I refused, insisting on joint custody with each of us having Sarah for equal time throughout the year.

4. At a court hearing to determine Sarah's custody arrangements, Jody accused me of hitting her and Sarah on several different occasions. I was shocked and appalled that Jody had told such a vicious lie to the court, under oath, just to obtain primary custody of Sarah. I told the judge that while Jody and I had argued loudly and often, there had never been any physical abuse between us. I also denied vehemently that I had abused Sarah.

5. Despite my denials, and a total lack of any evidence to support Jody's wild stories, the judge granted Jody's request—allowing me only four weeks of visitation per year. I admit that I was so angry and shocked by the judge's ruling that I shouted across the courtroom to Jody, "You are a fucking liar! You think you've won here?! One day, I'll pay you back for your lies! I'll pay you back good!" What I said that day was uttered in the heat of the moment. While I will never forgive Jody for her lies to the court in 19YR–9, I have no desire to satisfy any "vendetta" against Jody in this proceeding. I only want what is best for my daughter, Sarah.

6. Following my divorce from Jody and the court's 19YR–9 custody ruling, I was devastated. In order to ease the pain of losing Sarah, I

decided to move away. In early 19YR–8, I left the Morena area and moved to Coos Bay, Oregon. Each year since that time, I have followed the courts orders, limiting my visitation to the four weeks a year established by the court's order. In all honesty, I have several times thought several times about not bringing Sarah back to her mother. But I knew that would only create more problems, and probably result in losing the little time that I did share with Sarah.

7. I have a close relationship with my step-daughters, Regina Blackwell and Theresa Jones. Although Regina and Teri are not my biological children, we formed a close bond while I was married to Jody. Since my divorce from Jody, I have stayed in touch with both Regina and Teri by telephone, mail and e-mail.

8. Just before my divorce from Jody, Regina had a small problem with the law involving a minor case of shoplifting a blouse. Regina was about fifteen years old at the time. My ex-wife insisted that Regina "pay the price" for her actions by facing prosecution in juvenile court—even though the probation officer in the case had offered Jody the opportunity to handle the matter at home. Regina was frightened. She came to me in tears begging me to stop the court proceedings. I tried to reason with Jody and talk Jody into letting Regina just return the blouse. Jody refused, telling me, "Regina is my child, not yours. I know what's best for my children, not you, not anybody else!" I was very angry with Jody for blowing the situation out of all reasonable proportion. Still, I had to tell Regina that, as her step-father, there was nothing that I could do. Regina gave me a hug, and said that she understood. Then she told me that she would hate her mother forever. I remember that I told her, "You know, forever is an awful long time to hate somebody." Regina nodded her head and said quietly, "Yeah, I know, Harry, but I mean it. I'm just really scared. Why is she doing this to me? The probation officer told us that going to the judge isn't even necessary."

9. On April 5, 19YR–2, I called Jody to make arrangements for Sarah's three-week summer visit. During that phone call, Jody informed me that Sarah had recently taken ill with some sort of undefined stomach pains. Jody asked if she could call me back in a couple of weeks to finalize Sarah's summer arrangements. I agreed, with some hesitation.

10. Three weeks went by, and I did not hear back from Jody. I called her again on April 25, 19YR–2, to arrange Sarah's summer visitation. Jody informed me that Sarah was still sick, and that the doctors—even after several visits—were having trouble pinpointing the diagnosis. I spoke with Sarah during that phone call. In a halting manner Sarah said, "My tummy feels really bad, daddy." I told her that she shouldn't be afraid, and that the doctors would help her.

11. At the end of our April 25 phone conversation I told Jody that I would like to have my visitation with Sarah from August 23 through September 12, 19YR–2. I told Jody that I had planned a camping trip, and a road trip up the Pacific Coast and into Canada. Jody told me,

"Well, that shouldn't be a problem, as long as Sarah is feeling better." I assured Jody that four months ought to be plenty of time for Sarah to get over her stomachache.

12. About one month later, in early-June, I called Jody to let her know that I had made plane reservations for Sarah's visit in late August. Jody told me that Sarah's stomach pain was continuing and had not been diagnosed. I asked to speak with Sarah. Jody told me Sarah was sleeping.

13. On June 27, and again on July 12, 19YR–2, I called to check in on Sarah to make sure she was okay and that our August visitation plans were still on track. Each time, nobody answered. Each time, I left a message on the answering machine. Jody never returned my calls. I assumed that all was well, or that Jody would have called me otherwise.

14. On August 15, 19YR–2, I called to finalize plans for Sarah's visit at the end of the month. When Jody answered the phone, she sounded genuinely distraught—her voice was a bit shaky and she seemed on edge. I lived with Jody long enough to be able to tell when she's really upset. When I asked if things were looking okay for Sarah's visit, Jody told me that Sarah was still sick, and that Sarah's visit to Klamath Falls was probably going to have to be canceled. I was shocked and annoyed. I reminded Jody that I had already purchased the airplane tickets, which were non-refundable. Jody shouted at me, "Don't you hear me? You never pay attention. Your daughter is sick! She's not going anywhere until she is better! Do you just want her to get worse while you're out in the middle of God-knows-where camping?! Then what would you do?" For a moment, I became very angry because Jody had not told me about this decision sooner. But, then I reminded myself that Sarah's health was the most important thing. Reluctantly, I agreed with Jody that—for the first time since our divorce—my summer visit with Sarah should be canceled.

15. I continued to call once every three to four weeks to check in on Sarah's progress. Each time Jody told me that nothing had been resolved, but that the doctors were still conducting tests. Each time I talked to Sarah, she would say "My tummy still hurts, daddy," when I asked about her illness. She always said the same thing, almost as if it was a script. She never mentioned any other pain or symptoms during our short phone conversations, except in response to my direct questions.

16. By Christmas 19YR–2, my next scheduled visitation, Jody was still insisting that Sarah was as sick as ever. According to Jody, the doctors still had no explanation for Sarah's mystery illness. I told Jody that I would like to come down to Morena for Christmas, so I could at least be with Sarah. Jody told me that the doctors had advised against any added excitement for Sarah during the holidays. Jody suggested that I wait until after the beginning of the year to visit. Against my better judgment, I agreed. I told Jody that I had some vacation time in late-February 19YR–1, and that I would visit then.

17. On January 2, 19YR–1, I called Regina—who I knew visited with Jody and Sarah on occasion—to see if I could learn any more about Sarah's mystery illness. Regina told me that she had seen Sarah only a few times during the past year—once on July 4th, once at Thanksgiving, and again at Christmas. Regina told me that Sarah seemed to be fine whenever the two of them were alone together, but that Sarah would complain of stomach pains in the presence of her mother. Regina told me, "You know, if the doctors weren't taking this seriously, I'd almost think this was all in mom's head. Sarah really seems just fine to me, except for when mom's around." I told Regina that I'd have a talk with the doctors myself when I visited in February.

18. On February 17, 19YR–1 Regina called to let me know that Sarah had been diagnosed with appendicitis and that the doctors were going to operate that day. I was shocked and very concerned for Sarah's health. I had actually planned to visit during the following week.

19. After speaking with Regina on February 17, I immediately called Jody. She began to cry as soon as I asked her what was going on. Jody told me that Sarah had been diagnosed with appendicitis three days earlier in Jackson, and that Dr. Newsome had decided that emergency surgery was necessary to remove Sarah's appendix. I was stunned. I did my best to assure Jody that everything would work out fine with Sarah's operation. I then told her that I would fly down right away to be there for both her and Sarah. At that point, Jody quickly regained her composure. She coolly thanked me for my concern. However, she insisted that I should probably wait at least a few weeks so that Sarah could heal. Once again, I reluctantly agreed, but informed Jody that I planned on coming down as soon as Dr. Newsome thought that Sarah had recovered sufficiently recovered. By the beginning of March, I had not heard back from Jody.

20. In hindsight, I realize that I should never have listened to Jody's crazy stories. I should have involved myself directly with Dr. Newsome and the other doctors who were dealing with Sarah's mystery symptoms and Jody's irrational insistence on increasingly invasive medical procedures. If I had flown down to Morena on February 17, 19YR–1, I might have been able to intervene in a surgical procedure that nobody, except for my ex-wife, believed was medically justified or necessary.

21. Finally, on March 12, 19YR–1, I decided to take direct action. I called Dr. Newsome's office to find out how Sarah was doing. That was when I learned the horrible truth. Dr. Newsome informed me that he believed that Jody had been coaching and coercing Sarah's illnesses from the very beginning. Dr. Newsome informed me that Jody had insisted on all sorts of invasive medical tests and procedures during the previous year. Dr. Newsome also informed me that Jody had insisted on the appendectomy, even though she knew there was no evidence of appendicitis. Dr. Newsome added that Jody had recently manufactured a whole new set of symptoms for Sarah—coughing and fainting. Dr. Newsome stated that he was performing some basic tests to rule out actual illness.

He informed me that he fully expected the test results would be negative, and that he planned on notifying Morena County CWS of suspected child abuse. I asked him to also please call me if and when he notified CWS of his suspicions.

22. On March 17, 19YR–1, Dr. Newsome called to inform me that he had reported Jody to CWS for suspected child abuse. I immediately called CWS to inform them that I was Sarah's father, and that I would like to be directly involved in any proceedings involving Sarah from that point on. After a brief preliminary investigation, CWS filed a civil suit seeking immediate, temporary transfer of custody to me while they further investigated Jody's bizarre behavior for possible criminal prosecution. On April 5, 19YR–1, the Morena County Superior Court awarded me temporary custody of Sarah, pending resolution of CWS' criminal investigation.

23. My daughter Sarah has been living with me for one-and-one-half years. During this time CWS and my ex-wife have been engaged in a series of negotiations, motions and continuances, psychological evaluations and other preparation for this trial.

24. During the past eighteen months Sarah has had no stomach pains. She has had no coughing fits. She has not fainted. Sarah eats normal quantities of food, and eats all types of foods. Sarah has not had any illness since she came to live with me in Oregon. As far as I can tell, Sarah is a perfectly normal, healthy eleven-year old girl.

25. From my conversations with my step-daughter Regina and with Dr. Newsome—and from my own experience with Sarah over the past year-and-a-half—I have come to the conclusion that my ex-wife, Jody Cray, fabricated Sarah's "appendicitis" and her "asthma." Despite what I said in 19YR–9, I do not bear Jody any active ill-will or any desire to exact "revenge" for lying to the court and taking Sarah away from me. Nor do I think Jody is insane or anything like that. However, I do believe that Jody has caused our daughter to suffer emotional harm and physical disfigurement for no reason. I only wish I had involved myself earlier so that I could have prevented Jody from forcing needless medical procedures on my little girl.

STIPULATION OF EXPECTED TESTIMONY OF DR. ROBERT SUMMERS

It is hereby stipulated between the People and the defense, with the defendant's express consent, that if Dr. Robert Summers, M.D., 945 12th St., Mason, El Dorado, was present in court and sworn as witness, he would give the following testimony:

1. My name is Robert Summers. I am licensed to practice pediatric medicine and general psychiatry by the State of El Dorado. I have been actively practicing pediatric medicine and psychiatry in the Morena area for the past twelve years. My office is located at 3245 Broadway, in Mason, El Dorado.

2. I served as a court appointed medical and psychological expert witness in the civil case that determined Sarah Beringer's present custody status. I was appointed by the court to serve as an independent expert witness in Sarah's custody case in May of 19YR–1. I had never met or examined Sarah or Ms. Cray prior to May of 19YR–1.

3. I have served as a court appointed expert in five prior cases involving CWS investigations and custody procedings. In three of these cases I concurred with CWS' doctors, and rendered expert testimony that charges of parental incompetence brought by Child Welfare Services were well substantiated and indicated that the child should be separated from the custodial parent (two of these cases involved mother-child custody arrangements, the third involved a custodial father and his son). In one case, I disagreed with CWS' actual diagnosis, but, on independent grounds found that there were alternative conditions establishing that the custodial parent was incapable of rendering proper care for her child. In one case, I disagreed entirely with CWS' position, and testified that there was no valid medical or psychological reason for separating the mother and child.

4. I have examined Sarah on several occasions, both before and after she was removed from her mother's home and placed in her father's custody. On the basis of these examinations my professional opinion of Sarah's case is as follows:

- Prior to terminating Ms. Clay's custody, Sarah had been belligerent and acting out in school. Since she has gone to live with her father, her behavior has been exemplary, and Sarah has become an honor student.

- Since moving to live with her father, Sarah has not complained of any medical problems. Sarah eats normal foods in normal quantities. She has not fainted or suffered coughing fits, asthma, or any abdominal pain.

- Sarah has poor identity formation as a result of inadequate individuation from her mother. Her recognition of self has dramatically improved since she began living with her father.

- Sarah has visited with her mother twice since her father was awarded temporary custody. After each visit, Sarah's behavior regressed markedly. In each instance it took about two weeks for her behavior to return to normal.

5. I have personally conducted medical examinations of Sarah. I have also reviewed all of Sarah's medical history that is available from Dr. Newsome and the Sutter Morena Hospital. My professional opinion based on these examinations and records is that Sarah has no medical problems. Nor did she have any actual medical problems requiring surgery or other invasive testing procedures, such as barium enemas and multiple exposure to x-rays, between April of 19YR–2 and March of 19YR–1

6. After interviewing Sarah, Jody Cray, Regina Blackwell, Dr. Newsome and the physicians who examined and treated Sarah at Sutter Morena Hospital, I have reached the professional opinion—and testified to it at the civil hearing—that Jody Cray suffers from Munchausen Syndrome by Proxy. This condition causes Ms. Cray to convince Sarah that Sarah is sick. Munchausen Syndrome by Proxy is an "attention seeking" disorder, rooted in a desire by the affected parent to be recognized and praised by doctors as a good mother or father. The affected parent either coerces the child to believe that he or she is ill—or may even go so far as to inflict actual illness upon the child—and then seeks professional treatment for the child's "symptoms."

7. Based on these observations and conclusions, it is my expert opinion that Sarah's "appendicitis" and her "asthma" never existed. It is also my professional opinion that Ms. Cray has directly and substantially jeopardized Sarah's health and physical well being by subjecting her to numerous unnecessary tests and diagnostic procedures, and by insisting that Sarah's doctors perform unnecessary surgical procedures.

STIPULATION OF EXPECTED TESTIMONY
OF DR. GARY SNYDER

It is hereby stipulated between the People and the defense, with the defendant's express consent, that if Dr. Gary Snyder, M.D., 1224 Valley View Ln., Vacaville, El Dorado, was present in court and sworn as witness, he would give the following testimony:

1. My name is Gary Snyder. I am licensed to practice pediatric medicine by the State of El Dorado. My office is located at 924 Main Street, Suite A, in Fairfield, El Dorado.

2. My office records indicate that on March 2, 19YR–1, a same-day appointment was made for 1 p.m. for Sarah Beringer. The appointment was later canceled.

3. I have no written record or personal recollection of examining Sarah or prescribing medication for her.

4. I do not personally recall scheduling or canceling Sarah's appointment. Nor do any of my staff members. I do not personally remember having any direct phone conversation with Sarah's mother, Jody Cray.

5. I have a small staff in my office. On occasion—generally in the mornings before 10am—I do answer my own telephone and schedule appointments if my staff is busy handling other calls or patients. It is possible that I may have spoken with Ms. Cray on the morning of March 2, 19YR–1. I could simply have forgotten to note the call if it was a particularly busy morning. Things get pretty hectic sometimes.

*

Index

†